£9.95

D1086972

Germany and the Far Eastern Crisis
1931—1938

GERMANY AND THE FAR EASTERN CRISIS 1931-1938

A Study in Diplomacy and Ideology

JOHN P. FOX

CLARENDON PRESS · OXFORD
LONDON SCHOOL OF ECONOMICS AND
POLITICAL SCIENCE

Oxford University Press, Walton Street, Oxford OX2 6DP
London New York Toronto
Delhi Bombay Calcutta Madras Karachi
Kuala Lumpur Singapore Hong Kong Tokyo
Nairobi Dar es Salaam Cape Town
Melbourne Auckland
and associated companies in
Beirut Berlin Ibadan Mexico City

Oxford is a trade mark of Oxford University Press

Published in the United States by
Oxford University Press, New York

© John P. Fox 1982

First published 1982
Reprinted (new as paperback) 1985

All rights reserved. No part of this publication may be reproduced,
stored in a retrieval system, or transmitted, in any form or by any means,
electronic, mechanical, photocopying, recording, or otherwise, without
the prior permission of Oxford University Press

This book is sold subject to the condition that it shall not, by way
of trade or otherwise, be lent, re-sold, hired out or otherwise circulated
without the publisher's prior consent in any form of binding or cover
other than that in which it is published and without a similar condition
including this condition being imposed on the subsequent purchaser

British Library Cataloguing in Publication Data
Fox, John P.
Germany and the Far Eastern crisis 1931–1938.
1. Germany — Foreign relations — Far East
2. Far East — Foreign relations — Germany
I. Title
327.43'05   DD24.1.F/
ISBN 0-19-821975-X

Printed in Great Britain
at the University Press, Oxford
by David Stanford
Printer to the University

To my children
JANE and PAUL

'Hitherto we have pursued a German—Japanese and a German—Chinese policy but not a German Far Eastern policy. It is difficult to apply a common denominator to our Far Eastern policy. It moves like a pendulum, sometimes to the Chinese and sometimes to the Japanese side, and a strong inclination to the one side causes bad feeling on the other.'

Oskar Trautmann, January 1937

Acknowledgements

Since this book deals with Far Eastern and international affairs it may be appropriate to mention an old Chinese proverb. This says, in effect, that at the right time one's 'teacher' appears to offer guidance, encouragement, and support. Professor D. C. Watt, Professor in International History at the London School of Economics and Political Science, has been such to me and I owe him a great debt. I hope therefore, that he will consider this present study in diplomatic history a tribute and return, not only for his particular example and excellence in this field of study, but more especially for the encouragement and friendship he has shown me over the years during and since the time I was a part-time post-graduate student of his at the L.S.E. for my Master's degree and doctorate. When things became difficult, as more often than not they did, it was important to know that I had his invaluable support and encouragement to help me persevere in my efforts.

I should like to thank Professor John Erickson of Edinburgh University for also having read my doctoral dissertation, 'The Formulation of Germany's Far Eastern Policy 1933–1936' (University of London, 1972), on which this present study is based.

My thanks go to the staffs of the libraries and institutions in which I have worked while preparing this study: the British Library of Political and Economic Science at the L.S.E., where I am particularly grateful to Miss Deidre McKellar and Miss Susan Richards of the Inter-Library Loan desk for their cheerful endeavours on my behalf; the Institute of Historical Research and Senate House Library of the University of London; the Reading Room of the British Museum; the Public Record Office, London; the Foreign Documents Centre, Imperial War Museum, in particular the help afforded by Miss Angela Raspin when employed there, and her successors, Roderick Suddaby, Edward Inman, and Stephen Inwood; the late Mr Brian Melland of the Cabinet Office; the Politische Archiv of the Auswärtiges Amt in Bonn; the Press Library of the Royal Institute of International Affairs; and the staff of the Library and Records Department of the Foreign and Commonwealth Office, London.

I am especially grateful for the willing and constant help given by Mr Kenneth Hiscock of the German Documents Section of the Library and Records Department, Foreign and Commonwealth Office, London. He has been a veritable mine of information, and unstinting and uncomplaining in his assistance. This help is warmly remembered.

I should also like to express a word of thanks to my German colleague on Series B of *Akten zur deutschen auswärtigen Politik 1918–1945,* Dr Harald Schinkel, of the Auswärtiges Amt, Bonn. On a number of occasions he provided invaluable assistance by checking the daily Journals of the German Foreign Office records in order to verify the authorship of many unsigned memoranda, as well as helping to decipher otherwise illegible signatures.

For enabling me to purchase microfilm and other materials necessary for my research I am grateful both to the Central Research Fund, University of London, and the Institute of Historical Research, University of London, for the Lindley Studentship 1968–69.

I must also thank Professor Dr Bernd Martin of the University of Freiburg for very kindly sending me an outline of part of the contents of the private papers of one of von Ribbentrop's collaborators, Dr Friedrich Wilhelm Hack, and for allowing me to use this outline in my book. I am also extremely grateful to Dr Meier Michaelis, Research Associate at the University of Jerusalem, for extracts from a document from the Military Archives at Freiburg. I should also like to thank Matild E. Holomany, Director of the Berlin Document Centre, for interesting and useful information about Ambassador Oskar Trautmann.

A study such as this also requires two other kinds of acknowledgement. Firstly, to the lecturers who stimulated my interest in modern history: Dr John Lander and Dr Michael Fry (who subsequently moved to Canada and the United States) of the City of London College, now part of the City of London Polytechnic; Miss Hilda Lee, Mr George Grün, and Professor W. N. Medlicott of the L.S.E. To the latter, and his successor as Stevenson Professor of International History at the London School of Economics, Professor James Joll, I should like to express my thanks for the help and kindness I always found in the Department of International History.

Secondly, I must acknowledge my debt to the many other scholars who have worked in the field of Nazi Germany's relations with the countries of the Far East, their examples and scholarship having helped signpost my own path through this complicated subject.

Apart from the published series of German documents and other works in English, translations from the German are mine and any errors are therefore mine alone.

I owe an especial debt of gratitude to Mrs Gillian Bennett for having so willingly and ably undertaken the difficult task of reading this book in typescript form and suggesting stylistic and other improvements. She also provided invaluable help at subsequent stages.

I must also thank Miss Kathleen Jones for the assistance she provided.

I am particularly grateful to Mrs Pamela Sparks for stepping in at extremely short notice and taking over from me the final typing of the manuscript when other tasks ate away at my time.

I should also like to thank Mr Raymond M. Hyatt for having drawn the maps.

My thanks also go to Alfred Metzner Verlag, Frankfurt-am-Main for permission to use a slightly adapted and amended version of the chart on 'The Structure of National Socialist Foreign Policy 1933–1938' from Hans-Adolf Jacobsen, *Nationalsozialistische Aussenpolitik 1933–1938* (1968).

In conclusion, I should like to thank both the members of the Publications Committee of the London School of Economics & Political Science and the Isobel Thornley Bequest Fund Committee (University of London) for their generous assistance in ensuring publication of this book.

Contents

Illustrations

Abbreviations

AA	Auswärtiges Amt
ADAP	Akten zur deutschen auswärtigen Politik
AGK	Ausfuhrgemeinschaft für Kriegsgerät
AO	Auslandsorganisation der NSDAP
APA	Aussenpolitisches Amt der NSDAP
DBFP	Documents on British Foreign Policy
DDF	Documents diplomatiques français
DGFP	Documents on German Foreign Policy
DNB	Deutsches Nachrichtenbüro
FO	Foreign Office Correspondence 371
FO.646/TWC	Transcript Volumes and Document Books of Trials of War Criminals
FRUS	Foreign Relations of the United States
HAPRO	Handelsgesellschaft für industrielle Produkte
IMT	Trial of the Major War Criminals before the International Military Tribunal
IMTFE	International Military Tribunal for the Far East
NSDAP	Nationalsozialistische Deutsche Arbeiterpartei
OKW	Oberkommando der Wehrmacht
OKW/W-R	Oberkommando der Wehrmacht, Wehrwirtschafts- und Rüstungsamt
OR	Ostasiatische Rundschau
PA	Politische Archiv des Auswärtiges Amt
SIA	Survey of International Affairs
TC	Tsingtao Consulate
TWC	Trials of War Criminals before the Nuremberg Military Tribunals
VfZ	Vierteljahrshefte für Zeitgeschichte

Introduction

This book examines the part played by the German Foreign Office, the Wilhelmstrasse, in the making of Germany's Far Eastern policy from 1931 to 1938 with particular reference to the Nazi period. The history of Germany's position and relationships in the Far East,[1] from the outbreak of the Manchurian Crisis in September 1931 to the withdrawal of the German Ambassador to China in the summer of 1938, covers a progression from a situation of fairly equal and mutual relations with China and Japan, somewhat economically weighted in China's direction and from September 1931 termed 'neutrality', to one of gradual commitment to Japan.[2] How this occurred is examined here from the viewpoint of the Wilhelmstrasse, the Ministry usually but not always looked to for advice, guidance, and leadership in the making of German foreign policy.

In many respects the establishment of the National Socialist régime in Germany in 1933[3] presented the German Foreign Office with no new problems in so far as its constitutional function and political position regarding the formulation and execution of foreign policy was concerned. Its primary function was to proffer advice to the political leadership of the country and to execute the general lines of policy decided by that leadership. This had been its function before 1933, and the Hitler government was no exception to the general rule that overall lines of policy were decided and dictated at the top and left to others for detailed execution. Under democratic régimes this process of decision making in foreign and domestic policy — in which the officials of the Foreign Office expected to play their full part because of their professional experience, knowledge, and expertise — had often confronted the Foreign Office and other Ministries with the problem that 'outsiders' would be employed by the government for the formulation and even the execution of policies. From January 1933, with the institution of the 'anarchic-impulsive dictatorship',[4] when Hitler not only permitted but positively encouraged inter-personal and inter-departmental rivalry as a means of ensuring the maintenance of his authority and position, the Foreign Office in particular was confronted with the old problem in an accentuated form.

The relationship between the Foreign Office and the Nazi government was to be a strained and difficult one, not least because of differences in social background between the permanent officials and the general run of the Nazi leadership. Above all, though, there were major differences on foreign policy. One fundamental question confronted all German policy makers in the post-Versailles era: the definition of Germany's role in European and world affairs. In many respects the officials in the Wilhelmstrasse and the Nazi leadership were at one over many objectives to be pursued and attained in German foreign policy. On many others there were serious differences of opinion and for the moment one need only summarise the cause of such conflicts under the generic, Nazi ideology.[5] The importance of this subject and its connection with Far Eastern policy after 1933 is that it was a Party man and a Party organisation, Joachim von Ribbentrop and his Büro or Dienststelle, which tended to make the running in German–Japanese relations and concluded the Anti-Comintern Pact of 25 November 1936. To most observers, and certainly to the Japanese, this Pact signified a form of political commitment on the part of Germany towards Japan, something which the Japanese attempted to ensure was underwritten during 1937 and beyond. At the post-war Nuremberg Trials this development (among others) was used as evidence to prove the contentions of the German diplomats that the Foreign Office lost its 'traditional' powers over the formulation of German foreign policy in the Nazi era. It was submitted that proliferating para-diplomatic agencies eroded the power of the Foreign Office while Hitler made all the crucial decisions without consulting the professional diplomats. This argument found its apotheosis in the defence statement of Ernst von Weizsäcker, State Secretary in the Foreign Office from 1938 to 1945, at Nuremberg on 7 June 1948: '[in 1936] I found that in the Foreign Office the reins of government had slipped. Hitler had no great opinion of the Foreign Office. He preferred information from laymen to that obtained from us. Decisions were taken without the Foreign Office or even the Foreign Minister being heard on the subject . . . orders came to us out of a clear sky. Our Foreign Service had sunk to the level of a technical agency.'[6] This defence, intended to absolve the officials of the German Foreign Office from all responsibility for the steps which had led to war in 1939 and after, has been effectively demolished.[7]

In the final analysis, though, the Foreign Office's ability to deal with the difficulties it faced under the Nazis, and to maintain what it felt were its prerogatives in the making and execution of German foreign policy,[8] depended on how far its voice could be heard and paid attention to in the Nazi jungle. There were several reasons why its influence in the making of Far Eastern policy in particular, at least up to February 1938 when von Ribbentrop finally became Foreign Minister, gradually diminished. It was at a severe disadvantage, in the first place, in having as the Foreign Minister until then a fairly weak and irresolute character in the person of Constantin von Neurath. Completely unsuited for the rough and tumble of the gutter-like politics of the Nazi State,[9] he tended to reinforce the low opinion Hitler already had of his class and of members of the Foreign Office. The Foreign Office was further at a disadvantage since von Neurath did not belong to the Party élite, and almost automatically this put him and the Foreign Office on the level of 'outsiders' in the Nazi view of things. From the very beginning of the Nazi régime, therefore, the influence of the Foreign Office was weaker than it might otherwise have been. Thirdly, von Weizsäcker's statement at Nuremberg in 1948 was factually correct: the Nazi State did encourage the proliferation of many para-diplomatic, i.e. Nazi Party agencies active in the field of foreign policy, e.g. the *Aussenpolitisches Amt* (*APA*), the *Auslandsorganisation* (*AO*), and of course the Büro or Dienststelle Ribbentrop.[10] In addition, other individuals came to the fore and tried to be active in matters directly related to foreign policy. Little wonder that the Foreign Office continually operated under tremendous pressure and strain, and much nervous energy was expended in the struggle to be 'heard' where it mattered most.

Above all, though, the nature of the new Nazi State, with its increasingly dictatorial and radical characteristics, meant that Hitler's views on foreign policy, whatever they were (a subject which has most exercised historians in recent years),[11] became the norm by which most Party hacks at least set their own standards. So far as the Far East was concerned, Hitler and other leading Nazis were only interested in the situation there in so far as it was able to influence Germany's position in European and world affairs in a favourable manner. What particularly interested Hitler and his faithful follower, von Ribbentrop, was that the aggressive and apparently successful militarist Japan occupied a crucially strategic position in world affairs: vis-à-vis the Soviet Union on the one hand, and Britain's overseas interests on the other, both nations occupying important positions in Hitler's view of world affairs.[12]

Yet the Foreign Office's continual difficulties with the Nazi leadership over the question of whether or not Germany's Far Eastern policy should be oriented towards Japan were complemented by those it had with the German Army over the development of closer military links with China. Even here, though, some blame for this development can be laid at the door of the Nazi leadership. Although military links with China gradually increased after Max Bauer's important and pioneer work there from 1927 to 1929, they were not intensified until the deterioration of Nazi Germany's relations with Soviet Russia from 1933 had ensured that there could be no resuscitation of military collaboration between the Reichswehr and the Red Army. At the same time Hitler's foreign policy objectives required the speeding up of Germany's economic and military rearmament as a means of securing their ultimate execution. This, in fact, contributed to the confusion over Germany's position in the Far East. The deeper involvement of German military circles in China after 1933 was based on that country's role in being able to supply large quantities of raw materials absolutely vital for Germany's rearmament and which Hitler continually pressed forward as the most urgent task facing the country at the time. Like the Japanese, though, the German Foreign Office could only recognise closer Sino-German military relations as a form of political commitment to China. While the Wilhelmstrasse initially opposed this particular development, it could not deny the undoubted military and economic benefits that Germany obtained from China at a time of under-employment and other economic difficulties. The Foreign Office's opposition to the Army's activities in China goes some way towards disposing of the usual legend that it was completely pro-Chinese in its attitudes. It often showed a strong degree of cynicism and doubt about Sino-German economic relations, questioning the capabilities of the Chinese and their economy, especially when the question of government involvement in this trade in the form of Reich guarantees came up for discussion. Yet the Wilhelmstrasse also had to contend with Nazi Party efforts to swing Germany to Japan's side in the Far Eastern struggle for power in the hope of obtaining, in return, Japan's support for Germany's world position and policies.

A further problem which the Wilhelmstrasse faced in the formulation of Far Eastern policy, and indeed in its general struggle to maintain its authority in the Nazi State, was that affliction known to Foreign Ministries the world over, 'Ambassador's disease'. While Trautmann in China tended to represent the general line of policy favoured by the Wilhelmstrasse, that of uncommitted 'balance' — although more and more this came to mean a degree of defence of German interests in China against constant Japanese representations for their limitation or even removal — von Dirksen in Tokio tended to be swayed more by Nazi ideas and ideals and, like Hitler and von Ribbentrop, favoured much closer relations with Japan.

Of the two, von Dirksen was the more complex in temperament and character and, unlike Trautmann, close to the Nazis. He came from a line of bourgeois civil servants who were rewarded with a patent of nobility in 1887 for their loyal service to the Prussian State. Although von Dirksen became what his father wished him to be, a correct and proper aristocrat with all the right connections — a 'vain and pompous man'[13] — unlike the true aristocrat he had an uncommon respect for and fear of those who held authority and wielded power in the modern world. Not surprisingly, he became more than a loyal civil servant to the Nazis. By 1936 he had joined the Party and was genuinely impressed with its economic and political achievements.[14] Trautmann, on the other hand, was a completely different person and his attitude towards the Nazi Party was the antithesis of von Dirksen's. The records of the Berlin Documents Centre show that Trautmann was never a member of the Nazi Party and in fact the Party Chancellery issued a *Warnungskarte* stating that under no condition was he to be granted Party membership. Trautmann's own antipathy towards the régime was seen by the fact that he never used the salutation 'Heil Hitler', which was customary by the time he requested that he be exempted from having to become a member of the ubiquitous *Reichsschrifttumskammer* in connection with his book on Russian foreign policy from 1870 to 1914, *Die Sängerbrücke* (Stuttgart 1940).[15]

The difference of opinion over Far Eastern policy between Trautmann in China and von Dirksen in Japan was not, therefore, a new experience for the Foreign Office since it would have been a rather unique Ambassador who somehow did not tend to adopt the viewpoint, or at least the *Geist,* of the country he was posted to. In the Third Reich, though, the significance of this malady went beyond being an internal Foreign Office matter since it was often associated with the efforts of the political leadership to pursue a line of foreign policy opposed to that of the Wilhelmstrasse. Given von Neurath's rather weak leadership and von Dirksen's inclination to adopt Nazi-type views, the Foreign Office's position in the internecine quarrels in the Nazi State over Far Eastern policy was doubly weakened because of the personal characteristics of two of its influential members. Consequently, it could not present a strong and unified front to its opponents and enemies.

While von Ribbentrop and von Dirksen, and even von Neurath, emerge from this story with very little credit, other officials in the Wilhelmstrasse, and especially Oskar Trautmann, deserve some praise for the personal and professional qualities they tried to display at a time when the quality of public and private life in Germany deteriorated day by day. Even though he was the essential cause of this deterioration, nevertheless one must also recognise the fact that on Far Eastern issues Hitler's attitude was often a more reasonable and sensible one than that adopted by his loyal and slavish follower, von Ribbentrop. Hitler often decided in favour of those who, like many in the Wilhelmstrasse and the Wehrmacht, wished to see a 'balanced' policy pursued in the Far East, or at least one which defended Germany's important economic and military interests in China. For a time, then, Hitler was content to see only a limited kind of commitment undertaken with regard to Japan.

Yet while the pressures inside Germany mounted for a definite inclination towards either China or Japan — internal pressures which were all the time complemented by those exerted from Chinese and Japanese sources — only after the outbreak of the Sino-Japanese war in July 1937 could it be said that 'the essential dilemma' facing the western powers, 'to wit, whether to back China or Japan',[16] really came to the fore and confirmed that element of inflexibility in the whole range of Far Eastern international relationships which had been implicit since the outbreak of the Manchurian Crisis in September 1931. Yet the fact that there still remained an element of 'balance' in Germany's Far Eastern relations after November 1936 and July 1937, until von Ribbentrop assumed the mantle of Foreign Minister in February 1938, was due not only to the influence which the German Foreign Office still managed to retain in the policy making processes of Nazi Germany, supported by the extensive nature of Germany's military and economic interests in China, but by the fact that with the conclusion of the Anti-Comintern Pact Hitler himself believed that for the time being his Japanese policy had gone far enough. The important point was that increasingly this policy was predicated upon the nature of Anglo-German relations just as much as on Russo-German relations, and it is significant that the Sino-Japanese war was six months old before von Ribbentrop set in train, in January 1938, the first steps along the path to the agreements with Japan of the years 1940, 1941, and 1942. But it was not so much the exigencies of Japan's war in China which had prompted von Ribbentrop's solicitations but the deteriorating state of Anglo-German relations throughout 1937, culminating in Hitler's analysis in November 1937 that Britain was Germany's implacable enemy, to be echoed in January 1938 by the ever-faithful von Ribbentrop.

This development in Hitler's political and strategic thinking and the serious deterioration in European relations coincided with Japan's apparently increasing mastery of the situation in the Far East. It was perhaps inevitable, therefore, that after von Ribbentrop became Reich Foreign Minister on 4 February 1938 the German Foreign Office should so faithfully fulfil its constitutional role as to become the instrument of 'ideology' in creating a German policy of imbalance in the Far East under the general political leadership of Adolf Hitler. In the final event, therefore, Germany's interests in China were sacrificed on the altar of National Socialist *Weltanschauung*, while within the Wilhelmstrasse the views and policies of von Dirksen, and of course von Ribbentrop, triumphed over those of Oskar Trautmann and the German Army. This was signified in the summer of 1938 by the open declaration of support for Japan made clear by the withdrawal of the German Ambassador and the German military advisers from China. In this way German Far Eastern policy under the Nazis progressed from that of *Kontinuität* to that of *Bruch*[17] and saw the triumph of ideology over diplomacy. How it was done is the subject of this book.

I

Weimar Germany and the Manchurian Crisis 1931-1933

The Wilhelmstrasse's immediate response to the outbreak of the Sino-Japanese conflict in September 1931 and its consideration by the League of Nations[1] at Geneva was to adopt, in the name of Republican Germany, a policy of official neutrality but full cooperation with the due processes of the League.[2] Germany's participation in these processes was, however, intended to be such as to leave whatever blaze of glory or ignominy there might be on the shoulders of Britain and France. Consequently, the German delegation at Geneva was instructed to refrain from supporting any anti-Japanese front that might come into existence since Japan had proved accommodating to the German position on questions such as reparations and Memel. It was also felt that if Germany joined an anti-Japanese bloc she would be repeating the mistake made in 1895 with the intervention of Shimonoseki.[3] Nor did Germany feel any particular responsibility for securing the integrity of China. She had not been represented at the Washington Conference of 1921–22 and was not a signatory of the Nine Power Treaty of 6 February 1922 dealing with China's sovereignty and the maintenance of the 'Open Door'.[4] Responsibility for these matters was placed squarely on the shoulders of the signatory powers, not on Germany.[5]

Dr Julius Curtius, German Foreign Minister, made Germany's position quite clear at Geneva when he avoided taking any stand towards the conflict when approached by the Chinese for his support,[6] and in his short speech to the League Council on 22 September. In view of Germany's increasingly negative attitude towards the League and her membership of it,[7] it is interesting to note that in Curtius's speech and the conversations pursued by German diplomats with Chinese and Japanese officials great emphasis was placed on maintaining the integrity of the League in connection with the current crisis.[8] Germany did fulfil her function as an important member of the League Council and was chosen to be one of the Committee of Five, a select group of the Council composed of representatives from Great Britain, France, Italy,

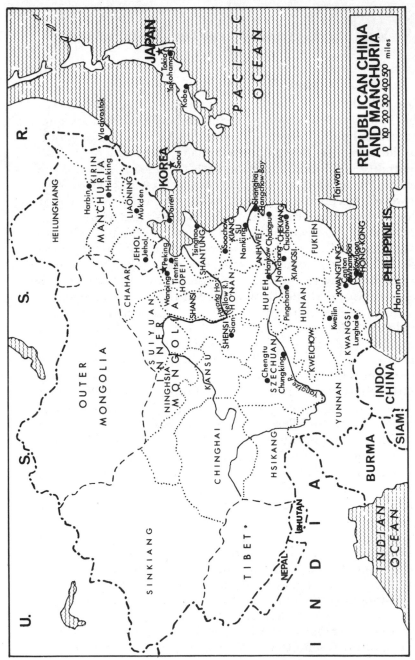

Map. 1.   Republican China and Manchuria

Germany and the President of the Council, established on 22 September 1931 to deal with the crisis and with Chinese and Japanese representatives outside the normal functions of the Council.[9] Furthermore, following the Council's resolution of 10 December 1931, Dr Heinrich Schnee, Governor of German East Africa 1912–19 and active in the German colonial movement, became the German representative on the five-man League Commission of Enquiry which was to visit the Far East and report.[10]

It was not to be expected, however, that Germany would escape either a degree of pressure from Chinese and Japanese sources, or a measure of publicity over her role in the crisis. Following the initial pressure exerted on Curtius by Chinese diplomats, loud complaints were soon expressed by the Chinese about what they regarded as Germany's apparent policy of self-effacement at Geneva. Chiang Kai-shek even sent a personal appeal to Curtius for his further attendance at the League Council.[11] The Chinese were also disappointed at Germany's reaffirmation of her neutral role in the dispute when they sought her support over the invocation of the Kellogg-Briand Pact.[12]

If this, in Chinese eyes, was bad enough there was worse to follow. While the Wilhelmstrasse continued to reaffirm the 'passive' nature of Germany's more general and political role in the crisis,[13] on 15 October she drew particular attention to herself by voting together with Japan at the Council which had before it a proposal by Briand, President of the Council, that the United States of America be invited to send an observer to the League Council. A Japanese proposal for the establishment of a committee of experts to study the constitutional difficulties of inviting a non-League power such as America was rejected, Germany and Japan voting together in support of that particular motion. Briand's proposal was then unanimously adopted, Japan casting the sole dissenting vote.

Surprising everyone, Germany's support of Japan was quickly explained in instructions to the German Minister in China, Oskar Trautmann, and on 19 October to the Chinese Chargé d'Affaires, Dr L Liang, by Erich Michelsen in charge of Far Eastern affairs in Department IV of the Wilhelmstrasse. He explained that Germany had acted in this manner for reasons unconnected with the present crisis and in order to facilitate a Japanese retreat on the question, but that Germany's behaviour in no way affected her neutral role in the crisis. Liang was not entirely convinced by these arguments and in turn emphasised that it was also in Germany's interest that the League remain an authoritative international body, taking the opportunity at the same time to express his concern at what appeared to be anti-League feeling in Germany.[14] Germany had, however, voted with Japan to emphasise her own opposition to any precedent being set of majority decisions in the Council on questions of substance. The Japanese argued that the invitation to America was one of substance and not of procedure, and only the latter, according to Article V of the League Covenant, allowed for majority decisions.[15]

Chinese pressure on Germany was counter-balanced by that from the Japanese who were similarly disappointed at some of the attitudes adopted by Berlin. It was not at all to the liking of Torikitchi Obata, Japanese Ambassador to Germany, to be told once again in November 1931 of Germany's neutral stance in the crisis by the State Secretary in the Foreign Office, Bernhard von Bülow, who also emphasised his concern that current events in the Far East should not lead to any derogation of the authority of the League of Nations.[16] An early indication of the kinds of pressures the Japanese could exert on Germany, whose role was a minor one compared to that of Britain and France, was seen over the question of nominations for membership of the League Commission of Enquiry. The Japanese made it clear that they would consider it an unfriendly act if members of the League Commission represented nations with large economic interests in China. Their own choice as Germany's representative was Wilhelm Solf, German Ambassador to Japan 1920—28, since they felt that his presence on the Commission would tend to offset what they saw as the pro-Chinese attitude of the German press.[17] One name put forward in the Foreign Office was that of General Hans von Seeckt, 'father' of the Reichswehr, and a person whom the Chinese fully expected to participate in the mission.[18] To a certain extent the Germans were influenced by the Japanese and consequently informed the Chinese that members of the Commission had to be people whose judgement was also valued in Japan.[19] Finally, though, even the Japanese had to accept the Secretary General's ruling that the Commission should exclude those who had been established diplomatic representatives at either Peking or Tokio.[20] The Japanese would have accepted this decision with more grace had they known that it was the Wilhelmstrasse's intention to repeat to Schnee the instructions already issued to the German delegation at Geneva, namely that his role on the Commission was to be a neutral, passive, and reserved one.[21]

Nevertheless, in view of the bad press they were getting throughout the world, what the Japanese most wanted was action on the part of any would-be supporter. Japanese pressure in Tokio seemed to have had some effect on the German Ambassador there, Ernst Voretzsch, who believed that Germany should accept the political changes occurring in the Far East and act accordingly since no German political interests were at stake. Japan could be of service to Germany in the difficult future but China could offer Germany nothing in the political field. He wanted this 'realistic' view publicised and the German press induced to curb their attacks on Japan 'since neither the people nor the government will forget it'.[22] The leader of the National Socialist Party, Adolf Hitler, also adopted a 'realistic' attitude when he stated that Japan had every right to secure her *Lebensfrage* in Manchuria, while there were even reports that he had volunteered the despatch of National Socialist *Freikorps* to Manchuria.[23] But in reply to a thinly-veiled hint of a better political relationship between Germany and Japan, even leading to Japan cancelling her reparations claims against Germany — expressed by the Japanese Ambassador in Moscow, Koki Hirota, to Germany's Ambassador, Herbert von Dirksen — von Bülow merely expressed his pleasure at Japan's appreciation of Germany's role in the crisis.[24]

There were, however, several important factors which acted as a brake on any inclination there might have been in the Wilhelmstrasse to pursue a policy of 'benevolent neutrality' in Japan's favour, and which raised such irritations in German–Japanese relations anyway as to vitiate somewhat the effects of the Foreign Office's carefully enunciated and executed policy of neutrality. These were Germany's economic and military interests in China, and the general problem of Manchuria and uncertainty about its political and economic future.

Germany's economic interests in China implied, at the very least, a certain orientation of German policy. Natural differences in terms of size and natural resources meant that Germany's economic interests were greater in China than in Japan. In 1932 it was estimated that there were in China about 350 German firms and about 4000 Germans, in Japan 60 and 1000 respectively.[25] Germany also occupied a special position in the China trade since she, unlike most of the other 'white' powers, did not enjoy the benefit of unequal treaties, having concluded 'equal' treaties with China in 1921 and 1928. The basis of Germany's Far East trade was the export of manufactured goods in return for raw materials, especially the soya bean from Manchuria. Germany's economic interests and participation in China increased after 1930 following the visit to China that year by a mission from the *Reichsverband der Deutschen Industrie*. In 1929 China had stood in seventh place among Germany's export markets outside Europe but by 1936 had risen to third place. Conversely, Germany stood fourth behind America, Japan, and Great Britain in China's export trade. In general, Germany's unfavourable balance of trade with China was offset by her favourable balance with Japan. The situation was complicated by the establishment of Manchukuo in 1932 as a separate entity from China, although official German trade statistics continued until 1937 to include the Manchukuo figures with the Chinese.[26]

Economics as well as politics were disturbed and shaken by Japan's military progress in Manchuria, and Germany's economic representatives in China soon complained about the threat posed by Japan to German interests in Manchuria. At the same time the German business community in Japan opposed the arguments of the China enthusiasts, that China was 'the market of the future', when they saw Dr Schnee in Tokio. They also complained of the damage caused to Germany's position in Japan by the anti-Japanese and pro-Chinese tone of most of the German press. Not surprisingly, they argued that Germany stood to gain economically in Manchuria as a result of the economic growth which could be expected there following the institution of Japan's policy of 'law and order'.[27]

While the German Foreign Office did not always adopt what could be described as a positive attitude towards economic relations with China there was, for a long time, little fear of this question becoming a serious irritant or issue in German—Japanese relations. The same could hardly be said

of the presence in China of German military advisers, principally to Chiang Kai-shek and the Kuomintang régime. Originating with the expulsion of the Russians in 1927 and Colonel
Max Bauer's visit to China that year, this group of German
ex-officers soon established their position in China. After
Bauer's death in 1929 his successors were Colonel Hermann
Kriebel (1929—30), later to be German Consul General at
Shanghai, Lieutenant General Georg Wetzell (1930—34), in a
temporary capacity General Hans von Seeckt (1934—35), and
finally General Alexander von Falkenhausen (1935—38), later
to be the German military commander of Belgium during the
Second World War.[28]

The presence of these military advisers in China was opposed
by the German Foreign Office and raised three issues which
directly concerned German foreign policy. The first involved
Germany's liability under Article 179 of the Treaty of
Versailles prohibiting her nationals from being employed in a
military capacity by other governments as well as the export
of arms from Germany. Already in 1929 the Wilhelmstrasse
had opposed the activity of German military advisers in China
on the grounds that their presence there would increase the
Sino-German arms trade, which soon began to involve large
organisations such as Krupps, Carlowitz, and Siemmsen.[29] It
tried to dissuade the ex-officers from going to China by
threatening the cancellation of their state pension, but it was
admitted that nothing much could be done to stop them.[30]
Apart from Article 179 of the Treaty of Versailles, Germany
itself had promulgated laws in 1921 and 1927 forbidding the
export of war material, and in that becoming effective on
27 April 1928 arms trade with China was specifically prohibited. This did not solve the problem, however, since the
law of 1928 expired in the summer of 1929 following the
termination on 26 April 1929 of the Arms Embargo Agreement of 5 May 1919 relating to China.

The second aspect of the question was the detrimental effect
the presence of the advisers was expected to have on Germany's
economic position in China. The remarks made in April 1929
by the German Chargé d'affaires at Peking, Otto von Erdmannsdorff, to a member of the British Legation were also
applicable in later years: 'the objection of the German government to Bauer's employment was that by assisting Chiang
Kai-shek he might prejudice German trade and relations in

parts of China controlled by other military and political leaders who at any time might be in open conflict with the Chiang Kai-shek faction of the Kuomintang'.[31] Indeed, anti-German feeling ran high in Canton during August and September 1931 because of German arms deliveries to Chiang Kai-shek, while German arms deliveries to Canton and other places raised difficulties in Germany's relations with the Nanking government.

Although German arms and chemicals were also delivered to Japan during the Manchurian Crisis,[32] it was the Japanese reaction which constituted the third and most troublesome aspect of this question for the Wilhelmstrasse. The Japanese regarded the training of Chinese soldiers by German military experts and the establishment of 'German' arsenals in China to supply arms for the Chinese army as signifying hostility by Germany towards Japan. Despite the efforts of the Wilhelmstrasse both to reassure the Japanese and to limit anti-Japanese expressions in the German press, Japanese anger and disquiet on this question reached a new height at the time of the fighting in Shanghai in February 1932 when rumours circulated that German advisers were involved in the Chinese defence of the city.[33]

Though these reports were denied, and a denial in turn issued to counter Chinese accusations that Germany was supplying Japan with war material,[34] the whole question of German military advisers in China and German arms deliveries to China was to plague German—Japanese relations right through to 1938. The Wilhelmstrasse continually pressed the Reichswehr Ministry to limit the scale of German military activity in China in order not to exacerbate relations with Japan. Another reason for its pressure was its objection to any German involvement in the confused nature of Chinese domestic politics, and in June 1932 it was alarmed to learn that Chiang Kai-shek wished to invite Reichswehr Minister Groener to visit China to advise on the reorganisation of the Chinese army. Groener, however, declined the invitation.[35] Until 1933, however, the role of the Reichswehr Ministry in China was ambivalent and unclear, its principal interests and those of the German armaments firms with whom it had close contacts being in Russian military affairs. But from 1933, when Russo-German military relations were wound up, the Wilhelmstrasse was to find that the Reichswehr Ministry (from

May 1935 the Ministry of War) was an important factor to be reckoned with in the formulation of its Chinese and general Far Eastern policy.

The third question which caused great difficulties in German–Japanese relations concerned Manchuria following the Japanese conquest and involved three main problems: firstly, German economic interests in Manchuria; secondly, the League's handling of the Sino-Japanese dispute; and thirdly, the possible *de jure* recognition of the new state of Manchukuo by other powers after its creation in March 1932 and Japan's recognition of it in September 1932.

The new situation in Manchuria greatly concerned Germany since in recent years she had become Manchuria's biggest customer for soya beans, relying on this commodity as her principal source of edible vegetable fats, especially margarine. Concern over developments and economic prospects in Manchukuo, as it came to be known, was to be fully justified.[36] Despite hopes, and even assurances, that Japan would maintain the principles of the Open Door in Manchukuo and welcome foreign business there, it was soon clear that economically and politically Manchukuo was being developed in Japanese interests alone. More specifically this meant development in the interests of the Kwantung Army so that the area could be regarded as a 'continental war base',[37] while in any case 'after the occupation of Manchuria the Kwantung Army was the real government there'.[38]

While Japanese administrators, business, and industry rapidly controlled all aspects of Manchukuo's economic life, the army planners also used foreign trade as a policy instrument. Conditions for foreign businesses became intolerable and the big American and British oil companies were forced out, a policy which also affected German enterprises.[39] By February 1932 Trautmann was reporting pessimistically on the prospects for German enterprises in the Three Eastern Provinces, placing no faith in Japanese assurances that the Open Door policy would be maintained. He even suggested that because of Japanese policy Manchukuo was as good as lost for German trade, especially in the important field of government orders and contracts.[40] Events confirmed Trautmann's analysis, and at the end of May 1932 the German Chamber of Commerce in Mukden compiled a detailed list of complaints regarding the exclusion of non-Japanese commercial undertakings to be presented to the German representative on the League Commission of Enquiry, Dr Schnee.[41] Schnee himself confirmed this depressing picture when he spoke of the new State as having been founded by the Japanese through force and that it would be maintained only by the Japanese.[42] On the other hand, the German Chamber of Commerce in Japan believed that a Japanese-controlled Manchukuo would afford Germany great economic opportunities.[43]

In the circumstances it was not surprising that the Wilhelm-strasse's reaction to Japanese hints — and they were no more than hints — of German–Japanese economic cooperation in Manchukuo was a decidedly cool one. The German Embassy in Tokio was instructed to respond to any such overtures with the comment that Germany needed to be approached with 'concrete proposals'. Nor could Germany's relations with China be ignored: 'we should require that the Chinese be informed directly the proposals have been formalised; China herself has an interest in the participation of third States in the development of Manchukuo based on her own claims for the maintenance of the principles of the Open Door'.[44] Perhaps the overriding consideration for the Wilhelmstrasse at the time was that any overt German–Japanese cooperation in Manchukuo would have implied a tacit recognition of that State at a time when Manchuria was *sub judice* so far as the League of Nations was concerned, and when the League Assembly's Resolution of 11 March 1932 had applied the non-recognition doctrine to Manchukuo. Nor were the Germans, or anybody else, allowed to forget Chinese feelings on the subject of Manchuria.[45]

The Wilhelmstrasse likewise viewed with reserve the idea of political cooperation with Japan, and when Japanese officials hinted at such cooperation, as Hirota did again in May 1932 to von Dirksen, with the addition of Russia in such a combination, the German Foreign Office was fully aware that Japan was less interested in Germany's particular friendship as such than in attempting to weaken the apparent unity of the League powers lined up against her. Von Dirksen was wisely non-committal in reply, pointing out to Hirota that difficulties in Russo-Japanese relations in any case militated against the im-mediate implementation of such a plan. Von Bülow approved von Dirksen's stance, especially since he was uncertain how far

these were Hirota's personal suggestions or whether he was
acting on instructions from Tokio. For the moment the
matter was left on the basis that von Dirksen was to maintain
his attitude of reserve and await any further Japanese proposals, should they be put to him. He was also to be on the
lookout for any Japanese suggestion that Germany act as a
go-between for Japan and Russia.[46]

A month later von Bülow returned to the subject, and for
von Dirksen spelt out some of the reasons for Germany's
attitude of reserve towards suggestions that she adopt a more
positive policy *vis-à-vis* Japan at that time. Berlin feared that
if she collaborated with Japan and Russia, and China was then
treated as 'a common colonial area', Germany's position in
the China market would be a disadvantageous one compared
to that of the other two powers. While the value of such a
political combination was recognised it was not envisaged that
it could take place at the time. Nor was much faith placed in
the effectiveness or consistency of Japanese promises of political support for Germany, so that von Bülow wanted
Germany's policy towards Japan to be similar to that pursued
towards Italy: one of friendly association without any close
or political commitments. Nevertheless, he also implied that
the time might not be too far distant when direct German—
Japanese collaboration would be feasible.[47] This admission
was probably less a statement of long-term intent than an
indication of the tremendous pressures the Wilhelmstrasse
felt itself to be under, both as regards its position in the Far
East and as a member of the League dealing with the Sino-
Japanese dispute, but more particularly *vis-à-vis* Britain and
France on the vital questions of disarmament and reparations.[48]

Germany's predicament was recognised, and used, by the
Japanese initially on the question of the recognition of
Manchukuo. On 14 September 1932 Obata, the Japanese
Ambassador, called on Foreign Minister von Neurath to inform
him of Japan's recognition of the new State the following
day and to request a statement of Germany's attitude on the
question. Von Neurath wisely reserved his position but took
the opportunity to press home complaints about the parlous
state of Germany's economic interests in Manchukuo. Six
days later Obata repeated his request for a German statement
to von Bülow. Following closely the arguments of a memorandum by Michelsen, von Bülow stated that Germany had no

political interests in Manchukuo except concern that the current crisis should be settled through the responsible authority, the League of Nations. Referring to the Lytton Report and the imminent League debate upon it, the State Secretary made it quite clear that Germany's attitude would be determined by her interests in the League and 'the attitude of other powers'. He, too, took up the theme of Germany's economic interests in Manchukuo, and pointed out that Germany's attitude towards the new government in that area would be determined by the treatment meted out to Germany's economic interests in the country. Obata therefore drew the only conclusion he could, that 'in the present situation' he could not expect a clear statement of German intent on the question of Manchukuo.[49]

Japan's intent, however, became increasingly clear in the weeks and months, and even years, that followed: not only to bring about Manchukuo's recognition by other powers, but to use their attitude on this question as a barometer or gauge for Japan's own relationship with any nation. Obata's interview with von Bülow was accompanied on the same day by one between Michelsen and a Dr Hack of the firm of Schinzinger, Hack & Co — the same Dr Hack who was later to be used by von Ribbentrop as his contact with the Japanese. Hack reported his conversation of the previous day with the Japanese Naval Attaché, Captain Yendo, and another member of the Japanese Embassy, Motoharu Shichida. Hack's conclusion was that there existed in Japan, particularly within the influential military and naval circles, a great deal of sympathy for Germany's demands at the disarmament conference. But unless Germany declared her friendship for Japan by an early recognition of Manchukuo, it was feared that Japanese policy would be aligned with that of France at Geneva, possibly as a price for obtaining a measure of French support in the Sino-Japanese dispute.[50] It was thought that Germany could be offered favourable economic terms in Manchukuo, while Hack warned that German policy must avoid a 'second Shimonoseki'. In this connection he expressed his concern at the anti-Japanese tone of the German press, mentioning in particular the *Deutsche Allgemeine Zeitung*.[51] Michelsen, in reply, could hardly do less than assure Hack that 'any fears that we should adopt an unfriendly attitude towards Japan were unfounded'.[52]

In view of Germany's strong stand at the disarmament

conference and her refusal to attend after 23 July 1932 until
the other powers accorded her 'equality of rights', it is doubtful whether these attempts to force a recognition of Manchukuo out of Germany were taken seriously in the Wilhelmstrasse. While the Foreign Office wished to maintain friendly
relations with Japan it was not intended to show her any
favours which, besides raising immense difficulties in Sino-
German relations, would have reduced Germany's chances of
obtaining from Britain and France her desiderata on the disarmament question. In any case, and as von Bülow had pointed
out to Obata, Germany's attitude on the recognition question
would be determined by the approach of the other powers
when the matter came before the League in November. It was
clear, therefore, that Germany was maintaining her loyalty to
the League Assembly's Resolution of 11 March 1932 which
formalised the League's non-recognition of Manchukuo.

For Germany and everyone else the League's handling of the
Sino-Japanese dispute was soon to reach its long-drawn out
conclusion. On 21 November the Lytton Report was considered by the League Council, while the Director of Department IV in the German Foreign Office, Richard Meyer, had
already recommended that everything should be done to
prevent Japan feeling that she had to withdraw from the
League, and indeed it was clearly stated that it was also in
Germany's interests that Japan remain in the League.[53]
Germany's policy at Geneva was thus to follow that laid down
by Sir John Simon for Great Britain, 'conciliation before
condemnation', and this was echoed in von Neurath's own
speech in the League Assembly debate on 7 December.[54]

Although this speech gave rise to speculation that Germany
was adopting an attitude of indulgence towards Japan's
conduct, the Wilhelmstrasse continued to impress upon both
Chinese and Japanese diplomats that Germany had not
departed from her official position of neutrality.[55] On the
other hand, von Bülow reacted more strongly when he received
the Japanese Chargé d'affaires, Keinosuke Fujii, on 9 January
1933. This was because Japanese troops had occupied Shan-
haikuan, immediately south of the Great Wall and in the
province of Jehol, six days previously, an action which tended
to compromise Germany's own efforts to be 'fair and impartial'
towards Japan's case at Geneva, while it was further and unwelcome evidence of Japan's aggressive designs on the mainland

of Asia. Apart from giving a veiled warning about further military adventures, von Bülow also declined to take any attitude on Japan's current demands that there should be direct negotiations with China.[56]

More publicly, Dr Rudolf Breitscheid of the Social Democratic Party tried to elicit from the German government a statement openly condemning Japan by submitting a suitably worded 'interpolation' in the Reichstag. While this step alarmed those pro-Japanese groups which thought it might harm German–Japanese relations, the interpolation was never officially answered in the Reichstag. However, von Neurath did refer to it in his speech of 20 January 1933 before the Foreign Policy Committee of the Reichstag. He reiterated the main lines of his speech at Geneva on 7 December 1932, refusing thereby to accuse Japan of aggression in the Far East. Yet he went beyond his Geneva speech by emphasising that Germany was not involved in the conflict since after the Treaty of Versailles her interests in the Far East had been restricted to economic ones only. Furthermore, Germany had no interest in action unless the other powers united in action as well. Since von Neurath knew full well that Germany was even less able than the other powers to consider 'action' in the Far East, this implied not only a reaffirmation of German neutrality in the dispute, if not benevolent neutrality, but also the clear desire to keep open the line to Tokio. Four days later, however, von Neurath was able to assure the Chinese Minister that Germany stood by her policy of neutrality and China need not fear that 'we would speak one-sidedly in favour of Japanese arguments'.[57]

By that time, however, it had become patently clear that only Japan would argue 'one-sidedly' in her favour. By the beginning of February 1933 the Special Committee of Nineteen had virtually abandoned its attempts to conciliate China and Japan, and had begun to prepare a Draft Report under paragraph 4 of Article 15. At the same time warnings were heard from Japan that if things went against her she might be forced to withdraw from the League. The Draft Report was circulated to League members on 16 February 1933, and it was clear why Japan raised so many objections to it. Part Four, the Statement of Recommendations, made it clear that sovereignty over Manchuria belonged to China and recommended 'an organisation under the sovereignty of, and compatible with, the administrative integrity of China'. The Report also reaffirmed the League's non-recognition doctrine.[58]

The vote in the League Assembly on this Report was therefore of great importance, and Japanese diplomats began their not unexpected round of the chancelleries in order to assess the likely outcome and to canvass support. On 20 February 1933 the Japanese Military Attaché, Lieutenant Colonel Banzai, called on Czibulinski of the Japanese Section in Department IV of the Wilhelmstrasse to request that Germany abstain from voting on the Report at Geneva. He argued that although previously ties with France had been close, in the future the pro-German tendency in Japanese policy could predominate. This feeling would be strengthened if Germany abstained during the forthcoming vote at the League of Nations. Banzai went beyond being a mere supplicant, though, when he warned that the 'favour asked would deserve thorough consideration in Germany's own interests in view of future developments'. This was a clear hint that henceforth Germany, among others, had to recognise the changed balance of power in the Far East and that Japan's friends would soon be listed and counted. Czibulinski, however, refrained from commenting on these remarks.[59]

The reason for Czibulinski's silence became clear four days later. On 24 February 1933 Germany joined the other powers, except of course, Japan (and Siam), in adopting the Draft Report at the League of Nations Assembly. On 27 March 1933 the Japanese government gave notice of its intention to withdraw from the League of Nations. Yet another phase in Far Eastern relations had begun.

Nearer home, however, in Berlin even more significant events for the course of world history had occurred: on 30 January 1933 Adolf Hitler had been appointed Chancellor of Weimar Germany. This was also to have far-reaching implications for Germany's Far Eastern situation and policies since it introduced into that complex a factor that was openly partisan in nature. This was the Nazis' desire for a closer political or even military relationship with Japan, an objective which was to cause tremendous difficulties because of Germany's important interests in China. Almost immediately the pro-Japanese views of the Nazi leadership made themselves felt in the fight over the precise nature of Germany's policy towards Japan's recent creation, Manchukuo.

II

The *Machtergreifung* and Policy Conflicts over Manchukuo 1933–1935

From January 1933 the German Foreign Office worked in an environment of hostility towards it on the part of Hitler and other leading Nazis. Hitler had a deep aversion for the Wilhelm-strasse and the social background of its officials, and once called it 'that omnium gatherum of creatures'.[1] Yet it has been argued that 'after 1932 . . . Hitler did not shove aside the diplomats; their labours were essential to his successes',[2] and that Hitler and von Ribbentrop agreed that the Foreign Office, 'in spite of its antiquated methods and lack of imagination of its leading officials was absolutely indispensable'.[3] This was because Hitler wanted to create the illusion, for some time at least, of a sense of 'continuity' in German foreign policy as a way of confusing his opponents within and without Germany. But the radical nature of the régime and the Party's programme and intentions raised two important issues for the diplomats and other civil servants. How were they to react to the new régime, and what effect would it have on their position and power to formulate or even influence policy?

Von Dirksen, at the time Ambassador to Moscow but later in the year appointed to the post at Tokio, a typical representative of the old ruling class, a faithful civil servant who was also inclined to be somewhat anti-Semitic,[4] wrote in March 1933 to a colleague in the Wilhelmstrasse that 'it is especially the task of us, the professional officials, to do everything in our power to facilitate the National Socialist movement becoming accustomed to government'.[5] Von Dirksen regarded the new situation with some equanimity, and even thought that the National Socialist régime would be good for Germany's internal situation, a view shared by many others in the Wilhelmstrasse who looked forward to a period of 'strong government'. Later, in accordance with his belief 'in German cooperation with whatever country he was assigned to at the moment',[6] he supported Hitler's attempts to culti-vate close relations with Japan in opposition to the basic lines of the Wilhelmstrasse's Far Eastern policy.

Other members of the Foreign Office were not so complacent

or optimistic. Von Prittwitz, German Ambassador to the United States, resigned while the State Secretary, von Bülow, hesitated before deciding to remain at his post in the hope that the worst excesses of National Socialist foreign policy aims could be tempered. Ex-Chancellor Brüning attempted to bring his influence to bear in this matter, and pointed out to von Bülow and others that it would be extremely dangerous for Germany's foreign policy situation if important members of the Foreign Office resigned at that critical period in Germany's history. Much play was made with reference to the situation in 1918.[7] Von Bülow therefore adopted the typically conservative attitude towards the new régime and its exponents when he wrote to von Dirksen that the retention in the government of such personalities as von Neurath as Foreign Minister and von Blomberg as Minister of Defence 'guaranteed the development of political relations as hitherto pursued'.[8] Nevertheless, it cannot be denied that many Wilhelmstrasse officials saw in the Nazis an excellent means of achieving their own heartfelt desire, the swift and decisive overthrow of the hated Versailles system. Von Bülow's own anti-Versailles attitude was well known, and one British report in 1934 spoke of him being *persona grata* with Hitler because, 'like his master, he usually prefers the policy which has "punch" in it'. By 1936 he was being described as an 'obstructionist' whose policy was a 'negative one of "no more concessions"'.[9]

The Foreign Office's ability to maintain its position and influence in the newly-established 'anarchic-impulsive dictatorship' depended to a large extent upon the personality and influence of the Foreign Minister himself. In von Neurath's case, however, the Foreign Office was handicapped in several respects. He was inclined to be 'indolent and leave things to Bülow', and to take 'his vacations more seriously than his official responsibilities'.[10] One authority has stated that his promotion to his office from the ranks of diplomacy was disastrous because it weakened the influence of the Foreign Office in political counsels, the appointment of a civil servant as Foreign Minister emphasising the civil service ideology of unquestioning submission to the authority of the State.[11] The general and widespread criticisms of von Neurath's personality and attitudes have been politely summed up in the phrase that he was not a 'strong defender of Foreign Office prerogatives',[12] although at Nuremberg von Neurath tried to present a picture of a strong Foreign Minister continually opposing Party influence in the formulation of German foreign policy.[13] Yet the basic factor affecting the attitude of the German Foreign Office towards the new German government that took office on 30 January 1933 was summed up by von Weizsäcker at Nuremberg: 'as a civil servant, one does not serve a constitution, but the Fatherland. One serves whichever government and constitution is given the country by the people'.[14] Germany, in particular, was a country where the bureaucracy were 'not educated to ignore and despise the political leadership',[15] and where to ensure their political reliability civil servants were required (after 1919) to swear an oath to the Republic and after the civil service law of 1937 to the 'Führer of the German Reich and People'.[16] Furthermore, after August 1934 Hitler was not only Führer of the Party but also Head of State.

So far as general policy matters were concerned, the Wilhelmstrasse found that the new régime and situation allowed, if not encouraged more than had previously been the case, the proliferation of various agencies and individuals active in the field of foreign policy competing and often in conflict with the established officials and lines of policy of the Foreign Office.[17] From 1933 such people could claim, in the absence of contrary statements from Hitler, that they possessed a *Führerbefehl* to pursue a particular aspect of foreign policy. Likewise, Hitler could use anybody and whichever channels of communication he wished in the field of foreign policy and not simply the usual government ministry, the German Foreign Office or Wilhelmstrasse. As von Weizsäcker put it at Nuremberg, 'in the Third Reich there wasn't really any outstanding personality who did not try to play a part in foreign policy and by his own connections with foreign policies, to impress Hitler and make an impression on him'.[18]

More specifically, the establishment of the Nazi régime was accompanied by a new departure in Far Eastern policy, an 'official', i.e. government inspired campaign of sympathy towards Japan, 'created and duly deepened by all the machinery of Party and propaganda'.[19] This complemented the interest shown in Nazi Germany by many circles in Japan and reflected their need to search for a 'like' nation, with equally revisionist and dynamic foreign policy aims, to share Japan's relative state of self-imposed isolation. As the Director of the

European—American Bureau in the Japanese Foreign Office, Shigenori Togo, put it in the spring of 1933, 'it is therefore advisable that, now the German rightist party is in power, we make efforts to have Germany understand our international position in the Far East, and at the same time promote closer contact in culture and science between the two nations, so that she may not deviate from her traditional neutral attitude towards Far Eastern problems'.[20]

The maintenance of a neutral attitude on Germany's part was not, however, the intention either of the Nazi leadership in Germany or those in Japan who were spreading the net far and wide for new — or even any — allies for Japan in the changed circumstances of 1933. Since 1932 Japan had made it quite clear to the international community that a test of their attitudes and intentions towards Japan lay in the policies which they adopted towards Manchukuo. Manchukuo was thus laid down as 'bait' on the path to the granting of Japan's own political favours, an attitude of mind which too readily presupposed that there might be other nations who could find an identity of interests with Imperial Japan.

An early start was made with Germany in this respect. Despite the Japanese attempt to exclude foreign business from Manchukuo — underlined by those sections of the Economic Construction Programme of 1 March 1933 which decreed that state control would be established in the case of 'important economic activities' and that due emphasis would be placed on cooperation between Manchukuo and Japan[21] — it was hoped to obtain Manchukuo's recognition, and therefore justification for the role Japan claimed in Far Eastern affairs, by holding out to certain countries the promise of particular economic gain in Manchukuo. Yosuke Matsuoka, Japan's erstwhile chief delegate to the League of Nations, went out of his way to praise the work of German industry and science in Manchukuo, and more importantly its prospects there in the future, when he was in Berlin from 3—6 March 1933.[22]

Coincidentally — or deliberately — Matsuoka's hints were accompanied by a visit to the Wilhelmstrasse on 6 March by one Ferdinand Heye, a Far Eastern businessman of some disrepute. It is difficult to judge whether Heye had any close relationship with the Nazi Party before 1933, although in 1931 he contacted Fritz Thyssen, the German industrialist who at the time strongly supported the National Socialists, and who then referred him to his friend Göring. In turn, Göring recommended Heye to the German Foreign Office.[23] Richard Meyer, Director of Department IV who received Heye, was not at all taken by his ambitious and far-reaching plans for an intensification of German economic activity in Manchukuo, based upon the premise of supporting Japan in her Far Eastern enterprises. Heye then astounded Meyer further by stating that he wished to go to the Far East 'as a kind of plenipotentiary and carry on the negotiations there'.[24]

Heye ignored Meyer's advice against going to the Far East but it was not until later that the Foreign Office learned that Heye's activities in Manchukuo during the summer of 1933 had impinged directly on matters of foreign policy. He had apparently offered German recognition of Manchukuo, which he said he could obtain on the strength of his connections with the Nazi Party, in exchange for agreements between German firms and Manchukuoan soya-bean exporters, while he would be granted an export monopoly for soya beans by the Japanese.[25] When he saw von Dirksen, the newly designated Ambassador to Japan, in Berlin upon his return in late September, Heye emphasised that 'keen interest was felt in high party circles in the commercial potentialities of Manchukuo'.[26]

It was only gradually, though, that the Wilhelmstrasse came to perceive that Heye constituted more than a mere irritant, and was in fact part of a much wider threat to its own power and influence in the foreign policy making process and to Germany's more general position and policies in the Far East. In the meantime, and still confident or hopeful that the reins of policy were in its hands, the Wilhelmstrasse continued to react coolly to persistent Japanese hints that Germany would find a fruitful field of economic activity in Manchukuo.[27] Furthermore, and in an obvious attempt to discredit Heye, all known unsavoury details about him were passed by the Wilhelmstrasse to Ministers and senior officials and, through Prince Waldeck, the representative of Hess, to Hitler.[28] When Germany's own withdrawal from the League of Nations on 14 October 1933 led the Japanese Ambassador in Berlin, Matsuzo Nagai, to suggest to von Dirksen that 'the moment had perhaps now come for Germany to recognise Manchukuo', the latter faithfully represented Wilhelmstrasse policy when he replied that Germany's relations with China 'imposed the utmost restraint on us in the question'.[29]

Restraint was not, however, the watchword of Hitler and other Nazi leaders. Hitler now made it clear that he wanted Germany to develop a closer relationship with Japan. On 17 October the Minister of Defence, Werner von Blomberg, indicated to von Dirksen what Hitler was to confirm on the 18th, that Dirksen was being sent to Japan 'to effect a consolidation and development of German–Japanese relations' since Hitler viewed Japan as an important counterweight to the Soviet Union. Hitler instructed von Dirksen to answer any approaches regarding the recognition of Manchukuo with the statement that he was authorised to negotiate on this question in return for economic advantages. The Wilhelmstrasse later disputed all this, but von Dirksen's own attitude during the winter of 1933–34 showed that he at least had no doubts as to the *Führerbefehl* he had received. Besides which, as he was to admit in his memoirs, he 'personally favoured the policy of friendship with Japan'.[30] He later claimed that he had received a similar authorisation from the Foreign Office since when he had reported the substance of his conversation with Hitler to von Neurath and von Bülow, the State Secretary was supposed to have stated that 'caution was necessary and that we should preferably give recognition only half an hour before the others'.[31] In his memoirs, though, von Dirksen stated that in his interview with Hitler the Führer merely 'confined himself to some general phrases without revealing his designs as to his policy towards Japan', and that it was only from von Blomberg that he learned of Hitler's intentions *vis-à-vis* Japan. More to the point was his complaint that 'as usual, the Foreign Office gave me no specific instructions when I took my leave of Berlin'.[32]

Whatever the truth about von Dirksen's interviews with Hitler and von Blomberg, subsequent events made it clear that Hitler had certain positive ideas about German–Japanese relations and that after Germany's withdrawal from the League of Nations he expressed these in such a way as to encourage others to work for their realisation. One month later, involving Thyssen and undoubtedly at the instigation of Werner Daitz, head of the Foreign Trade Section of the Foreign Policy Office of the National Socialist Party (*Aussenpolitisches Amt* or *APA*),[33] the German–Manchurian Import and Export Company was established. Ostensibly intended to coordinate the exchange of German industrial goods for Manchukuoan soya beans, the real purpose of the company was to work towards a German recognition of Manchukuo as a means of improving German–Japanese relations, upon which basis other things might then become possible. Heye was also involved in the enterprise, as were senior Party members such as Göring and Wilhelm Keppler, Hitler's Plenipotentiary for Economic Questions.[34]

Whatever the company's pedigree, and the Party nature of this naturally gave it that much more weight in the Germany of 1933, the Wilhelmstrasse could do nothing to hinder it and its operatives so long as their activity remained in the field of private economics. But Party plans were more ambitious than this. While Daitz claimed to have Hitler's support for the whole enterprise, so far reaching were the company's plans that reference had to be made to the Reichsbank and the Ministries of Food and Economics to discuss the use of foreign exchange and the expected totals of soya bean imports from Manchukuo within the context of Germany's more general economic policies. Of greater political significance for the Wilhelmstrasse was the suggestion by Daitz, based upon his reference to Hitler's support, of the appointment of both an independent Consul General in Manchukuo and a German economic 'overlord'. Daitz and Heye immediately assumed that they had obtained von Neurath's approval, not only for the project itself but also for Heye's elevation to the role of special trade commissioner.[35]

The attempt by Daitz and Heye to obtain some kind of official standing for their new enterprise and plans from the Wilhelmstrasse was supported shortly afterwards by Keppler, who confirmed Hitler's support for the project. He also told Karl Ritter, Director of the Economic Department in the Foreign Office, of Hitler's instructions to enquire whether Germany should continue to treat Manchukuo as part of China and to allow official German representation in Manchukuo to be supervised by the Legation at Peking. Ritter pointed out that to all intents and purposes the Consulate in Manchukuo was independent of Peking's control, but since he knew what Hitler and Keppler were really getting at he emphasised that the Foreign Office's view regarding political relations with Manchukuo was to continue the policy adopted by the other great powers. He made it quite clear to Keppler that while a German recognition of Manchukuo would obviously be welcomed in Japan it would seriously affect Germany's position in China, similar considerations applying also to any large-scale economic agreement with Manchukuo.[36]

The Wilhelmstrasse could hardly fail to recognise either the trend of events or the implications for its own position and that of Germany in the Far East. Von Neurath now decided to step in with his authority as Foreign Minister to deny absolutely the grant of any official authorisation for Heye's activities in Manchukuo. Henceforth Heye was to negotiate simply as a private businessman.[37] Not surprisingly, Daitz tried to circumvent this ruling, which would have an obvious effect on Heye's status and the possible success of his 'mission', by asking Ritter to instruct the Consuls in Manchukuo to refrain from any activity connected with the soya bean trade until Heye had concluded his own negotiations. The Wilhelmstrasse's confidence about its own position in the matter was reflected in Ritter's emphatic refusal of this request,[38] although events in 1934 were to show that this was a Pyrrhic victory. As it was, almost immediately it had to deny a report in the *Journal des Nations* at Geneva on 21 December 1933 which stated that 'an official German representative' was negotiating with Japan and Manchukuo on economic questions and that Germany would be the next country to recognise Manchukuo.[39]

Meanwhile, the Foreign Office had been attempting to develop Germany's economic interests in Manchukuo through more usual and official channels, but without the obviously political overtones of the Heye undertaking. But so difficult was the situation that Meyer wanted Keppler informed of this activity on the part of the Wilhelmstrasse, undoubtedly to deflect any criticisms of 'obstructionism' that Party quarters might direct at the Foreign Office.[40] At the same time, though, the Foreign Office could not deny that the economic aspects of Heye's efforts in the Far East coincided with Germany's economic needs at the time. Germany was struggling to overcome the debilitating effects of the world economic crisis, while her problems were accentuated by a refusal to devalue the mark. This had the effect of over-pricing German manufactured goods in the world's markets at a time when world trade had fallen, along with a fall in the price of primary products. The fact that in the period 1933–39 Germany's foreign trade was to be about one-third of that in the years 1928–29 obviously increased her foreign exchange difficulties,[41] while this situation was naturally reflected in her trade with Japan and Manchukuo.[42]

Apart from a reduction in German exports to Manchukuo, another factor in the relative decline in German—Manchukuoan trade was the imposition of heavy duties on imported lard and margarine, while in 1934 a special permit was required for soya bean imports into Germany. The Balkans also began to play a larger role in Germany's bean-oil trade.[43] Ritter felt that this shift away from total dependence on Manchukuo for soya beans in fact strengthened Germany's position *vis-à-vis* Manchukuoan or Japanese authorities since, he suggested, they would be mistaken 'if they felt that because of Germany's need for soya beans they could treat Germany's demand for increased exports [to Manchukuo] coolly'. But at the same time he did not want any talks on this question to become involved in a wider discussion of Japanese claims respecting the total of trade between Germany, Japan, and Manchukuo.[44]

The Wilhelmstrasse's difficulties with Party officials and hangers-on over policy towards Manchukuo raised more than enough problems of their own, but these were compounded in the winter of 1933/34 by problems from within the diplomatic service. In December 1933 von Dirksen reported from Tokio that Hirota, now Japanese Foreign Minister, had suggested that he might undertake a trip to Manchukuo 'for information at an early date'. While von Dirksen recognised that it was Hirota's ultimate intention 'to bring the Reich Government gradually around to recognising Manchukuo', he recommended the suggestion to the Foreign Office on the grounds of the economic advantages Germany might gain in Manchukuo. In particular, he thought 'it would be a unique opportunity which we should exploit in the interest of the development of German—Japanese relations'. To impress upon the Wilhelmstrasse what he took to be the urgency of the matter, von Dirksen referred to the possibility that France and other countries might recognise Manchukuo and obtain an advantageous position there instead of Germany. He did not think such a visit would 'commit us definitely in any way', while he discounted Chinese susceptibilities in the matter because of her 'offence' in employing emigré Social Democratic officials. Von Dirksen then played what he thought was his most telling card when he referred to 'the Chancellor's

express instructions to indicate, in the course of my endeavours to develop and deepen the German–Japanese relationship, that we are willing to negotiate on the recognition of
Manchukuo'. As von Dirksen later commented, this set off
what was to be 'a somewhat lively exchange of letters'.[45]

Senior Foreign Office officials unanimously and totally
opposed the idea of such a trip, and von Dirksen received
several instructions to treat the matter in a dilatory fashion.
In order not to totally offend Japanese feelings, von Neurath
suggested that the Embassy's economic expert, Secretary of
Legation Karl Knoll, be sent to Manchukuo instead. Hirota
reluctantly agreed to this, while Meyer emphasised to Peking
the purely economic nature of Knoll's projected journey, an
undertaking which the Chinese were bound to take an extraordinary interest in.[46] Having just opposed Heye's pretensions
to official or semi-official status, the Foreign Office could not
allow its policy on Manchukuo to be compromised altogether
by the visit there of somebody with the standing of an
Ambassador. Just what the Wilhelmstrasse was afraid of soon
became clear, and intensified its opposition to von Dirksen's
ideas of closer German–Japanese relations and the political
pretensions of Heye and his Party supporters. Early in January
1934 *Izvestia,* the mouthpiece of the Russian government,
linked the von Dirksen–Hirota meetings with the imminent
recognition of Manchukuo by Germany, and by implication
the gradual alignment of Germany and Japan in world affairs.
Other rumours that Germany was about to recognise Manchukuo, or that through the activities of Heye and Knoll she
was taking preliminary steps towards recognition, were quickly
denied by the Foreign Office.[47] In turn, Keppler denied the
truth of a report from von Dirksen which stated that Heye had
been 'officially empowered' by Hitler and the Economics
Minister, Kurt Schmitt, to negotiate economic questions with
Manchukuo. Keppler's denial to Ritter nevertheless gave the
Foreign Office little comfort since the day after their interview
Alfred Rosenberg, leader of the APA, the Party's chief racialist
theorist, and editor of the Party newspaper *Völkischer Beobachter,* together with Daitz, tried again to obtain official authorisation for Heye from von Neurath. This was refused, and further
instructions to the diplomats in the Far East emphasised both
the private nature of Heye's activities and the Wilhelmstrasse's
opposition to any official pretensions on his part.[48]

Expressions of Chinese concern about the possible effect upon Sino—German relations of a German recognition of Manchukuo,[49] supported by the *Ostasiatische Rundschau* in February and March 1934, tended to reinforce the arguments of the Foreign Office in the somewhat contentious correspondence which, meanwhile, it had been conducting with von Dirksen. The essential point of Foreign Office policy on the subjects of Manchukuo and Japan was stated by von Bülow on 10 January to be that for a long time Germany's rapprochement with Japan 'must lead neither to a common policy which is outwardly recognisable nor to any agreements that are in the nature of an alliance'. This stricture, in turn, dictated a reserved policy with regard to Manchukuo. Further arguments adduced by von Neurath and von Bülow in support of their opposition to von Dirksen's proposed visit to Manchukuo were its possible and deleterious effect upon Sino—German and even upon Russo—German relations, and that everywhere it would be taken as evidence of German support for Japan's expansionist policies. Von Bülow emphasised that while Germany could herself endure a temporary isolation she must avoid the risk of being connected with Japan's policies. Von Dirksen's plea that Japan would 'register the temperature of her relations to third powers' on the basis of their attitude on the subject of the recognition of Manchukuo fell on deaf ears in the Wilhelmstrasse. Nor was the Wilhelmstrasse over-impressed by von Dirksen's arguments about the economic opportunities open to Germany in Manchukuo, its evidence being to the contrary while Knoll's trip would make it 'clear what the Japanese can actually offer us in Manchukuo, and whether they seriously want to do so'. In this correspondence von Dirksen raised the contentious question of the racial issue in German—Japanese relations,[50] and thought that a positive German policy on Manchukuo would go some way towards dispelling Japanese ill-feeling, but von Bülow thought that the Ambassador was over-estimating this resentment. In general, though, what particularly irritated those in the Wilhelmstrasse were von Dirksen's continual references to the instructions he had received from Hitler on 18 October 1933 and he was left in no doubt that his superiors in the Foreign Office considered that not only had he overstepped Hitler's instructions but had even misunderstood them.

Two guide-lines were then laid down for von Dirksen on the

policy to be adopted with regard to Japan and Manchukuo. The most that von Bülow would concede to Japan was 'unobtrusive rapprochement and moderate demonstrations of friendship', but certainly 'no compromising of us by Japan'. On Manchukuo, von Neurath argued that Japan's strong desires to see Manchukuo recognised in fact enabled Germany to judge when the time was right for this and that the question had to be dealt with 'entirely from the point of view of our interests'. In other words, German recognition ought to be 'a trump which we are ready to play at the right time in the political game'. That the Wilhelmstrasse was particularly concerned about Sino–German economic relations was made plain by von Bülow on 9 February 1934: 'it is not possible at present to opt for Japan when one is not sure that she will be the better customer in the long run, and when, on the contrary one definitely knows that with such an option one would seriously alienate the other good customer, China, and possibly lose her'.[51]

While the Foreign Office thus remained unyielding on the recognition issue, totally rejected von Dirksen's attempts to shift German policy and attitudes into a distinctly pro-Japanese direction, and wisely preferred to wait upon Knoll's report before proceeding further, by February 1934 it appeared that the APA had stolen a march upon the Wilhelmstrasse. Although at the beginning of February von Dirksen was once more instructed to emphasise to Heye in Tokio the unofficial and economic nature of his enterprises in Manchukuo[52] – Dirksen himself saw Heye's activities in Manchukuo in a more personal light and saw him as a rival who was trying to bring about the very thing he was, a German recognition of Manchukuo[53] – on 16 February von Neurath informed Ulrich, Deputy Director of the Economic Department in the Wilhelmstrasse, that following representations by Thyssen, Daitz, and Rosenberg, Hitler had empowered Heye to conduct negotiations for the restoration of trade relations with Manchukuo. It appears that Rudolf Hess was the intermediary used by Daitz and the others to obtain Hitler's authorisation for Heye.[54] It was clear that this manoeuvre was intended to pave the way for Germany's eventual recognition of Manchukuo, while Daitz, in conversation with the United States Ambassador, Dodd, thought this might occur sooner rather than later if the United States recognised Manchukuo. Dodd was astonished by this

Party foray into the question and later confirmed with the Wilhelmstrasse that Daitz was, in fact, speaking 'privately'. To Washington, Dodd commented that: 'the party organs are more exercised over the "Manchukuo" question than the Foreign Office. It may also well be that the Japanese considered that their persuasive powers would be better spent on the Nazi Party organs than on the Foreign Office'.[55]

Although von Neurath tried to retain some vestige of Foreign Office authority in the matter by insisting that the telegram investing Heye with authority as Provisional Trade Commissioner should stipulate that agreements he negotiated required the prior approval of the Reich Government before their formal conclusion,[56] it now appeared that the Wilhelmstrasse could do little to hinder Heye, especially if he limited himself to economic affairs. It was hoped, however, that Knoll's journey to Manchukuo and the announcement in February that Germany would establish a trade commissioner's office in Muken on 1 March 1934, with Knoll in charge,[57] would restore to the Foreign Office some measure of influence in the handling of Germany's economic relations with Manchukuo and, by implication, political affairs with Japan.

Surprisingly, the Foreign Office found itself supported by an unexpected ally, Adolf Hitler, in its running difficulties with various Party hacks. Following the publication of a statement on 20 February 1934 in the *Deutsche Diplomatisch Politische Korrespondenz,* the official organ of the German Foreign Office, deprecating attempts to describe Germany's relations with the Far East as anything but normal, particularly with reference to the question of the recognition of Manchukuo and Germany's economic interests there,[58] a less ambiguous and more authoritative statement was issued by the *Deutsches Nachrichtenbüro* (DNB), the official German news agency, on 24 February. Evidently published at the instigation of Hitler, this stated quite clearly that there were no grounds for widely spread reports that Germany was about to recognise Manchukuo. Apart from strengthening the position of the Wilhelmstrasse, it so weakened the position of Heye with Manchukuoan and Japanese officials as to discredit entirely any official pretensions on his part.[59]

While Chinese and Italian enquiries met with a restatement of Germany's non-recognition policy,[60] a report from Trautmann of 2 February and its submission to Hitler by von

Neurath, through Keppler, on the 26th appeared to clinch
the matter for the Wilhelmstrasse. Trautmann (also) totally
dismissed von Dirksen's arguments that Germany would win
Japan's unfailing political support in return for recognising
Manchukuo, that she would be able to reap untold economic
benefits in Manchukuo, and that one did not have to worry
too much about Chinese susceptibilities. Trautmann's view
was that 'even a beginning of negotiations with Japan on the
basis of a political quid pro quo in Manchukuo for economic
advantages would be a step in the wrong direction', and
would place Germany in the position of the 'Moor of Venice
who is advised to go when he had discharged his obligations'.
He thought that Germany should refrain from an active political policy in the Far East, and only in this way did Trautmann feel that Sino—German relations at least would remain
stable while offering the chance of restoring 'sensible' relations
with Russia.[61]

Received on 26 February, Trautmann's report obviously
had no influence on the decision to issue the DNB communique of 24 February. Nevertheless, his arguments about the
maintenance of good Sino—German relations were fundamentally those which had led to that statement, and which
on 27 February forced Hitler to concede that the question
of Manchukuo's recognition was not 'at all acute'.[62] It has
also been suggested that Hitler was influenced against recognition by Rosenberg's arguments that closer cooperation with
Japan would alienate Britain at a time when Germany still
hoped to woo her.[63] The Foreign Office itself not only
maintained, but emphasised, its policy of non-recognition
when it refused to answer a communication of 1 March 1934
from Hsieh Chieh-shih, the Foreign Minister of Manchukuo,
announcing Pu Yi's assumption of the monarchy and expressing a wish for the maintenance of friendly relations with
Germany.[64]

A restatement of the Foreign Office position on the question, which was also intended to wind up the rather lengthy
and contentious discussion between Berlin and the Embassy
at Tokio, was then issued by von Neurath to von Dirksen on
6 March. The instruction makes it clear that the Foreign
Minister probably doubted whether the Ambassador understood or accepted the Wilhelmstrasse's standpoint. So impassioned had von Dirksen's plea been in his eleven-page report

of 15 January for a more positive approach to Manchukuo
and Japan, a report which had crossed in the post with von
Neurath's instructions of 18 January, that on 6 March the
Foreign Minister made it as plain as possible that the instruction of 18 January 'lays down the guiding principles for the
question of recognition of Manchuria (sic); these guiding
principles remain in force until further instructions'. Previous
arguments were repeated, while as he put it, 'a thorough and
cool weighing of all political and economic aspects at this
time speak against recognition'. Irritated by von Dirksen's
constant assertions that Hitler's authorisation for him to
negotiate with the Japanese Government for the recognition
of Manchukuo in return for economic concessions overrode
anything that came from the Wilhelmstrasse, von Neurath
took great pleasure in pointing out that 'I have once again
broached the matter to the Chancellor, and the Chancellor
has once again stated that "the question of the recognition
of Manchuria (sic) so far as he was concerned was not yet at
all acute"'.

But more important were the wider political and strategic
implications for Germany of the steps she took in the Far
East. Von Neurath repeated von Bülow's argument of 10
January that Germany had to avoid any appearance of collaboration with Japan because of unfavourable reactions
elsewhere. Von Dirksen, though, on 15 January had spoken
almost like a true Nazi: 'in our international situation we
must join with those countries which like us are dissatisfied
with the present pattern in which power is distributed. . . .
Since now the premises of the Rapallo policy have disappeared
in consequence of the attitude of the Soviet Union, Germany
will be able to attain a similar success through a rapprochement with Japan, without having to assume the political onus
of the Communist machinations'. Von Neurath rejected this
since it would 'act as a spur to the tendency to place Germany
in the line-up with Japan and to direct the general hostility
towards Japan also against us. In no circumstances must we
expose ourselves to this'. In his view as well the close relationship with Japan desired by Hitler and von Dirksen raised the
risk for Germany of becoming involved in any future war in
the Far East. Like Trautmann, von Neurath felt that both
the Nazi Party and von Dirksen were allowing themselves to
be stampeded in Japan's direction when — from the Foreign

Office point of view — there was no need to be.

Furthermore, von Neurath and the Wilhelmstrasse preferred to secure Germany's economic interests in China by non-recognition than to go for the chimera of economic benefits in a Manchukuo controlled by the Japanese. Von Neurath put at 70 million Reichsmarks annually the expected loss of exports to China through Chinese boycotts if Germany recognised Manchukuo, and this would have to be added to the 'losses which are inflicted on Germany in all markets by Japanese competition'.

Finally, and in no uncertain terms, von Dirksen was told to refrain from pursuing the question of the recognition of Manchukuo any further, although von Neurath did concede that the Ambassador had to follow Hitler's instructions to make it 'your mission to follow attentively the question, keeping yourself informed as to what economic opportunities Manchuria (sic) could offer us and how these could be realised, even without granting long-term credits'. Nevertheless, von Neurath's concluding remarks made it clear that von Dirksen should devote his future energies to following the Wilhelm-strasse's line of thought on Far Eastern matters: 'in any event we intend to retain the initiative in our hands and be in a position to treat the matter dilatorily as we desire, without breaking the threads. It would be the wrong tactic to rush into paying with the hard cash of recognition, which could not be regained, for a promise of dubious economic and political value'.[65] The fact that Germany did not recognise Manchukuo until 1938 is an indication that the Wilhelmstrasse was able to hold its own on this issue for some time and in extremely difficult circumstances.

Although not a great deal was expected from Knoll's report of his trip to Manchukuo from 16 January to 1 February, received in the Foreign Office on 12 March with a covering letter from von Dirksen,[66] the Wilhelmstrasse awaited it with some interest since it was hoped it would provide some points of reference as guidance for future policy on Manchukuo. In several respects the report was a disappointment. Although it contained up-to-date observations there was nothing new or very hopeful in it. Familiar facts and themes were repeated: Japanese control of Manchukuo's economic and political life, references to the fields of trade in which it was thought that Germany could prosper, and the delicate question of how

Germany's trade with Manchukuo could be improved if only she were to grant recognition, and so on. Even von Dirksen had to admit a number of difficulties in the way of pursuing the more favourable aspects of Knoll's report: that the Manchukuoan government would be hard put to institute even a limited programme of expansion, the opposition of Japanese business circles to any improvement of Germany's position in Manchukuo, while any attempt to improve the German—Manchukuo trade balance would be accompanied by Japanese demands for a similar improvement in German—Japanese trade. Another difficulty Knoll referred to was that associated with Heye's suggestion of increasing German exports to Manchukuo in return for soya beans by means of a system of blocked accounts or currency. Knoll pointed out that Manchukuo had no specific foreign currency bank, while the chief banks were owned or controlled by the Japanese.

Although von Dirksen was less pessimistic than Knoll about the prospects for an improvement in German—Manchukuoan economic relations, of greater interest to the Wilhelmstrasse was the not entirely unexpected pressure which had been put on Knoll regarding the association between economic negotiations and the issue of recognition, while some Japanese and Manchukuoan officials in Manchukuo had even gone so far as to suggest the desirability of a closer economic and even political relationship between Germany and Japan.

If things were really as difficult as they appeared to be from Knoll's report and as politically sensitive, then the Wilhelmstrasse felt it was impossible that negotiations with Manchukuo should remain in the hands of someone as disreputable as Heye and who, as Ambassador Nagai pointed out to von Bülow on 9 March 1934, no longer had the confidence of the Japanese authorities. And in fact, it was the contentious question of Heye's status — for the Japanese as much as for the more directly affected officials in the Wilhelmstrasse — which was to bedevil Germany's attempts to resolve her own economic and political dilemma *vis-à-vis* Manchukuo in the following months without at the same time upsetting either the Chinese by appearing to go too far and too fast in Japan's direction, or the Japanese by not going far and fast enough along the path towards Tokio.

Nagai confirmed what von Dirksen had already told the Wilhelmstrasse, that Heye had been spreading stories in 1933 of his ability to obtain Manchukuo's recognition if at the same time firm economic agreements were arrived at. For his part, von Bülow attempted to undermine Heye's position further in Japanese eyes by insisting that Heye was merely the representative of German economic interests and was negotiating with the knowledge but not on instructions of the Reich government, and that in any case Heye's negotiations had nothing to do with the issue of recognition. Two days after Nagai's visit the Commercial Secretary of the Japanese Embassy, Alexander Nagai, made no secret of Japan's desire to see Germany politically compromised over Manchukuo when he rather innocently wondered why Heye's investigations and negotiations could not be transferred to von Dirksen or Knoll. As Strachwitz pointed out, and Nagai knew the answer already, the presence in Manchukuo of either one 'could be politically misconstrued'.[67]

For the moment, in 1934, the Wilhelmstrasse's chief concern remained to avoid upsetting the Chinese because of the expected repercussions in Sino–German economic relations of a premature recognition of Manchukuo. An indication of the possible Chinese reaction to such a step by Germany was signalled by the fact that Chinese firms at Shanghai warned that they were prepared to insert clauses in new contracts with German businesses making such agreements dependent upon the maintenance of Germany's non-recognition policy.[68] The association of German commercial interests in the Far East, the *Ostasiatischer Verein,* also wanted Heye withdrawn since this would 'unquestionably remove any doubt about Germany's position in the Manchukuoan question'. It was also pointed out that 'while Herr Heye . . . is not authorised to negotiate for a commercial treaty, still the distinction between negotiations for a commercial treaty and business negotiations is not understood in China'. The association also felt that the appointment of a trade commissioner in Manchukuo had been unnecessary, and suggested that trade relations with Manchukuo could just as well be improved through diplomatic negotiations with Japan, which in turn would avoid the political disadvantages of something as spectacular or at least noticeable as Heye's enterprise.[69]

No less a person than von Dirksen supported the burden of these complaints. He again informed the Wilhelmstrasse of Heye's promises of recognition during 1933 in return for an export monopoly of soya beans, but his chief complaint concerned Heye's method of negotiating without informing the Embassy and wanted instructions issued that would correct a situation which he felt was 'untenable in the long run'. Shortly afterwards the Consul at Harbin, Balser, went further by suggesting that the mistrust of economic circles in the Far East had to be considered and that Heye had to be recalled.[70]

It was, however, easier to decide that Heye had to be recalled than to put such sentiments into effect. In any case, and as the Wilhelmstrasse was fully aware, theirs was hardly the deciding voice in the matter. When von Dirksen pointed out on 7 April that for the sake of German prestige in the Far East the matter had to be handled rather delicately,[71] he could just as well have been describing the sentiments of the officials in the German Foreign Office. As a preliminary step in the direction of effecting Heye's removal, and based on the reams of complaints the Wilhelmstrasse had received about him, approaches were finally made to Keppler. Interestingly enough, Keppler seemed to share the general misgivings about Heye, and even agreed with Ritter on 19 March about the necessity of his recall from the Far East. But then Keppler criticised the Foreign Office's handling of the matter and suggested that had he been consulted about the telegram of 17 February containing Heye's authorisation he might well have been successful in stopping it. But he seemed more disturbed by the Wilhelmstrasse's apparent laxity in handling Daitz's 'continuous meddling in foreign policy and foreign trade policy'. Ritter had sparked off this complaint by mentioning Daitz's conversation with Ambassador Dodd on the recognition issue,[72] but then tried to defend the Foreign Office's difficult position by the counter-argument that as Party spokesman in the Reich Chancellery it was Keppler's job to keep Party members in line. Finally, though, it seemed as though Ritter had made the Wilhelmstrasse's point forcefully enough since Keppler went so far as to suggest that if von Neurath wished to raise the matter with Hitler he would speak jointly with the Foreign Minister at such a meeting.[73]

By the spring of 1934 complaints about Heye from all sources had even begun to embarrass the Party, so much so that it instigated an investigation by Rudolf Hess. The Foreign Office was only too pleased to provide Hess with all the

damaging material it could find, but in doing so still emphasised its somewhat passive attitude *vis-à-vis* the Party authorities.[74] Apart from numerous and urgent calls from von
Dirksen for Heye's recall, even if only for 'discussions' in
Berlin, there was the more damaging (for Germany's position
and prestige) report from Balser at Harbin received on 18 April.
This contained the written reply of the Manchukuoan Government to Heye's offers, a reply which von Dirksen characterised
as so evasive 'as to approach ridiculing of the German negotiator'. Balser reported the unanimous wish of the Manchukuoan authorities that Heye be recalled and replaced by
somebody else. As H. Kita, the Secretary of the Manchukuoan
Ministry of Trade and Industry commented, they could have
no confidence in Heye who repeatedly combined economic
negotiations with the recognition question and when they
were perfectly aware that Germany had no intention of
recognising Manchukuo in the immediate future. As it was,
on 18 April von Neurath again emphasised to Ambassador
Nagai that Heye had no competence to speak on the political
question of the possible recognition of Manchukuo by
Germany.[75]

Some notion of protocol in the new Nazi State at least
demanded that in its attempts to unseat Heye the Wilhelmstrasse also approached one of Heye's more influential, or at
least well-known, mentors, Fritz Thyssen. Ritter attempted
the impossible on 26 April when, hardly surprisingly, he failed
to persuade Thyssen of the necessity to recall Heye even
though it was obvious that the Manchukuoan and Japanese
authorities had let Heye 'fall' after the DNB communique of
24 February disclaiming any German intention to recognise
Manchukuo. On the contrary, Thyssen maintained his position
and asserted that Heye's action was 'not a matter of private
business but of general policy and power politics'. He went
further when he claimed that closer economic relations
between Manchukuo and Germany was only a 'side issue'
compared to the greater task of aligning Germany with Japan,
a subject he had discussed with Hitler and von Blomberg and
with which Hitler had agreed. Thyssen was probably unaware
of the Wilhelmstrasse's sensitivity on this particular point, and
almost certainly failed to grasp the nuances in Ritter's point
that while the Foreign Office did not want 'to lean one-
sidedly on China in the Far East' it wished, nevertheless, 'to

keep ourselves completely apart from the political tensions there and to maintain our economic position in both countries'. Recognising that the cards were being increasingly stacked against Heye, Thyssen tried a rather desperate throw by suggesting that the Military Attaché at Tokio (Ott) be instructed to report on what he (Thyssen) suggested were the good relations between Heye and the Japanese military authorities. This was to counter Ritter's charges that Heye had even lost the support of the Japanese authorities. Thyssen went further by suggesting that if Heye faced any difficulties in the Far East this had been due to the uncooperative attitude of the German officials there, mentioning in particular the 'bias' shown against Heye by Knoll. That inverterate diarist, Alfred Rosenberg, also took this point up later when he wrote that Knoll's actions constituted the 'plainest treason'.[76] Finally, Thyssen took refuge in the statement that his own attitude on the question would depend upon the results of Hess's investigation into the Heye case.[77]

Unfortunately for Thyssen, Lieutenant Colonel Ott's report on Heye was unfavourable in the extreme. The Military Attaché at the Tokio Embassy detailed the objections of the Japanese General Staff and War Ministry to Heye on the grounds of his general incompetence and, most important of all for an Asiatic people, his clumsy and ill-mannered way of conducting his business. Von Dirksen supported Ott's remarks by stating that 'the foregoing report strengthens me in the conviction that an early recall of Heye is extremely desirable in the interest of German prestige . . . Negotiations have bogged down completely and I am convinced they can no longer be reactivated by Heye'.[78] Yet Dirksen's motives were not entirely altruistic: the 'prestige' he was referring to was that of *Nazi* Germany, not of Germany's more general reputation in the Far East. Once Heye had been removed Nazi Germany would gain some measure of respect in Japanese eyes, thus clearing the path (possibly) for a closer political relationship between the new Germany and the 'new' Japan. This was neither the Wilhelmstrasse's view nor its hope, and it regarded Heye's removal in the more limited sense of being a means towards restoring some semblance of normality and stability to Germany's general position and policies in the Far East.

Yet since it was a *Nazi* Germany after 1933, and given both the character of the Foreign Minister and the nature of Party

support for Heye, it is hardly surprising that the Wilhelmstrasse found it difficult to effect the removal of even a
nonentity such as Heye. Although the Foreign Office possessed
sufficient evidence to damn Heye beyond any doubt, von
Neurath failed to demand unequivocally that the Party
authorities recall Heye and merely requested from Hess a
statement of opinion on his observations that Heye was un-
suitable to conduct the negotiations with Manchukuo. This
was a less explicit statement of anti-Heye views than had
been prepared in the Wilhelmstrasse, while the tendency
simply to let the evidence against Heye speak for itself and
for the Wilhelmstrasse's case against him, was seen yet again
when von Neurath merely forwarded to Hess a copy of von
Dirksen's telegram of 25 May in which it was stated that
Kurusu, the Director of the Commercial Department of the
Japanese Foreign Office, had expressed further disapproval
of Heye's activities.[79]

Matters really came to a head in June 1934 when, for
once, von Neurath stood firm in the face of pressure by
Daitz that a form of confirmation be issued for Heye's
appointment on the grounds of his recent 'success' in concluding a provisional economic agreement with the Manchukuoan
government. While Heye's actions went beyond the limited
authority by which the Wilhelmstrasse felt it had somehow
managed to restrict him, the repercussions and implications
of what he had done were more wide-sweeping. The text of
Heye's agreement was received in the Foreign Office on
12 June, accompanied by telegrams from China and Japan
which added to the wholesale condemnation it met with in
Berlin. It was rejected on both political and economic grounds:
any increase in German imports of Manchukuoan soya beans
was dependent upon an increase of German exports to that
country, and nobody apart from the ever prescient Heye had
the least idea how this could be brought about, particularly
at the rumoured level of over a 100 million Reichsmark trade
agreement. Politically, the chief fear was that China would
regard it as the first step towards a German recognition of
Manchukuo, but the expected complaint on this score by the
Chinese Minister in Berlin was speedily rejected.[80]

On 11 June von Dirksen, while commenting that the agreement was totally useless, ventured the opinion that it had
only been concluded on the Manchukuoan side in order to get

rid of Heye. He also thought that the German government could not possibly accept the agreement and again pressed for the recall of Heye. Meyer supported these views and in turn suggested to Ritter that any agreement concluded would have to be between an agency for oils and fats and the South Manchurian Railway since state treaties between the German and Manchukuoan governments were out of the question.[81]

The straight fight between the Wilhelmstrasse and the *APA* now became much clearer. On 21 June von Dirksen was told to inform Heye that there could be no approval for his agreement and that he should refrain from any further negotiations. Nor was Daitz's telegram of confirmation about Heye's appointment authorised by the Foreign Office, while in any case the termination of his so-called appointment as Reich Commissar was imminent. Von Neurath also felt in a strong enough position to be able to write to Hess on the same day that 'I regret, therefore, that I cannot give the agreement my approval. The way matters are developing definitely requires the cessation of Herr Heye's activities which are politically and economically just as useless as they are harmful'. Apart from elaborating the political and economic arguments against Heye's agreement, von Neurath bitterly complained about Daitz's action in telegraphing Heye about his position against the express wishes of the Foreign Office: 'I must emphatically protest against this manner of conducting official business', and in view of the 'urgency of the matter' asked for an early decision by Hess on his request 'for the termination of the activities of Herr Heye as Reich Commissar'. Ritter supported von Neurath's action by speaking with Thyssen on the necessity for Heye's recall but failed, not unexpectedly, to receive a clear answer. Instead, the industrialist said he first wished to discuss the matter with Zores of the German–Manchukuo Export Company, a colleague of Heye's who had been recalled to Germany to report on developments in the Far East.[82]

Although Ritter was disappointed at Keppler's news on 30 June that he had been unable to discuss the Heye case with Hitler before the latter's departure from Berlin[83] — Hitler was absent from Berlin on more pressing matters, the imminent murder of Ernst Roehm and other S.A. leaders — it is clear that the efforts of the Foreign Office to establish, or at the very least maintain, its authority in a particular field of foreign policy, were having some effect. On 28 June Rosenberg complained to his diary about the Wilhelmstrasse's role in the Manchukuoan question and particularly about Ritter's pressure on Daitz: 'eight months' work, Thyssen's 200,000 RM for nothing, the Führer's authorisation pushed aside'. The following day he went further by blaming Ritter for the 'sabotage action' of the Foreign Office in the matter and stating that 'Ritter is over-ripe for a concentration camp where he could find honest work'.[84]

Nevertheless, the *APA* still seemed confident of its position, and on 29 June Daitz telegraphed Heye describing the instructions issued to von Dirksen on the 21st as 'incomprehensible'. Daitz's telegram ended with the cryptic message: 'continue working'.[85] Thyssen, however, seemed 'much milder and less aggressive' when Ritter and Erdmannsdorff met him and Zores on 20 July. Ritter emphasised the Foreign Office's willingness to be 'reasonable' once it had achieved the termination of Heye's appointment, and if then Thyssen wished to leave him in the Far East as his personal representative instructions would be issued granting assistance to Heye as a private businessman. Thyssen remarked that he had no particular regard for Heye personally, but that he would accept the result of Reich Minister Kerrl's enquiry into the Heye case 'without further ado'. Ritter also promised Zores that his account of the business opportunities open to Germany in Manchukuo would be discussed immediately by the relevant Ministries.[86]

The Foreign Office hoped that the arrangement agreed upon at a Ministerial meeting on 27 July would finally help to clarify the situation. On the basis of a memorandum from the German–Manchukuo Export Company it was agreed that it should negotiate a compensation agreement with Manchukuo, but that it should not claim a monopoly of business there but was to represent German interests generally. So far as the Foreign Office was concerned the important principle was established that Heye and Zores were to negotiate with Manchukuo as private agents of the Company. This in their view effectively ruled out Heye acting as Reich Commissar.[87]

Nevertheless, the general situation remained confused and rather uncertain since it was not until February 1935 that the Wilhelmstrasse obtained the official cancellation of Heye's appointment as Reich Commissar. As it was, the general air of uncertainty only seemed to be exacerbated by repeated and

'urgent' feelers from Manchukuoan sources for the commencement of 'authorised' negotiations with Germany, discussions
which were not to include Heye.[88] By the late autumn of
1934, therefore, two problems still required a solution: the
necessity for a formal and official decision on Heye's status;
and how best to initiate serious economic negotiations with
Manchukuo without infringing the policy of non-recognition
and avoiding the use of Heye as an intermediary.

If, for the time being, the first problem remained unresolved,
despite further Japanese pressure (this time on Hjalmar
Schacht, Minister of Economics and President of the Reichsbank) and with von Neurath once more communicating with
Hess but not being vouchsafed a reply,[89] a way of approaching the second was suggested by von Dirksen in a private letter
to von Erdmannsdorff on 2 November: 'the despatch of a
German economic delegation analogous to the English one'.
This was a reference to the impending visit to Manchukuo of
a British economic mission under the leadership of Lord
Barnby. He thought this would be the best way of bringing
about 'an informal improvement of our trade with Manchukuo
and an analysis of German–Japanese relations; at the same
time it will be the best means of dealing with restrictive intentions [by the Japanese] against our imports'.[90]

This suggestion underlined what was already being admitted
in Berlin, that the Heye–Zores negotiations were not the best
way of taking up Manchukuoan feelers for serious trade talks.
As it was, on 10 November the semi-official Manchukuo News
Service reported that Heye's negotiations for a barter system
between Germany and Manchukuo were 'not progressing
favourably'. This went further by remarking that Manchukuo
could buy better and cheaper manufactured goods from Japan
than from Germany, so why consider purchasing German
goods? The report went on to state that 'certain circles here
are said to believe that Mr Heye represents a certain German
financial group which is supporting President Hitler, and that
he is not a trade representative of the German government'.[91]

But it was only after further reports from von Dirksen in
December 1934 that a way out of the maze that engulfed
Germany's Manchukuoan policy was at last seen and pursued.
On 5 December von Dirksen once more posed the question of
the future course of German policy towards Manchukuo:
'there are two possibilities: either we wait upon a successful

outcome of the Heye–Zores negotiations, and in the case of their failure show the cold shoulder to Manchukuo by limiting German purchases of soya beans and expanding purchases elsewhere; or alternatively, attempt to improve the trade balance by means of talks of any kind with Manchukuo'. He clearly considered the second to be the more viable proposition, but in turn this raised further questions: how to pursue discussion with Manchukuo so that influential Japanese economic circles in Manchukuo were also involved, and in this way avoid possible Japanese counter-measures in German–Japanese trade relations; and secondly, how to conduct the talks without compromising Germany on the recognition issue, especially *vis-à-vis* China.

Von Dirksen thought the answer lay in sending an economic mission to the Far East, led by a private businessman who would, nevertheless, represent the whole of German industry and commerce, to discuss issues of German–Japanese as well as German–Manchukuoan trade. In his view such a mission would be ideal for discussing these involved questions 'in a flexible manner without requiring an official commitment on either side'. Although he considered the matter to be an urgent one, he was still worried in case it appeared as though Germany was treading in the footsteps of Britain and France. As a further argument in support of his proposals, he stated that Japanese military authorities in Manchukuo had more influence there than Japanese economic interests, and the former were favourably inclined towards an increase of German activity in Manchukuo.[92]

More telling arguments were contained in von Dirksen's report of 8 December in which he described the 'situation of total confusion' surrounding Heye and the question of his status, while a 'new jolt' had been given to his personal position and his negotiations in Manchukuo because of his journey to Berlin to report 'to his Berlin department' on his position as Reich Commissar. In these circumstances no progress could be expected in the Heye–Zores negotiations for a compensation agreement. Nor had matters been helped by the great enmity which existed between Heye and Zores, while Heye's exclusion from the aviation negotiations in Tokio and their handling by Zores had certainly exacerbated this aspect of the matter. Once more Dirksen emphasised that there were opportunities open to Germany in Manchukuo, if only definitive negotiations were begun and without the meddling hands of Heye. Von Dirksen therefore urged the Wilhelm-strasse to act fast and firmly, to take the matter up with the relevant Ministries before Heye arrived in Hamburg on 18 January 1935 when he could be expected to set out to justify his own position and so discredit that of his opponents.[93]

While von Dirksen further reported on Japanese feelers to Krupp's representative in Japan, Herr Lemke, about participation in an industrial project at Mukden with a Japanese concern, Iyogumi,[94] his report of 5 December was discussed at a Ministerial meeting on 22 January 1935. It was agreed that since Germany was not in a position to state definitely what levels of soya bean she could import from Manchukuo, while on the other hand there existed no reason to limit such imports, there was to be no new German initiative but that proposals would be awaited from the Manchukuoans and Japanese. In his telegram of 25 January to von Dirksen, Ulrich emphasised that there was no intention to show Manchukuo the 'cold shoulder' but that Germany's attitude was based on her lack of foreign exchange, although she still wished to continue her purchases of Manchukuoan soya beans. As to the despatch of a German economic mission to Japan and Manchukuo, again Ulrich emphasised that it was intended to await further proposals from the other side. Moreover, 'the predominant feeling here is that although a private journey of influential economic personalities to Japan and Manchukuo is extremely desirable, the combination of such private journeys in a formal German economic mission would have, at the least, a semi-official character and would not facilitate the achievement of their purpose'. In accordance with this attitude of reserve Ulrich further informed von Dirksen on 30 January that the suggested visit of an expert to the Far East in connection with the Iyogumi business could perhaps be taken up once it was clear who was behind the proposals and what the attitude was of official Japanese and Manchukuoan circles.[95]

Finally, though, the general situation was to be changed by the information contained in the letter which Foreign Minister von Neurath sent Reich Minister Hess on 4 February 1935: 'the Führer and Chancellor has informed me that he is completely withdrawing his support from Herr Heye . . . the Commission granted to Herr Heye in February 1934 as temporary German Commissar to initiate commercial relations between Germany and Manchukuo is therefore to be regarded as terminated with immediate effect'.[96] Although the evidence is lacking, it must be presumed that von Neurath had obtained this decision from Hitler through the intermediary of Keppler. By that time nobody, including Hitler, could ignore the absurdities and difficulties caused by Heye, but as will be shown there were other considerations in German—Japanese relations which influenced him in the direction of support for the stand so long advocated by the Wilhelmstrasse.

The Foreign Office thus gained its victory over the *APA* in the matter, but almost immediately the latter tried to get another Reich Commissar sent out in Heye's place. This attempt was immediately squashed by von Erdmannsdorff. Von Dirksen followed up this success by repeating his suggestion that an economic mission be sent to Manchukuo; or, if it was desired that contact with Manchukuo should be of a more permanent nature, such contact should be made through an official of the Foreign Office.[97]

By the beginning of 1935, therefore, the general direction of German policy towards Manchukuo was once more firmly in the hands of the Foreign Office. As von Dirksen later noted, 'from that time onward Manchukuoan affairs were dealt with in the regular way'.[98] In the final analysis, though, Heye's removal from 'office' had been due more to his own personal inadequacies and the storm of criticism he had aroused in the Far East than to the efforts of the Foreign Office alone. These efforts, both intense and persistent, had been insufficient by themselves to effect Heye's removal. Even allowing for the difficulties of the Wilhelmstrasse's position in the Nazi State, and with respect to the complex of Germany's Far Eastern relations, these efforts might have had a better chance of success had they not suffered from the burden of the personality and official attitude of the Foreign Minister, von Neurath. As it was, the *raison d'être* of the Wilhelmstrasse's careful handling of the Manchukuoan issue, the avoidance of a closer German—Japanese relationship, was to be nullified from 1935 by the 'amateur' diplomacy of its *bête noir*, von Ribbentrop, with the Japanese military authorities.

III

German Interests in China 1933-1935

The conflict which ensued after January 1933 over the nature of Germany's policy towards Manchukuo — a struggle more about policy towards Japan — highlighted some of the differences between the German Foreign Office and the Nazi leadership over what constituted Germany's political interests and intentions in the world (and the Far East) after the Nazi *Machtergreifung*. In opposing what it regarded as the headlong rush of the Nazi leaders into the arms of Japan, the Wilhelmstrasse argued that Germany had to avoid any political commitments in the Far East. In practice this only meant avoiding a political commitment to Japan since Germany, like any other western nation, would have regarded the notion of a political agreement or alliance with Republican China as absurd in the extreme. But there was much more to it than the simple desire to remain a kind of 'neutral' in the Far Eastern maelstrom, as everybody concerned knew full well. The Wilhelmstrasse argued that Germany had an important economic basis in China whose excellent prospects for the future could not — indeed should not — be jeopardised for the chimera of a possible future German–Japanese agreement, alliance, understanding, or whatever else was envisaged by those who desired such a thing. Nor was the Wilhelmstrasse alone in arguing the case for a special consideration for China in Germany's foreign relations. The Reichswehr Ministry likewise argued that Germany's increasingly involved and important military commitments with China would also be threatened by any untoward political move or gesture in Japan's direction. Interestingly enough, it was the Wilhelmstrasse which often opposed the Reichswehr Ministry over that Ministry's involvement in China, because the Foreign Office feared that such activity would disturb the more normal pattern of German–Japanese relations.

The arguments propounded in turn by the Wilhelmstrasse and the Bendlerstrasse themselves raised a legitimate question often posed by the Nazi leadership: what benefits, political and practical, did Germany's interests and involvements in China actually gain her in the real world of 1933 and beyond which seemed to outweigh the benefits which might accrue from a closer German–Japanese relationship, especially given Germany's apparent state of isolation on the one hand and the long-term political aims and ambitions of the Nazi leaders on the other?

Any answer clearly lay in the specifics of the relationship between Germany and China. But from the beginning of 1933 two further questions came to affect and therefore shape the individual issues in Sino–German relations in addition to those normally posed in any set of foreign relations: how did the management and development of those particular issues serve the special interests and purposes of either country? The two additional considerations to be taken into account were, firstly, the effects on Germany's foreign policy of the Nazi assumption of power, and secondly, Japan's new status and possible ambitions in the Far East. The two main points of focus to Sino–German relations, economic and military matters, were directly and especially affected by these new developments in the international positions of Germany and Japan.

The economies of Germany and China naturally complemented each other in that one was largely industrial and the other agricultural and a supplier of raw materials, much of which the German army and arms manufacturers required for the rearmament of the Reichswehr. After January 1933 and Hitler's statement in February that for the next four to five years 'the main principle must be everything for the armed forces',[1] a country like China which could supply such vital ores for rearmament as antimony and wolfram (for tungsten) became of even greater importance to Germany. But there were problems. One consequence for Germany of the domestic and international economic crises since 1929 was ever increasing difficulty in being able to pay her way in the world market, with exports failing to keep pace with imports. With a consequent diminution of her reserves of foreign exchange this posed an ever present threat to essential imports, especially to those which the Nazi leadership regarded as more vital than anything else, imports of raw materials vital for Germany's rapid rearmament.

Whether the solution which emerged under the Nazis as a means of dealing with Germany's chronic economic state in the wake of the world economic crisis was one which would have been attempted under any other form of government in Germany is hard to determine. It is a fact, however, that the advent of the Nazi régime affected the management of Germany's foreign trade (including that with China) in several significant ways and was designed to bring about a 'defence economy' situation. By 1934 control boards had been authorised to fix quotas for the purchase of foreign raw materials, while later that year the Reichsbank applied a system of foreign exchange allocations. By this method imports of materials needed for rearmament were safeguarded at the expense of supplies for consumer industries, the Reichsbank thus disposing of foreign exchange according to the government's list of priorities. But in order to obtain the essential imports it was necessary to maintain exports at all costs, and this was achieved with the development of a system of export subsidies, barter agreements and clearing arrangements. This was the essential element of Schacht's New Plan of September 1934, a monopolistic foreign trade scheme designed to maintain the import of raw materials in the face of the depletion of Germany's foreign exchange, which had reached crisis proportions by 1934.[2]

These methods were generously applied in the China trade, including two variants of the barter trade: compensation arrangements and the use of ASKI (*Ausländersonderkonte für Inlandszahlungen*) marks. These allowed for the payment of subsidies as compensation for low prices, and for the direct control and utilisation of foreign exchange. Trautmann, however, warned against a policy of sanctioning too many barter agreements and a too ready policy of Reich guarantees against loss since he felt this was not in the interests of 'the normal trade of German businessmen in China', particularly in those areas of trade not covered by such guarantees. Yet by 1935 both the Shanghai Chamber of Commerce and Kriebel, the Consul General at Shanghai, were claiming that 'compensation allowances' had made possible the success of German exports to China and that the elimination of such arrangements would paralyse this trade.[3]

Despite many difficulties and uncertainties Sino—German trade and German economic activity in China increased after 1933. Although German exports to China declined in value during 1933 and part of 1934, by 1937 they had more than doubled those of 1933; by 1936 China rose to third place of all Germany's export markets outside Europe. Furthermore, while the value of German exports to China almost doubled between 1933 and 1936, Germany's total exports in 1936 were less in value than those of 1933.[4] It would be hard to determine how much of this success story was due to mutual need and how much to Nazi methods of foreign trade policy, but the benefits to both countries of the combination of these elements became increasingly obvious.

In 1933 and beyond, though, the question of Sino–German economic relations was also connected with China's attempt to internationalise her own 'reconstruction' or efforts to leap into the twentieth century. Germany, like Britain and America, was also seen as a suitable and prospective partner for this ambitious enterprise, so that for a number of reasons Germany and China had cause to pay some special regard to each other in the field of economic cooperation. As part of the continuing efforts of the Chiang Kai-shek régime to combine attempts to gain economic as well as political support from the rest of the world, excluding Japan, the Chinese Minister of Trade and Industry, Dr H. H. Kung, visited Germany in January 1933. Given his political position in China the German authorities acceded to Chinese requests that he be received by President Hindenburg and Foreign Minister von Neurath. Efforts were made to see that he met a wide circle of economic and industrial leaders, while from the Chinese side it was repeatedly emphasised that Germany could play an important role in China's industrial redevelopment. Yet von Bülow tried to keep this aspect of Germany's relations with China separate from more contentious issues, and consequently adopted an attitude of reserve with Kung over Germany's policy towards current developments at Geneva in connection with the Manchurian Crisis.[5]

At the same time the Germans also felt it politic to invite the Chinese Finance Minister, T. V. Soong, brother-in-law of Chiang Kai-shek, to visit Germany later in the year on the occasion of his journey to London for the World Economic Conference, the intention being to reinforce the effects of Kung's visit by emphasising Germany's interest in the maintenance of good Sino–German relations in the wake of the difficulties caused by the Manchurian Crisis. The Foreign Office made careful preparations for Soong's visit, and as Altenburg wrote to Dr Mohr, President of the *Ostasiatischer*

Verein, because of the shortness of the visit the contacts with economic and industrial leaders would have to be limited to the 'cream of the cream'. Soong himself expressed a wish to meet Schacht and to be informed about the reorganisation and re-equipment of the Reichswehr. As it was, Trautmann recommended that any negotiations pursued in Berlin with Soong should be conducted by Schacht because of the contact already made between the two men in London.[6]

There were two points to be considered in Berlin: what did the Chinese expect of the visit, and what did the Germans expect? An opportunity to examine these questions was provided by a report from Trautmann received in Berlin on 12 June 1933. It appeared that while Soong was prepared to discuss China's industrial reconstruction with the relevant German authorities, his real purpose was to obtain long-term credits. Since this would deeply involve the German government, Trautmann expressed his reservations about the advisability of such a course, based on the uncertainties of the situation in China: the 'critical' situation in North China where Japanese troops were 'pacifying' Jehol (Trautmann wrote on 19 May, twelve days before the Tangku Truce of 31 May 1933), the divided state of the Chinese Government itself, the split between the northern and southern factions of the government, and the continuing anti-communist campaigns of the government. Trautmann felt it important that the Berlin conversations with Soong should be limited to 'practical' matters, i.e. those with some chance of success or realisation, with there being only a brief mention of other and wider fields of cooperation, e.g. the credits question. But he was clearly concerned about the pressure that would be exerted over the credits question, and warned the Wilhelmstrasse about 'the danger of allowing ourselves to be driven further and further by interested circles (as happened with the Russian credits) into a situation where, in order to avoid political bad feeling, we must finally accept what the interested parties of both nations desire'.[7]

These points were taken up in a departmental discussion in Berlin on 27 June when it was agreed that concrete business arrangements with China were possible so long as the stability of the Nanking régime was assured, and that sufficient security was offered for German capital. Technical questions regarding Chinese security for credits and the length of the period of credit were also to be discussed with Soong, while Michelsen, Deputy Director of Department IV, believed that the government should adopt a positive approach towards these questions. In any case, it appeared that Soong himself thought the moment opportune for approaching Germany on economic questions since the Chinese felt that Germany was searching for a 'substitute for the Russian market' as a result of the noticeable worsening of Russo–German relations consequent to January 1933.[8]

T. V. Soong visited Germany from 21–26 July 1933 and during that time held discussions with officials from various Ministries and with industrial leaders but, interestingly enough, was unable to meet any Reich Ministers. At the Foreign Office Soong raised the question of his recent proposals for a 'consultative committee' for the reconstruction of China by obtaining further credits for China, which was to consist of prominent financiers and businessmen divided evenly between Chinese and foreigners; he also intended it to replace the Banking Consortium organised in 1920 for the same purpose. Soong was told that the German Government was prepared to cooperate with the new committee, as was the Reichsbank. Both sides expressed willingness to cooperate in the future reconstruction of China, while the Germans impressed upon Soong and his associates that their greatest concern was for the security of any credits granted to China. It was finally suggested that Soong draw up a memorandum setting out his proposals so that the German government could consider its attitude towards them.[9]

The Foreign Office admitted that the visit had achieved very little in the way of practical results except to have impressed upon Soong evidence of Germany's goodwill towards China.[10] But even this was no small achievement given the almost universal Chinese attitude of suspicion towards all western powers throughout the Manchurian Crisis, while early Chinese reaction to the nature of the Nazi régime in Germany during 1933 had been rather critical although public comment in China on the new Germany gradually became more favourable.[11] Interestingly enough, when Germany withdrew from the League of Nations and the Disarmament Conference in October 1933, some Chinese argued that any blame for this action rested not with Germany but with the League Powers for denying her legitimate demands for equality. On

16 October 1933 Trautmann was assured of China's sympathy for Germany's difficulties in international affairs by no less a person than Wang Ching-wei, President of the Executive Yuan.[12]

Despite the increasing importance of China to Germany's foreign trade, the Foreign Office adopted an attitude of extreme reserve towards the idea of state guarantees for far-reaching German undertakings in China. The reason for this was less a degree of apprehension about possible Japanese reactions, for as Trautmann was to point out later to the Japanese Consul General, Suma: 'Japan . . . could not really have any objections to the economic activity of other powers here. This resulted from the policy of the Open Door and was important to us in this period of the severest economic depression, when Japan was the only power that was prospering, while the trade of the others was declining more and more. This argument had to apply principally to such powers, like ourselves, who pursued no political aims in the Far East'.[13]

As von Bülow explained on 27 September 1933 to Gustav Krupp von Bohlen, President of the *Reichsverband der Deutschen Industrie,* the Foreign Office's attitude of reserve was based on a fear of radical changes in internal conditions in China affecting the country's economic stability and foreign investments. Not that this could be said to the Chinese, for when the Chinese Minister had visited von Bülow on 18 September to inform him of the exchange of letters between T. V. Soong and Krupp von Bohlen regarding Sino–German economic cooperation, the State Secretary added that 'a participation of the Reich Government in the agreements was inevitable later on because of the credit and currency questions involved'.[14]

Nevertheless, Foreign Office approval of Reich guarantees for trade with China was one of its main weapons against what it regarded as the distinctly political – and implicitly anti-Japanese – question of Germany's participation in China's rearmament. Not only was China important to the German armaments industry as a supplier of vital raw materials, but she rapidly became a ready market for the products of the German armaments industry, which in turn helped to maintain employment and develop technical excellence in that industry in Germany which had suffered from a lack of domestic orders under the restrictions imposed by the Treaty of Versailles — and in exchange for which important raw materials were obtained. But the ability of the Foreign Office to block, or at least restrict, this trade in armaments and therefore Germany's involvement in China's military affairs by opposing Reich guarantees for it depended, in the final analysis, upon wider issues in Germany. And the wider scene, and therefore limitations upon the Foreign Office's freedom to act in this particular respect, had already been set earlier in the year when Hitler, on 3 February, outlined his political ideas to Germany's military leaders, emphasising his intention to rearm on a large scale, reintroduce conscription and establish an authoritarian state in which the military would enjoy their old privileged position. Five days later he emphasised to the Reich Cabinet that for the next four to five years 'the main principle must be everything for the armed forces'. He also made the point that Germany's standing in the world was 'decisively conditioned upon the position of the German armed forces' and that, therefore, 'the position of the German economy in the world was also dependent on that'.[15]

It was perhaps fortuitous for German military interests that the winding-up of military collaboration with Russia during 1933 coincided with serious Chinese efforts in the direction of rearmament and economic reconstruction. Already in the spring of 1933 the ground was explored by Vice-Admiral Kinzel, a specialist in naval weapons recently retired from the Reichswehr Ministry, who had been sent to China on behalf of several German firms to investigate the possibilities of trade in weapons with the Nanking Government and the supply of arsenals. He explained to Trautmann that there were two serious difficulties in the way of an expansion of German arms exports to China: Germany's official representatives appeared to give no help in the matter, while German arms were more expensive than those from other countries.[16]

Kinzel elaborated these points in a report for the Foreign Office, and emphasised that because of the officially restricted nature of Germany's armed forces the German arms industry could not maintain its technical development without the aid of regular orders from abroad. The report was received in the Wilhelmstrasse on 9 August 1933 and rejected,[17] but by this time the question of German arms deliveries to China had taken a more official turn with requests by German firms for

Reich guarantees for this trade, to which the Foreign Office had responded coolly. On 30 June Director General Eltze and Major Pabst (one of the leaders of the Kapp Putsch of March 1920) of the Rheinmetall concern, an armaments firm controlled by the Reichswehr Ministry, approached Michelsen about a Reich guarantee to cover part of the delivery to China of an order for machine guns to the value of 10 million Reichsmarks, the initiative for the order apparently having come from T. V. Soong. This fact, and Soong's impending official visit to Germany a few weeks later in July, made any German failure to meet the order extremely awkward and Eltze and Pabst made it quite clear to the Wilhelmstrasse that 'the Reichswehr Ministry took great interest in the delivery being affected'. For his part Michelsen explained the Foreign Office's objections to German arms deliveries to China and to the grant of Reich guarantees for such trade: they involved Germany, officially, in the vagaries of China's domestic politics and perennial civil wars, while Japan's reactions had to be taken into account. He also emphasised that a recent inter-departmental meeting had agreed that deliveries of war material 'must remain excluded, as in the past, from the granting of Reich guarantees against loss'.

This did not deter the gentlemen from Rheinmetall and on 6 July Major Pabst suggested a possible compromise to Michelsen. Following talks between Eltze and State Secretary Feder of the Reich Economics Ministry it was proposed that the Solothurn Company appear to the Chinese as the seller of the arms, with Rheinmetall selling the materials to Solothurn and the Reich guarantee covering only the issue of promissory notes from Solothurn to Rheinmetall. Solothurn was a Swiss firm controlled by Rheinmetall to provide a convenient cover for its various and often 'illegal' activities, but given the Reichswehr Ministry's control of Rheinmetall this showed just how far that Ministry's influence extended. Michelsen promised to put this suggestion to 'a higher authority' for a decision, but in his memorandum to the Acting State Secretary at the time, Gerhard Köpke, he opposed this course: he did not want the Foreign Office to become involved in the arms trade since this would make it impossible for it to continue to deny any official support for the trade, while approval in this case would, it was felt, open the floodgates to other similar requests. Michelsen asked for and obtained Köpke's approval to refuse Rheinmetall's request.[18]

Trautmann was equally guarded about the whole subject of arms trade with China and its proposed financing by credit agreements. His doubts were intensified following Consul Wagner's report of his journey through Kwangsi Province, and where the question of German participation in arsenal plans was discussed. Wagner's findings, that because of its relative poverty the province was not in a good position to offer Germany the necessary financial security needed for credit agreements, were later complemented by Kriebel's negative conclusions after investigating the situation in Fukien, Kiangsu, Kiangsi and Anhwei.[19] On 24 August Trautmann wrote to von Bülow supporting the Foreign Office stand by arguing that the Wilhelmstrasse should keep its distance from the arms trade since this business annoyed the Japanese. Furthermore, he admitted that 'our ideas of economic expansion cause me some anxiety here too', and again referred to his opposition to the previous policy of granting credits to Russia. He agreed with the conclusions reluctantly arrived at in Berlin, that the greatest concern was to find 'positive guarantees' for the trade with China, and as he concluded, 'I take the stand: rather a small but sound deal, than a risk that robs one of one's sleep. If for reasons of internal policy you wish it otherwise, you must so command'.[20]

In the meantime the Reichswehr Ministry returned to the attack and on 26 September informed the Wilhelmstrasse of its own reply to Admiral Kinzel's letter of 10 July. Up to a point this satisfied the Foreign Office since it was pointed out to Kinzel that so long as the laws against the export of arms remained in force Germany's diplomatic representatives could not officially support the arms trade. There then followed an important and significant claim, and one which gave the Foreign Office clear warning of the firm attitude which the Reichswehr Ministry was clearly going to adopt with regard to Germany's military interests in China: 'they could, nevertheless, through confidential discussions with influential personalities promote orders, but only when the mediation has been suggested by the Reichswehr Ministry'.[21]

Not only was this meant to underline the role of the Reichswehr Ministry in the question of arms sales to China, but virtually implied that the initiative for diplomatic support of this trade rested with it and not the Foreign Office. This was clear evidence of the army's growing strength and confidence in

German politics. It also placed the Foreign Office in a difficult position over its reservations about diplomatic support for arms sales to China since even it could not deny the economic and military benefits for Germany from such trade. When, additionally, the Chinese government expressed great interest in the conclusion of arms deals with German firms, this further embarrassed the Foreign Office. As it was, the day after the Foreign Office learned of the Reichswehr Ministry's standpoint was the day (27 September) that von Bülow explained to Krupp von Bohlen the Wilhelmstrasse's attitude of reserve over credits for the China trade. But Krupp von Bohlen had visited the Foreign Office to obtain official reactions to his exchange of letters with T. V. Soong about trade with China, which included the delivery of an arsenal by the Krupp organisation to the Chinese government, as well as to enquire about the prospects of obtaining government credits to facilitate the export of a whole host of German industrial products to China.[22] In reply, von Bülow repeated the arguments put foward in a memorandum by Michelsen of 25 September which criticised Chinese requests for a credit period of ten years and doubted the value of guarantees offered by the Central Bank of China, an institution closely involved with the Chinese government. If Krupps persisted in the arsenal project it was suggested that security be obtained from other Chinese sources such as the Bank of China, an independent bank. Von Bülow therefore argued with Krupp von Bohlen for the individual treatment of each enterprise, for a limitation of their scope, and for great caution in negotiating the necessary guarantees.[23]

An attitude of caution was also seen on the Chinese side. Since many of the matters discussed between Soong and Krupp von Bohlen concerned China's 'national defence', Soong refrained from giving the German government an official memorandum because 'Japan might easily take umbrage at German—Chinese governmental negotiations'. Instead, individual questions would be taken up 'at the proper time'.[24]

By November 1933, though, the Foreign Office was again under pressure from the Reichswehr Ministry which, in pursuance of its letter of 26 September, again pressed for Foreign Office support for the sale of arms from Rheinmetall to the Chinese Central Government. This time Trautmann was instructed to support the idea of such sales in his talks, but although he carried them out Trautmann thought the instructions were superfluous in view of the favourable position the German arms firms had already established for themselves in China, reinforced by and reinforcing the (contentious) position of the German military advisory staff at Nanking.[25]

At the same time the Foreign Office felt that its policy of reserve on the arms question was justified by an official Note from the Nanking Government requesting that no arms be delivered to the rebellious régime of Ch'en Ming-shu, Ts'ai T'ing-k'ai and Li Chi-shen in Fukien which had been set up in November 1933, and which was crushed by Chiang Kai-shek's forces in January 1934. The incident clearly underlined the Foreign Office's point about the dangers of becoming involved in Chinese domestic affairs through the arms trade. This point was again underlined by another Chinese Government Note of 21 April 1934 requesting foreign governments to ensure that all arms shipments to China had previously received the approval of official Chinese representatives abroad. This Note went further by requesting foreign governments to forbid any 'unauthorised' arms shipments to China, but this was dismissed out of hand by Kühlborn, by then responsible for China in Department IV, in a marginal comment on the communication from the Chinese Legation in Berlin.[26]

None of this altered the fact that the big German armaments firms were pursuing arms deals with China, and that if matters were not handled carefully enough there could be serious repercussions in German—Japanese relations, a constant concern of the Wilhelmstrasse (something the Nazi leadership often overlooked in their criticism of the diplomats for being too pro-Chinese in outlook). That this complex situation could work both ways was seen by the complaints from Krupp representatives in China that rumours of Germany's recognition of Manchukuo were damaging the prospects for the arsenal project with the Nanking Government which that firm and the Reichswehr Ministry were intent on pursuing. Even Keppler was brought into the matter and on 13 March 1934 requested von Neurath to inform the Chinese government of the lack of truth of such rumours. Keppler, like Trautmann was also concerned at the effect of such rumours on the more normal pattern of German trade with China.[27] Nevertheless, and undoubtedly influenced by the Amau statement of 17 April 1934, a clear warning by Japan to the other powers not to support China against Japan,[28] the Foreign Office maintained its previous policy of reserve and opposition and in April 1934 declined to support attempts by Solothurn to conclude an arms credit deal worth 20 million Reichsmarks with the Chinese government.[29] That the Foreign Office's power to influence such matters was limited was shown by the fact that on 17 May Trautmann reported on Chiang Kai-shek's decision to purchase only German arms, and on negotiations between him and Solothurn for the sale of twenty-four 15cm heavy field howitzers which had been released by the Reichswehr Ministry for China. Although von Seeckt was then in China to promote closer military relations with Germany, he too expressed his opposition to such arrangements.[30]

For its part, the Reichswehr Ministry left the Foreign Office in no doubt about its responsibility for arms deals with China and its determination to see them executed. On 15 September 1934 Major-General Liese, Chief of the Army Ordnance Office (*Heereswaffenamts*) informed the Foreign Office that on 11 September he had been told by the Chinese Legation in Berlin that the Chinese Government had finally awarded the howitzer contract to Rheinmetall. Of equal importance was Liese's reply to points raised in Meyer's letter of 11 September concerning a division of the arms trade in China between Rheinmetall and other interests. Meyer had approved the division suggested to Trautmann by representatives of Krupps-Bofors, the Swedish part of Krupp, for whom the German firm of Carlowitz had been promoting arms talks with Chiang Kai-shek. Carlowitz had apparently argued that Rheinmetall were unable to produce 15cm howitzers, and that in any case such arms deliveries were prohibited to Germany under the terms of the Treaty of Versailles.[31] While the suggested division of the arms market in China was to leave Rheinmetall without any competition on the howitzer contract, Liese emphasised to Meyer that despite its links with Krupp, the Bofors Company had to be considered a foreign firm.[32] As it was, the matter of competition in the Chinese arms market had to be thrashed out at a meeting at the Reichswehr Ministry between Rheinmetall, Krupp, and Carlowitz.[33]

Given the Reichswehr Ministry's support of the Rheinmetall contract and the Foreign Office's reserve towards official

support for such arrangements, it was clear that great difficulties were going to be raised by the letter of 21 September
1934 from the *Deutsche Revisions-und Treuhand-Aktiengesellschaft* to the Foreign Office. This forwarded Rheinmetall's
application of 20 September for a Reich guarantee covering
the delivery of the twenty-four howitzers with 24000 rounds
of ammunition.[34] Von Erdmannsdorff, Deputy Director for
Far Eastern Affairs in Department IV, opposed any official
participation in the transaction for a number of reasons: the
Law on War Material of 1927, expected Japanese protests
and particularly as a consequence of the Amau statement,
and the repercussions on German economic interests in those
areas of China where Chiang Kai-shek's writ did not run. He
also expressed doubt about the validity of the guarantees
offered by the Central Bank of China since this amounted
'to no more than the Minister of Finance's signature, since
the bank is an organ of the government'. Nor could the
delivery of such weapons from Germany remain a secret
since Solothurn, through whom the contract was to be
implemented, were said to be unable to produce the howitzers.
These objections were then communicated to the Ministries
of Economics and Finance, and to Reichsbank Director
Blessing.[35]

A hint that the Foreign Office recognised and even accepted
its subordinate role in the arms trade with China was given by
Senior Counsellor Frohwein, responsible for military and
disarmament questions in Department II, to Lieutenant
Colonel von Böckman of the Foreign Intelligence Branch
(*Auslandsabteilung*) of the Reichswehr Ministry, when he
pointed out that the objections of the Foreign Office applied
to the guarantee and not to the transaction as such.[36] But
any authority which the Foreign Office felt it had in the
matter had already been undermined. Liese had spoken to
Schacht about the question of a Reich guarantee for the
transaction and Schacht had insisted that the Foreign Office
would have to withdraw its objections, otherwise he would
place the matter before Hitler for a decision.[37] Already on
16 April 1934 Liese's Chief of Staff in the Ordnance Office,
Colonel Georg Thomas, had recommended that the arms
trade with China be encouraged and supported by Reich
guarantees.[38]

Schacht's strong attitude appeared to influence the Foreign

Office. Although Voss of Department IV argued at length with Reichsbank Director Blessing about the possible reactions if a Reich guarantee was granted — Japanese protests and demands for similar facilities from Chiang Kai-shek's domestic rivals — he finally admitted that if Schacht stood his ground the Foreign Office 'would make no further difficulties'. Blessing suggested that one way out of the difficulty would be to obtain support from the Golddiskontbank, and although this was an important subsidiary of the Reichsbank it was felt that this would help disguise the problem of 'formal' government participation in the transaction.[39]

On 16 October 1934 the matter was taken up directly with representatives from the Reichswehr Ministry, General von Reichenau, Head of the Armed Forces Office (*Wehrmachtsamt*) and an enthusiastic follower of Hitler and the Nazi revolution, and Lieutenant Colonel von Böckman. Reichenau stressed the support which the Rheinmetall's howitzer transaction received from the Reichswehr Ministry and from Schacht, and suggested that the Foreign Office should allow Ministries to assume responsibility for the relevant financial arrangements. Nor did he think there was much to worry about from Japan. Having thus seen von Erdmannsdorff's arguments simply dismissed, Frohwein tried to retrieve something out of the discussion by emphasising that a Reich guarantee for the howitzers could be expected to lead to further similar demands, and that in any case the matter was 'a serious question of foreign policy, as under the present procedures the Reich guarantee, which usually became known abroad, involved the Reich Government directly in individual transactions and in certain circumstances this might create awkward situations as regards our foreign policy'. Nevertheless, both sides seemed willing to compromise. The Foreign Office would be satisfied if government assistance was granted in such a way as to remain entirely unremarked abroad, an indication that Blessing's suggestion to Voss had had some effect in the Wilhelmstrasse; while von Reichenau admitted that the procedure for assistance by the Reich in the form of credits might be reviewed, particularly in the case of arms transactions. Three days later Frohwein suggested a meeting between representatives of the Ministries and agencies concerned to discuss the problems involved in the guarantee of arms exports.[40]

Before that meeting, which took place on 22 November, the howitzer question was placed before Hitler by General von Reichenau at two meetings on 18 October, with von Neurath present at the second. In view of Nazi inclinations towards Japan it was not surprising that Hitler carried Foreign Office arguments further by stating that the howitzer transaction with China should not be carried out. But after a compromise proposal from von Neurath, Hitler decided that the field howitzers should not be delivered in 1935 and reserved to himself the decision as to whether they should be delivered later. Even this did not finally decide the matter since in a letter of 19 October von Reichenau informed von Bülow that it had been agreed that Rheinmetall could fulfil their contract if they agreed to forgo the Reich guarantee and if delivery was made as late as possible. Schacht would be supervising the transaction, while delivery would commence nine months later at the earliest and end about 1937, a procedure which took into account von Neurath's points of view. Von Neurath himself noted on this letter that 'the Führer told me quite categorically that he forbade delivery in 1925 (sic)'. On the 25th von Bülow drew von Reichenau's attention to the discrepancy between the two accounts of Hitler's decision.[41]

At the meeting on 22 November 1934 Frohwein maintained the Wilhelmstrasse's opposition to Reich guarantees for arms exports but admitted that the government had to ensure its control over this trade since for political reasons it might become necessary to prohibit the export of arms to certain countries and to encourage their export elsewhere. He then went further by repeating the compromise which the Wilhelmstrasse had only recently accepted, namely that if the government was forced to intervene with its own financial backing this should be done 'in such a way as to give the maximum guarantee that the participation of the Reich would not become known'. Frohwein's demand about the political control of arms exports was to some extent met by statements from Reichswehr Ministry representatives who stated that such control was in any case exercised through the Ordnance Office, while he also received the promise from those present to use their influence to prevent armaments firms from applying for Reich guarantees or credits for armaments orders from abroad. Nevertheless, it was also generally agreed that very often Reich financial assistance was the only means by which valuable arms orders from abroad could be met, and apart from providing employment within Germany such transactions would also enable the country to obtain valuable foreign exchange. Finally, the general consensus of opinion was that as much secrecy as possible should be maintained over such transactions and to disguise the part played by the Ministries of Economics and Finance.[42]

But even in China there appeared to be difficulties. Finance Minister Kung seemed to be delaying the signing of the Rheinmetall contract because of cheaper competition from the Skoda Company of Czechoslovakia. He also hinted to Krupp's representative that because of the troublesome Klein projects in the south and Rheinmetall's own connections with Canton, Nanking's interest in the howitzer deal might be threatened.[43]

The matter seemed to rest there until 2 April 1935 when Soltau of the Ministry of Economics approached Frohwein to enquire whether the Foreign Office's previous opposition could not be rescinded in view of the new procedures for granting a credit to Rheinmetall suggested as a result of the meeting of 22 November 1934. Frohwein reserved his position and passed the matter to Department IV for a decision. Both Rohde and Kühlborn thought that events had overtaken Hitler's decision of 18 October 1934 and that the restriction should be lifted. In his memorandum of 4 April 1935, therefore, Kühlborn appeared satisfied that the suggested credit was to be granted by the *Reichskreditgesellschaft,* a State bank functioning like a private bank, and not by the *Revisions- und Treuhand-Aktiengesellschaft.* He also thought that Klein's activities in Canton removed any political objections there might be to such a transaction with the Central Government of China. There were still doubts on the economic side of the matter, but these too had been somewhat reduced by recent experiences with the Chinese Government, while the credit period was only to be a short one. More significantly Kühlborn wondered whether Germany's recently changed national defence situation, following the announcements of 9 and 16 March 1935 that the German air force officially existed and that conscription was to be reintroduced, required a new decision in the case.[44] In May 1935 Trautmann reported that these developments, and the changes in the European situation envisaged as a result of the Franco-Russian Pact of 2 May caused some Chinese Ministers to think that Germany might shortly be involved in war. Finance Minister Kung had again opposed orders being placed with Rheinmetall since he feared that in the event of war Germany would be unable to make deliveries to China.[45]

Von Neurath also raised no objections, so that when Soltau wrote on 13 April requesting the Foreign Office's formal answer on the question of a Reich guarantee to Rheinmetall, Meyer was able to reply on 18 April in the required sense.[46] Nevertheless, it still took until the end of 1935 for the Reich guarantee to be finalised,[47] and even then Rheinmetall's troubles were not over. At the beginning of January 1936 von Falkenhausen, leader of the German military advisory staff at Nanking, wrote to his friend Lieutenant Colonel Brinckmann, that the Chinese were particularly upset at news that a Japanese Commission had visited Rheinmetall's works at Düsseldorf and had been allowed to see secret weapons assigned to China. This was of course quickly denied by the War Ministry, and appropriate instructions were quickly sent to Nanking.[48]

While the purely military characteristics of arms deliveries to China could never be disguised, the Wilhelmstrasse's opposition to certain other military activity in China tended to be less fierce because their civilian aspects could always legitimately be emphasised. As Kühlborn admitted in April 1934, it was not the task of the Foreign Office to draw attention to the military characteristics of such enterprises, e.g. the establishment of aircraft factories and their ancillary organisations in China and which, in any case, benefited the infant aircraft industry in Germany.[49]

Compared to other countries, Germany lagged behind in the Chinese aviation market, and Trautmann supported all efforts to rectify the situation. His only concern about the negotiations begun in 1933 between the Junkers and Otto Wolff concerns and the Chinese Government for the construction of an aircraft factory was 'the purely military character of the enterprise . . . and Japanese opposition to the building up of the Chinese aircraft industry by third power'. In March, Consul General Suma warned Trautmann about the Japanese position, while on 18 April Wang Ching-wei, President of the Executive Yuan and acting Foreign Minister, was warned by the

Japanese Minister to China, Ariyoshi, about China's policy of 'favouring Europeans and Americans' in the further development of her air force and aviation industry.[50]

Since the Wilhelmstrasse felt that these enterprises were such as to warrant greater concern for Germany's economic interests than for specific political objections from Tokio, von Dirksen got short shrift from Meyer when he complained in April 1934 that 'the building of an aircraft factory in China by German economic interests would do irreparable harm to German—Japanese relations which are already under a continuous burden because of the presence of German military advisers in Nanking'. In reply, Meyer warned von Dirksen against making the aircraft factory a 'to be or not to be' issue in German—Japanese relations, and emphasised that Germany's relations with China or even Russia (interestingly enough) were not to be subordinated 'simply to Japanese points of view'.[51]

Nevertheless, the Foreign Office pursued the matter in Berlin in an attempt to find a form for these undertakings which would satisfy not only Chinese and German aviation interests but also Japanese susceptibilities.[52] By May 1934 the Otto Wolff group had abandoned its plans for an aircraft factory and instead arranged for a contract for delivery, cooperating in this with other countries.[53] Finally, on 29 September and 2 October 1934 contracts were signed between the Junkers Werke and the National Government of China for the establishment of an aircraft factory, together with the delivery of German aviation materials, as well for the closest German participation in the establishment, administration, and technical and training aspects of the new enterprise. Trautmann expressed his satisfaction with the arrangments for two reasons: German technique and German technicians would be utilised in China, and Germany's financial risk in this instance was less than that involved in other enterprises.[54]

The German aircraft industry thus became increasingly involved in China, in both the civilian and the military fields. The Reich Air Ministry's involvement was less than that of the Reichswehr Ministry's, but even so it too attempted to express views on policy towards China which did not always accord with the policy of the Foreign Office. In May 1935 it entered into the discussion of the status of Germany's diplomatic relations with China when it was suggested that the

German Mission in China be raised to the status of an embassy since this would help boost Germany's share of the Chinese aviation market by strengthening the hands of those Germans thus involved in China.[55] It also seemed that the Reich Air Ministry was thinking of having an advisory staff at Canton as well as at Nanking. Lieutenant General Streccius, the German aviation adviser with the Nanking Government since 1934, denied this and pointed out to Trautmann who raised the matter with him that he would have nothing to do with such plans. Yet Trautmann informed the Wilhelmstrasse that the plans originated with the Reich Air Ministry which had requested von Falkenhausen to sound out the possibility of the delivery of 100 aircraft to Canton, and had ordered Streccius to report on the relations between Nanking and Canton. When forwarding the report by Streccius, Trautmann made it clear that the Reichswehr Ministry was not alone in attempting to pursue policies in China contrary to those desired or recommended by the Foreign Office, a point well taken by von Bülow in a comment on Trautmann's letter.[56]

German arms deliveries to China, whatever their form, were only part of the wide range of Germany's military interests in that country. Of particular significance were the German military advisory staff at Nanking, and in connection with this the visits of General von Seeckt to China in 1933 and from 1934 to 1935. Following letters in 1932 from General Wetzell, German Military Adviser to the Chinese National Government, and a direct invitation from Chiang Kai-shek in September 1932, General von Seeckt left Marseilles on 14 April 1933 for what was supposedly a 'private' visit. This euphemism covered a multitude of intentions since he had intimated to von Neurath on 3 April that his visits would strengthen General Wetzell's somewhat shaky position with Chiang Kai-shek. The Foreign Office also learned that following Chiang Kai-shek's offer during 1932 to Reichswehr Minister Groener to visit China to reorganise the Chinese army and of Groener's refusal, von Seeckt was now expected to be offered the position of military adviser to Chiang Kai-shek.[57] Apart from the reputation he had gained during the First World War, von Seeckt was also renowned for his work for the Reichswehr during his appointment as Chief of the Army Command 1920–26.

Although von Seeckt emphasised the private nature of his

visit to China to both von Neurath and von Blomberg, the Reichswehr Minister,[58] Foreign Office fears were soon justified by signs of Japanese concern that Seeckt might be going to China as military adviser and in order to make the German military advisory staff at Nanking more of an 'official' body.[59] Von Neurath wanted a denial issued to assuage Japanese fears that Germany might be abandoning her 'neutrality' in Far Eastern affairs but Altenburg opposed this as being 'dangerous'. Apparently, however, von Seeckt had other more personal aims in view. He had a Jewish wife while it seemed that on his part there was a distinct 'lack of sympathy with various recent developments' in Nazi Germany.[60] Any denial about the purposes of von Seeckt's visit to China would, however, have created a very bad impression in China, particularly with Chiang Kai-shek. However, Meyer suggested to Trautmann that Japanese susceptibilities might be appeased if von Seeckt was able to visit Japan on his return journey. While Trautmann also tried to emphasise the private nature of the visit during von Seeckt's presence in China, in the event the General felt it impossible to visit Japan. Trautmann considered that apart from not wishing to upset official Chinese circles, von Seeckt was also suffering from the effects of what was a strenuous journey for an old man. Later, von Seeckt made the interesting observation that Trautmann was secretly pleased that Japan had not been on his return itinerary.[61]

Trautmann's report of 26 August 1933 also made it clear that von Seeckt's visit would undoubtedly lead to an intensification of German military activity in China. He described von Seeckt's activities and conversations while in China, including the General's visit to the Canton Marshals already reported on 19 July, a visit that had apparently been prepared in Berlin by a representative of the Canton régime.[62] Trautmann drew particular attention to the memorandum which von Seeckt had given to Chiang Kai-shek, outlining his impressions of the trip and setting out his proposals for the improvement of China's military establishment. An important section of this report dealt with the inadequacies of Chinese war material and arsenals, and von Seeckt therefore recommended great European, i.e. German participation in this field. His other recommendations for the restructuring of the Chinese army could also have been expected to have led to greater German involvement through the appointment of more German advisers.[63]

While von Seeckt's relationship with the Reichswehr Ministry was a shadowy one and only became clearer in connection with the Klein enterprises,[64] there is no doubt that he was as keen as that Ministry to see closer military ties between Germany and China. The Foreign Office and Trautmann opposed this, and when von Seeckt informed von Neurath on 19 October 1933 that Chiang Kai-shek had invited him to China for a further visit, this time as military adviser, von Neurath pointed out that 'such activity was politically incompatible' for Germany and asked him to decline the offer, a step which showed that the Wilhelmstrasse was just as keen on maintaining good German–Japanese relations as it was on maintaining good Sino–German ones. An awkward situation could have arisen if von Seeckt had declined to follow this advice, but he did so, having already expressed his own doubts about the advisability of such a course in his correspondence with the Chinese. In declining Chiang Kai-shek's offer, von Seeckt recommended Generals von Falkenhausen and Faupel for the positions of military adviser and adviser to the war ministry respectively.[65]

Chiang Kai-shek, not surprisingly, did not take kindly to this proposal. Through the Chinese Minister of Communications, Chu Chia-hua, he continued to exert pressure on von Seeckt, while Chinese diplomats in Berlin expressed great concern that a refusal by the General would be taken as a personal affront to the Generalissimo. Besides which, such a refusal might jeopardise the position of the German military advisers in China, along with the military and economic advantages their work was bringing to Germany. In these circumstances, the French might then replace the Germans. These points had already been recognised in the Wilhelmstrasse and one solution to the problem appeared to be the suggestion that von Seeckt undertake only a short winter trip to China in order to introduce General Wetzell's successor, von Falkenhausen, after which he could return to Germany.[66]

This compromise was accepted by the Chinese Chargé d'affaires,[67] and then put to von Seeckt by von Neurath. The document recording their conversation of 11 November 1933 omits this point,[68] the record simply stating that although the General had reservations about accepting Chiang Kai-shek's renewed offer, he recognised that his refusal could mean the German military position in China being lost to the French.

Although the Reichswehr Ministry approved the journey, as a marginal note by von Bülow indicated, the Foreign Office was at pains to emphasise to that Ministry, and particularly to the officer most concerned with the China enterprises, Colonel von Reichenau, that foreign policy considerations dictated that von Seeckt only undertake a temporary visit and enter into no contract of employment.[69] Von Seeckt finally wrote on 22 November 1933 accepting Chiang Kai-shek's invitation, and informed him that he would be travelling to China the following spring together with the other two Generals.[70]

While the motives of the Reichswehr Ministry in the matter were obvious enough, those of the Foreign Office were more mixed. As the 'guardian' of German interests abroad it could not adopt an overtly obstructionist attitude, particularly on a matter where the advantages to Germany were becoming increasingly clear. Even Trautmann had to admit that von Seeckt's journey would consolidate the German position in China. He was, however, extremely disturbed about the effect of this second trip on the Japanese, and urged on the Wilhelm-strasse a course that had already been put into effect, namely, that von Seeckt should avoid giving any impression of going to China as the new military adviser. Yet the problem was further complicated when he reported at the beginning of 1934 that the Chinese did not count on a short visit by von Seeckt.[71]

Not surprisingly, von Dirksen was especially worried about Japanese reactions and particularly so when he was doing his level best to persuade the Wilhelmstrasse that it was Hitler's intention to pursue the closest possible relationship with Japan.[72] On 19 January 1934 he asked for von Neurath to intercede with von Blomberg to prevent von Seeckt's second visit to China. Apparently, von Blomberg had been prepared to accede to this request in October 1933 and it is likely that his meeting with von Seeckt on 18 October 1933 influenced the latter's attitude when he spoke with von Neurath on 19 October.[73] Von Neurath, however, seemed to have so much confidence in the strength and stability of German—Japanese relations that he was able to comment on von Dirksen's request that 'the apprehension [is] exaggerated'.[74]

Prompted by this disquiet from Germany's diplomatic representatives in China and Japan, even though Trautmann and von Dirksen were motivated by different reasons, von Bülow wrote to von Blomberg on 29 January 1934 to impress upon him the possible foreign policy repercussions of von Seeckt's trip to China, mainly with reference to Japan. He also asked the Reichswehr Minister to emphasise to von Seeckt that the position of military adviser should be declined and to stress the political necessity of undertaking only a short trip. Von Dirksen was given instructions to pursue his conversation in Tokio along the lines of von Bülow's letter to von Blomberg, while the matter was considered to be so important, and indeed delicate, that on 20 February 1934 the *Völkischer Beobachter,* the NSDAP newspaper, issued an 'explanatory' notice about von Seeckt's imminent visit to China.[75]

The Wilhelmstrasse's fears about the possible repercussions the visit might raise were soon realised. The Japanese press adopted an extremely hostile attitude towards von Seeckt's return to China, although if von Neurath had been able to persuade the old General to visit Japan on the outward journey this reaction might have been less strong.[76] Ambassador Nagai also went to the Foreign Office for an explanation. While von Bülow instructed von Dirksen to deny all tendentious reports that Germany intended to rearm China against Japan, he informed Nagai of the facts of the case and explained that 'we would not have sanctioned the trip of Seeckt . . . had we not been certain that he would not engage in any sort of adventure'.[77]

For the Wilhelmstrasse this particular issue and its consequent publicity could not have come at a worse time for German–Japanese relations. Apart from the difficulties caused by Nazi Germany's avowedly racialist basis and legislation,[78] the Japanese, and certainly the Nazi leadership, were becoming aware that a German recognition of Manchukuo and therefore a closer German–Japanese relationship would never be forged through the portals of the Wilhelmstrasse.[79] Although Ambassador Nagai appeared satisfied, von Dirksen, disappointed and frustrated over the cool reception from the Wilhelmstrasse over his (and Hitler's) proposals for an early recognition of Manchukuo hopefully paving the way for the millenium in German–Japanese relations, adopted an extremely critical attitude in a report of 13 March 1934 on the Seeckt issue. He appeared to argue along the lines of the Japanese press reports which he enclosed, namely, that the political and military importance of von Seeckt's visit to China implied that Germany was making a political choice in the Far East for China. In any case, von Dirksen thought the issue would inevitably 'stir up again the whole complex of the German military advisers to China', as sore a point with him as it was with the Japanese military and political authorities who still suspected that German military advisers may have been active in the Shanghai operations of 1932. Finally, and with particular reference to German—Japanese relations, von Dirksen raised the general implications of von Seeckt's visit for Germany's Far Eastern policy as a whole, that is as he saw them: 'if it is the intention of German policy with respect to Japan merely to play the role of the interested but inactive spectator and observer, we shall not need to take into consideration any Japanese sensibilities. Should we intend, however, to introduce Japan as an active factor in our general policy and create accordingly a friendlier and more cordial atmosphere, undertakings should be avoided in the future which — such as the journey of General von Seeckt — are certainly the cause of ill-feeling and pessimism'.[80] Von Dirksen's concern for Japanese sensibilities also caused him to press, successfully, for the cancellation of the Reichwehr Ministry's instructions to Colonel Eugen Ott, the newly appointed Military Attaché to the German Embassy at Tokio, to use a pause in his journey to Tokio at Shanghai to visit General Wetzell. Von Dirksen feared that such an ostentatious gesture would compromise Ott's future relationship with Japanese military circles and suggested instead that Wetzell could visit Ott in Shanghai.[81]

With the military activities in China of von Seeckt and those of Hans Klein, supported by the Reichswehr Ministry,[82] it was not surprising that von Dirksen and the Japanese should have drawn the correct conclusion that Germany was increasing her military, and perhaps political, commitment to China, at a time when Germany's official line over Manchukuo — despite whatever else was being said or intimated at an unofficial level — was an extremely cool one and which indicated to those circles desirous of a closer German—Japanese relationship that success was not going to be an easy matter. These and other developments in Sino—German relations, on the other hand, not only pleased the Chinese but encouraged them to think that Germany was a friend that could perhaps be relied upon in the difficult and uncertain future. Apart from economic and military relations, careful attention was also paid to cultural links between the two countries, while Nazi Germany received a number of important and prominent Chinese visitors, including the Young Marshal, Chang Hsueh-liang, and Wang Ching-wei.

These developments also helped to maintain and strengthen this important relationship for Germany which, in 1933 at least, had been subjected to certain strains because of the avowedly authoritarian and racialist nature of Nazi policies and the Nazi régime. Apart from the episode involving Adolf Grimme, Albert Grzesinski, and Bernhard Weiss,[83] there was the case of a Dr Jaenicke who had gone to China in 1933 from the League of Nations as adviser for administrative reform, with the approval of the German government. When in 1933 and 1934 the Ministry of the Interior raised the question of his retirement under paragraph 6 of the Civil Service Law of 7 April 1933 and enquired of the Foreign Office regarding possible foreign policy repercussions,[84] it was a report from Trautmann on 10 July 1934 which finally decided the issue in Jaenicke's favour. Because of the nature of his work in China and his relations with the Chinese government, Trautmann warned that the enforced retirement of Jaenicke would have a detrimental effect on Sino–German relations. A month later Meyer informed Trautmann that Jaenicke's retirement was to be postponed.[85]

At the same time Japanese complaints and concern about Nazi Germany's racial ideologies and practices were complemented by similar expressions by the Chinese, so that the Wilhelmstrasse found it necessary to have to assure Chinese diplomats that Nazi policies were not intended to discriminate against the 'old cultural races of the Far East, in particular the Chinese'.[86] Nor was the Wilhelmstrasse pleased to have to handle the delicate question of a Chinese professor, one Dr Shen Tung-hui, who was having difficulty in obtaining official permission to marry a German citizen, Gertrud Schulz. As Felix Altenburg of Department IV noted on 15 November 1933, the Chinese were making this question a 'test case' for the future handling of the race problem.[87] Later, following representations by the Chinese Minister in Berlin, State Secretary Funk of the Reich Ministry of Propaganda promised that paragraphs referring to Negroes and Chinese would be altered or deleted in future editions of *Mein Kampf*. Funk emphasised that Hitler had no wish to offend the susceptibilities of 'the great Chinese people'.[88]

In fact, earlier in 1935 Germany's stock with China rose when, on 17 May, von Neurath informed the Chinese Minister that Germany had decided to raise the German Mission at Peking to the status of an Embassy, a move quickly reciprocated by the Chinese. Later, in June 1935, Hitler acceded to a request from Chiang Kai-shek that the German Embassy be sited at Nanking.[89] Nevertheless, and in the final analysis, the Chinese rested uneasily about one thing in particular: the true nature of German attitudes towards Japan and therefore of the German—Japanese relationship during the first years of the Third Reich. But Chinese uncertainty on this question simply reflected the confusion which existed within policy-making circles in Nazi Germany on the very same issue.

IV

Diplomacy and Japanese Issues 1933–1935

The policy of the German Foreign Office towards Japan, unlike that of the Nazi leadership, was one of extreme caution for two reasons: Japan was universally considered to be a danger to peace in the Far East under its Panasian legend of 'Asia for the Asians'; while this, and Japan's withdrawal from the League of Nations in 1933 implied that the interests of other nations in the Far East might be at risk as a result of Japan's political and military ambitions.[1] While it was the appearance of Japanese 'dynamism' which so attracted the Nazis towards Japan, the German Foreign Office had to take a wider view of the situation — at what the Nazis considered to be a 'lower' level of political activity — and take into account the fact that in a sense it acted *in loco parentis* to Germany's economic and other interests in the Far East, the greater part of which were in China. Although this attitude of reserve gave the impression that the Wilhelmstrasse paid greater attention to China in its Far Eastern policy, nevertheless it continually showed concern for Japanese susceptibilities in the formulation and execution of its China policy. But while there was little chance of a directly political agreement being concluded with China, the Foreign Office was at one with the Nazi leadership in recognising the political importance of Japan. As Michelsen wrote on 5 July 1933, 'as a great power and factor of world politics, Japan will be able to strongly influence the international situation through its conduct, particularly *vis-à-vis* the Soviet Union, and thereby Germany's political position'.[2] Consequently, the Wilhelmstrasse too desired to maintain and foster good and normal working relations with Japan, but it had no intention whatsoever of closing the political gap between Berlin and Tokio.

The differences between the Wilhelmstrasse and the Nazis towards the Japanese became quite clear in the winter of 1933–34 over the closely connected issue of policy towards Manchukuo.[3] The Foreign Office's restraint in this matter hardly enhanced its reputation with Hitler, showing the Führer that the path to a closer German–Japanese relationship was not to be found through the portals of 76 Wilhelmstrasse.

Furthermore, the episode had a disturbing effect on morale and relationships within the Foreign Office since, to some of the diplomats and officials at least, von Dirksen's attitude and behaviour must have reminded them strongly of the ploy used by Greece finally to defeat Troy. Even after the Foreign Minister's 'final' despatch of 6 March 1934, von Dirksen continued to be 'lectured' to by his colleagues in the diplomatic service. At the end of March 1934 Trautmann wrote a 'frank' letter to the Ambassador at Tokio in which he argued that instead of pursuing a German–Japanese policy or a German–Chinese policy, Germany should instead attempt to execute a comprehensive Far Eastern policy of friendship to both China and Japan. He argued that Germany had no political interests in the Far East and should remain neutral in any Far Eastern conflict except when 'we have vital interests' that might justify a policy of support for one side or the other. Nevertheless, he opposed any one-sided agreement with Japan, especially since he had grave doubts as to the kind of political support that Germany could expect from her even if she abandoned her policy of neutrality in the Far East. In addition, Trautmann thought that a closer German–Japanese relationship would have the effect of increasing the intimacy between France and Poland, and between these countries and Russia, thereby worsening Germany's position in Europe. Finally, Trautmann's total lack of trust in Japan expressed itself in his apposite comment that Japan's attitude towards Germany was always likely to be that signified by the 'Heine-like tip off: "My lovely child, when you meet me in public, pretend you don't know me" '.[4] Not surprisingly, Trautmann's major concern was for Sino–German relations, and the effect on these of either the fact or rumour of a closer political relationship between Germany and Japan.[5]

Two weeks later Meyer reinforced this general standpoint in a communication to von Dirksen. Taking up von Dirksen's concern at von Seeckt's visit to China,[6] Meyer assured him that the Foreign Office paid equal attention to German–Japanese relations in the formulation and execution of its Far Eastern policy. Nevertheless, he made it quite clear that relations with Japan were to be limited 'by the political exigencies in regard to the other Far Eastern powers and European, or American, conditions'. Meyer then underlined the point which had continually been impressed upon von Dirksen: 'if we promote and cultivate German–Japanese relations with cool realism and do nothing that might tend to disturb them, this must not, on the other hand, be a licence to the Japanese to demand that all measures be considered only from Japan's point of view'.[7]

If the Wilhelmstrasse reacted coolly to early Nazi efforts to close the political gap between Berlin and Tokio, efforts which were as much public as private,[8] it was equally reserved towards Japanese attempts to achieve the same result. In March 1934 the Japanese Assistant Military Attaché in Berlin, Major Ishii, disingenuously suggested that Japanese concern for the subject Russian nationalities within Soviet Russia might be the subject of discussions with the Wilhelmstrasse. Heye, the Deputy Director of Department IV, rejected this since he felt the Japanese could make political capital out of such conversations.[9] That this was not an isolated incident appeared to be borne out by a letter of 19 March 1934 from von Dirksen to von Bülow. Referring to reports of an attempted rapprochement with England on the initiative of the former Japanese Minister of War, Lieutenant General Sadao Araki, von Dirksen stated that 'the matter is of immediate interest to us, inasmuch as the same Japanese circles would like to draw Germany into this combination'.[10] A month later, and the day after the Amau Statement of 17 April, Ambassador Nagai pointedly remarked to von Neurath that 'Germany and Japan were the real bulwarks against Bolshevism, and for this reason a common German–Japanese basis of interest had already been formed'.[11]

The Amau Statement, a renewal of Japanese opposition to foreign aid to China 'in a manner that transformed it into an issue of major international importance' and a reaffirmation of Japanese claims to be responsible for the maintenance of peace in the Far East,[12] appeared to confirm Foreign Office doubts about the widsom of any close political relationship with Japan. As it was, on 18 April Ambassador Nagai warned von Neurath that Japan 'could by no means permit China to summon foreign powers to aid her against Japan. Japan would most decidedly oppose this attempt'. As if to emphasise Germany's own misdemeanours in this respect, Nagai referred to von Seeckt's visit to China.

While Germany was obviously interested in the principles of

the Open Door with regard to China, she was not a signatory of the Nine Power Treaty. Since it was argued that Germany had no political interests in the Far East and consequently no political issues with Japan, the Wilhelmstrasse decided that any reaction to the Amau Statement could safely be left to the United States and Britain.[13] Had the Wilhelmstrasse protested to Japan it would have appeared to have been defending the very things about which the Japanese were complaining, and would most certainly have given Germany's military activity in China a mark of respectability which the Foreign Office was continually at pains to deny. Nevertheless, an answer of sorts was given by the *Ostasiatische Rundschau* on 1 May 1934 which carried a full summary of the Chinese Government's reply to the Amau Statement. This emphasised that China's rearmament with the help of foreign powers implied no aggressive designs on the part of China against Japan. Although it is not clear whether the coverage given to the Chinese reply was meant to indicate Germany's 'freedom of action' in the whole question, the Japanese may well have read it in this light.

Of particular significance was von Dirksen's response to the Japanese declaration. He accepted the fact that implicit in the Japanese warnings was concern at Germany's military activity in China and other 'pending' plans. Although Foreign Minister Hirota and the Japanese Foreign Office studiously avoided referring directly to Germany in this connection, von Dirksen felt that the subject would become even more of a sensitive topic in German–Japanese relations. He therefore renewed his attack on Germany's military activity in China, and ended his report of 23 April on a somewhat peevish note by emphasising that his opposition to this activity was one of long standing, so that he felt 'above the suspicion that my proposals were a result of the pressure of the Japanese statement'.[14] Shortly afterwards he informed the Wilhelmstrasse that he and the Military Attaché, Ott, would do their utmost in Japan to counter any bad feeling there might be about Germany's military activities in China.[15] A few months later the Japanese appeared to be changing their tactics over the question of foreign aid to China. In August Trautmann informed the Foreign Office of his impression that the 'sharp Japanese policy of "hands off"' had ended but that 'the same policy will be pursued with more dissembling and on the basis of influencing other powers diplomatically'.[16]

Concern about this and other factors in the international arena prompted von Bülow to write to von Dirksen in October about the encirclement of Japan 'which must be taken seriously', but instructing him to avoid 'any close relations with Japan which might lay us open to being suspected of wishing to render assistance against Russia'. While the Foreign Office itself did not believe in the imminence of a Far Eastern war, nevertheless, it took the view that 'the encirclement of Japan may, however, easily result in unforeseen and undesirable developments'. Von Dirksen replied that he was restricting relations with Hirota to a minimum, and that the Military and Naval Attachés were doing the same with regard to the Japanese Service departments. Similarly, in October 1934 Trautmann disregarded feelers by Suma, the Japanese Consul General in Nanking, for cooperation between Germany and Japan in the Far East, initially on economic matters.[17]

The Wilhelmstrasse was under constant pressure, therefore, to modify its general stance towards Japan. But since the day-to-day relationship with Japan was still conducted through normal diplomatic channels, the Foreign Office was not entirely without means to influence the general pattern and tenor of German–Japanese relations after 1933. Although the Anti-Comintern Pact of November 1936 was concluded by Ribbentrop and appeared to commit Germany to a pro-Japanese course of action and policy, it could be argued (although the point must not be taken too far) that the existence of a whole range of issues which had to be conducted through diplomatic channels still meant that it was Nazi policy towards Japan which laboured under the burdens imposed by the diplomats, and not the other way around. One issue which illustrated only too well the dilemmas posed for both the Nazi leadership and the Wilhelmstrasse by the existence and policies of the Nazi régime, internally and externally, was the potentially explosive issue of race.

On 7 April 1933 Nazi Germany introduced the Law for the Restoration of the Professional Civil Service. Its key stipulation, article 3, stated that 'officials of non-Aryan origin are to be retired'. This measure was soon followed by others designed to cleanse the 'Jewish contagion' from every aspect of German life. Yet the law of 7 April posed a difficult question: who was to be classed as 'non-Aryan'? Four days later the Minister of the Interior, Wilhelm Frick, answered this question by declaring that 'anyone is considered non-Aryan who is descended from non-Aryan and in particular Jewish parents or grandparents. It suffices for one parent or one grandparent to be non-Aryan'. Despite the fact that this Nazi legislation was aimed at German Jews, the Japanese were particularly concerned since such policies were reminiscent of the racialist 'Yellow Peril' warnings of the ex-Kaiser earlier in the century. The domestic implications of the *Arierparagraph* therefore had serious external repercussions for the Nazi State, not only with respect to Japan but also to China.[18] And the Ministry which had to cope with this added strain on Nazi Germany's foreign relations was the Foreign Office.[19]

In an obvious attempt to mitigate the serious international resentment aroused against Nazi Germany because of this question, particularly in Japan, the question of innate racial quality was one of the most persistent themes in Nazi speeches and writings from 1933. The reasons for this were finally summed up in a press directive of February 1935: 'the Yellow Peril must no longer be made out as a picture of horror, for Germany's attitude toward other races leaves completely open the question of the worth of other races — especially when these races must not, for political reasons, be offended'.[20] As seen later, the timing and intended purpose of that directive was extremely significant.

The most notable contribution towards an easing of Japanese susceptibilities on the racial question came from no less a person than Alfred Rosenberg. In numerous speeches during 1933 and 1934 he emphasised the need to dwell on the diversity of races rather than their disparate qualities (*Verschiedenartigkeit der Rassen* rather than *Verschiedenwertigkeit der Rassen*). At the Nuremberg Party Rally in September 1933 he stated that 'we acknowledge the destiny of the Yellow Race and hope that in its own *Lebensraum* it will develop the specific culture born of its racial soul'. Rosenberg pursued this theme on 30 October 1933 at the Berlin Sportpalast when he pointed out that the white man's endeavour to improve his own qualities in no way denigrated other races; in fact, a similar effort on the part of the Japanese and Chinese would be welcomed. In 1935 the achievements of Japan were singled out for special praise as evidence of Japan's particular racial genius.[21] In addition, the Germans were also warned by Dr Johann von Leers, a prolific writer on the subject of race, not to rely on other white races for support. The Treaty of Versailles was a good example of what could be expected from such quarters. Instead, he argued that Nazi Germany and Japan complemented each other in international affairs, and underlined this by pointing out that in politics Germany could not expect all her friends to have blue eyes and blonde hair.[22]

Hitler himself added his authoritative voice in an attempt to soothe international and Japanese misgivings. In his Reichstag speech of 30 January 1934 — at a time when he was hoping to move closer to Japan by a positive approach on the Manchukuoan question, only to be opposed in this by the Wilhelmstrasse — he explained that 'the National Socialist racial idea and the science underlying it do not lead to the underrating or disparagement of other nations but rather to the recognition of the duty to preserve and maintain the life of our own people'. As late as February 1945 Hitler stated: 'I have never regarded the Chinese or Japanese as being inferior to ourselves. They belong to ancient civilisations, and I admit freely that their past history is superior to our own. They have the right to be proud of their past, just as we have the right to be proud of the civilisation to which we belong.'[23] Nevertheless, Hitler's basic attitude towards the Japanese was an ambivalent one. His public references to the 'innate superiority' of the white man continually upset the Japanese, as at Munich on 26 January 1936 when he stated that only the white race was capable of colonisation.[24]

The major theme of German propaganda on this question in Europe and the Far East, therefore, was that Germany's overriding problem was not the racial worth or purity of the Far Eastern peoples but the Jewish question.[25] Yet all efforts failed to persuade the Japanese that Germany could pursue a discriminatory policy at home and quite another abroad, and in fact it was the racial question which at this time most persistently vitiated official relations between the two countries. Two specific issues upset the Japanese: Germany's refusal to state whether the Japanese were to be included in the classification of 'coloured races', and the prohibition of marriages between 'coloured' people and other non-Aryans and Germans. Their misgivings — and those of the Chinese — were particularly aroused by a memorandum published on 29 September 1933 in which the Prussian Minister of Justice,

Hanns Kerrl, had suggested that in order to combat the 'erosion of the German race' the Government should make 'race treason' a punishable offence and prohibit mixed marriages. Although Rosenberg had emphasised the legitimacy of such legislation in a speech at Nuremberg by drawing attention to Japanese provisions under which the Emperor could prohibit similar marriages in Japan, the Japanese press reacted strongly and said that the proposed ban on a marriage with a 'coloured person' was an insult to Japan.[26]

So seriously did the Japanese regard the question that it was soon taken up diplomatically with Germany. On 11 October 1933 Ambassador Nagai demanded clarification from the Foreign Office on the official German attitude towards the Japanese within the context of the *Rassenproblem*. Von Bülow emphasised that Germany was legislating against the mixing of race, nothing else, and although this seemed to satisfy Nagai he warned about the detrimental effect on German–Japanese relations if the Japanese ever came to be regarded by the Germans officially as 'coloured', and made his point by referring to the prevailing bitterness which this issue had introduced into American–Japanese relations. Von Bülow limited himself to promising that efforts would be made to limit or prevent the use of offensive expressions.[27]

Yet nine days later, when Voretzsch informed the Foreign Office of the hostile attitude of the Japanese press on the question, Nagai again appeared at the Foreign Office, this time asking von Neurath for an unequivocal statement as to whether the term 'coloured' was to apply to the Japanese and whether the prohibition of mixed marriages in the new laws would affect Japanese citizens. The memorandum recording this conversation does not give von Neurath's answer,[28] but in London *The Times* of 24 October carried a report from Tokio, datelined 23 October, which stated that von Neurath apologised to the Japanese Embassy in Berlin for an attack by Nazi youths on a Japanese schoolgirl. More significantly, it also stated that he had given the assurance that in Germany the Japanese were not considered as 'coloured' and promised to rectify the supposed inclusion of the Japanese in the proposed legislation prohibiting Germans from marrying Jews or coloured people. A Russian press report also stated that von Neurath had told Nagai that the German Government had decided that the Japanese race could be recognised as the equivalent of the Nordic—Germanic races.[29]

But when three Japanese correspondents, Suzuki, Tamaki, and Professor Masuda asked the same questions at the Ministry of the Interior, it seems that Dr Gehrke, a specialist on race research, answered 'unhesitatingly' in the affirmative, i.e. the Japanese would not be given any particular consideration. The incensed Japanese promptly informed Tokio, while Dr von Leers had the difficult task of trying to calm Professor Masuda and of convincing him that the proposed legislation would not in fact apply to the Japanese but only to Jews, Negroes, and 'primitive races'. On 25 October von Leers informed Altenburg of his initiative, and was in turn informed of the Foreign Office's attitude as explained to the Japanese Ambassador on 11 October by von Bülow.[30] It was then suggested that von Leers might contact the Ministry of Justice through Dr Gaus of the Foreign Office's Legal Department, who had discussed the racial issue with them, and in this way add the weight of his reputation and his standing as an old member of the Nazi Party to the views of the Foreign Office.[31]

At the same time the Foreign Office lost no time in approaching Dr Gehrke, who in turn maintained to Meyer that his answer to the three Japanese had been 'extremely cautious and interspersed with various reservations'. Meyer's concern about the foreign policy implications of 'careless statements about the race problem' appeared to have had some effect on Dr Gehrke since he promised that this would be passed immediately to the relevant officials in the Ministries of the Interior and Justice.[32] But how far the Foreign Office thought it had gained its point is hard to tell. The Japanese at any rate were still beset by doubts about the German attitude and continued to pursue the matter elsewhere. On 21 November Counsellor Fujii of the Japanese Embassy complained to Admiral Behncke, President of the German—Japanese Association, and again asked for definite assurances that the Japanese would not, under the terms of the proposed legislation, be regarded as non-Aryans. He warned about the current effects of this issue on German—Japanese relations and stated that Ambassador Nagai had received specific assurances in his talks with von Bülow and von Neurath during October that the term 'coloured' did not apply to the Japanese.[33]

By then the Wilhelmstrasse was so disturbed by Far Eastern and world reactions to Germany's racial legislation and the

general practices of the régime that on 21 November it convened an inter-Ministerial conference to draft a government
statement on the subject. The Foreign Office view was that
'if we do not succeed in dispelling the distrust of the coloured
world, our political and cultural relations with the countries
in question will deteriorate acutely, our trade will suffer great
losses, and our Germans abroad possibly lose their livelihood
in these countries'. The Wilhelmstrasse's memorandum for
the meeting of 21 November then continued:

the Departments must therefore be clear as to whether this loss should
be accepted or whether there are perhaps ways which, without harming
our foreign relations, allow the aim of the racial renewal of the German
people to be attained. This important question obviously cannot be
decided by the Foreign Office alone. We must establish with the participating Departments whether and in which direction the German standpoint can be defined with regard to the coloured races. The matter has
become urgent because both Japanese and Chinese diplomats have
continually pressed for a definitive answer. We should also not forget
that since the hostility against Germany as a result of the Jewish question
has begun to abate somewhat, we must not offer fresh material for the
propaganda campaign against the new Germany by means of the colour
question.[34]

Although von Bülow was to admit to Trautmann the difficulties of finding a formula which would at the same time
satisfy internal necessities and Chinese and Japanese susceptibilities, nevertheless there can be no doubt that Nazi views on
race and the Jewish question found a ready and sympathetic
response in many quarters of the German Foreign Office.[35]
It is hard to tell, of course, how much of this may indeed
have been due to considerations of political expediency.

Following two meetings on 21 and 29 November, a formula
of sorts was worked out and then stated by the Minister of
the Interior, Wilhelm Frick, in an interview with a representative of the *Wolffs Telegraphisches Büro* on 5 December 1933.
Although less explicit than the Foreign Office might have
desired, Frick's statement nevertheless went beyond what
certain sections of the Nazi Party would have wished to be
publicly stated, and demonstrated the impact of foreign policy
considerations on what had been regarded, certainly by the
hard-liners in the Party, as purely domestic matters. Frick
categorically denied Far Eastern press reports that the German
Government intended to discriminate against the members of
other races, but emphasised that its chief aim in framing this

legislation was to maintain the racial purity of the German people, that the Jews were the most numerous alien race in Germany, and that German racial legislation had to be understood as 'a defensive rather than a racial measure'. He insisted that these laws did not imply any value judgement on other races, while he felt that the implications of the laws controlling mixed marriages in Germany had been distorted by alarmist rumours from abroad.[36]

If the Germans thought that such general statements would suffice to dispel Japanese misgivings, they were sadly mistaken. The reaction in Japan was one of extreme dismay since it was felt that the German Government had not gone far enough on the question of mixed marriages. Ambassador Nagai also expressed his disappointment, but recognising the difficulties of Germany's internal situation admitted that it could be regarded as a 'beginning'.[37] For his part, von Dirksen suggested that Japanese resentment on the question might be overcome by a more positive approach to the Manchukuo problem by Germany, as well as a policy of avoiding such terms as 'Yellow' and 'coloured' in connection or in conjunction with the 'Aryan question'. Although von Bülow thought that von Dirksen overestimated 'this resentment',[38] it was still felt necessary to get Frick to make another speech on Germany's racial legislation and policies. On 15 February 1934, in an address to the Diplomatic Corps, he again emphasised that the German Government intended no reflection on other peoples and races by this legislation.[39]

By May 1934 it was being suggested in the Wilhelmstrasse that one answer to the problem might be an internal German decree excluding Chinese and Japanese from the Aryan laws, and if this was not yet possible specific cases of complaint should be handled with especial regard to foreign policy considerations.[40] It appeared that Frick accepted the importance of this point since he emphasised to the Foreign Office that National Socialist ideology proceeded on the assumption of the *Verschiedenartigkeit* and not of the *Verschiedenwertigkeit* of the races, and that the racial laws implied no attack on other races. While he was prepared to recommend to the authorities the suggestion made by von Dirksen, he did not think it was possible to exclude the Japanese from the Aryan laws, although this would of course be done in particular cases.[41]

Nevertheless, the problem was kept alive by individual cases of discrimination in Germany and by the lack of a legal as opposed to a political statement regarding the position of the Japanese under the racial laws of Nazi Germany. By 7 August 1934 it had been agreed between the Referat Deutschland department in the Foreign Office, headed by Vicco von Bülow-Schwante and responsible for the foreign policy repercussions of internal German affairs, and the Racial Policy Office of the NSDAP (*Rassenpolitisches Amt*) headed by Dr Walter Gross, that there should be an inter-Ministerial meeting to discuss the whole question. It was hoped that ways and means would be found of eliminating undesirable international reactions to Germany's racial policies. Of particular significance was the suggestion of possibly separating the Jewish question from the racial problem in general. In his memorandum of 7 August von Bülow-Schwante recorded the Party's agreement to support the Foreign Office in its endeavours to avoid foreign policy difficulties over the racial legislation, an indication that the Party was also worried about Germany's image abroad, certainly in politically sensitive areas. Suitable instructions were to be issued within the Party, and Dr Gross also agreed to impress on German public opinion the need to respect the susceptibilities of other races.[42]

In a memorandum of 29 August for the forthcoming conference von Erdmannsdorff accurately described the central problem when he stated that the extent of the difficulty 'leads one to wonder whether it would not now appear desirable to have a decision as to what races should be affected by the restrictions of the Aryan legislation'. He accepted the application of this legislation to Jews and 'members of the primitive races (Negroes, Polynesians, etc)' but not to 'peoples of a high racial and cultural standard such as the Japanese and Chinese who, moreover, in the view of many scholars, are, since they belong to the Turanian group of races, closely related to the Germanic peoples'. It was his view that until the concept 'Aryan' had been defined in principle the measures suggested by von Dirksen and taken up since then in the Foreign Office and the Ministry of the Interior, and more recently in the conversation between von Bülow-Schwante and Dr Gross, should be applied. Of these it was most important to get the press to refrain from using the terms 'yellow races' or 'coloured races' or linking up the problem of 'coloured peoples' with the German Aryan legislation.[43] Von Erdmanns-dorff's views and recommendations in effect amounted to classifying the Japanese as 'honorary Aryans'.

The Foreign Office invitation to the inter-Ministerial meeting on 15 November emphasised that its purpose would be to discuss the effect of Germany's racial policies on her foreign relations, and although it was admitted that the question naturally touched on a basic principle of National Socialist ideology which could not be abandoned, nevertheless it was argued that this should not be allowed to impair relationships with other countries. As a point of discussion, it was suggested that the Aryan legislation might be so phrased as to apply to Jews only and not to other non-Aryans such as the Chinese, Japanese, and South Americans.[44] Admiral Behncke voiced similar views, and he too felt that a government statement was needed to indicate whether and how Japanese citizens would be affected by proposed race laws.[45]

The inter-Ministerial meeting of 15 November 1934 yielded two important results: the Foreign Office's point of view was successfully carried, and some of the proposals discussed although not finally decided upon, were to form the nucleus of the Nuremberg laws of September 1935. Von Bülow-Schwante suggested that local authorities and Party offices should be instructed to limit the Aryan legislation to Jews and grant exceptions to non-Aryans of foreign nationality or parentage. Dr Gross, speaking for Rudolf Hess, explained that although the Party was not in a position to depart from its basic attitude to the racial question, he was authorised to state that it would cooperate in ensuring exceptional treatment in cases where foreign relations would be impaired by decisions taken in domestic policy. Ministerialdirektor Nicolai of the Ministry of the Interior made a suggestion which had already been mooted for some time and which carried von Bülow-Schwante's proposals a stage further: he wondered whether existing ambiguities would not be eliminated if in the Civil Service Code and other legislation the word 'Jewish' was substituted for the term 'non-Aryan'. Although agreed to in principle, it was felt that this important and far-reaching step required further study. Finally the meeting accepted proposals put forward by the Foreign Office: henceforth the Ministry of the Interior was to be responsible for decisions under the Aryan Laws which involved foreigners or people of foreign non-Aryan parentage; that the cases transferred to the Ministry of the Interior would be decided by that Ministry in consultation with Reich Minister Hess (Racial Policy Office) and with the Foreign Office. It was also agreed that the guiding principles for granting exceptions to the Aryan legislation should be that the disadvantages in foreign policy would considerably outweigh any success achieved in internal policy.[46]

While the Foreign Office thus succeeded in getting its arguments accepted, it was not expected that the conclusions of this meeting would be speedily or even totally implemented. In fact, in a lengthy reply on 30 January 1935 to the communication from Admiral Behncke of the previous October, the NSDAP *Rassenpolitisches Amt* fiercely opposed any suggestion of classifying the Japanese as Aryans, a proposition it considered tantamount to the abandonment of a fundamental National Socialist principle. The fact that there seemed to be a genuine conflict of interests in reconciling basic ideological assumptions with the exigencies of politics in general and foreign policy in particular, merely convinced the Party of the primacy of the racial concept and the need to confine Aryan status to Germans only. The Party also failed to see why, in view of earlier explanations, the introduction of Germany's racial laws should cause any resentment, while it warned that in any further discussions, particularly with the Japanese, such 'weakening' on racial issues as Admiral Behncke had displayed must not be repeated.[47]

In Tokio Legation Counsellor Kolb welcomed the news that Germany's racial laws were to be applied only to Jews since he believed the Japanese would conclude that Germany did not intend to judge them in racial terms and they would therefore lose interest in what was essentially a domestic German issue. But he advised repeated explanations to the Japanese on the need for, and objectives of, Germany's racial legislation, basing this on a Ministry of the Interior aide-mémoire for the Foreign Office, part of which ran as follows: 'the difficulties foreign countries have in understanding Germany's racial policies lie not so much in the direction of this policy as in ignorance of the aims pursued by the German Government'.[48] Kolb therefore suggested that it be emphasised in Japan that 'Germany's only racial problem was a Jewish one', and other races had nothing to fear from Germany's racial laws. Finally, he urged that Japan's own demand for equality of treatment — *Gleichberechtigung* — in world affairs might be suitably supported.[49]

The success of these proposals depended entirely upon what happened in Germany and whether inferior racial status was applied to Jews rather than to non-Aryans in future legislation. Although Counsellor Rohde of the Far Eastern section in the Wilhelmstrasse doubted whether the Party would approve so radical a semantic departure,[50] it was in actual fact carried out within six months. At Nuremberg on 13 September 1935 Hitler ordered that a 'Law for the Protection of German Blood and Honour' be drawn up in two days. From the point of view of the Wilhelmstrasse the Nuremberg Laws represented a great step forward by basing definitions of race on Jewish rather than non-Aryan criteria.[51]

In both Foreign Office and Party circles it was felt that the new laws would remove most of the misunderstandings which had hitherto exacerbated German–Japanese relations because of this particular question. The law of 15 September therefore removed legalistic irritations even if it could not entirely remove individual instances of racial discrimination and prejudice against Japanese domiciled in Germany. Yet what had happened significantly demonstrated how sensitive even the Nazi State was to external pressures, and the strength of foreign policy considerations on matters of domestic policy. The issue had also shown the undoubted influence of the Foreign Office in the decision-making process, besides indicating the degree to which Nazi racialist attitudes were shared by some members of the German Foreign Office. The Nuremberg Laws, resolving as they did a contentious issue between Germany and Japan, came just in time to allow negotiations for the crucial Anti-Comintern Pact to proceed without undue difficulties of this kind in the background.

Another question which tended to disturb German–Japanese relations was Germany's apparent attitude of ambivalence towards the former German colonies in the North Pacific, now mandated to Japan. While the colonial issue had never died down in Germany after the Treaty of Versailles in 1919 and was used by Hitler in varying degrees and for different purposes, what concerned the Japanese in 1933 was the conjunction of German colonial demands with their own withdrawal from the League of Nations. This raised the pertinent question of whether or not Japan had to 'return' to the League the mandated territories she administered, with the possibility that the original colonial powers might then have a claim for the return of their former colonial territory.[52] The Germans thought the issue could only be settled through the League of Nations, and not solely by Japan who argued that it was one for discussion between the ex-Principal Allied and Associated Powers.[53] The Japanese, and particularly the Japanese naval authorities, reacted very strongly to any suggestion that the German Government had a justifiable claim to the Pacific Islands, regarded as 'Japan's life-line by sea as Manchukuo is the life-line by land'.[54] On 24 March 1933 Voretzsch reported from Tokio on this concern, but also complained about former Ambassador Solf's statements to Japanese officials in Berlin that Germany placed little value on a return of the Pacific Islands as compared with the former African territories. Voretzsch was concerned in case such talk impaired Germany's general position on the colonial question.[55]

Great excitement was caused, however, by reports of what was supposed to have transpired at a *Bierabend* at the Japanese Embassy in Berlin on 24 March 1933 before the arrival of the new Japanese Ambassador, Matsuzo Nagai, thus leading to a veritable 'storm in a beer mug' in German–Japanese relations. Goebbels, Minister of Propaganda, Rosenberg, Head of the APA, and Funk, Chief of the Reich Press Bureau, were all reported as having suggested to the Japanese Chargé d'Affaires that Japan should formally return the Pacific Islands to Germany but that she would be allowed to continue her occupation of them. These reports were denied, it being emphasised that there had been only private and unofficial conversations. It was also reported that Hitler had instructed the leaders of the Nazi Party to refrain from issuing any unauthorised statements on the question in future in order to avoid the risk of disturbing relations with Japan.[56]

Thereafter, and particularly while the legal issues regarding Mandatory Powers who were no longer members of the League of Nations remained unresolved, all parties involved attempted to play down the question. In Shanghai the Japanese Secretary of Legation, Ota, was assured by a member of the German Consulate that recent reports did not imply a systematic anti-Japanese campaign on the question but were intended, in his view, to draw attention to Germany's more general claims regarding colonies.[57] Likewise, and especially following Hitler's

orders to the Party, the Wilhelmstrasse also avoided any unnecessary mention of the subject when Ambassador Nagai
was received at the Foreign Office for the first time.[58] Its
embarrassment was all the greater, therefore, when on 6 April
1933 the *Deutsche Allgemeine Zeitung* published an open
letter from a section of the German Colonial League which
demanded that Japan should return the former German
colonies.[59] Similar efforts to reduce the temperature of this
issue were also made in Japan. Although the Navy Ministry
continued to be suspicious whenever the question was raised,
Shigenori Togo thought that Japan had nothing to fear from
Germany: 'as these islands are not politically or economically
of any vital importance to present-day Germany, it may be
presumed that she will not insist in regaining them in the face
of our objections thereto'.[60]

Interestingly enough, a Foreign Office meeting on 25 April
1933 was in favour of maintaining the Mandates system since
this (ostensibly) avoided the annexation of former colonial
territories by the Mandatory Powers. This meeting also reaffirmed the view that the whole question had to be dealt
with by the League of Nations and not by the Principal Allied
and Associated Powers as the Japanese seemed to think, and
implied that any legal decision should be in the direction of the
'return' of a mandated territory to the League of Nations by a
Mandatory Power that left the League. But as to the German
attitude should this ever be put to the test, this was left open.[61]

The whole issue was again raised towards the end of 1934
when it was reported that the United States was about to
make a move regarding Japan's fortification of the Pacific
Islands. The Japanese were afraid that Germany would be
asked to support American efforts to remove these islands
from Japan's control and authority. While these reports were
denied, the Wilhelmstrasse insisted on maintaining an open-
ended attitude on the issue: 'in order to maintain our basic
standpoint in the mandates question, we do not intend to
interfere in any discussion of the Pacific Mandates'.[62]

Japan's increased nervousness was due to the imminence of
her formal withdrawal from the League of Nations in 1935,
and to some extent this was appreciated in Germany. In March
1935 Dr Heinrich Schnee suggested to Hitler that Germany
should accept the permanent loss of the Pacific territories to
Japan, and that perhaps compensation could be arranged

between the two countries.[63] More positive, and controversial, was von Dirksen's response in Tokio. In reply to a query from Foreign Minister Hirota, he stated that according to his knowledge Germany did not intend to raise the mandates question with Japan. On 23 March Hirota put this more forcefully in the Japanese Diet when he stated that he had been assured by von Dirksen that Germany did not intend to demand the return of the Pacific Islands.[64] Von Bülow, however, complained that von Dirksen had been too specific in his statement to Hirota and suggested that he should have ignored Hirota's mention of the mandates question. Somewhat peevishly, von Dirksen justified his action by referring to Dieckhoff's telegram of 10 November 1934. It was clear that von Dirksen thought the time had arrived to make a formal statement expressing Germany's disinterestedness in the Pacific Islands, and as if to reinforce this idea he included yet another strong statement from the Japanese naval authorities expressing the view that these islands clearly belonged to Japan.[65]

Yet on 25 and 26 March Hitler complained bitterly to the British Foreign Secretary, Sir John Simon, about the fact that although Japan had left the League of Nations she would still be able to retain former German territory which Germany herself would not get back even if she returned to the League.[66] Reports then began to circulate that Britain and Germany were arranging their own *Kuhhandel* in the colonial field at Japan's expense, but this was quickly denied by the Germans.[67] When von Neurath gave Ambassador Nagai an account of these talks he referred directly to Germany's demands for the return of colonies, but left open the question of exactly what Germany might or might not do in this connection. The question was also discussed in a general way between the two men on 6 May 1935.[68]

Intermittently, then, the question remained an irritating side-issue in German–Japanese relations, and was raised in diplomatic conversations and the Japanese press whenever speeches were delivered in Germany on the colonial issue. Even during 1936, when serious negotiations were under way for the Anti-Comintern Pact, and even after its conclusion, the Japanese still waxed nervously on the subject.[69]

German–Japanese relations were also disturbed by economic issues. Two problems in particular caused great difficulty:

German accusations of Japanese 'dumping' of cheaply made and lower priced goods in overseas markets, thus competing 'unfairly' with better quality and higher priced German manufactured goods; and the disparity in the balance of trade between the two countries in Germany's favour. A public reference to Japan's desire that this imbalance be rectified was made by Ambassador Nagai when visiting Hamburg in September 1933.[70]

Although much of the hostile opinion expressed in Germany against Japanese trade practices originated from economic circles, there were nevertheless political overtones to many of the comments because of the linking together of Japan's economic aims with her political ambitions. Werner Daitz of the *APA* came out strongly against 'dumping' practices, and emphasised that National Socialist foreign trade policy was guided by the principles of 'fair play'.[71] This point was also echoed by Robert Ley, Director of the Party Organisation of the Nazi Party, in a speech at Cologne on 9 April 1934. Ambassador Nagai complained bitterly about this speech to von Neurath on 18 April because of reports that Ley had used the offensive term 'coolies'.[72]

Yet the question of competition and alleged dumping was only the symptom of a deeper malaise in German—Japanese relations. Japanese complaints about the prevailing pattern of trade with Germany were accentuated after 1933 by the changes introduced into the management of Germany's foreign trade designed to bring about a 'defence economy'.[73] The Japanese felt that the imposition of import quotas and the raising of tariffs on imported raw materials was particularly directed at them, although some Japanese comment on the situation expressed more sorrow than anger.[74] This was not the mood, however, of Saburo Kurusu, head of the economic division of the Japanese Foreign Office, when in May 1934 he met the new economic expert at the German Embassy in Tokio, Secretary of Legation Haas. He even threatened that Japan would retaliate by cutting off imports from Germany. Haas vigorously denied the accusation of unilateral measures against Japanese trade and warned Kurusu against making the temporary stringency resulting from the shortage of foreign exchange the basis for a general judgement about developments in German—Japanese trade. Von Dirksen in turn explained to Berlin that Japanese anxiety was due to uncertainty over

Britain's quota policies, while he expected that the Japanese would shortly ask for negotiations to settle the trade question between Berlin and Tokio. But his request for instructions was not answered until a month later when he was finally told to wait and see whether the Japanese actually requested negotiations with Germany.[75]

Although a step towards reducing the tension appeared to have been taken by the agreement signed in Tokio on 25 July 1934 by which Germany and Japan agreed to avoid the double taxation of shipping profits in both countries,[76] the optimism was short-lived. Kurusu's threats to Haas appeared to be substantiated by von Dirksen's communication of 7 August 1934 in which he forwarded a confidential memorandum detailing the Japanese Ministry of Trade's proposed counter-measures against German trade with Japan.[77] This coincided with the preparations in Germany for the introduction of Schacht's New Plan the following month, with its stricter control of foreign exchange and imports. Taking note of Japanese hints, Benzler of the Economic Department in the Wilhelmstrasse suggested to von Dirksen in a telegram of 25 August that the Foreign Office was prepared to consider adjustments should it be found that the new measures led to a disproportionate deterioration in Japanese imports. A few days later von Bülow likewise assured the Japanese Ambassador that the new measures would really apply to countries with which Germany already had trade agreements and he doubted whether they would affect German–Japanese trade.[78] There were difficulties, however, for as von Dirksen reported in September, Germany's introduction of quotas on imports of Japanese artificial silks was going to be countered by increased duties in Japan on imports of drugs and chemicals from Germany.[79]

The introduction of the New Plan meant that price connections with other countries were severed or greatly modified and foreign exchange governed by an extensive clearing system, so that by 1938 about forty clearing agreements existed covering about 80 per cent of German imports.[80] Bilateral clearing agreements determined the total of goods that could be exchanged with other countries within a specified period of time, as well as outlawing the conversion of money between the countries involved. But the Foreign Office opposed any idea of applying such agreements to German–Japanese trade since, in von Bülow's words, it was felt to be 'a dangerous experiment'. Ambassador Nagai was also opposed to any clearing agreements between Germany and Japan.[81]

The discussions that ensued over the following months and years were primarily concerned, therefore, with the technical details of reconciling Japanese demands for a greater share of the German market with Germany's foreign trade restrictions. Threats of restrictive counter-measures against German imports into Japan prompted the Foreign Office in October 1934 to impress upon the Ministry of Economics that the application of the New Plan should not lead to a worsening of Japan's already poor balance of trade with Germany through a further reduction of Japanese imports into Germany. It was requested that suitable sums of foreign exchange be allocated to prevent this.[82] This principle was accepted and the technical details of foreign exchange allocation for specific Japanese imports were agreed to at meetings in the Ministry of Economics on 8 November and 4 December 1934. It was also agreed that trade with Japan was to be regulated on the basis of mutual understanding and not by means of any special agreements, while to the Japanese it was to be pointed out that these arrangements and the maintenance of the trade relationship of 5:1 (German exports to Japan: Japanese imports into Germany) could not be pursued if the Japanese imposed restrictions on German imports into Japan. Von Dirksen was also instructed to stress Germany's foreign exchange difficulties, but emphasise that everybody concerned with German–Japanese trade in Germany intended to develop these relations.[83]

Under Japanese pressure the trade ratio between the two countries was changed during 1935 to 4:1,[84] but even this did not remove all difficulties. The Japanese continually pressed for a relaxation of controls on their exports to Germany, as well as assurances that these exports would not suddenly be affected or restricted by Germany's foreign exchange difficulties or regulations. The Wilhelmstrasse supported Japanese efforts to have regulations applying to Japan's trade fixed for a twelve-month period instead of a six-month one,[85] while at an inter-Ministerial meeting on 11 May 1935 Knoll explained that the Japanese were complaining that they were being denied foreign exchange certificates for the import of Japanese goods into Germany by the control boards set up under the New Plan. Knoll emphasised that there was a risk of counter-measures against German goods, while he pointed out that Japan had to be given special consideration because of the forthcoming mission to Manchukuo, and on that question 'one was entirely dependent upon the goodwill of the Japanese'. The meeting did agree to increased foreign exchange allowances for Japanese imports into Germany, and from this point on German–Japanese trade relations operated within limits that were more or less acceptable to both sides, even though the Japanese still tried to remove all restrictions while the Germans had no wish to commit themselves too far ahead in their own regulations and arrangements.[86] Although there was a basic and natural conflict of interests, the air of extreme tension on this question gradually evaporated, although the question was to be an important part of the negotiations conducted by the Kiep Mission during its visit to the Far East in 1935 and 1936.[87] It was an interesting pointer to political developments that after the conclusion of the Anti-Comintern Pact the *Ostasiatische Rundschau* published an article which referred to the mutual understanding and economic interests of Germany and Japan, despite their economic rivalry.[88]

Until after the conclusion of the Anti-Comintern Pact there were no close military relations between Germany and Japan, and what existed was based on the usual type of commercial-technical agreements that Germany had with many other countries. Since nothing like the situation existing between the Reichswehr and China was to be found between Germany and Japan, the Foreign Office was less involved in such developments as occurred in military relations with Tokio, particularly in the period up to 1938.[89] On the other hand, it was the Foreign Office which made the arrangements for Colonel Eugene Ott's trip to Japan as a military observer during 1933 when he was given 'special facilities' for studying the Japanese Army in Japan and in Manchukuo. Von Bülow's telegram of 17 March 1933 to the Embassy at Tokio makes it clear that the trip was arranged at the same time as German military attachés were being sent to other missions, and Ott's trip was seen as a way of avoiding the appointment of such an attaché at Tokio but at the same time of not offending Japanese susceptibilities.[90] By 1934, when Ott was finally sent to Japan as military attaché, it appeared that the Japanese Army would restrict the facilities it afforded him. At the same time it emerged that Major Komatsu, the private secretary to the new Minister of War, General Senjuro Hayashi, knew only one foreign language and that was German.[91]

While Germany's increasing military-political involvement in China precluded similar links with Japan, the Reichswehr and the Foreign Office discounted Japan as a useful factor for Germany in world politics, especially with regard to any Russo—Japanese or even Russo—German conflict, Japan's weaknesses in the economic sphere being especially remarked upon.[92] Before his second departure for Japan in March 1934, this time as Military Attaché, Ott displeased Hitler by agreeing with a despatch from the Military Attaché at Moscow, Colonel Otto Hartmann,[93] which had declared that a Japanese attack on Russia would have no effect on the European situation. It seemed that the Japanese army was behind the times in training and equipment, a point taken up by von Dirksen as evidence that an imminent Russo—Japanese war was unlikely.[94] It also appeared that the Soviet Far Eastern Army was developing an increasingly independent position *vis-à-vis* European Russia. Ott's conclusion was that distances were too great in Russia for a Far Eastern war to have an influence on the European situation. Hitler disagreed and promptly terminated the interview.[95] Hartmann's general end of the year survey for 1933 concluded that in the event of war with Japan, Russia would employ 20—30 divisions in the Far East, leaving 120—30 divisions in the west which were more than sufficient to deal with Poland's 50—60 divisions. Hartmann admitted, however, that the situation could change in the event of a long-drawn out war in the Far East or in the case of a more general war.[96]

While informed observers entertained no doubts about the difficulties facing Soviet Russia in developing a relatively 'independent' and efficient Far Eastern Army,[97] the trend for the future accorded more with the analysis put forward by Hartmann and Ott. There were two reasons for Hitler's angry reaction on this subject: disappointment at concrete evidence of Russian preparations in case of war on her most vulnerable frontier; and secondly, continual reports of a temporary stabilisation of the uneasy relations between Soviet Russia and Japan.[98] As it was, Hartmann reported on 10 January 1934 that there would be no advantage to Germany from any Far Eastern war.[99] These developments obviously brought into question the whole *raison d'être* of Nazi leanings towards Japan which aimed to exert additional pressure on Soviet Russia. There was also the notion of reversing Japan's role during the First World War by turning Japanese strength against Britain's position in world affairs. Already in October 1933 von Blomberg had hinted to von Dirksen that it was Hitler's intention to endeavour to find in Japan a substitute for Russia, especially in military affairs.[100]

There was a third reason for Hitler's anger. The arguments put forward by Hartmann and Ott reminded him of the Reichswehr's lack of enthusiasm for the winding-up during 1933 of the long and fruitful period of military cooperation with Soviet Russia which had ensued during the 1920s.[101] In 1933 General von Seeckt published a pamphlet in which he emphasised that Germany should not join the ranks of Russia's enemies. Colonel Georg Thomas, later head of the German Armed Forces Economic and Armaments Office, agreed with this view, especially after his visit to Russia during 1933 with General von Vollard-Bockelberg.[102] Hartmann also warned that should Germany opt for Japan in world affairs, this would eventually push Russia into the waiting and willing arms of France.[103]

In general, though, there proceeded the development of a relationship between the Reichswehr — after May 1935 the Wehrmacht[104] — and the Japanese Army, links between the two going back to before the turn of the century.[105] Ott made a point of developing good relations with the Japanese Army, efforts which began to be reciprocated during 1935 because by then the Japanese gradually came to be impressed by Germany's military and political recovery in Europe at the time.[106] Tentative steps were also taken to improve technical cooperation with the Japanese Army. While technical facilities and information were made available to the large number of Japanese army and naval officers who visited Germany from 1933, in October 1935 Ott suggested that in return Germany should demand certain technical information, that the Japanese army should give information about Russia, and support the German Economic Mission that was about to visit the Far East.[107] It seems that little came of these proposals. In the autumn of 1936 Ott told Hitler that he was unable to form an opinion on the value or worth of the Japanese army since the Japanese were sparing with the necessary information. He suggested that if Hitler sent a mission of technical experts to Japan to instruct its army in Germany's latest techniques he might be able to obtain military information in return. While Hitler evidently agreed to this suggestion, General von Fritsch, the Commander-in-Chief of the Army, opposed it since he felt unable to spare any officers for such an assignment. The real reason, though, was undoubtedly his concern for Germany's military interests in China, especially the position of the military advisers, and no military mission was sent to Japan. This incident served only to heighten Hitler's long-term dislike of Fritsch, the epitome of the type of Prussian officer he detested. Moreover, Fritsch seemed to go out of his way to make his independence of, and antipathy towards the Nazi régime, well known. In turn this laid him open to the kinds of intrigues and hatred of the SS and other rivals that finally led to his downfall at the beginning of 1938.[108]

The idea of closer military-political relations between the armed forces of Germany and Japan was also taken up by Admiral Behncke, President of the German–Japanese Association, who canvassed leading personalities and Ministries during 1935, suggesting ways in which this could be done. On 10 October he wrote to the War Minister, General von Blomberg, suggesting that language and other courses should be established in the armed forces, and that employees of German firms in Japan should be utilised for service in the Wehrmacht. While he only received a negative reply from von Blomberg, and not until 24 April 1936 at that, both the Navy and Air Force promised to pursue Behncke's suggestions further.[109]

Although a German Naval Attaché, Commander Paul Wenneker, was appointed to the German Embassy at Tokio in the autumn of 1933, German–Japanese naval relations seemed as distant and troubled as were military relations. While there had been some close technical cooperation during the 1920s, particularly on submarines,[110] von Dirksen later complained that this good foundation was not built upon because of the 'customary secretiveness' of the Japanese Navy.[111] Similarly, Wenneker complained that during his period of service in Japan from 1934 to 1937 he had 'absolutely no instruction of any kind with reference to military collaboration with Japan', and that he and other naval attachés had been treated with 'like suspicion and distrust by Japanese naval officers'.[112] Yet according to a British report of January 1934, Wenneker also boasted that he expected that the Japanese naval authorities would allow him to see everything 'as there is very close understanding between Japan and Germany now'. It was also learnt that the Japanese Naval Attaché at Berlin had been allowed to go to sea in German ships and witness gunnery and torpedo practices.[113]

Yet there was some technical cooperation in the naval sphere. On 23 January 1935 Wenneker reported that the inspection of aircraft carriers was going according to plan and that the greatest cooperation was being afforded by the Japanese authorities. By July 1935 the Japanese Navy was proposing an expansion of this kind of cooperation to cover the exchange of information on such matters as aircraft and submarines, while they were even prepared to advise the Germans on the question of aircraft carriers. The Japanese Naval Attaché in Berlin would be instructed to approach the Marineleitung on these matters. Later, von Dirksen wrote approvingly of the Japanese Navy's help to a mission of German naval technicians who visited Japan during 1935.[114] However in August 1935 German naval authorities admitted that they were more interested in Japanese tactics than technical knowledge.[115]

Nevertheless, by April 1936 Wenneker was complaining to the British Assistant Naval Attaché at Tokio that the German Navy could never consider any agreement with the Japanese to exchange information on technical subjects. According to Wenneker, the exchanges of information on the basis of details of Japanese submarines and aircraft carriers had come to a halt, principally because the Japanese had been so vague about what they would offer in the way of submarines and because the German Admiralty had decided that the aircraft carrier had no place in the German Navy. Wenneker also complained about the fact that unlike Japanese naval officers in Germany, he was allowed no opportunity to visit military or naval establishments. He had therefore presented what had amounted to an ultimatum to Captain Tayui, the Ministry of Marine's Adjutant. It was later learned that the naval authorities in Germany had begun to crack down on what they showed Japanese officers until similar facilities were afforded to Wenneker. In any case, the mutual suspicion shown by German and Japanese naval officers on the occasion of the visit of the cruiser *Karlsruhe* to Japan in March 1936 demonstrated the great gap still existing between the German and Japanese navies.[116]

But there were also political problems associated with German—Japanese naval relations. In June 1934 the Wilhelmstrasse and the Marineleitung denied the veracity of reports that the Japanese Navy would support Germany if she wished to participate in the preliminary and naval conferences, especially the Naval Conference of 1935. The Foreign Office's information was that the Japanese Government opposed German participation since this would inevitably lead to demands for Russia's participation, thus ensuring a full discussion of Far Eastern problems.[117] It also appears that the Japanese Foreign Office initially persuaded the Japanese Navy, without too much effort of course, to adopt a less favourable and more critical attitude towards the Anglo—German Naval Agreement of 18 June 1935.[118]

The Japanese Ministry of Marine was also closely involved in several aviation questions between the two countries, much to the discomfort of the German Foreign Office in the winter of 1934—35. It seemed that the negotiations by Zores and Breithaupt for the sale of Zeppelins to the Pacific Air Transport Company for an air service covering Manchukuo, Japan and the Pacific Islands, the exchange of 'Zeppelins for soya beans' which caused such a furore in China, were being regarded in Japan almost as official negotiations, despite the Wilhelmstrasse's request to the contrary.[119] This was because the principal parties were the German—Manchukuo Export and Import Company, in agreement with the *Luftschiffbau* Zeppelin Company and the Japanese Ministry of Marine. Von Dirksen also emphasised that if the negotiations were not successfully concluded or satisfactory reasons put forward for any German withdrawal from them, this would be detrimental to good German—Japanese political relations.[120] However, the Foreign Office was assured by the Reich Air Ministry that official negotiations were not taking place.[121] In addition, mutual study tours for air force officers took place during 1934 and 1935 while in September 1935 a three-man mission from the German Air and Navy Ministries went to Japan to study the whole problem of developing Germany's air and naval links with Japan. Later, the Heinkel Aircraft Company allowed the Japanese to manufacture Heinkel engines on licence.[122]

The appointment of a German air attaché at Tokio was also discussed during 1934 and 1935, but von Dirksen was worried lest Germany went ahead of other countries in this respect. Similarly, in June 1935 the Japanese Ministry of Marine was concerned in case Japan precipitately 'recognised' Germany's rearmament in the air. Although the Foreign Office in Berlin thought that this attitude was 'unsatisfactory and unnecessary', Japanese suggestions were in fact taken up by the Reich Air Ministry and a junior officer was sent out as Ott's assistant.[123]

From 1933 to 1935, therefore, these developments in German–Japanese relations, and the whole range and variety of developments in Sino–German and German–Manchukuoan relations meant that Germany's involvement and commitments in the Far East grew deeper and more complicated. But during these years, and whatever the nature of Germany's relations with the three countries of the Far East, no important or overtly political agreements or arrangements were arrived at. Obvious difficulties were involved in pursuing these different sets of relationships at the same time, which were far from being complementary to each other in the tense Far Eastern situation. Nevertheless, and despite the fierce conflict of interests inside Germany itself, the German Foreign Office, up to 1935 that is, could still congratulate itself that the Far Eastern policy of balance and of political non-involvement which it constantly recommended and attempted to pursue, still remained relatively intact and somewhat successful.

From 1935, however, this situation changed. Negotiations set on foot by the Reichswehr Ministry in China, the German Foreign Office in Manchukuo, and the Nazi leadership through Herr von Ribbentrop, were to lead to the three separate and important agreements of 1936 with China, Manchukuo, and Japan. The fact that negotiations (and agreements) proceeded with the three Far Eastern countries at the same time might have been taken to mean that Germany was in fact formalising her policy of balance and neutrality in Far Eastern affairs. Nothing of the sort. The formal and serious nature of these negotiations served only to intensify and not mollify the conflict of purpose between the various German interests involved in Far Eastern affairs from 1935. They did nothing to resolve the basic dichotomy in Germany's Far Eastern policy and situation which had been implicit since 18 September 1931, nor could they given the state of affairs existing between China and Japan. On the contrary, by involving Germany so deeply and so variously in the Far East by the end of 1936, these negotiations and agreements ensured that when the perhaps inevitable war between China and Japan erupted, Germany especially would be confronted by the uncomfortable necessity of having to make some kind of choice in the Far East involving serious losses in one direction or the other. The course, progress, and results of the three sets of negotiations and agreements of 1935 and 1936 help to explain, therefore, the nature of the problems and dilemmas confronting the German policy-makers during the first year of the Sino–Japanese war which finally erupted in the summer of 1937.

V

Agreement with China: The Army, HAPRO, and China 1933-1936

The Klein—HAPRO agreement of 9 April 1936 between Germany and the Nanking Government, providing for the exchange of German armaments for Chinese raw materials vital for German rearmament, was the first of Germany's three Far Eastern agreements of 1936,[1] and the culminating point of the German Army's work in China over previous years. Confirmed by General von Reichenau's visit to China two months later the agreement marked the formal commitment of the Ministry of War to Germany's military work in China begun by Colonel Max Bauer's activities between 1927 and 1929. The Chinese undoubtedly saw the agreement as a political commitment on the part of Germany, giving China a much-needed boost in her struggle with Japan. For its part the Ministry of War encouraged the Chinese in this interpretation so as to ensure the fruits of the agreement and other enterprises. Yet the agreement's undeniably political character ran counter to the wishes of the German Foreign Office since it threatened to compromise Germany's political 'neutrality' in Far Eastern affairs by deeply involving and committing Germany on the Chinese side. Likewise, the Foreign Office was concerned by von Ribbentrop's negotiations with the Japanese military authorities since these too were intended to 'commit' Germany in the Far East, this time to the other side in the Far Eastern struggle for power. The Army's work in China, and the Nazi leadership's attempts to reach an agreement with the Japanese, underlined and reflected the basic dichotomy in Germany's Far Eastern policy and relationships in the first years of the Third Reich.

The fact was that by 1936 the Army's commitments and interests in China provided a serious challenge to the Foreign Office's policy of 'no Far Eastern entanglements' and to Nazi dreams of a closer relationship with Japan. This was due to their complexity, extent, and increasing importance to Germany's economic and military rearmament since China supplied Germany with wolfram and other high-quality ores vital for rearmament. The paradox was that this situation derived from the accelerated pace of rearmament brought about by direct and urgent pressure from Hitler because of his general and long-term foreign policy aims for Germany. The pace of rearmament desired by Hitler might well have been impossible without the supplies of raw materials obtained from China, and even he conceded the importance of Germany's military relations with China. Yet the development of these relations, especially after the establishment of the Nazi régime, raised two points of controversy between the Foreign Office on the one hand and the Reichswehr Ministry on the other, directly linked to the former's opposition to any German involvement in the labyrinth of Chinese domestic politics and its desire to avoid Japanese accusations of 'support' of China in the Far Eastern struggle. The first was how far German military interests in China were to be developed *per se,* and the second concerned the degree and nature of official support for them. From 1933 these and associated policy issues revolved around the activities of Hans Klein, previously active in Africa before 1914, who involved himself in matters pertaining to foreign policy, a situation encouraged by the 'anarchic-impulsive dictatorship' that was the Third Reich,[2] and behind whom loomed the shadow of the Reichswehr Ministry.

While Klein's own character contributed much to the political storms which raged about him in Berlin and China (he gave Trautmann a 'feeling of uneasiness and mystery'),[3] his pursuit of arms deals between Germany and China — or more precisely, between certain sectional interests in China and Germany — was bound to raise serious issues of foreign policy in both countries. Yet by the time that Klein's presence in China was first brought to the notice of the Foreign Office in Berlin in 1933 the nature of many of these issues had been clear for some time. The furore caused in Berlin by his work in China with different régimes therefore reflected the inter-action of the three complicated situations which affected or involved Germany in the Far East: the struggle for power within China itself; Japan's attempt to establish a position of mastery in that part of the world; and Germany's attempt to re-establish her interests, if not influence, in the Far East after her defeat and losses in the First World War and the serious blow this had dealt to her prestige as a Great Power.

The Foreign Office first learned of Hans Klein in November

1933 when Trautmann forwarded to Berlin a report from the Consul-General at Shanghai, Dr Wagner, that in the summer Klein had signed contracts with Marshals Chen Chi-tang and Li Tsung-jen for the establishment of an armaments industry in Canton. These had been negotiated in cooperation with a Major Preu who had accompanied General von Seeckt from Germany to China as far as Nanking, and had then parted from him to visit Canton. Von Seeckt had also called at Canton on his way back to Germany for confidential discussions with the Canton Marshals.[4] Klein had airily dismissed such important questions as Nanking's and Tokio's reactions to these contracts, emphasising instead that 'the leading circles at home had considered this carefully.' and had in turn discounted them, while he appeared confident that the financial arrangements would be secured by his application for a Reich guarantee. Trautmann, however, was horrified by 'such arrangements with a local government whose relations with the central government are entirely unstable', and he strongly recommended the 'exercise of extreme caution in so far as official support of Klein's plans is concerned'.[5]

Two things concerned the Wilhelmstrasse in Berlin: the fact of the contracts with Nanking's chief rivals, and Wagner's assumption that the Reichswehr was behind Klein. The Foreign Office later established that Klein was head of a trading organisation, STAMAG, and had received support from the Reichswehr Ministry, particularly the Ordnance Office. But although the Foreign Office agreed with Trautmann that Germany's sole concern should be with the Nanking Government,[6] pressure from the Nanking régime was needed before it decided to confront the Reichswehr Ministry with economic and political objections to the Klein project. In fact, the Chinese Counsellor of Legation, Tann, visited both the Reichswehr Ministry and the Foreign Office to emphasise that the appointment of military advisers to Canton and the establishment there of arsenals required the prior approval of the Nanking Government. Tann was so disappointed that General von Reichenau, Head of the Armed Forces Office (*Wehrmachtamt*) in the Reichswehr Ministry appeared to lack understanding of the delicate situation existing between Nanking and Canton that an informant suggested that the Wilhelmstrasse might 'educate' the Reichswehr Ministry in this respect.[7]

On 1 February 1934 Tann appeared at the Foreign Office to request just this. Some measure of success in the direction of blocking Klein's Canton projects seemed possible since General von Reichenau had just intimated to the Chinese authorities in Berlin that he would refrain from sending military advisers to Canton. Tann assumed that this was as a result of advice from General von Seeckt, although he was unclear about von Seeckt's role with respect to Klein's dealing with Canton.[8] Shortly afterwards, on 7 February, von Bülow wrote to General von Blomberg, Reichswehr Minister, and tentatively stated the Foreign Office's opinion that 'with regard to the [Chinese] Central Government's attitude it appears that Klein's plans are hardly feasible'. He therefore suggested a meeting of the Ministries concerned to discuss the matter.[9]

At this meeting on 16 February Altenburg, Kühlborn, and Stoller for the Foreign Office emphasised two things: that no confidence was placed in Klein's statements concerning the guarantees for the payments to be credited since the economy of the province of Kwantung was thought to be unsound; secondly, that the execution of the Klein project in Canton could jeopardise Germany's good relations with the central government and Chiang Kai-shek. It was emphasised that Germany had no interests in maintaining China's national disunity by supporting provincial régimes against the central authorities, or in maintaining that disunion as a permanent state as, for example, the Japanese might desire. The Reichswehr Ministry case was forcibly put by General von Reichenau, who argued that such orders from abroad would strengthen the productive capacity of the armaments industry particularly since it was not kept sufficiently employed by domestic orders.[10] The financial guarantees promised appeared to him to be sufficient, and he suggested that a successful execution of the project would result in increased sales of German industrial products in one of China's richest provinces. He took the opportunity to criticise the paucity of military orders from Nanking, nor did he believe that Nanking would retaliate against German trade should the project go ahead. Von Reichenau also felt that Nanking's objections were weakened by current discussions in Berlin on plans for a similar project for Nanking.[11] The General therefore recommended that the 'Nanking request that the Klein project be abandoned should not be acceded to without a corresponding *quid pro quo*'. Although he believed that they should stand firm he was, nevertheless, prepared to handle the Klein project in a dilatory manner for a time and to limit its scope because of the obvious political difficulties that would arise elsewhere in China for Germany. He agreed that the final decision should be made dependent upon von Seeckt's securing Chiang Kai-shek's agreement to the project, a suggestion accepted by Altenburg. But von Reichenau's parting shot seemed to confirm Klein's statement that his project had the support of 'leading circles at home', for he remarked that 'the financial part of the project had been settled through an agreement between the Reichswehr Ministry and the Reichsbank'.[12]

Subsequent developments served only to increase the Foreign Office's suspicion that its advice on matters crucial to Germany's foreign policy situation in the Far East was being ignored by the Reichswehr Ministry. While the Chinese Foreign Office denied Klein's assertions that Nanking had expressed 'understanding' for his Canton plans, the Wilhelm-strasse learned that Klein was the agent of a recently formed syndicate designed to facilitate the export of war material and arsenals to Canton. This was HAPRO (*Handelsgesell-schaft für industrielle Produkte mbH*) registered in the Greater Berlin Trade Registry on 21 January 1934 and apparently subordinate to the Reichswehr Ministry.[13] As disturbing to the Foreign Office was the news that von Seeckt had asked for more officers to be sent to China, while it appeared that the Reichswehr Ministry was granting leave of absence to active Reichswehr officers for service in China and offering immediate reintegration into the Reichswehr to some of the younger officers. Lieutenant-General Kurt Schonheinz, Director of the Foreign Department (*Abteilung Ausland*) in the Reichswehr Ministry, dismissed Meyer's objections by pointing out that the Reichswehr Minister himself supported von Seeckt's request. Faced with such authority, Meyer had no alternative but to suggest that von Blomberg's support of von Seeckt's request be acceded to, provided that this was the last request of this nature. Yet at the end of the month it was reported from China that von Seeckt had received an evasive reply to his request for more officers.[14] This general air of uncertainty was then compounded by information received from Canton at the end of May: that four new military advisers would shortly be going to Canton, more or less at the same time as the first deliveries of machinery for the new arsenal were expected. Klein was also expected in Canton at the beginning of June to undertake further negotiations. It also transpired that Klein's name was apparently suggested to Chiang Kai-shek by von Seeckt as a suitable person to organise the procurement of war material essential for the reconstruction of China's armed forces. But von Seeckt had not as yet, in May, spoken to Chiang Kai-shek about the Canton projects.[15]

While Klein signed further trade and military agreements with Canton in July and on 8 September 1934 contracted with Marshal Chen Chi-tang, Commander-in-Chief of the First Army Group at Canton, for the construction of armaments factories and an arsenal,[16] von Seeckt was proving himself a diligent servant both of Chiang Kai-shek and the Reichswehr Ministry. Evidently as a result of his efforts an important Chinese Government military–civilian commission was sent to Germany in the summer of 1934, arriving there on 28 July. The military section was led by the Commander of the Seventeenth Army, General Hsü Ting-yao, while the Vice-Minister of Communications, Yu Fei-peng, led the civilian section. Its purpose was to study communications systems and purchase material for the motorisation of the Chinese army and for the creation of an army intelligence service. The Chinese Legation in Berlin emphasised that this offered great opportunities to German industry.[17]

The most interesting thing to emerge from this visit was the subordination of the Foreign Office to the *Aussenpolitisches Amt* of the NSDAP regarding the programme and organisation of the visit, von Seeckt's agent, Major Pirner, approaching the Party and not the Foreign Office on this matter.[18] Although von Neurath received the leaders of the Commission on 20 September, Hitler did not receive them until 17 October. Hitler's reluctance was only overcome after it was repeatedly pointed out that the Commission had been received by Mussolini while in Italy, and that Chiang Kai-shek thought it only right that Hitler should accord the Commission the same honour in Germany. But even Hitler had finally to admit the economic gains to Germany in the form of contracts and orders as a result of the Commission's visit.[19] Surprisingly enough, the *APA*'s solicitous concern for this Chinese Commission came at a time when it was attempting to pursue very different foreign policy objectives in Manchukuo and *vis-à-vis* Japan.[20]

For their part von Seeckt and the Reichswehr Ministry were determined to do nothing *vis-à-vis* Japan that could compromise the position of the German military advisers with the Nanking Government. Both rejected a suggestion by the Japanese General Staff that Ott, the Military Attaché at Tokio, should mediate between the Japanese and the military staff at Nanking with a view to influencing Chiang Kai-shek in the direction of a Sino—Japanese rapprochement. Although it was agreed with the Foreign Office that Japanese suspicions of the German military advisers should be dispelled, mediation by Ott was rejected and the most that von Seeckt promised was to receive the Japanese Military Attaché, stipulating that he would inform Chiang Kai-shek beforehand. In the event, nothing came of these suggestions because the Japanese finally rejected them.[21]

What continued to disturb the Foreign Office, however, was not only the obvious expansion of the interests of the Reichswehr Ministry and the German armaments industry in China, the 16 February meeting notwithstanding, but also evidence of the way in which foreign policy initiatives in China were apparently being taken out of its hands. Besides informing Trautmann that Klein's contracts with Canton were in accordance with the plans of certain National Socialist circles in Germany to relieve Germany's raw materials shortages, von Seeckt also informed the German Minister in China that he had introduced Klein to Chiang Kai-shek so that similar plans could be pursued with Nanking but that he, von Seeckt, had emphasised that negotiations with Canton would continue as before. The Klein projects were also evidently going ahead without Trautmann or the Foreign Office being consulted about either their economic viability or possible effect on more usual trading channels and practices, let alone their political repercussions. Trautmann in particular was especially concerned by Chiang Kai-shek's suggestions that this business be organised at a government level and not through the private firms active in the China trade — which Trautmann considered to be 'the basis of our commercial activities in China' — and that negotiations on these matters should avoid the usual diplomatic channels. Trautmann also doubted whether barter agreements could be the means of exchanging German industrial and military products for Chinese raw materials since an essentially agricultural economy, managed as it was in the Chinese manner, could hardly complement such a strictly organised industrial economy as Germany's. Nevertheless, on 23 August 1934 Klein concluded a contract with the Nanking Government for the exchange of raw materials for German industrial products, while in October it was learned that in Canton he had begun to exclude German firms from participating in his business, especially the arsenal question. It also appeared that General von Reichenau's brother was active in the Canton area as a technical adviser.[22]

Trautmann's hope that this 'will not develop into a second Heye case' was undoubtedly shared by the Foreign Office. Yet von Seeckt and his mentors had one argument whose validity even the Wilhelmstrasse found it hard to deny by the end of the second year of the Nazi régime, which was that 'the question of the supply of raw materials was the focal point of our policy'. While this certainly reflected the feelings of Colonel Georg Thomas of the Army Ordnance Office, the fact that China could supply high quality ores clearly marked that country for an important place in the drive for a German 'defence economy'.[23] Seeckt claimed that: 'we needed 2,000 million Marks worth of raw materials and that we did not know where we could obtain them. There was in China a possible way out of our situation'. Against such 'life or death' considerations which would help to determine the nature of Germany's role in European affairs, Foreign Office arguments about the niceties of the political situation between Nanking and Canton, or even *vis-à-vis* Japan, appeared somewhat academic. By the end of 1934, therefore, the retreat of the Foreign Office in the face of the Reichswehr Ministry's determination to see the Klein projects through to their conclusion was evidenced by its willingness to reply to complaints about Klein by the Chinese Minister in Berlin — who had already been told by Meyer, Director of Department IV, that Klein's activities in Canton were purely private transactions which did not involve the German Government — to the effect that the question of arms deliveries to Canton was the subject of negotiations between von Seeckt and Chiang Kai-shek but that it was unable to interfere in the matter. This followed a meeting on 6 November between Meyer, General

von Reichenau and Klein. Von Reichenau emphasised that
the Ordnance Office place great importance on the completion of Klein's transactions and that Schacht, who had been
dealing with the question, had given his approval. Furthermore, negotiations were also in progress for a compensation
agreement for the exchange of raw materials with China. It is
hardly surprising that in the event the Foreign Office did
'interfere', for on 12 November 1934 Trautmann was instructed
by von Bülow to suggest to Generals von Seeckt and von
Falkenhausen, the former's designated successor, that because
of the great interest of the Reichswehr Ministry in the Klein
projects they should speak to Chiang Kai-shek about them.[24]

Chiang Kai-shek's refusal in November 1934 to sanction
Klein's munitions transactions with Canton — at one point
the Nanking Government had even threatened to withdraw
from the controversial howitzer deal because of Klein's
activities in the south[25] — and the fact that Klein was now to
concentrate his efforts on Nanking, at least encouraged the
Foreign Office to hope that if it continued its opposition to
Klein's work, especially in the south of China, a speedy
solution might soon be found which satisfied all of the
Wilhelmstrasse's (and perhaps even Chiang Kai-shek's) requirements. Yet whatever political and economic arguments the
Foreign Office might use against the Klein projects, the fact
remained that it was confronted by three factors over which
it had very little direct influence: the fact that Klein was
actually at work in China and signing contracts there; that
the other 'interested' parties in the Klein negotiations were
the Chinese authorities in Nanking and Canton; while in Berlin
it became increasingly evident that Klein was receiving support
from people like Hjalmar Schacht, President of the Reichsbank
and acting Reich Minister of Economics, Colonel Georg
Thomas, Wilhelm Keppler, the Führer's Commissioner for
Economic Affairs in the Reich Chancellery, and even apparently from Hitler himself. But while the Foreign Office was
especially concerned by the impression being created in China
and Germany that Klein was an 'agent in disguise of the
Reich Government, and in particular of the Reichswehr
Ministry',[26] it appears that even Hitler appreciated the delicate
nature of the issues raised by Klein's activities and accepted
the point that arms transactions in China should not involve
the government.[27]

By the end of 1934, therefore, the Foreign Office was faced
with as many dilemmas in its China policy and relationships
as confronted it in the Far East as a whole. On the one hand
it was hardly in a position to 'sabotage' the activities of Klein
and von Seeckt because of the economic and military benefits
they brought to Germany; while on the other it felt it had to
continue to pursue the general lines of Chinese and Far
Eastern policy which it saw as the only means of maintaining
Germany's position and freedom of choice in the Far East. In
any case, if it was to retain some credibility as a decision-
making body in the discussion on German foreign policy, a
moot point in the Nazi State, it could not simply let the
matter pass by default. Trautmann's complaints that the scale
of Klein's negotiations with Nanking and the status of the
Chinese officials he was dealing with signified that much
more than a purely private compensation agreement was
under discussion appeared to conflict with instructions he
had received in October that official trade negotiations with
China were not envisaged, although this did not exclude the
negotiation of private compensation agreements.[28] At the
beginning of 1935, therefore, the extent of Klein's economic
activities and his claims for their potential success were carefully examined in the Wilhelmstrasse and found to be wanting in almost every respect, particularly his exaggerated claims
about the expected scale of deliveries of wolfram he could
arrange from Canton.[29] Voss concluded that Klein's contracts
were 'in their present form, economically unacceptable and
politically undesirable, and that the more so the greater the
extent of the German contribution', especially since the
Chinese Governments were to be given German State credits
without any security, a step 'without precedent'. Because of
Klein's claims to Chiang Kai-shek and Marshal Chen Chi-tang
that he was acting on the instructions of 'the highest German
authorities', Voss wanted it established how far these authorities were prepared to back Klein and recommended that the
Foreign Office repeat its objections to these agreements.
Voss's concern that Germany should do nothing to compromise its position either with Nanking or Canton, and its
position of 'neutrality' between China and Japan, was then
reflected in his suggestion that the German contribution
should be as limited as possible and that 'in so far as it is
thought essential to fulfil' the contracts, this should be done

'in as inconspicuous, innocuous and non-military a manner as possible'.[30]

It was one thing for Voss to make such recommendations; it was another thing entirely to get them implemented by the Foreign Office without raising accusations of obstructionism from Reichswehr Ministry and other circles. In any case, the Foreign Office was faced by an established policy that it could only hope to alter or influence in a marginal way. Klein's representative, Prince Reuss, emphasised this to Voss and von Erdmannsdorff when he rejected their complaints about Klein's activities, and calmly informed them that the Reichswehr Ministry was primarily interested in the Canton projects and that 'the parallel contract with Nanking would only be accepted in order to allay Chiang Kai-shek's suspicions'.[31]

The relative weakness of the Foreign Office's position was further underlined when Reichsbankdirektor Jünne of the Golddiskontbank informed Meyer and von Erdmannsdorff of the support Klein had from leading circles and that even Hitler was interesting himself in the projects. He also stressed a point which the Foreign Office could not fail to be impressed with, that the plans were to be welcomed on the grounds of the 'general national economy'. Although he too admitted to 'serious misgivings' on business grounds about Klein's contracts, his news that credits of 20 million Reichsmarks each for Nanking and Canton were being considered in connection with these plans placed the Foreign Office in a very difficult position.

Meyer's reply showed both the Foreign Office's desire not to appear obstructionist on such issues of national importance and, more significantly, the degree to which these questions began to influence attitudes within the Foreign Office. He pointed out that the Foreign Office 'warmly supported' all plans designed to produce an additional exchange of goods with China, and continued: 'the Foreign Office had also no objection, in cases where things necessary for the army's requirements are concerned, to greater risks being taken than was generally the case in private business. A precondition was, however, that the raw materials could actually be delivered within the prescribed period and that there was a guarantee for their delivery, further that there should be a certain financial guarantee and, finally, that the carrying out of the transactions would not lead to political complications (between Nanking and Canton, and between China and Japan) and to its being dropped afterwards for that reason'. It was then emphasised that Germany could not afford a financial débâcle in China and that certain questions would have to be clarified with Klein. As if to assert some measure of Foreign Office authority in the matter, Meyer then informed Jünne of the incorrectness of Klein's statements regarding deliveries of wolfram ores from Canton.[32]

The Foreign Office now decided that it had to circulate its views on the Klein project in an official *Stellungnahme*, although whether the motive was one of window dressing for the Wilhelmstrasse's alleged position of 'authority' or whether it genuinely thought that some degree of pressure could still be brought to bear on the Reichswehr Ministry is hard to tell. What it required most of all was up-to-date and authoritative information on Chiang Kai-shek's views on the Klein projects in Nanking and Canton, but unfortunately the person most able to supply the Wilhelmstrasse with this information at the beginning of February 1935, von Seeckt, had a vested interest in the Klein projects. This was recognised in the Foreign Office, so that Colonel Thomas, from October 1934 Head of the Military Economics and Ordnance Branch (*Wehrwirtschafts-und Waffenwesen*) in the Reichswehr Ministry, was also quietly sounded out by Meyer as to whether Chiang Kai-shek approved of Klein's enterprise or alternatively would quietly tolerate it. Meyer emphasised the seriousness of the case since the impression had been created in China and Germany that Klein was 'an agent . . . of the Reich Government', and suggested an inter-Ministerial conference to discuss the whole issue of Klein's enterprises in China. Meyer was at least encouraged by Colonel Thomas's comment that Klein's claim would also have to be examined by the Army as well.[33]

Von Seeckt's reply to Foreign Minister von Neurath's request for information about the Generalissimo's standpoint was hardly an encouraging or hopeful one for the Wilhelmstrasse. It confirmed the fact that the focus of Klein's work was now Nanking and that while Chiang Kai-shek had not given his express approval for Klein's Canton projects, 'unless he is compelled to define his attitude, the Marshal will make no difficulties apart from perhaps, occasional formal protests'. Von Seeckt recommended that the execution of further Canton plans be postponed until after the conclusion of Klein's negotiations with Nanking in March, but that a start could be made with such non-military works as shipyards, railways, and dock construction, and that these operations be supported by the grant of German credits providing the Chinese could give satisfactory assurances regarding deliveries of raw materials. The General also forwarded the Marshal's request that the diplomatic representation of both countries be advanced to Embassy status, and that an office be established in Germany through which all German business would pass, thus excluding private German firms from direct negotiations with the Chinese. Apart from anything else, it was obvious that the Marshal wished to make military relations between China and Germany as 'official' as possible in order to 'commit' Germany to China's side in her long-running feud with Japan, particularly when such a step, if achieved, was made public.

Von Seeckt's support of this suggestion and the proposal to exclude the 'China Firmen' from the trade in arms with China brought an immediate and angry riposte from Trautmann, who was in any case critical of von Seeckt's excursion into the field of trade and foreign policy and still extremely sceptical as to the viability of the Chinese economy in connection with the Klein enterprises: 'the trade in arms with China has very often caused diplomatic complications. It should therefore be quietly left to private enterprises. The Klein—von Seeckt scheme would, if carried out, do grave damage to German trade in China. Do we wish to dig the grave of our trade out here, which is practically our only source of strength?'.[34] Reichsbankdirektor Jünne also had his doubts and thought that the Klein plans ought to be changed so that the Chinese began delivery immediately instead of first obtaining long-term credits, while Prince Reuss suggested that before credits were granted to Canton a commission of experts should be sent out to establish just what raw materials Canton could deliver.[35] But the more 'official' nature of the projects seemed assured when it was learned that Schacht had decided to recommend the granting of unsecured credits of 20 million Reichsmarks each to Nanking and Canton a guarantee being issued to the Golddiskontbank by the Ministry of Finance to cover the credits. According to Ministerialrat Nasse of that Ministry, however, they regarded the whole affair 'extremely sceptically'.[36]

In these circumstances it was not surprising that the Foreign

Office was forced to accept the series of *faits accomplis* by the Klein—Reichswehr Ministry partnership and its supporters with as much grace as it could. On 27 February 1935 von Neurath informed the Reich Finance Minister, the President of the Reichsbank, General von Reichenau and Reichsbank-direktor of the Wilhelmstrasse's official attitude on the important question of granting credits to Klein. Based on a draft by Richard Meyer, the memorandum which was circulated admitted that the Foreign Office supported all efforts to obtain raw materials, particularly when such materials were 'necessary for the defence of the country'. As opposed to Trautmann's opinion,[37] the bald statement was made that 'every endeavour to extend Sino—German economic relations on the basis of barter transactions will be heartily welcome by the Auswärtiges Amt', an indication of the extent to which the change in Germany's international trading practices had become a necessary article of faith in government circles. The usual Foreign Office objections to the various Reichswehr Ministry projects in China were put in the form of statements rather than objections, particular emphasis being placed upon the relatively poor financial standing of the Nanking and Canton governments, their political and economic rivalry, and Japan's continual pressure to bring China into her sphere of influence by attempting to exclude all foreign influences from the mainland. Mention was also made of von Seeckt's suggestion for delaying further plans with Canton until negotiations with Nanking had been concluded, and that in any case they should only compromise non-military undertakings in the first place.

So far as the credits for Klein were concerned, von Neurath emphasised several points which has already emerged from within the Wilhelmstrasse and in the discussions with Jünne, von Seeckt and Klein's representative, Prince Reuss. While it was admitted that the Foreign Office recognised the necessity of accepting unusual financial risks in cases where the Reichswehr Ministry's interests were involved, it suggested that before all the credits were finally granted the situation in China regarding deliveries of raw materials should be thoroughly investigated, so that 'on the conclusion of the preliminary work it will then be seen whether and to what extent Herr Klein's plans are practicable'. From the Foreign Office's point of view, however, its final point went to the crux of the differences between it and the Reichswehr Ministry, and even between it and what Chiang Kai-shek apparently intended: 'in carrying out Klein's projects everything will have to be avoided which might give the impression that Herr Klein has any official or semi-official assignment. All political complications and any danger to normal German– Chinese commercial relations must be most scrupulously avoided'.[38] Yet given Klein's ambitious plans for obtaining raw materials from the Canton area, it was rather paradoxical that news was received that Canton's own influence over the wolfram producing areas of the Province of Kwangsi had been reduced and that of Nanking increased.[39]

The Foreign Office was mistaken, however, if it thought that its 'reserved agreement' to the Klein Projects would remove all difficulties with the Reichswehr Ministry regarding mutual policies towards China since military links of all kinds, including Klein's, continued to be developed with Canton. Reports of the appointment of further military advisers to Canton, including that of General Hans Selmsdorff as general adviser, prompted Trautmann and von Falkenhausen to express their fears about Chiang Kai-shek's reaction and the possible repercussions on the position of the advisory group with the Nanking Government.[40] Von Neurath immediately demanded an explanation from von Blomberg,[41] while Voss restated the Foreign Office's general attitude on the question in a six-page memorandum. He emphasised the importance of maintaining Chiang Kai-shek's confidence in the loyalty of the German military advisory group at Nanking, and in the loyalty of the German Government. Voss felt this confidence would disappear if the Reichswehr Ministry cooperated in the military reconstruction of Canton without Chiang Kai-shek's approval, which obviously had not been given. He argued that the aims being pursued in Canton were not 'important and secure enough to compensate for the damage to our advisory group in Nanking', while in view of the spread of Nanking's influence in the Province of Kwangsi he felt that a military defeat at the hands of Nanking was in the offing for Canton. Voss concluded that it was essential to restrict military cooperation with Canton to that approved of by Chiang Kai-shek.[42]

Von Blomberg's reply of 23 March 1935 certainly confirmed the worst fears of the Foreign Office. He emphasised the private nature of any contracts concluded with Canton by retired officers, and discounted reports that any of the officers came from the Ordnance Office. He then put the Reichswehr Ministry's attitude in no uncertain terms: 'there can hardly be any objections on the part of Nanking to retired officers being employed in an advisory capacity, when Nanking itself requested and obtained permission for a Cantonese military study commission to come to Germany.[43] The right to send advisers to Canton too, in order to establish relations, must be maintained in face of Nanking's objections, particularly as the Reich Minister of Economics will doubtless attach great importance to the establishment of trade relations with Canton too'. Von Blomberg then requested that this standpoint be transmitted to the Nanking Government, a communication having already been sent to von Falkenhausen.[44]

An indication of the relative positions of strength and authority of the various Ministries in the Nazi State, especially at the time of the Reichwehr's practical and psychological triumph in March 1935 with the reintroduction of conscription in defiance of the Treaty of Versailles, can be seen in the fact that Meyer simply forwarded von Blomberg's request to Trautmann without raising any further issues with the military authorities in Berlin. In addition, Trautmann was told to cooperate with von Falkenhausen in safeguarding German 'interests' in Canton and to forestall any possible complications with Nanking. Consul General Kriebel at Shanghai was also instructed to give Klein all the assistance he requested.[45] Following Hitler's reception of Klein in February and the latter's return to China with letters of greeting to the Chinese Marshals from Hitler and von Blomberg, and a recommendation from Schacht,[46] the Foreign Office had thus been manoeuvred into a position where — albeit reluctantly — it was having to support Reichswehr Ministry plans in China.

What especially concerned the Wilhelmstrasse was that this intensification of German military activity in China coincided with an extension of Japanese influence in North China following the Japanese occupation of Kuyuan in Eastern Chahar in January. This raised the frightful spectre of the German-trained Chinese Army clashing with Japanese forces and possibly, involving the German advisers in a Sino–Japanese conflict. Rumours that Japan wanted the German military advisers replaced by Japanese advisers were, however, denied by the Japanese.[47]

Although the officials in the Wilhelmstrasse apparently failed to stand up to those in the Bendlerstrasse, the diplomats in China continued to make free with their criticisms of the further development of Reichswehr Ministry and Klein's plans at Canton and the possible effect of these upon Germany's relations with the Nanking Government and the position of the German military advisers there. Even Chiang Kai-shek complained directly to Berlin that everywhere Klein was allowing it to be known that he had the Marshal's express permission for his Canton plans, which was denied.[48] By April 1935, in an attempt to clarify the situation by 'drawing' Klein further away from Canton, the Legation of Nanking even expressed its willingness, along with von Falkenhausen, to support Klein's Nanking projects with Chiang Kai-shek, thus providing a neat twist to the Wilhelmstrasse's basic attitude of hostility towards Reichswehr Ministry plans in China. The legitimate point was also made that in China there did not exist two independent and equal governments, and that arms deliveries to a provincial régime such as Canton required the prior approval and permission of the National Government at Nanking.[49]

It was, in fact, pressure from German diplomatic sources in China which finally achieved some measure of success for the Foreign Office's point of view in the Klein affair. The Canton issue was only resolved when Kriebel appealed directly to Hitler to wind-up the Canton enterprises. Coming as this did from an old Party comrade and one who could impress the Führer with his first-hand experience and knowledge, it succeeded where the more usual opposition of the Foreign Office had failed. He emphasised that the military enterprises in Canton raised the danger that the military mission at Nanking might have to be recalled at the request of Chiang Kai-shek.[50] Kriebel then plainly indicated the mistakes which he felt were being made in German policy, and the correctives that were required:

I am very much concerned lest the Reichswehr Ministry, as an interested party, may be misjudging the realities of this situation and the relations between the recognised Nanking Goverment and Canton. . . . We are destroying the Nanking Government's confidence in us and are running the risk of falling between two stools if we believe that we can support the recognition of the Government on the one hand and at the same time their potential enemy of tomorrow on the other. I suggest a generous settlement: the recall of the German military advisers from Canton or their transfer to Nanking, and the abandonment of the Klein's arms and ordnance transactions in Canton, in exchange for larger-scale transactions with Nanking which, in accordance with your instruction would receive full support from here.

Trautmann, who forwarded this appeal, agreed with it but thought that any cessation of military involvement with Canton 'would . . . have to be done slowly, unobtrusively and with the greatest caution, in order to avoid the danger of a boycott of the resident German nationals'.[51]

Coincidentally, Kriebel's telegram was despatched and received in Berlin on the very day that von Neurath informed the Chinese Minister that Germany had decided to raise the German Mission in Peking to the status of an Embassy.[52] The German Government would thus have appeared to have been pursuing an extremely nebulous policy in China had it persisted in supporting Klein's military activities in Canton. Even Lieutenant-General Streccius, the German aviation adviser with the Nanking Government, called it 'double-dealing' when he heard of a similar post being established at Canton, although Trautmann pointed out that these plans originated with the Reich Air Ministry. More significantly, Trautmann's report on this question made it clear that the army authorities were not alone in pursuing policies in China contrary to those desired or recommended by the Foreign Office.[53]

The deciding factor for Hitler and the Reichswehr Ministry appears to have been Kriebel's reference to the large-scale transactions of raw materials vital for rearmament that could be obtained from Nanking. On 24 May 1935 Meyer informed Trautmann that Klein would be transferring his work from Canton to Nanking while the Canton plans were to be gradually abandoned. No further arms were to be supplied to Canton, while the fate of what had already been started there would be decided by Chiang Kai-shek. The German military advisers at Canton, again depending on the Marshal's decision, would gradually be withdrawn and absorbed into the staff of General von Falkenhausen. Meyer then instructed Trautmann to assist Klein with the future development of his enterprises at Nanking.[54] A fortnight later Frohwein informed von Bülow that the Reich Air Ministry had apparently abandoned its plans of large-scale exports of air and war material to Canton.[55] This change of plans and the instructions regarding Foreign Office support for Klein went some way towards answering

Chinese criticisms about Klein's uncertain status, which Trautmann had again reported on 23 May.

Although discussions between Klein and Chinese officials at Nanking for a large-scale arms agreement began in June 1935,[56] and the Foreign Office instructed Trautmann to keep clear of the actual details of what was now clearly admitted to be outside its sphere of authority,[57] Klein's still nebulous relationship with the Canton authorities continued to irritate Chiang Kai-shek, the War Ministry, and the Foreign Office. In addition, Klein's somewhat uncertain position *vis-à-vis* the German authorities continued to bother the Chinese authorities, and when von Seeckt reported to the Führer on 26 June in the presence of von Neurath, von Blomberg and Schacht, he tried to persuade Hitler of the necessity of pursuing a clear-cut policy in China as a means of reinforcing the efforts of those (e.g. Klein) whose principal aim was to obtain the raw materials vital for Germany's military and economic rearmament. But von Seeckt's suggestion obviously meant much more than this. It implied an end to the policy of balance in the Far East by openly designating Germany's military-economic interests in China as political interests which had to be secured by a closer Sino—German relationship. In view of Nazi aspirations and plans *vis-à-vis* Japan[58] it is not surprising that Hitler contented himself with listening politely for over an hour to the old General. Hitler's only positive reaction was to accede to Chiang Kai-shek's request, transmitted by von Seeckt — for which he apologised to von Neurath for 'interfering' — that the German Embassy be transferred from Peking to Nanking.[59]

This was one of those rare occasions when the views of Hitler and the Foreign Office on Far Eastern policy coincided. Not that Hitler would have decided otherwise than to deny, or disregard, von Seeckt's suggestions in view of Nazi inclinations towards Japan. Nevertheless, the Foreign Office was undoubtedly relieved by the Führer's response since it avoided, for a time at least, the possibility of yet further complications in Germany's relations with Japan which the Wilhelmstrasse would have had to deal with. As it was, Japan had only recently consolidated her position on the mainland of Asia by scoring an undeniable victory over Chiang Kai-shek by the Ho-Umetsu and Ching-Doihara agreements of 10 and 23 June 1935 by which Kuomintang authority over the Provinces of Hopei

and Chahar virtually disappeared.[60] Although Hitler had
saved the Foreign Office from further complications with
Japan, Japan's actions in the Far East still led to difficulties
for the Wilhelmstrasse in China *vis-à-vis* the War Ministry. While
Klein's efforts at Nanking began to be reciprocated in the
discussions which began in June 1935 with the Chinese
Government, relations between Canton and Nanking grew
daily more bitter because of the latter's supposed 'appeasement' of the Japanese. This represented the widespread dis-
affection with Nanking's policy towards Japan, and resulted
in the attempted assassination of Wang Ching-wei on 1 November 1935 at the opening meeting of the Sixth Plenary Session
of the Kuomintang.

The complexity of this situation was compounded for the
Foreign Office at the end of November 1935 when Trautmann
forwarded (from Canton) Marshal Chen Chi-tang's request to
von Blomberg that Klein should be instructed to go to Canton
immediately to complete the arsenal project there. As Trautmann commented, 'the Marshal is taking this matter very
seriously and . . . his attitude towards us more or less depends
on whether Klein, to whose initiative we owe this unpleasant
matter, carries through the undertaking which has been begun
and the contract regarding the shipyard'.[61] Trautmann's
concern for the continued livelihood of German businessmen
in the Canton area and his comments again underlined the
extreme difficulty of the Foreign Office's position. On the
other hand, the War Ministry could only have been encouraged
by Chiang Kai-shek's admission to von Falkenhausen that he
could not really prevent the rearming of Canton by the
delivery of war material from abroad.[62]

The Foreign Office hoped that matters would be clarified
somewhat by the meeting scheduled for 24 January 1936
between Hitler, von Blomberg, von Neurath, and Klein himself.
When Klein then attempted to set out his plans 'at epic length'
von Neurath interrupted him and said that what most interested him was how far Klein had obtained the Nanking
Government's approval for his Canton projects. At this Klein
produced a letter from Chiang Kai-shek to Hitler which stated
that Klein enjoyed his full confidence. Klein then said that a
Chinese commission would shortly be arriving in Germany to
negotiate an exchange of goods,[63] while he pointed out
that the Chinese would deliver to Germany the valuable raw

materials, including wolfram, that she so desperately needed. He finally got around to answering von Neurath's point by stating that he possessed a document from Chiang Kai-shek approving the Canton projects. Klein also stated that the arsenal at Canton had been completed, which as von Neurath knew full well did not accord with Trautmann's report of 28 November 1935.

Von Neurath's irritation with Klein finally boiled over when the latter complained about the poor treatment he had received from the missions at Nanking and Canton. The Foreign Minister pointedly remarked that these had been instructed to support Klein, but that he had carefully avoided visiting them. Von Neurath promised that when Klein again went out to China he would be given letters of introduction to the missions, that the Foreign Office was at his disposal for further discussions but that he, von Neurath, wished to see as little of Klein as possible.[64]

That there were ample grounds for von Neurath's distrust was further confirmed when Trautmann reported on 8 February that Chiang Kai-shek did not believe Klein's denials that he had sold to Canton a poison-gas installation and a gun factory. On being informed about this, the War Ministry asked for the following telegram to be sent to Trautmann: 'all the projects which Klein has promised to Canton have been reported to Marshal Chiang Kai-shek. The arsenal is under construction, poison-gas installation is planned but not yet delivered. Delivery will only take place subject to Marshal Chiang Kai-shek's agreement'.[65]

It was obvious that the War Ministry shared the Foreign Office's concern at Chiang Kai-shek's distrust of Klein, though for different reasons. The Foreign Office was concerned lest this should affect Germany's general political and economic relations with China; the War Ministry was more concerned for the particular projects it had under consideration in China. Although by this time it was obvious that the Foreign Office would never be able to stem the tide of the War Ministry's advance in China, it was nevertheless able to advise it of the political impossibility of allowing General Lindemann to accept the post of military adviser to General Sung Che-yuan, leader of the Twenty-Ninth Army and Chairman of the Hopei—Chahar Political Affairs Council. Both Trautmann and von Falkenhausen emphasised that Germany should in no way become involved in Sino—Japanese differences, while it was clear from Trautmann's telegram that recent experiences with Canton had severely shaken the confidence of both the diplomats and military advisers in China.[66]

By February 1936 the Wilhelmstrasse learned from the War Ministry that, according to Klein, what was required was a formal agreement between Germany and China under which Germany would supply military and other materials to the extent of 250 million Reichsmarks, and later to an annual level of 100 million Reichsmarks. In return, China would deliver raw materials and other products, for which various schemes of redevelopment would begin in several provinces. Schacht was supposed to have agreed to all this. However, this would do exactly what von Seeckt had hinted at in his talk with Hitler on 26 June 1935[67] and openly designate Germany's military-economic activities in China as political interests. The War Ministry was warned that such a development could hardly fail to affect Germany's relations with Japan.[68] Afterwards, it was learned that the sum of 100 million Reichsmarks made available for the proposed delivery of war materials to Chiang Kai-shek, in accordance with the Klein plans and without the knowledge of von Falkenhausen, came from War Ministry funds.[69]

The War Ministry intended that the agreement was to take the form of a 'barter' arrangement, thus securing the interests of rearmament at a time of serious difficulties for the German economy. Rearmament, like everything else in Germany at the time, was seriously affected by the foreign exchange crisis which reached its high point during 1936. The War Ministry was therefore faced with the problem of how to maintain or increase levels of rearmament, based on the supply of foreign raw materials, at a time of extreme shortages in foreign exchange which inevitably restricted Germany's ability to purchase in overseas markets. The situation had been building up for a long time due to the pressures imposed on Germany's precariously balanced economy by Hitler's demand for the major part of the country's resources to be devoted to rearmament purposes. By 1936 the economy was unable to cope with these demands, while Germany was finding it increasingly difficult to pay her way in the world. Exports for 1935—36 fell below the 1933 level precisely at the time when demand for food and raw material was growing at an unprecedented rate. Germany thus found it increasingly difficult to obtain the raw materials needed for rearmament on the scale demanded by Hitler by normal trading methods. The foreign exchange crisis of 1936, the constant bickering and fighting between the War Ministry and the Reichsbank and the Ministry of Economics, especially in the winter of 1935—36, and between the different branches of the Wehrmacht over the important question of the allocation of the raw materials so painfully short in supply, as well as the contemporaneous development of Hitler's ideas on foreign policy, led ultimately to Hitler's fateful conference of 5 November 1937.[70]

The War Ministry's view was that the urgency of the rearmament/raw materials situation dictated the necessity of pursuing the Klein projects to their logical conclusion. But in March 1936 Chiang Kai-shek's own attitude and distrust of Klein posed a threat to these plans, and he complained to Trautmann that Klein had misled him about the size of the arsenal project at Canton. Since it transpired that it was a large undertaking, he now threatened to stop delivery of 300 tons of wolfram which had been prepared for Germany and to sabotage the work of the mission he had sent to Germany under Chen Ku, Director of the Keiluan Mines, unless Klein's activities at Canton finally ceased. The War Ministry at Berlin had to take Chiang's threat seriously since this mission's task was to conclude the barter transactions begun by Klein in Nanking.[71]

The Chinese authorities also complained about the fact that, despite von Blomberg's promise a fortnight earlier that no arms deliveries would be made to other provincial governments without Nanking's express approval, it appeared that HAPRO was making such deliveries to Canton, and that the amount of wolfram ready for delivery to Germany was only 200 tons. Dr Yue, Chief of the Ordnance Office in Nanking, complained to von Falkenhausen and Dr Kiep, Head of the German Economic Mission to the Far East that the deliveries of material to Canton signified Germany's 'disloyalty' towards the Nanking Government, but this was emphatically denied.[72]

Von Blomberg quickly reacted to this evidence of Chinese disquiet. On 24 March 1936 he telegraphed Chiang Kai-shek to confirm his telegram of 14 February[73] that arms deliveries to Canton through HAPRO only took place with his agreement; to explain the limited . . . quantities of arms and arsenal plans that were being delivered to Canton under an agreement which had been submitted to Chiang Kai-shek; and to request confirmation of Chiang Kai-shek's support for the commission visiting Germany to conclude a credit agreement.[74] He then took the matter up directly with von Neurath, complaining on 25 March that 'both the Ambassador and the Staff advisers held views on the Klein plans which cannot meet with our approval. Now that the Führer and Chancellor has approved the Klein project and the conclusion of the credits agreement will take place within the next few days, it is absolutely essential that the Ambassador and the Staff advisers should further the matter by every possible means and should not, as previously, rouse Marshal Chiang Kai-shek's suspicions of Klein anew'. Von Blomberg demanded that Trautmann be given as 'firm instructions' as he had himself sent to von Falkenhausen encouraging all authorities to support 'in every way' the execution of the plan for the exchange of goods.[75]

Despite the reference to Hitler's approval of the Klein projects, von Neurath, to his credit, immediately took up this challenge to his prerogatives as Foreign Minister and to the integrity of the diplomatic service. At a meeting with the Minister of War the following day he completely rejected von Blomberg's reproaches against Trautmann, underlining his defence of the Ambassador by pointing out that Klein had deliberately avoided calling on the Embassy and informing the officials about his plans. As to the question of Foreign Office support, von Neurath tartly pointed out that 'it is above all necessary for this that we be informed about these plans'. Although von Blomberg promised that Klein would visit the Foreign Office and impart the required information, the War Ministry had still managed to retain its initiative over the Canton question.[76]

While the War Ministry resolutely pursued its plans in China, the members of the reorganised Department III in the Foreign Office responsible for Far Eastern affairs[77] returned to the attack with political and economic objections to the Klein plans. In a memorandum of 31 March 1936 which he submitted to the State Secretary, von Erdmannsdorff drew attention to the important question of Japan's position in the Far East and its foreign policy objectives:

if the Japanese are regarding even the granting of financial aid to China by other powers as an unfriendly act, it seems even more doubtful whether they will quietly acquiesce in the equipment of the Chinese Army with war materials on a scale as large as is apparently intended under the Klein plans or in the installation of war industries in China, particularly since we would thereby, in conjuction with the activities of the German Advisory Staff in Nanking, be making it possible for the Chinese to intervene in a Russo–Japanese war on the side of the Soviet Union against Japan.

He then went on to complain that the War Ministry, like Klein, continued to impute to von Neurath and Chiang Kai-shek support for the Klein plans which did not exist. It also appeared that instructions had been issued in the Reich Ministry of Economics 'to hold aloof from the Klein plans and to attribute the responsibility for them solely to the Reich War Ministry'.[78]

Von Erdmannnsdorff's political arguments were complemented by economic ones. He made it plain that the Foreign Office recognised that the War Ministry was about to present it with a *fait accompli* in the form of a definite agreement with China, but attempted to put the best face possible on this situation when he remarked that 'the Foreign Office must draw attention to the economic difficulties associated with the Klein plans in good time if they do not wish to lay themselves open, as has happened before, to suspicion that these inevitable difficulties have been caused by a lack of official support'. He therefore suggested that the revolving credit of 100 million Reichsmarks outweighed the previous pattern of the value of German exports to China and could be expected to create difficulties in normal trade relations with China; that the Nanking Government enjoyed no creditworthiness abroad; and that the offer of unsecured credits to the sum envisaged would create insuperable difficulties for the arrangements of large German firms and organisations, whose principal difficulty was to conclude agreements on the basis of secured credits. If the Nanking Government did not have to promise tax revenue or bank guarantees to obtain the supplies they required, it could be expected that they would immediately abandon difficult negotiations with such firms as Otto Wolff and Krupp in favour of the Klein plans. He also cast doubt on the ability of the Nanking Government to obtain the requisite amount of raw materials from Chinese suppliers, on China's production levels of raw materials, and the general honesty of China in her economic relations with Germany.[79]

In reality, though, these continued expressions of Foreign

Office disquiet were a waste of time and effort. Chiang Kai-
shek himself removed what props remained to support the
Foreign Office's position when he replied favourably to von
Blomberg on 3 April.[80] Six days later, on 9 April 1936, a
credit agreement for 100 million Reichsmarks was concluded
between von Blomberg and Chen Ku, Director of the Keiluan
Mines and leader of the mission sent to Germany by Chiang.
While the agreement had the approval of the President of the
Reichsbank and the Reich Minister of Finance, Count Schwerin
von Krosigk, von Blomberg emphasised whose authority was
paramount in this matter when he informed the Wilhelmstrasse that the direction of HAPRO, which had been founded
to carry out the exchange of goods between Germany and
China, lay with the Chief of the Military Economics Staff
(*Wehrwirtschaftsstab*) of the Reich War Ministry, Colonel
Georg Thomas. He also stated that Klein had withdrawn from
HAPRO but was returning to China to organise the supply of
goods there. However, neither this news nor von Blomberg's
statement that Klein would visit the Auswärtiges Amt to
discuss his future plans was calculated to endear the War
Ministry or Klein to the officials in the Wilhelmstrasse.
Although the agreement spoke of the exchange of German
'industrial and other products' for Chinese agricultural
products and mineral raw materials, the bulk of the goods to
be supplied from Germany were armaments of all kinds while
the raw materials from China, such as wolfram and iron, were
to contribute to Germany's rearmament. The Chinese were
also to establish a corollary to HAPRO in order to organise
the trade from China, a so-called 'Defence Office'. Colonel
Thomas's statement on all this to Dr Nolte of the firm of
Carolowitz & Co. and of the *Ostasiatischer Verein* on 22 April
1936 in Berlin only confirmed the worst fears of German
commercial circles, that what had been concluded was a monopolistic state treaty which was bound to have a detrimental
effect on the position of the private German trading firms in
the general field of Sino—German economic relations.[81]

The War Ministry could congratulate itself for two reasons:
it had secured an important source of raw materials vital for
Germany's rearmament at a crucial juncture in Germany's
international relations, and this had been achieved in the face
of continual opposition from the Foreign Office. What most
concerned the Foreign Office however, was that the agreement

would everywhere be taken as a political one. The most sensitive — or vehement — reactions could be expected from
Japan. For the Foreign Office, von Blomberg's agreement
with China complicated an already difficult situation by
making it certain that von Ribbentrop would intensify his
efforts to reach his own 'balancing' agreement with Japan.
But how far Hitler really expected this to be compatible
with his approval of the Klein projects, or vice-versa, is hard
to tell.

Intent upon securing the fruits of its 'victory', the War
Ministry arranged for Lieutenant-General von Reichenau,
then Commander-in-Chief of Wehrkreis VII (Munich) to visit
China to confirm Klein's treaties and to ascertain Chinese
intentions regarding their implementation. His main task,
however, was to cultivate relations with Chiang Kai-shek. He
also strengthened the War Ministry's case *vis-à-vis* the Foreign
Office by informing von Bülow on 4 May that Schacht had
made available a revolving credit of 100 million Reichsmarks,
while von Bülow's doubts about the economic validity of
Klein's agreements were simply brushed aside. On the other
hand, von Reichenau had warned von Blomberg that the
rearmament of China by Germany would be a protracted
business that could not show quick results. Most significantly,
he had warned the Minister of War that 'it would not be
compatible with a German–Japanese rapprochement'. Von
Blomberg's not unexpected reply had been that a rapprochement with Japan was out of the question and that the Japanese
negotiations with von Ribbentrop had been broken off. This
gave von Bülow the opportunity to hint at the Foreign Office's
general dissatisfaction with its own role in the formulation of
Far Eastern policy, to imply that not only was the War
Ministry not in a position to complain about von Ribbentrop's
negotiations but because of its commitments in China could
even be partly blamed for their inauguration. He sharply
pointed out to von Reichenau that the Army had deeply
involved itself in the Japanese negotiations, and that in von
Dirksen's opinion it was quite impossible to break them off.
Von Bülow made quite clear his scepticism regarding the
Army's plans in China and, while he thought that most of the
money made available would be lost, his chief concern was
for 'the disorganisation and risk involved for our China trade'.
A week later the Foreign Office forwarded to Nanking von

Blomberg's request to von Falkenhausen to support von
Reichenau in his task, one which stood 'at present in the
forefront of Sino—German collaboration'. Although von
Blomberg mentioned that von Reichenau's appointment had
been agreed with Hitler, it must be assumed that the latter's
agreement was more of a formal than a political nature.[82]

By now, however, the Foreign Office itself was in no position to complain or influence matters. Voss virtually admitted
as such a fortnight later when Römmer of the Reich Finance
Ministry called to ask for the Foreign Office's views of the
Klein agreements, particularly with regard to the position of
the 'China Firmen', in preparation for a meeting that afternoon at his Ministry to discuss the credit agreement with
China and the grant of a guarantee to the Golddiskontbank
for the 100 million Reichsmarks credit. Voss repeated the
Foreign Office's usual complaints, but his general attitude
implied that all the various Ministries could do was to accept
the *fait accompli*, especially since Hitler had placed the weight
of his authority behind the agreement.[83]

For his part, von Dirksen admitted to von Blomberg that
while the technical questions involved did not fall within his
competence, he had 'to ensure that the strain placed on
German—Japanese relations by the HAPRO—Reichenau
complex of questions was kept to a minimum'. To this end
he suggested that von Reichenau should also visit Japan and
that the competent Japanese authorities should be fully
informed about War Ministry plans in China. Von Blomberg
agreed to the first proposal on condition that it did not
endanger the real purpose of the journey, to achieve closer
contact with Chiang Kai-shek and the Chinese authorities,
and so long as Chiang Kai-shek also approved. As to the second
proposal, von Blomberg 'agreed without any reservation and
promised to do what was necessary'.[84] But like von Seeckt
before him, and out of a similar regard for Chinese susceptibilities,[85] von Reichenau refrained from visiting Japan, a decision supported by Hans Dieckhoff, Director of the newly
organised Political Department from 15 May to 21 June 1936,
after which he became acting and then substantive State
Secretary.[86]

While von Reichenau prepared for his trip to China to secure
the Klein projects on the spot, von Blomberg tried to secure
them in Berlin. At a conference on 27 May with Göring,

Schacht, the Reich Finance Minister von Krosigk, the Prussian
Finance Minister Dr Popitz, and Lieutenant-Colonel Wilhelm
Löb of the General Staff of the Air Force of Göring's recent
creation, the Raw Materials and Foreign Exchange Staff
(*Rohstoff- und Devisenstab*),[87] von Blomberg emphasised
the importance of China as a source of the ores and other raw
materials which were essential for the Army's rearmament.
He warned against a 'brusque political treatment' of China by
a political, alignment with Japan and the recognition of
Manchukuo, both of which could be expected to damage
the Klein plans. When Göring tried to point out the value of a
common front involving China and Japan against Soviet
Russia, von Blomberg repeated the Army's doubts about
Japan as a military factor in the Far East. Göring's response
to this was to draw attention to widespread doubts about the
value of the Army's China enterprises because of the uncertain
internal situation in that country, a direct reference to the
difficulties which existed between Nanking and Canton and
to the Chinese communist movement, a point which had
some relevance in Hitler's and von Ribbentrop's pursuit of a
pact with Japan.[88]

While von Blomberg obtained Schacht's support at this
meeting, Germany's relations with Japan and von Ribbentrop's
negotiations with Tokio nevertheless raised a large question
mark over the Klein enterprises. In these circumstances it was
in the obvious interest of the War Ministry to press ahead in
China and show, particularly in the event of a political pact
with Japan, that the Chinese enterprises were equally if not
more so a question of *Lebensbedingung* for Germany. In
China, therefore, it was General von Reichenau's task to assure
the Chinese of the War Ministry's fidelity to the cause of
Sino—German military relations, particularly in view of
constant rumours of certain developments in German—
Japanese relations. He appeared to be successful in this
because on 2 July the Chinese Finance Minister, H. H. Kung,
with whom he had carried out the final negotiations, replied
to a speech by von Reichenau and pointed out that 'for a
long time disturbing news had circulated here about German—
Japanese relations. But now all doubts have been removed,
and we know that Germany is our true friend'. Von Falkenhausen, however, complained to his friend, Lieutenant-
Colonel Brinckmann, that the Klein—HAPRO agreements and

von Reichenau's visit to China signified the loss of his own 'control' over military matters in the relations between Germany and China.[89]

In Berlin von Blomberg was adamant that the new situation was so important that it allowed of no opposition or questioning by other quarters. In a letter of 10 July to Emil Helfferich, President of the *Ostasiatischer Verein,* who had requested a meeting to discuss the concern of the China Firmen regarding the new agreements, von Blomberg emphasised that the Klein agreement was a State agreement, concluded with the approval of the Führer, to alleviate Germany's raw material shortages in the interests of Germany's rearmament. The responsibility for the conclusion and implementation of the agreement was the German Government's alone, and von Blomberg did not intend to engage in any discussion with economic circles whose interests lay in China. Von Reichenau adopted a similar attitude in China and argued that he was under no obligation to 'explain' himself or the agreement to German businessmen. While Helfferich continued to press the War Ministry on this matter and Dr Nolte was sent to China to sound German commercial opinion on the spot, a representative from Carlowitz & Co., Major Rüdorff, approached Wilhelm Keitel, Head of the *Wehrmachtsamt,* in Thomas's absence. Keitel said that he found von Reichenau's attitude 'understandable' but that on Thomas's return he would recommend that a telegram be sent to China suggesting that von Reichenau meet members of the German business community.[90]

Although von Blomberg stated that Schacht and Reich Minister Göring had been informed of his attitude, Göring was more forthcoming in his letter to Helfferich on 1 August. He at least was prepared to give assurances regarding the position of the 'China Firmen', that their interests would not be infringed and that perhaps some kind of collaboration could be worked out *vis-à-vis* the Klein—HAPRO contracts.[91]

The more official development of the Army's interests in China strengthened not only the resolve of von Ribbentrop to conclude an agreement with Japan but also Japan's opposition to Germany's military enterprises in China. Japanese enquiries at the Foreign Office were accompanied by extensive press reports in Europe and the Far East speculating on the extent of Germany's obligations to supply war material to China. These prompted Göring, through the Raw Materials and Foreign Exchange Staff, to enquire about raw materials actually en-route from China and to suggest that all German deliveries not yet on their way to China be stopped.[92] This evidence of embarrassment on the part of the Nazi leadership in its relations with Japan in some way recompensed the Foreign Office for its own embarrassment with China caused by the positive Nazi attitude towards Japan. Nevertheless, the Foreign Office still had to deal with a stream of Japanese complaints about the matter, when it was denied that the agreement was in any way 'directed' against Japan.[93]

Interestingly, Japanese enquiries in Berlin and the loud complaints of the Japanese press led several members of the Foreign Office in Berlin and China to place a fair degree of emphasis on the importance of German–Japanese relations during the second half of 1936. One could argue, of course, that with the War Ministry's relationship with China now safely formalised in an official agreement the Foreign Office felt freer than before to give vent to its concern for German–Japanese relations. At the same time, however, von Ribbentrop's negotiations with the Japanese military authorities, negotiations undertaken on behalf of the Nazi leadership, were now moving to a crucial stage. In a memorandum of 18 July Voss, now of the newly reorganised Economic Policy Department, carried von Dirksen's suggestion of relieving Japanese fears to a point which, if pursued, at the very least would have resulted in a reversal of Foreign Office support, reluctant as this was, for War Ministry plans in China. After describing Japan's recent policy towards China as based on her 'ineluctable aim to acquire predominance over China and thus hegemony in the entire Far Eastern living space', he warned of the effect Germany's military policy in China was having on Japan's position and on German–Japanese relations: 'thus, as a result of the German contracts, Japan has been placed in the dilemma of either having passively to watch a development that will cause her China policy to spring a leak or of falling out with a friendly power on whom she thought she could count *vis-à-vis* Russia. We have given evasive answers to every Japanese enquiry about the HAPRO contracts, and Japan is asking herself whether we wish to pursue our China policy without Japan and against her'. Voss's phrasing is interesting and revealing since it cannot really be said that Germany's policy in China was ever carried out *with* Japan in the first place. As significant was the reference to Russia since this hinted more at a Nazi than a Wilhelmstrasse view of *German* (not Japanese) attitudes towards the Soviet Union.

Voss then pointed out that Japan could exert pressure on Germany in two ways: by a policy towards China designed to secure the removal of the German military advisers, and by hinting that an alignment with Russia was a feasible project in Japanese foreign policy. Voss's apparent willingness to accede to expected Japanese arguments regarding the extent and intensity of War Ministry plans in China was then clearly indicated in his final paragraph: 'in any event a policy of rearming China will become all the less acceptable to Japan the longer it continues, and it is not possible for us to pursue a policy against Japan in China such as even America and Britain are unable to undertake. We can only conduct a policy in China on the basis of an understanding with Japan — or at least without harming Japanese interests. Since the HAPRO contracts are extremely harmful to Japanese interests, the day will come when Japan will confront us with a choice of alternatives. In that case we could only retreat. Whilst there is still time and whilst a conciliatory step on our part will still be valued as such by Japan, it would be better to reach an understanding with her. And for this there must be a frank discussion'.[94]

Although realistic in its assessment of Japan's role and power in the Far East, Voss was hopelessly wrong in thinking that Germany could negotiate with Japan on her military interests in China and still expect to retain anything of them. He ought to have realised that such an approach to Japan, particularly if carried out with the 'appeasement' mentality his memorandum betrayed, would have resulted in the very thing that so many people in Germany were trying to avoid, namely the loss of German interests and influence in China.

Von Reichenau's arrival in China to ratify the Klein agreement (25 July 1936) and his stay there until September provided an opportunity for the diplomats on the spot to express to him their concern about the economic and political effects of the agreement. The attitude of Counsellor of Legation Fischer of the Nanking Embassy was much less defeatist than that of Voss, though no less realistic. Fischer also saw the Klein agreement in a political light and conse-quently as a form of commitment which would 'of necessity lead to obligations which, in contrast to our policy hitherto, would commit us much too strongly to the weakest factor in Far Eastern politics'. He also cast doubt on von Reichenau's assertion that 'one need only traverse a short danger zone in order to make China a significant military factor, also where Japan is concerned'. An indication of the War Ministry's desire to extend its control over all aspects of German military activity in China was von Reichenau's suggestion that this aim could best be achieved by the participation of German officers on the active list. This development would inevitably affect von Falkenhausen's position, but as Fischer pointed out to von Erdmannsdorff in his report, 'that the Commission is actually excluding him completely and is not even informing him of what is contained in the new rearmament programme is an open secret here and might sooner or later lead to General von Falkenhausen making it a question of confidence with Field Marshal von Blomberg'. As it was, Trautmann later complained that the Nanking Embassy was completely by-passed by the Ministry of War in its dealings with the Chinese Government over military matters connected with the Klein— HAPRO agreements.[95]

Fischer was particularly concerned at the increased pace and intensity of Germany's military involvement in China hinted at by von Reichenau, and insisted that one simply had to take cognisance of Japan's position in the Far East and as a factor in Germany's Far Eastern policy:

the Japanese had become accustomed to the existence of the Advisory Staff in its present form, a fact which did not exclude the unobstrusive addition of officers on the active list as well, in order to preclude outdating and superannuation. A radical transformation from top to bottom, on the other hand, seemed to me a two-edged sword; possible military wishes in this matter ought to be subordinated to political necessities.

Although von Reichenau admitted that an intensification of German military activity in China carried the risk of Japanese reactions, and that if this took the form of a threatened intervention there was nothing that Germany could do to help China, nevertheless what the Foreign Office was up against was the War Ministry's basic argument that 'political necessities' had to be subordinated to those of Germany's economic and military rearmament.[96] This was something the Foreign Office could neither deny nor overcome, while even its own responsibility in this respect was underlined by a circular instruction from von Neurath at the end of July. In this he drew the attention of Germany's representatives abroad to the work they should be doing in connection with the fact that 'the great upsurge in the German domestic economy during the last two years had made the *supply of indispensable foreign raw materials* the most important task for German economic policy'.[97]

Japanese reactions to the Klein agreement were only one aspect of the problem. Before and after the ratification of 25 July 1936 the Foreign Office received numerous complaints and expressions of fear about the future position of the 'China Firmen' in the face of the monopolistic position that HAPRO had apparently abrogated to itself in the China trade. This question had already given rise to correspondence between Emil Helfferich, President of the *Ostasiatischer Verein,* von Blomberg and Göring, the latter replying in a more positive manner than von Blomberg.[98] These complaints were put to Colonel Georg Thomas by Voss on 8 August, who also suggested ways in which the situation could perhaps be improved, that HAPRO should abandon its previous reserve and enter into discussions with the 'China Firmen'. Thomas answered that he had already instructed von Reichenau to contact the Chamber of Commerce in Shanghai and receive Herr Nolte of Carlowitz & Co. This had been on instructions from von Blomberg. He also agreed that to counter the impression in Japan that HAPRO was only supplying military equipment, it should emphasise its non-military projects in China. It was also proposed that an agreement be arrived at regarding 'spheres of interest' in China between HAPRO and other German businesses. Discussions on the question then took place on 27 August between Colonel Thomas and members of HAPRO and the *Ausfuhrgemeinschaft für Kriegsgerät,* while Helfferich was at last permitted to attend an inter-Ministerial meeting on 21 December. To emphasise whose interests were paramount in this case, however, both meetings took place in Colonel Thomas's office at the War Ministry.[99]

Thomas's agreement to the suggestions put forward by Voss was confirmed by General von Blomberg in his talk with Dr Kiep, Head of the German Economic Mission to the Far East, upon the latter's return from Asia. Von Blomberg,

however, emphasised that the War Ministry rejected suggestions to replace the military advisers at Nanking by officers
on the active list, while there was to be close cooperation
with von Falkenhausen on matters connected with the HAPRO
agreements.[100] This showed how far von Blomberg was prepared to take Japanese reactions into account and was ready
to compromise on incidentals in order not to endanger the
total of War Ministry operations in China.

The War Ministry also faced other problems in the form of
doubts about the extent and reliability to China's contribution and completion of the Klein agreements, especially since
it was learned that Kung had again opposed any agreement
with Germany and had had to be ordered by Chiang Kai-shek
to pursue the contracts so far concluded.[101] These difficulties
were, however overshadowed in the final months of 1936 by
two considerations relating to German—Japanese relations:
Foreign Office exhortations to the War Ministry not to allow
its agreements with China unduly to disturb relations with
Japan; and the fact that von Ribbentrop's negotiations with
Japan for the Anti-Comintern Pact had reached a decisive
stage. The Wilhelmstrasse's concern for German—Japanese
relations and expressions of doubt regarding China's ability
to maintain the HAPRO agreement in the face of Japanese
pressures,[102] produced different reactions from the Army.
Captain Voelter, von Reichenau's Adjutant, completely
exasperated by the attitude of such diplomats in China as
Fischer, remarked that 'one must decide, either Japan or
China. Our diplomatic representatives here are too sceptical
with regard to China'. Yet so involved were the ramifications
of War Ministry and Foreign Office interests and objectives in
the Far East that when the *New York Herald Tribune* of
26 August reported that von Reichenau had visited Japan for
secret military talks, Noebel of the German Embassy at Tokio
had no choice other than to 'catergorically' deny the allega-
tion.[103]

Apart from anything else, Voelter's remark pinpointed the
cause of the Foreign Office's dissatisfaction at the way things
had gone in Far Eastern policy. By late 1936 it could only
stand and watch its policy of political uninvolvement in the
Far East compromised, first by the Army in China and second
by the Nazi leadership with Japan. The fact that obviously
political agreements were being concluded with both China

and Japan by different German groups naturally did nothing to enhance Germany's supposed 'neutrality' in Far Eastern affairs. At least von Blomberg appeared to recognise the important foreign policy implications of the War Ministry's obvious political agreement with China. Even before Dr Kiep informed him that the Foreign Office took 'a very serious view' of the whole matter, he had had 'an exhaustive conversation' with the Japanese Military Attaché, General Oshima, about the agreement with China.[104] Nevertheless, the Foreign Office did not go so far as to accede to Japanese requests that it should issue a statement in Tokio that 'this was not a matter of a treaty concluded between the German Government and the Chinese Government for the supply of war material.[105] Not only would this have flown in the face of the facts of the case, but would have resulted in a serious breach of confidence in Sino—German relations.

The Japanese question came to affect the Chinese enterprises of the War Ministry in a more direct manner when the Japanese hinted that the final success of the Anti-Comintern Pact negotiations depended upon a satisfactory settlement of their demands regarding certain aspects of these enterprises. On 30 October Ambassador Mushakoji explained to the Acting Secretary of State, Hans Dieckhoff that 'a certain danger' to the Anti Comintern Pact, then under consideration in Tokio, arose from reports that the Klein group had promised to install fortification on the Yangtse and to set up a military arsenal in Pingchan (Hunan Province) in return for Chinese supplies of wolfram and antimony. The Ambassador then spelt out the dilemma confronting the Foreign Office: 'such reports . . . were calculated to endanger the agreement or at least to make it difficult for the Government to get it through the Privy Council'.[106]

This presented the Foreign Office with an extremely neat problem. After its previous general 'warnings' to the War Ministry about Japanese reactions to its military activities in China, it was now confronted with a situation where a certain political agreement — but one not of its making and to which it was generally opposed — might be in danger of rejection by the Japanese unless the War Ministry could give satisfaction on the points raised. That the two were really connected is doubtful, but Mushakoji used an obvious ploy in order to pursue two particular Japanese interests. Not entirely unforeseen, the incident nevertheless indicated what could be expected once Japan had achieved a real position of mastery in the Far East.

Strictly speaking, of course, there was nothing the Foreign Office could do but pursue the Japanese Ambassador's points, and in this way it could be said to have contributed towards the final acceptance of the Anti-Comintern Pact. On 4 November, therefore, Colonel Thomas explained to the Foreign Office the changed extent of the War Ministry's recent plans in China, particularly concerning the delivery of some war material. Colonel Thomas repeated von Blomberg's point that the War Ministry would not be sending active officers to Nanking, nor would the Advisory Staff be strengthened, as von Reichenau had originally intended as part of his proposals for intensifying Germany's military links with China. Most illuminating was Thomas's admission that these decisions had been taken 'with regard to German–Japanese relations'. Von Erdmannsdorff concluded that 'Colonel Thomas . . . showed complete understanding that the export of German war material which would particularly disturb the Japanese – in particular coastal guns for the mouth of the Yangtse and fast boats for coastal defence – must be postponed because of the current German–Japanese negotiations known to him, while in view of China's insignificant deliveries this can be explained to the Chinese without further ado'. Nevertheless, von Erdmannsdorff must have been taken aback by Thomas's account of the extensive and expensive programme of German arms supplies in China, those delivered and en route to the value of 10 million Reichsmarks while more deliveries were planned for the immediate future.[107]

Six days later, Hans Dieckhoff received Ambassador Mushakoji and in a memorandum brought in during the interview it was explained that there was no grounds for the fears which he had expressed on 30 October. The memorandum stated that German war material was being sent to China in so far as it was necessary to purchase in this way Chinese raw materials which Germany needed. It was also pointed out that the Japanese Government could rest assured that Germany 'would not undertake the delivery of German war material [to China] which exceeded that necessary to keep our armaments industry fully occupied after our own requirements had been met, or what was exported to many other countries'.[108]

Fears were expressed, however, by the War Ministry and by

China on the occasion of the signature of the Anti-Comintern Pact on 25 November 1936. Colonel Thomas complained to von Erdmannsdorff that the agreement might adversely affect China's willingness to deliver the raw materials promised under the Klein agreements, while von Blomberg requested that instructions be sent to Ambassador Trautmann to 'pacify' the Chinese.[109] Chiang Kai-shek also demanded to know the attitude of von Blomberg to the Pact, and was given the stock answer that it was simply a form of defensive cooperation against the subversive activity of Comintern and that in no way would it affect the relations existing between Germany and China.[110] According to Klein this met with a mixed reception on the part of Chiang Kai-shek. Although von Blomberg's telegram of assurance prompted the Marshal to quash a boycott of German goods instituted in protest against the Anti-Comintern Pact, nevertheless Chiang Kai-shek seemed intent on sending a mission to von Blomberg to clarify and establish the basis of Sino—German relations in the light of the new circumstances in German—Japanese relations. It also appeared that on 3 December the Chinese Ambassador raised the whole question with von Blomberg personally.[111]

These new circumstances undoubtedly increased the general political difficulties of the War Ministry's operations in China. When the Sino—Japanese war began in 1937 it could only be a matter of time before the War Ministry's interests in China, and most particularly the work of the Military Advisory Staff at Nanking, clashed in an obvious manner with the political and military interests of the Nazi—Japanese alignment. The War Ministry had only to wait until the middle of 1938 for ten years' careful work to be sabotaged for political considerations. At the behest of the Nazi leadership China was thus to join Russia in the War Ministry's roll of 'dishonour'.

VI

Agreement with Manchukuo: The Kiep Mission 1935-1936

The intensification of the Reichswehr's interests in China was in a sense 'balanced' by the contemporaneous development of Germany's economic relations with Manchukuo, through the efforts of the Foreign Office, formalised by the German—Manchukuoan Agreement of 30 April 1936. Yet there was no deliberate policy of 'balance' as such on the part of the Foreign Office to offset Reichswehr interests in China and Nazi interests in Japan. Not only did German—Manchukuoan economic relations have a history of their own, but the Foreign Office was the obvious body to handle such questions. Since Manchukuo had emerged as a kind of 'test case', both for the nature of the policy-making process in Berlin and for Germany's general position in the Far East, it is interesting that it was not until April 1935, several months after Heye's removal as Reich Commissar on 4 February, that the Foreign Office began to consider responding to feelers from Manchukuo for the regularisation of German—Manchukuoan economic relations. These feelers and suggestions came from a variety of Japanese and Manchukuoan sources, each emphasising the keen desire for a normalisation of trade relations with Germany and for German participation in industrial projects in Manchukuo. In connection with the Iyogumi plans,[1] Herr Lemke's discussions in Manchukuo went so far that Takahashi, Chief of the Industrial Department in the Manchukuoan Ministry of Trade, suggested that perhaps Germany could send a special mission to Manchukuo.[2] This was particularly interesting in view of von Dirksen's own suggestions.[3]

The Foreign Office could not for long ignore the persistent nature of these approaches, while they went some way towards meeting Ulrich's point in his telegram of 25 January 1935 to von Dirksen that no new German initiative would be undertaken but that proposals would be awaited from the other side.[4] Finally, in a memorandum written in April 1935 Karl Ritter, Director of the Economic Department, carefully analysed the whole question. Ritter first of all noted Manchukuoan and

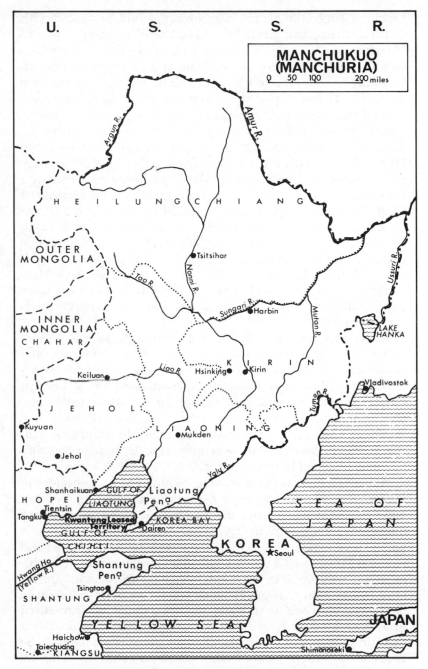

Map. 2.   Manchukuo (Manchuria)

Japanese suggestions that large orders would be placed with German firms, and that these could send representatives to Manchukuo. It had also been made clear that Manchukuo would prefer Germany to send an official representative to Hsinking to coordinate economic relations between the two countries. It was hoped that from this there might emerge a general delivery, credit, and compensation plan for German–Manchukuoan trade relations. Ritter admitted that many uncertainties needed to be resolved, particularly since 'what the Manchukuoan authorities expect from us is not yet completely clear'. Since, however, Manchukuo was aware of Germany's foreign exchange difficulties it was assumed that they realised what Germany's own demands would be, i.e. a like increase of German exports to balance Manchukuo's exports to Germany. Ritter assumed that Manchukuoan and Japanese demands would consist of requests for credit, that the proceeds of the bilateral trade be used to purchase more Manchukuoan products, and that the imports of Manchukuoan soya beans be given a privileged position in Germany's bean-import trade.

Ritter accepted that Germany should begin to play a more active role in German–Manchukuoan trade relations, and suggested that by the middle of September a suitable representative of German industry, accompanied by a Foreign Office official, be sent to Hsinking to negotiate with Manchukuoan and Japanese authorities. He also recommended that the Manchukuoan Minister of Trade be informed that the German Government was prepared to finance the Silo business that had been suggested.[5]

Another consideration leading to this renewed interest in Manchukuo appears to have been the visit there in October 1934 of the mission from the Federation of British Industry under the leadership of Lord Barnby. Following this, and with Heye's removal, Ritter suggested to von Bülow and Richard Meyer on 25 April 1935 that Germany should testify in some way to her economic interests in Manchukuo by sending her own mission. He added that one of its tasks would be to establish whether trade relations could be formalised in a loose kind of treaty without at the same time involving the formal recognition of Manchukuo, an obvious point to be considered with regard to Sino–German relations. This required that the mission had no official character, that it would be composed of representatives of German industry having interests in Manchukuo, and that it be accompanied by Dr Knoll, and in a more senior position Minister Kiep, one-time Consul General at New York.[6]

There was a third consideration behind the Foreign Office's more positive but still rather cautious interest in furthering economic relations with Manchukuo. Nazi plans for autarky had also affected German agriculture, and Walter Darré, the Minister of Agriculture, had succeeded in cutting food imports substantially. But production declined steadily, partly because of poor harvests and partly because of the Ministry of Agriculture's faulty pricing policy. As consumer demand increased with the economic revival, difficulties were unavoidable. Schacht attempted to keep food imports to a bare minimum to ease the strain on foreign exchange, but came under increasing pressure to modify his position. It is significant that Ritter's memorandum on economic relations with Manchukuo, whose staple export to Germany was the soya bean, an important source of edible fats, came at a time when Schacht reluctantly authorised additional oilseed imports in order to overcome Germany's fats shortages.[7]

Ritter obtained the approval of von Bülow and Meyer for his proposals and the interest of Sarnow of the Ministry of Economics. On 9 May the matter was officially taken up with that Ministry, while a request was put forward concerning the financing of the Silo transactions. While von Dirksen was informed of these developments, the Silo project was developed in discussions with the civil and military authorities in Manchukuo.[8]

Although von Dirksen was pleased that things seemed to be progressing in Berlin, nevertheless he warned the Foreign Office of something that was undoubtedly being considered in the Wilhelmstrasse: 'the leader of the delegation should be completely authorised to conclude agreements, so that it is possible to achieve positive results and the damage caused to Germany's reputation through Heye's negotiating methods, which still rankle, and the distrust of Manchukuoan as well as of Japanese authorities, will be avoided'. He also suggested that it would be necessary for a member of the mission to visit Tokio to reach full agreement with the Japanese central authorities responsible for Manchukuoan affairs.[9]

Von Dirksen had raised not only an important tactical point

regarding the work of any German mission, but also a vital economic and political consideration: the position of Japan *vis-à-vis* German—Manchukuoan relations. By the winter of 1934—35 both Japan and Manchukuo were extremely worried by the unhealthy state of the latter's soya bean export trade. In 1934 a general import prohibition was issued barring soya beans from the German market unless imported by special permit; furthermore, early in 1935 Great Britain removed soya beans from the import list, with the result that soya bean prices slumped heavily. Japanese efforts to improve German—Manchukuoan trade relations would thus help Japan's own position in the triangular economic relationship of the three countries.[10] There was, of course, another side to the question. If Germany was 'won' for Manchukuo in this way, Japan herself could expect to begin to reap some more general political benefits. Not only would it give the appearance that somehow Japan had managed to 'balance' or even offset the German Army's work in China, but it would also (hopefully) provide some further encouragement to those Nazi circles who wished to pursue a political agreement with Japan. Both reasons of course, explain the Wilhelmstrasse's caution in handling the delicate question of regularising economic relations with Manchukuo. Nevertheless, the Foreign Office was impelled towards seeking such a regularisation because of the slump in the price of Manchukuoan soya beans and as a result of Germany's chronic and perennial shortage of edible fats at a time of extreme difficulty in the foreign exchange field.[11]

Preparations for the Far Eastern mission then went quickly ahead. Early in June 1935 Ritter obtained Schacht's agreement to the proposal of Kiep's leadership of the mission, while he accepted the Minister's suggestion that it should include members of the Reichsbank who were familiar with the Far East. Although Schacht expressed his confidence in Kiep because of his recent mission to South America, Ritter pointed out that the Economics Ministry was of the opposite opinion. Shortly afterwards, however, on 15 June the Ministry of Economics informed the Foreign Office of its agreement to the mission and the financing of the MIAG—Silo projects subject to preliminary discussions. It was also suggested that the mission should begin its work in Hsinking by the middle of October, while Kiep was fully informed of what was proposed regarding the purpose and tasks of the mission.[12]

Kiep himself also contributed to the discussion on the important question of the form, nature and purpose of the proposed mission. In a memorandum of 22 June he suggested that undue publicity be avoided for two reasons: Manchukuo's special political position *vis-à-vis* China and Japan, and the risk that the mission would be classified as an official one. The mission's chief task was to examine how far a regular German–Manchukuoan compensation trade could be built up, through the conclusion of a formal treaty if necessary or by some other means. To avoid public discussion and speculation Kiep suggested that the presence of officials such as Knoll and representatives of the Reichsbank be justified by statements that they were visiting Germany's diplomatic representatives and Chambers of Commerce in the Far East to explain the details of the 'New Plan'. He also proposed that the non-governmental side of the mission be dispensed with altogether on the grounds of cost, again to avoid undue publicity, and to avoid difficulties in choosing between competing economic interests for representation. He recommended instead that a general economic representative be appointed, but somebody connected with the bean-oil trade. Should other economic interests still claim representation, he proposed that their representatives in Manchukuo could participate in the work of the mission once it was in the Far East. Kiep also thought the mission should avoid visiting China on its outward journey to Japan and Manchukuo, while on the homeward journey the non-political and purely economic nature of the mission was to be emphasised. The Chinese Government could be informed of the Mission's general task, while only later could it be told of major tasks.[13]

The preparations for the mission were supposed to be strictly confidential so that von Erdmannsdorff was somewhat taken aback to learn on 27 June from the Japanese Ambassador that Schacht had that same day informed a Mr Genda, a Japanese official in the Manchukuoan Ministry of Finance, of the mission's impending departure for Manchukuo in the autumn. Mushakoji expressed his pleasure at this news, and hoped that the mission would visit Japan as well as Shanghai where good relations existed between German and Japanese firms. But any hope that this information would remain strictly within diplomatic circles was dashed by Oshima's statement to Knoll that he had transmitted this news to the Japanese Ministry of War.[14]

By the time the Chinese Embassy was informed about the mission at the end of June the Foreign Office felt it politic to have designated the mission as one to the Far East generally and not one simply to Manchukuo. Although an unsigned memorandum of July emphasised that this had been the Foreign Office's intention for some time, it was admitted that the intention to have a Far Eastern mission visit China to show Germany's 'visiting card' had been strengthened by Great Britain's decision at the beginning of June to send the Government's Chief Economic Adviser, Sir Frederick Leith-Ross, to advise on the reconstruction of the Chinese economy. Ritter, however, denied to the Chinese Minister on 4 July that this was Germany's motive in sending the mission and emphasised instead its general duties, but admitted that special trade agreements might be arrived at where opportune.[15]

Kiep's suggestion for abandoning the idea of including representatives of German industry in the mission was finally accepted. He was to lead an essentially official and Foreign Office mission, although instructions sent out on 10 July which also covered many of the points raised by von Dirksen,[16] stated that all enquiries should be answered with an affirmation of its unofficial character. Kiep was to be supported by Dr Knoll, while following Schacht's suggestion Herr Rosenbruch of the Reichsbank would be included in the mission. It was not known whether the Ministry of Economics would participate, although the Foreign Office had made it clear that it would welcome a Far Eastern specialist from that Ministry. It appeared, however, that Ritter was opposed to such participation although the Ministry of Economics desired it. Knoll himself thought that Ritter's attitude might create difficulties with the Ministry.[17]

Apart from studying the possibility of increasing trade with Manchukuo and pursuing the large industrial projects which had Government approval such as MIAG, Krupp and Iyogumi, the mission was also to examine the relationships between the Manchukuoan authorities, the Japanese civil and military authorities, and the Japanese business giants, although the Foreign Office had already received many reports on this question. General discussions but not negotiations were to take place with Japanese and Chinese authorities on trade relations with Germany when explanations would also be given about recent developments in the management of Germany's foreign trade.[18]

Two problems then arose which underlined not only the complex nature of Germany's position in the Far East but also the difficult position of the Foreign Office in Berlin. The first concerned the decidedly unwelcome publicity given in the Japanese and Manchukuoan press to the mission, particularly since these reports raised the question of Germany's recognition of Manchukuo in connection with her impending definitive withdrawal from the League of Nations. There was also talk that the recognition of Manchukuo 'would result in a new orientation of Germany's Far Eastern policy'. Trautmann's warnings about the effect of this upon China were probably expected by the Wilhelmstrasse, as was his suggestion that the mission should first visit China on its outward journey. But it also seemed that Trautmann was personally opposed to the whole idea of the mission: 'it would be unfortunate if, through an *experiment* [my italics] we should damage our China business which has been well maintained in spite of the economic crisis'. On 30 July Ritter instructed Trautmann to reassure the Chinese Government that the mission would have nothing to do with the recognition issue, and that the wilder Japanese press stories should be disregarded.[19]

It was clear, however, that the recognition issue would be a troublesome one. In Berlin the Japanese Chargé d'Affaires tried to suggest that any economic agreement with Manchukuo would automatically involve the *de jure* recognition of the country, and that consequently such an agreement must be of a political nature. Ritter then had to repeat to von Dirksen the instructions he had sent to Trautmann about the recognition question, this time for the benefit of the Japanese Government. The Foreign Office also tried to play down the whole matter by refusing Trautmann's request for a semi-official statement on the matter to be issued through the German news agency in China, *Transozean*. It was feared that such a statement would only lead to fresh speculation in the Japanese press. As it was, in July the British Consul General at Mukden had reported to London that:

in its usual irresponsible fashion, the local Japanese press had rushed to the conclusion that the visit of the mission will be promptly followed by formal German recognition of Manchukuo. Mr Tigges (the German Consul) said that, so far as he was aware, this assumption was ground-less but I am told that the step is generally anticipated by the German community in Mukden, the members of which, being mostly ardent Nazis, may conceivably be better informed than their Consul.[20]

The other problem concerned Germany's relations with China and centred round the attitude adopted by Hjalmar Schacht, President of the Reichsbank and Minister of Economics. Despite what he had said to Ritter in June,[21] at the end of July he expressed grave doubts about the dispatch of the Economic Mission. This was because of his talks with General von Seeckt upon the latter's return from China. He told Ritter that he would have no objections to Dr Knoll travelling to the Far East 'to explore the ground', but that he was now opposed to Kiep's journey. The real reason for Schacht's *volte-face* was then made clear: he was afraid of undesirable repercussions on German interests in China, particularly the War Ministry's current projects in the hands of Herr Klein. In reply, Ritter made the interesting point that:

if he had said this to us four or five weeks previously, I would have immediately agreed since we had certainly considered whether it was not politic first of all to send Herr Knoll alone on a kind of 'patrol'. Since, however, the mission had been announced, first to the Japanese Ambassador and then to the Chinese Ministers, and had then been widely reported in the Far Eastern press, it was hardly possible to alter present plans.

Schacht had to accept this point, but in turn recommended that the mission be kept as small as possible. To this end he said that nobody from the Ministry of Economics or the Reichsbank would participate. Schacht went so far as to imply that Herr Rosenbruch, previously promised for the mission, would work instead at Klein's side. In conclusion, Schacht stated that he would speak once again with the War Minister, von Blomberg, while Ritter responded by saying that in the final resort the whole question depended upon a decision by the Foreign Minister, von Neurath. Schacht promptly answered that this was 'obvious'.[22]

While the Foreign Office was perfectly aware of the force of Schacht's arguments regarding China, it was rather surprised at his general attitude since the overriding purpose of the forth-coming Economic Mission was to help overcome Germany's difficult economic situation. On the other hand, under tremendous and continued pressure from military sources,

Schacht was doing what he felt was necessary to protect an important source of Germany's rearmament. Nevertheless, the Foreign Office felt obliged to try and overcome his opposition. Without even Schacht's tacit approval it was expected that the fundamental purpose of the mission would be nullified since any positive outcome of its work could not be expected or implemented without the full cooperation of the economic authorities in Germany. On 2 August von Bülow wrote to von Neurath at his country estate, requesting the Foreign Minister's support: 'in these questions we cannot progress further with Herr Schacht without your intervention.' Von Bülow admitted that the Foreign Office was prepared to accede to his request that the mission be kept as small as possible, but as Ritter had emphasised to Schacht, he argued that any other alterations in plans were now out of the question.[23]

Prompted by this request, von Neurath wrote to Schacht on 3 August, pointing out that:

as regards the mission to the Far East, I cannot share your concern regarding an unfavourable reaction on the trade with China. The mission has never been thought of by the Foreign Office as one to Japan or to Manchukuo, but always as a mission to the Far East. From the outset it has been provided that the greatest part of the mission's time will be spent in China.

Von Neurath insisted that circumstances made it impossible either to cancel the mission or to send Dr Knoll alone to the Far East, but in an attempt to overcome Schacht's reluctance regarding Herr Rosenbruch's participation he promised to keep the mission as small as possible and to avoid any undue publicity. He was also prepared to allow Kiep and Knoll to travel to the Far East alone, and to emphasise the mission's unofficial character until it was established that the Far Eastern Governments wished to negotiate officially with it.[24]

While von Neurath was attempting to clarify matters with Schacht, Ritter cleared up a misunderstanding with the Ministry of War which apparently was under the impression that the Foreign Office desired its participation in the forth-coming mission. On 3 August Ritter made it clear to Lieutenant Colonel von Böckmann that the Foreign Office had taken no initiative on this question, but that naturally it would be prepared to discuss such participation. Böckmann ignored this hint and in doing so made it clear that the Ministry of War was not interested in associating itself with the mission, for obvious reasons. Yet the Ministry of War's surreptitious interest in business with Japan and Manchukuo (and surreptitious it needed to be in view of the fuss the Klein projects in China were causing) slipped out when Böckmann wondered whether the mission could not contact Colonel Ott when it was in Japan. It was finally agreed that the Ministry of War should make preliminary enquiries of Ott regarding such business, and before the departure of the mission Knoll should contact it for instructions.[25] Two months later Ott recommended that the Japanese Army be requested to support the work of the mission as part of a package deal in return for facilities accorded to Japanese officers and missions in Germany.[26]

Yet the Foreign Office still faced the difficulties raised by Schacht's attitude. On 8 August he suggested to von Neurath that the outward journey of the mission be arranged so as not to 'disturb' the talks Ambassador Mushakoji would be having in Manchukuo, along with Shoji Kaisha, the Berlin representative of Mitsubishi, to prepare the ground for the work of the mission. Schacht also suggested an inter-departmental meeting before the departure of the mission. Von Bülow's reply firmly but politely dismissed Schacht's concern regarding Mushakoji's talks in Manchukuo, but he did agree to an inter-departmental meeting and promised that discussions could take place with the Reichsbank over any treaty to be concluded with Manchukuo.[27]

Although Kiep finally obtained Schacht's general support for the mission and his assurance that Herr Rosenbruch would cooperate with the mission once it was in the Far East,[28] Schacht was not to be moved from his stand that no representative of the Ministry of Economics would be involved in the work of the mission. When Ritter wrote to von Dirksen on 15 August this point was judiciously 'explained': 'unfortunately, the Reich Ministry of Economics will not be sending a representative. This does not mean that that Ministry or the Reichsbank President take no interest in the mission. It is simply that a suitable personality could not be found who could be spared for so long in view of that Ministry's current work'.[29]

The inter-departmental meeting suggested by Schacht took place on 16 August 1935, with representatives from the Foreign

Office and the Ministries of Economics, Finance, Agriculture
and War, the Reichsbank and the Reich Agency for Foreign
Exchange Control. While Kiep outlined the mission's purpose,
the attitude of reserve on the part of the Ministry of Economics
was repeated by Ministerialrat Mossdorf when he stated that
they wished to await the result of Mushakoji's exploratory
talks in Manchukuo. He confirmed that both Mushakoji and
Kaisha had spoken with Helmuth Wohlthat, Ministerialdirektor in the Reich Agency for Foreign Exchange Control
before their departure and had promised to communicate
directly with him about the results of their survey. With this
reservation, Mossdorf explained that the Ministry of Economics was prepared to support the mission's work. He also
repeated Schacht's point that the mission should remain as
small as possible. An attitude of reserve was also adopted by
Reichsbankdirektor Puhl who only appeared satisfied when
Kiep assured him that the Foreign Office only expected a
general form of cooperation from the Reichsbank. Lieutenant
Colonel Warlimont of the War Ministry also explained its
reasons for not wishing to be associated with the mission: the
poor prospects of business with Japan and the activity of
Klein and the German military advisers in China.[30]

This meeting emphasised two things already clear to the
Foreign Office: its initial and, ultimately, final responsibility
for the forthcoming mission; and the attitude of reserve on
the part of other Ministries and Reich Agencies. Yet their
cooperation was essential to the success of this mission, and
this was reflected in the close consultation the Foreign Office
maintained with them as the final arrangements and plans for
the mission materialised. How far one can argue from all this
that the Foreign Office was deliberately attempting to secure
a measure of success for itself in Manchukuo in order to
'balance' the efforts of the Army in China and the Nazi
leadership in Japan is hard to tell. Nevertheless, Manchukuo
was an area where the Foreign Office was able to pursue its
policy after 4 February 1935 without overt intervention
from other Reich personalities or agencies. A Japanese press
suggestion that the forthcoming mission should work with
Herr Heye was therefore dismissed by Knoll as 'fantasy'.[31]

Just before the final instructions about the mission were
issued on 18 and 19 September 1935 the Foreign Office was
again reminded that the recognition issue was bound to be a

question overshadowing the mission's work in the Far East. At Harbin the Japanese Vice-Foreign Minister of Manchukuo, Ohashi suggested to Consul Balser that the imminence of Germany's formal withdrawal from the League of Nations made the time right for Germany to recognise Manchukuo. He thought this would constitute a friendly gesture towards Japan, and while it would not lead to immediate economic advantages for Germany in Manchukuo, it could later on. As if to underline the practical situation Germany should recognise and accommodate herself to in the Far East, he emphasised that 'North China is already a Japanese sphere of influence and Central China will be by and by'.[32] The instructions of 18 and 19 September therefore emphasised that although the major part of the mission's work would concern Manchukuo this did not signify any change in Germany's position on the recognition question.[33] Yet the recognition issue was to provide a continual source of difficulty and even some embarrassment for Germany during the mission's work in the Far East.

The Economic Study Mission of Kiep and Knoll, to be joined later by Herr Rosenbruch, left Germany at the beginning of October 1935, just when the Japanese began exerting pressure in Berlin to alter the 4:1 trade relationship, due to expire in January 1936, with a view to increasing Japanese exports to Germany.[34] Travelling via Canada, the mission arrived in Japan at the end of the month where it met a friendly reception, and preliminary discussions were carried out in a favourable atmosphere. In reporting this at the beginning of November, von Dirksen added that the War Minister, General Yoshiyuki Kuwashima, had expressed the hope that 'the cooperation on economic and other matters would be fruitful'. Von Dirksen also stated that Balser now had a more favourable impression of the attitudes of the authorities in Manchukuo towards the mission that had been reported in October.[35] According to the American representative at Harbin, the Hsinking authorities had placed so much emphasis on the recognition issue that Balser had finally warned that 'if they insisted upon it he would be forced to recommend that the German Economic Mission avoid visiting Manchukuo'. At this the Manchukuoan authorities withdrew somewhat and assured Balser that 'the question of recognition need not be taken up at present and that they by all means desired the mission to visit Manchukuo'.[36]

The basis of the mission's discussions with Japanese officials was a memorandum dated 4 November 1935. This explained the necessity for the restrictions on Germany's foreign trade as implemented in the New Plan, particular emphasis being placed on Germany's difficult foreign exchange situation. These difficulties had affected Germany's ability to maintain its imports of Manchukuoan soya beans, so that the talks in Manchukuo were to explore the possibility of increasing German soya bean imports 'beyond the limits set through the exchange problem, by enabling the payment of a part thereof through German exports'. Additional imports of soya beans into Germany beyond the purchase paid for with the available foreign exchange could be achieved through the participation of German firms in the reconstruction programme of Manchukuo, while Manchukuoan soya beans would be given a 'favoured' position in Germany's bean import trade. German participation in the reconstruction of Manchukuo would also be in those areas in which there was no Japanese competition.

When these proposals had been agreed to in Berlin during September, Wohlthat had informed Kiep that foreign exchange could be made available for the importation of up to 300,000 tons of Manchukuoan soya beans during 1936. An interesting stipulation was that such an arrangement was out of the question if the problem of the German–Japanese trade balance was included.[37] It was hardly to be expected, however, that the Japanese, in view of their close relationship with Manchukuo and with the German Economic Mission actually in their capital city, would refrain from discussing not only the whole complex of German–Japanese–Manchukuoan trade but the more specific question of German–Japanese trade relations. This was pointed out in the Japanese reply of 11 November 1935 from Kurusu, head of the Trade Section of the Japanese Foreign Office. The reply also stated that points relating to German–Manchukuoan trade would have to be discussed directly between the mission and the authorities in Manchukuo. However, in view of Japan's general interest it was explained that the Japanese authorities would be prepared to discuss such questions with the mission. More importantly, the Japanese reply stated that discussions would take place with the mission on German–Japanese trade relations, the Japanese approach being indicated by reference to their dissatisfaction with Germany's policy of restricting Japanese imports because of Germany's foreign exchange difficulties. Reference was also made to supposed German 'dumping' in Japanese markets. It appears, however, that the mission 'found it difficult to make the Japanese understand the German financial position as affecting trade exchanges'.[38]

During the conversations with Kurusu it emerged that the Japanese were concerned that out of the direct German–Manchukuoan negotiations nothing should emerge which would affect Japanese exports to Manchukuo. It was also emphasised that should an arrangement be arrived at between Germany and Manchukuo along the lines of the German memorandum, Japanese desiderata regarding developments in German–Japanese trade should also be taken into account. These included the financing of Germany's trade with Manchukuo through the foreign exchange surplus she had in her trade with Japan. In any case, the Japanese made it plain that they would await the final outcome of the German–Manchukuoan negotiations before formulating their own definite proposals regarding German–Japanese trade. For this reason the German Mission proposed to return to Tokio after the completion of negotiations with Manchukuo.

Although these were early days yet, Kiep was cautious but optimistic. He had been favourably impressed by his conversations with the Ministers of Foreign Affairs, Economics, Finance, War, and with the President of the South Manchuria Railway, Yosuko Matsuoka, Japan's representative of the League of Nations during the Manchurian crisis. The Japanese Ministers expressed the hope of more general cooperation with Germany, and that the planned regulation of trade with Manchukuo was proof of such cooperation in the economic field. During his talks with Matsuoka, Kiep had discussed the use of German technical processes and assistance in connection with coal liquefaction, the treatment of low grade iron ore, the manufacture of alcohol from kaolin, and of food products from the soya bean, besides more general assistance in the development of Manchukuo's natural resources in return for continued German imports of soya beans. German constructional material and machinery for railways, harbours and other undertakings were also offered. Kiep appeared to have been so impressed by his reception in Japan that by the end of November 1935 he was suggesting to the Wilhelmstrasse that one way of ensuring the mission's success in Manchukuo would be for Germany to adopt a more accommodating attitude towards Japanese requests for an improvement on their trade position *vis-à-vis* Germany.[39]

By 1 December 1935 the mission had arrived in Mukden, from where Kiep reported that he had agreed to the suggestion of the Manchukuoan authorities that the mission be received by Emperor Kang-te (Henry Pu-yi) of Manchukuo. He thought this would advance its work, while he discounted any political repercussions since the Emperor had received the Barnby Mission.[40]

Kiep's continual insistence in the Far East that no political significance should be attached to the mission was in accordance with Foreign Office policy. When the Foreign Office itself acceded to Japanese requests in December 1935 that a trade commissioner from Manchukuo be resident in Berlin, it was emphasised that this decision in no way compromised Germany's stand on the recognition question. It was also felt that such a move would complement Germany's own efforts to increase trade with Manchukuo, while it appeared that von Dirksen would propose that a German Consulate General be opened in the Capital city of Hsinking, or at least that a trade expert be sent there.[41] Any change of policy on recognition was also denied when the Foreign Office decided to rationalise its administrative arrangement in the Far East. From December 1935 the Consulates at Harbin and Mukden, previously under the control of the Embassy at Nanking, were to join the Consulate at Dairen in being under the control of the Embassy at Tokio. This decision was to remain secret and was not to be communicated to either the Chinese or Japanese Governments since it was a 'purely internal measure'.[42]

The mission, meanwhile, had been steadily at work in Manchukuo. German businessmen in Mukden and Harbin complained that conditions in Manchukuo were difficult for them because of competition from cheaper Japanese goods and because of the predominant position which the Japanese had in all aspects of the country's life. Such complaints were complemented by those raised in the official discussions in Hsinking with a (predominantly Japanese) Manchukuoan delegation led by the Japanese Vice-Foreign Minister for Manchukuo, Ohashi. He expressed interest in an agreement with Germany, but emphasised that this should serve to improve Manchukuo's trade position *vis-à-vis* that of Germany. It was suggested that Germany utilise more foreign exchange to improve the total of Manchukuoan imports into Germany since, as the Manchukuoan delegates argued, such an increase through a compensation agreement would merely result in a corresponding increase in German exports to Manchukuo, thus intensifying the already dissatisfactory situation.

German suggestions that the import of increased amounts of Manchukuoan soya beans into Germany be paid for by German participation in the reconstruction of Manchukuo were dismissed because of the uncertain nature of such projects as were envisaged, and because in any case the Manchukuoan delegation was not authorised to negotiate on this question. Von Dirksen had already raised doubts about this approach to the question in his letter to von Erdmannsdorff on 28 November. The principal difficulty appeared to be the character of the contract partner for the German firms engaged in such reconstruction projects. The Manchukuoan Government was out of the question, while the South Manchurian Railway was only partially suitable for this purpose. He therefore suggested a consortium as the best solution.[43]

As was to be expected, the Manchukuoan delegates could not for long refrain from raising political questions. In reply Kiep maintained the economic purpose of the mission, although he had to admit that in view of Germany's expected cooperation with Japan in the development of Manchukuo this attached a considerable political significance to Germany's role. Even more encouraging for the Manchukuoans was Kiep's further admission that the execution of the programme proposed by Germany was unthinkable without some form of cooperation between German and Manchukuoan Government departments. It was suggested that from the German side this could take the form of a German economic representative in Manchukuo or the establishment of a Consulate in Hsinking.[44]

By the end of 1935 several problems of both an economic and a political nature had thus emerged from Kiep's negotiations in Manchukuo. The economic ones revolved around the fact that while both the German and Manchukuoan delegations wished to increase their own country's exports, this raised the problem of payment and, consequently, the level of imports to be allowed from the other country. To this had been added a Manchukuoan suggestion of a triangular relationship between Germany, Manchukuo and Japan on a basis of 1:1.[45]

The political questions concerned Kiep's suggestion of an economic representative from Germany being sent to Hsinking and Ohashi's that the final conclusion and signature of the expected German–Manchukuoan agreement be pursued through the German Ambassador at Tokio. Knoll had already urged on von Erdmansdorff that the idea of a German economic representative in Hsinking be given serious consideration in Berlin. He also stated that a failure of Germany's plans in Manchukuo and Japan would be of greater importance and significance in the political than in the economic field, and that this be kept in mind when the levels of foreign exchange available for Far Eastern trade were discussed in Berlin.[46]

In view of Manchukuo's nebulous position in the international community and Germany's relations with China the point regarding procedures for concluding an agreement with Manchukuo was an important one. Kiep thought that any difficulties could be overcome by explaining that such an agreement and the final procedures employed were technical matters connected with German–Japanese trade.[47] On 31 December 1935 Dieckhoff telegraphed Peking to ascertain Trautmann's views on this question, emphasising that von Dirksen had no objection to such a procedure and that Kiep had pointed out that while this recognised the *de facto* situation between Japan and Manchukuo, it was also a means of using Japanese influence in Manchukuo to further German wishes.[48]

Even before Trautmann's own negative reply had been received, Ritter informed Kiep on 3 January 1936 that 'considerable objections exist here against the conclusion of an agreement through the Ambassador'. It was also explained that a decision about sending an economic representative to Hsinking would have to wait on further developments.[49] Trautmann's reply on 4 January 1936 also emphasised that the Chinese were watching Germany's negotiations with Manchukuo and Japan with the greatest attention and that if an official agreement was signed with Manchukuo it would be assumed that Germany was in reality pursuing a political agreement with Japan. This was important given the persistent rumours of such German–Japanese negotiations and Ministerialdirektor Wohlthat's suggestion to Ritter that Kiep be informed of the Ribbentrop–Oshima negotiations 'otherwise he could not conduct his discussions in Manchukuo properly'.[50] Trautmann's views simply confirmed the doubts already held in the Foreign Office, and on 7 January von Dirksen was informed of the objections to his involvement in the conclusion of an agreement with Manchukuo. Foreign Office annoyance at Manchukuoan efforts to impute a political significance to the negotiations was also made clear.[51]

Nevertheless, the purely economic details of the negotiations were still the major concern of those involved. By the middle of January 1936 Kiep and von Dirksen thought that the German delegation should be authorised to conclude an agreement on the points agreed so far, while von Dirksen thought that 'the psychological moment' in which to finalise arrangements had arrived.[52] This was not Ritter's view, and on 17 January he declined to issue such authorisation. The Foreign Office still required clarification on such technical matters as the levels and values of Manchukuoan soya beans that Germany would be committed to importing and the kind of foreign exchange surplus Germany would have in her trade with Japan which might then be used to finance more Manchukuoan imports into Germany. Nor was Ritter pleased by anything which emphasised the unity of the Japanese–Manchukuoan bloc against the individual position of Germany. He was agreeable, however, to suggestions which maintained the 4:1 arrangements in German–Japanese trade, and that for the purpose of financing the expected increase in trade with the Far East an arrangement should be arrived at between the Reichsbank and the Yokohama Specie Bank, the dominant Japanese financial institution in Manchukuo and responsible for financing the bean export trade. Kiep was also authorised to conclude any agreement with Manchukuo on behalf of the 'German Administration of Foreign Exchange', a ploy designed to avoid any use of the word 'Government'. Ritter then made it quite clear that the Foreign Office wished to exercise greater control over the mission by demanding that Kiep keep it supplied with drafts of any final agreement, a move to ensure Foreign Office influence in the final drafting of the agreement.[53] Later, Kiep informed Ritter that these instructions, among other factors, contributed to an extension of the negotiations with Manchukuo and Japan.[54]

By this time Kiep was back in Tokio where he held further talks with Kurusu. He explained that for obvious political reasons Germany could not conclude a State treaty with Manchukuo but merely a technical one, and stressed that in any case Germany's relations with China were being compromised by the propaganda and tendentious reports from Hsinking regarding the political significance of an agreement with Germany. He also emphasised that the acceptance of a Manchukuoan economic representative in Berlin was 'purely a technical-economic measure, which in no way had any political significance'. Much to his gratification this approach was recognised and accepted by Kurusu and Hirota, the Foreign Minister.[55]

While Knoll remained behind in Tokio to continue technical discussions and negotiations, which appeared to progress satisfactorily, much to the pleasure of von Dirksen who was critical of what he thought was Ritter's over-cautious and sceptical attitude,[56] Kiep left Tokio on 18 January 1936 for China. This journey to China — after which Kiep was due to return to Japan — was to provide some semblance of 'balance' in the mission's activities in the Far East and to explain to the Chinese authorities and German businessmen the general economic purposes of the mission.

Kiep's visit to China came at an opportune moment. While the German Army was developing its plans in China, Chinese suspicions about the economic negotiations with Manchukuo and Japan had been compounded by continual rumours of negotiations between Germany and Japan for a political agreement. Nor was the situation improved by the kind of propaganda which Hsinking was releasing about the significance to be attached to the future German—Manchukuoan agreement, the *Manchurian Daily News* reporting from Tokio that a trade treaty with Hsinking 'means the virtual recognition of Manchukuo as a State on the part of Germany'.[57] In Nanking and Shanghai Kiep faced complaints on all these questions by Chinese Government Ministers and officials. However, in return and after explaining the purely economic aspects of his negotiations, he at least obtained the admission that Germany had every right to pursue her own economic interests. Since it was also admitted that in Manchukuo they did not conflict directly with Chinese interests, the Chinese Ministers went so far as to say that by improving economic conditions in Manchukuo Germany would be contributing to the economic well-being of the Chinese people there.

Kiep also reassured the Chinese in positive terms about the effects on Sino–German economic relations of Germany's policies under the New Plan. In an address at Shanghai he emphasised that 'the trade relations between Germany and China seem particularly adapted to reciprocal supplementation and expansive development', and asserted that mutual trade relations had maintained their buoyancy despite the economic crisis. He went further by praising China's role and contribution to the particular needs and requirements of the German economy at that time.[58]

The extent to which Kiep had been influenced by his experiences in China was seen in two recommendations he put forward at the conclusion of his long report of 3 February 1936 and in his covering letter of 8 February to von Dirksen. In view of Germany's interests in China and the risks they could be liable to if the Manchukuoan and Japanese authorities insisted on linking economic and political questions together, he suggested that it be repeated to them that any agreement should avoid reference to political issues. Should they refuse to accept such a condition, Kiep went so far as to recommend that negotiations be broken off, or at least delayed until the return of the mission to Berlin or the appearance there of the Manchukuoan Trade Commissioner. Kiep's own impatience with recent developments then made itself clear: 'in any case the Japanese cannot reproach us. We have negotiated with them for twelve weeks, visited Manchukuo, shown the patience of Job with the officiousness of Ohashi and agreed to the Trade Commissioner without anything in return'. By this time he felt that a return visit by him to Tokio would simply renew Chinese press speculations about a possible German–Japanese alliance, and suggested that it would be better if the final negotiations were left in the capable hands of Knoll in Tokio.[59]

While Ritter was concerned in case Kiep and Knoll went too far and fast in their negotiations,[60] von Dirksen's chief worry was that they might not go far enough. He was sufficiently concerned to take up with the Foreign Office Kiep's report of 3 February, particularly the suggestions for breaking off the negotiations. Von Dirksen totally dismissed Kiep's fears regarding the effect of the negotiations with Manchukuo and Japan on Germany's interests in China, particularly since the week before the Japanese had put a press ban on the negotiations. Although he could not deny Kiep's argument of what might happen in China if he returned to Tokio, von Dirksen admitted that Knoll could sign the eventual agreement but warned that 'our relations as a whole with Japan would be shaken to their foundations if we were now to withdraw without cogent and material reasons. At the present stage, the negotiations (could) fail only for material reasons, for which, however, I see no occasion'. Von Dirksen also thought that any withdrawal on Germany's part would raise insuperable difficulties for her future trade relations with Manchukuo and Japan. Commendable as it was, this concern for Germany's economic position in the Far East was motivated by other factors, for von Dirksen was especially concerned that nothing else in German–Japanese relations should be allowed to threaten the Ribbentrop–Oshima negotiations.[61]

Kiep's position at this juncture was an unhappy one. Despite his fears of the repercussions in China, the Foreign Office decided that he should, after all, return to Tokio since the situation there was still 'unclear'.[62] At the same time Kiep was perfectly aware of what would happen in Tokio – or rather, what would *not* happen – if he acceded to Chinese approaches regarding greater governmental control and management of Sino–German trade relations.[63]

As to the negotiations in Tokio, by early March 1936 the Foreign Office shared Kiep's dissatisfaction to the extent that on 6 March von Bülow instructed von Dirksen to obtain satisfaction from the Japanese on certain technical points, and that if this was not forthcoming the negotiations were to be broken off. It was explained that such a break could be disguised by emphasising the preliminary nature of the negotiations so far as that the mission had returned to Berlin to report, where negotiations could be resumed either with the Manchukuoan Trade Commissioner or by some other means.[64]

Chinese pressure on Germany probably contributed to this hardening of the German attitude in the negotiations with Manchukuo and Japan. In conversations in Nanking on

13 February and 21 March with Chiang Kai-shek and Foreign
Minister Chang Chun, Kiep himself was reminded of the effect
rumours of a German—Japanese agreement were having on
Chinese confidence in Germany's good faith. Chiang Kai-shek
accepted Kiep's explanations regarding the mission's purpose
in Manchukuo, but gave a clear hint that its work there and
in Japan should be limited to economic matters. This led the
Marshal to ask Kiep whether it was true that Germany was
building an aircraft factory in Mukden and whether similar
material was being exported to Japan. Kiep denied any knowledge of such activity, but rejoined that if there was talk of a
special orientation in Germany's Far Eastern policy this
could only be in the direction of China in view of the activity
of the German military advisers and the amount of war
material delivered from Germany. Because of this, he explained that he found it all the more surprising that there
should be so much talk and excitement in China, particularly
in the press, of a German—Japanese agreement. In any case,
he emphasised that Germany's principal interests in the Far
East were economic ones and that she wished to stay clear of
all political conflicts. Chiang Kai-shek agreed and then closed
the conversation by stating that China could only welcome
improved German—Japanese relations, a point which Kiep
remarked upon by stating that before his departure from
Tokio the Japanese Foreign Minister, Hirota, had said exactly
the same thing regarding Sino—German relations.

   That there appeared to be more to Chiang Kai-shek's final
remarks than mere politeness seemed to be borne out by
Kiep's conversations with Foreign Minister Chang Chun. After
discussing Germany's intention to create a technical-economic
organisation in Manchukuo, which Kiep emphasised would
have no political character or significance, the Chinese Foreign
Minister expressed the wish to speak 'personally and confi-
dentially'. He wondered whether there could not be a form
of political cooperation between China and Germany, and
intrigued Kiep by repeating the question at the end of their
interview. Kiep replied that he thought that the major problem
in China's foreign policy was Japan, and in his report to
Berlin raised the question whether this was a hint that
Germany should mediate between China and Japan.[65]

   Von Dirksen, meanwhile, continued to urge on the Foreign
Office the necessity for a more flexible approach to the

economic negotiations in Tokio. In view of Kurusu's concern about Kiep's intentions and fears that the German Government would delay the agreement under discussion, von Dirksen emphasised that any break in the negotiations would be seen by Manchukuo and Japan as a German 'capitulation' to China. By the beginning of April 1936 he was warning the Foreign Office that the Japanese Foreign Office and War Ministry were coming to regard Germany's economic agreement with Manchukuo largely as a political agreement and proof of the possibility of a later political understanding between Germany and Japan. Von Dirksen showed himself fully sympathetic to this interpretation when he pointed out that 'we should emphasise to internal departments that an over-rigid adherence to certain princples of immediate economic policy can threaten possibilities whose realisation would perhaps later greatly suit us'.[66]

While Kiep returned to Tokio and advised the Foreign Office of an early conclusion to the negotiations because of the renewed campaign by the Chinese press against his work in Japan,[67] the Foreign Office gradually came to admit that all that remained to be settled were relatively minor questions. By 28 April 1936, therefore, Benzler was able to instruct the Embassy at Nanking to inform the Chinese Government of the imminence of the signature of the agreement with Manchukuo, and to stress the purely economic nature of the agreement. This concern to avoid any political overtones being imputed to the agreement was also reflected in instructions to Tokio that same day for transmission to the Manchukuoan and Japanese authorities.[68]

The 'Arrangement for German–Manchukuo Trade' was finally signed by Kiep and the Manchukuoan Ambassador to Tokio, Hsieh Chieh-shih, on 30 April 1936 in the presence of Shikao Matsushima, the Director of the Commercial Affairs Bureau of the Japanese Foreign Office, coming into force on 1 June 1936. The agreement provided that Germany should 'admit the importation of products of Manchukuo to the amount of 100 million Yuan' in value during the period of one year (Article 1); that payment should be in the ratio of three-quarters in foreign exchange and one-quarter in Reichsmarks (Article 2); that should Germany's foreign exchange situation worsen, the level of imports into Germany to be paid for by foreign exchange could then be reduced from

75 to not less than 65 million Yuan, while any surplus of foreign exchange accruing to Germany from her trade with Japan above the level of 63.75 million Yuan was to be utilised for further German imports of Manchukuoan products (Article 3); and the 'competent authorities of Manchukuo' undertook to ensure 'sufficient importation . . . into Manchukuo of products of Germany during the period of one year, to utilise the whole amount of Reichsmarks paid into a special account in accordance with Article 2' (Article 4). An important role in the credit financing of this trade was allotted to the Yokohama Specie Bank. Signed for one year, the agreement was renewed in 1937 while a new one was concluded in September 1938 which was to run until May 1940. An exchange of resident trade commissioners was also agreed to.[69]

The Germans could feel satisfied on several points.[70] An agreement had been concluded which regularised Germany's important trade with Manchukuo without at the same time compromising her official position on the recognition issue or admitting too openly to the Japanese—Manchukuoan economic-political bloc. On the German side Kiep had signed the agreement 'For the German Administration of Foreign Exchange', while the Manchukuoan Ambassador to Tokio had signed 'For the Competent Authorities of Manchukuo'. In this way any mention of 'Governments' was avoided. Germany had also managed to avoid being committed to utilising a specific sum from German—Japanese trade to boost German—Manchukuoan trade, the final figure being left to any surplus over 63.75 million Yuan.[71] She had also ensured that provision was made for flexible treatment of her commitment to accept Manchukuoan goods, due allowance being made for Germany's foreign exchange situation. But as the British Ambassador to Berlin observed:

the special characteristic of this affair is that the German Economic Mission unlike the F.B.I. Mission and other missions of a similar sort, were less preoccupied with the stimulation of German exports to Manchukuo than of Manchukuoan exports to Germany. In a recent memorandum, the Commercial Counsellor at Berlin stated that a shortage of fats was the Achilles heel of German economic autarchy; perhaps the new arrangement is designed in some sort to strengthen that heel.[72]

It was not to be expected that such an agreement would be allowed to pass without world-wide comment. In view of

Japan's dominant position in Manchukuo it was natural that the agreement was seen as further evidence of Germany's political inclinations towards Japan. Such speculation was reinforced by reports that Germany next intended to conclude an economic agreement with Japan.[73] The Foreign Office, however, was particularly concerned about Chinese reactions, and immediately on 30 April Ritter received the Chinese Ambassador to explain the agreement and to reassure him as to its purely economic nature. Ritter emphasised that the agreement in no way signified Germany's recognition of Manchukuo nor did it compromise her on this question.[74] Ritter's assurances regarding the recognition issue were somewhat offset, however, by elements of the Japanese press giving the agreement such an interpretation in their paean of triumph.[75]

This point was in fact taken up by the Chinese Ambassador on 4 May when he communicated to von Bülow the Chinese Government's protest that by concluding such an agreement Germany had made it appear as though she had recognised Manchukuo. Von Bülow, somewhat on the defensive, protested that Germany had done everything to avoid being compromised over this question. He also emphasised that the agreement was, strictly speaking, not a trade agreement as such but simply a technical agreement designed to regulate payment in German—Manchukuoan trade. Von Bülow's explanations were to no avail since the Chinese Ambassador obviously remained dissatisfied about the whole affair.[76]

In an attempt to remove all uncertainties and to deflate polemical Japanese comment, the Foreign Office decided to publish the full text of the German—Manchukuoan Agreement. Von Bülow also impressed on Ambassador Mushakoji that there was no parallel between the cases of the Italian annexation of Abyssinia on 9 May 1936 and Manchukuo.[77] This was meant to imply that even if, as was expected, Germany formally recognised Italy's action it did not follow that she would similarly recognise Manchukuo. In these circumstances, and given Germany's own economic difficulties, it may be concluded (contrary to one writer's assertion) that the Foreign Office was *not* 'belatedly trying to modify its earlier anti-Japanese stand' through its economic agreement with Manchukuo.[78] As Kiep had remarked earlier to the American Ambassador to China concerning rumours of a German—Japanese alliance:

Germany's trade with China was too important to Germany for Germany
to enter into any kind of arrangement of a cooperative character with
Japan. Germany was not interested in mixing up in the situation here in
the Far East and thus sacrificing her hard-won share of world commerce.[79]

The Chinese, however, continued to make the Foreign Office
fully aware of their concern at the conclusion of the agreement and their dissatisfaction with the explanations given,
especially so far as the recognition question was concerned,
although by mid-June 1936 Fischer reported from Nanking
that the Chinese would probably drop the matter.[80] Such
complaints about the German—Manchukuoan agreement
signified in equal measure irritation and uncertainty about
the future course of German policy in the Far East. Unmol-
lified by the extensive military agreement it had concluded
with Germany at the beginning of April 1936, the Chinese
Government was more concerned for the wider political
implications of Germany's most recent act in the Far East
since it could not, particularly in Chinese eyes, be divorced
from the substantial rumours regarding negotiations for a
German—Japanese political or military agreement. It was
inevitable, therefore, that the Chinese should suspect that the
Germans were abandoning their policy of political neutrality
in the Far East, although for their part the Japanese levelled
similar charges at Germany because of the military agreement
with China.

The uncertainty felt by the Chinese about one aspect of
the German—Manchukuoan agreement was also shared by the
Manchukuoan authorities although for different reasons. This
concerned the exchange of resident trade commissioners, the
Chinese regarding this as further evidence of the political
importance of the trade agreement. Although Hiyoshi Kato,
Director of the Commercial Affairs Bureau of the Manchukuoan Department of Foreign Affairs was appointed
Manchukuoan Trade Commissioner in Germany in June 1936
and immediately took up his appointment, there were delays
regarding the German appointment which tended to displease
the Manchukuoan authorities. Fischer at Nanking recommended that the despatch of the German commissioner to
Manchukuo be handled in a dilatory manner since this would
help him to reassure the Chinese as to the real significance of
the agreement with Manchukuo.[81] This question was also
raised by the Chinese Ambassador during an interview with

von Bülow on 20 May. Von Bülow tried, without much success, to emphasise that Commissioner Kato's position in Germany would be an unofficial one and that he would be treated as a private person by the officials he dealt with. As to the question of the German representative, the State Secretary explained that a final decision had not yet been arrived at.[82] The Wilhelmstrasse could be in no doubt, therefore, that the Chinese especially distrusted this part of the agreement as signifying the *de facto,* if not the *de jure,* recognition of Manchukuo by Germany.

The Foreign Office was obviously worried in case China's hostile reaction manifested itself in attacks on the Wehrmacht's growing and increasingly important links with China. But by the beginning of August 1936 it had been decided to send Dr Schiller, the Agricultural Attaché at the German Embassy at Moscow, to Japan and Manchukuo on a private and unofficial journey to decide whether to accept the post of Germany's trade commissioner at Hsinking. Von Dirksen thought he was a highly gifted person and 'came to be the foremost authority on Russian agriculture'.[83] Schiller's professional qualifications appeared to be a necessary requisite, therefore, for the person appointed to supervise the soya bean trade between Germany and Manchukuo.

By the time Schiller arrived in Tokio on 3 September from Moscow via Vladivostock, the situation had changed somewhat. Although Kato and the Manchukuoan authorities had been informed of the nature of Schiller's journey and came to regard the matter more officially, the latter wanted specific instructions from the Foreign Office before making contact with the authorities in Tokio and Hsinking. These were readily given, while he could allow it to be known that he would be Germany's new trade commissioner at Hsinking.[84] But things did not turn out as planned in Hsinking. The irrepressible Ohashi accused him of being off-hand, evasive and not interested in the important questions at issue between Germany and Manchukuo, and consequently not the right person for Hsinking. On 9 November, however, Knoll told Kato that the nature of Schiller's journey had precluded any technical discussions, but he then placed the blame squarely with Ohashi for any difficulties that may have arisen over Dr Schiller. He then stated that it had been decided not to appoint Schiller to the post at Hsinking, and that a decision on another person for the post would be taken shortly.[85]

To mitigate the obvious effects in Manchukuo and Japan of these delays, von Dirksen immediately recommended that the consul at Mukden, Kühlborn, be appointed to the post.[86] Kühlborn had the particular advantage of being on the spot and familiar with local matters. Yet he was opposed to such a post being created and thought that the trading firms in Manchukuo could best look after matters at that end. He also thought that the essential points of policy could only be decided in Berlin, so that a trade commissioner at Hsinking would be a superflous appointment. Nor was he satisfied with the working and living conditions in Hsinking that a European would have to contend with. He thought that if it was necessary to make such an appointment, the place of residence should be Mukden and not Hsinking where 'it would be hopeless for a non-Japanese speaking person to work'.[87]

In the final event, though, Dr Knoll, another Far Eastern economic expert, was appointed Germany's Trade Commissioner to Manchukuo in December 1936. A public announcement was delayed, however, one of the reasons being that the agreement of the Party authorities had to be obtained.[88] So far as the Foreign Office was concerned, though, this exactly suited their purposes *vis-à-vis* China since it was intended at all times to deny or play down any political significance that was attached to the new relationship existing between Germany and Manchukuo. After the conclusion of the Anti-Comintern Pact on 25 November 1936 between Germany and Japan, this aspect of the question became even more imperative.

Agreement with Japan: The Wilhelmstrasse and von Ribbentrop's Anti-Comintern Pact Negotiations 1935-1936

At his trial at Nuremberg in 1946 von Neurath attempted to explain the Foreign Office's position with respect to von Ribbentrop's Anti-Comintern Pact negotiations[1] and Nazi policy towards Japan in the following words:

Hitler pursued this plan stubbornly, and Ribbentrop supported him in this. I rejected this policy, as I considered it detrimental and in some ways fantastic, and I refused to allow my staff to carry this through. Ribbentrop, therefore, in his capacity as Ambassador with a special mission, carried on these negotiations independently, and on Hitler's instructions, concluded the so-called Anti-Comintern Pact. Hence this Pact bore Ribbentrop's signature not my own, even though I was still Foreign Minister at that time and in the ordinary way would have had to sign the pact.[2]

Von Neurath's main purpose at Nuremberg in presenting the Wilhelmstrasse's role *vis-à-vis* Japan as such a passive one was, quite simply, to save his neck. Along with other defendants, he faced charges which carried the death penalty.[3] Although, von Neurath's statment in 1946 accorded with the general policy of reserve which the Auswärtiges Amt pursued towards Japan, nevertheless it tends to give a somewhat misleading picture of the Wilhelmstrasse's situation with regard to Hitler's policy towards Japan as it eventually formalised itself in von Ribbentrop's negotiations with the Japanese military authorities. Apart from general indications in the winter of 1933–34 of the direction in which he *hoped* that Germany's Far Eastern policy would develop under the auspices of the Foreign Office, particularly with respect to Japan,[4] there is no evidence to suggest that Hitler ever 'offered' the Foreign Office the 'opportunity' of conducting negotiations with Japan for an agreement or alliance. Since von Ribbentrop testified later that it was in 1933 that Hitler first approached him on the subject of establishing closer relations with Japan,[5] and bearing in mind von Dirksen's own conversation with Hitler on 18 October 1933 and the intentions behind the *APA*'s policy towards Manchukuo,[6] it is clear that in the period 1933 to 1934 Hitler was prepared to use any means possible to approach Japan, and when the Foreign Office made known its opposition to a policy of closer relations with Japan by its rejection of virtually all of von Dirksen's policy recommendations at the beginning of 1934 the Führer quietly dropped it from his list. From von Ribbentrop's testimony it also appears that Hitler wished to avoid using official channels since he envisaged a predominantly ideological agreement with Japan.[7]

When von Ribbentrop's negotiations with Japan commenced in 1935 the Foreign Office was therefore faced with a situation which it could neither oppose nor sabotage. The negotiations were being undertaken on behalf of the political leadership of the country and by an agency, the Büro Ribbentrop, whose leader had made it quite clear that he was more than willing to work for the fulfilment of the Führer's wishes for closer political relations with Japan. More important, however, was von Ribbentrop's more 'official' position after his appointment on 1 June 1935 as Ambassador Extraordinary and Plenipotentiary on Special Mission. Ostensibly this placed him under the authority of the Foreign Minister, von Neurath,[8] but in practice he continued to go his own way while the officials of the Foreign Office refused to recognise his 'attachment' to the Foreign Office as von Dirksen was to do so in March 1936. It was, therefore, less a case of the Büro Ribbentrop pushing the Foreign Office aside and grasping the initiative in German–Japanese political relations than the Foreign Office simply playing itself out of this particular game. But neither could the Foreign Office welcome a situation whereby obviously important political negotiations with Japan were being undertaken by what it regarded as a group of crass 'amateurs'. Foreign Office disdain increased when it learnt of the 'Anti-Comintern' nature of the proposed agreement, this 'empty sham' in German–Japanese relations,[9] but one which was to have tremendous repercussions on Germany's more general position in the Far East.

There is no doubt that the Foreign Office was informed of the multifarious — and nefarious — activities of the Büro Ribbentrop because around the time when von Ribbentrop was appointed Commissioner for Disarmament Questions on 24 April 1934, the Foreign Office managed to appoint a 'liasion officer' with the Büro. This was Erich Kordt, brother of Theo Kordt, secretary to the Secretary of State in the Foreign Office, Bernhard von Bülow. It appears that it was von Bülow who suggested this 'clever' move.[10] Gerhard Köpke, Director of Department II, told Erich Kordt of Foreign Office fears that von Ribbentrop might achieve too great an influence with Hitler in matters of foreign policy, and Kordt was being appointed to keep the Foreign Office, in particular von Bülow, informed of von Ribbentrop's activities. While Kordt reluctantly accepted the post, von Bülow instructed him to refrain from interfering in any way with von Ribbentrop's reports to Berlin when they visited foreign capitals. Since von Ribbentrop could hardly draft an intelligible report, this was meant to show up his stupidity to Hitler and President von Hindenburg.[11]

Typical of the long-running feud that emerged between the Foreign Office and the Büro Ribbentrop, this situation had a direct bearing on the Foreign Office's attitude during von Ribbentrop's negotiations for the Anti-Comintern Pact. Inhibited as it was in its criticisms of this 'adventure' in diplomacy by Party amateurs who were negotiating on behalf of the political leadership of the country, the Foreign Office still regarded the situation with some degree of equanimity and, in the long run, could adopt an attitude of expediency. Should the negotiations fail this would prove the Foreign Office's argument about its 'inherent superiority' over the 'amateurs' in foreign policy, while to the Chinese and Japanese it could argue that it had never compromised its own position and policies. If, on the other hand, the negotiations were to succeed it could be argued to the Chinese that the negotiations had been undertaken for the political leadership of Germany and that, consequently, the Foreign Office had no choice in the matter but to act accordingly. As to Japan, subsequent Foreign Office attitudes and policies could be adjusted accordingly.

As to the Anti-Comintern Pact negotiations themselves, there is no doubt that *Realpolitik* as well as ideological, i.e. anti-communist, considerations were involved.[12] Both the Nazi leadership and the Japanese army, particularly the Kodo-ha or Imperial Way School faction,[13] were concerned with, if not obsessed by, Soviet Russia. Developments in Europe and the Far East showed that Soviet Russia's position in world affairs was growing more influential and in an anti-German and anti-Japanese direction, although much of this complemented the anti-Russian direction of a great deal of German and Japanese policy. Japan felt threatened by the Far Eastern 'encirclement' that seemed to be heralded by America's recognition of Russia in November 1933, thus adding to the 'normal' state of tension in Russo—Japanese relations. Hitler was especially concerned at Russia's apparent willingness to cooperate more closely with the Western democracies: Russia's entry into the League of Nations in September 1934, the Franco—Russian Protocol of 4 December 1934 which in its turn led to the Franco—Russian and Russo—Czech Treaties of 2 and 16 May 1935. Japan also felt threatened by the supposed 'freedom' granted to Russia in the Far East by the Franco—Russian Pact.

Political or military cooperation between Germany and Japan was expected to relieve their mutual anxieties about Soviet Russia and to bring more positive benefits affecting their positions and policies in Europe and Asia generally. Exactly what form the projected German—Japanese cooperation was to take remained unclear for some time, particularly since there were obvious political and strategic difficulties in the way of direct military cooperation between the two countries. Hitler's preliminary consideration of an ideological agreement with Japan, whatever else might be added to it, appears to have been motivated by a desire to counter Russia's new respectability in international affairs through the creation of an anti-communist bloc of powers. It was also hoped that Great Britain would join such a crusade, thus complementing Hitler's aims and ideals in Anglo—German relations. Such an agreement would also tend to alleviate Nazi Germany's relative isolation in world affairs. Similar motives were present on the Japanese side, while added to their anti-Russian requirements was a desire to embarrass Germany's economic and military relations with China. Later, however, when it became clear that Hitler had failed to achieve his original intentions in Anglo—German relations, the arrangement with Japan was also intended to exert pressure on Britain and her world-wide interests.

It has been suggested that von Ribbentrop's visit to London in November 1934 for naval talks and his attempt to contact the chief Japanese delegate to these talks, Vice-Admiral Isoroku Yamamoto, were connected with Hitler's idea of implementing his anti-communist crusade with respect to Great Britain and Japan.[14] Von Ribbentrop's approach to the Japanese Navy was rebuffed, and it was not until after Germany had announced the restoration of her military sovereignty in March 1935, giving clear evidence to Japan and the other powers of her potential viability as a military and political force, and following Russia's pacts with France and Czecho-slovakia in May 1935, that approaches were then made to General Hiroshi Oshima, Japanese Military Attaché at Berlin.

There was, therefore, a certain significance to the timing of the preliminary contacts between Oshima and Ribbentrop's intermediary, Dr Friedrich Wilhelm Hack who, according to Oshima's post-war testimony, first approached the Japanese Military Attaché in May or June 1935 about the possibility of a defensive alliance between Germany and Japan against Russia. Hack emphasised that the idea was von Ribbentrop's alone and had nothing to do with the policy of the German Government. Oshima reserved his position and said that he could not say anything until he had ascertained the views of the Army headquarters in Japan.[15] Even allowing for the usual myth of Oriental inscrutability, Oshima must have been hard put to it to maintain his composure in the face of Hack's suggestions. Upon his appointment as Military Attaché in March 1934, he had received instructions from the Chief of the Japanese General Staff, Prince Kanin, to study in parti-cular Russo—German relations and more specifically relations between the two armies. He was also to collect information and report on Soviet Russia, and to this end he had made contact with Admiral Wilhelm Canaris, Chief of Military Intelligence.[16]

While von Ribbentrop made his first moves, the Foreign Office maintained its opposition to any form of cooperation with Japan which would compromise Germany's general posi-tion in the Far East. In April 1935 the Foreign Office repeated its opposition of 1934[17] to a request by Colonel Eugen Ott, Military Attaché at Tokio, to undertake a fact-finding mission to Shanghai. This mission was to be on behalf of the Japanese General Staff who wanted contacts established between the German Military Mission in Nanking and the Japanese military authorities there, while Ott was expected to persuade the Nanking Mission to exert influence on Chiang Kai-shek in favour of Sino—Japanese rapprochement. Meyer told Colonel von Stülpnagel, Director of Military Intelligence in the Reichs-wehr Ministry, that previous objections still stood, i.e., that such a step would harm both Germany's relations with China and the position of the German Military Mission at Nanking. He emphasised that it was essential that German authorities should not become involved in Sino–Japanese affairs, while the fact that Ott had had detailed discussions with the Japanese General Staff could attach political consideration to the visit.[18]

Such hints of a German mediation between China and Japan were connected with the tortuous attempts during 1935 to find a *modus vivendi* in Sino–Japanese relations,[19] and were to be complemented later in the year by Chinese suggestions of a similar nature. An important aspect of Japanese policy towards China at this time was the creation of an anti-communist bloc in the Far East, and while the Kuomintang was obviously concerned about the Chinese Communist Party the Japanese were increasingly troubled by armed communist bands in North China.[20] From this it is easy to see the interest of the Japanese Army in Nazi suggestions for a defensive alliance against the Soviet Union, which were to be given added point with the eventual failure of any real agreement or peace in Sino–Japanese relations.

An added impetus was provided by the Seventh World Congress of the Communist International held in Moscow from 25 July to 20 August 1935, which passed resolutions accusing Germany and Japan together as the most likely instigators of war in the future.[21] While such attacks merely intensified Hitler's own hatred of communism, Lieutenant Colonel Wakamatsu of the German division of the Japanese General Staff had emphasised to Ott that, 'for Japan the most important question in Europe is that Germany exerts as much pressure as possible on Russia'.[22] In fact it was Wakamatsu who was sent to Berlin at the end of 1935 to follow up the further contacts between Hack, von Ribbentrop, and Oshima.

Previous accounts of these negotiations have emphasised two things: firstly, that the initiative for them came more from the German than from the Japanese side; and secondly, that the first serious discussions between Hack, von Ribben-trop and Oshima took place during October 1935. From the Hack papers it now appears that the Japanese military autho-rities may have been the real instigators of the talks, or at least were the first to put vague ideas into concrete terms which provided the necessary basis for serious negotiations. If we accept as correct Oshima's post-war testimony that the initiative for the talks came from the German side and that his immediate response in May or June was to state that the development of the matter depended upon the attitude of the Japanese General Staff, new evidence from the Hack papers that Oshima approached Hack on 17 September 1935 to discuss the possibility of a close form of German—Japanese collaboration to be achieved without involving their respective Foreign Offices may be taken as indicating that Oshima did contact his superiors and was given permission to develop the matter further.[23] Whatever the case may be regarding the ultimate responsibility for the initiation of the talks, and recent Japanese research suggests that it was in fact Oshima who was the prime instigator of the Anti-Comintern Pact,[24] there is no doubt that von Ribbentrop welcomed this positive reaction by the Japanese military authorities. If he achieved such a coup this would undoubtedly advance and strengthen his own political position in Germany. He also thought that such an arrangement might include Great Britain and even Poland and thus help to achieve the Führer's heartfelt wishes in this direction. Von Ribbentrop may have been encouraged in this respect by his success a few months previously in concluding the Anglo—German Naval Agreement on 18 June 1935. So great seemed to be the confidence in the Ribbentrop camp that on 25 September Hack informed Admiral Canaris and von Blomberg of what was afoot, but while the former accepted the idea of a common anti-Soviet front formed by Germany, Japan, Great Britain, and Poland, the Minister of War expressed his concern that nothing should be done to prejudice the German position in China. A fortnight later on 4 October Oshima presented a first draft of a possible agreement between Germany and Japan.[25]

The matter was pursued further between the three principal negotiators, but von Ribbentrop was careful to prepare the ground in case Hitler should change his mind about the idea of an agreement or alliance with Japan; or alternatively, that the opposition from other domestic quarters in Germany (or even in Japan) might prove too overwhelming. It was also essential that he establish Oshima's *bona fides* in the matter. At Hack's home on 15 October 1935[26] von Ribbentrop emphasised that he was acting on his own and wished to know exactly how the Japanese General Staff felt about the suggestion for an alliance between the two countries. Again he insisted that the idea was his alone, and that Oshima should not bear him any ill feelings if the German Government did not support him in this project. At the Tokio trials the Japanese witnesses argued that this was proof of Germany's initiative and original responsibility for the Anti-Comintern Pact. From the Hack evidence this may now be taken as an indication of von Ribbentrop's well advised caution in the affair. Both parties agreed on the necessity for the strictest secrecy, while according to Wakamatsu's testimony Ribbentrop requested Oshima to transmit to Tokio the suggestion of an agreement between Germany and Japan providing that neither country would help Soviet Russia if a war should break out between either of them and Russia. This was to lead to Wakamatsu's visit to Germany shortly afterwards to investigate the views of the German Army and Government as to the form of the agreement proposed by von Ribbentrop, the possibility of concluding an anti-Comintern agreement between Germany and Japan, and who von Ribbentrop was and what his position was in Germany.[27]

It is now clear that the German Foreign Office learned of these negotiations during November 1935, if not in October. By October the War Ministry was fully informed of developments, and following a request from von Blomberg and Admiral Canaris the National Defence Branch of that Ministry produced a highly secret report on the subject of an 'Agreement with the Japanese General Staff' on 30 October 1935. Unfortunately, its contents remain unknown.[28] Given the War Ministry's concern with its interests in China, and its knowledge of the Foreign Office's opposition to any overtly political arrangement with either of the Far Eastern protagonists, it is reasonable to assume that an intimation of what was afoot was passed from one Ministry to the other. If Ott's recollections in 1955 are to be accepted as accurate, then in October 1935 at least one member of the German diplomatic service was also informed since he stated that it was at that time that he had informed von Dirksen of the news he had received from Wakamatsu. According to his memoirs von Dirksen states that it was in November 1935 that he first learned of the existence of the Nazi–Japanese negotiations from the Japanese General Staff, through Ott.[29]

Similarly, during October or November 1935 von Ribben-trop himself indicated to the Foreign Office, presumably von Neurath, the course of action he was undertaking. Not surprisingly, he found that the Wilhelmstrasse opposed his plans.[30] What is clear from the Foreign Office records for November 1935 is that it was Hermann Kriebel, German Consul General at Shanghai and at that time in Germany, who informed the Wilhelmstrasse of the Ribbentrop—Oshima negotiations. This important news emerged in connection with a secret Chinese approach to Hitler through Kriebel and Edmund Fürholzer, the *Transozean* representative in Shanghai. Following a three-day discussion between Wang Ching-wei, President of the Executive Yuan and acting Foreign Minister, and Chiang Kai-shek in mid-October, Wang Ching-wei requested Fürholzer at the end of October to go to Germany to deliver a memorandum to Kriebel and that Hitler's views be ascertained. If Hitler were to state that he agreed in principle with the Chinese proposal, the Chinese Government would then approach the German Government through official diplomatic channels.

The memorandum contained three major suggestions: a compromise between Japan and China; cooperation between Germany, China and Japan in the economic and anti-communist spheres; that a prominent German, e.g. retired Ambassador Solf, undertake soundings with the Japanese on the first two points; and finally, that China would welcome such a step on Germany's part.

Von Erdmannsdorff's memorandum of 18 November 1935 on this matter then states quite clearly:

according to Consul General Kriebel, discussions with Japanese military representatives here about German—Japanese cooperation have been in progress for some time. But no agreements are being considered that would go beyond the promise of benevolent neutrality in a conflict between Japan and the Soviet Union and/or between Germany and the Soviet Union, for the purpose of preventing the Russians from being able to denude their Western and/or Eastern front of troops. It was intended in the further course of the discussions to inform Poland and Britain too, and possibly to make them parties to this combination.

The Chinese feeler seemed like an unexpected bonus to von Ribbentrop since it offered the possibility of avoiding all the unpleasantness in Sino—German relations that could be expected from an obviously political German–Japanese agreement. On the other hand it is difficult to judge whether Hitler and von Ribbentrop really considered the effect a German–Japanese agreement might have on Sino–German relations and consequently for Germany's extensive economic and military interests in China, and whose importance Hitler certainly recognised. Their main objective was to secure an agreement with Japan; the possible repercussions of such an agreement were of secondary importance, and were probably not even fully considered at that time. Since Hitler only envisaged a 'limited' i.e. ideological agreement with Japan, he probably thought that there was little risk of Japan being willing or able to put any pressure on Germany because of her important interests in China. In any case, that problem could be dealt with as and when it arose, if ever.

Von Ribbentrop took up the Chinese feeler and, without divulging his source, asked Oshima what Japan would think about including China in the German–Japanese agreement directed against the Soviet Union. Oshima's favourable reply enabled Ribbentrop and Kriebel to take the Chinese memorandum to Hitler at the beginning of November and obtain his agreement to it. On 15 November therefore Fürholzer sent a message to Wang Ching-wei informing him that Hitler 'took the warmest interest in a Sino–Japanese settlement' and that consultations had already been set in train, but it was requested that diplomatic channels should be avoided. Kriebel, moreover, advised against using Ambassador Solf, while he wanted to know from Wang Ching-wei what practical form China thought the proposed cooperation should take and in what way Germany could be useful to the Chinese in the matter.[31]

It appeared, therefore, that Nazi 'diplomacy' was making contact with both China and Japan in the pursuit of its anti-Soviet policy. However, the success of the notion — if it was at all seriously entertained by von Ribbentrop and his aides — of incorporating China in the projected anti-Comintern agreement with Japan,[32] depended on circumstances entirely beyond the control of anyone in Germany and which, on the contrary, militated in the opposite direction. These circumstances were the apparently unbridgeable gap in Sino–Japanese diplomatic relations, the political intrigues of the Japanese Army in North China, and the increasing domestic opposition in China to any semblance of an agreement with Japan shown by the attempted assassination of Wang Ching-wei on 1 November 1935 at the opening meeting of the Sixth Plenary Session of the Kuomintang, Wang being accused of having adopted a 'soft' policy towards Japan.

In Berlin, meanwhile, opposition was mounting against the form which Nazi diplomacy towards Japan was taking. Von Blomberg, the War Minister, heeded warnings from Ott and made it quite clear to von Ribbentrop on 22 November that the Army was against any military agreement with Japan. Ott was particularly worried because he considered Japan to be weak and unprepared in the military sphere and erratic in the political, and in view of the state of tension in Manchukuo was apprehensive in case an open-ended commitment was entered into by Germany. Later he claimed that the Army's opposition to the agreement ensured that it took the form not of a military agreement but that of the political and ideological anti-Comintern one.[33] At the end of November or the beginning of December 1935 von Neurath warned Hitler of the consequences of this policy on Germany's interests in China, and argued that 'there is nothing the Japanese can give us', while he felt that after the Ethiopian question Britain would direct the whole of her pressure against Germany and/or Japan.[34] Such opposition was, however, futile since Hitler's mind appeared to be set on arriving at some form of arrangement with Japan, and following his approval on 25 November of von Raumer's draft to an agreement with Japan, on 27 November 1935 he confirmed von Ribbentrop's actions in the direction of Japan.[35]

Von Dirksen's foray into Sino–German–Japanese relations in November and December 1935 went some way towards confirming both the doubts about the role of China held by some elements of the Nazi leadership and the correctness (as they saw it) of Ribbentrop's initiatives in Japan's direction. On 28 November he referred to the crisis in Sino–Japanese relations and warned the Foreign Office in Berlin that:

in view of this strained and unpredictable situation, all proposals of the Nanking Government concerning the inclusion of Germany in economic or any other developments in East Asian questions are viewed here with extreme distrust; besides, in the improbable event of their realisation, they would involve Germany in the Japanese–Chinese quarrel. Please bear this consideration in mind in respect of the Nanking Government's proposals transmitted by Herr Fürholzer of which I was informed by a German confidant.[36]

There was, however, more to von Dirksen's remarks than a simple explanation of the Japanese position. Assuming by this time knowledge on his part of the Ribbentrop–Oshima negotiations,[37] it is easy to see how these fitted in with his own views regarding the 'correct' course for German–Japanese relations and how the Chinese proposals threatened to weaken or impede progress in this direction. In fact, his own inclinations were those of the Japanese General Staff, for Wakamatsu admitted later that von Ribbentrop's approaches to Japan offered the possibility of drawing Germany away from China.[38]

In view of the tense situation in the Far East and Lieutenant Colonel Wakamatsu's presence in Berlin in December 1935 in pursuance of the Ribbentrop–Oshima negotiations, when he also met von Blomberg, it is perhaps not surprising that on 7 December 1935 von Ribbentrop ordered Kriebel, by then on his way back to China, to indicate to Chiang Kai-shek that mediation by Germany at that time was virtually impossible. At the same time, by getting Kriebel to block any official Chinese démarches von Ribbentrop was also ensuring that neither would the question of an arrangement *à trois* arise for the purpose of combating communism.[39] From von Ribbentrop's point of view the embarrassment of the Chinese approach appeared to be finally removed with Kriebel's news on 16 December, from a confidant of Wang Ching-wei, that a communication to Chiang Kai-shek was not advisable as it would then go to the new Foreign Minister, Chang Chun, and thus through diplomatic channels, and that because of Wang's convalescence it would be at least two months before further mediation proposals were received.[40] Although Kriebel kept in touch with Wang Ching-wei on this question, by mid-January 1936 Dieckhoff was able to comment that 'nothing is to be done for the time being', which really meant not at all.[41]

By this time von Ribbentrop's negotiations were an open secret in governmental circles. The Foreign Office, however, remained excluded from them and was only brought into the picture as and when the 'inner circle' felt it necessary. On 7 December 1935 Ritter noted that Wohlthat of the Ministry of Economics had suggested that Kiep, leader of the German Economic Mission to the Far East, should be informed of the Ribbentrop–Oshima negotiations, 'otherwise he could not conduct his discussions in Manchukuo properly'.[42] How far

Kiep was in fact brought into the general picture is not known, but this was more than a clear hint to the Foreign Office that nothing that came within its sphere of authority should spoil the chances of the German—Japanese détente desired by the Nazi leadership.

The open secret also appeared to extend to the Japanese Embassy in Berlin. On 26 November Counseller Inoue wrote to the Far Eastern section of the *APA* requesting that the Embassy be supplied with a copy of the draft text of a German—Japanese agreement which he had heard was being circulated. This was passed to the Foreign Office for information, with the intimation that the *APA* would reply that no such draft text was known to them.[43]

This came at a time when further rumours of a German— Japanese alliance began circulating in the world's press, apparently instigated by the Soviet Government which had learned of the negotiations and wished to issue a 'warning' to Germany and Japan. On 2 December Counsellor Tann of the Chinese Embassy handed von Erdmannsdorff a copy of an article taken from the *Basler Nachrichten* of 29 November with the title, 'German—Japanese Alliance in Sight?'. Remarkably accurate, this stated that a Japanese delegation was shortly expected in Berlin for negotiations for such an alliance, the German side being represented by von Ribbentrop.[44] The question of whether a denial was to be issued was passed by Gottfried Aschmann, Head of the Press Department in the Foreign Office, not to von Neurath but to von Ribbentrop for a decision. His answer was a negative one, for the time being.[45]

In view of this and of Dieckhoff's role as the intermediary for the Ribbentrop/Kriebel telegrams, it can be seen that with respect to von Ribbentrop's new position of 'authority' in Japanese questions, the Foreign Office had in part been reduced to the level of a 'technical apparatus'. Only in part, however, since von Neurath had already made it clear to Hitler that the Foreign Office opposed von Ribbentrop's negotiations. For his part von Dirksen went to the other extreme in a letter of 1 January 1936 to von Erdmannsdorff with which he enclosed a memorandum dated 28 December 1935 entitled 'Memorandum on 'the Possibilities of German—Japanese Military and Political Cooperation'. Von Dirksen's letter was in reply to one from von Erdmannsdorff, dated 9 December

1935, in which he had been informed of the Oshima and Kriebel negotiations as well as of von Neurath's interview with Hitler, and was his way of intervening 'in this very involved matter, in which nobody knows what anybody else knows'.

Although representative of his own convictions, von Dirksen's clear and strong support of von Ribbentrop's negotiations in this letter was an attempt to overcome the opposition and reluctance of the Foreign Office on the matter. Von Erdmannsdorff's letter of 9 December 1935 is no longer available, but from the wording of von Dirksen's reply it is obvious that apart from informing the Ambassador at Tokio of recent developments it gave an indication of the strength of the opposition within the Foreign Office to the secret negotiations. More importantly, it seems that von Erdmannsdorff had hinted to von Dirksen that the Foreign Office felt itself in a position to be able to 'disavow' the negotiations as and when necessary. Von Dirksen's answer to this was clear and simple:

> the Oshima negotiations were not begun on Japanese initiative but, quite unmistakably and clearly, on official German initiative by two high-ranking German Officials, Ribbentrop and Canaris. It is utterly impossible in any way to disavow these two gentlemen because we have meanwhile got cold feet, or to conduct the negotiations in such a way that they are bound to fail. We cannot go back now; if you say A, you must go on to say B.

This argument was used to justify his memorandum which 'contradicts the arguments [employed by the Foreign Minister with the Führer] which you mentioned'. He suggested that his presence might be required in Berlin for the further discussions on this question, but his request for an early leave as well as his more general analysis of German—Japanese relations were rejected in the Foreign Office in marginal comments on his letter by von Neurath, von Bülow and Dieckhoff.

It appears, however, that some misunderstanding had crept into the von Erdmannsdorff—von Dirksen exchange of letters. Through von Erdmansdorff's claim to be able to 'disavow' the negotiations and von Dirksen's response to this, it seems that von Dirksen was under the mistaken impression that not only was the Foreign Office involved in some way in the negotiations but, as a consequence, was able to influence their outcome. On the other hand, he was perfectly correct in pointing out that the Foreign Office was in no position to disavow the German negotiators.

In his Memorandum von Dirksen argued in great detail in favour of a German—Japanese combination on the grounds of the mutual antipathy of the new Germany and Japan to Soviet Russia. While he dismissed the possible reactions to such a German—Japanese alignment from the Soviet Union, France, Italy, and the United States, he admitted that Great Britain's response was of the greatest importance. This was because of her significance in Germany's foreign policy, her position as a Pacific Power, and finally because of the possibility that she might join a German—Japanese combination. He recognised however, that the British attitude was uncertain, and that there was no guarantee that she would either consider a German—Japanese—British combination or even welcome a German—Japanese one. This led him to consider two connected questions: 'Should German—Japanese cooperation be postponed until the British attitude is clear?'; and, 'Is it possible for Germany and Japan to come to terms without the risk of alienating Britain?'.

Given the extent of the German—Japanese talks so far and the personalities involved on the German side, von Dirksen's answer to the first was a decided 'No', while as an answer to the second he suggested putting the German—Japanese agreements in a form that would alienate Britain as little as possible. While he accepted that these could be of a military and/or political nature, he argued that they should not be such as to draw Germany automatically into a war with the Soviet Union, particularly since he thought that the dangers of a bilateral war with Russia were greater for Japan than for Germany. He thought the significance of any German—Japanese political convention would be, therefore, 'in its laying down the fact of political cooperation between the two Powers and bringing it to public knowledge'.

Von Dirksen dismissed any idea of including China in the negotiations. As he had commented in his letter, the Oshima—Kriebel 'twins' had to be kept strictly apart since the Fürholzer—Kriebel one was 'a still-born child, whereas the other, the Oshima twin, is by no means so'. He emphasised this by pointing out that Japan regarded China as her sphere of interest, although he felt that later German—Japanese talks could take place about German participation in the exploitation of China.

This was, however, to presume an inevitable Japanese over-lordship of China, a prospect which was certainly recognised by the Foreign Office as being within the bounds of possibility but was not regarded with the same degree of equanimity as von Dirksen appeared to view the matter.

Von Dirksen's conclusions were perhaps read with some surprise in the Foreign Office since they went beyond anything which officials in the Wilhelmstrasse felt were either desirable or required:

from the seething cauldron of Europe the new Germany stands out, united, consolidated, untouched by the false mentality of the post-war decades, shortly to be the strongest military Power in the world. On the other side of the globe, Japan, in ideology, in power politics and geo-politics,[46] is assuming a corresponding position. It seems to be both a psychological imperative and one dictated by reasons of state that these two Powers, who are combating the status quo and promoting the dynamism of living forces, should reach common agreement.[47]

Obviously influenced by Nazi ideas, these views worried the Foreign Office because they were at direct variance with its Far Eastern policy and because they cast doubt upon the Ambassador's fitness to represent *its* views abroad and within Germany's foreign policy-making processes generally. An essential part of this policy was consideration for China, or more particularly for German interests in China, and any German commitment to Japan was expected to harm them.

This was the theme of the many warnings and evidence of Chinese disquiet which the Foreign Office continued to receive because of the persistent rumours that negotiations for a German–Japanese alliance were in progress.[48] The Chinese were particularly upset at the fact that a denial of these rumours had been issued in Tokio but not in Berlin. On 13 January 1936, therefore, von Bülow authorised Trautmann to deny such reports in his conversations,[49] while even von Ribbentrop was eventually forced to issue a denial in Berlin after consultations with Hitler. It appears that the decisive factors for this decision were the reactions to the rumours in the British and French press, interestingly enough just when, in January 1936, Hack had been sent to Japan to pursue the negotiations there.[50] On the other hand, during a conversation with the British Ambassador on 23 January 1936 Göring indiscreetly hinted 'at the possibility at some future date of Germany being driven to conclude an alliance with Japan', although interestingly enough he added that this would be personally distasteful to him because of the differences in race.[51]

The attitude of the Foreign Office, meanwhile, continued to go beyond one simply of suspicion and hostility towards von Ribbentrop's negotiations. According to Erich Kordt the State Secretary, von Bülow, had shown no concern (at some unspecified time) when informed of the Ribbentrop–Oshima negotiations and of the anxiety felt by the Japanese General Staff about Germany's commitments towards Soviet Russia under the Treaty of Berlin of 1926.[52] When von Bülow replied on 15 February 1936 to von Dirksen's letter of 1 January to von Erdmannsdorff, he maintained the Foreign Office's viewpoint that Admiral Canaris and von Ribbentrop *could* be disowned at any time. He also instructed von Dirksen to ensure that no suspicions arose that he was in any way initiated into the secret negotiations.[53] Meant as evidence of Foreign Office 'strength', von Bülow's statement only succeeded in sounding defensive in the face of the undeniable fact that the secret negotiations were being undertaken on behalf of the political leadership of Nazi Germany by persons other than members of the Foreign Office.[54]

For his part von Dirksen continued to misjudge the role of the Foreign Office in the affair. When he replied to von Bülow after the army mutiny in Tokio on 26 February 1936, which still left him convinced that Japan remained a viable and reliable factor in the fight against bolshevism, i.e. Soviet Russia, although he reassured his superiors in the Wilhelmstrasse that the new government of Hirota signified no military adventures against China or Russia,[55] he argued that, 'if we, for our part, only wanted to take soundings, we ought not to have allowed that competent official here to travel to Berlin solely for this purpose. We ought to have stopped the discussions long ago'.

An obvious and informed reference to Wakamatsu's trip to Berlin, it underlined nevertheless von Dirksen's own lack of knowledge about the true state of affairs existing in Berlin. His use of 'we' accorded neither with the influence or role of the Foreign Office in the matter, while there was certainly no unity of purpose and intention between the Foreign Office and the Büro Ribbentrop regarding policy towards Japan. On the other hand, he had a most telling argument when he pointed out, with particular reference to von Ribbentrop's appointment as leader of the German Delegation to the London meeting of the Council of the League of Nations called to discuss Germany's re-militarisation of the Rhineland on 7 March 1936, that 'politically speaking, we should no longer be taken seriously here if we were simply to disown Ribbentrop, who is now the representative of the Reich Government in London'. He expressed the hope, therefore, that nothing precipitate would be done in Berlin while he warned that he would wish to discuss the matter when he was in Berlin on leave.[56]

Von Dirksen's letter, however, contains the clue for the misunderstanding between him and the officials of the Foreign Office regarding von Ribbentrop's position in the whole affair and, consequently, the interpretations placed upon the Foreign Office's degree of authority in the matter. In referring to von Ribbentrop and the impossibility of the Foreign Office disowning him and his negotiations with Japan, von Dirksen described him as 'a high-ranking official of the Foreign Office'. This was to accept as *de jure* a situation that the Foreign Office hardly recognised as *de facto*.[57]

The gap between the Foreign Office and von Dirksen regarding the nature of Germany's Far Eastern policy remained as wide as ever. In the view of the Foreign Office the only good thing which von Dirksen had to report was that Ott had telegraphed his superiors in the Reich War Ministry on 15 January 1936 suggesting that in view of the far-reaching plans of the Japanese General Staff with regard to Outer Mongolia the Germans should proceed with caution in the discussions in Berlin. Ott had been mentioned in the correspondence because von Bülow had wanted to establish whether he was in direct communications with Admiral Canaris and von Ribbentrop by means of a private cipher. Von Dirksen denied this, but told von Bülow that Ott had obtained information about the secret negotiations from the Japanese military authorities, and apart from informing him had also reported the news to the War Ministry.

While the burden of von Dirksen's arguments was that the Foreign Office should take a risk on the reactions of the Chinese or simply ignore them, and wholeheartedly support von Ribbentrop's negotiations, his more routine reports contained hints that Japanese inclinations towards Germany for an anti-Soviet purpose were not confined to the Japanese Army. On 10 March the Japanese Vice-Minister for Foreign Affairs, Mamoru Shigemitsu, expressed to von Dirksen his 'profound anxiety lest Eastern Asia be affected by the Russo—French Pact', a point taken up by Prime Minister Hirota when von Dirksen called to congratulate him on his new office following the events of 26 February.[58] Japanese press reactions to Germany's action on 7 March were more than positive, with Hitler being described as a 'great diplomat and tactician'.[59] But as von Dirksen pointed out, this support of Germany and of her arguments about the incompatibility of the Franco—Russian Pact with the Locarno Treaty was determined largely by Japan's anxiety about the pact's effect on Russia's position in the Far East.

What could not be denied in the Wilhelmstrasse was that there now appeared to be in Japan a more general acceptance of arguments that had been propagated in Germany since 1933, namely, that the simplest way to deal with the very real cause of mutual concern to the two countries, Soviet Russia and international communism, would be for them to 'join together'. Whether Japanese fears about Russia's supposed new 'freedom' *vis-à-vis* Japan in the Far East would actually be translated into a policy of alignment or alliance with Germany that the German Foreign Office itself would have to deal with remained to be seen, but the possibility provided yet another inhibiting factor in the Wilhelmstrasse's approach to von Ribbentrop's negotiations with the Japanese Army. In fact, hints of official sanction for the policy of drawing closer to Germany were given out by Shigemitsu on 30 March 1936 at a reception on the occasion of Ambassador Mushakoji's return to Berlin and von Dirksen's imminent leave of absence.[60] Such hints were to be confirmed when the Foreign Office was informed of Mushakoji's interview with Hitler on 9 June 1936.[61] These tendencies in Japanese policy were confirmed by the ratification on 27 March 1936 of the Franco—Russian Pact and the publication on 8 April of a Pact of Mutual Assistance between Soviet Russia and Outer Mongolia, the latter being a clear warning to Japan in view of the state of undeclared war which existed along the Mongolian—Manchukuoan border.[62]

How far these developments in Japan affected the attitude of the German Foreign Office is hard to tell. What cannot be denied was the feeling of anger and frustration in the Wilhelm-strasse at the situation of virtual impotence in which it found itself with respect to von Ribbentrop's negotiations. This is the most likely explanation for von Bülow's rather surprising attitude and statements on 4 May 1936 when he received Lieutenant General von Reichenau before the latter's journey to China to ratify the Klein–HAPRO agreement of April.[63] Von Reichenau emphasised that it was General von Blomberg's view that the War Ministry's interests in China were not compatible with a German–Japanese rapprochement, and that von Blomberg had also stated that von Ribbentrop's negotiations had been broken off. Von Bülow quickly reported that the Army had heavily engaged itself in the Japanese negotiations, which showed that he was still not sure of Ott's role in the matter,[64] while more surprising was his statement that 'in the opinion of our Ambassador [von Dirksen] it was quite impossible to break off these negotiations'.[65] By not adding any comment of his own to this bald statement von Bülow made it appear as though the Foreign Office shared von Dirksen's views, and this could only have created the impression with von Reichenau that the Foreign Office would not *actively* oppose a political or military agreement with Japan that was desired by the Nazi leadership.

In view of von Reichenau's imminent visit to China and the reasons for it, it is significant that on 12 May the Foreign Intelligence Branch in the War Ministry, the *Auslandsabteilung,* requested reports on the subject of 'Japan as a Power Factor in the Far East'. A fortnight later it forwarded to the Head of the Armed Forces Office, the *Wehrmachtsamt*, then Lieutenant General Wilhelm Keitel, and to the National Defence Branch, the *Landesverteidigungsabteilung* the reports from the three branches of the Armed Forces and from the Military Economics Staff, the *Wehrwirtschaftsstab.*

The conclusion is inescapable that these reports were called for to substantiate and support the Army's arguments against any pact with Japan. Their clear message was that Japan could *not* be considered a viable military partner for Germany. Compared to the Soviet Far Eastern Army, Japan's Army was inadequately armed and it was expected that it would be two years at least before it was equipped with modern weapons. The rivalry between the Japanese Army and Navy created doubts about the stability and effectiveness of Japan's armed forces, while the Japanese Army was considered to be still in a state of ferment and unrest after the abortive uprising of 26 February 1936. Strategic and tactical considerations in the Far East were considered to be unfavourable to Japan *vis-à-vis* Soviet Russia, while her well-known reliance on the import of many and vital raw materials was thought to be an inhibiting factor on her ability to pursue a long and drawn-out war. Nor was there any other Great Power on which Japan could rely for support in any struggle with the Soviet Union, the clear implication being that if Germany allowed herself to become involved with Japan she ran the risk of becoming isolated herself in world affairs. Furthermore, Japan's advances and activities in North China gave a clear warning of her ultimate intentions concerning other foreign capital interests in the rest of China, including those of Germany.

Two main conclusions were drawn. The first was that for Japan a war against the Soviet Union at that point would be a dangerous undertaking. Secondly, and more pertinent to current considerations in German foreign policy, was the conclusion that 'it does not seem probable that a Russo–Japanese war would have decisive reactions on the power-political position of the Soviet Union in Europe, while a European partner of Japan would then be brought into conflict with England and America'. This was because the size of the Soviet Union meant that the Soviet Far Eastern Army could be strengthened without weakening the strength of the Red Army in Europe.[66] There were, therefore, good grounds for von Blomberg's dismissal of Japan as a military factor in the Far East at the conference on 27 May 1936 with Göring.[67]

It is reasonable to assume that these reports were forwarded to Hitler and von Ribbentrop for their further consideration of the negotiations with Japan. The Army's intention was to continue to ensure that whatever kind of pact the Nazi leadership concluded with Japan, it was one that did not bind Germany in a military sense. These indications of the Army's views came at a crucial time for in June and July 1936, after a gap of several months following Wakamatsu's return to Japan at the beginning of the year, Hitler and von Ribbentrop again turned their attention to the question of negotiations with Japan and the problem of Soviet Russia and international communism. It was at this time also, according to one source,

that von Ribbentrop sent his agent, Friedrich Hack, to Japan
to discover how far Japan could be regarded as a reliable military partner in an alliance.[68]

Nazi inclinations towards Japan were encouraged as a result
of Ambassador Mushakoji's interview with Hitler on 9 June
1936. For the Ambassador's part, this was in execution of
the orders he had received from Foreign Minister Arita before
he left Japan in April[69] and Arita's telegraphed orders of
8 May 1936:

various conditions indicate the necessity for closer relations between
Japan and Germany. It is considered proper, if Germany desires it, to
make a vague engagement without limiting the matter for the present,
as I charged you before you left Japan. As for the details of the engagement, they are now under consideration. But before everything, it is
necessary for Japan to discern the limit and substance of the German
claim. In this connection, you are requested to shun courting attitudes,
and promptly report the result of your investigation closely keeping
in touch with the leading figure of the German Foreign Office and the
NSDAP.[70]

Mushakoji emphasised that during his long stay of nine
months in Japan he had noticed an increased sympathy and
understanding for Germany, while the Japanese form of
government had changed to become like that of Nazi Germany,
an authoritarian one. Most significant of all was his statement
that 'Japan regarded Bolshevism and the Communist idea as
her great enemies; holding this view, she looked with great
respect on Germany who, as Russia's western neighbour, had
overcome this danger. Japan, as a spiritually related country,
was in the fullest sympathy with Germany and her Führer
and desired the closest cooperation with Germany'. Hitler
needed no prompting and replied that he was 'happy to take
note of this and was prepared for this cooperation'. He then
treated Mushakoji to a lecture on the evils of communism
and the necessity to combat both it and Soviet Russia, and
was pleased that according to a report from von Ribbentrop
the danger of communism was beginning to be increasingly
understood in Britain. Mushakoji said he shared Hitler's
general views and expressed the hope that 'a common attitude
on the part of Japan and Germany would be of value'.[71]

While German and Japanese records show that Mushakoji
kept in close touch with von Ribbentrop in pursuit of an anti-
Comintern pact[72] it does not appear that he showed a similar
effort in the direction of the Wilhelmstrasse. It may be, of

course, that like von Dirksen the Japanese considered von Ribbentrop 'a high-ranking official of the German Foreign Office'. Von Neurath's record of his conversation with Mushakoji on 6 May 1936 shows that nothing of substance was discussed, or at least recorded in the memorandum, a not entirely unusual phenomenon where von Neurath was concerned.[73]

Although excluded from deliberations at the highest level on the subject of an agreement with Japan, the Foreign Office continued to be informed of developments. But as with Otto Meissner's action in forwarding a copy of the record of the Hitler–Mushakoji interview, often this served to underline the Foreign Office's 'minor' role. In fact, its position in the affair was highlighted by Mushakoji's interview with Hitler since this showed how far the Japanese Foreign Office had become involved in the secret negotiations. Yet while the officials in the Wilhelmstrasse appeared to be rather passive in the face of this situation, in the middle of 1936 the two German Ambassadors in the Far East, in Berlin on leave, adopted a rather different attitude but with important differences between them.

On 9 June Ambassador Trautmann was received by Hitler and then by von Ribbentrop. Writing to Dieckhoff on 10 June, Trautmann explained that he had intended giving Hitler his views on Far Eastern policy in a written form but had been unable to do so. Instead, he had given von Ribbentrop a memorandum on the subject and had enclosed a copy for Dieckhoff's information. From Trautmann's covering letter to Dieckhoff it seems as though von Ribbentrop had not been interested in listening at length to Trautmann's arguments since their discussions had been 'very short'.

Trautmann's memorandum set out in no uncertain terms the well-known arguments of the Foreign Office against a one-sided policy of political friendship in the Far East, especially if this was in the direction of Japan because of the deleterious effects this would have on Germany's interests in China. He thought Germany should try 'to pursue a policy which cultivates uniformly friendship with both countries, China and Japan, and to make no choice in favour of either country'. He also felt that a German understanding with Japan would disturb Britain who did not want to see Japan become too strong, besides encouraging an Anglo–Russian rapprochement without having obtained for Germany the advantage of involving Japan in European politics: 'Japan has no interests in Europe and will run no risks there. We shall thus have gained nothing for our policy in Europe if we come to an understanding with Japan.'

Trautmann next argued — and one has the impression that he had perhaps been well briefed in the Bendlerstrasse — that in the event of any conflict in Europe it was doubtful whether Germany's military situation would be 'appreciably eased even by an understanding with Japan'. This was because of the strength of the Soviet Far Eastern Army and Air Force *vis-à-vis* Japanese forces in the area. Finally, and in an attempt to stem what he thought was the Nazi stampede towards Japan, he argued that while China was experiencing great economic and political difficulties its future could be viewed with some degree of optimism.[74]

Von Dirksen, on the other hand, pursued his activities and inquiries in Berlin in a different manner, including, it seems, talks on a closer German—Japanese relationship *vis-à-vis* Soviet Russia with the Japanese Ambassador to Sweden, Toshio Shiratori.[75] Far from attempting to dissuade the Nazi leadership from its intentions in the direction of Japan, von Dirksen was intent on confirming them. As he was to admit later: 'I was definitely in favour of the basic political idea of a closer understanding with Japan'.[76]

To this end he saw von Ribbentrop and gave a detailed explanation of the political situation within Japan. In return, von Ribbentrop allowed von Dirksen some details of his negotiations with the Japanese, although later he wrote that he received more detailed information from Ambassador Mushakoji. Von Ribbentrop agreed that this information could be passed to von Neurath, and according to his memoirs this at least made von Dirksen aware of the situation existing in Berlin:

when I communicated these facts to the Foreign Office I was effusively thanked for having procured such extremely valuable information. This made me realise to what extent the Foreign Office had allowed itself to be excluded from knowledge of what was going on. It need hardly be mentioned that the Foreign Office was dead against the pact with Japan.[77]

In particular, von Neurath and von Bülow were 'very sceptical and antagonistic' to the idea of a political liaison with Japan.[78] However, while the Foreign Office may not have been fully informed about such important details as the obligations to be assumed by Germany and Japan under the pact, e.g., of a consultative kind *vis-à-vis* Soviet Russia and undertaking that in the case of one party being involved in a war with Russia the other was to abstain from acts likely to assist the enemy, this was not the same thing as saying that the Foreign Office was 'in no way informed about the Ribbentrop—Oshima negotiations'.[79] On the other hand, Kordt insists that he kept his superiors in the Foreign Office informed, particularly when he heard of references to a secret agreement being concluded against the Soviet Union.[80]

Following a rather unsatisfactory interview with Hitler shortly after his arrival in Berlin, von Dirksen had a more fruitful meeting with the Führer and Göring on 8 July 1936. Von Dirksen considered whether 'the structure of the Japanese State was being undermined by the revolutionary uprisings of the Army or whether Japan could be trusted as a partner to the Anti-Comintern Pact. My answer to this question was in the affirmative.' Both Hitler and Göring shared these views.[81]

Von Dirksen's views undoubtedly confirmed Hitler's and von Ribbentrop's intentions to conclude a pact with Japan, particularly since they came from the one official German representative most likely to have arrived at an accurate and informed judgement about political developments within Japan. It was precisely for this reason that von Dirksen did the Foreign Office a disservice by propounding such views at the fountainhead of its opposition. He knew full well that the consensus of opinion and policy within the Foreign Office was to avoid any form of political entanglement with Japan, and that consequently his own views on policy towards Japan were not accepted. He must have realised, therefore, that by representing Japan in a favourable light to Hitler and von Ribbentrop this would weaken still further the position of the Foreign Office in Berlin and its policy of 'balance' in the Far East. One cannot dismiss either the notion that von Dirksen had other motives as well for behaving as he did. It is more than likely that he wished to impress the political leadership with his political acumen in the hope that this would mark him out for some promotion or higher office in the Nazi State. At another and more human level it may be that von Dirksen was simply 'getting back' at his superiors in the Wilhelmstrasse for his own isolated position with regard to Far

Eastern policy. As it was, von Dirksen's account of the Japanese political scene and his conclusion that Japan was a worthy partner for Germany against the Soviet Union provided a welcome antidote for Hitler and von Ribbentrop to the dose of gloom that had been presented to them by the War Ministry.[82]

International developments also served to undermine the force of the War Ministry's objections and those expressed by Trautmann. Just one week after the Japanese Army had proposed to the Nazi leadership that the pact under discussion be not merely an anti-Comintern pact but a secret neutrality agreement directed against the Soviet Union — something which initially disturbed von Ribbentrop since he was afraid that the English line of German policy might be disturbed through Japanese indiscretions[83] — the Spanish Civil War broke out on 18 July 1936. This made a deep impression on Hitler and reinforced his anti-Bolshevist and anti-Russian views to such an extent that when he received Oshima four days later at Bayreuth in the presence of von Ribbentrop and von Raumer, the Japanese negotiator was able to obtain not only full agreement to the further and serious pursuit of the negotiations but also to the secret addendum requested by the Japanese General Staff.[84] As Hitler remarked a month later in his memorandum on the Four Year Plan, 'apart from Germany and Italy, only Japan can be regarded as a Power standing firm in the face of the world peril' of bolshevism.[85] In the hands of von Ribbentrop on the German side, the negotiations went ahead to the initialling of the Anti-Comintern Pact on 23 October 1936[86] and its final signature in Berlin on 25 November 1936.

During this time the Foreign Office was kept firmly in the background and only came into the picture intermittently. In 1937 Knoll told the British Consul at Mukden that 'a few days before the agreement was initialled [he] was sent for by von Ribbentrop and asked to give purely technical assistance in comparing the texts of the Japanese and German drafts'. Knoll also emphasised that the Foreign Office had been kept completely in the dark about the agreement.[87] However, it has been suggested that towards the end of the negotiations the Foreign Office was consulted about the compatibility of the projected pact with the Russo–German Treaties of Rapallo and Berlin of 1922 and 1926 respectively.[88]

This background role did not imply any lack of general knowledge of events, and if Count Ciano's record of his conversations with von Neurath on 21 October is to be believed the Foreign Minister was certainly better informed of details of the German–Japanese negotiations in October than he had been in July. Von Neurath told him that Hitler wished to recognise Manchukuo but intended to delay the gesture for some time so as not to compromise certain German economic interests in China. Nevertheless:

relations of close collaboration have, however, been established between Germany and Japan, and . . . shortly they will proceed to the signature of two protocols — one public, containing an anti-Bolshevist agreement, and another, secret, containing a clause guaranteeing benevolent neutrality in any eventuality.[89]

The significance of Ciano's record is that von Neurath's memorandum of the talk makes no mention of the projected German–Japanese agreement.[90] On 24 October Hitler remarked to Ciano that one purpose of his efforts to form a group of powers under the banner of anti-bolshevism was to impress England in the hope that she would 'seek means of agreement and common ground with this new political system'.[91]

On 30 October 1936 the Foreign Office was given a clear warning by Ambassador Mushakoji of the effects of recent reports of closer Sino–German military collaboration on the chances of the anti-Comintern Pact being accepted in Tokio: 'such reports . . . were calculated to endanger the agreement or at least to make it difficult for the Government to get it through the Privy Council'. Dieckhoff denied any knowledge of such reports, but Mushakoji 'insisted very strongly' that the point be clarified so that he could 'reassure' Tokio.[92] The Foreign Office's position was such that it could not do otherwise than pursue Mushakoji's demands, even though what appeared to be at stake was a political agreement not of its making and to which it was opposed. On 4 November Colonel Thomas explained to von Erdmannsdorff and von Weizsäcker how the Army's plans in China were being adjusted in accordance with current political requirements, and six days later Mushakoji was informed of this by Dieckhoff.[93] In this way the Wilhelmstrasse could be said to have contributed towards the final acceptance of the Anti-Comintern Pact in Tokio. The extent of the deliberations on the pact in Tokio,

involving as they did the senior members of the Hirota Cabinet
and the Privy Council, provided a sharp contrast with the
nature of policy-making in Berlin on the subject.[94]

While the Wilhelmstrasse maintained its position of reserve
and hostility by casting doubt on whether the Japanese
Government would persevere with the anti-Comintern Pact
and accused Tokio of deliberate indiscretions regarding the
negotiations in order to strengthen Japan's position *vis-à-vis*
England,[95] it was again subjected to Chinese complaints and
inquiries about the rumours of an imminent German—Japanese
military or political alliance. Following an inquiry from the
Chinese Foreign Minister, Chang Chun, Trautmann requested
that he be allowed to inform the Minister of the negotiations
with Japan, but this was refused.[96] Trautmann was also
worried in case reports of Italy's expected recognition of
Manchukuo raised fears in China that part of the supposed
deal with Japan involved a similar step on Germany's part. He
suggested that if Italy recognised Manchukuo a statement
should be issued emphasising that Germany's policy on this
question remained unaltered.[97] A more personal expression
of Chinese concern was made clear to Herr Klein on 17 November by the Chinese Finance Minister, Dr H. H. Kung, a report
on this conversation being delivered to the Foreign Office on
25 November by Colonel Thomas who also communicated
the War Ministry's fears at the effect of the anti-Comintern
pact on its interests in China.[98] Taking up the anti-communist
basis of the reported German—Japanese agreement, Kung
warned Klein about the effect of this on Sino—German relations, on Germany in the world at large, and that such an
agreement would give Japan a free hand against China. In a
desperate and last-minute attempt to deflect what he correctly
saw as a disastrous course of policy in the Far East, Kung
suggested that Germany should continue her anti-communist
propaganda but use England or China to reassure Soviet Russia
that she intended no warlike action against her and could
guarantee peace for a period of time. Kung thought that this
would ensure that Russia turned her attention towards the
Far East and Japan, particularly since she herself had no warlike intentions in the direction of Germany.[99] Kung's suggested 'mediation' was, however, as untimely as it was
inappropriate.

The Foreign Office again appeared to be relegated to the

lowly status of a 'technical apparatus' in connection with the 'explanations' about the new pact which had to be issued to missions. These emphasised its defensive nature as a measure for domestic police protection against communism, as were the recent agreements between Germany and Italy and between Italy, Austria, and Hungary,[100] that it was not directed against any third state, and that the agreements contained nothing about the supply of war materials.[101] Nevertheless, the Foreign Office appears to have played an important part in the precise formulation of a secret and extremely important addendum to the pact that was signed on 25 November 1936. This took the form of a letter from von Ribbentrop to Ambassador Mushakoji on 25 November, one of several exchanged that day, which stated that the German Government did not regard the provisions of the Treaties of Rapallo and Berlin of 1922 and 1926 as being in contradiction to the spirit and obligations of the Anti-Comintern Pact 'in so far as they have not become null and void under the conditions existing at the time of the coming into effect of this Agreeement'.[102] One authority accepts that it was the German Foreign Office which was thus responsible for keeping the 'back door to Rapallo open'.[103]

This is an important point since Article II of the Secret Supplementary Agreement to the Anti-Comintern Pact implied a new coordination of Germany and Japan's *Russlandpolitik*,[104] for under its terms both countries agreed not to conclude treaties with Soviet Russia 'contrary to the spirit of this Agreement without mutual consent'.[105] On 23 October von Ribbentrop had confirmed as correct a telegram from Ambassador Mushakoji to Foreign Minister Arita which stated the Ambassador's 'firm convictions' that the spirit of the Secret Supplementary Agreement 'is alone decisive for the future policy of Germany towards the USSR'.[106] While this continued to be Japan's interpretation of the Anti-Comintern Pact,[107] Japan had also reserved her position regarding certain treaties with Russia.[108]

The final result, therefore, was 'a form of anti-Soviet alliance' which had been converted into 'an association of dubious strength by a variety of reservations'. On the basis of the agreement Germany and Japan could move jointly *vis-à-vis* the Soviet Union. On the basis of the reservations 'each could go its own way', as Germany was certainly to do in August 1939.

Equally, the pact or alliance could be used against the Western powers. Despite the 'anodyne' qualities of the Pact,[109] therefore, the important fact was that the two most powerful disturbers of the peace in Europe and Asia had drawn together, with Italy in attendance, and this point of *Realpolitik* could not be ignored by Britain, China, France, the Soviet Union or the United States of America.[110]

Several things concerned the German Foreign Office about this development. The first and most immediate was that this well publicised and in its view useless act of foreign policy had been concluded by von Ribbentrop, who regarded it as his 'special contribution to the world's wisdom'.[111] While von Dirksen reported the mixed reception which the Pact received in Japan,[112] the Foreign Office's greatest and justifiable concern was for its effect in China. The Chinese certainly lost no time in communicating their concern to the Germans. Following a meeting held in the Chinese Foreign Office on 26 November to discuss the Pact, the Chinese Foreign Minister, Chang Chun, warned Trautmann on 27 November during a 'long and serious conversation' of two hours of the effects of Germany's 'inexplicable' action on Sino–German relations, while he wanted clarification on several questions relating to the German–Japanese agreement. In particular, the Chinese wanted to know whether the new agreement would be used against China because of her domestic communist problem, and whether China was to be one of those 'third States' that would be invited to join the Anti-Comintern Pact under the terms of Article II. The Chinese were obviously afraid that this could only weaken their position *vis-à-vis* Japan, while Chang Chun and Trautmann made it quite clear to the Foreign Office that any improvement in Sino–German relations was dependent upon what Germany's future policy was, particularly with regard to Japan.[113]

In Berlin the Chinese Military Attaché, Colonel Feng Te, had already asked similar questions at the War Ministry, drawing particular attention to the fears of the Chinese General Staff that German officers in China might find themselves in the service of the Japanese in their fight against communism, and that in any case the Pact provided evidence of Germany's moral support for Japan's expansionist plans in the Far East. The Chinese General Staff requested assurances that the Pact would not affect adversely the hitherto close relations between

China and Germany. Von Pappenheim of the War Ministry was unable to give these since, as he pointed out, the Pact appeared to him to be a purely political agreement and he felt it was not within the competence of the military authorities to answer questions upon it.[114]

Both the Foreign Office and the War Minister were at pains, however, to ensure that Sino–German relations were not unduly disturbed by the agreement with Japan. On 30 November the Acting Director of the Political Department, von Weizsäcker, instructed Trautmann to reassure the Chinese Government about Germany's intentions towards China. Trautmann was also to emphasise that there was nothing in the agreement with Japan that could be directed against Chinese interests or be connected with Sino–Japanese questions, that Chiang Kai-shek had already received assurances from von Blomberg,[115] and that a formal request to other States to join the anti-comintern bloc was not intended at the moment. It appears that von Ribbentrop was also concerned about Chinese reactions since marginal comments indicate that he agreed with these instructions.[116] Yet they did not go far enough for Trautmann, and following a further telegram from him von Weizsäcker finally agreed on 2 December that he could state to the Chinese Government that no secret military agreement or alliance existed between Germany and Japan.[117]

The War Ministry, too, adopted a more positive response to Chinese approaches. By 2 December the *Auslandsabteilung* was proposing that Colonel Feng Te be given general assurances regarding Germany's military relations with China, in particular that while German officers remained in Chinese service they would never be used in undertakings not commensurate with Chinese interests. Assurances could also be given that no secret military arrangements existed between Germany and Japan. On the other hand, it had been agreed with the Foreign Office that all questions of a political nature relating to the recent agreement had to be referred to it.[118] However, these recommendations were overtaken by von Blomberg's interview with the Chinese Ambassador about the Pact since the War Ministry felt that this obviated any necessity to answer the Chinese Military Attaché's questions.[119]

Efforts to assuage the feelings of the Chinese were continued by von Neurath's reception of the Chinese Ambassador, Cheng Tien-fang on 3 December and by Trautmann with

Chang Chun.[120] Kiep also spoke favourably about the 'new China' on 7 December in the presence of Cheng Tien-fong.[121] These efforts were, however, somewhat offset by the public welcome given to the Pact by von Dirksen's statement to the Japanese press,[122] and by the difficulties associated with Chinese requests for a public statement from the Foreign Office on Sino—German relations. The Chinese wanted this to include favourable references to China's own fight against her domestic communism,[123] and that because of this it would be unnecessary for her to join the Anti-Comintern Pact, but this would have meant the Foreign Office making public the kind of statements which it felt it could only make privately. The most that von Neurath would agree to was that the Chinese Government could issue a statement on his conversation with Cheng Tien-fong, while he put a complete veto on the Ambassador's wish to issue a statement in Germany.[124]

It was clear that the Anti-Comintern Pact had introduced a new and disturbing factor into the complex of Germany's Far Eastern policy and relationships. How it would affect Germany's position *vis-à-vis* China and Japan in the long run had to wait upon developments. The *Japan Times* advised everybody to suspend judgement 'until the agreement had been given a decent chance to operate in the world of actual affairs',[125] but neither the Foreign Office nor the two Ambassadors in the Far East followed this advice. For his part, von Dirksen welcomed the new agreement on three grounds. In view of the world political situation and the tendency towards new and, to Germany, dangerous political groupings he thought it was right that Germany should move quickly to establish her own groupings with powers in a similar situation, e.g. Japan. Secondly, he felt that the anti-communist alliance with Japan was 'a matter of course' since in both countries the feelings against bolshevism 'is combined with an established political attitude against Russia'. Finally, and despite his references to the very real political, military and economic difficulties that Japan was facing, von Dirksen thought that she was well on her way to becoming a powerful and united State.[126]

If von Dirksen's attitude of support for the Pact was not entirely unexpected, the somewhat subdued tone of Trautmann's Political Report of 27 January 1937 was. This was a comprehensive survey of political conditions in the Far East and Germany's Far Eastern policy. Unlike many of his previous reports on the subject, Trautmann allowed no direct criticism on this occasion of the pro-Japanese policy favoured by the Nazi leadership. Instead, in his conclusion he accepted the fact of the German–Japanese agreement and simply pointed out that 'no grumbling after the event is intended'. As he explained, his main purpose was rather to draw particular attention to how the situation was viewed in China and to warn against any 'exaggerated expectations' from the Anti-Comintern Pact. In this connection he referred to the cool welcome given to the Pact in Japan, and to von Falkenhausen's observations that in the event of a European conflict and a Russo–Japanese war occurring at the same time, Russia's strength in the Far East was such that she would not need to send any forces from Europe to the east.

Trautmann expressed his concern at the recent turn of events and what it meant for Germany's future position in the Far East more indirectly and subtly by commenting on the nature, control and direction of Germany's Far Eastern policy. What particularly concerned him was that Germany's position in the Far East appeared to be weakened by the divided nature of the policy-making processes in Berlin, resulting not in a *German Far Eastern policy* but rather in the pursuit of German–Chinese and German–Japanese policies:

hitherto we have pursued a German–Japanese and a German–Chinese policy but not a German Far Eastern policy. It is difficult to apply a common denominator to our Far Eastern policy. It moves like a pendulum, sometimes to the Chinese and sometimes to the Japanese side, and a strong inclination to the one side causes bad feeling on the other.

He blamed this on the fact that 'the mainspring of our Chinese policy is to be found in one Ministry, and that of our Japanese policy in other quarters', and that this exposed Germany to the charge of 'political unreliability' in the Far East. As he had argued before, it was necessary for Germany to pursue a policy of friendly relations with both China and Japan but in such a manner as to avoid impinging upon the 'difficult relations' between the two countries through any agreements that Germany might conclude with either country. He felt, therefore, that this wisdom of Solomon could only be applied and executed if Germany's Far Eastern policy was directed and coordinated by one central authority in Berlin, and that if this was not done Germany's policy in the Far East would remain uncoordinated, ineffective and liable 'to disappointments'. It was obvious who Trautmann regarded as the obvious authority for this task but his assumption that 'only the Foreign Office can be successful in bringing about an adherence to the general framework of our policy and prevent the exaggeration of departmental points of view' betrayed an optimistic evaluation of the Foreign Office's authority and competence at the end of 1936, let alone for the future.[127]

VIII
The Period of Tenuous Balance, January–June 1937

One common problem affecting mutual relations faced the policy-makers in Germany, China and Japan after 25 November 1936: 'What now?'. Almost immediately von Ribbentrop, von Dirksen and the Japanese General Staff tried to ensure that the question did not remain an academic one. On 27 November von Ribbentrop intimated to von Raumer that he was hoping to expand the membership of the Pact to include Italy, Poland, Bulgaria, Latvia, Rumania and even some South American States. As early as January and February 1937 he began work through von Raumer to bring about Italy's accession to the Pact. Despite the Foreign Office's opposition, this was finally achieved on 6 November 1937, superseding Italo–Japanese negotiations for a bilateral agreement.[1] The Foreign Office was especially perturbed, therefore, when it also had to contend with von Dirksen's support for attempts to give some form and substance to the 'cooperation' envisaged under the terms of the Pact, by means for example of the establishment of a joint commission in Tokio.[2]

Nor were the Japanese military leaders slow to act. In December 1936 Oshima approached the military authorities in Germany with a draft of a German–Japanese military agreement to supplement the Anti-Comintern Pact. This proposed exchanges of information about Soviet Russia, cooperation in the intelligence field, delivery of war material, especially raw materials in the event of one party to the agreement being involved in war. Of greater military and political significance was the proposal for 'general consultation'. Oshima met General Keitel on 14 December and, with Hitler's approval, was given General von Blomberg's answer by Admiral Canaris on the 17th. Von Blomberg argued that such an agreement was a political matter and therefore the concern of the political leadership of Germany. There was no objection to exchanges of information about Russia and cooperation in the intelligence field, areas where there was already some contact between Germany and Japan, while even the proposal for general consultation in the sphere of *grossen Politik* was agreed to. However, von Blomberg made it quite clear that Oshima had to return to Japan to establish the standpoint of the Japanese Government 'so that after his return from Japan the whole complex can be discussed further'.[3]

This attitude of reserve was consistent with the Army's general policy towards Japan, based upon its concern to protect and even expand its military interests in China, particularly with the events of November 1936 in mind. Of particular interest is Hitler's approval for this attitude of caution less than a month after the conclusion of the Anti-Comintern Pact. It must be concluded that he considered the Pact to be sufficient for his immediate and general purposes, namely as a counter-balance to Russia and as a further means of pressure on Great Britain for some form of *Ausgleich*. There was also another, perhaps more compelling, argument in favour of a policy of restraint towards Japan at this time. Despite the Spanish Civil War in Europe, the Far East remained the most likely spot for the outbreak and development of a serious international conflict, and one which would naturally involve Japan either with Soviet Russia or with China, or with both at the same time. A military agreement with Japan at that stage carried the risk for Germany that the initiative in the German—Japanese relationship would rest with Japan, and any involvement with a Japanese quarrel or conflict in the Far East would involve a consequent loss of manoeuvre and strength for Germany in European affairs.

Following the conclusion of the Anti-Comintern Pact, the Wilhelmstrasse was faced by several more problems in the formulation and execution of Germany's Far Eastern policy, not least of which was its apparent lack of control over the general direction in which this policy appeared to be moving. The conclusion of the Pact had shown the authority and power of the Nazi political leadership, and if for some time an attitude of reserve towards Japan became a feature of German policy the Wilhelmstrasse was the first to recognise that its influence on this matter was not always very great. Besides which, should European or Far Eastern circumstances alter significantly, the political leadership could change its mind and advocate a policy of even closer political and perhaps military collaboration with Japan, with consequent and far-reaching effects on Germany's relations with China.

The Wilhelmstrasse's major concern was still to maintain a

kind of 'balance' between China and Japan and avoid any firm political commitment to either power. The problem was that the Anti-Comintern Pact implied a one-sided and public commitment to Japan. The Japanese could always argue that it was Germany's military agreements with China which implied a political commitment on her part to that country. The difficulties in this situation were compounded by the uncertain, and even dangerous situation in Sino—Japanese relations, any developments there being bound to affect Germany's own position and policies.[4] Von Falkenhausen, however, was confident that the balance of military effectiveness was gradually moving in China's favour.[5]

At the beginning of 1937, therefore, two basic problems confronted the Wilhelmstrasse: the effect of Germany's new relationship with Japan on the delicate balance of relations between Germany and China, Manchukuo and Japan; and, depending on what actually happened in these relationships, whether the Foreign Office would regain some, or lose more, of its authority in Berlin in the making of Far Eastern policy. While Trautmann's point regarding the bilateral and even multilateral nature of Germany's Far Eastern policy was only too well taken in the Foreign Office,[6] the new and disturbing element which had been thrown into the complex of Germany's Far Eastern relations merely intensified the Foreign Office's opposition to closer links with either China or Japan. A suggestion by the Air Ministry that a military mission be sent to Japan was opposed since it was feared that this would confirm recent reports of a secret German—Japanese military agreement.[7] Yet steps were taken to promote the sale of military aircraft to Japan, von Ribbentrop's collaborator, Dr Hack, being sent on a special mission to Japan for this purpose. It also seems that he was given the additional task of overcoming the final opposition of Japanese Navy circles to the Anti-Comintern Pact. On 14 March von Dirksen admitted that the Japanese Naval authorities, among others, had still not abandoned their attitude of reserve towards the Pact.[8]

The Pact made it extremely difficult for the Chinese to accept at face value Wilhelmstrasse protestations of unbroken German friendship for China, while from the Chinese Ambassador at Rome came the first clear warning that the new situation might strengthen the hands of those who, like the

Young Marshal, Chang Hsueh-liang, favoured an orientation of China's policy towards Soviet Russia.[9] Further problems for Germany were hinted at when a member of the Executive Yuan warned Trautmann on 18 February 1937 of the propaganda being conducted in China against the German military advisers. It was felt that their position would become untenable in the event of a conflict with Japan. Trautmann strongly denied any pro-Japanese direction to German policy, and referred instead to the positive work being done by Klein and the advisers in the field of Sino—German relations.[10] To impress upon the Chinese Government his own and Germany's good faith, he then made a suggestion which was to give the Foreign Office a much needed lever in its own policy struggles in Berlin: that the Minister of Finance, H. H. Kung, should meet von Neurath, von Blomberg, and if possible Hitler, after Kung's visit to Britain for the coronation of King George VI in May and when Kung went to Bad Nauheim for a cure. Eight days later Schacht requested the Foreign Office to pass on his own invitation to Kung.[11]

Von Dirksen made a similar suggestion regarding the younger brother of Emperor Hirohito, Prince Chichibu, who was also travelling to Europe for the coronation. Although the Foreign Office supported von Dirksen's request that an invitation be issued by Hitler, to which the Führer agreed,[12] and which von Ribbentrop also wanted his Büro associated with,[13] it was clearly understood that Kung's visit could be of the utmost political importance. The Foreign Office especially hoped to demonstrate to the Nazi leadership the necessity of cultivating good relations with China in spite of, or even because of, the Anti-Comintern Pact with Japan. Kung's acceptance of the invitation to visit Berlin and the preparations for this at least provided a positive point of contact between Germany and China which the Foreign Office hoped might cushion some of the shocks still reverberating from 26 November 1936. Von Blomberg also extended his own invitation to General Ho Ying-chin and Chen-cheng, the Chinese Minister and Vice-Minister of War respectively.[14]

Nevertheless, Chinese doubts about Germany's intentions in the Far East grew when an official announcement was finally made at the beginning of March about the appointment of a German trade commissioner to Hsinking. Although by December 1936 it had been decided that Dr Knoll, and not the less politically important figure of Dr Schiller, was to be appointed to the new post, a public announcement was delayed for technical reasons.[15] It was not until 9 March that Dr Knoll was formally appointed to the new post at Hsinking, and the telegram sent to Trautmann the following day clearly indicated the Wilhelmstrasse's concern about China's reaction to the news. Trautmann was told to emphasise the economic nature of Knoll's appointment and that it related only to German—Manchukuoan trade relations.[16] That there were grounds for the Wilhelmstrasse's apprehension was confirmed when Trautmann reported that the Chinese Vice-Minister of Foreign Affairs had expressed his Government's disappointment and hoped that Knoll would not be concerned with political questions. Trautmann therefore recommended that the Wilhelmstrasse should treat the matter as unobtrusively as possible because of Chinese public opinion. In Berlin the Chinese Ambassador, Cheng Tien-fong, was more pointed in his response. On information he had received about Germany's disappointment with the outcome of the agreement of April 1936 with Manchukuo, he wondered why Germany was not considering annulling it.[17]

In fact, Ritter had already suggested to the Manchukuoan Trade Commissioner in Berlin, Hiyoshi Kato, that before Knoll left for Manchukuo the two should meet to begin discussions on the renewal of the 1936 agreement, such talks to include Voss and if necessary Wohlthat. Kato agreed, and wanted the talks to begin before the arrival in Germany at the end of the month of Manchukuo's Vice-Minister of Foreign Affairs, Ohashi.[18] Whether Kato wanted to avoid too much interference from Ohashi because he had the same reputation among Manchukuoan circles that he had among German ones,[19] or because Kato genuinely wanted to prepare the ground for Ohashi is not known. Nevertheless, when Ohashi met Ritter at the end of March 1937 he immediately rushed into political matters by suggesting that Manchukuo be allowed to establish a consulate in Germany. From the discussion it was clear that Ohashi's real purpose was in this way to exert pressure on Russia to permit Manchukuoan consulates, and for obvious reasons Ritter quickly stamped on the idea.[20]

In addition to this problem, by mid-March 1937 the Wilhelmstrasse had to contend with Chiang Kai-shek's fears that Germany planned to extend the Anti-Comintern Pact to include Italy and other states. The Foreign Office and War Ministry were forced to send a joint denial of the reports, as well as a reaffirmation of Germany's fidelity to the cause of good relations with China. Although welcomed by the Generalissimo and the Chinese Foreign Minister, Wang Chung-hui,[21] nevertheless the Marshal warned Trautmann of the effect on Chinese feelings of Germany's seemingly closer relationship with Japan. In his conversation with Trautmann on 20 March Chiang Kai-shek complained that his remarks on the Anti-Comintern Pact during the débâcle at Sian,[22] when he stated that it would have no effect on Far Eastern politics, had in fact worsened his own domestic situation. It had played an important part in the propaganda of Chang Hsueh-liang and the communists who accused him of aligning China with the Fascist Powers. Although Chiang Kai-shek denied that China's policy would be oriented more towards Russia after the events in Sian, Trautmann thought that the Marshal's recent abandonment of his previous Foreign Minister, General Chang Chun, indicated that he was having to make concessions to the pro-Russian and pro-Western groups within the Kuomintang.[23] Despite emphasising Hitler's hopes that China would understand that Germany's policy towards Japan was dictated by general and not Far Eastern considerations, Trautmann was finally put into the position of having to 'defend' the Anti-Comintern Pact as a simple kind of 'police' agreement designed to fight international communism, although he emphasised that it was not an alliance as such.[24]

If Trautmann appeared to be on the defensive in Nanking about the changes brought about in German—Japanese relations, in Tokio von Dirksen went on the offensive. Annoyed by Foreign Minister Sato's somewhat negative remarks about the Pact in several Parliamentary speeches during early March[25] he took it upon himself, without instructions from the Wilhelmstrasse, to approach Sato on the matter. There was, however, a particular reason for Dirksen's concern. Naotake Sato, appointed Foreign Minister on 1 March 1937 in the moderate Hayashi Cabinet, was a 'strong advocate of friendly relations with the Anglo—American nations',[26] and von Dirksen was clearly afraid that not only German—Japanese relations but more specifically the Anti-Comintern Pact would be thrown to the winds if such tendencies ever became the maxim in Japanese foreign policy.

The Foreign Minister was therefore subjected to a long and rather peevish lecture on his supposed shortcomings regarding the Pact and German—Japanese relations. In particular von Dirksen's tirade was prompted by Sato's comment in the Japanese Diet on 11 March during a discussion on Russo—Japanese relations, that 'it would not have been necessary to have considered something like the Anti-Comintern Pact if the Comintern had not existed'. Von Dirksen was concerned that foreign observers might deduce from this and previous attacks on the Pact in the Diet and Japanese press that certain political circles in Japan rejected 'not only the Pact but above all a policy of friendship towards Germany'. He was also worried in case an overestimation of the political importance of these circles created the impression in Europe that Japan was 'moving away' from the Anti-Comintern Pact, and virtually accused the Foreign Minister outright of favouring Soviet Russia rather than Germany in his foreign policy. As it was, on 12 March the *Japan Chronicle* had quoted from a new French weekly journal in which Sato had said that he had been one of the first to 'regret' the new agreement with Germany. Von Dirksen relented somewhat towards the end by admitting that privately Sato had previously assured him of his loyalty towards the Pact.[27] But what concerned the German Ambassador above all was the impression created abroad and in the press, and he suggested that it would be a good thing if the Foreign Minister could issue a statement through *DNB* clarifying the matter. Sato agreed to this.

Von Dirksen's singular and individual attempt to 'correct' the supposed misdemeanours of Foreign Minister Sato can also be seen as yet another milestone in his rather unhappy relationship with the Wilhelmstrasse. The tenor of his report to Berlin implied that it was he, the Ambassador, and not his superiors in the Wilhelmstrasse who was most keenly aware both of the requirements and shortcomings in German—Japanese relations. He pointedly drew Berlin's attention to the fact that the Japanese military authorities, who favoured and supported the Anti-Comintern Pact, were the authoritative political force in Japan. Although he discounted Sato's importance he had felt it necessary to 'stop the rot' regarding what he thought was the public disparagement of the

Anti-Comintern Pact and German—Japanese relations by certain sections of the Japanese Government. It was a measure of von Dirksen's self-assurance that he felt he had succeeded in his self-appointed task.

Despite this emphasis on the Anti-Comintern Pact von Dirksen, probably like Hitler, obviously thought that Germany could run in harness with Japan at the same time as she developed her various interests in a China that remained free from outside threats, especially from Japan. When Sato talked about Japan's other foreign relations, von Dirksen recommended a Sino—Japanese *Ausgleich,* primarily for the sake of Sino—German relations. As he explained to Sato 'just as Germany would very much welcome a Sino—Japanese *Ausgleich* since she stands in very friendly relations with Japan, she also wishes to maintain good relations with China because of Germany's numerous interests in China'.[28]

Six days later von Dirksen again reported critically on Sato, this time because of the Foreign Minister's answers to questions submitted by Yukio Ozaki, an independent member of the Lower House of the Japanese Parliament. Sato had declared that 'the Government has no intention whatever of considering the return to Germany of the South Sea Mandated Islands'. Nor did Sato's rather general comments on the Anti-Comintern Pact do much to redeem his reputation in von Dirksen's eyes.[29]

While von Dirksen seemed intent upon keeping the Pact issue alive, the Wilhelmstrasse hoped that there would be a period of relative quiet in German—Japanese relations in which there would be no more diplomatic or ideological 'surprises', and which would enable the world-wide excitement raised against Germany by the Anti-Comintern Pact to die down. Its attitude was epitomised by von Neurath's confrontation with von Raumer on 23 April when, with Hitler's approval, he ordered him to cease any activity against the Comintern which went beyond the terms of the Pact, especially where this concerned the accession of third States to the agreement. Von Neurath emphasised instead that the fight against communism and 'Russian bolshevism' was the responsibility of Alfred Rosenberg. Directed against von Raumer's efforts with respect to Italy this thrust was, nevertheless, part of the long-running feud between von Neurath and von Ribbentrop.[30]

In Tokio, however, von Dirksen persisted in his efforts. As

a result of his complaints to the Japanese Foreign Office and Army, instructions were issued to the Japanese press and to the Berlin correspondents of Japanese newspapers to limit their criticisms of the Anti-Comintern Pact and the German tendency in Japanese foreign policy. This seemed to have had some effect since towards the end of April von Dirksen was informed that at a confidential meeting between Sato, General Kotaro Nakamura, Minister of War, and Admiral Mitsumasa Yonai, Navy Minister, the Anti-Comintern Pact was confirmed as an element of Japanese foreign policy. This meeting, at which Nakamura and Yonai affirmed their support for an extension of the Pact with Germany, had been called to discuss Japan's response to Russian pressure, based on what the Russians claimed was their knowledge of the full text of the Anti-Comintern Pact, designed to prevent any further collaboration between Japan and Germany. Von Dirksen contemptuously dismissed the Russian move as 'a sign of weakness'.[31]

Yet by 10 May von Dirksen was reporting on differences with Sato regarding the establishment of a German—Japanese Commission in Tokio under the terms of the Anti-Comintern Pact. Sato obviously hoped to shelve the issue since he suggested that preliminary talks take place with von Dirksen. This would avoid the immediate establishment of such a Commission which, he argued, would only lead to further domestic and foreign policy problems for the Japanese Government. Von Dirksen tried to argue that the Commission was an accepted and publicised part of the Anti-Comintern Pact, but Sato countered by stating that on the German side the intention was to use the Commission for secret talks to harmonise German and Japanese policies towards Russia. In desperation, von Dirksen appealed to the Wilhelmstrasse for instructions.[32] At that time, however, the Foreign Office was pursuing its own policy of obstruction on this very question. At the end of April a delay occurred in the despatch to von Raumer of a draft programme of work for the permanent commission within the framework of the Anti-Comintern Pact. Whether the delay was due to uncertainty as to von Raumer's position and role in the struggle against the Comintern, or because von Erdmannsdorff, who had been handling these questions, was due to take up his new post as German Minister to Hungary on 11 May 1937, is not known.[33]

The Foreign Office's attempts to play down the importance — to the Chinese at least — of Germany's supposedly new 'orientation' in the Far East was also seen at the time of the negotiations in March and April for the renewal of the German—Manchukuoan trade agreement of 1936. By early April these negotiations had reached a successful conclusion with the Germans gaining their point that the agreement was to remain virtually unaltered. The final protocol, which was eventually signed on 21 May 1937 by Wohlthat and Kato, provided for a renewal of the agreement until 31 May 1940, although from January 1938 both parties were free to open negotiations for its alteration.[34] On 7 April Ritter was able to assure Cheng Tien-fong that the negotiations with Manchukuo were being conducted by Wohlthat with Kato, and certainly not with Ohashi. As Ritter then pointed out, this showed that 'as before we are treating this matter only as an economic question'.[35] The Wilhelmstrasse's desire to avoid any political complications arising out of relations with Manchukuo again showed itself on 20 May when Ritter once more blocked the suggestion, this time brought by Kato, that Manchukuo be allowed to establish a consulate in Germany.[36]

Several factors were currently at work, however, which not only strengthened ties between Germany and China but helped to alleviate some of the anxieties in Sino—German relations caused by the Anti-Comintern Pact. While Kung's pending visit to Germany was made more official by the fact that von Blomberg and Göring associated themselves with Schacht's invitation,[37] the most important questions in Sino—German relations remained, as always, military and economic ones. Klein continued to sing the praises of the Chinese and Hapro agreements because of the scale of deliveries of Chinese raw materials and goods to Germany, evincing optimism about overcoming the difficulties with the German firms in China and dismissing reports of problems in the execution of the arms agreement. He also supported Chiang Kai-shek's proposals in a letter to Hitler that the Chinese Army should undergo even further reorganisation by German officers. Klein went so far as to suggest that von Falkenhausen be put back on the active list and that his work as adviser be additionally supported by the despatch of other senior officers to China. Klein countered Trautmann's objections by suggesting that these moves be kept secret, while he further suggested that the military mission should be given a more official status by allowing the German advisers to be paid from Germany. The extent of the rivalry between the 'Chinese' and the 'Japanese' influences in the formulation of Germany's Far Eastern policy was then seen when Klein told Trautmann that he had suggested to Chiang Kai-shek that the Chinese Ambassador in Berlin should be able to stand up to the Japanese and capable of countering Japanese influence in Berlin. He should also be able to speak German, and Chiang Kai-shek's agreement made it appear as though Cheng Tien-fong's days in Berlin were numbered, although in fact he stayed for more than another year.[38]

Trautmann notwithstanding, it appears that the War Ministry was quick to respond to suggestions from China for an intensification of its work there. Rumours soon circulated that a mixed military economic mission under the leadership of General von Reichenau would visit China at the beginning of May. Following the lead of the Berlin correspondent of the *Daily Telegraph,* the Tokio press suggested that part of the mission's task would be to work for a form of German—Chinese—Japanese cooperation.[39] Trautmann opposed these plans, and used von Falkenhausen's appointment on 23 April 1937 as Chiang Kai-shek's chief adviser as an argument for suggesting that the visit and other far-reaching plans be cancelled. Even von Falkenhausen appeared concerned in case Klein's suggestions for changes in the nature of the German military advisory staff were adopted in Berlin for they implied increased War Ministry as opposed to Chinese control and direction over the officers in China. On the other hand, Trautmann was pleased with the more official nature of von Falkenhausen's position with Chiang Kai-shek since he thought this would block Italian aspirations to build up an Italian advisory group in competition with the Germans.[40]

Trautmann's concern at the extent of Germany's military relations with China was complemented by the reserve which von Neurath, Hitler, and the military authorities still maintained towards Japan. On 7 June Keitel informed China of von Blomberg's rejection of another draft military agreement which Oshima had presented in April. Containing three articles, this proposed exchanges of information about Russia and the Red Army; discussions for granting mutual relief measures *vis-à-vis* Russia; and possible annual consultations between the German and Japanese armies about mutual objectives respecting Russia as part of a strengthening of the secret supplement to the Anti-Comintern Pact. Such a general 'consultation' was also recommended should Germany's and Japan's international positions be drastically threatened.[41]

The meeting on 7 June in fact showed how wide the gap remained between the German and Japanese General Staffs. Oshima tried his hardest to convince Keitel of the necessity of a formal and written agreement between the two armies, but admitted that grave doubts existed in Japan, especially within army circles, about the wisdom of the Anti-Comintern Pact with Germany. Significantly, he stressed that a written agreement would serve to remove the doubts about Germany's sincerity respecting the new situation in German—Japanese relations. Although Oshima did not explain what he meant by this, he was obviously referring to the German military advisory staff in China and the rumours in May about von Reichenau's visit. Another consideration was the fact that nothing 'spectacular' had happened in German—Japanese relations during the previous six months, while such a military agreement would help the Japanese Army authorities to counteract what they feared was a drift in their own Cabinet's policy towards the Anglo-Saxon powers.

Keitel, undoubtedly aware of these factors and suspicious of the rather vague commitment in Article 2 of the draft regarding mutual aid, emphasised to Oshima that a written agreement was unnecessary. He failed to see why the existing consulation and cooperation between Oshima, himself, and Admiral Canaris in Berlin, and between Ott and the Japanese General Staff in Tokio, should not continue and suffice for their mutual purpose. Besides which, he argued, such an agreement was a political matter and in Germany this was the Führer's responsibility since the German Army was not such a political force as was the Japanese Army. That Britain's position loomed as large in German thinking as in Japanese was clear from Keitel's remarks that news of such an agreement would only lead to further attacks on Germany and Japan by other powers and so worsen their respective positions in international affairs.[42]

In view of Oshima's impassioned pleas for a reconsideration of the matter the Minister of War, von Blomberg, discussed the matter on 24 June with Keitel and the leaders of the

Army, Navy and Air Force, von Fritsch, Admiral Raeder, and Göring.[43] Following this and other discussions, Keitel told Oshima on 6 July that the German position was unchanged and there could be no written agreement between the two armies, but that the existing verbal exchanges should continue. Nor was Keitel any more forthcoming over the suggestion for fixed consultations between the respective General Staffs, wanting this question treated on an *ad hoc* basis. The most that Keitel would admit was that Oshima should work more closely with Admiral Canaris about respective spheres and exchanges of intelligence. Oshima at least salvaged something from his largely unsuccessful efforts since the following day, 7 July 1937, an agreement on intelligence matters was concluded between the Abwehr and Oshima. To set the record absolutely right on the outcome of these important talks, Ott was instructed to deliver a verbal declaration to the Japanese General Staff in Tokio outlining the attitude of the Wehrmacht to Oshima's proposals.[44]

Von Blomberg's refusal to countenance any form of written commitment between the armed forces of Germany and Japan was accompanied in the same period by von Neurath's refusal to sanction anything which even hinted at an extension of Germany's political interests or responsibilities *vis-à-vis* Japan. Basing himself on Hitler's authority, von Neurath rejected on 2 June 1937 a proposal by Schumberg of Referat Deutschland in the Foreign Office that it would be in Germany's interest to support Italo—Japanese negotiations for an Anti-Comintern Pact. Only two months previously he had confronted von Ribbentrop's aide, von Raumer, on the same question.[45]

Schumberg's memorandum on 1 June, which raised the issue of political relations with Japan in two forms, had been prompted by telegrams from von Dirksen in Tokio and von Hassell in Rome. Both Ambassadors had requested instructions from the Foreign Office regarding their attitude concerning Germany's political relations with Japan. On 10 May von Dirksen reported Foreign Minister Sato's request for confidential discussions with him about the establishment in Tokio of a mixed commission in connection with the Anti-Comintern Pact. These were to complement similar conversations that Mushakoji had recently had in Berlin, undoubtedly with members of the Büro Ribbentrop. Von Dirksen was concerned at Sato's request for secrecy because of possible foreign policy repercussions and pointed out that the matter was known publicly in connection with the Anti-Comintern Pact. Sato's answer particularly interested the Foreign Office in Berlin since he explained that the German intention appeared to be the initiation of secret talks about the co-ordination of German and Japanese policies against Russia. Von Hassell's telegram of 26 May reported the opposition of the Japanese Ambassador to Italy, Sugimura, to negotiations for an Italo—Japanese Anti-Comintern Pact because he feared it would worsen Japan's relations with Britain and the United States.

Schumberg accepted the evidence of von Schmieden, Head of the Far Eastern section of the Political Department, that the political situation in Japan and the widespread criticisms there of the Anti-Comintern Pact meant that cooperation between the two countries would have to be limited to administrative or police matters arising out of the Pact. Any discussion concerning mutual foreign policies was out of the question, as was the establishment in Japan of a special commission for Pact purposes. On the other hand, he recommended that von Hassell should be instructed to support negotiations between Rome and Tokio by conferring with Ciano and Sugimura since he, Schumberg, doubted the possibility of repercussions by Britain or Russia against Germany.[46]

Von Neurath's acceptance of the proposal to limit German—Japanese cooperation under the Pact to administrative or police matters and his rejection of support for the Italo—Japanese negotiations, a rejection he based on the Führer's authority,[47] made it quite clear that, for at least a short while in the summer of 1937, some degree of unanimity about German policy towards Japan existed between Hitler, the Army and the Foreign Office. There were different reasons for this unanimity but at least one idea was common: not to allow Germany to become closely involved, militarily or politically, with Japan at that particular time. Germany's own position in Europe was an uncertain one, and while hopes of an *Ausgleich* with Britain were rapidly vanishing any open alliance with Japan could be expected to disturb to an unknown degree the precarious line that still existed between Berlin and London. Similarly, the continuing uncertainties in Japan's relations with China and Russia heightened the risk of an outbreak of armed conflict in the Far East of unknown extent, consequences, and duration. Militarily and politically Nazi Germany was in no position to wish upon herself the extra burdens involved in further formalising the relationship with Japan. The arguments for a policy of reserve on Germany's part were also strengthened by the evidence of policy conflicts in Japan over attitudes towards Germany and the Anti-Comintern Pact. This evidence encouraged the Wilhelmstrasse since it appeared to strengthen its continual arguments that Germany's role in the Far East should be a non-political one.[48]

While this consensus of opinion encouraged the Foreign Office to think that the 'battle' over the control of Far Eastern policy was at least being held and stabilised, if not won, von Dirksen's telegram of 10 May had raised a point which cast doubts over the whole picture. This concerned the secret talks that had been taking place in Berlin about joint policies against Russia, although in his answer of 4 June to Tokio von Neurath denied all knowledge of these. On 7 June von Dirksen explained that Foreign Minister Sato had said that there had been talks in Berlin with von Neurath *or* von Ribbentrop about the formation of a mixed commission. From Director Togo of the Gaimusho, von Dirksen established that von Ribbentrop had been involved in talks about a commission whose primary task was to be the examination of joint German—Japanese policies against the Soviet Union. This commission, which could be established in Berlin alone if necessary, was to be secret and known as Commission B while that concerned with police matters and openly provided for in the Anti-Comintern Pact could freely meet as Commission A.[49]

Although von Neurath thought it might have been von Raumer rather than von Ribbentrop who was involved, von Dirksen's information showed that even if Hitler, the Army, and the Foreign Office were following a policy of circumspection towards Japan, the Büro Ribbentrop was not. At the end of June, von Neurath emphasised to von Raumer that the Foreign Office opposed any Japanese wish to publish a notice on the creation of the joint commission on the basis of the Anti-Comintern Pact, and in turn pointed out to Mushakoji that any talks about Russia desired by the Japanese should be established between the Japanese Embassy and the Foreign Office.[50] Von Neurath, knew of course, what the Foreign

Office's reaction would be to any suggestions of a joint policy against Russia and this was his way of pointing out the 'correct' procedures for such political discussions. He may even have hoped that the Japanese would raise the matter with the Foreign Office since this would bring it and not the Büro Ribbentrop more into the picture. A later telegram to Tokio made it clear that von Neurath had been quite specific that any discussions between the Foreign Office and the Japanese Embassy about Russia were to be limited to an exchange of information only.[51]

Apart from anything else there was a particular reason for the Foreign Office's reserve towards Japan in June 1937: from 9 to 14 June the Finance Minister of the Chinese Republic, H. H. Kung, was to pay an official visit to Nazi Germany. From the Foreign Office's point of view it was unfortunate that this coincided with von Neurath's own visits to the capitals of Yugoslavia, Bulgaria and Hungary,[52] even though arrangements were made for Kung to be received by Hitler. Not surprisingly, the Foreign Office's preparations for the visit were based on the premise that the chief topic of conversation would be the effect of the Anti-Comintern Pact on Germany's general Far Eastern policies.[53] Mushakoji, who made an 'obvious' appearance at the Wilhelmstrasse on 7 June, need have had no fear then that Japan would be 'ignored' while Kung was being fêted in Germany.[54]

H. H. Kung and his companions arrived in Berlin on the morning of 9 June 1937, and during the following six days were received by Schacht, the State Secretary at the Foreign Office, von Mackensen (von Neurath's son-in-law), the War Minister von Blomberg, Reich Air Minister Göring, the *Ostasiatischer Verein*, and finally on 13 June by Hitler himself. The visit also included trips to an aircraft factory at Dessau and the Infantry School at Döberitz, while a contract was concluded for the construction of an iron and steel works at Chuchow under the terms of the Reichenau agreement. An indication of the importance the Chinese attached to the visit could be seen in the composition of the group which accompanied Kung, which included the Chinese Minister of Marine, Chen Shao-kuan, Rear-Admiral Liu Hsien-hui, the Vice-Minister of Railways, Tseng Yang-fu, the General Secretary of the State Office of the Executive Yuan, Wong Wen-hao, Lieutenant-General Kuei Yung-chin and Major-General

Wen Ying-ching of the Army. When it came to choose those to be received by Hitler, both the War Ministry and the Foreign Office suggested that Kuei Yung-chin be included since he was Commander of the Training Brigade at Nanking and was consequently in close contact with von Falkenhausen and the German military advisers.[55]

Not surprisingly, the Anti-Comintern Pact emerged as the chief topic of discussion in Kung's meetings in Berlin. In all cases, though, previous German arguments were repeated and emphasised, that China need have no fear either for the future amity of Sino—German relations or about the nature of Germany's supposedly new relationship with Japan. Both von Mackensen[56] and Schacht emphasised that Germany's policy towards Japan was based on general political considerations and not Far Eastern ones as such. As Schacht put it, Germany's interest in the Spanish Civil War and the conclusion of the Anti-Comintern Pact were to be viewed from the standpoint of Germany's struggle against international bolshevism and the Comintern. He tried to explain to Kung that the ideological nature of the Pact with Japan meant that it had been von Ribbentrop and not von Neurath who had concluded it, and this very fact showed that no far-reaching commitments were involved. He also made the interesting observation that 'during the dangerous phase of Germany's rapid rearmament we had had a natural interest in showing our opponents that we also had friends, and that in this policy the great military power which Japan represents had been a factor for us against the appearance of isolation'.

In an attempt to convince Kung of Germany's faithful adherence to a policy of 'balance' in the Far East, Schacht restated the familiar refrain that Germany had no political interests in that region of the world. Instead, he emphasised that Germany regarded China from a long-term point of view, while in any case Germany's regard for China could be seen by the recently concluded 100 million Reichsmark credit agreement. As Schacht then confirmed, German trade with Japan was pursued on an entirely different basis, cash only. The interview ended, however, on rather an unhappy note since Schacht complained of shortcomings on the Chinese side in Sino—German trade relations, while Kung appeared to be unhappy with the quality and price of much .of the military equipment that was offered to China.[57]

The following day Kung was received by Göring who, as Commissioner for the Four Year Plan, was especially interested in the strategic raw materials that China supplied Germany with under the HAPRO treaties. The anti-communist theme emerged again with reference to German—Japanese relations, but this time Göring stated that Germany wished to see a strong and efficient Chinese army in order to fight communism in China. For this purpose, Göring continued, Germany was prepared to help China's communications and railway systems by the supply of manufactured goods, but in return she was more interested in receiving iron-ore than supplies of wool. As a reflection upon the internal German struggle for the control of various spheres of policy, Göring made the interesting remark that he thought that the whole question of the Klein agreements should be removed from the competence of the Ministry of War. He also emphasised his own concern that the 'normal' channels of Sino—German trade should not be unduly disturbed by such inter-State agreements which he appeared to think would be of increasing importance in the future, but like Schacht also expressed some concern about the future management of Sino—German trade relations, especially from the Chinese side. He made it quite clear that Germany could only continue to supply China with manufactured goods if a policy of long-term planning was instituted with respect to Chinese orders to Germany, otherwise Germany would be forced to adopt a 'cash down' policy.[58]

The high point of Kung's visit to Germany was undoubtedly his trip to the Obersalzberg on Sunday 13 June to be received by the Führer and Reich Chancellor. In view of what was to happen in the Far East only a month later, Hitler's comments to Kung and of Kung to von Schmieden of the Foreign Office are of great interest. Not surprisingly, the anti-communist theme dominated Hitler's views, although he prefaced these by remarking on the complementary nature of Sino—German relations in the economic sphere and the fact that Germany pursued no political aim in the Far East. Nevertheless, his portrayal of the communist threat to Western Europe — he dismissed out of hand the military value of the Red Army — was designed to justify the fact that Germany had concluded an obviously political agreement with Japan. Given Hitler's own responsibility for the pro-Japanese aspects of Germany's Far Eastern policy and the reserve so recently shown towards that country, his remarks to Kung regarding Sino—German—Japanese relations are of some interest. He hoped that some form of détente would be arrived at in the relations between Nanking and Tokio, and offered German mediation should it be required.[59]

One can take this as clear evidence of Hitler's acceptance of the importance of maintaining the German Army's important interests in China and awareness of the fact that they could only be run in harness so long as the two Far Eastern powers remained at peace, and while for her part Germany had only a limited and ideological agreement with Japan. Hitler was only too well aware that this twofold policy in the Far East carried tremendous risks of all kinds for Germany but that for the sake of expediency — while his own foreign policy objectives were unfolding and Germany's position in Europe was being stabilised and strengthened — he was prepared to run these risks. This meant that he was prepared to wait for the day when a necessary choice would have to be made in the Far East, but probably reasoned that the time to worry about that would be when the choice actually confronted him. One further point is also perfectly clear: Hitler, unlike the universally disliked von Ribbentrop, at least took a broader and more common-sense view of Far Eastern affairs generally and towards the role which Germany played there.

According to von Schmieden, Head of the Far Eastern Section of the Foreign Office and who accompanied the Chinese guests to Bavaria, it appeared that the cumulative effect of Kung's talks in Berlin and at the Obersalzberg was such as to convince him and his companions that German denials of an anti-Chinese tendency in German—Japanese relations were genuine. Hitler's comments on Sino—German economic relations made it appear that Germany could pursue a predominantly economic policy in China and a political one in Japan without the two clashing. Nevertheless, almost everyone recognised that the future pattern of events would be determined by the outcome of the uncertain and complicated political manoeuvres in Tokio and North China. Whatever the result, there could be no doubt that Germany's position and policy in the Far East would be greatly affected.

When Mushakoji enquired on 18 June about the results of Kung's talks, von Mackensen again and emphatically rejected his suggestions for the establishment in Berlin of a 'German—

Manchukuo' Chamber of Commerce. The State Secretary emphasised that Germany's requirements of raw materials from China made it essential to consider Chinese feelings in this respect, besides which there could be no question of the recognition of Manchukuo. Since Mushakoji's main objective was to lead Germany along the path to recognition it is not surprising that he rejected von Mackensen's alternative proposal of a 'German—Japanese' title for any such commercial establishment. Although only a brief reference was made during this conversation to the question of an aviation contract for an airline between Germany and Japan via the Near East and China, von Schmieden's memorandum for the State Secretary had expressed his section's opposition to the idea because of Chinese susceptibilities and concern for German industrial and military undertakings in China.[60] Three weeks later Mushakoji was faced with yet another example of what he probably considered to be the Foreign Office's obstructionist policy towards Japan, a statement of von Neurath's clear objection and doubts about a mixed commission under the terms of the Anti-Comintern Pact.[61]

Germany and the Sino-Japanese War.

1. July—September 1937

The uneasy peace of the Far East was shattered in the summer of 1937 by the events of 7—8 July at Lukouchiao, or Marco Polo Bridge, south of Peking. Concentrated on the nearby walled town of Wanping, the local clash of Chinese and Japanese troops soon developed into a full-scale military and political confrontation between Nanking and Tokio with reverberations throughout the world.[1]

Germany was especially embarrassed by the new situation, and two sides of the same question came to dominate the discussion about her role in the conflict: could she remain neutral and yet maintain good relations with both belligerents; or would a choice between China and Japan finally have to be made in view of the special relationships which had been developed with both countries? These were difficult, if not impossible, decisions to make in view of the complex nature of Germany's position in the Far East. Neither the pro-Chinese nor the pro-Japanese factions in Germany welcomed the new situation since it placed their special interests and relationships at risk and could provide the opportunity for the policy of the opposing group to dominate. Even the exponents of the Anti-Comintern Pact were perturbed that Japan's new and increasingly wholesale involvement in China might reduce her value as a means of pressure on Soviet Russia. As von Dirksen later wrote, 'the effect of a certain pressure on Russia, which was certainly welcome to Hitler, was reduced to insignificance by this adventure'. This was also the view of von Mackensen, the State Secretary in the Wilhelmstrasse.[2] On the other hand, the pressures the new conflict exerted on Britain's interests in the Far East were likely to serve Hitler's purposes when Anglo—German relations deteriorated and tension heightened in Europe. Meanwhile, the Wehrmacht's leaders could only congratulate themselves for having declined Oshima's pressure earlier in the year for a formal and written commitment between the German and Japanese armies. The Wilhelmstrasse's chief concern, though, was its role in the formulation of Germany's policy as yet another

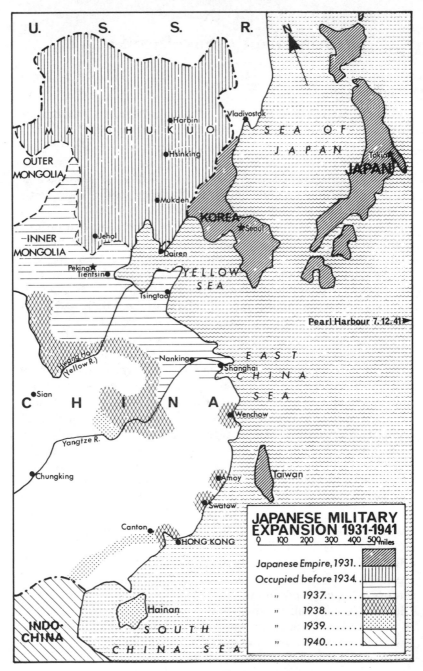

Map. 3.   Japanese Military Expansion 1931—1941

and potentially more serious crisis unfolded in the Far East.

An omen of sorts for the future could be seen in Hitler's letter of 10 July to Foreign Minister Hirota, in which he stated that 'in clear recognition of our common aims Germany will do all that it can to strengthen the cooperation initiated by the [Anti-Comintern] agreement'. Significantly, the draft for this letter, a reply to one from Hirota to Hitler on 1 April 1937, came from the Wilhelmstrasse. The final form of the letter was extremely skilful since it encouraged Japan while ensuring that Germany had an escape clause from unwelcome demands by Japan — i.e. the phrase 'Germany will do all that it can'. It was Prince von Bismarck, deputy leader of the Political Department, who had altered the original draft, which read that 'Germany will remain true to the [Anti-Comintern] agreement', probably because he thought that this form implied too definite an undertaking towards Tokio. Of particular interest and significance was the fact that this change was accepted by Hitler.[3]

Von Neurath's first inclination was to blame the Russians for having instigated, through the Chinese communists, the clash between China and Japan as a means of diverting Japan's attention from Russia when the latter was especially weak because of Stalin's extensive purges. To the Chinese Ambassador he emphasised Germany's 'strict impartiality' in the affair, but warned Mushakoji that the only beneficiary of the incident would be the Soviet Union. According to Ambassador Dodd's diary (but not von Neurath's record of their conversation), the Foreign Minister informed him that Germany would support England and the United States if they were able to negotiate a peace in the Far East. Yet, von Neurath rejected the Chinese Ambassador's view, as recounted by Dodd, that Japan had chosen that time to attack China because Russia was too weak to come to its aid.[4] Nevertheless, the Foreign Office thought it would be a mistake to discount the military value of the Red Army in an emergency, despite Stalin's purges. It considered that the Soviet Far Eastern Army had escaped the worst excesses of the purges, while the reported return of Marshal Blücher to the Far East indicated that the situation there would be stabilised.[5]

Initially, both China and Japan expressed the wish for a peaceful settlement of the conflict, while China issued a memorandum to the signatories of the Nine Power Treaty setting out her case against Japan. Although not a signatory, Germany received a copy of the document.[6] Nevertheless, while urging moderation on both parties,[7] the Wilhelmstrasse's main concern was that both China and Japan could be expected to exert pressure on Germany for more than a token declaration of support for one or the other power. Yet the first tentative step in Germany's direction took a different form. Ambassador Mushakoji sent his First Secretary, Koda, to London to approach Ambassador von Ribbentrop about the possibility of mediation by Germany. Because of his negotiation of the Anti-Comintern Pact, the Japanese probably considered him to be the best person to approach in the first place. It is not clear, however, what von Ribbentrop's response was; nor is it certain whether the hopes he expressed for a speedy Japanese military solution to the 'police action' in North China really signified an earnest wish for international peace, the avoidance of a position of embarrassment for Germany in the Far East, or a speedy return of Japan to her assigned role (in Nazi eyes) as a lever on the Soviet Union and Britain in world affairs. Apparently, he showed only perfunctory interest in the whole question and sent Koda on his way with the remark, 'keep me informed through von Raumer'. Evidently this was Mushakoji's first and only approach to von Ribbentrop on this matter. Assuming knowledge on von Ribbentrop's part of the lack of unity in Tokio between the civil and military authorities, it is quite possible that von Ribbentrop was embarrassed at being approached in this way by a member of the Japanese diplomatic establishment at the same time as he was maintaining contacts with Oshima, the Military Attaché.[8]

Yet when the Chinese Finance Minister, H. H. Kung, and the Chinese Ambassador to London met him on 22 July, von Ribbentrop expressed the hope for a peaceful solution of the problem in terms which probably impressed his Chinese visitors with the honesty of his views. He emphasised the friendly nature of Germany's relations with both China and Japan, her neutrality in the present conflict, and that after the conclusion of the Anti-Comintern Pact he had intimated to the Japanese that they should establish good relations with China. His statement that he had hoped that China would enter the Anti-Comintern Pact was rejected by Kung on the grounds of the opportunities it would offer Japan to meddle in Chinese affairs under the pretext of fighting communism.[9]

The first hint of direct pressure on Germany came on 16 July when Mushakoji tried to imply to von Neurath that Japan's action in North China was connected with the Anti-Comintern Pact since it was part of the fight against bolshevism.[10] The Foreign Minister quickly rejected any such implications since he realised that it could only lead to a discussion of Germany's obligations and responsibilities, if any, in the matter.[11] It was afterwards realised that Mushakoji had probably (and wilfully) misinterpreted von Neurath's statement of 14 July regarding Russia's role in the affair as implying German approval for Japan's actions against China which, through skilful diplomacy, could be converted into a public statement of support for Japan. The State Secretary subsequently emphasised to von Dirksen that this could not be the case since it was the Wilhelmstrasse's view that the Anti-Comintern Pact was not designed to combat bolshevism on the territory of a third state.[12] Von Mackensen had in fact already instructed him to impress upon the Japanese the difficulties of Germany's position, and that any reticence regarding certain Japanese wishes did not signify that 'we want to depart from the line of policy inaugurated by the Anti-Comintern Pact'. Nevertheless, von Dirksen was told to make it quite clear that Germany's position did not allow of one-sided demonstrations in Japan's favour, while Japan did not seem to take account of Germany's own interests in North China or of the fact that Japan's recent actions reduced the pressure on Russia and increased that on China, with whom Germany had to maintain good relations for economic reasons. Eugen Ott also adopted a critical attitude when speaking with members of the Japanese General Staff, rejecting their arguments that Japan's actions would help to strengthen Germany's anti-Comintern partner.[13]

The Foreign Office's circular to missions of 20 July therefore emphasised Germany's 'strict neutrality' in the Far Eastern conflict, and pointed out that Germany hoped for an early peaceful settlement because of her economic interests in the area and her anti-Comintern policy. This latter point was not to be used in diplomatic conversations, although free rein was given to von Neurath's views regarding Russia's supposed role in the affair. At the same time a special instruction was sent to Trautmann urging moderation on the Chinese, thus complementing von Dirksen's efforts in Tokio.[14]

Yet the moderation urged by the other world powers[15] seemed doomed to failure when Japan publicly announced that massive reinforcements would be sent to North China and Ambassador Sugimura admitted to von Hassell in Rome that although Japan did not want a conflict with Russia at that time, her aim was the large-scale and definitive disruption of all lines of communication between Soviet Russia and China, thus necessitating the advance of Japanese troops as far as the Hwang Ho river. The prospects of a localisation of the conflict or of immediate peace seemed dim, von Dirksen's optimism notwithstanding.[16]

Nor was the news from Nanking any better. Although Chiang Kai-shek said he wanted a peaceful settlement, he had no intention of sacrificing vital Chinese interests. Von Falkenhausen thought that Chiang rather preferred to have a military showdown since 'the hatred of Japan holds the nation together, and capitulation to Japan by his government would lead to personal attacks on him and to serious internal political conflicts'. Apparently, the Chinese strategy for an all-out war was already prepared, while von Falkenhausen thought that China's chances were 'not at all unfavourable', despite her lack of heavy artillery and specialist weapons, and that if the advice of the German advisers was followed the Chinese Army was 'capable of driving the Japanese over the Great Wall'. This view evidently influenced Chiang Kai-shek towards adopting a strong stand in the summer of 1937. Recognising that there was bound to be a struggle in Berlin between the pro-Chinese and pro-Japanese factions, von Falkenhausen thought it essential that von Blomberg should not be swayed by those who thought that a Japanese victory was certain: he felt that any Sino—Japanese war would turn into a struggle to the death.[17]

Japan's determination to have a 'clear ring' in which to pursue her ambitions in China was soon made plain to Berlin in two ways: rejection of intervention by third powers or offers of good offices, even by Germany, a standpoint supported by von Dirksen;[18] and constant reference to the sensitive question of German arms shipments to China.[19] On 22 July Yanai, the Counsellor of the Japanese Embassy at Berlin, complained to von Weizsäcker, Head of the Political Department in the Wilhelmstrasse, that despite von Neurath's promises to

Ambassador Mushakoji nothing had been done to stop the supply of German arms to China. According to Mushakoji's report to Tokio of his conversation with von Neurath on 14 July, the Foreign Minister had said that Germany did not intend to carry out any further deliveries of arms to China, although no mention of this fact appears in von Neurath's record of the conversation.[20] While the Japanese Ministry of Marine appeared to be considering a blockade of China which excluded Hong Kong, Yanai virtually threatened action at sea if the practice continued. While von Weizsäcker promised to look into the matter, although he pointed out that he had no personal knowledge of any such promises to Mushakoji, von Schmieden noted that the Ministry of War had ordered the cessation of deliveries of war material to China. Yet in view of what emerged subsequently one must assume that the order was issued more for form's sake than for anything else. From Tokio, however, von Dirksen reported Japanese complaints that it had taken protests from them to achieve this much, the implication being that because of the new and special relationship between Berlin and Tokio the Germans themselves should have acted independently on the matter.[21]

That other contentious issue, the German military advisers in China, was raised with Ott by the Aide of the Japanese War Minister, it being suggested that Germany could remove certain anti-German sentiments in the Japanese Army 'by a friendly gesture', an obvious euphemism for their removal from China. While Ott tried to emphasise the policy of active friendship followed by the German military authorities towards their Japanese counterparts, and echoed the Wilhelmstrasse by pointing out that the Anti-Comintern Pact was designed only to meet situations created by Russia, von Dirksen wanted to meet Japanese complaints on this score more than halfway.[22]

By this time, though, von Weizsäcker's patience with the Japanese attitude was wearing rather thin. Both to von Dirksen and Ambassador Mushakoji he set out at length a clear statement of Germany's policy and attitude of neutrality at that juncture of the Far Eastern conflict, a position which had already been made public on 22 July in the *Berliner Börsenzeitung* and the following day in the *Deutsche Diplomatisch-Politische Korrespondenz,* along with the disclaimer that the Anti-Comintern Pact had anything to do with current events in the Far East.[23]

Von Weizsäcker contested Japanese claims that the action in North China was in pursuance of the Anti-Comintern Pact by repeating the argument that the Pact was *not* designed to fight bolshevism on the territory of a third State, and that by preventing the consolidation of China, Japan itself would only further the spread of communism and increase the risk that China would turn towards Russia, a conclusion attested to by reports from Trautmann. As he put it to Mushakoji, 'we did not assume, on the basis of our contractual relationship, that we had to approve or give moral support to a Japanese action that might very well lead to the opposite of the aim pursued by both of us'. Von Weizsäcker also doubted whether the creation of a 'strategically clear situation' in North China would bring Japan any advantages *vis-à-vis* Russia because of the hatred that would be engendered in China, thus raising the possibility that Japan might find herself involved in a two-front war. Von Dirksen, however, disagreed with this and even questioned Germany's right to pass judgement on Japan's actions in North China: 'the obligations entered into refer only to the fight against the Comintern; in other respects the freedom of both States in foreign policy is by no means limited. Japan has no right to forbid Germany from concluding a naval agreement with England or a new Locarno treaty; nor has Germany the right to forbid Japan from an action in North China'. He admitted, though, that Germany's task at that moment was to urge caution and moderation on both China and Japan.[24]

Von Weizsäcker also impressed on von Dirksen that the recall of the German military advisers from China was out of the question for two reasons: it would signify that Germany was supporting Japan and abandoning her position of neutrality. It also carried the risk that the Russians would re-establish in China the position they had lost in 1927. He might also have added that their removal would have had an immediate and disastrous effect on the complex of important military and economic relations between China and Germany. As it was, Mushakoji and Oshima seemed satisfied with assurances from the Ministry of War that the military advisers would take no active part in military operations. On the other hand, Weizsäcker was adamant that German arms shipments to China could not be made the subject of German—Japanese negotiations. Nevertheless, he explained that von Neurath had told Mushakoji some time before that arms shipments had not been and were not being made to China in any considerable quantities. Furthermore, since a virtual state of war now existed in the Far East, Germany would cease further delivery of war material to China because of her own policy of neutrality. That this question would remain a contentious issue with Japan was clear from the general attitudes of von Neurath and von Weizsäcker: both were adamant that not only did the Japanese have no right to control or question German arms shipments to China, but that the German Government had no authority over the private trade in arms. Von Dirksen quickly informed Hirota of the main points of Weizsäcker's instruction.[25]

In view of the many warnings about Russia which the Wilhelmstrasse continued to give the Japanese, the Foreign Office's dismay was understandable when it received Trautmann's view that Japan's actions and policy were probably driving China in the direction of Soviet Russia. So far as Russia was concerned, Chiang Kai-shek now felt himself to be a 'free agent' and as a consequence Sun Fo, Chairman of the Legislative Yuan and member of the Standing Committee of the Central Executive Committee of the Kuomintang, now felt he could agitate openly for an alliance with the Soviet Union.[26]

Nor were the Japanese averse to using the Russian card. Tokio soon began to complain about what it thought was Germany's rather uncertain attitude towards Japan in the present conflict and warned that 'Germany's "support" of China by arms deliveries and the activities of the German military advisers might lead to intervention by Soviet Russia, in which case the Japanese would request a broadening of the Anti-Comintern Pact'. A restatement of the Wilhelmstrasse's position on all these points had therefore to be given to Yanai by von Schmieden on 30 July. Yanai finally admitted that the Japanese authorities were satisfied with the orders issued that the military advisers should take no part in military operations, and agreed with von Schmieden that it was better that the German advisers remain in China since their recall would mean their places being taken by 'nationals of another power whose presence in China would be less agreeable to Japan', an obvious reference to the Soviet Union. Finally, von Schmieden repeated the Wilhelmstrasse's standpoint on the inapplicability of the Anti-Comintern Pact to the Far Eastern conflict. None of this could have been very encouraging for the Japanese, though, while on 31 July von Dirksen also reported further on Japan's disappointment at Germany's attitude since the outbreak of the China Incident; 'more had been hoped for from Germany, at the very least an expression of sympathy or even a word of warning to the Soviet Union'.[27]

While the Wilhelmstrasse acknowledged the frankly propagandistic nature of Japanese claims that their actions in North China were in pursuit of anti-Comintern aims, the threat to demand an extension of the Anti-Comintern Pact should Soviet Russia intervene could not be entirely disregarded in view of Chiang Kai-shek's recent statement to Trautmann. Von Weizsäcker accordingly requested from Trautmann and von Dirksen an assessment of Soviet influence in the Far East at the time. In British, French, and American diplomatic circles the rumour spread that German diplomats at Moscow had warned the Chinese Ambassador there that if the Soviet Union intervened on China's side, then Germany would be compelled to go to Japan's assistance. While Trautmann dismissed as Japanese propaganda reports of increased communist activity in North China, von Dirksen claimed that the Japanese authorities possessed 'allegedly unimpeachable evidence . . . of intensified communist activity in China on the part of the Chinese communists as well as of the Comintern and the Soviet Government'.[28]

Interestingly enough, it was at this time that Chiang hinted to Trautmann that Germany should use her special relationship with Japan through the Anti-Comintern Pact to influence her towards moderation. Trautmann's answer, that although Germany was already working for peace in Tokio she could not use the Pact for this purpose, was approved of by von Weizsäcker. This tendency to regard Germany as perhaps an obvious and even sympathetic channel of communication with Japan seemed to be confirmed a fortnight later when Wang Ching-wei, Chairman of the Central Political Council, wondered whether Germany could not obtain Japan's maximum demands on China and communicate these to the Chinese authorities. Trautmann carefully replied that he had heard nothing from Tokio, and pointed out that Japan would not tolerate any interference from third parties.[29]

Japanese complaints that in spite of the Anti-Comintern Pact Germany had not shown any particular evidence of good feeling or faith towards Japan were complemented by Chinese fears that *because* of the Pact German policy would become increasingly pro-Japanese. The Chinese Minister of Finance, H. H. Kung, on a visit to Germany in August 1937 for a *Kur,* wanted to establish 'where Germany stands politically'. On 10 August, however, Kung appeared dissatisfied with the explanations given about Germany's position by Schacht, von Blomberg, and von Weizsäcker, while he was warned that any intervention by Russia could seriously affect and compli- cate Sino—German relations. On the other hand, Kung could not complain when von Blomberg raised the question of continued arms deliveries to China by suggesting that the best way round the Japanese problem would be to camouflage the deliveries and to use third parties. But both he and Schacht urged the Chinese to consider a political solution to the Far Eastern conflict. Kung had in fact suggested a conference to include Germany, Great Britain, France, and the United States 'to bring the Japanese to reason'. Afterwards, von Blomberg told von Weizsäcker that he agreed with the Foreign Office's approach on the Far Eastern question, but then, significantly, suggested that this policy be confirmed by Hitler since he was 'not entirely certain of the Führer's complete support for the official policy hitherto pursued'. In this way he probably hoped to block the attempts of the pro-Japanese circles for a policy of commitment to Japan.[30]

Two days later Kung spoke with von Blomberg again and set out China's case at length. He explained that any improve- ment of relations with Russia would be based on the neces- sities of China's political and strategical position but that Chiang Kai-shek rather hoped for support from Europe. That this was a clear hint to von Blomberg of what the Chinese required of Germany was virtually confirmed by Kung's statement that China would do all in its power to continue to supply Germany with its requirements of vital raw materials. Von Blomberg explained that the outbreak of the Far Eastern conflict had placed Germany in an extremely difficult posi- tion but that she had to maintain her policy of neutrality. On the other hand, he was prepared 'to intercede with the Führer, *who alone in our State makes foreign policy,* so that the good relations with China will not be disturbed' [my italics]. He therefore assured Kung that the arms trade would continue, so long as Hitler gave him no express orders to the contrary, while there was no question of the recall of the military advisers from China. He also informed Kung of Germany's policy of opposing Japanese pretensions that the current conflict was in any way connected with the Anti-Comintern Pact. From information given to the Foreign Office by Colonel Thomas, it appeared that Göring also approved of continued arms deliveries to China in a camouflaged form. The following day, 13 August, Kung had a final conversation with the State Secretary, von Mackensen, in which familiar ground was again covered.[31]

It was at this point that Hitler made his first pronouncement about Germany's position in the Sino—Japanese conflict. His meeting with von Neurath and von Blomberg at Nuremberg on 16 August undoubtedly arose from the latter's remark to von Weizsäcker six days previously. Although Hitler stated that he adhered in principle to the idea of cooperating with Japan, he emphasised that Germany must remain neutral in the present circumstances. This statement was especially important for von Neurath since it confirmed the policy of the Foreign Office. Of particular interest to von Blomberg, though, was Hitler's assertion that arms deliveries to China already contracted for should continue, so long as China covered these by foreign exchange or raw materials and that they were camouflaged as much as possible, but that further Chinese orders for military equipment should not be accepted.[32] It was Colonel Thomas's view, however, that this last injunction did *not* apply to further contracts and orders under the HAPRO agreements, which were paid for by foreign exchange, but only to transactions, for example, involving steelworks which were arranged on a credit basis with private firms.[33]

Hitler's pronouncements, cautious though they were, showed that for the moment at least the Wilhelmstrasse and the Wehrmacht were maintaining their influence in the formulation of Germany's Far Eastern policy against that of the pro-Japanese elements, especially von Ribbentrop. Apart from Japan's actions confirming Hitler's and von Blomberg's doubts about the wisdom of a military alliance with her, considerations of overriding military and practical importance dictated the maintenance of close military relations with China.

The 1937 annual report of the *Ausfuhrgemeinschaft für Kriegsgerät* (*AGK*) showed that China received approximately 37 per cent of Germany's total exports of arms for that year. During 1936 Chinese orders amounted to 64,581,000 million Reichsmarks, and actual deliveries to 23,748,000 million Reichsmarks; for 1937 the figures were 60,983,000 and 82,788,600 million Reichsmarks respectively. Before 17 August 1937 contracts worth 223 million Reichsmarks had been concluded under the HAPRO agreement and with several German armaments firms, contracts after that date amounting to 59 million Reichsmarks. There can be no doubt that the HAPRO agreements were of fundamental importance in boosting this trade with China, and ensuring that Germany continued to receive much needed supplies of raw materials for rearmament. By comparison, the arms trade with Japan was lightweight, during 1937 orders amounted to 16.8 million Reichsmarks and deliveries to 10.9 million Reichsmarks.[34]

Since the Wilhelmstrasse was especially concerned that nothing should compromise Germany's position of neutrality – Trautmann sharply opposed a suggestion by Knoll in Hsinking that Germany should seriously consider the recognition of Manchukuo in the near future[35] – von Mackensen was understandably annoyed when Alfred Berndt of the Reich Propaganda Ministry took a distinctly pro-Japanese stand on the Sino–Japanese conflict at a press conference on 17 August. This came four days after the opening of hostilities in the Shanghai area on 13 August, when 'China and Japan were now at war, in all but name', and while Trautmann and von Dirksen were playing their part in attempts to limit the fighting in China's commercial capital.[36] The State Secretary impressed upon Walter Funk, Chief of the Press Section and State Secretary in the Propaganda Ministry, that this was contrary to the Führer's decision on Germany's neutrality on 16 August. He hoped that Funk would settle the matter to avoid the necessity of a meeting between von Neurath and Goebbels. Von Mackensen followed this up by requesting the aid of General Keitel, Chief of the *Wehrmachtamt,* in influencing the attitude of the Propaganda Ministry. Keitel said he had in fact given his own press chief instructions which accorded with the view of the Foreign Office. Although Funk admitted that Hitler's recent statement, which had been unknown to him, changed matters it appears that he was unable to alter anything. He told von Mackensen that it was Reich Press Chief Otto Dietrich who had issued instructions that the press should write in a more friendly manner about Japan than had hitherto been the case in some instances. As *The Times* in London put it on 28 August, 'under Party influence some newspapers are obviously straining at the neutrality leash imposed at the outset of the conflict in the interests of Germany's commercial and industrial interests in the Far East, and are seeking every pretext to come down on the side of Japan'. Both von Mackensen and Funk agreed, therefore, that unless von Neurath intervened the new instructions would have to stand.[37] Not surprisingly, the changed tone of the German press led to bitter protests by the Chinese, including one from Kung to Hitler.[38]

If the fighting at Shanghai was a turning point for the development of the military situation in the Far East, a turning point in the political arena came with the conclusion on 21 August 1937 of a non-aggression pact between China and Soviet Russia. The Wilhelmstrasse was particularly concerned for two reasons: it could be expected to lead to increased Japanese pressure on Berlin claiming that their 'anti-Comintern' actions in North China were fully justified and that accordingly Berlin should adopt a policy of 'cooperation' with Tokio; and secondly, increased demands by the pro-Japanese circles in Germany for an orientation of German policy towards Japan. That there were good grounds for such fears was evident from what had happened in 1936 when Japanese suggestions for a pact coincided with the clear threat that Soviet influence might make itself felt in Spain. Whether China would ever lean on Russia for military advisers and supplies in competition with those she obtained from Germany was another worrying question for the Wilhelmstrasse and the Bendlerstrasse. Reports soon came in that Soviet Russia had offered China 400 heavy bombers for use against the Japanese. It seems that the news of the Sino—Soviet agreement prompted the War Ministry to enquire of Hitler whether this new situation affected his decision of 16 August regarding arms deliveries to China. On Friday 27 August Hitler confirmed that his decision of eleven days before still stood.[39]

There were, therefore, domestic political as well as foreign policy reasons for the extreme reserve with which the Wilhelmstrasse received Chinese explanations about their recent actions, and the strength of its reaction was probably attributable to a fear of Hitler's possible reaction to the news. When Friedrich Gaus, Director of the Legal Department, received the Chinese Ambassador he made no secret of the fact that 'serious misgivings' would be felt in Germany at this new development: 'Germany had learned from experience that in the case of such treaties it was not so much a question of the concrete contents as of the political aims and background'.[40] When Kung sent his general appeal of 3 September to Hitler he also emphasised that for China the pact had been a strategic necessity in the war against Japan. Although the pact was to lead to 'a formidable array of Soviet talent in China',[41] the general feeling was that the Soviet Union would refrain from military operations in the Far East because of her relative weakness there and because she feared such an involvement would endanger the European part of her security problem. Nevertheless, thereafter Trautmann tried to dissuade the Chinese from too much reliance upon Russia.[42]

It was at this time that the Wilhelmstrasse began to perceive that of all the Great Powers, Germany might be in a position to play a special role in the Far Eastern conflict. A hint of this was contained in a report from von Dirksen on 23 August. Worried by the scale of the fighting on the mainland, he feared that 'our neutral position must, in my opinion, be expected to become more difficult' because of the risk that the German advisers would be involved in the fighting and the feeling in Japan that German neutrality was being modified in China's favour. He admitted that the withdrawal of the advisers would worsen relations with China, a point confirmed by Trautmann, while in Berlin the War Ministry categorically rejected Oshima's request for their removal.[43] As a compromise, therefore, von Dirksen suggested that the advisers be ordered to exercise the greatest restraint and not participate in any way in the fighting. More significantly, he proposed that Berlin should consider the idea of German mediation, perhaps through the German military advisory staff, should the war continue and reach a position of stalemate. He thought mediation would offer the chance of extricating Germany 'from the difficulties of neutrality', and that suitable pressure should be exerted on Chiang Kai-shek by the advisers if the situation warranted it. Von Dirksen's own pro-Japanese predilections emerged quite strongly when he suggested that it should be China's responsibility to offer such concessions as to make the Japanese think that peace would be worth while. The German advisers were also to be given the unenviable task of warning Chiang Kai-shek against any continuation of the struggle that would bleed China white. In this way, von Dirksen thought that the advisers might pave the way for mediation.[44]

Von Dirksen's suggestion of German mediation was an important proposal, but at a time when the overall situation was still unclear it was premature — although evidence presented at the post-war Tokio trials makes it appear that the suggestion for German mediation at this point originated with Hirota.[45] Instead, the escalation of the fighting in China during August and September 1937 focused attention on reports that von Falkenhausen and other German advisers had been actively involved in directing Chinese military operations against Japanese forces at Shanghai and elsewhere. These reports were denied, although Trautmann admitted that he had had to warn von Falkenhausen about his activities because of a recent trip to the war front.[46] Trautmann raised the matter with Chiang Kai-shek and again with von Falkenhausen, and insisted that no German advisers were to be employed at the front, although he pointed out to the Wilhelmstrasse that 'formally we are covered by the fact that no war had been declared'. While von Dirksen was informed of this, von Neurath was concerned enough to issue instructions that close contact was to be maintained with the War Ministry on this question.[47]

Yet the fact was that much of the planning and direction of the operations of the Chinese Army against the Japanese was the responsibility of von Falkenhausen and other German officers. With a total of seventy-one German military and other advisers in China by September 1937, it would have been surprising if these experts had not been used in their various fields. This seemed to be an open secret, and as one British report put it:

not only is Germany supplying arms and ammunition more abundantly than any other country but her military advisers are virtually running the war. . . As a result of their attitude there is no doubt that Germans have more than regained the confidence in them lost at the time of the signature of the German—Japanese anti-communist pact.

It also alluded to the important political point that one reason for the strength of German military support for Chiang

Kai-shek was to prevent Chinese reliance on Soviet aid. Von Falkenhausen's command of operations on the Shanghai front was also well known in British circles, while it appeared that Chiang Kai-shek appreciated to the full the loyalty shown towards the Chinese Government by the German advisers. Some of the German advisers even expressed interest in the Chinese Navy, much to the concern of the British who suspected that the Germans wished to replace them in this sphere.[48]

The Japanese, meanwhile, remained concerned by the further delivery of German war material to China, especially after what they felt had been the supposedly firm assurances to the contrary given by von Neurath to Mushakoji, to Oshima on 20 August by Admiral Canaris and General Milch, the Deputy Air Minister, and on 24 August by Major-General Udet, Göring's representative, who had also promised that military aircraft would be delivered to Japan so long as this did not interfere with Germany's own rearmament requirements. According to Oshima, Canaris had further informed him on 27 August of von Blomberg's assurances that in the Sino—Japanese conflict the German Armed Forces would grant extensive support to Japan. While this gave the false impression that the Wehrmacht was trying to run with the hare while hunting with the hounds — von Blomberg certainly believed that the Chinese were capable of sustaining a long war, and that the Japanese might have to break off hostilities without achieving any real objective because their resources were limited and dwindling rapidly — Admiral Canaris later denied that he had spoken with Oshima on 20 August, claiming that on that day he had been absent from Berlin. Furthermore, the reference to 'support' on the 27th referred only to the development of the exchange of information about Russia already taking place between the armed forces of Germany and Japan.[49]

Arms deliveries to China was likely to become more than a diplomatic problem, however, with the progressive blockade of the Chinese coast by the Japanese navy after 25 August 1937, despite Japanese protests that 'peaceful commerce carried on by third Powers' would be respected.[50] A British suggestion that Germany should also request elaboration of the Japanese statement of 23 August to the Powers was rejected after a long discussion in the Wilhelmstrasse. The

German argument was that this statement had not been communicated to the German Government while virtually all German shipping was avoiding the Far Eastern danger zone. Emphasis was also placed on the fact that no German ships were delivering German arms to China.[51] To avoid obvious 'embarrassments' over interpretations of Japan's 'assurances' regarding the sea-going traffic of other nations, most of China's arms imports increasingly made their way into the country via Hong Kong. It was estimated that during the first sixteen months of the Sino—Japanese war 60,000 tons of arms each month entered China by this route, with Germany supplying around 60 per cent of China's total arms imports.[52] A specific case during August and September involving the German merchantman *Gneisenau* served to highlight both the degree of irritation which Germany's activities caused in Japan and the possible dangers to German shipping in the Far East at the time.

This ship was suspected of carrying German arms for China while on general passage in Far Eastern waters. Von Dirksen and Behrend, the Consul at Shanghai, urged the Wilhelmstrasse to prevent these and other German arms from falling into the hands of the Chinese. Trautmann equally strongly warned of the deleterious effects on Sino—German relations if the arms did not reach their objective.[53] Von Bismarck's statement of 30 August that the orders issued by the *Norddeutscher Lloyd* for the *Gneisenau* to unload in Hong Kong and not Shanghai would mean that the arms would not get into Chinese hands was, however, sharply disputed by von Dirksen. By that time the ship had been held up by the Japanese authorities at the port of Kobe because several cases marked HAPRO were discovered on board, but von Bismarck insisted to von Dirksen that no further restrictions should be placed upon its movements.[54] Following careful examination of the ship's papers that described the contents of the HAPRO cases as machinery of various kinds, the Japanese let the ship proceed.

Von Dirksen, however, seemed to prefer Japanese statements that the *Gneisenau* was carrying German war supplies for China to contrary ones from the Wilhelmstrasse, and adopted an attitude of annoyance with Berlin accordingly, especially since later it transpired that the ship had been carrying false papers. He felt that this compromised his position with the Japanese, particularly since he had worked to secure the release of the ship on the grounds of the 'innocent' nature of its cargo. He was also perturbed since he guessed that the Japanese assumed that he knew of the Foreign Office's admission to the Japanese Embassy in Berlin that the HAPRO cases on board the *Gneisenau* actually carried war material for China. At least this was the information given to von Dirksen in Tokio, although he appears not to have been given any information of this nature from the Wilhelmstrasse. Above all, von Dirksen expressed his strong opposition to continued German arms deliveries to China, especially since this conflicted with the assurances given to Oshima by Göring. He also wanted a thorough investigation into how the Captain of the *Gneisenau* came to be issued with false papers, implying that the responsibility for this lay somewhere in the Bendlerstrasse.[55]

Von Dirksen was right to doubt his superiors on this question. The Wilhelmstrasse not only knew about this trade but in a sense defended it, especially those orders already contracted and paid for, on the grounds of Germany's need for foreign exchange and raw materials, an argument repeated to the Ministry of Economics on 9 September by the industrialist Otto Wolff.[56] Von Schmieden warned Colonel Thomas of Japanese operations in Europe and Egypt in cooperation with the Italians to spy on the arms trade between Germany and China, and suggested that the Chinese authorities in Berlin responsible for this question, the trade section of the Chinese Embassy,[57] be alerted accordingly. The Foreign Office also argued that it had no responsibility for the transport of German arms in neutral ships, foreign arms in German ships, or even for the export of arms from Germany by private firms, in the absence of laws to the contrary in the formal state of 'no war' that existed in the Far East. None of this satisfied von Dirksen, who continued to press for the strict control, if not the total cessation, of the German arms trade with China.[58]

In these circumstances it was not surprising that the Japanese dubbed the Far Eastern conflict 'the German war'[59] when they had failed to obtain corresponding political advantages from Germany under the Anti-Comintern Pact. What they did not seem to understand was that even by September 1937 Germany's policy of neutrality still meant the maintenance of previous patterns in the relations with

China and Japan. Even the credit agreement for 100 million Reichsmarks that the Otto Wolff concern concluded with the Manchukuoan Government on 4 September could be defended on the grounds of Germany's previous economic relations with Manchukuo. This policy of neutrality was that pursued by the Wilhelmstrasse, approved of by Hitler and reinterpreted by Colonel Thomas. Given the pressures exerted on Germany after 7 July, and because the intensity and scale of the fighting in China indicated a long and terrible struggle, the crucial question confronting the Wilhelmstrasse from September 1937 was: how long could this policy be maintained? Would the pressures from within and without Germany for a one-sided Far Eastern policy in either direction prove too great to deny any longer?

There was no denying the frequency and intensity of these pressures. At the beginning of September H. H. Kung sent an impassioned letter to Hitler outlining China's case and denying Japan's, as well as highlighting the factors making for good Sino—German relations. Again he spoke of the economic opportunities China could offer Germany, but although he did not suggest any pro-Chinese course of action that Germany might follow this was the hope behind his letter.[60] However, Kung could not have been too pleased at Hitler's favourable mention of Japan in connection with the fight against international bolshevism in his Proclamation to the Party at Nuremberg four days later. Hitler also assured Prince Chichibu, the younger brother of Emperor Hirohito, at that time on a visit to Germany, of his adherence to the principles of German—Japanese cooperation in world affairs.[61] According to von Dirksen, the Prince's visit to Europe brought to the fore again the struggle between the pro-German and pro-English groups in Japanese politics.[62]

The Japanese also tried to influence German policy in a pro-Japanese direction by suggesting that Trautmann be withdrawn from Nanking. There was a practical side to Mushakoji's suggestion of 22 September since it was on that day that the Japanese began a massive aerial bombardment of Nanking, which in any case led to German protests in Tokio. A few days later the Foreign Office received an irate telegram from Trautmann, describing how on the 25th Japanese bombers had attacked the railway and Ministry of War 'in the immediate vicinity of my house'.[63] Not unexpectedly, considering the dire consequences that would result for Germany in China should she accede to this Japanese request, von Neurath rejected Mushakoji's proposal, and the further suggestion that Trautmann keep the Japanese informed about conditions in Shanghai. Von Neurath gave equally short shrift to the Ambassador's talk of a joint German—Italian—Japanese agreement. By then, protests were being made in Tokio about Japanese interference with German commercial activities in the Shanghai area.[64]

So long as the mainstream of Far Eastern policy seemed to be in its hands the Wilhelmstrasse managed to cope fairly successfully with such pressures. Yet there were also those within the Wilhelmstrasse and the foreign service who wished to see Germany play a more positive role in the crisis. Von Dirksen's suggestion of German mediation in his report of 23 August was taken up by the Head of Section VIII, von Schmieden, who also felt this might be the means of bringing peace to the Far East 'with the least possible alteration of the status quo'. While von Dirksen was undoubtedly concerned about Japan's value as an anti-Russian ally being diminished the further she became embroiled in the Chinese struggle, von Schmieden was worried about the effects of the war, and especially of the prospects of a Japanese victory, on Germany's general and economic interests in China. In this respect he referred to Oshima's statement that 'we now seek our Königgrätz in China'. Von Schmieden opposed a one-sided declaration for Japan as offering Germany no political or economic advantages, while such a step was bound to react adversely on Sino—German relations, and probably influence China more in the direction of Russia. Besides which, he thought that the situation in Sino—Japanese relations was still so fluid that a choice for Japan was even less necessary at that point. He therefore supported the idea of German mediation on the grounds that the resulting settlement or adjustment of the Far Eastern balance, which would correspond with her political views, would also further Germany's own aims *vis-à-vis* Russia and the communist danger, besides removing the Japanese threat from China and Germany's interests in that area. He also felt that mediation by Germany would enhance her international reputation, especially *vis-à-vis* England. Von Schmieden accepted that one element of a Sino—Japanese agreement would have to be a declaration about the common enemy, communism, but whether he meant that China would have to join the Anti-Comintern Pact is not clear.[65]

On 29 August von Weizsäcker rejected von Schmieden's arguments: he felt that they would gain Germany nothing with Japan, while nothing should be done which risked the loss of Germany's interests in China. By this he really meant two things: a German offer of mediation at that time could only have been interpreted as serving China's interests since the momentum in military affairs was clearly in Japan's favour; while Japan's final conditions might be so severe as to affect Germany's interests in China because of the inevitable fierce reaction which could be expected. Weizsäcker feared that such a German initiative would detract from Germany's position of neutrality while carrying too much of a risk for her vital military-economic interests in China. However, he made the important and valid point that German mediation could only arise when it was suggested by the parties involved and not by Germany, who would only then take the matter up if conditions seemed to offer a chance of success. Weizsäcker, too, was interested in England's reaction to such a German move, but unlike von Schmieden he considered that England and America would be unlikely to remain passive in the face of such a German initiative.[66]

Von Schmieden countered with further arguments, but to no avail. His anti-Japanese tendencies were even more pronounced in his reply of 4 September, and in this respect one section is particularly revealing:

Finally, one could argue further from the necessity of maintaining the solidarity of the white race. In a sense our interests are similar to those of the other Western powers. Our generation does not yet need to abandon completely the notion of white supremacy in the face of the demand of 'Asia for the Asians', while a premature abandonment of our position would react adversely on our economic situation.

He also informed von Weizsäcker that this view was shared by Alfred Rosenberg's *APA*, with which he kept in close contact.[67]

Von Neurath himself stated the Wilhelmstrasse's attitude on German mediation on 12 September. Replying to an enquiry by Trautmann about reports that Hitler had declared himself ready to mediate, the Foreign Minister emphatically denied that mediation was being considered in Berlin. Trautmann's telegram also mentioned the important point that the intervention of third parties would be impossible if peace proposals from Tokio meant only the defeat of China. He felt that the only prospects for peace lay in a revision of Japanese demands upon China or if China suffered an outright military defeat forcing her to sue for peace. Alternatively, 'should the Chinese forces stand firm, mediation would only be possible if, after a certain time, the feeling gained ground in Japan that the game was not worth the candle'.[68] But it was not until the last week of October 1937 that the Foreign Office's conditions about its participation in peace moves in the Far East began to be met. Meanwhile the war continued, with the added risk that both sides would adopt more inflexible attitudes towards conditions for an armistice or peace.

2. October 1937—January 1938

The month of October 1937 was to prove a crucial one for the development of the Far Eastern crisis. Four distinct but closely related and contemporaneous developments were at work at this time: China's appeal to the League of Nations in September and the calling of the Nine-Power Conference at Brussels in November; Japan's willingness to negotiate with China through the intermediary of Germany, thus excluding and preempting anything which came from the Brussels Conference which it twice refused to attend; von Ribbentrop's efforts to establish a closer relationship with Japan and to influence German policy into a more pro-Japanese direction; and the decision by Hitler and von Ribbentrop to persuade Italy to join the Anti-Comintern Pact, superseding Italo—Japanese negotiations for another bilateral pact.

Germany refused to participate in the Far Eastern Advisory Committee set up by the League Council on 16 September following China's appeal to the League of Nations on 12 September, a refusal which the Chinese Ambassador professed as understanding because of Germany's position *vis-à-vis* the League. Not that Cheng Tien-fong appeared to place much faith in the efforts of this committee since he doubted whether Japan was 'ready for an attempt at mediation'.[69] The Wilhelmstrasse was also opposed to participation in the Nine-Power Conference that was to meet at Brussels from 3—24 November. Although the Chinese wanted Germany to attend, despite her non-membership of the treaty, the Foreign Office doubted whether it could achieve anything in view of Japan's expected absence. In any case, it was inclined to consider sympathetically Japanese approaches that Germany should also not attend. Yet when reports were received that Japan was still undecided about participation, the Foreign Office left its options open.[70] The news of Germany's probable non-attendance at the conference was an obvious disappointment to the Chinese and Trautmann,[71] besides which it was expected to lead to public speculation that Germany was supporting Japan in the Far Eastern conflict. Yet Kung was apparently told that Germany's absence from the Brussels Conference would actually help China since if Germany attended she would be obliged to side with Japan in a most public manner.[72] The Chinese were probably grateful enough to Germany for the practical support received and for the fact that she had not yet invoked the Anti-Comintern Pact, despite Japanese radio propaganda in China that the Pact meant that Germany stood beside Japan in her military enterprise.[73]

In the meantime the Wilhelmstrasse's *bête noire,* von Ribbentrop, had been in contact with Hitler about Far Eastern affairs. He and the members of his Büro also maintained close contact with the Japanese Ambassador and Military Attaché, and while a great deal of their activity in this direction remains unknown the inescapable conclusion is that they were working towards such a strengthening of German—Japanese relations as to commit Germany to a pro-Japanese course of action in the Far East.[74] While von Raumer discussed with the Japanese the possibility of strengthening the Anti-Comintern Pact by drawing Rumania and Poland into it,[75] von Ribbentrop was kept up to date on the latest developments by Oshima. The Ambassador to London in turn utilised his various trips to Berlin and relatively easy access to Hitler to present an obviously one-sided view of the Far Eastern situation, complete with charts and maps, representing Japan's chances of a complete military victory over China in the best possible light, an attitude that directly conflicted with the policy and objectives of the Wilhelmstrasse. For his part, Hitler seemed pleased with the progress of the Japanese forces in North China. In a memorandum of 19 September for the Führer, von Ribbentrop supplemented his pro-Japanese reporting by stating that Oshima had 'again mentioned the proposal for an early agreement on a joint economic programme with Japan in China'. This makes it clear that shortly after the outbreak of the Far Eastern war the Japanese were attempting to influence von Ribbentrop with familiar arguments. Unlike the Wilhelmstrasse, which had rejected previous and similar Japanese blandishments as being totally worthless, von Ribbentrop accepted Oshima's promise at face value and immediately contacted Göring who promised to appoint a special representative for negotiations on this question.[76]

Von Dirksen also appeared to accept the validity of Japanese claims about the prospects of such German—Japanese co-operation in the future.[77] Yet in view of the difficulties that were once more making themselves felt in the sphere of 'normal' German—Japanese trade relations, such expectations were rather optimistic to say the least. There was also a certain irony in the situation since it was as a direct result of Japanese actions that Germany began to experience serious losses in her economic relations with North China and Shanghai.[78]

The fact was, as the British Foreign Secretary, Anthony Eden, remarked after a meeting with the German Ambassador in October, von Ribbentrop:

saw Far Eastern affairs solely through the same anti-Communist glass as other international problems. . . . He [von Ribbentrop] added that he had nothing against the Chinese people, but since Japan was the enemy of Russia and Russia was the fount of all evil, it was clearly desirable that Japan should be strengthened against Russia. Herr von Ribbentrop seemed to be quite unaware of the importance of the Chinese market to Germany, still less of the prospects which it offered as one of the few expanding markets.[79]

Later, on 24 January 1939 von Ribbentrop told an audience of Admirals and Generals at Berlin:

It was well known by everybody that from time immemorial China has lain in a deep sleep and was weak, and it was just as clear that in the next few years, which will be decisive ones for Germany's future, this weak China would not be able suddenly to dispose of a strong army against Russia or produce a fleet of Dreadnoughts. There was no choice for Germany other than Japan.

At this meeting von Ribbentrop also argued that Germany's strengthened relationship with Japan would actually improve Germany's economic situation in China, given the establishment of a pro-Japanese régime there, compared to the difficulties which he suggested had hitherto existed in normal Sino—German economic relations.[80]

Hitler and von Ribbentrop also thought it was a question

of strengthening Germany's position against Britain, and while it was still felt to be too early to consider a direct alliance with Japan[81] an alternative which would serve both purposes was under serious consideration. The bilateral Italo—Japanese negotiations were to be superseded by Italy's accession to the Anti-Comintern Pact, a development opposed by the Foreign Office on the very grounds that von Ribbentrop supported the idea: the threat to Anglo—German relations and to Germany's policy of neutrality in the Far Eastern conflict.[82] Given Hitler's recent authorisation for the maintenance of arms deliveries to China, it is clear that von Ribbentrop was not only less aware of the added complications that would be imposed upon Germany's position in the Far Eastern conflict by associating Italy with the German—Japanese ideological bloc, but he probably did not care either. How far Hitler himself thought that this intensification of the two separate strands of Germany's Far Eastern policy could be developed, let alone maintained and for how long, without a fatal clash occurring at some time is hard to tell. Nevertheless, the issue once again underlined the kaleidoscopic nature of the policy-making processes of the Third Reich. In Rome, Ciano criticised the hostile attitudes adopted by von Neurath and von Hassell and remarked that 'they don't want to do something which will disturb London, and then they are afraid of Ribbentrop's personal success'.[83]

By early October the decision was taken, probably by von Ribbentrop and Oshima,[84] and certainly with Hitler's approval, to impress upon the Italians that their negotiations with Japan should be converted into an Italian accession to the Anti-Comintern Pact. According to von Raumer's later testimony, von Ribbentrop told him that 'the Führer wants the accession of Italy to the Anti-Comintern Pact to hit the Brussels Nine-Power Conference like a bomb', and Italy's accession actually occurred three days after that conference opened.[85] It has also been suggested that two other motives for Hitler's action were the obvious failure of Ribbentrop's 'mission' in London and the desire to bind Italy further to Germany's side rather than see her conclude an independent act of foreign policy with Japan.[86]

Significantly enough, Hitler wanted von Ribbentrop to work on this matter with von Neurath, but since the latter opposed this policy von Ribbentrop sent von Raumer post haste to Rome on 18 October to negotiate with Ciano. It appears that on 21 October von Neurath made a last-minute attempt to get this policy reversed by flying to Berchtesgaden for an interview with Hitler, but to no avail. On 22 October von Ribbentrop flew to Rome to reinforce von Raumer's presence there with his own august body and to take charge of the final negotiations.[87]

To von Ribbentrop Italy's accession to the German—Japanese pact was, as he intimated to Ciano on 22 and 23 October, simply a stage on the path to a military alliance between Germany, Italy and Japan 'in anticipation of the inevitable conflict with the western powers'. As he also told Mussolini, 'when negotiations between Germany and Japan began it was said that it was a question of constructing a small wooden bridge so as to be able to build later a great permanent iron bridge between the two nations'. Von Ribbentrop informed Ciano of the existing 'technical liaison' between the German and Japanese General Staffs and that he had suggested to Tokio that the relationship between Germany, Italy and Japan be transformed by a 'political undertaking' on the part of Japan to the other two.[88] This was an indication of the wide-ranging and ambitious plans he entertained in the direction of Japan. China, of course, did not enter into his scheme of things. In addition, von Ribbentrop intended his success in this enterprise to substantiate his claim to be nominated as von Neurath's successor.[89]

The first intimation the Foreign Office had that the scheming of its *bête noire* was also taking other forms came on 19 October when Colonel Thomas telephoned von Mackensen to enquire whether the Foreign Office was aware of Göring's instructions to industry to stop all deliveries of arms to China on Hitler's express orders. Von Mackensen conferred with von Weizsäcker, only to discover that nothing was known about the matter. It was clear that something else was being decided without reference to the Foreign Office and the War Ministry. Thomas said he would raise the matter with Keitel in von Blomberg's absence, while von Mackensen asked him to maintain contact and to take no step without first discussing it with the Wilhelmstrasse since it was a question which was 'also of vital concern' to the Foreign Office.[90]

Later that same day the matter was somewhat clarified. Keitel informed von der Heyden-Rynsch of telephone calls he had received the previous Saturday and Monday from von Raumer and Göring. Through his aide, von Ribbentrop wanted Keitel told of Hitler's decision that in the Far Eastern conflict the Wehrmacht was to avoid doing anything which might 'in any way hinder or obstruct Japanese aims'. On Monday 18 October Göring also informed Keitel that the Führer had decided that 'an unequivocal attitude was to be adopted towards Japan' because they had threatened to withdraw from the Anti-Comintern Pact if 'the support of the Chinese by Germany was continued in its present form', a reference to arms deliveries and the activities of the German advisers in China. On 18 October Göring had also received Oshima at Karinhall and assured him that negotiations with Japan about the purchase of German military aircraft could be finalised. Without doubt this was an attempt to counter Oshima's representations about Germany's continuing arms trade with China.[91]

The background to Hitler's important statement of policy was a week of intense pressure by Mushakoji and Oshima on von Ribbentrop. On 7 October Mushakoji informed Hirota of assurances received from von Ribbentrop, on orders from Hitler, about the 'inactive' role to be adopted by the German advisers in China. Given the fierce internal struggle which proceeded over the whole question of the advisers this is evidence, nevertheless, of the strength of the Army's opposition to any talks of their premature withdrawal.[92] Hitler also wanted it known that 'Germany had the deepest understanding for Japan in the North China conflict'.[93]

Yet Oshima's strong representations to von Ribbentrop on 12 October about the true nature of Germany's position in the Far Eastern conflict seem to have been prompted by the denial, published on Hitler's orders, of Japanese press reports that he would support Japan to the extent of sacrificing Germany's rights in China. Through the Ministry of Propaganda Hitler also wanted the Japanese Embassy informed that on the German side such a report was considered to be inappropriate.[94] Von Ribbentrop immediately laid Oshima's complaints before Hitler at the Obersalzberg, and on 14 October was able to inform the Japanese Military Attaché of Hitler's orders to von Blomberg to limit the role of the advisers in China and that stricter orders would be issued on the arms question. Oshima also informed his superiors that both Hitler and Göring admitted that the Sino—Japanese conflict came within the context of the Anti-Comintern Pact.[95]

On the 18th, therefore, Göring requested Keitel to issue instructions that no further supplies of military materials were to be made to China while he, Göring, had already given similar instructions to HAPRO which that month had come under the auspices of his Office of the Commissioner for the Four Year Plan. Keitel admitted to Heyden-Rynsch that because these orders had come from 'the highest level' he had no alternative but to carry them out. Nevertheless, he thought certain practical difficulties would arise because foreign exchange had already been received from China for a number of orders, which had been distributed to industry and which was working on them. Keitel made it clear that the War Ministry would fight on this issue. Colonel Thomas would collate the necessary data about the arms trade, while Keitel himself would take the matter up with von Blomberg on the 19th. The latter would undoubtedly go to the Obersalzberg to establish whether the new instructions regarding Germany's 'changed' attitude in the Far Eastern conflict were 'really in accordance with the intentions of the Führer'.[96]

Exactly what transpired between the 19th and 20th of October is not clear, although from later developments one can surmise that Keitel saw von Blomberg on the 19th and that the latter used Ribbentrop's absence in London before flying off to Rome as an opportunity to press the War Ministry's case with Hitler. It appears that this case was pressed successfully since Göring not only contacted von Ribbentrop to discuss the matter further but on the 20th instructed Colonel Thomas to continue business with China 'in its present form'. At this von Blomberg decided to set down in writing for Göring's benefit the War Ministry's stand, i.e. the Army offices concerned should continue the business with China in its camouflaged form. Keitel informed Heyden-Rynsch of this and added that China could not utilise a three-million dollar credit she had obtained, although he then referred to a delicate aspect of the question by stating that the German goods were being delivered to a British firm in Singapore on Danish ships, all participants being 'enjoined to the strictest secrecy'.[97] Göring's position in this affair seemed to be that of the proverbial straw in the wind since it later emerged that although

Klein was no longer directly associated with HAPRO, he had been requested by Göring to use his influence in China to ensure the continued cooperation of the Chinese authorities with the HAPRO agreements.[98]

Interesting information about the fierce battle over the control of Far Eastern policy being waged in Berlin was passed at that time to the American Chargé d'Affaires, Prentiss Gilbert, by a leading member of the German—Chinese Society for Economic Cooperation who had just returned from a visit to Berchtesgaden. Gilbert's informant stated that apparently Hitler's policy was 'to remain friendly to Japan but not be against China'. He had not urged a definitely pro-Chinese policy but insisted that Germany should adopt a more strictly neutral position. Hitler's belief that communism existed to a 'menacing' extent in China was probably attributable to von Ribbentrop's efforts with the Führer. Gilbert was then told of the line-up of the pro-Chinese and pro-Japanese factions in the German Government, but that the Party was 'not solid in this matter' because many people did not believe in the communist threat in China while it was thought that Japan's actions would only push China into the waiting arms of Russia. It even seemed that Alfred Rosenberg 'was now convinced that the German pro-Japanese policy was a mistake'. Gilbert's friend also pointed out that Germany's military involvement in China seemed to be on the increase since three additional officers were on their way to China and that one would go in November. He also suspected that German munitions were being moved to China, 'possibly in part by the Richmer line of ships'.[99]

The confusion over Far Eastern policy certainly affected the Foreign Office. On the troubled day of 19 October von Schmieden drafted a reply to Herr Jannings of Siemssen & Co., about the latter's complaints of the difficulties under which the German arms firms were labouring in their trade with China, especially the orders from the Military Economics Branch of the War Ministry as distributed through Rheinmetall. While von Schmieden could offer no help over specifics, he made an extremely significant remark which indicated the extent of the general uncertainty in government circles as to the final direction of Germany's Far Eastern policy: 'the situation in the Far East had become more hazy, especially since the Sino—Soviet détente, *so that in the long run our policy cannot be determined*'. [my italics.] [100]

An obvious cry of exasperation, von Schmieden's remark
nevertheless showed an acute awareness of the frailty of the
policy of neutrality as pursued by the Foreign Office. It was
obvious that the longer the Far Eastern conflict continued
the more it could act as a catalyst for the strengthening of
the position and influence of the pro-Japanese circles in
Germany, especially if the Japanese army was victorious. A
cessation of hostilities would not only serve to further the
cause of international peace but might even strengthen the
policy and position of the German Foreign Office: by restoring some semblance of the *status quo ante bellum* it would
(perhaps) draw the claws of Japanese expansionism and so
take something away from the dramatic image of Japan's
'dynamic' role in world affairs which so attracted the Nazi
leadership.

Although the fighting in the Far East had been accompanied
by tentative steps towards a political compromise in Sino—
Japanese relations and in the relations between the Japanese
military and civilian authorities,[101] it was not until the latter
part of October 1937 that these involved the Wilhelmstrasse.
The most that came to be agreed by the Japanese Government was that the good offices of other governments might
be used to facilitate direct negotiations with China, but that
arbitration, mediation, or conciliation were excluded, all of
which the Japanese regarded as forms of active intervention.[102]
On 1 October the Inner Cabinet of the Konoye Government
approved yet another statement of its desiderata *vis-à-vis* the
Nationalist Government of China,[103] but in view of the
arrangements for the Brussels Conference, which the Japanese
regarded as yet another line-up of the Powers against them,
Army feeling especially was against using the Western Powers
as letter carrier to Chiang Kai-shek. Instead, by 11 October
the Ministry of War had decided that if Germany and Italy
were to offer their services for the purpose of instituting
Sino—Japanese negotiations at the request of China, these
should be accepted 'on account of their relations with us'.[104]
On 21 October this policy was accepted by Foreign Minister
Hirota and formally adopted by the Ministries of Foreign
Affairs, War and Navy the following day.[105] While these steps
also involved getting Ott to visit Shanghai, it has been suggested
that what caused the Army to 'reconsider mediation in a more
favourable light' was the surprising and unexpected extent of

the fighting on the mainland which 'involved the Japanese far beyond their original calculations'.[106]

While these aspects of Japan's policy were also intended to pre-empt the Brussels Conference, Chiang Kai-shek's intention was to obtain as much practical and moral support as he could from the Powers. In September China wanted an outright condemnation of Japan by the League, and hoped that the Brussels Conference would institute a comprehensive boycott of the Japanese Empire. The Chinese probably hoped to achieve more from such international diplomacy than from direct Sino—Japanese negotiations, and certainly during November this viewpoint influenced (perhaps fatally) their attitude to the Japanese proposals they then received.[107]

In this very difficult situation the Wilhelmstrasse recognised the significance of Japan's initiative in involving Germany in the opening of peace negotiations with China. On the day that Hirota approved the War Ministry's suggestion of utilising the good offices of Germany and Italy, 21 October, he received von Dirksen to discuss Japan's expected refusal of the invitation to attend the Brussels Conference. In conclusion Hirota remarked that Japan opposed such conferences and would prefer direct Sino—Japanese negotiations, especially 'if a power friendly to China, such as Germany or Italy, should persuade the Nanking Government to seek a settlement'.[108]

The Wilhelmstrasse immediately seized upon this. On 22 October von Mackensen instructed Trautmann to impress on the Chinese Government that Germany's probable refusal to attend the Brussels Conference would not be based on any dislike for China or special sympathy for Japan but on the 'futility' of such an undertaking if Japan did not participate. More important was the statement that was to be given to the Chinese Government: 'We consider direct negotiations more promising for the present and would, if the occasion arose, be prepared to serve as a channel of communication'. Von Mackensen's clear intention was to make Germany's own moves dependent upon China's reaction, for he then told Trautmann to use his discretion as to the use made of the final section of von Dirksen's telegram of the 21st, a copy of which had been sent direct to Trautmann from Tokio.[109]

The Japanese General Staff seemed to desire a settlement with China so strongly that they also attempted to make

contact with the Chinese through Eugen Ott. At the instigation of General Shun Tada, Vice-Chief of the Japanese General
Staff, Ott was persuaded to visit Shanghai so that an outline
of their terms could be given either to Trautmann, who himself visited Shanghai while Ott was there from 22 to 28 October, or to von Falkenhausen for communication to Chaing
Kai-shek.[110]

The Japanese General Staff also wanted to impress on Ott
the extreme dissatisfaction of the Japanese forces in China at
what they felt was Germany's rather nebulous role in the Far
Eastern conflict because of the nature of Sino—German military relations.[111] It was implied that this bitterness might
disappear if Germany successfully fulfilled her role as mediator
or letter carrier. Von Dirksen agreed that because of their
'special relationship' with the Chinese, the German military
advisory staff were in the best position to impress upon the
Chinese the futility of a long drawn-out war of resistance
against the Japanese, a decidedly pro-Japanese turn of phrase.
Von Dirksen also warned the Wilhelmstrasse of the particular
dangers relating to any act of mediation, but that with China
suspicious of Germany's role because of the Anti-Comintern
Pact and supported as she was by the Soviet Union and the
Western Powers, Germany would be accused of acting as
Japan's tool. To avoid 'falling between two stools' he recommended that Germany should 'in case of doubt march with
the strongest battalions and decide for the Japanese side'. He
argued that Japan had proved to be Germany's staunchest
friend, besides which a policy of friendship on the part of
Germany would lead to Japanese offers of economic advantages for her in the occupied territories of North China.[112]

On the same day that von Dirksen sent this pro-Japanese
missive to the Wilhelmstrasse, Japan formally refused to attend
the Brussels Conference and Hitler made known his decision
that Germany should also not attend. Yet since the Brussels
Conference was held on China's behalf, Germany's absence
was taken to be anti-Chinese and pro-Japanese in intent: 'she
could not satisfy both powers, and her position in relations
to the meeting was an illustration of her dilemma in the Far
East'.[113] Little came of the Brussels conference, and it has
been described as 'worse than a fiasco, it was a disaster'.[114]

In Shanghai, meanwhile, Trautmann and Ott had met. Ott
gave the Ambassador a memorandum from General Homa,

Chief of the Intelligence Division of the Japanese General Staff, while Trautmann also received another from the officer accompanying Ott, Lieutenant-Colonel Manaki, both documents outlining Japan's war aims. Trautmann was surprised since it appeared that the Japanese General Staff no longer seemed to demand the complete overthrow of Chiang Kai-shek or the total separation of North China. He agreed with Ott that although the terms were obscure they constituted a basis for discussion. According to other evidence, it appears that General Homa was probably playing a double game for he was one of those officers 'who challenged the propriety and wisdom of the cautious military and political plans sanctioned by Generals Tada and Ishiwara'.[115]

Peace moves were not the only topics that Trautmann discussed with the Japanese officers. Manaki complained about difficulties over the delivery of German aircraft to Japan and about the military advisers in China. Trautmann in turn emphasised the relatively 'harmless' part they played, and countered by arguing that it was probably better for Japan that the Chinese had German and not Russian advisers. He also, naturally enough, rejected Manaki's suggestion that he maintain some form of contact with the Japanese General Staff through the Japanese Consul at Shanghai to transmit news of any military help that Russia was giving to China. Prompted by representations from German business circles, Trautmann and Ott also raised with the Japanese Embassy and military authorities the question of Japanese interference with German trade, especially in the Shanghai area. Involved in the discussions on this question were the Landesgruppenleiter of the Auslandsorganisation of the NSDAP, Herr Lahrmann and the economic expert of the Landesgruppe, Dr Woidt.

The overriding question remained that of establishing peace negotiations between China and Japan. There can be no doubt of the importance of Trautmann's role in this respect, nor of the enormous difficulties facing him in trying to persuade the Chinese to adopt a more positive attitude towards Japan. One major difficulty seemed to be that the Chinese did not know the conditions under which Japan would be prepared for peace, but when he mentioned this to Shigeru Kawagoe, the Japanese Ambassador to China who was at Shanghai, the latter remarked that the Chinese knew what these were and they could only be modified in a small way. He asked Trautmann to carry a personal message to Chiang Kai-shek about the Japanese position, but explained that even if Japan revised her position *vis-à-vis* China, she would have to take note of Japan's growing strength. Before leaving Shanghai, and in an effort to temper Chinese uncertainty as to the significance of Ott's presence in Shanghai, Trautmann gave a reception at the Park Hotel for Shanghai's Chinese civil, military and business authorities, and for a number of Germans resident in the city.

When he returned to Nanking Trautmann informed the Chinese authorities of his talks in Shanghai. To Chiang Kai-shek, Wang Ching-wei, the Vice-Minister of Foreign Affairs, Chen Chieh, and the Minister of Railways, Trautmann emphasised that what China seemed to require most of all in her struggle was a clear political programme, and that she would do well to take note of Germany's example during the 1914–18 war. This showed that 'under certain conditions it is better to conclude an honourable and not too costly a peace in order to obtain a respite for the restoration of the country than to wait until one is completely exhausted'.[116] By the time Trautmann reported to the Wilhelmstrasse on 29 October that he had carried out von Mackensen's instructions of 22 October,[117] news had been received on the 28th from von Dirksen that the Japanese Vice-Minister of Foreign Affairs had again spoken of Japan welcoming German efforts to influence China in the direction of opening peace negotiations.[118]

Trautmann's report of the 29th of his conversation with Chen Chieh, during which he again criticised China's policy towards Russia and suggested that this ought to be revised, showed that the Chinese wanted to know Japan's conditions before they responded in any way, or even to Trautmann's arguments that 'the first step would have to be taken now for this was the psychological moment for peace . . . nothing would come of the Brussels Conference'. He stated that Germany was prepared to serve as a channel of communication with Japan, and suggested that authorisation be obtained for him to inform the Japanese Government that China was ready for a settlement. From the Wilhelmstrasse he requested more information about the Japanese attitude to present to Chiang Kai-shek.[119]

The Wilhelmstrasse, however, adopted an attitude of reserve at this stage. Although for the sake of Germany's important

interests in China it desired an early end to the Far Eastern
war it realised only too well the danger that mediators lay
themselves open to, the dissatisfaction generally felt by
warring parties at any compromise peace that falls short of
original objectives. Acutely aware of Germany's delicate situation between China and Japan, the Wilhelmstrasse particularly
wished to avoid being used as a tool by the Japanese since
this would inevitably compromise Germany's important position in China, especially if any peace negotiations failed or
resulted in humiliating conditions being presented to China.
It was, of course, recognised that because of the Anti-
Comintern Pact and Germany's interests in China the Japanese
probably expected great things of Germany in respect of
possible mediation with China. Von Mackensen therefore
showed the same reserve towards the Japanese hint of the
28th that he had showed in his instructions to Trautmann on
the 22nd. On 30 October he told von Dirksen to inform the
Japanese that Germany had done everything possible to exert
a friendly influence on China and that a 'more far-reaching and
pointed move' was considered premature. More importantly,
he wanted to establish just how genuine Japanese protestations for peace were, or whether these were being played
only for their propaganda effect. In his opinion the initiative
for peace moves had to come from Japan and not from China.
As it was, in Nanking Kung admitted to a British diplomat
that 'China could not . . . speaking personally, accept such
mediation even by the Germans. It would merely mean that
Germany would act as Japan's "second" '.[120]

Von Mackensen also warned Trautmann not to allow any
impression to be created that Germany's role would go
beyond that of 'letter carrier',[121] Japan's own condition for
a go-between with China.[122] Von Mackensen's reservation
was directed towards Trautmann's report of the 29th, and
the Ambassador admitted that it had been his intention to
give Chiang Kai-shek an outline of the Japanese terms he had
received from Ott in Shanghai but that he would now 'withdraw' to the role of a letter carrier. As to the Japanese proposals, he felt they were obscure but could provide a bridge
for China, but that he would now do nothing further except to
inform Chiang Kai-shek of his conversations with the Japanese
in Shanghai 'which contained nothing very positive'.[123]

Trautmann was received by Chiang Kai-shek and Finance

Minister Kung on 3 November and informed them of Kawagoe's message, that the Marshal knew what Japan's conditions for peace were and which could only marginally be modified. While Chiang Kai-shek emphasised that any solution involving the abandonment of North China was unacceptable, and Kung spoke of a long-drawn out war of resistance that Japan would find too costly in the long run, Trautmann warned against too much optimism and pointed out that in the North Japan wanted her 'pound of flesh'. He also tried to assure Chiang that Italy's imminent accession to the Anti-Comintern Pact had nothing to do with the Far Eastern conflict.[124]

That same day, 3 November 1937, Foreign Minister Hirota gave von Dirksen the Japanese terms for peace. These proposed an autonomous Inner Mongolia; a demilitarised zone in North China, with North China administered by the Nanking Government so long as a pro-Japanese official was appointed; the creation of a larger demilitarised zone in Shanghai; the cessation of anti-Japanese policy on matters arising out of the Nanking negotiations of 1935; a common fight against bolshevism; reduction of customs duties on Japanese goods; and respect for the rights of aliens. Hirota made it quiet clear that if Japan was forced to continue the conflict, she would do so to the point of China's total defeat when she would then exact harsher terms. Von Dirksen felt that Nanking could accept these proposals without loss of face and urged the Wilhelmstrasse to exert pressure on the Chinese Government to accept the terms. He again suggested using the military advisers who, 'by their appraisal of the war situation', could encourage peace negotiations.[125] From Rome, though, it was learned that the Japanese military authorities did not agree with Hirota's policy.[126]

Trautmann, who received a copy of this communication direct from Tokio, was immediately instructed by von Neurath to inform Chiang Kai-shek of the Japanese terms and to state that in Germany's view they appeared to be quite acceptable as the basis for the opening of peace negotiations.[127] This was not the Marshal's view and on 5 November told Trautmann that he could not accept any Japanese terms, a copy of which Trautmann handed over, unless they were prepared to restore the *status quo ante*. No discussion of the individual terms could take place until after this had been done; any other course would result in a revolution in China that would allow the communists to come to power. Nor could he take official cognisance of the Japanese demands because China 'was now the concern of the powers at the Brussels Conference, and they had the intention, for their part, to work for peace on the basis of the Washington Treaty'. It was clear that Chiang Kai-shek was looking to the Nine-Power Treaty Powers for support and expected to gain more from them than from direct negotiations with Japan. Trautmann was well aware of the prevalence of this view in China and of the fact that many important Chinese favoured the idea of Anglo—American mediation in the conflict.[128]

A more definite Chinese response to the Japanese terms did not emerge until the beginning of December 1937, by which time the atmosphere in Berlin, Tokio and the Far East generally had worsened. Italy's accession to the Anti-Comintern Pact on 6 November did nothing to increase Chinese confidence in Germany's role in the Far East, while world opinion did not take kindly to this latest example of cooperation between the three outcast powers of the world,[129] especially since it was recognised that the new arrangement was predicated just as much upon European, i.e. anti-British considerations as anti-Russian ones, if not more so.[130] Trautmann had already warned the Foreign Office against any association with Italy on Far Eastern questions because of her reputation as Japan's ally, and he urged the Foreign Office to use its influence with the German press to limit praise for Japan on the occasion of Italy's accession to the Anti-Comintern Pact. He also wanted it emphasised that the new arrangement had nothing to do with the Sino—Japanese conflict, as he himself had pointed out to Chiang Kai-shek and the Propaganda Minister on 3 and 4 November. The Political Department in the Foreign Office noted its agreement to this suggestion, which was carried out.[131] In mid-November the Chinese Minister of Propaganda, Chen Kung-po, spoke in Rome of China's loss of confidence in Germany and Italy because of their 'pact' relationships with Japan.[132]

There was no doubt that the driving force behind the new development in Germany's relations with Japan and Italy was von Ribbentrop. However, Erich Kordt has suggested that because it coincided with Hirota's approach to von Dirksen of 3 November this public declaration for Japan upset Hitler and put von Ribbentrop temporarily out of favour since it appeared to reduce the value of Germany's 'neutral' role in the Far Eastern conflict, especially so far as world opinion was concerned. Von Ribbentrop was also criticised for not having acquainted the Foreign Office in time with these developments.[133] If so, and one authority had expressed his doubts about this,[134] Hitler was ignoring a multitude of other factors which militated against the success of such a venture undertaken by Germany or any other power for that matter. Yet apparently he genuinely desired peace in the Far East and was quite taken with the idea of German mediation. Not only might this achieve a form of *modus vivendi* between the two protagonists in the Orient, but an important and useful by-product would be an easing of the pressures upon the Führer by the Wilhelmstrasse, the Wehrmacht and the Büro Ribbentrop for a particular emphasis to Germany's Far Eastern policy.[135] Furthermore, should Hitler be the instrument of an 'honourable' peace in the Far East, his international reputation would be enhanced accordingly. According to von Ribbentrop, in conversation with Mussolini (who himself wished to see a German—Italian form of mediation) and Ciano on 6 November in Rome, Hitler's view was that any such mediation would have to be based on two points: China's adherence to the Tripartite Anti-Comintern Pact, and a Japanese undertaking to respect all foreign interests in China.[136] The latter stipulation was of particular significance since it showed that Hitler still placed some importance on the maintenance and integrity of German interests in China,[137] and that an out-and-out declaration of political support for Japan was still not yet his policy. Yet the arguments of those in Germany who wanted such a declaration seemed to be strengthened by the changes which occurred in the Far Eastern military situation following the landings on 5 November of the Japanese Sixteenth Division in Hangchow Bay, south of Shanghai. This led to a Chinese rout by the third week of November, with Nanking in danger by the end of the month.[138]

The Wilhelmstrasse's disappointment at Chiang Kai-shek's negative response of 5 November was all the greater given the worsening military situation. Hirota's immediate response, that China was playing a tactical game because of the Brussels Conference, was probably agreed with in the Foreign Office,[139] although it was still hoped that the Chinese might be persuaded

to adopt a more positive attitude. Von Dirksen again suggested
using the military advisers for this purpose and admitted, in
agreement with Ott, that their withdrawal from China was
neither 'expedient or necessary' at that time since the complaints of the Japanese General Staff appeared to have
subsided for the moment. Again he wanted them to warn
Chiang Kai-shek of 'the consequences for China of prolonged
war', but warned the Foreign Office that failure of the current
peace effort could be expected to lead to an intensification
of Japanese pressure for the withdrawal of the advisers.[140]
There had even been talk that Hitler wanted the advisers
withdrawn from China, and the subject was expected to be
raised at the meeting between the Führer and von Blomberg
(who opposed the idea) scheduled for 4 November. But
neither broached the subject, Hitler merely pointing out that
the Ministry of War should 'rid itself of the reputation of
having a pro-China attitude'.[141]

Trautmann immediately acted upon von Dirksen's suggestion. At his request von Falkenhausen warned Chiang Kai-
shek, Finance Minister Kung, and General Pai Chung-hsi, the
Chief of the Chinese General Staff, of the gravity of the
military situation.[142] But the Chinese could not be moved.
After a further unsuccesful talk with Minister Kung on
9 November, Trautmann reluctantly came to share Hirota's
opinion, and warned the Wilhelmstrasse that China's attitude,
and her hope for intervention by Russia or the Western
Powers, could only mean a continuation of the Far Eastern
war.[143] Von Neurath agreed with this, but also saw that there
could be no peace while the Japanese 'have not yet completely
achieved their military aims'. He also blamed press indiscretions about Germany's possible role as 'peacemaker' on those
Japanese military circles who wished to sabotage negotiations
with Chiang Kai-shek. In the circumstances he felt there was
nothing further Germany could do except 'to wait for a clearing of the atmosphere'.[144]

It was the military situation in China that eventually resolved most of the diplomatic uncertainties. On 19 November
this changed dramatically when Japanese forces captured
Changshu and Soochow before beginning their march towards
Nanking. Before that, and with some apparent stabilisation of
the Chinese front, Trautmann agreed with von Falkenhausen,[145] in thinking that now was perhaps as good a time as

any to exert further pressure on the Chinese to conclude a peace with Japan. But his suggestion that Germany could perhaps cooperate with Britain and America, and that Lord Halifax's visit to Germany that month be utilised for this purpose, was rejected by von Neurath.[146] On the other hand, Trautmann firmly opposed any joint mediation with Italy, reflecting a fairly common anti-Italian viewpoint in the Wilhelmstrasse.[147] But just as the military balance seemed to be swinging most definitely in Japan's favour, von Dirksen received information that both the Japanese Foreign Office and the Ministry of War counted on the assistance of Germany to expedite the opening of peace talks with China. Despite their recent successes the Japanese declared there would be no hardening of their demands, while as before the autonomy of North China would not figure in their conditions. This was immediately transmitted to Trautmann for communication to the Chinese.[148]

While the Foreign Office waited for the Chinese response, another matter had arisen and been settled in Berlin in a manner which encouraged the Wilhelmstrasse to think that its influence on Far Eastern policy was still considerable. Italy suggested to Berlin that both countries should recognise Manchukuo simultaneously, or at least that she should be 'permitted' to act alone. Von Weizsäcker was especially concerned to be told by the Italian Ambassador, Bernardo Attolico, of von Ribbentrop's statement to Rome that Hitler agreed to Germany's recognition without any return favours being demanded.[149] It required none of Trautmann's arguments[150] to persuade the Wilhelmstrasse against such a step. On 22 November von Neurath informed Attolico that Germany considered the move 'inexpedient' since it would indicate an abandonment of her neutrality in the Far Eastern conflict, while more sharply he emphasised a long established Foreign Office viewpoint: 'we were not prepared to make the Japanese a gift without something in return'. He added that the Japanese had been pressing Berlin for a statement of recognition to coincide with the first anniversary of the Anti-Comintern Pact, but that Hitler had declined this.[151] This did not satisfy Attolico who, hard-pressed by Ciano, saw Hitler on the 24th. But Hitler reserved his position and instructed von Neurath to inform Attolico that although Germany was prepared in principle to recognise Manchukuo no date could be set for this. At the same time Japan would have to give definite guarantees about German trade in Manchukuo 'but also in whatever other Chinese areas Japan might occupy', a prescient point indeed. There was, nevertheless, no objection to Italy recognising Manchukuo, which she did on 29 November.[152]

Hitler also explained to the Japanese Ambassador that a formal recognition of Manchukuo was not yet possible, despite his own inclinations, because this would lead to a rupture of trade relations with China and create tremendous difficulties for Germany's raw materials situation. The only hopeful thing he could say was that the matter would be kept under continuous review.[153] Even at that late stage Hitler still recognised the importance of maintaining good relations with China, something which cannot be said of von Ribbentrop.

As it was, Knoll reported from Hsinking that anti-German feeling was gaining ground in the Manchukuoan Government and leading circles of the Kwantung Army because of Germany's non-recognition stand. He warned the Wilhelmstrasse that Germany's economic and political position *vis-à-vis* Manchukuo and Japan could be endangered by such a negative attitude, but von Neurath's reaction was that 'we will not let that scare us'.[154] For the moment, therefore, Germany's Manchukuoan policy remained unchanged. Ciano, however, blamed the baleful influence of von Neurath and the Wilhelmstrasse for this 'wavering' policy. In describing the 'anomalies in the Reich's foreign policy' Ciano spoke of there being 'too many cocks in the hen-house', i.e. the foreign policies of Hitler, Göring, von Neurath and von Ribbentrop, that it was 'difficult to coordinate them all properly', and that the Wilhelmstrasse was 'the most obstinately *ancien régime* organisation'.[155]

The failure of the Brussels Conference to achieve anything positive except 'a platonic declaration of sympathy for China'[156] underlined the fact that the military situation in China would perhaps be the decisive element in the situation. The breakthrough the Wilhelmstrasse was looking for seemed to be heralded by news received on 30 November from Trautmann in Hankow. On 28 and 29 November he had informed Finance Minister Kung and Foreign Minister Wang Chung-hui of what appeared to be the urgent desire of the Japanese for peace talks with China.[157] Although Kung still hoped for Russia's entry into the war, he telephoned Chiang Kai-shek at Nanking three times to persuade him to agree to the opening of negotiations with Japan. Without committing himself, the Marshal asked that Trautmann go immediately to Nanking for discussions with him. Kung also wondered whether the Japanese could be persuaded to halt their progress and warned Trautmann that nobody would understand it if the Marshal undertook negotiations while the Japanese persisted in their advance on Nanking.[158]

This was a valid point since no Chinese Government could be seen to sue for peace under the threat of Japanese military action. But while von Falkenhausen and von Neurath spoke of the military situation dictating the necessity of positive peace moves by China herself,[159] an added inducement prompting the Chinese to reconsider the question of peace with Japan through the mediation of Germany was the lack of any practical help from the Brussels Conference. Moreover, unlike Britain or the United States, Germany was not tainted in Japan's eyes with the 'odour' of Brussels. Even Wang Ching-wei, during a speech at the Whampoa Military Academy on 30 November in which he discounted Soviet aid to China, recommended that China should look more towards Germany and Italy for help.[160]

Accompanied by Counsellor Lautenschlager and Hsu Mo, Vice-Minister of Foreign Affairs, Trautmann left Hankow on 1 December and arrived at Nanking the following morning at 9.00 a.m., to be received by Chiang Kai-shek at about 5.00 p.m. During that day the Marshal held a conference with the leading Generals still in Nanking, the sense of the meeting being in favour of peace.[161] Although it appeared that Chiang Kai-shek and other leaders had no doubt about the unity of the Chinese people in the face of the Japanese threat, nor about the capability of the Chinese economy and armed forces to pursue the war as compared with the position in Japan,[162] the fact had to be faced that China, for all intents and purposes, was facing her old enemy alone. Recent evidence also showed that the Japanese Army in China was far from being a negligible quantity. Furthermore, continuation of the war increased the risk that the Chinese communists would strengthen their position, especially if China should be defeated. Yet any weakness on the part of the government in the face of Japan's demands could also be expected to lead to difficulties for the régime, if not its overthrow. Chiang Kai-shek's position at the beginning of December 1937 was a far from enviable one.

After initial prevarication Chiang Kai-shek finally conceded to Trautmann at their afternoon meeting that the Japanese terms previously communicated to him could serve as a basis for a discussion on peace. He demanded, however, that North China's independence be maintained, that Germany act as mediator in the negotiations, and that China's agreements with third Powers, not be affected, an obvious reference to the Sino—Soviet agreement of 21 August. The extreme delicacy of the situation was underlined for the Wilhelmstrasse by Trautmann's support of Chiang's request for total secrecy. It was feared that premature or untoward disclosures of the terms and fact of the negotiations with Japan would result in the pro-Russian group coming to power in China, while Trautmann had twice warned the Foreign Office that many people in China hoped for Soviet intervention. The Japanese General Staff also worried about this and on 2 December Oshima told Keitel that if Chiang Kai-shek was removed there could be no negotiations with China and chaos would result.[163]

In Nanking, Trautmann correctly represented the Wilhelmstrasse's policy to Chiang Kai-shek when he insisted that Germany could not participate directly in the peace negotiations or even conduct them, but he probably went a little beyond its standpoint when he explained that 'we would rather try to do what we could behind the scenes to help China'. In another effort to persuade Chiang Kai-shek to adopt a positive attitude towards Japan's terms, he remarked that he did not think that the condition that China should join the fight against communism was incompatible with the Sino—Soviet Non-Aggression Treaty. Rather cryptically, Trautmann pointed out to the Wilhelmstrasse, 'Chiang Kai-shek did not contradict me'.[164]

The domestic political situation regarding peace was just as complex in Japan. The Japanese General Staff wanted to conclude peace with China at that time because of the favourable military situation and to avoid being dragged into a costly campaign of unknown duration, but this was opposed by those groups who wished to eliminate Chiang Kai-shek completely. The General Staff therefore looked to Germany, and in particular to Hitler, for a way out of their own dilemma in a situation of total dilemma for all participants.[165] According to Oshima's post-war testimony, at the end of December 1937 he was instructed by the Japanese General Staff to request the German Army to offer peace to Chiang Kai-shek through von Falkenhausen. Apparently Keitel agreed and initiated some action but 'this attempt at peace did not materialise and had to be abandoned when the efforts of mediation by Ambassador Trautmann were terminated'.[166] In fact, it was on 3 December 1937 when Keitel suggested to von Mackensen that von Falkenhausen could be asked for his opinion of China's military situation, with a view to an ultimate settlement of the Sino—Japanese conflict. As opposed to Oshima's later testimony, Keitel explained to von Mackensen that since he no longer had any contact with the advisory staff his request would have to go through the Foreign Office and Trautmann to von Falkenhausen. The State Secretary told him of Trautmann's meeting with Chiang Kai-shek but that the Ambassador's report would determine whether reports from von Falkenhausen were necessary. Mackensen subsequently passed Trautmann's report to Keitel for information,[167] a significant step of communication between two Ministries in the suspicion-ridden atmosphere that was Nazi Germany.

At this point the Wilhelmstrasse wished to establish, formally and in writing, progress so far with Germany acting only as the transmission agent and not as mediator. Chiang's statements of 2 December were therefore incorporated in a document which von Dirksen was instructed to hand to the Japanese Government, the latter to be asked whether they agreed to begin negotiations on this basis. Once an affirmative answer was received, Trautmann would ask the Chinese Government the same question on the basis of the same document. Hopefully, Hitler would then be able to issue an appeal for a cease-fire and the commencement of peace negotiations.[168] To make the position even clearer von Dirksen was instructed to make appropriate use of the Chinese synopsis of the Trautmann—Chiang Kai-shek conversation, especially the point that the terms communicated by Trautmann to the Chinese were not to be considered 'as unalterable demands in the form of an ultimatum'. Another and extremely important point was that the Chinese could not consider peace negotiations unless hostilities had ceased, a point that was bound to raise difficulties with the Japanese.[169]

However, all hopes were to be disappointed when von Dirksen reported Hirota's negative response to the German memorandum on the current state of the peace talks,[170] while Trautmann had warned that any extension of Japanese aims in North China should immediately result in an end to Germany's peace activity: 'otherwise even we will be tainted with Japan's double-dealing'.[171] Yet it was on the basis of Japan's recent military successes in China and the pressures exerted by the Field Army that Hirota justified a significant change in Japan's position by casting doubt on the possibility of negotiations on the basis of the previous month's terms. He maintained that these had only been main points which required further definition. Even von Dirksen appeared sympathetic to this approach: 'a certain broadening of the main point of the Japanese [terms] is unavoidable, considering the extraordinary military successes and the serious Chinese collapse of the last few days'.[172]

While von Neurath accepted the logic of this point, he insisted to von Dirksen that Germany could not be expected to transmit humiliating or unacceptable demands to China, nor any which the Japanese would feel free to broaden in scope at some later date. Despite von Neurath's admonition that this instruction was to be taken as a guide for von Dirksen's language should Hirota give him a set of broader terms and was not to indicate any German intention to influence Japanese thinking, this was the Foreign Minister's undoubted intention although he probably realised that no outsider would be able to exert any such influence on Japanese policy.[173]

This point was especially pertinent at a time when Japanese advances made it clear that the fall of Nanking was imminent. Hirota's attitude on 7 December simply reflected the tremendous conflict between the army leaders, the Japanese General Staff, and the Japanese Cabinet about the policy to be adopted towards China and the Government of Chiang Kai-shek. While General Tada, the Vice-Chief and real head of the General Staff, thought that Japan should concede generous terms to her beaten foe and thus effect a reconciliation to leave Japan free to face her real enemy, the Soviet Union, Konoye and Hirota thought of imposing harsher terms once Nanking had fallen as a means of blocking more extremist demands for the complete overthrow of the Kuomintang régime. An added factor in the calculations of the extremists in Tokio seemed to be the suspicion that the Chinese Government had agreed to 'mediation' by Germany to stimulate the rivalry between the Fascists and democratic Powers in order to secure positive intervention on China's side by the latter group. The real conflict in Japan therefore, was not so much between the advocates of moderate or severe peace terms, but between those who still wished to offer terms of some kind and those who wished to see the complete collapse of Chiang Kai-shek and the establishment in China proper of various Japanese-orientated administrations.[174]

While Trautmann seemed to be aware of the fierce struggle in Tokio and had little doubt that the extremist viewpoint would finally prevail,[175] the stark choice facing China in this event was made clear by General Chang Chun, the former Foreign Minister, in a speech at the Cosmopolitan Club in Hankow on 9 December. He was adamant, though, that if China could not obtain an honourable peace and maintain her territorial and administrative integrity, this would mean a fight 'to the bitter end'. A British report of the same day spoke of Chiang Kai-shek having finally refused 'point blank' to consider the Japanese terms which Trautmann had discussed with him on 2 December. The Mayor of Hankow thought this step was taken 'after the receipt by Chiang Kai-shek of a wire from his military agent in Moscow giving optimistic reports regarding the possibility of direct Soviet intervention in the near future'. According to General Wu Te-chen, Chairman of the Kwantung Provincial Government, member of the Central Executive Committee of the Kuomintang and of the Central Political Council, Chiang Kai-shek refused the terms presented to him because there had been no confirmation from Japanese quarters and because of imprecise expressions such as 'economic cooperation in North China' or 'joining the Anti-Comintern Pact'. Of particular interest was Wu Te-chen's third reason for Chiang's action: that Chiang Kai-shek had 'distrusted German motives'.[176]

The turning point finally came on the night of 12—13 December 1937 when Japanese troops entered Nanking and began the 'rape' of the city.[177] On the 14 December the Japanese-influenced 'Provisional Government of the Chinese Republic' was inaugurated at Peking, a step which led the Chinese

Ambassador at Berlin to seek assurances from the Foreign Office that Germany would not recognise this 'fraudulent government'. Von Mackensen promised to forward the Chinese memorandum on the subject to von Neurath, but limited himself to remarking that Germany had not recognised Manchukuo.[178]

A compromise between China and Japan now seemed unlikely, but on 13 December Trautmann warned the Wilhelmstrasse that should further terms from Japan prove to be unacceptable the war would continue, while if arms supplies still came through Hong Kong the Chinese could pursue the war until well into the summer of 1938. Von Weizsäcker tried to temper this optimism by instructing Trautmann to inform the Chinese Government and military advisers that Japanese military operations in the direction of the Kowloon—Canton railway or even Canton would mean the virtual end of supplies of war material to China.[179] Nor could the Wilhelmstrasse be entirely happy with the many indications received that China was thinking of turning towards Russia in her hour of need. Trautmann soon received instructions to point out to the Chinese Government that any further rapprochement in Sino—Soviet relations might force Germany to re-examine the nature of Sino—German relations.[180]

Nevertheless, the Foreign Office was left in no doubt as to the temper of Chinese feeling since General Chang Chun emphasised to Trautmann that after the fall of Nanking no Chinese Government could accept humiliating terms from the Japanese and survive, while on 16 December Chiang Kai-shek issued a manifesto calling on the Chinese nation to continue its resistance to Japan.[181] Trautmann was also worried since certain sections of the Chinese press seemed to be adopting a hyper-critical attitude towards Germany because of her relationship with Japan. As he commented to the Wilhelmstrasse, 'we have slid so close to the danger of being considered as Japan's tool'.[182]

From Tokio, however, von Dirksen foresaw a sharpening of the terms to be presented to China, a point that Trautmann did not fail to emphasise to Chiang Kai-shek when informing him of von Neurath's recent instructions to Tokio. While it appeared that the Japanese General Staff opposed an extension of the peace terms, they were under pressure by the victorious armies in the field. The Cabinet also seemed to be influenced towards a hard line by the extreme nationalist views of Admiral Suetsugu, Minister of the Interior.[183] These divisions about the form and nature of Japan's China policy were fully revealed at the Cabinet meeting of 17 December and the Liaison Committee on the 20th.[184] Marquis Kido, the Minister of Education, had the gravest doubts about approaching China through Germany: 'What need is there to obligate ourselves by asking Germany?'. He was also extremely suspicious of the contacts between the Japanese General Staff and Ott, wondering if the former had not made 'various commitments in concrete terms through the German Military Attaché in Tokio'.[185]

Von Dirksen's forecast proved to be correct. On 22 December 1937 Hirota revealed to him Japan's new terms, and his opening remarks served only to prepare the German Ambassador for the worst. Hirota stated that Japan's stand now took into account the 'recent rapid developments in hostilities and the great change in the general situation', and that if China 'should not be able to accept these terms, Japan — though reluctantly — would be forced to treat the present situation from an entirely different point of view from that maintained hitherto'. The new terms covered the abandonment of China's pro-communist, anti-Japanese and anti-Manchukuoan policies; full cooperation with Japan and Manchukuo in an anti-communist direction; demilitarised zones and régimes to be established where necessary; close economic cooperation between China, Japan and Manchukuo; and that China should pay Japan the required indemnity. Just as ominous were Hirota's additional remarks. He explained that Japan did *not* want Germany to recommend the cessation of hostilities once Chiang Kai-shek had accepted the Japanese terms and wished to negotiate — military operations would continue during the peace negotiations and would only cease once peace had been concluded. He also elaborated on Japan's basic conditions, but emphasised that his comments were not to be communicated to the Chinese. Point one implied the recognition of Manchukuo, and although the termination of the Sino—Soviet agreement and China's accession to the Anti-Comintern Pact were not being demanded it would be desirable if these could be effected. As for point two, apart from the demilitarised zones in the North one was now contemplated in the Yangtze Valley. Although a 'special régime' was contemplated only for Mongolia, it was expected that the government of North China would have extensive powers and not be dependent upon the Central Government, although it would be under Chinese Sovereignty. The third stipulation involved a general tariff and trade agreement. Beyond all this, however, Hirota explained that Japan expected China's answer by the end of the year.

While Hirota tried to defend these terms as being a compromise in the face of severe demands presented by elements in the Army and government, von Dirksen considered acceptance by the Chinese Government as 'extremely improbable'. He warned the Wilhelmstrasse however, of a strong feeling in the Japanese Cabinet and Army that the terms were too mild and that it was hoped that China would reject them 'in order to make it possible to carry through the war of annihilation against Chiang Kai-shek'.[186]

Although forewarned by von Dirksen, the Foreign Office was still taken aback by Japan's new conditions. Serious doubts were now entertained about the advisability of transmitting to China what now appeared to be a Japanese ultimatum.[187] While it was admitted that they deviated considerably from the terms previously received from Tokio, von Neurath decided that Germany should still maintain her role as letter carrier and immediately transmit them to China. Trautmann was told, in the strictest confidence, of Hirota's supplementary remarks to von Dirksen, as well as of von Dirksen's information regarding attitudes in the Japanese Government but that these comments were not to be passed to the Chinese. Germany would still act as letter carrier but would pass no comment on the latest terms. As to the time-limit imposed by the Japanese, von Dirksen was being instructed to draw the attention of the Japanese Government to the time-lag involved in communicating with China through Berlin.[188]

Since Chiang Kai-shek was ill Trautmann informed Madame Chiang Kai-shek and Finance Minister Kung of Japan's new proposals at 7.00 p.m., on 26 December.[189] Their shock and consternation were reinforced the following day when Trautmann had to inform Kung of Hirota's refusal to accede to von Dirksen's representation for an extension of the time period set out for the acceptance of the Japanese terms, or for a cease-fire while negotiations were in progress. Hirota suspected that the

Chinese were set only on gaining time, but conceded that if bilateral negotiations began and proceeded satisfactorily army leaders of both sides could discuss an end to the fighting. Trautmann also told the Minister of Railways of Hirota's response, but declined to offer any advice as to whether China should accept Japan's conditions. Instead, he pointed out to the Minister that 'there are two sides even to an armistice, as was shown by the armistice which we were forced to conclude in 1918'.[190] In fact, it was China's current economic and political position, and the consequences of a refusal to accept the conditions, that persuaded Lautenschlarger, Counsellor at the Embassy, that it was in China's best interests to accept the terms now presented. His only reservation was that such an acceptance should be based on the ability of the Chinese Government to overcome with force any internal opposition to such a peace.[191]

The Chinese leaders immediately discussed the Japanese demands but quickly came to the conclusion, as Chang Chiangao informed Trautmann by telephone, that they meant not only the recognition of Manchukuo but the rest of China being treated like a second Manchukuo, so that China's political, economic, and financial independence would disappear. Trautmann thought this interpretation too pessimistic but understandable in view of Japan's previous policies. Nevertheless, he suggested to the Wilhelmstrasse that it would help if the Chinese were informed of Hirota's supplementary remarks to von Dirksen, especially those relating to North China.[192]

Trautmann sent a copy of this telegram direct to von Dirksen late on 28 December. By the 29th the latter had also been instructed by von Mackensen to warn the Japanese Government of recent indications that China was seeking the support of the Soviet Union. Although Germany had warned China against this, the Japanese Government ought to be quite clear of the consequences of a prolongation of the conflict: the Bolshevisation of China which the Wilhelmstrasse considered to be inconsistent with the purposes of the Anti-Comintern Pact. Instead, the Foreign Office's view was that 'the common interest of Germany and Japan directed against the Comintern requires that normal conditions in China be restored as soon as possible, even if this could be done only by peace terms which did not meet all the Japanese aspirations.

The lessons derived from the history of the Treaty of Versailles should be pondered by Japan'.[193] These comments, indicative of a deep concern for the state of impasse, gave the lie, at an appropriately critical time, to the Wilhelmstrasse's oft-repeated statement that its role was limited to that of letter-carrier.

Since the Military and Naval Attachés meanwhile had established from their conversations with the General Staff and leading Admiralty officers that the central military authorities in Tokio strongly desired the initiation of peace negotiations with China, von Dirksen was in a good position to impress on Hirota on the 30th the necessity for moderation on Japan's part, especially allowing China some knowledge of the further details of Japan's conditions and a consideration of at least a partial cessation of hostilities after the beginning of negotiations. Hirota went so far as to agree that his confidential supplementary remarks of 22 December could be given to Chiang Kai-shek, not as a statement of Japanese policy but only as von Dirksen's personal impressions of his talks in Tokio. Hirota also elaborated further on his previous supplementary points, but failed to say anything about Japan's time-limit for China's acceptance of the terms presented to her. It was obvious, therefore, that this particular condition had been quietly dropped, despite Hirota's adamant stand on 26 December.[194]

Small enough, this gain appeared to confirm the impression of a slightly more relaxed attitude on the part of the Japanese in the previous 48 hours. On the 28th news had been received that the Japanese General Staff was willing to stop hostilities once negotiations had begun and if the Chinese gave a guarantee to fulfil the peace terms.[195] On the 30th as well Ott was told that the General Staff were thinking that this 'guarantee' could take the form of a control commission to prevent China's rearmament, and it was hoped that this would obviate the necessity of continuing hostilities after direct negotiations had begun.[196] On 29 and 31 December Trautmann was therefore instructed to inform the Chinese of von Dirksen's personal 'impressions' of the broader picture of Japan's position which had emerged from his talks with Hirota and Ott's with the General Staff.[197] It was hoped that this would persuade the Chinese to formulate an early and positive reply to Japan, but the feeling in the Embassy at Hankow was against 'pressing' the Chinese to avoid an over-hasty refusal on their part.[198]

While General Tada seemed to be fighting a rearguard action in Tokio for a definite and positive approach to a negotiated peace with Chiang Kai-shek,[199] the onus of responsibility for the cessation of hostilities now appeared to rest squarely on the Marshal's shoulders. But the immediate signs from China were hardly encouraging. Von Mackensen's instructions to Trautmann of the 31st crossed a Trautmann telegram giving China's negative response to the attitude of the Japanese General Staff as reported on the 28th. The Chinese Vice-Minister of Foreign Affairs seemed so upset at the suggestion that China should guarantee to fulfil the peace terms that he complained that neither Germany nor Italy had exercised a moderating influence on Japan. Prime Minister Kung's response was more pointed: Japan's terms were a 'blank cheque with which Japan could do what it liked. Japan will drive China to despair and towards bolshevism'.[200]

By 1 January 1938 Trautmann informed Foreign Minister Wang Chung-hui of von Dirksen's 'impressions', and when communicating them to Kung the following day attempted to draw him on the possibility of an answer to Japan, besides warning him of Germany's concern for aspects of Sino—Soviet relations. While Kung wanted Hitler to press the Japanese to moderate their stand, Trautmann felt that the Japanese demands would not be rejected out of hand. Yet Kung's protestations that the Japanese were mistaken in thinking that China's military power was broken and his information that two of the country's leading Generals, Yen Hsi-shan and Pai Chung-hsi, were involved in the government's latest discussions did nothing to convince either Trautmann or the Wilhelmstrasse that the Chinese would be open to much persuasion. As it was, on 3 January the Chinese Vice-Minister of Foreign Affairs informed a British diplomat that 'it had not yet been decided whether a blanket refusal should be returned or further details of Japanese peace terms [be] called for'. It was little wonder that by this time Trautmann was feeling 'depressed'.[201]

The pressures were now all on China to respond positively to Japan. Although the Japanese General Staff professed themselves ready to answer questions about Japan's basic conditions,[202] Hirota pressed von Dirksen strongly for a quick answer from China, especially since new military operations were planned. He also appeared upset by reports that Chiang

Kai-shek was approaching Britain and the United States for help.[203] On 5 January 1938 von Dirksen urged the Wilhelm-strasse to obtain an immediate reply from China, even if this only took the form of a further enquiry about Japan's terms as a means of maintaining contact. His basic attitude, however, was that of Japan's advocate. He was far more impressed by Japan's military resources than by von Falkenhausen's optimistic views of China's chances in a long-drawn out war.[204] Again, he suggested involving the military advisers in the peace negotiations, which would help confirm their position in China after the conclusion of peace, a possibility mentioned by military circles in Tokio. But more to the point, he wanted them to impress upon the Chinese leaders a more 'realistic' view of the situation, even though he had been told by the Japanese General Staff that it would not demand any kind of Chinese disarmament in spite of strong pressure to the contrary. It refused to follow the Treaty of Versailles in this sense. But Ott had also been given to understand that the General Staff could not for long withstand the intense pressure being exerted for a rupture of both negotiations and relations with Chiang Kai-shek.[205]

This information was immediately passed to Trautmann for the Chinese and von Falkenhausen, with von Mackensen adding the weight of his authority behind the request for an early reply or even further enquiry. It was also hoped that Hirota's agreement to direct contacts between the German Embassies at Hankow and Tokio without having to wait for instructions from Berlin would help to overcome any last-minute difficulties.[206] At almost the same time, though, information was received that the Japanese had now imposed a time-limit of 10 January, although this was not to be considered an ultimatum.[207]

Although Trautmann received this news direct from Tokio,[208] there was surprisingly little evidence of a sense of urgency in Hankow. When informing Foreign Minister Wang Chung-hui at 5.00 p.m., on the 7th of von Mackensen's instructions of the 5th, Trautmann simply remarked that the suggestion of a further enquiry 'would make it easier for the Chinese Government to give an answer, if they wished to do so'. There was no hint of urgency in this, nor in Trautmann's further comment to the Wilhelmstrasse that he had refrained from pressing for a speedy reply from the Chinese side. Not that one seemed to be in the offing since Wang Chung-hui told him that there had not yet been a formal meeting of the Chinese Cabinet, only an informal exchange of views having taken place. Even three days later Trautmann reported that as of the 9th the Chinese were still studying the Japanese terms, although von Falkenhausen had again emphasised to them it was better to conclude an 'acceptable peace' than to fight an extensive war.[209]

Trautmann's reluctance to press the Chinese at this point was undoubtedly due to his feeling that, morally at least, it was the Japanese who were completely in the wrong and who ought to be subjected to intense pressure to modify their terms. Yet he was spurred to action when he received a copy of von Dirksen's telegram number 13 of 10 January to Berlin and numbered 10 direct to Hankow, stating that Hirota was pressing hard for a definite reply from China, although he too affirmed that the time-limit of 10 January was no ultimatum. But what especially concerned Trautmann was Hirota's confirmation of semi-official press reports that a continuation of the war and the rupture of negotiations with China were measures envisaged by the Government in the case of a negative reply from China. Hirota's explanations that it was the militarists who were insisting upon an immediate and clear-cut reply led von Dirksen to conclude that 'the pressure of the Nationalist wing has increased to such an extent that the moderate wing will give in, if a positive answer of the Chinese Government does not arrive soon'.[210] Trautmann was so taken aback by this important new shift in Japan's position that he wanted official instructions from the Wilhelmstrasse before communicating this information to the Chinese. He feared they would regard it as a 'dirty trick' which the Japanese had played on the Germans as well, who would then lose face with the Chinese. These instructions were quickly given.[211]

From now on matters proceeded quickly to a final dénouement. While the new Japanese Ambassador to Berlin, Shigenori Togo, informed von Neurath of the hardening of Japan's position,[212] in Tokio the fierce struggle over the final formulation of Japan's China policy continued unrelentlessly. A third session of the Liaison Conference met on 10 January for the specific purpose of deciding the basic question, peace or war. General Tada, though, hoped to delay things further by using his influence in getting an Imperial Conference convened for the following day. At 1.40 p.m., on the 11th von Dirksen warned the Wilhelmstrasse in telegram number 14 that the Imperial Conference was expected to decide that if China declined to accept the Japanese terms war would be declared and military operations extended, while the Central Government would be denied and the Peking régime recognised instead.[213]

The Imperial Conference, presided over by Emperor Hirohito, began at 2.00 p.m., on 11 January and finished fifty-five minutes later with Hirohito silent throughout. While the Conference approved the Cabinet's policy aims agreed that morning, an extensive programme of nine conditions that China had to accept, Hirota conceded China another seventy-two hours in which to request a settlement of the incident. Failing this the Chinese Central Government would be annihilated and a 'new China' be rejuvenated by the promotion of new governments on the mainland.[214] Apart from Hirota's concession of an extension of the time-limit this extensive list of conditions was never officially communicated to the Chinese Government, so that as far as they were concerned they still had to decide whether to accept 'final' negotiations on the basis of the first and second sets of Japanese terms presented in November and December. By now the Japanese position had shifted so much that it was probably realised that if China was suddenly presented with this latest set of conditions there could be no hope of even a façade of negotiations. The Japanese Government probably hoped to get the Nationalist Government to begin negotiations on the basis of the now superseded terms and then suddenly spring the up-to-date conditions on them, terms which would have meant the virtual occupation of China and an end to her independence. Either way, the intention was to burden China with the responsibility for any break in negotiations, a ploy the Nazi leadership was to use so well against Poland in 1939.

In the meantime the Chinese Government was only too aware that the pressures from Tokio were reaching unacceptable levels of intensity. At 10.30 on the morning of 12 January Trautmann informed Foreign Minister Wang Chung-hui of von Dirksen's telegrams from Tokio of 10 January (number 13 to Berlin, number 10 to Hankow) and of the 11th (number 14 to Berlin) which clearly indicated that Japan was moving rapidly along the path to an all-out war with China. It was quite clear that the situation was reaching crisis point, and Trautmann emphasised to Wang that the Chinese 'had to act immediately if the Chinese Government still intended to send an answer. It was five minutes to twelve, if it was not already too late'. In reply he was told that a Cabinet meeting would be immediately convened to discuss the matter. Later the same day Trautmann and von Falkenhausen impressed on General Chang-chun, Vice-President of the Executive Yuan, the necessity for a positive and speedy answer to Japan.[215]

On 12 January von Mackensen tried to set the record straight so far as Germany's position was concerned by explaining to Trautmann that although it was recognised that the Japanese appeared to be shifting their position, Germany's role as letter-carrier imposed on her the obligation to transmit the information contained in von Dirksen's telegram 13 of the 10th. It was the Wilhelmstrasse's view, however, that while the Japanese Foreign Office was maintaining its previous standpoint, it was the Japanese military authorities who were shifting theirs. More to the point was his comment that while he hoped that Trautmann had, as usual, avoided making any official or personal interpretation of the news from Tokio, he had however 'spoken in such a manner that there can be no suspicion against us as if we had made ourselves a tool of an unclear or unclean Japanese trick'. Von Neurath was also concerned at Japan's tactics, and on 13 January he informed Sir Nevile Henderson, the British Ambassador, that he was perturbed lest Japan 'might be constrained to settle affairs with Northern China separately, leaving Chiang Kai-shek to carry on guerrilla warfare indefinitely, thus leaving China in [a] state of perpetual turmoil'.[216]

Later in the evening of the 12th Trautmann received more disturbing news from von Dirksen in Tokio telegram 13 (number 16 to Berlin). This contained the information that if Japan had not received an answer by 15 January, 'the Japanese Government would have to reserve the right to freedom of action', a phrase that needed no elucidation. It was made quite clear that China's response had to be a positive one, even if this took the form of specific enquiries concerning individual points, but that a reply 'to the effect that they were still considering the matter would not suffice'.[217] Trautmann was not able to inform the Foreign Minister and his

General Staff Headquarters has already informed China through the German Military Attaché.[224] At any rate China is generally well aware of our concrete proposals. In spite of this, however, she feigns ignorance and is saying, "that cannot be understood" '. He argued that 'there is no alternative but to proceed with our alternative plan. This is to transfer the present hostilities into a long-term warfare'. General Tada's last-minute efforts to obtain sanction for immediate and direct negotiations of his own with Chiang Kai-shek at least forced a two-hour recess, but to no avail. The Liaison Conference of the 14th and the Cabinet meeting of the 15th therefore agreed to cease negotiations with China and to annihilate the Chiang Kai-shek Government, and to formulate Japan's position in a statement that was to be handed to von Dirksen at 10.30 on the morning of 16 January and published later the same day.[225]

Sometime during the afternoon or evening of the 15th von Dirksen managed to learn the main points of the Government's decision through Ott's contacts with the Japanese General Staff. The Germans were told that even at this late stage the execution of the Cabinet's decision could be avoided if, before the statement was actually handed over to von Dirksen, an unconditional acceptance of Japan's 'terms' was received from China.[226] In view of the stage that Japanese policy had then reached this really meant that China should signify her willingness to negotiate 'blind' as it were. As it happened, Prime Minister Kung asked Trautmann on 15 January to communicate a further message to Tokio. A plea for 'understanding' and peace between China and Japan, Kung's message again spoke of China's wishes to be informed of the nature and content of the basic conditions proposed by Japan 'because we want to use every sincere effort to seek the sign of restoring peace between the two countries'. Kung suggested that 'with this additional information . . . we shall be in a better position to express our views concerning the terms offered by Japan.'[227]

Although Trautmann had pointed out to the Chinese that to insist on great precision in the Japanese terms might render continuation of the discussions more difficult, he transmitted Kung's statement from Hankow at 3.50 p.m., on 15 January, although it appears not to have reached Tokio until late in the morning of the 16th.[228] Similarly, it was not until

11.00 a.m. on the 16th that von Dirksen transmitted the important news obtained the previous evening about the Japanese Cabinet's probable decision, his communication arriving in Hankow during the afternoon of the same day. Either way, it is doubtful whether the course of events and decisions arrived at in Hankow and Tokio would have been changed or influenced had these communications been sent hours earlier. At 10.30 on the morning of 16 January 1938, while Kung's message was being decoded in the German Embassy at Tokio,[229] Hirota gave von Dirksen the decision of the Japanese Government. This was that the Chinese reply dated 13 January and received on the 14th led the Japanese to conclude 'that the attitude of procrastination on the part of the Chinese Government reveals no intention to sue for peace by accepting in their entirety the basic conditions for peace negotiations, which I had previously made known'. Japan therefore abandoned the current peace negotiations, at the same time expressing many thanks to the German Government for its efforts in the enterprise.[230] This decision was immediately communicated to Trautmann for the Chinese Government, Trautmann being told to state the attitude of the German Government in the following words: 'In view of the Japanese statement we consider our role of letter carrier ended for the time being'.[231]

Yet even at this late hour both Trautmann and von Dirksen tried to salvage something out of the wreck. Trautmann delayed communicating the Japanese Note 'in order to give the Chinese one more chance to reconsider Kung's statement'.[232] For his part, von Dirksen expressed his regret to Hirota at what he hinted was a hasty decision and warned that Japan would incur world condemnation for breaking off the peace overtures. He also thought a continuation of the war would adversely affect German—Japanese relations in three ways: by worsening Anglo-Japanese relations, by ensuring the bolshevisation of China, and by the weakening of Japan *vis-à-vis* Russia through the tying down of Japan's military strength against China.[233] Even Kung expressed the hope that the cessation of Germany's mediation was only temporary.[234] But it really was too late. On 18 January 1938 both China and Japan recalled their Ambassadors and the war was pursued in earnest.

Another casualty at the time was the Wilhelmstrasse. While

contact was maintained between the Nationalist and Imperial Governments, despite the fact of a full-scale war, it could still argue forcefully that Germany was under no compulsion to make a political choice in the Far East, nor to abandon its position of official neutrality. This situation strengthened the Wilhelmstrasse's position in the policy-making processes of Nazi Germany, especially once it became 'responsible' for the tentative Sino—Japanese negotiations in the winter of 1937—38. Yet their failure marked not only the conversion of the Sino—Japanese conflict from a *de facto* to a *de jure* war but also the swan song of the Wilhelmstrasse's policy of neutrality in Far Eastern affairs which it had attempted to follow since at least the end of the First World War. When von Ribbentrop became Reich Foreign Minister on 4 February 1938, the Far Eastern policy of the Wilhelmstrasse, and hence of Germany, became distinctly partisan and pro-Japanese. But because of von Ribbentrop's political position in the Nazi State, from February 1938 the Wilhelmstrasse found itself assured of an increased authority in the formulation of Germany's Far Eastern policy, albeit one that differed from that pursued in previous years.

X

The 'Balance' Abandoned: Von Ribbentrop and Far Eastern Policy, February–July 1938

The future pattern of Germany's Far Eastern policy was forecast at the beginning of 1938 by von Dirksen in a report dated
26 January. His analysis was based on the twofold assumption that Japan would emerge the victor from the war and
that China would drift further into the Russian orbit. He
recommended a complete reorientation of German policy in
the direction of Japan, by the withdrawal of the military
advisers from China, total suspension of deliveries of war
material to China, the recognition of Manchukuo, and a
radical shift of Germany's economic and political policies
away from Nationalist China towards the Japanese occupied
and influenced areas of North China.

Von Dirksen was especially concerned that following the
recent unsuccessful efforts at peace, Japan 'in her deep ill-
humour [will] confront us with unpleasant decisions at an
inopportune moment'. Previously Japan had had 'no choice
but to let Germany wear a halo of innocence' because of her
role in the Sino–Japanese peace negotiations and because she
appeared to be Japan's only support in the world. While
summaries of German arms deliveries to China were given to
German authorities with an obvious and implied reproach,
Japanese spokesmen had denied British and American suggestions that Germany's arms trade with China was still continuing. Von Dirksen now warned Berlin that this situation would
no longer prevail, and that 'we shall therefore do well, precisely
on the most thorny problems of military advisers and deliveries
of war material, to redefine our position now in good time,
and, if occasion arises, to explain it to the Japanese'.

He thought the failure of the peace negotiations nullified
all previous arguments in favour of retaining the military
advisers in China. As to their withdrawal leading to a loss of
Chinese confidence in Germany, he considered the days of
the present régime numbered. He felt that the military advisers
were so pro-Chinese as to be incapable of impressing on the
Chinese authorities the hopelessness of their military situation,
while he was especially concerned that the continual defeats

suffered by the Chinese army would harm the reputation of
the military advisers and that of Germany.[1] Nor did he relish
the idea that they might find themselves working in close
collaboration with such Russian advisers as China might
employ.[2] Because so much of China was now in Japanese
hands he also dismissed the argument that their retention
helped German trade. Ott also felt that they should be
recalled.

Von Dirksen further argued that there could no longer be
any objections to the total cessation of deliveries of war
material to China nor of Germany's long-overdue recognition
of Manchukuo, which he thought would 'serve as a friendly
gesture towards Japan'. Given the expected growth of Japanese
influence in China he felt that 'we shall have to consider our
China problem more from the vantage point of Peking than
of Shanghai, Hankow or Chungking', and to this end recommended 'the establishment of a close liaison with the Japanese
military and civil authorities. This will be easily accomplished
by expanding the mission at Peking and by appointing to it a
mature official experienced in Japanese affairs'. Finally, he
considered it a matter of urgency that 'the possibilities of an
economic development of North China, as well as collaboration in this matter, should, in agreement with the Japanese
authorities, be examined by some prominent German experts
or by a small, specially constituted delegation'.[3]

Von Dirksen's recommendations were the practical measure
for the execution of the pro-Japanese policy already proposed
by von Ribbentrop on 2 January in a memorandum for
Hitler. Echoing his Führer's pronouncements of 5 November
1937, and indeed taking them further, von Ribbentrop argued
at length that Britain was Germany's implacable enemy, that
conflict between the two would come sooner or later, and
that one of Germany's prime tasks in foreign affairs should
be the 'quiet but determined establishment of alliance against
England, i.e. in practice, strengthening our friendship with
Italy and Japan and in addition winning over all countries
whose interests conform directly or indirectly with ours. For
this purpose the diplomats of the three great powers are to
cooperate closely and intimately'.[4] This was all part of the
'grand design' of Nazi foreign policy during 1938 and 1939
to neutralise Great Britain, and in this way to bring about the
changes required in Central and Eastern Europe as a necessary

preliminary to that great and final enterprise, the 'Holy War' against the Soviet Union.[5]

As usual, though, von Ribbentrop ignored certain of his precepts and those of the Wilhelmstrasse, and in January 1938 asked Oshima whether 'there was not some way in which Germany and Japan might be brought closer together by means of a treaty or otherwise'.[6] Oshima's consequent communication to the Japanese General Staff in Tokio and the first Japanese reply in June 1938 laid the somewhat uncertain foundations for the agreements finally concluded in 1940, 1941 and 1942. Von Ribbentrop approached Oshima and not Ambassador Togo because he wished to sound out the intentions of the Japanese military authorities, while he was correct in supposing that Togo would oppose the idea if approached first.[7] Togo's reasons for opposing an alliance with Germany were the very obverse of those which motivated von Ribbentrop. Togo was afraid that a closer liaison with Germany would involve Japan in conflict with Britain, France and the Soviet Union because of Germany's general policies, besides which such a development would contribute nothing to a solution of the China problem.[8] In this he provided a remarkable echo (or mirror) of the attitudes adopted in the German Foreign Office.

This situation was a neat reversal of that which had prevailed in German—Japanese relations only a year previously. Then Japanese proposals for a closer relationship in the wake of the Anti-Comintern Pact, predicated upon the situation prevailing in Sino—Japanese relations, met with a cool response from Germany because it wished to remain free of Far Eastern entanglements. To the Japanese it now appeared that Germany wanted a form of reinsurance treaty against the eventuality of war in Europe resulting from German actions and policies. This time the whip hand was undoubtedly held by Tokio, and the Japanese were not averse to exerting pressure of their own. Before a reply was finally given to von Ribbentrop in June 1938, the Japanese made it absolutely clear that they were set upon liquidating as much of the practical and moral support China still received from Germany. From von Ribbentrop's appointment as Foreign Minister of 4 February 1938 this support was weakened and indeed finally liquidated.

Until then, the Foreign Office under von Neurath — with the notable exception of von Dirksen — attempted to maintain its previous policy of balance in the Far East. But while the Chinese pleaded for Germany to abandon her policy of neutrality, it was clear that some sections of Chinese opinion had become increasingly distrustful of Germany.[9] Nor were German—Japanese relations entirely harmonious. At the beginning of 1938 the colonial question again emerged as a contentious issue. Following the denial on 27 November 1937 of the Japanese Colonial Vice-Minister Hagiwara, that Japan intended to return her Pacific mandates to Germany, discussions about a possible solution to the problem ensued. A complicated procedure for the sale of the islands by Japan with their immediate re-sale by Germany back to Tokio, suggested by the Japanese naval authorities, was accepted by von Neurath with reservations. But he wanted the matter dealt with diplomatically and discussed with Hirota. He suggested a secret purchase agreement with certain safeguards for Germany, while Japan should publicly announce that she was prepared to discuss the colonial question with Germany, a ploy designed as much for Western as for Eastern eyes and ears.[10] Von Neurath considered these exchanges to be so secret that he wanted them kept under lock and key and not to be shown to anybody else, presumably von Ribbentrop and members of his Büro. As it was, Oshima informed von Ribbentrop on 18 January that the Japanese Army was prepared to support Germany's colonial claims with the Japanese Government. Besides informing Hitler, von Ribbentrop was gracious enough to inform von Neurath.[11]

Von Neurath's rather involved manoeuvre was rejected, however, by von Dirksen. Since the islands question had been discussed between the Japanese Army, Navy and Foreign Office authorities he thought Germany should wait for Hirota to raise the question first. Von Neurath agreed, but impressed upon von Dirksen that when Hirota raised the issue he was to maintain a non-committal attitude.[12] By the time Hirota mentioned the subject on 5 February 1938 a new era in German foreign policy had been ushered in.

That 'new era' was marked by the appointment of Joachim von Ribbentrop as Reich Foreign Minister on 4 February 1938, an elevation which did nothing to improve the low opinion many people inside and out of the Wilhelmstrasse had of him. Although it was no secret that von Ribbentrop had long aspired to von Neurath's office — one of the many reasons for the long-running feud between the two men — it seems that when von Ribbentrop's hour finally struck he was as surprised as von Neurath. This much at least can be accepted from von Ribbentrop's memoirs.[13] Just when Hitler finally decided upon the change of Foreign Minister is hard to tell. On the other hand, it can safely be assumed that von Neurath's days were numbered — as were those of von Fritsch and von Blomberg — by the critical attitudes these three adopted at Hitler's conference of 5 November and afterwards. Together they represented the face of traditional conservatism that Hitler found so repugnant and unacceptable in the Nazi State, and after November 1937 a positive hindrance to his grandiose and far-reaching plans. In this way von Neurath's fate came to be bound up with those of the Minister of War and the Commander-in-Chief of the Army when, through von Blomberg's scandalous second marriage to a prostitute in January 1938 (at which Hitler and Göring acted as witnesses) and the secret machinations of Göring, Himmler and Heydrich which resulted in fabricated charges of homo-sexuality being brought against von Fritsch, Hitler took the opportunity to sweep the board clean of the most important and concerted opposition to his plans that he had yet faced. Thereafter, 'it was merely a question of when it might be accomplished with a minimum of international attention'.[14] There can be no doubt that von Ribbentrop's appointment as Reich Foreign Minister on 4 February 1938 dramatically altered the whole basis of Germany's Far Eastern policy as hitherto pursued — or at least recommended — by the Wilhelm-strasse. The arch-apostle of the pro-Japanese course in foreign policy now took the helm of the German Foreign Office at a decisive moment in Germany's history and in the Sino—Japanese conflict.

Although the German press maintained its strong emphasis on German—Japanese relations, articles appeared which warned Japan that she faced a long and costly struggle if she continued to pursue her war in China. Great concern was felt in government circles because of the expected losses in the Chinese market due to Japan's actions, while it was felt that Japan was reducing her value as an Anti-Comintern Pact partner by weakening herself militarily in China. Some observers even thought that Hitler's rather casual reply to Shigenori Togo's enthusiastic speech about German—Japanese relations when the latter presented his credentials, and the lack of prominence given to this reception in the German press, indicated the severity of the crisis over Far Eastern policy which the events of December and January had forced upon those in Berlin.[15] Taken in conjunction with Hitler's refusal on 14 January to accept von Neurath's resignation in the course of their rather difficult meeting, this raises the interesting question of whether had it not been for the Fritsch—Blomberg crisis von Ribbentrop might not have been appointed Foreign Minister in February 1938, so that Germany's Far Eastern policy might have continued, for a while at least, along the path charted for it by von Neurath and even Oskar Trautmann.

The manner in which von Ribbentrop's influence on Far Eastern policy came to be felt during the first half of 1938, when the policy of balance that Germany had pursued in the Far East since at least the end of the First World War, brought out two important points concerning the Wilhelmstrasse's position. Firstly, despite the appearance of total Nazi 'control' over the Foreign Office because of von Ribbentrop's political position in the Nazi State, the Nazi line of Far Eastern policy continued to be resisted within the foreign service. Secondly, the final result was a vindication, if one may call it that, of the Wilhelmstrasse's strictly constitutional position since it (eventually) acceded to the wishes of the political leadership of the country, and of the new Foreign Minister. As von Ribbentrop continually emphasised to his new subordinates in the Foreign Office, 'only Hitler made foreign policy, that this was Hitler's affair and that the employees of the Foreign Office therefore should not concern themselves with it but restrict themselves to mere routine and administrative work'. At the same time, von Ribbentrop lacked confidence in the old professional civil servants and doubted whether they could ever work for Hitler. Even after von Ribbentrop's appointment, Hitler still retained his suspicions about the Foreign Office and classed it with the Army and Justice as an 'uncertain element' in the Nazi State.[16]

Von Ribbentrop's appointment as Foreign Minister can therefore be viewed as 'the formal re-establishment of control over the bureaucratic apparatus by the German political leadership'.[17] Nevertheless, the Wilhelmstrasse did not view von Ribbentrop's appointment as a complete disaster since the

Foreign Minister's own organisation would finally be brought within the control of the bureaucracy, and it was felt that the Wilhelmstrasse's voice in foreign policy would now be heard more clearly by Hitler than that of its rivals. As it was, 'after February 1938 the Foreign Office was extremely busy with major affairs of state, accomplished many of Germany's most important objectives and was curiously effective in a way that Hitler may not have recognised'.[18]

Von Ribbentrop realised that he would never achieve a more wide-ranging agreement with Japan unless Germany's obvious politico-military interests in China were abandoned and other evidence given that Germany was more politically inclined towards Japan. The onus of establishing an iron bridge and not merely a wooden one between Berlin and Tokio[19] was clearly seen to be Germany's responsibility. Furthermore, as the European situation deteriorated rapidly during 1938 the urgency of improving relations with Japan at China's expense became even more pronounced. Tokio was fully aware of this and it is not surprising that the Japanese leaders felt themselves in a strong position to demand concessions over Chinese questions. As early as 5 February Hirota and the Vice-Minister of Foreign Affairs, Horinouchi emphasised to von Dirksen that it was Berlin's responsibility to improve German—Japanese relations, and this could only occur if Germany terminated both the export of war material to China and the activities of the military advisers there. It was obvious why these two issues in particular irritated the Japanese. By contributing to China's war effort they stiffened her resolve and prolonged the war. Besides which, their abrogation and removal would benefit Japan politically as well as militarily by signifying German support for her and not China in the Far Eastern struggle. As it was, during January 1938 30,000 tons of munitions were imported into China, the greater part of these coming from Germany. A month later twelve Henschel HS.123s, German single-seater dive-bomber/fighters arrived in Hong Kong for the Chinese. Although the bill of lading showed the port of origin as Stockholm, it was established that the aircraft were in fact embarked at Hamburg.[20] Hirota also thought it time that Germany recognised Manchukuo 'since [German] considerations with respect to China probably no longer applied'. Rather cautiously he also broached the colonial question, wanting it resolved 'for the sake of the further strengthening of German—Japanese relations'. He wanted Ambassador Togo informed of the German position and the matter could proceed from there, but warned von Dirksen that the mandate islands were of the greatest strategic importance to Japan. For his part, but rather late in the day, von Dirksen pointed out to Hirota that the Anti-Comintern Pact was designed to proceed jointly against Russia's Comintern, not to fight China.[21]

Berlin was now being asked to make fundamental and far-reaching decisions about its position in the Far East. It could either abandon those aspects of its policy in China which were militarily and politically offensive to Japan and hope thereby to purchase some (as yet intangible) form of political and perhaps economic advantage. Alternatively, it could maintain those interests and take the risk that Japan would move further away from Germany, reducing the degree of pressure brought to bear upon Britain's world position that Hitler and von Ribbentrop considered to be so essential for their plans in Europe. It was obvious that the colonial issue was being used by the Japanese as a form of 'sweetener' for the main objective of removing completely what practical and moral help China still received from her most obvious supporter, Nazi Germany. Of the three claims now put forward by Japan as test-cases for the sincerity of Germany's intentions towards her, the easiest one for Germany to consider immediately and perhaps accede to was the recognition of Manchukuo. There could be no doubt where the sympathies of Hitler and von Ribbentrop lay, the latter having already assured Admiral Godo that he would support Japan's request on the question with Hitler,[22] or that the future pattern of Germany's policy towards China hinged upon the decisions arrived at on this question. Now that von Ribbentrop was Foreign Minister it is not surprising that the discussions which took place in the Foreign Office after von Dirksen's telegram of 5 February tended towards an acceptance of what appeared to be the inevitable.

Although the basis of the discussion in the Foreign Office on 7 February was the examination of conditions to be demanded from Japan in return for Germany's politically significant act of recognition, Germany's position was undeniably a defensive one. A demand for economic concessions

in Manchukuo and North China was rejected, undoubtedly
on the grounds of past experience, but also from a somewhat
naive belief that if Germany avoided obvious 'horse trading'
this would actually help to improve 'normal' economic negotiations with the Japanese authorities. Instead, it was agreed
that 'recognition should be a politically friendly gesture from
which it can be *expected* [my italics] that in Japan favourable
consideration will be given to our economic hopes and that
our negotiations are advanced'. This referred to the continuing problems in economic relations with Manchukuo and
Japan. Economic relations with Manchukuo appeared to have
been strengthened by the credit agreement signed on 4 September 1937 between the Otto Wolff concern and the Central
Bank of Manchukuo, initially to the value of 35 million Yen
and principally to enable Manchukuo to buy German machinery. The agreement was part of Manchukuo's programme of
industrialisation since German industry received important
orders, while the Showa Steel Works, the most important
subsidiary of the South Manchurian Railway Company, was
established by German engineers with German machinery.
More generally, there was the continual problem of trade
ratios between Germany and Manchukuo, and the proportion
of this trade which had to be paid for in foreign exchange.[23]

As to economic relations with Japan, trade questions again
became an issue following the visit of Admiral Godo to
Germany in November 1937. Formerly Japanese Minister of
Commerce and then President of the Showa Steel Works,
Godo arrived in Berlin in November 1937 as head of a mission
which remained until the following April and was designed
to foster in a practical manner the relations between Germany
and Japan, Godo's mission being only one of several that
Japan sent out on 'goodwill' visits to the major powers. For
its part the Foreign Office wanted detailed negotiations on
Japanese demands for further credits and German demands
for the fulfilment of agreed quotas for German exports to
Japan to be conducted with the Japanese Embassy and not
with Admiral Godo. In December 1937 the Foreign Office
had been concerned that Japan's tactics seemed to be for the
Embassy to handle things in a dilatory manner while Godo
obtained the necessary credits from private industry and banks,
thus circumventing Germany's official demands for concessions from Japan. This practice was opposed and by the end

of the month von Dirksen was informed that negotiations had now been taken up officially with the Japanese Embassy, although in the latter part of January 1938 von Neurath informed Ambassador Togo that 'even with the best intentions we were not in a position to grant large, long-term credits'.[24]

By then Germany was particularly concerned about the disturbances caused to the normal flow of trade with China in those areas occupied by Japanese forces. While the number of complaints on this score increased in proportion to Japanese advances, analyses made of Germany's trade figures show that from the latter part of 1937 there was a slight, if discernible, change of emphasis in the pattern of Germany's Far Eastern trade, away from China and towards the Japan—Manchukuo trade bloc.[25] This tendency is of particular interest when related to von Ribbentrop's attempts to obtain from Japan assurances regarding Germany's economic interests in North China, and despite the consensus of opinion in the Foreign Office on 7 February there is no doubt that he wished to use this question as a lever on the Japanese in connection with the recognition issue. The Japanese played the same game in reverse by holding out the promise of economic advances and opportunities for Germany after she had recognised Manchukuo.[26]

While the Foreign Office meeting of 7 February agreed that Germany was in no position to demand special economic privileges of Japan, it was recognised that the same consideration applied to the Pacific Islands now controlled by Japan. Nevertheless, and virtually as an afterthought after this meeting, the Foreign Office felt that Germany should demand something from Japan in return for her act of recognition. It was proposed to obtain from Japan 'in advance a blanket recognition of such acquisitions as we might actually be in a position to make (i.e. in Europe)', especially as regards Austria and Czechoslovakia, Danzig and Memel, a move that would effectively prevent (it was hoped) any tendency towards an Anglo—Japanese understanding that was bound to have an anti-German direction to it. It was felt this would bind Japan to Germany's side and create even more of an anti-British bloc.[27] The Foreign Office seemed fairly confident that it could hold up the German recognition of Manchukuo until such a declaration had been obtained from Japan.[28]

Yet by 9 February a different counsel had prevailed and this stipulation was abandoned. In the draft telegram to Trautmann drawn up that day and initialled by von Mackensen, von Schmeiden and von Strachwitz, informing him that recognition of Manchukuo was imminent and asking for an analysis of the reaction that could be expected in China, the point that Germany intended to negotiate for 'valuable Japanese compensations in the sphere of European politics' in return for the grant of recognition was crossed through. Instead, the statement that 'compensation' was to be sought from Japan 'in another sphere' was substituted. This meant that concessions were to be demanded of Japan in North China and Manchukuo, especially since the instruction mentioned the economic difficulties Germany was facing in Manchukuo as a result of withholding her recognition. One draft for this contingency also mentions the pre-war German Colonies, Japan being asked to recognise Germany's rightful claims and to enter into negotiations for their return, so long as 'such negotiations with other mandate powers had begun'. Von Mackensen's instructions to Trautmann, despatched on the 10th, made it clear that the decision to recognise Manchukuo in principle had been taken in Berlin, although it would be emphasised to China that this was not to be taken as signifying any alteration of Germany's policy of neutrality in Far Eastern affairs.[29]

Shortly after this telegram had been drafted one was received from Trautmann commenting on the Hirota—von Dirksen interview of 5 February. Not surprisingly, Trautmann warned against any change in German policy which could be taken by the Chinese to mean that Germany was abandoning her policy of neutrality. He emphasised the extensive nature of Germany's interests in Nationalist China and repeated previous warnings that a recognition of Manchukuo would result in a boycott of German goods. He also recommended continuing the supply of war material in exchange for foreign exchange, such transactions to be undertaken by private firms. Again he opposed the withdrawal of the German advisers from China because 'the effect here would be catastrophic and would result in their replacement by Soviet advisers; the Chinese army would then become a Soviet army'. More strongly, he repeated his opposition to any economic co-operation with Japan in the north, saying that this was simply 'a myth'. What particularly concerned Trautmann, though, was increasing suspicion of Germany's policy and motives in the ruling circles, especially among the members of the Sung family, and he therefore requested an instruction from von Ribbentrop in order to assure the Chinese that Germany's policy towards China had not altered. Such a directive was not given.[30]

The reactions of Trautmann and the Consuls at Shanghai and Canton to the instructions from Berlin could have been no surprise to the Wilhelmstrasse, that recognition of Manchukuo would have a disastrous effect on Germany's economic position in China and on the standing of the German Government with the government and peoples of China. Trautmann's immediate response on 13 February was to counsel caution by pointing out that 'for our purpose the military situation should first of all be considered'. By this he meant it was wrong to dismiss China as a military factor and quoted from a report by an adviser, Colonel Newiger, which emphasised that since the fall of Nanking the Chinese army had regrouped and reformed and had therefore strengthened its position against the Japanese. Von Falkenhausen was also optimistic about the prospects for the Chinese army and considered that it could pursue the war for some time.[31]

In his formal reply of 16 February to Berlin's instructions of the 10th, Trautmann again opposed the imminent recognition of Manchukuo, especially since China would hardly accept Germany's explanations that it signified no change in her position of neutrality in the Far East. In von Ribbentrop's eyes he probably made himself a marked man by referring to von Neurath's comment of the previous November, that recognition would only be taken to mean the abandonment of that neutrality in Japan's favour.[32] As Trautmann pointed out, the Chinese were fighting for their very existence and the recognition of Manchukuo would be seen as sanctioning one of Japan's main war aims. As the Japanese had never forgotten Shimonoseki, neither would the Chinese ever forget if Germany now recognised Japan's puppet-state. He was again sceptical about any economic advantages that Germany would receive in return from Japan, and warned that basic principles should not be sacrificed for such intangible gains. He also warned that because of Germany's position in Far Eastern affairs the reaction against her if she recognised

Manchukuo would be greater than that experienced by Italy. By this time, however, Trautmann undoubtedly realised that he was fighting a rearguard, and probably losing, action to keep some semblance of balance in Germany's Far Eastern policy. He could only warn the Wilhelmstrasse that 'the nervousness of the Chinese at Germany's attitude is increasing', while his personal view was that 'we should wait until the war in China is ended before linking ourselves politically with Japan'.[33]

However, the aims of the Nazi leaders in Europe brooked no delay in the cementing of German–Japanese relations. Von Ribbentrop submitted to Hitler the reports from von Dirksen on 5 February and those from Trautmann describing the responses of the Consuls at Shanghai and Canton. Not surprisingly he failed to submit Trautmann's eloquent telegram of opposition of the 16th. The result was that on 17 February Dr Hans Lammers, Reich Minister and Chief of the Reich Chancellery, told von Ribbentrop that Hitler now wished to recognise Manchukuo.[34] Although Trautmann informed the Wilhelmstrasse on the 19th that Chiang Kai-shek and the Chinese Government hoped that Germany would refrain from this step and maintain its policy of neutrality,[35] Hitler declared his intent in his Reichstag speech of 20 February 1938.

His audience was probably surprised at the attention paid to the Far East in this speech, which amounted to an open declaration of support for Japan in the arena of world politics, but given the overall strategy postulated for Germany by Hitler and von Ribbentrop there were good reasons for this. He stated that he had now decided to recognise Manchukuo, although he failed to set a date for it. This was a clear indication to Japan that Germany would still require something in return for her action. Nevertheless, the rest of this section was virtually a paean of praise for Japan's political ideology and position. He made a particular point of contrasting Japan's value as an anti-bolshevist ally with China's relatively weak position. This amounted to a public acceptance of Japan's arguments that she was fighting communism in China within the terms of the Anti-Comintern Pact, a point the Foreign Office under von Neurath had always been at pains to avoid. But Hitler also showed himself sensitive to foreign and domestic criticisms of his policies towards Japan as signifying a betrayal of the tenets of Nazi racial doctrines when he stated that 'Japan's greatest victory would not affect the civilisation of the white races in the very least'. Yet another step towards Japan was his comment that Germany had no territorial interests in the Far East, a point the Japanese could take as referring to the colonial issue.[36]

Von Ribbentrop now had two immediate tasks on hand: to pacify the Chinese and to negotiate with the Japanese. One of the German military advisers in China later told the Wilhelmstrasse that if anything had turned China against Germany, it was the moral support given to Japan's undertakings in China epitomised by Hitler's speech on 20 February 1938: this 'would never be forgotten by the Chinese people'.[37] Although it was emphasised to Hankow that the forthcoming act of recognition implied no change in Germany's attitude towards China, a point brought out in the statement issued by the German Embassy at Hankow, the Chinese believed otherwise. Chiang Kai-shek complained that it would 'always remain a blemish on the relations between the two countries'.[38] Trautmann thought that the blow could have been softened by statements that military supplies to China would continue, that the military advisers would remain there, and that Germany would not recognise the Peking régime. Von Ribbentrop rejected this suggestion for obvious reasons: the Chinese would have taken such a statement as a firm political commitment on the part of Germany, besides which it hardly accorded with the Foreign Minister's pro-Japanese policy. Instead Trautmann was told to stand by the Führer's reasons for recognition, that recognition was only to be considered from the point of view of Germany's general foreign policy situation and had nothing to do as such with Germany's attitude towards the Far Eastern conflict.[39] Nevertheless, a severe blow had been struck at the Sino—German relationship, and one immediate consequence was a strengthening of the pro-Soviet faction in the Chinese Government.[40]

The future direction and pattern of Germany's Far Eastern policy also depended on what emerged from the complex of negotiations that von Ribbentrop was about to undertake with the Japanese. He thought that even without hurrying, the details connected with the formal recognition of Manchukuo could be completed within a period of three weeks, and it is significant that he wanted to discuss this with the Japanese

Ambassador and not with Kato.[41] Von Ribbentrop's immediate aims were made clear in von Mackensen's instructions to Tokio of 21 February informing the Japanese Government officially of Hitler's Reichstag speech: concessions for German trade in North China. The immediate signs seemed encouraging since on the 22nd Noebel reported from Tokio that Hirota had said it was a fixed part of Japanese policy not to exclude foreign powers from the economic development of North China, and the participation of a friendly state such as Germany was especially welcome to the Japanese. He also explained that the economic plans for North China were only in their first stages, but he hoped that as soon as they had been formulated 'it would be possible to present to Germany in a concrete form proposals for cooperation'. In the Political Department in the Wilhelmstrasse, however, this section of the telegram was side-lined with a large exclamation mark.[42]

Von Ribbentrop appointed Wohlthat of the Ministry of Economics to lead the talks with Japan, although it was accepted that he would be 'speaking' for the Economics Section of the Foreign Office. Because of their political significance, the Foreign Minister also appointed von Raumer as well as ensuring that the Director of the Economic Policy Department in the Foreign Office, Emil Wiehl, would cooperate.[43] Whether von Ribbentrop thought he would be able to keep the talks on a straightforward basis of economic gains against recognition without becoming involved in a discussion of Germany's politico-military involvement in China is not clear.

When Ambassador Togo called on von Ribbentrop on 22 February to express the 'deepest gratitude' of his Government for Germany's willingness to recognise Manchukuo, economic questions were touched upon in a general manner. Von Ribbentrop emphasised that he had always felt that the recognition of Manchukuo should be kept a separate issue from any economic negotiations that ensued. On the other hand, and Togo could hardly have failed to grasp his point, he emphasised that the war in China and Germany's imminent recognition of Manchukuo would result in serious economic losses for her in the Far East (in China) and it would be appreciated if 'by a generous agreement a certain compensation were provided for the losses incurred by the business interests'. This point had been made in a memorandum by

Voss of the Economic Policy Department. But as von Schmieden remarked when forwarding this memorandum to the senior member of the Political Department, 'if the economic consequences of a recognition of Manchukuo actually occur as shown in the enclosed memorandum . . . then not only the position of German businessmen but also Germany's reputation [in China] will be brought into question'.[44]

Von Ribbentrop also pointed out to Togo that during conversations in connection with the Anti-Comintern Pact he had explained that 'in case of cooperation in China he expected Germany to have complete equality with the Japanese in business transactions'. Togo promised to inform Hirota of this, but emphasised that he and not Admiral Godo had been officially authorised by the Japanese Government to negotiate with Germany. The question of frozen credits in Japan was also mentioned by von Ribbentrop, while Togo referred to the international commission provided for in the supplementary protocol to the Anti-Comintern Pact. He also suggested the establishment of a commission in Italy, but this was rejected by von Raumer in a later comment.[45]

Although Togo was quite encouraging on the colonial question during this conversation, the subject was left in abeyance for the time being. While the Japanese themselves again returned to the theme of the purchase of the Pacific islands from Germany, at the same time emphasising their strategic importance to the Japanese Empire, by the end of February 1938 it was von Ribbentrop who ordered that the matter should not be pursued since it could prejudice Germany's general and more widespread claims in the colonial sphere.[46]

It was to be six weeks, however, before Togo brought Japan's answer to von Ribbentrop's request. But von Ribbentrop was not only waiting for an answer about economic cooperation but also one to his enquiry to Oshima in January for a closer political and military relationship between the two countries. In the meantime Germany's European position changed dramatically after the *Anschluss* with Austria in March 1938,[47] a step that focused attention on Germany's unsettled relations with Czechoslovakia. These developments, and the intensification of the anti-British course in German foreign policy, again raised the value of the link with Japan in the eyes of Hitler and von Ribbentrop. The question, as always, was what Japan would demand in return for the grant of her political 'favours'.

The obvious answer was the liquidation of Germany's politico-military interests in China. Von Dirksen had already mapped the course in January, while Hitler's declaration on Manchukuo on 20 February showed that the first steps in this direction had already been taken. Furthermore, in certain government circles there was strong talk of removing the military advisers from China. Only eight days after von Ribbentrop's appointment as Foreign Minister and his own as Head of the Armed Forces High Command (*Oberkommando der Wehrmacht, OKW*) Wilhelm Keitel informed von Mackensen that 'should a withdrawal of these military advisers become advisable or necessary on political grounds, no objections of a military nature will be raised'. At the same time he emphasised the private nature of the German military advisory group in China and pointed out that the *OKW* could have nothing to do with its removal. Nevertheless, there could be no doubt as to the accommodating political attitude of the new leadership of the High Command of the Armed Forces, especially now that after 4 February 1938 von Blomberg and von Fritsch had been removed and Hitler had assumed personal command, dispensing with the post of Minister of War and C-in-C of the Armed Forces. This was made clear from Keitel's opening remarks when he expressed concern that the continued presence of the advisers in China could be taken to mean that the army leadership of Germany subscribed to a one-sided pro-Chinese policy in the Far East.[48] Yet a fortnight later von Raumer denied it when Voss of the Far Eastern section of the Economic Policy Department asked him whether recognition of Manchukuo would be followed by the withdrawal of the advisers and the cessation of military supplies to China.[49] On the other hand, and surprisingly enough, it was von Raumer who warned von Ribbentrop against a policy of concessions to Japan without obtaining sufficient advantages in return — only to be threatened with incarceration in a concentration camp later in the year for his troubles.[50]

In view of the undeniable tendency taking shape in Germany's Far Eastern policy Trautmann's report of 8 March (received in the Foreign Office on the 21st) advocating the opposite course, the maintenance of a policy of balance and

non-commitment, was decidedly unwelcome. A critique of
von Dirksen's report of 26 January, his remarks were even
more pointed because of the content and effects of Hitler's
speech of 20 February. Trautmann disputed von Dirksen's
basic argument, that following the new situation that had
arisen since mid-January it was now necessary to reconsider
(and liquidate) the fundamental bases of Germany's Far
Eastern i.e. China, policy. What particularly concerned him
was that Japan appeared to be using Germany to strengthen
her own position in the Far East and world politics generally,
and that Germany would be playing Japan's game for her by
abandoning her own position in China: 'from the report of
the Embassy in Tokio, it appears that Japan has thus far been
in a predicament which has prevented her from clearly expressing her dissatisfaction with Germany, because she needed
Germany as her only support in the world. I believe that we
ourselves are releasing Japan from this predicament if we
simply grant her demands one after another without asking
anything in return . . . with our help she could emerge from
her isolation and adjust her relations with England and
Russia. Japan would then, from the standpoint of realistic
policy, have even less interest in us than heretofore'. It was
to prevent such a development that von Ribbentrop was
intent, ultimately, on a policy of concession towards Japan,
the difference between the Foreign Minister and Trautmann
being the degree of faith each placed in Japan's probity. Only
two days previously the latter had reported that accounts of
a deliberate avoidance of tension in Russo—Japanese relations
'support the view that it is by no means certain whether
Japan, if one day it should become necessary for us to turn
against Russia, will also do the same. Even if Japan had the
intention to do so, apparently she will not be in such a position for some time to come'.[51]

Trautmann's intention, as always, was to impress on those
in Berlin the advisability, or necessity, of maintaining a
balanced policy in the Far East. As he put it, 'if the recognition of Manchukuo was only the first act directed against
China and the two other acts [withdrawal of advisers and
cessation of military supplies] are to follow, then we can only
liquidate our position here'. He virtually accused von Dirksen
of pandering to the worst of Japanese propaganda, arguing
against the notion that China was slipping further into the

Russian orbit by referring to what he thought was the failure
of Sun Fo's recent mission to Moscow. He also disputed von
Dirksen's analysis of the fighting on the mainland and disregard for the Chinese Army while he took particular exception to his criticisms of the position and standing of the
military advisers in China.

Trautmann was equally scathing about von Dirksen's recommendations concerning a shift of German interests and activity to North China, pointing out the anti-foreign drift of
Japan's economic policies in that region: 'any Japanese régime
in China will shut the door to foreign trade, all official
Japanese assurances to the contrary; we have been able to
observe for ourselves just how things are going in Manchukuo'.[52] He also warned that Germany would damage her
present and future prospects in the rest of China if she now
concluded an agreement covering North China similar to that
already concluded with Manchukuo, while again doubting the
economic advantages to be gained from such an agreement.

Trautmann also opposed the suggestions that diplomatic
appointments should be made at Peking, and that a German
delegation should be sent to North China. Again he warned
against the policy of haste:

In politics too much zeal is never advisable, and if there is anything I
fear it is a new edition of the Hcyc Mission, which at the time kicked
up so much dust in Manchukuo. I recommend that the files on it be
re-read. At this juncture we ought to avoid any conspicuous or provoca-
tive appearance in North China, which, despite the kick of the Japanese
boot, has by no means abandoned its patriotism. We would wound
Chinese sensibilities even more than we have done heretofore.[53]

Trautmann's words fell on deaf ears in Berlin. By the time
this report arrived on 21 March the complex of discussions
and negotiations with Japan and Manchukuo initiated by
von Ribbentrop were well under way. These seemed to show
that von Ribbentrop (rather belatedly) was aware of the
importance of securing Germany's economic interests in
the Far East, especially in view of her political and military
plans in Europe, and was therefore intent on striking as hard
a practical bargain as possible regarding Germany's economic
position in North China and Manchukuo in return for
Germany's grant of recognition of Manchukuo. Yet his
actions still begged the question: what economic advantages
did North China under the Japanese heel offer that free

Nationalist China could not provide in greater abundance?

While Voss urged on von Raumer the need for caution in the negotiations about North China because of Germany's relations with Nationalist China and doubts about the advantages to be gained in that region given Japan's control there,[54] von Ribbentrop's intention was also to conclude an economic agreement with Japan which protected the scale of German exports to Japan in the face of that country's regulation of her foreign exchange situation. It was also intended to maintain the export—import ratio of 4:1 in Germany's favour, while outstanding claims and debts had to be settled by Japan. It appeared that Japanese proposals for a compensation agreement by which Germany would supply war material in exchange for Japanese and Manchukuoan products to the value of 100 million Yen would be resisted until agreement had been reached on methods of financial settlement between the two countries and Germany's outstanding claims against Japan had been resolved.[55]

The negotiations with Kato about the details of Germany's formal recognition of Manchukuo proved to be difficult. On 4 March Kato handed to Wiehl, Director of the Economic Policy Department, his personal draft of a German—Manchukuoan Commercial Treaty which incorporated the diplomatic measures associated with recognition in a general economic agreement. Article 16 covering the most favoured nation clause made it clear that any future agreement between Germany and Manchukuo was not to touch upon Japan's privileged position in Manchukuo.[56] The difficulties which prolonged the negotiations until an agreement was finally signed on 12 May 1938 revolved around the precise definition and meaning of the grounds on which such an economic treaty was to be concluded, 'reciprocity' and the 'most favoured nation' clause, Article III. Matters were not helped by supplementary protocols from the Manchukuoan Government which virtually protected Japan's privileged position in the country, a point that Germany was bound to contest or reject because of her demands for parity with Japan. The manner in which these problems were resolved was extremely important for Germany. Voss was particularly concerned about safe-guarding Germany's economic demands on Manchukuo as against recognition since, as he put it, '*after* [italics in original] recognition we would not have this means of pressure any longer'.[57] Germany's general approach certainly displeased Ambassador Togo, who made it clear to von Mackensen that recognition should be a one-sided act not involving a whole host of other demands.[58]

April 1938 marked the beginning of the end of what semblance of balance there still remained in Germany's Far Eastern policy, despite Trautmann's continual efforts to halt the drift towards Japan.[59] The Foreign Office was soon made aware of the fact that Japan would not remain passive in the face of Germany's demands over North China without presenting her own conditions in return. Not surprisingly, the question of the military advisers in China was at the forefront. Admiral Koga, Vice-Chief of the Navy Staff, asked the Naval Attaché in Tokio, Captain Lietzmann, to use his influence with his superiors in Berlin to effect their withdrawal, whose work he described as that 'unnatural and anti-Japanese support of China . . . in cooperation with the Russians'. It is quite probable that this plea was connected with the fact that during March and April in the small Shantung town of Taiehchuang 'Japanese detachments suffered a stinging setback for the first time in modern history' at the hands of German-trained Chinese forces operating with German-made guns.[60]

Although this request was not entirely unexpected, von Ribbentrop was disturbed by Ambassador Togo's news on 8 April that Japan objected to Germany's requests for complete parity with Japan in North China since if this was granted on the basis of the 'most favoured nation' clause it could be expected that all other nations would demand similar treatment. Although he professed to understand Japan's special military and other interests in the area von Ribbentrop was, nevertheless, insistent that Germany must obtain 'a certain measure of equality with Japan and a privileged position as compared with all other countries, because of our good relations in other respects resulting from the Anti-Comintern Agreement, *and because of the closer cooperation that might prove necessary in the future'* [my italics]. He therefore suggested that Togo should take the matter further with von Raumer.[61] Apart from Japan's natural reluctance to grant special economic privileges to foreign powers in the occupied areas of mainland Asia, there were other political reasons for this attitude of reserve towards Germany's demands for *Gleichberechtigung.* Hirota was afraid that special privileges granted to Germany or Italy 'would threaten to cut off entirely the economic participation of England and America in the future' in North China, as well as affecting Japan's political relations with these countries. So far as the co-operation of Germany was concerned, he thought this could lie in her 'cooperative investment in various important industries'.[62]

It was becoming increasingly clear to von Ribbentrop that the two main parts to his Japanese policy, a closer political or military relationship between the two countries[63] and equality for Germany in Japanese-occupied North China would remain stillborn unless and until Germany proffered her own form of 'reciprocity', the liquidation of her politico-military interests in China. One step in this direction had already been taken early in March, Hitler's decision to cease the practice of allowing military personnel from China and Japan to complete their training and military education with Germany's armed forces. This greatly upset the Chinese despite the fact that it was emphasised that both Far Eastern countries would be equally affected by the new measures and that the decision had been taken to underline Germany's official position of neutrality in the Far Eastern conflict. When complaining about this at the Wilhelmstrasse Chinese diplomats wondered whether the next step would be the withdrawal of the German advisers from China, but on this question they failed to receive a clear reply.[64]

During the second or third week of April, however, the decision to withdraw the advisers from China was taken in Berlin, undoubtedly by von Ribbentrop himself and obviously in conjunction with Hitler. On 22 April, by which date the Foreign Office confirmed Japan's rejection of recent Italian attempts, at the behest of Wang Ching-wei and Prime Minister Kung, to promote further peace negotiations between China and Japan, and indeed of Germany's own transmission in mid-April of Chinese expressions of a willingness for peace,[65] Trautmann was instructed to enquire just how quickly the work of the advisers in China could be terminated, and the kind of personal and political effects this would have. While Trautmann was pursuing this matter, reports appeared in the European press that the advisers had been recalled from China. Ambassador Cheng Tien-fong immediately called on State Secretary von Weizsäcker for an explanation. The latter confirmed the accuracy of the reports and stated that it was Germany's wish to maintain a neutral attitude in the struggle between China and Japan: 'in the long run it was inconsistent with this attitude if, as a result of the presence and assistance of some thirty former German officers, the world should believe, rightly or wrongly, that we were actively influencing the Chinese conduct of the war'. Von Weizsäcker added that the instruction was not a military order 'but it was a definite wish of the German Government', although he did not know whether the officers concerned knew about the decision. He neatly side-stepped further discussion of the subject by recommending that they wait until the reaction of the advisers to these instructions had been received.[66] The Chinese Ambassador would have been even more concerned had he realised that this blow was being reinforced by yet another, Göring's order forbidding the further export of war material to China, a decision that had undoubtedly been taken as a result of pressure by von Ribbentrop.[67]

The first indication that matters would not go smoothly was received in the Foreign Office on 30 April, in a report from von Falkenhausen which set out at length the financial and employment problems the advisory staff and others employed by them would have to face if they had to leave China suddenly. Of particular importance was his point that 'the private contracts of the individual advisers, which run until 1939 and 1940, cannot be terminated unilaterally'. Although he clarified this by stating that unilateral notice of termination would lay the advisers open to claims for damages, who would then claim more general compensation from the Reich Government, it can be safely assumed that von Falkenhausen's real point was to warn the Foreign Office, and especially von Ribbentrop, that the matter was more complicated than Berlin perhaps thought it was. His reference to the private nature of the advisers' contracts was meant to cast doubt on the ability or authority of the German Government to effect the withdrawal of the advisers from China, many of whom had grave doubts about returning to a Nazi Germany and whom the régime likewise disowned.[68] *The Times* of 24 May 1938 reported that the 'categorical' orders for the return of the advisers was 'based on a law promulgated in Germany some months ago, by which the Führer's authority is absolute over all ex-army officers'. This probably referred to an order issued by Keitel on 22 February 1938 extending liability to military service for the Reich to all former officers.[69]

Nor was the question of German arms deliveries any easier to deal with. During May the Foreign Office and the Ministry of Economics appeared to be at cross-purposes as to what Göring's prohibition order of 27 April actually involved. Von Ribbentrop suspected that his interpretation of the order forbidding the further export of war material to China was a great deal stricter than Göring's, whose influence on the Ministry of Economics appeared to be greater than that of the Foreign Minister. What really concerned Göring, his subordinates in the Four Year Plan office and the Ministry of Economics with whom they worked closely, were the economic losses which the Reich and the German armaments industry would have to sustain if the outstanding contracts with China were not fulfilled. This loss was put at around 282 million Reichmarks.

The seriousness of this matter was underlined for the Foreign Office and for Göring, who also received a copy, by Trautmann's report of 20 April which arrived in Berlin on 3 May. This enclosed an analysis by Colonel Preu of the current state of the admittedly difficult negotiations between HAPRO, or rather Göring's office, and the Chinese Government. Both Trautmann and Preu argued strongly in favour of a compromise solution on the technical points of detail at issue (the reports were written and transmitted to Berlin before Göring's order of 27 April was made known). Preu also recommended that a positive attitude be adopted in Berlin towards Professor Durrer's negotiations for the establishment of a German ironworks in China, it being feared that if these collapsed the order would go to another country as well as affecting the HAPRO contracts. Trautmann's main purpose was still to stem what he thought was Berlin's policy of haste in the direction of Japan. Taking up von Falkenhausen's favourable comments on China's chances in the war with Japan, he pointed out that since neither China nor Japan seemed likely to collapse completely the greater danger lay in a protracted war. In these circumstances, he felt that Germany should try to convince both States that a compromise peace must be concluded. But even if Japan managed to force China to conclude a hard peace this would still leave a considerable part of

China under purely Chinese control and Trautmann warned the Wilhelmstrasse that:

until the outcome can be seen more clearly, we should not fundamentally alter our economic and political relations with China. After the war comes the period of reconstruction. We should also participate in that and not give the whole field over to the Anglo-Saxon powers. If we now abandon our economic cooperation with China and it leads to irreconcilable mutual ill-feeling, so we shall make it extraordinarily difficult for cooperation [to take place] after the war.[70]

Trautmann's efforts were to no avail. Two days after this report was written he was told by the Wilhelmstrasse that the Japanese were not interested in vague expressions of peaceful intentions from China,[71] while by the time his report arrived in Berlin on 3 May the decisions regarding the liquidation of Germany's military interests in China had already been taken and orders issued.

Nevertheless, there is no doubt that Trautmann's reports immediately affected Göring. On 7 May he wrote to Oshima and made no secret of the fact that Germany would expect Japan to free the foreign exchange she currently owed Germany as recompense for the losses that would be sustained because of the disruption of the arms contracts with China, which he put at 100 million Reichmarks. Göring also emphasised what the alternative might be if Japan proved obdurate: Germany would have to deliver to China 'so far as possible unimportant weapons' to the value of the foreign exchange involved. This was a clear hint that Germany not only reserved the right to resume regular arms deliveries to China in case difficulties should arise in the complex of economic negotiations with Japan, but that such deliveries might not be restricted to 'unimportant' weapons. There was a further barb in Göring's final point when he said that 'as it is, just now there are supplies [of arms] *en route* to China which I could not recall after the issue of the prohibition order'.[72]

Trautmann delayed informing the Chinese of the arms prohibition order because he wanted to know whether the restriction would also apply to Japan, while he warned the Wilhelmstrasse that the conjunction of the arms question with that of the military advisers could only create the impression 'of a sudden demonstrative withdrawal from China' on the part of Germany.[73] Nevertheless, Chiang Kai-shek received information from Berlin that Germany intended to stop deliveries of war material to China, and on 9 May warned Trautmann that if other countries, including Italy, continued to supply China with arms while Germany terminated her existing contracts, the effect on Sino—German relations would be severe. Trautmann tried to explain that Germany's position was particularly affected by the nature of German—Japanese relations, but Chiang Kai-shek insisted that his views be brought to the attention of the German Government. By now Trautmann undoubtedly realised that Germany's policy of balance in the Far East was nearly at an end, and his final remarks to Berlin, although intended to influence policy there, really betrayed his own anxieties: 'from Chiang Kai-shek's very earnest statements I gained the impression that we have now reached the decisive turning-point in our relations with China, and that we are risking all our constructive work in China since the war and perhaps in the future if we now act abruptly in regard to the question of the military advisers and the deliveries of war material. I shall also discuss this question fully with Ambassador Ott in Hong Kong'.[74]

That same day Trautmann forwarded to the Wilhelmstrasse a copy of a memorandum on 'The Situation in the Far East: the China Factor' he intended utilising for his talk with Ott who had been appointed German Ambassador to Japan on 5 April 1938.[75] He wanted the Wilhelmstrasse to consider whether Germany's *actual* interests in China should be abandoned in favour of *possible* advantages with Japan. The cessation of German arms deliveries to China or the withdrawal of the advisers could only be taken as an indication that Germany had decided in favour of Japan. More practically, Trautmann emphasised the importance of Germany's economic relations with China by estimating her investments in that country to be around 400 million Reichsmarks. Furthermore:

China is the only free great market which is still open to us. The question is, whether all these possibilities, expectations and interests [in Nationalist China] should be sacrificed for general political considerations, i.e. practically through an option in favour of Japan, which would also intensify our opposition to England and America in Far Eastern politics.[76]

An answer of sorts to Trautmann's arguments was almost immediately given by the signature on 12 May 1938 by von Weizsäcker and Kato of a Treaty of Friendship between

Germany and Manchukuo which came into force on 22 July. This provided for the immediate establishment of diplomatic and consular relations, and later the opening of negotiations for a consular, commercial and navigation agreement which was actually signed on 14 September 1938. The difficulties associated with Article III of the agreement[77] had not been resolved until late in April or early May,[78] and the final result showed that both the German and Manchukuoan authorities had been forced to accept a compromise solution. In its final version Article III stated that as soon as possible negotiations would be entered into for a general commercial and shipping treaty and that 'each part of the conditions of the other side will be met so far as is possible'. Although the Germans had succeeded in removing the supplementary protocol defending Japan's privileged position in Manchukuo they had had to accept a much less definite commitment regarding the position they themselves hoped to achieve in that country.[79] Manchukuo's first Minister to Germany, Lu I-wen, arrived in Berlin on 7 November 1938, while Hiyoshi Kato became Counsellor of the Manchukuoan Legation. Germany's first envoy to Manchukuo was Dr Wilhelm Wagner, the ambitious Dr Knoll being appointed as Counsellor of Legation.

Germany's formal recognition of Manchukuo was a serious enough blow to Sino—German relations, but there was more to come. After returning from the State visit to Italy with Hitler from 3 to 10 May, von Ribbentrop again pressed the question of the withdrawal of the advisers from China.[80] Desperate (because of the European situation) to present the Japanese with yet another striking indication of his fidelity to the cause of German—Japanese friendship,[81] von Ribbentrop insisted on 13 May that von Falkenhausen and the advisory staff comply with the German Government's request for their return 'as speedily as possible'. To overcome von Falkenhausen's arguments about the legal and contractual difficulties, he ordered Trautmann and the advisers themselves to intervene with the Chinese Government to effect their premature release from employment. They were to argue that it was 'inconsistent with neutrality for former German officers to be in the Chinese service, thus creating the impression in the world that we were actively influencing the conduct of the war by the Chinese'. Von Ribbentrop's complete and probably wilful lack of understanding for Chinese sensibilities was betrayed by his remark, 'we expected the Chinese Government, in view of the traditional friendship existing between the two countries, to give due consideration to those well-founded German wishes'. Although he admitted that the German Government was willing to pay the costs of the return journey and any other necessary compensation required by the advisers, von Ribbentrop made no secret of the seriousness of the matter in a 'strictly secret' section of his instructions to Trautmann: 'strict measures' were contemplated against officers who refused to comply with the Government's request for their return.[82]

But Trautmann still tried to delay the inevitable. In agreement with Ott whom he met in Hong Kong on or before 15 May while the latter was returning to Germany, he suggested that one way of avoiding too brusque a treatment of the Chinese would be a gradual rather than a sudden withdrawal of the advisers.[83] Von Ribbentrop, infuriated by this proposal, immediately replied that a gradual withdrawal of the advisers was out of the question and that he expected 'immediate' compliance with the instructions of the 13th and those to be issued on the 19th. So angry was he at the delay that now, for the first time, he stated that it was Hitler's 'express order' that the advisers return immediately. Even more disturbing for Trautmann was the new twist that matters now took. Von Ribbentrop wanted the Chinese Government to terminate the contracts straight away, but that if they made difficulties regarding this 'you may hint that your position in China would then become untenable'.[84]

Von Ribbentrop sent a more moderate instruction to Trautmann on the 19th, emphasising that the whole matter had to be considered in the light of Germany's neutrality in the Far Eastern conflict while defending at length Germany's relations with Japan because of their mutual struggle against bolshevism.[85] Nevertheless, there was no doubt that the Foreign Minister, extremely worried about his position *vis-à-vis* the Japanese, had taken Germany's policy of withdrawal from China an important stage further by threatening the removal of the German Ambassador if the military advisers did not abandon their contracts with the Chinese Government. At some point the Japanese authorities were informed of the proceedings, and von Ribbentrop was encouraged in his hard line by their response.[86]

Although he informed von Falkenhausen of Hitler's orders, Trautmann had still not communicated the German decision to the Chinese Government. Given the urgent tone of von Ribbentrop's communications and his emphasis that it was the Führer's wish that the advisers relinquish their posts, and because of Chiang Kai-shek's presence at the North front, he requested permission to bring the matter to the attention of the Chinese Foreign Minister.[87] Of particular interest was his inquiry as to whether the non-Aryans in the advisory group should also return to Germany. Evidently three of the advisers came into this category, but von Ribbentrop avoided a direct answer and simply said they should cease work as military advisers in China. Some officials in the Wilhelmstrasse, however, expected that some of the advisers would wish to remain behind in China since they were obviously *persona non grata* to the German Government. It also appears that these officials had hoped that if the Sino—Japanese conflict had somehow been resolved it would not have been necessary to recall the advisers. But as von Schmieden informed the American Ambassador at the beginning of June, 'now that hostilities had assumed proportions of large-scale warfare, the problem of neutrality became more definite'.[88]

Trautmann did not wait for von Ribbentrop's permission before talking with Wang Chung-hui. He was also afraid of press indiscretions because the advisers had already been informed of the decision regarding their future. When told of Germany's decision, the Foreign Minister expressed his 'utter astonishment' and warned that 'the people would interpret the new German measure as indirect aid to Japan'. Like von Falkenhausen, he also stressed the private nature of the advisers' contracts and emphasised that the German advisers were in a similar position to their British, French and American counterparts, who did not obligate their Governments in any way. He also emphasised that they had had no influence on the actual conduct of military operations, while he defended China's own role in the fight against communism. However, he warned Trautmann that if the position of the Central Government was jeopardised China might be forced into the arms of Soviet Russia. Although in an embarrassing position, Trautmann had to follow von Ribbentrop's instructions and ask Wang Chung-hui to do everything possible to avoid any worsening of Sino—German relations. But as he and the Chinese Foreign Minister fully realised, the real responsibility for this lay elsewhere. For the moment, though, Wang reserved China's reply on the question.[89]

There was, however, to be further delay before this question was finally resolved, although pressure from Berlin was maintained. Wang Chung-hui emphasised that the final answer had to come from Chiang Kai-shek himself, and although Trautmann continually pressed for an answer from the Chinese he wanted to avoid linking the advisers' questions with any threat of his own removal from China. Despite his own opposition to the recall of the advisers, in the circumstances Trautmann was forced to admit that their withdrawal was preferable to the shock that would be caused to Sino—German relations if he himself was removed from Hankow. On 25 May, therefore, he allowed a press statement to be issued that the German Government had in fact expressed a desire to the Chinese Government that the advisers should be allowed to cancel their contracts with the Chinese Government and return to Germany, a means by which Germany would be able to maintain her neutrality in the Far Eastern conflict. He followed this up four days later by confirming with the Chinese Foreign Office that notifications for the withdrawal of the German military advisers had been issued, a step which prompted the Chinese Government to lodge a protest in Berlin. At the same time, von Ribbentrop admitted that if Chiang Kai-shek made no difficulty about the withdrawal of the advisers, Trautmann need make no use of the part of the instructions of 17 May referring to his own withdrawal. If the Marshal proved obdurate, however, then Trautmann was to make this point.[90]

Yet if von Ribbentrop was finding it difficult to liquidate the military enterprises in China, his progress in the negotiations with the Japanese was no easier. By the 20 May the complex of negotiations pursued by von Ribbentrop, von Raumer, Wohlthat and Schlotterer of the Ministry of Economics with Ambassador Togo and other members of the Japanese Embassy, had reached the point when each side felt it could define its own position on the various points at issue. When he received the Japanese Ambassador that day von Ribbentrop complained that despite Germany's own positive policies of recognising Manchukuo, issuing orders for the recall of the advisers and banning the further export of war material to China, and the consequent sacrifices and losses which Germany would have to sustain following their implementation, Japan had still not been forthcoming on several points at issue in their mutual economic relations. He emphasised that Germany expected to be granted a *preferential* position in North China and wanted Japan to grant Germany more foreign exchange from German—Japanese trade and to release frozen credits. Togo tried to deflect von Ribbentrop's obvious anger by admitting Germany's various services to Japan, and explaining that it was not until Göring had written to Oshima[91] that the Japanese had learned of the extent of Germany's deliveries of war material to China.[92] Von Ribbentrop rightly doubted this conclusion, and then disputed Togo's assertions regarding the extent of Japan's concessions to Germany on the release of frozen credits. Nor did anything positive emerge from the further discussion of Germany's claims for more foreign exchange, the award of government contracts in Manchukuo, interference with German trade in North China by Japanese monopolies, and German claims for war damages.

The discussion of Germany's claims for a special status in North China at least produced something positive, the presentation of a *Pro Memoria* by Ambassador Togo which outlined the Japanese position as a result of the negotiations pursued so far in Berlin, and which he said was authorised by Tokio. Apart from repeating German and Japanese expressions of willingness to cooperate on economic questions in North China, which included von Ribbentrop's statement of his 'recognition' of the 'special position of Japan in China', the memorandum set out Japan's policy in two very carefully worded paragraphs which appeared to adopt a positive approach to Germany's wishes but in reality defended Japan's own interests to the hilt. The first paragraph stated that Japan would not give Germany the subordinate position of a third power in North China but 'will favourably consider German interests *where possible* [author's italics] in individual cases in which proposals may in future be made by Germany'. The sting came in the next sentence which pointed out that any 'benevolent treatment' thus granted to Germany could not preclude cooperation with third powers, an obvious hint that Germany might have to share her 'special' position with a country like Italy. The second paragraph dealt with the actual treatment of German trade in North China, and likewise stated that it would be on the same footing and receive the same treatment as Japan's trade, except that 'it should be emphasised that it will be necessary to safeguard any special position of Japan resulting for instance, from the necessity of preserving the monetary system in North China which is inseparably connected with the Japanese monetary system'.[93]

The Japanese *Pro Memoria,* which at least gave the German— Japanese negotiations a more substantive basis on which to work, was to cause tremendous difficulties over the ensuing months. The key problem was the precise definition of the position or status to be granted to Germany in the Japanese-controlled area of North China. According to Ambassador Togo's post-war testimony the Japanese memorandum was a direct response to two memoranda presented by von Ribbentrop which emphasised that Germany's demand was for 'preferential treatment' in North China. Togo opposed this on the rather surprising grounds that 'it would naturally result in violation of existing treaty obligations (I had in mind the Nine-Power Treaty) to grant Germany anything other than most-favoured-nation treatment in China'. He therefore narrowed down his instructions from Tokio, which had spoken of Germany being offered 'the best possible preference' in economic matters in North China and promising that Germany's interests would be given preference over those of any third country, to defining Japan's offer as being based on 'benevolent treatment' for Germany on an equal basis with third countries.[94]

A foretaste of the difficulties ahead was soon provided. On 28 May von Ribbentrop and Ambassador Togo clashed over the German demand for the provision of more foreign exchange by Japan, Togo objecting to Germany's apparent attempt to link this question with Germany's demands regarding North China. Von Ribbentrop denied this, but pointed out that Germany's foreign exchange losses in China were so serious they forced her to attach greater importance than before to increased foreign exchange revenue in all economic negotiations, a fact which applied just as much to the talks with Japan.[95] A week later Togo crossed swords with von Raumer and Wiehl on several aspects of the Japanese *Pro Memoria* of 20 May. The Germans now proposed to insert the words, 'concerning the economic development of the areas of China under Japanese influence', in place of China or North China. The intention was to ensure the protection of German interests in the future, as and when Japanese forces conquered more of the mainland. Not surprisingly, Togo rejected this proposal. As much difficulty was experienced in the discussion on the form in which Germany's future position in North China was to be admitted or granted by Japan. Togo was adamant that the Japanese Government would not agree specifically in the *Pro Memoria* to German demands for the insertion of 'preferential treatment', but insisted that Japan was prepared to treat Germany in the 'best manner possible'. After two hours of what was probably a frustrating experience for them, von Raumer and Wiehl withdrew on the premise that they would submit later a text covering their demand that 'Germany, as compared with third powers, should be accorded treatment in keeping with the particularly friendly relations existing between Germany and Japan'.[96]

Although the Japanese gave no definite indication that their attitude towards the German demands would be improved by the final withdrawal of the German advisers from China and the total liquidation of other military links between the two countries, von Ribbentrop undoubtedly believed that once these matters had been dispensed with the Japanese would prove more amenable. On the other hand, Germany would then be in a stronger position to demand concessions from Japan. Yet there was no guarantee that once Germany had satisfied Japan in these respects she would then prove any more accommodating in the economic negotiations than she had been hitherto. Not surprisingly, von Ribbentrop's position on the military questions still at issue in Sino—German relations was an extreme one. Furthermore, after the week-end crisis of 20—21 May 1938 and the rapidly worsening situation in German—Czech and Anglo—German relations, Japan's value as a political and strategic ally increased in the eyes of Hitler and von Ribbentrop. Hence the importance of von Ribbentrop's negotiations with Rome in May and Tokio from June 1938 onwards.[97]

Von Ribbentrop's policy of sacrificing Germany's politico-military interests in China appeared to be partially vindicated by the interview Eugen Ott, the newly appointed Ambassador to Japan, had with Hirota on 5 May before his departure for

Berlin. Ott's promotion from Military Attaché to Ambassador on 5 April had caused some surprise abroad and was taken as evidence of the increasing militancy of Germany's role in world affairs, besides having an obvious significance for German—Japanese relations. Following his appointment as Ambassador, Ott was ordered home for discussions with Hitler. According to Kordt's memoirs, Hitler seems to have been impressed by the intimate relations established between Ott and the Japanese General Staff. Kordt also suggests that by appointing a Military Attaché as Ambassador it was hoped to present the Japanese with a precedent that they themselves could follow in the case of Oshima, which happened shortly afterwards.[98]

The discussion between Ott and Hirota centred around the contents of a memorandum which Hirota wanted transmitted to Berlin. This stated that the recent decision of the German Government to withdraw the military advisers from China 'is highly appreciated'; that the Japanese Government had 'full confidence' in the attitude of the German Government regarding the reports of further arms deliveries to China; and that the German Government was invited to despatch an economic mission to North China to investigate matters on the spot which would enable Germany to arrive 'at some concrete decision with regard to methods of promoting them and approach the Japanese Government on individual questions'. Once this had been done 'the Japanese Government would be fully prepared to give favourable consideration' to such proposals as were presented by Germany.

It was clear that the Japanese Government regarded the future withdrawal of the German advisers from China as a great personal victory, while Hirota's statements about North China made it appear as though Tokio recognised the gesture which Germany had made in her direction. It was, however, the question of Germany's reported arms deliveries to China which Ott directly related to Germany's search for 'compensations' in North China, and in this stand he was complementing that adopted by Göring in Berlin. Ott denied reports that German arms were still being shipped through Hong Kong, but argued that because there had been no declaration of war in the Far East the Reich Government could not cancel previous commercial agreements by business firms without having to assume full financial liability for them which, if it did, would hamper the 'great task of developing and strengthening the German economy and the Wehrmacht'. Ott made it quite clear that 'the situation would be different if compensations were found in the Far East. The Embassy, therefore, was following the Commercial Attaché's investigations of business prospects in North China with great interest'. Hirota accepted Ott's arguments and expressed the hope that 'compensations would be found for Germany in North China. As to the outstanding issue of colonies, the Foreign Minister repeated the views he had outlined to von Dirksen on 5 February, while he also pressed for the establishment of additional Anti-Comintern committees in Rome and Tokio. He also repeated his statement of a fortnight earlier to Noebel, that Japan's statement of 16 January 1938 remained in force and that negotiations with Chiang Kai-shek were out of the question.[99]

When Ott saw Hitler in Berlin at the end of May the Führer explained to him that it would be his concern to remedy the Japanese aversion to Soviet Russia and to convince them instead that it was England which ought to be opposed. Ott raised objections by saying that Japanese policy was chiefly determined by her relations with the United States, and that she should only be considered a strategic factor for Germany if America remained neutral. Hitler rejected this notion as too pessimistic.[100]

On the question of arms deliveries to China it appears that other people in the Foreign Office and certainly the Ministry of Economics were inclined to adopt a fairly flexible attitude. On 27 May, around which time Ott's report of his interview with Hirota was received in the Foreign Office, the two Ministries came to an agreement on the interpretation to be given to Göring's prohibition order of the previous month, that it was not to apply to old contracts with China, i.e. those concluded prior to August 1937. On the basis of this 'understanding', and in reply to Trautmann's inquiry of 5 May, Wiehl telegraphed Hankow on 4 June with the news that Göring's order applied to the export of essential war material but that the old contracts would be honoured. HAPRO contracts for which immediate foreign exchange had been arranged would also be excluded from the prohibition, while it was thought that the iron and steelwork projects would go ahead. Wiehl emphasised that war material was not being delivered to Japan, only machine tools and other industrial goods.[101]

Ten days later, however, von Ribbentrop insisted that this loophole be closed. On 14 June, therefore, Wiehl impressed on Schlotterer of the Ministry of Economics von Ribbentrop's view that all deliveries of actual war material to China would have to cease, regardless of when the contract for delivery had been concluded. Wiehl also pointed out that the agreement of 27 May had been the result of 'a misunderstanding'. This makes it appear as though von Ribbentrop did not know of the understanding with the Ministry of Economics, which is unlikely, or that he did not grasp its full significance, a more likely explanation. Either way, his reaction to the idea that some arms were still getting through to China must have been a strong one for Wiehl now compounded his retreat from his position of 4 June by noting that Göring's instructions to the Ministry of Economics were obviously 'not so strict as the position now taken by the Foreign Minister, and that, particularly in certain cases, they still permitted the delivery of outright military equipment'. Strachwitz was therefore instructed to clarify the situation with Lieutenant Commander Schottky of the Ministry of Economics. Schottky's replies appeared to satisfy Wiehl, and presumably von Ribbentrop, since they emphasised that the Ministry of Economics had speedily and strictly executed Göring's prohibition order of 27 April: that since the end of May no deliveries of outright military equipment had been permitted and although work was continuing on certain other orders, eg. for submarines and torpedoes, delivery to China would not be made. Of particular interest to von Ribbentrop in his negotiations with the Japanese was the figure given of the Reich's expected losses as a result of not fulfilling the contracts with China, 282 million Reichsmarks, a far cry from Göring's figure of 100 million. In any case, as the Ministry of Economics emphasised, this loss 'could cripple our armament industry'.[102]

Von Ribbentrop's impatience with things Chinese was even more pronounced over the lack of progress on the question of the advisers in China. That he might be forced to use the threat of Trautmann's removal sooner rather than later[103] became clear from a telegram from Trautmann on 4 June. Chiang Kai-shek had said he was unable to give an answer on the question since he had had no opportunity to discuss the matter with the advisers themselves. Moreover, he wanted to know whether German officers working with the Japanese Navy and Air Force as advisers would also be withdrawn. Trautmann forcefully denied the truth of such reports and pressed for a definite answer on the position of the advisers in China. This was not because he wished to see the ultimate execution of the order but because he was well aware of the consequences for Sino—German relations and Germany's general position in the Far East if von Ribbentrop felt he had to implement his threat to withdraw Trautmann from Hankow. To the Foreign Office, however, Trautmann expressed the opinion that Chiang Kai-shek and the advisers ought to be given an opportunity to discuss the question, although von Falkenhausen also said that such a chance had not yet arisen. On the other hand, Trautmann made it quite clear to Chiang Kai-shek that ultimately the advisers would have to follow the dictates of the German Government.[104]

There can be no doubt as to the nature of von Ribbentrop's reaction to this news, and Trautmann was probably vilified as much as Chiang Kai-shek. From this point on the pressure on the Chinese Government was intensified. When denying the veracity of reports of German advisers in Japan to the Chinese Ambassador in Berlin, von Weizsäcker emphasised that there should be no further delay on this question 'in the interests of our friendly relations'.[105] By 10 June Trautmann was told that a definite reply about the departure of the advisers was expected by 13 June.[106] Trautmann had still not seen Chiang Kai-shek, but was hard put to it to deny to the Chinese officials he met that this was in fact an ultimatum. Nevertheless, he insisted that an immediate reply was necessary. He also cast doubt on the feasibility of Chiang Kai-shek's suggestion that a small number of the advisers remain in China, and that von Falkenhausen should stay behind as German Military Attaché, a question that had prompted itself as soon as it was known the advisers would be withdrawn.[107] Trautmann was right to have his doubts since these proposals were rejected out of hand by von Ribbentrop in another stiffly worded instruction of 13 June insisting on the immediate departure of the advisers. Once again reference was made to Hitler's wishes in the matter, but by this time von Ribbentrop's patience was obviously at an end since Trautmann was now told to inform Chiang Kai-shek that if he continued his opposition to the release of the advisers he would have to expect Trautmann's 'immediate recall'.[108]

By the following day, 14 June, it appeared to the Wilhelmstrasse that the whole question was well on the way to a solution. Before receiving von Ribbentrop's latest instructions Trautmann had already seen Chiang Kai-shek to impress on him that it was Hitler's wish that the advisers should leave China. To Trautmann's surprise, the Marshal said that in consideration of this he would now release the military advisers and allow the majority of them to leave immediately. Orders would be issued immediately to von Falkenhausen, and in this way he thought that Germany's neutrality would be preserved. Much to Trautmann's discomfort, though, Chiang Kai-shek insisted that his request for the retention of four or five advisers be passed to Berlin, despite the fact that he probably knew further difficulties over the withdrawal of all the advisers would endanger Trautmann's own position. It was clear, though, that the Marshal had spoken to von Falkenhausen as promised. When Trautmann informed the chief adviser of von Ribbentrop's instructions of 13 June he had the impression that the advisers would obey Hitler's orders. But in view of the nature of his own talk with Chiang Kai-shek, Trautmann now wondered whether he ought to present the threat of his withdrawal from China. However, he preferred to wait for the Marshal's instructions to von Falkenhausen before so acting, if Berlin thought this was necessary.[109]

Not surprisingly, von Ribbentrop thought such a step would be necessary if *all* the advisers did not leave China in the shortest possible time. At first Trautmann only hinted at this when he confirmed to the Vice Foreign Minister that the retention of any advisers was out of the question. But when the latter then told him that Chiang Kai-shek was insisting on retaining five or six advisers, Trautmann said that Chiang Kai-shek must now be told that if he persisted in this attitude his own immediate recall would have to be expected.[110] Following further indications that Chiang Kai-shek was maintaining his strong attitude, von Ribbentrop intensified his pressure. On 20 June Trautmann was instructed to tell the Chinese Government it had three days in which to confirm that all the advisers would leave. Failing this, Trautmann would have to turn all his affairs over to the Chargé d'Affaires and return to Germany with the real risk that a severance of diplomatic relations would be the consequence. Pressure was also to be exerted on the advisers themselves. They were now to be told they risked losing their German citizenship and the confiscation of their property if they did not comply with Hitler's wishes, while von Falkenhausen was to accompany Trautmann when the instructions were carried out. Immediately both men saw Hsu Mo, the Vice Foreign Minister and gave him this rather depressing and extremely important news.[111]

The Chinese Government met this ultimatum, for such it was, with a memorandum which expressed more sorrow than anger at the turn of events. This stated that because of the friendly relations with Germany it was not proposed to take a stand on the strictly legal viewpoint of the issue of the private nature of the adviser's contracts and Germany's request for the termination of the contracts would be complied with. Nevertheless, it was emphasised that the Chinese Government intended to retain the services of five or six advisers 'temporarily in order to wind up their affairs'. When this had been done, they too would be allowed to leave China.

It was apparent that the latter suggestion was Chiang Kai-shek's personal doing, and was based on two reasons. The first concerned military-technical factors. The war against Japan was still proceeding, and appeared likely to do so for a considerable time to come. Not only was the retention of a number of German advisers important to Chiang Kai-shek for this purpose, but because they possessed intimate knowledge of the fortifications at Hankow and on the Yangtse he was afraid that if they returned to Germany 'pressure would be put on them to reveal what they knew for transmission to Japan'.[112] Secondly, the issue had obviously and rapidly become one of prestige for both Berlin and Hankow. Chiang Kai-shek had evidently been infuriated when he learned of von Ribbentrop's instructions to Trautmann of 20 June and had threatened to intern the advisers rather than let them go.[113]

Trautmann was told that when the Prime Minister and Vice-Chancellor attempted to intercede with Chiang Kai-shek for a modification of his extreme attitude 'he gave them the devil'. On the other hand, it was also clear that as far as possible the Chinese Government was meeting Germany's wishes. On 22 June Prime Minister Kung gave a farewell dinner for the

advisers at which he spoke warmly about Sino—German relations and thanked the advisers for their valuable work in China.
For his part, von Falkenhausen told Trautmann that by 23 June
the advisers' office would be closed and an official communication made to Chiang Kai-shek that this work was at an end.[114]

Von Ribbentrop, however, did not accept that the attitude
of the Chinese Government as at 23 June constituted a complete acceptance of his conditions of 20 June. On 24 June,
therefore, Trautmann was instructed to take his leave of
China and hand over his affairs to his Chargé d'Affaire. Five
days later von Weizsäcker admitted that if the advisers left
Hankow on 5 July as arranged there was the possibility that
diplomatic relations between the two countries would be
maintained.[115] As it was, at their farewell meeting on 25 June
Chiang Kai-shek had assured Trautmann that all the advisers
would be released, although it was still to be a fortnight before
they actually departed from China.[116]

On 26 June 1938, therefore, Trautmann left his post, never
to return, while following banquets given in their honour on
2 July by Chiang Kai-shek and on the 4th by the Minister of
War, General Ho Ying-chin, von Falkenhausen and the other
advisers caught a special train at 9 o'clock on the morning of
5 July from Hankow to Canton. Their departure, witnessed
by the War Minister and other Chinese leaders, brought to an
end an important epoch in Germany's relations with China.
Already on 24 May *The Times* of London had written an
epitaph for the work the advisers left behind them in China:

thus ends . . . a record of nearly 10 years' fine work under often exaspe-
rating and always difficult conditions. Quietly, patiently, through
wearisome and disillusioning years of civil war against the Communists,
the Germans have transformed the Chinese Armed Forces from a mass
into something like a machine; and when Japan put the machine to the
test, the Germans, though always in the background, provided China's
new-found will to resist with an effectively adapted strategy. There is
no such thing in China as a trained General Staff, and the Germans,
besides their work at training depots, supplied the High Command with
invaluable guidance in the conduct of the war. It is probable, also, that
they acted as a unifying force on the heterogeneous and not normally
reconcilable military elements: General A, for instance, who has never
liked General B, will take B's orders less reluctantly if he understands
that foreign experts had a hand in their drafting. The recall of the
German advisers is a serious matter to China . . . the High Command
will miss them badly. From the point of view of German prestige and
trade in China Herr Hitler's gesture is likely to prove disastrous . . .

The departure of Trautmann and the military advisers showed that there no longer existed any semblance of 'balance' in Germany's Far Eastern policy, despite von Ribbentrop's request to Ambassador Togo that influence be exerted on the Japanese press to refrain from conjecture about a severance of Sino—German relations and a German recognition of the Peking régime.[117] The final and *de jure* break in Sino—German relations did not occur until 2 July 1941, the day after Germany formally recognised the pro-Japanese régime of Wang Ching-wei.[118] Nevertheless, there could be no doubt that from the summer of 1938 economic, military, and political relations with Japan would be developed post haste — in so far as this was possible, given the difficulties and constant reserve which still existed between the two countries — at the expense of those with China, and *pari passu* with developments in Europe which brought that continent to the edge of war in the autumn of 1938, actual war in 1939, and Germany's war with Soviet Russia in the summer of 1941.[119]

'By July 1938 Japan had charged her toll, and Germany had paid in full the price of the Anti-Comintern Pact . . . Germany deserted the "weaker" power for the "stronger" but in the end she failed to profit from either'.[120] In the final event, therefore, the policies of Trautmann (and even of von Neurath) had had to succumb to those of von Dirksen and von Ribbentrop. The paradox was that it was the Wilhelmstrasse, that previous exponent of the policy of balance — in its ideal form a chimera, a fact recognised in the Wilhelmstrasse — which now executed the policy of imbalance in the Far East continually proposed and worked for by the Nazi leadership. But since von Ribbentrop was now Foreign Minister that paradox was understandable.

Conclusion

The examination of Germany's Far Eastern policy from 1931 to 1938 provides a useful microcosm of German foreign policy making processes as a whole in a period of rapid and far-reaching change in Germany, Europe, and the Far East. It is a period which opens with Japan's first tentative advances in Manchuria and closes with her increasing dominance in China and poised on the path that was to take her to Pearl Harbor (and Hiroshima). In Europe the period marked the transformation of Germany from a republic assailed by internal conflict and economic crisis to a would-be totalitarian state ruled by Adolf Hitler and the National Socialist Party. From 1931 to 1938 Germany's international position was transformed from one of tentative participation in the post-1918 and post-Locarno power constellation into that of a nation seen as the real threat to the peace of Europe and the likely cause of any subsequent European war. Internally, the régime undoubtedly affected all aspects of the nation's life, but did so in varying degrees and at different times, and historians are now generally agreed that Nazi Germany was something less than a truly totalitarian state. Far Eastern policy, then, is a useful case study of how far and when Nazi lines of foreign policy were accepted — or resisted and even rejected — by other German policy makers. Immediately this raises one fundamental question: to what extent, if any, could 'Nazi' foreign policy be described as being different from 'German' foreign policy? Where, if at all, did the two coincide so that one also came to serve the interests of the other?

Much more was involved in Germany in January 1933 than simply a change of Chancellor and government. Apart from the fundamental changes in the practices and principles of German society which it was intended to institute, Adolf Hitler and the Nazi régime put into even sharper focus the question which had dominated German domestic and foreign policies ever since Compiègne and Versailles: whither Germany, and how? Most historians agree that with Nazism the questions posed about German foreign policy are not so much those of *Kontinuität oder Diskontinuität* with the emphasis on the *oder*, but rather the degrees to which each of these elements was to be found in the whole range of German foreign policy after January 1933. As from that date what could still be described as 'traditional' in that policy, and what was new or novel in it? Was there simply to be a revived, strengthened, and newly-respected Germany which the diplomats, soldiers, and industrialists wanted in order to overthrow the final vestiges of the Treaty of Versailles and aiming, at the very least, for a position of *primus inter pares* in European affairs? Such policies, which one might well describe as in the tradition of *Grossdeutschlandspolitik*, were such as to have involved Germany, almost inevitably at some time or the other, in armed conflict with one or more of her immediate neighbours and most certainly with Poland. There can be no doubt, though, that such a conflict would have been completely different, both in character and intent, from the war which Hitler eventually brought about.

Or was Germany and German foreign policy to be something entirely and uniquely different and was Hitler's philosophy of foreign policy to be the only or dominant one? Hitler saw revision simply as the stepping-stone towards his *jihad,* the holy and racial war against Jewish-Bolshevism with its power base for world domination in Soviet Russia, where he also intended to gain *Lebensraum im Osten* for the superior German Aryan *Volk* at Russia's expense.

Where, then, did the Far East come into the application of these different political concepts? Hitler was as much an astute *Politiker* as he was a *Programmatiker*, always ready to take advantage of current situations if they could help him achieve his long-term aims. Militarist Japan, clearly embarked on her own policy of aggression and expansion, occupied a crucial strategic and political situation in the Far East *vis-à-vis* the interests and position of the two countries which dominated Hitler's political philosophy and foreign policy: Great Britain and the Soviet Union. An alignment of sorts between Germany and Japan — and initially Hitler envisaged only a limited and ideological agreement as finally manifested in the Anti-Comintern Pact of November 1936 — would help serve the aims and intent of German policy in Europe, as Hitler saw these.

While political developments in Europe led Hitler to pursue an increasingly pro-Japanese line of policy, nevertheless and *pari passu* Germany became closely involved with China. Arising out of Germany's general economic situation and trade requirements, and further based on military links between the two countries going back to 1927, this involvement was intensified because of Hitler's insistence on 'everything for the armed forces'. Gradually, China became one of Germany's most important suppliers of raw materials essential for Germany's rearmament, while in turn that level of rearmament constituted an important and obvious determinant of Hitler's European policies. Sino—German relations were also underlined by the involvement of German military advisers in China's own rearmament and military retraining processes. Additionally, though, the Sino—German relationship had political overtones within the context of the Far Eastern struggle for power between China and Japan. Certainly, neither China nor Japan were entirely content with Germany's separate but quite different relationship with the other, although on balance Japanese complaints on this score were louder and more insistent than Chinese ones.

The crucial question of whether and for how long these two separate German policies in the Far East could actually be pursued, or whether one would finally have to succumb to the other, depended not only on developments in the Far East but also upon the complex power structure and struggle within Nazi Germany. The subject of Germany's Far Eastern policy from 1931 to 1938 is therefore an excellent illustration of the fascinating interaction of personalities and policies within the whole of the Nazi system of government and society. Like the study of all other policies, the Far Eastern one too can be reduced to that simple but apposite trinity: people, power, and policies. Who were the people involved in making policy and what were their characters? What positions of power did they hold or aspire to? How did they relate to each other? What were the factors contributing to the formulation of their policies? What policies did they finally aim to implement? Finally, who really was 'master' in the hothouse that was Nazi Germany? Was it Hitler alone, or other component parts of the State system? Or, more sensibly, was it some combination of all these elements which produced the policies Germany ultimately followed in the Far East and elsewhere?

As much depended on political or ideological conviction as on other factors. In this respect Hitler and some of the other

Nazi leaders had the edge over their more conservative opponents, or at least over those who whilst not actively opposing
them did not entirely support them either. Hitler at least
knew where he wanted to go. At the same time, as with the
Nazi régime and German society as a whole, much of what
Hitler and the Nazis were attempting in foreign policy found
a ready response and support in many diplomatic, military,
and economic circles. So that, for example, the German
Army's goals in China, gradually and almost imperceptibly,
came to serve *Nazi* as much as *German* goals. But then the
paradox: *Nazi* goals in and with Japan, because of the prevailing situation of tension and near-war between China and
Japan, were bound eventually to run counter to *German* goals
in China.

That Germany's Far Eastern policy still retained its double
aspect until the summer of 1938 when the choice was made
for Japan, despite all the pressures to the contrary exerted
long before, says a great deal for the nature and strength of
the other policy-making personalities and bodies in Nazi
Germany which Hitler and von Ribbentrop had to contend
with. That Hitler did not completely 'Nazify' the leadership
of the German Foreign Office and Armed Forces until
4 February 1938 also says a great deal for Hitler's own
attitudes and position *vis-à-vis* these pillars of State in Nazi
Germany. The Wilhelmstrasse's role in this power struggle,
even after 4 February 1938, was a mixed one, as was its
contribution to Far Eastern policy. In principle, the policies
of 'balance' in the Far East advocated under von Neurath
were maintained until the summer of 1938. Not that there
could ever be a true policy of balance since the different parts
of Germany's Far Eastern policy – or policies – originated
with different policy-making bodies within Germany who
were often in conflict with each other. In practice, the
Wilhelmstrasse saw its ideal policy of 'equal but uncomitted'
relations with both China and Japan eroded long before 1938,
firstly by the German Army in China and then by the Nazi
leadership in Japan. Yet while its voice was never omnipotent,
neither was it insignificant. Nevertheless, its position and
influence in the Nazi jungle was hardly helped by the character
of the man who was Foreign Minister until February 1938,
Constantin von Neurath. Personally weak, his was a civil service
and not a political appointment. Consequently, not only did

he practice the German civil servant's creed of unquestioning obedience to the legitimate government of the day — and constitutionally Hitler's was a legitimate government — but it also meant that he had no real *entrée* to the inner sanctum of political power in Nazi Germany. Together with the weaknesses of von Neurath's character, this situation placed the Wilhelmstrasse at a double disadvantage until February 1938. But if the authority and influence of the Wilhelmstrasse was already weakened by the character of von Neurath, exacerbated by Hitler's own dislike for diplomats and the civil service class as a whole, its reputation could hardly have been enhanced by the actions of von Dirksen who espoused Nazi and not Wilhelmstrasse policy for Germany in the Far East whilst serving as Ambassador to Japan. Nor, in von Dirksen's case, was it merely an unexceptional example of 'Ambassador's disease' but rather one of attempted self-seeking in the Nazi hierarchy compounded by a degree of disloyalty towards his diplomatic colleagues. Across the water of the Japan and Yellow Seas, however, one can only praise the professional and personal qualities of the Ambassador to China, Oskar Trautmann, and from what one gathers from the diplomatic evidence at least the strong impression gained is of that rarity at a time when the quality of public and private life in Germany was daily being debased, a gentleman.

Nevertheless, for all its personal and political difficulties, and notwithstanding post-war claims that under the Nazis the Wilhelmstrasse lost all power and influence, that department of State constantly maintained some voice of authority in the discussions and making of Far Eastern policy. This was true even with regard to the diplomatic handling of the Army's interests in China, as well as the involvement of German economic circles in the Chinese economy. While the Wilhelmstrasse came to recognise the undoubted military and economic benefits that Germany obtained from China, nevertheless its members often showed a strong degree of cynicism and doubt about the capabilities of the Chinese and the Chinese economy, especially when the question of German government financial involvement in this trade came up for discussion. This goes some way towards disposing of the usual legend that the Wilhelmstrasse was completely pro-Chinese in its attitudes. It was not. It was entirely pro-German and attempted to serve and protect Germany's interests, whatever and wherever they were and however it saw them. Yet despite its doubts about China, it was always quick to defend German interests and activity in China against any Japanese criticism, pointing out that Germany had the right to pursue her interests in that country without having to contend with complaints from Japan. While this was easier said than done with regard to economic interests, Germany's military relations with China obviously caused more difficulty in German–Japanese relations because they implied more than a degree of political support of China by Germany in the Far Eastern struggle for power. Not surprisingly, one of Japan's chief objectives was to get all forms of German 'support' for China reduced or even withdrawn altogether.

Despite Hitler's ideological interest in Japan and von Ribbentrop's individual negotiations with the Japanese military authorities, the Wilhelmstrasse's authority and experience in the field of 'normal' diplomatic relations with Japan was generally recognised to be paramount, even by the Nazi leadership. Nor was there any direct interference from Hitler in this direction. When the Foreign Office made it clear in the winter of 1933–34 that it would not work to achieve Hitler's desire of a closer German–Japanese relationship, he simply left it to get on with its business of diplomacy while he quietly used para-diplomatic channels to get what he wanted. Although official and unofficial channels of communication were both important in the general field of German–Japanese relations during the Nazi régime, it was the Wilhelmstrasse's contribution towards an easing of tension in those relations, because of Nazi Germany's racial legislation and the possible effects or consequences for the Japanese, that helped ease the way for von Ribbentrop's secret negotiations which were to lead to the Anti-Comintern Pact. Without the Wilhelmstrasse's contribution in an area of activity generally despised by Hitler and the other Nazis, diplomacy, von Ribbentrop's own negotiations might have proved even more difficult if not downright impossible. So far as Manchukuo was concerned, it was in fact the German Foreign Office which was most influential in bringing about the important economic agreement of 1936. In turn, this agreement could only signify something positive and certainly not negative for German–Japanese relations.

The making of German Far Eastern policy in the 1930s was

an exceptionally complex and difficult process. It involved personal reputations and positions of authority as much as substantive issues of policy. Little wonder, then, that in his report of 27 January 1937 Ambassador Trautmann should have felt it necessary to spell out both the cause and effect of Germany's difficulties in the Far East at the time, although the Wilhelmstrasse had been made painfully aware of the situation for some time past. Trautmann pointed out that the root cause of Germany's difficulties was that there was no single German Far Eastern policy as such (nor indeed could there be), directed or organised through one government department, e.g. the Foreign Office. Instead, there existed a series of different and hardly coordinated policies because the mainsprings of Germany's Chinese and Japanese policies were to be found in different Ministries and Party groups. Thus, the inherent conflict in the Far East was duplicated inside Germany.

It would be wrong to assume, however, that the existence of this conflict in Germany over policy towards the Far East meant that there was a 'dilemma' in this policy in the years 1931 to 1937 and then to 1938. In any situation a dilemma only arises when it becomes a matter of deciding between finely balanced and possibly equally advantageous interests, which however can still be in conflict with each other. However, none of the major foreign policy making groups in Germany ever felt the necessity of having to admit such niceties in their assessment of Germany's position and policies in the Far East. The German Army, economic, and industrial interests certainly had no doubt that for their purposes there was no alternative to China. For their part the Nazi leadership was equally convinced that there could be no alternative to Japan. If either group ever thought about Japan or China respectively, it was only in a negative or passive sense. Both seemed to feel that their particular interests could be pursued without it mattering what the effect would be on the other Far Eastern power and, consequently, on Germany's position in the Far East. Even Hitler seemed to think that he could run with both the hounds and the hare: while he pursued Japan, he also recognised the crucial importance of Germany's military interests in China.

In this complex situation the Wilhelmstrasse's role was sometimes that of fireman or policeman, sometimes that of honest broker, but always the unenviable one of being the middle-man in a vortex of constant activity. Certainly, it was the Wilhelmstrasse which had to bear the brunt of any and all brickbats thrown by the Chinese and Japanese because of their dissatisfaction with particular parts of German activity and policy in the Far East. In the final analysis, though, the Wilhelmstrasse's ability and power to maintain what precarious balance there was in German Far Eastern policy was strictly limited. While peace ruled in the Far East, however uneasy it may have been, the Wilhelmstrasse (and some others, includ-ing even Hitler) felt that the situation of inherent conflict which existed between the different parts of Germany's Far Eastern policy within Germany could be contained. It had, of course, absolutely no control over events in the Far East, so that when war finally erupted in the summer of 1937 it was only a matter of time before this event would have its inevit-able and disruptive effect upon the precarious balance of forces inside Germany. It was, of course, the Anti-Comintern Pact of November 1936, which von Ribbentrop and not the Wilhelmstrasse had negotiated, that marked the beginning of the end for Germany's more general and 'balanced' position in the Far East. Although the German Army had also concluded its own agreement with China earlier in 1936, it was von Ribbentrop's contribution to the world's wisdom (as Professor Gerhard Weinberg has so aptly described it) which publicly and politically signified a form of commitment to Japan on Germany's part — whatever the real truth of the situation was behind the scenes and away from the public gaze. Moreover, not only was it more in Japan's and not Germany's interest to 'call in' this particular card, but given all the circumstances the initiative for doing so at any particular time was bound to be Japan's alone. In a sense, then, von Ribbentrop had mortgaged Germany's interests in China to Japan and had made their future absolutely dependent upon Japanese policy and Japanese whims. Not surprisingly, after July 1937 Japan tried desperately to call Germany to account by attempting to get her to withdraw completely from China. Given Japan's military advances in the Far Eastern war, Germany's own manoeuvring in Europe ready to take advantage of any situa-tion that might present itself in 1938 and beyond (viz., the important meeting of 5 November 1937), and von Ribben-trop's appointment as Foreign Minister in February 1938, it was not surprising that by the summer of 1938 Germany's policy of precarious balance had been replaced by one of commitment to Japan. But even that process still took almost six difficult months to achieve after von Ribbentrop's elevation to the office he had so long coveted, showing yet again that the course of Nazi policy in Germany was still hardly straightforward or particularly easy even five years after the *Machtergreifung*. The paradox was, of course, that in the final event it was that previous exponent of the policy of balance, the Wilhelmstrasse, which brought about that policy of imbalance in the summer of 1938 so long desired by the Nazi leadership, or at least by von Ribbentrop himself. But since von Ribbentrop was now Foreign Minister that paradox was understandable, while in pursuing this particular policy the Wilhelmstrasse merely confirmed the practices and traditions of its constitutional position *vis-à-vis* the legitimate government of Germany. Nevertheless, and in the final analysis, one can still argue that in the Far East it was Nazi ideology which finally triumphed over German diplomacy in the formulation and execution of Germany's Far Eastern policy in the years 1931 to 1938.

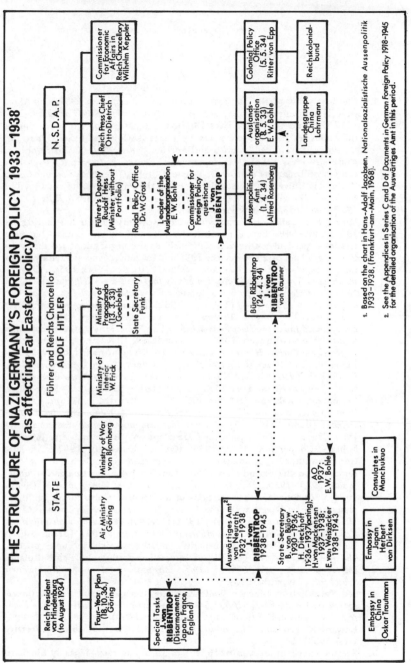

The Structure of Nazi Germany's Foreign Policy 1933–1938[1] (as affecting Far Eastern policy)

Notes

Introduction

1. The best study of the Far East in international affairs to 1931 is by Akira Iriye, *After Imperialism: The Search for a New Order in the Far East 1921–1931* (Harvard University Press 1965). For Japanese foreign policy during the 1930s see the excellent study by James B. Crowley, *Japan's Quest for Autonomy: National Security and Foreign Policy 1930–1938* (Princeton University Press 1966). A useful survey of Chinese history in the twentieth century still remains that by O. Edmund Clubb, *Twentieth Century China* (Columbia University Press 1964). See also the important study by Lloyd E. Eastman, *The Abortive Revolution: China under Nationalist Rule 1927–1937* (Harvard University Press 1974).

2. Most other studies on Germany's 'policy' towards the Far East during the 1930s (and 1940s) have concentrated almost entirely on German–Japanese relations, particular attention being paid to the negotiations for the Anti-Comintern Pact of 25 November 1936 and its consequences: Frank William Iklé, *German–Japanese Relations 1936–1940* (New York 1956); Ernst L. Presseisen, *Germany and Japan: A Study in Totalitarian Diplomacy 1933–1941* (The Hague 1958); Theo Sommer, *Deutschland und Japan zwischen den Mächten 1935–1940* (Tübingen 1962); Johanna Menzel Meskill, *Hitler and Japan: The Hollow Alliance* (New York 1966); Bernd Martin, *Deutschland und Japan im Zweiten Weltkrieg: Von Pearl Harbor bis zur deutschen Kapitulation* (Göttingen, 1969); V. Issraeljan & L. Kutakov, *Diplomacy of Aggression: Berlin–Rome–Tokio Axis, Its Rise and Fall* (Moscow 1970); James William Morley (ed.), *Deterrent Diplomacy, Japan, Germany, and the USSR 1935–1940. Selected translations from Taiheiyo senso e no michi: kaisen gaiko shi* (New York 1976); Bernd Martin, 'Die deutsch–japanischen Beziehungen während des Dritten Reiches', in Manfred Funke (ed.), *Hitler, Deutschland, und die Mächte. Materialien zur Aussenpolitik des Dritten Reiches* (Bonn 1976), 454–70. See also the unpublished dissertation by John Chapman, 'The Origins and Development of German and Japanese Military Cooperation 1936–1945' (Oxford University 1967). An East German author has approached the subject more generally but he too concentrates on the period after 1936: Karl Drechsler, *Deutschland–China–Japan 1933–1939: Das Dilemma der deutschen Fernostpolitik* (Berlin 1964). For Sino–German relations in the 1930s see also the unpublished dissertation by Beverley Douglas Causey Jr, 'German Policy towards China 1918–1941' (Harvard University 1942); Joachim Peck, *Kolonialismus ohne Kolonien: der deutsche Imperialismus und China 1937* (Berlin 1961); Hartmut Bloss, 'Deutsche Chinapolitik im Dritten Reich', in Funke, op. cit., 407–29. See also the general but interesting account by Bernd Ruland, *Deutsche Botschaft Peking. Das Jahrhundert deutsch–chinesischen Schicksals* (Bayreuth 1973).

3. See Karl Dietrich Bracher, Wolfgang Sauer, Gerhard Schulz, *Die nationalsozialistische Machtergreifung: Studien zur Errichtung des totalitären Herrschaftssystems in Deutschland 1933/34* (Köln 1960).

4. Edward N. Peterson, *The Limits of Hitler's Power* (Princeton University Press 1969), 48.

5. See the excellent analysis of Hitler's political and racial ideas by Eberhard Jäckel, *Hitlers Weltanschauung. Entwurf einer Herrschaft* (Tübingen 1969).

6. Nuremberg Military Tribunals. *Trials of War Criminals Before the Nuremberg Military Tribunals Under Control Council Law No. 10* (Washington D.C., 1949–53, 15 Vols. Green Series. Hereafter cited as *TWC*), Case II, The Ministries Case: U.S. versus von Weizsäcker, Vol. XII, 920; *Foreign Office 646*, Case II, Transcripts Vol. 217, 7604 (Imperial War Museum, London. Hereafter cited as *FO.646/TWC*).
7. See Donald C. Watt, 'The German Diplomats and the Nazi Leaders 1933–1939', *Journal of Central European Affairs*, XV, July 1955, 148–60; Leonidas E. Hill, 'The Wilhelmstrasse in the Nazi Era', *Political Science Quarterly*, LXXXII, December 1967, 546–70.
8. For an analysis and account of German foreign policy in the first years of the Nazi State see Gerhard L. Weinberg, *The Foreign Policy of Hitler's Germany: Diplomatic Revolution in Europe 1933–36* (University of Chicago Press 1970).
9. See Alan Bullock, *Hitler: A Study in Tyranny* (London 1952), 245: 'the street gangs had seized control of the resources of a great modern State, the gutter had come to power'.
10. For a structural analysis of the many factors involved in National Socialist foreign policy see the study by Hans-Adolf Jacobsen, *Nationalsozialistische Aussenpolitik 1933–1938* (Frankfurt-am-Main 1968).
11. See, for example, A. J. P. Taylor, *The Origins of the Second World War* (London 1961); W. N. Medlicott, *The Coming of War in 1939* (Historical Association Pamphlet G.52, 1963); E. M. Robertson, *Hitler's Pre-War Policy and Military Plans 1933–1939* (London 1963); Alan Bullock, *Hitler and the Origins of the Second World War* (The Raleigh Lecture on History, British Academy 1967); Andreas Hillgruber, *Kontinuität und Diskontinuität in der deutschen Aussenpolitik von Bismarck bis Hitler* (Düsseldorf 1969); Klaus Hildebrand, *Deutsche Aussenpolitik 1933–1945: Kalkül oder Dogma?* (Stuttgart 1971); E. M. Robertson (ed.), *The Origins of the Second World War: Historical Interpretations* (London 1971); William Carr, *Arms, Autarky and Aggression: A Study in German Foreign Policy 1933–1939* (London 1972); David Irving, *Hitler's War* (London 1977); idem, *The War Path: Hitler's Germany 1933–39* (London 1978); Wilhelm Deist, Manfred Messerschmidt, Hans-Erich Volkmann, *Das Deutsche Reich und der Zweite Weltkrieg*. Band 1: *Ursachen und Voraussetzungen der Deutschen Kriegspolitik* (Stuttgart 1979). See also other references in, John P. Fox, 'Adolf Hitler: The Continuing Debate', *International Affairs*, Vol. 55, No. 2, April 1979, 252–64.
12. See Jäckel, n. 5 above.
13. Weinberg, op. cit., 65.
14. Gordon A. Craig and Felix Gilbert (eds.), *The Diplomats 1919–1939* (Princeton University Press 1953), 478–81.
15. Letter to the author from Matild E. Holomany, Director, Berlin Documents Centre.
16. D. C. Watt, 'Japan in the Anti-Comintern Pact: Dilemmas and Hesitations', *Wiener Library Bulletin*, XIII, Nos. 5 & 6, 1959, 46, 54.
17. See Charles Bloch, *Hitler und die europäischen Mächte 1933–1934. Kontinuität oder Bruch?* (Frankfurt-am-Main 1966).

Chapter I

1. See the most recent and authoritative study of the Manchurian Crisis by Christopher Thorne. *The Limits of Foreign Policy: The West, the League and the Far Eastern Crisis of 1931–1933* (London 1972). For an analysis of Japanese policy see Sadako N. Ogata, *Defiance in Manchuria. The Making of Japanese Foreign Policy 1931–1932* (University of California Press 1964).

2. Almost the only study so far of Germany's role during this crisis takes an extreme position on Germany's alleged support of Japan: Renate Wünsche, 'Die Haltung des deutschen Imperialismus zum japanisch—chinesischen Konflikt von 1931—1933 und der Kampf der Kommunistischen Partei Deutschlands gegen die Fernöstliche Kriegsgefahr' (unpublished dissertation, Deutschen Akademie für Staats-und Rechtswissenschaft, 'Walter Ulbricht', Potsdam 1961). The evidence for the years 1931—38 hardly supports this author's contention that 'the tactic of German imperialism was to strengthen its own position in China with the help of Japanese aggression', op. cit., 74. Even when this *may* have been true after 4 February 1938, conditions in the Japanese-occupied parts of China proved that Japan's policy was to exclude, or put at a disadvantage, all foreign interests, including those even of Germany.

3. The Treaty of Shimonoseki of 17 April 1895 ended the Sino—Japanese war, while strong diplomatic representations by Russia, France, and Germany forced Japan to withdraw her claim to the Liaotung Peninsula within a fortnight of the signing of the treaty. Later, von Ribbentrop was to parade his wide knowledge of foreign affairs when he asked Erich Kordt, 'Shimonoseki? Now *who* was that?', Erich Kordt, *Nicht aus den Akten: Die Wilhelmstrasse in Frieden und Krieg; Erlebnisse, Begegnungen und Eindrücke 1928—1945* (Stuttgart 1950), 123.

4. In reply to an American invitation on 1 October 1925 to adhere to the treaty, Germany agreed to sign 'subject to ratification'. This ratification was never put into effect because of Chinese and domestic German opposition: Beverley Douglas Causey Jr, 'Why Germany Never Signed the Nine-Power Treaty', *Far Eastern Quarterly*, 1, No. 4, August 1942, 364—77. For a selection of German Foreign Office correspondence on this question early in 1926 see *Akten zur deutschen auswärtigen Politik 1918—1945*, Series B, Vol. III (Göttingen 1968. Hereafter cited as *ADAP*).

5. *Documents of the German Foreign Office*, Foreign and Commonwealth Office Library, London: K2088/K555400—01, von Schoen/Geneva, 22 September 1931; ibid., K555438, von Bülow/Count Bernstorff, 24 September 1931 (hereafter cited as *AA* — Auswärtiges Amt).

6. Ibid., K2088/K555391—391/1, Curtius/AA, Geneva, 21 September 1931.

7. 'The Germans did not make the League's cause their own. . . . Germany and the League were incompatible', Christoph M. Kimmich, *Germany and the League of Nations* (University of Chicago Press 1976), 201.

8. *League of Nations Official Journal*, July—December 1931, 2272.

9. Westel W. Willoughby, *The Sino—Japanese Controversy and the League of Nations* (Baltimore 1935), 55; Thorne, op. cit., 135.

10. For comments on members of the Commission and its work in the Far East, see Thorne, op. cit., 278—83.

11. *AA*.K2088/K555483—84, Memorandum by Curtius, 29 September 1931; 'Deutschlands Vertretung im Völkerbundsrat', *Ostasiatische Rundschau*, 12, 16 November 1931, 547—48.

12. Wünsche, op. cit., 70—71.

13. *AA*.K2088/K555855, Memorandum by Meyer, 12 October 1931.

14. *AA*.K2088/K556005—06, von Bülow/Peking, 16 October 1931; ibid., K556097—98, Memorandum by Michelsen, 19 October 1931.

15. See F. P. Walters, *A History of the League of Nations* (London 1965 [reprinted]).

16. *AA*.K2088/K557358—59, Memorandum by von Bülow, 12 November 1931.

17. *AA*.3088/D624432, Voretzsch/AA, Tokio, 4 December 1931; 3147/D662950, Mutius/AA, Paris, 5 December 1931. The Reichswehr rather pointedly referred to the *Deutsche Allgemeine Zeitung* as the *Chines.Allg. Ztg*: Thilo Vogelsang, 'Neue Dokumente zur Geschichte der Reichswehr 1930—1933', *Vierteljahrshefte für Zeitgeschichte*, 2 October 1954, 419.

18. *AA*.K2088/K558339, Memorandum by Meyer, 7 December 1931; Hans Meier-Welcker, *Seeckt* (Frankfurt-am-Main 1967), 641.
19. *AA*.3147/D662958—59, Mutius/AA, Paris, 8 December 1931.
20. *AA*.3147/D662960, Mutius/AA, Paris, 9 December 1931. Elsewhere it was argued that it was not necessary for Germany to participate in the Commission and that she would gain nothing by her action: 'Die Studien-kommission des Völkerbundes und Deutschlands Stellung zu ihr', *OR*, 12, 16 December 1931, 595—96.
21. *AA*.L1780/L518093, Köpke/Peking, 2 July 1932.
22. *AA*.L1780/L517445—53, Voretzsch/AA, Tokio, 8 January 1932.
23. *AA*.K2264/K625474—78, Voretzsch/AA, Tokio, 11 January 1932; ibid., K625528, von Dirksen/AA, Moscow, 4 May 1932.
24. *AA*.K2264/K625486—87, von Dirksen/AA, Moscow, 23 February 1932; ibid., E625489—90, von Bülow/von Dirksen, 27 February 1932.
25. *AA*.7072/E526615—26, Memorandum by Gipperich, 8 November 1932.
26. See *Bericht der China Studienkommission des Reichsverbandes der Deutschen Industrie* (Berlin 1930). The leader of this mission, Admiral Retzmann, later published a plea to his countrymen for greater interest and participation in China's economic affairs: 'Industrielle Beziehungen zwischen Deutschland und China', *OR*, 7, 1 April 1931, 177—78. For the trade figures and more on the subject of Sino—German economic relations see Karl Casper, 'Deutschland und China im gegenseitigen Warenaustausch', *Weltwirtschaftliches Archiv*, XLV, March 1937, 414—15; Pang Bin-Chin, *Der Aussenhandel zwischen Deutschland und China und die deutsch—chinesischen Aussenhandelspolitik* (Erlangen 1937); Hou Chi-Ming, *Foreign Investment and Economic Development in China 1840—1937* (Harvard University Press 1965).
27. *AA*.L1780/L517580—83, Voretzsch/AA, Tokio, 7 March 1932.
28. See F. F. Liu, *A Military History of Modern China 1924—1949* (Princeton University Press 1956); Karl Mehner, 'Die Rolle deutscher Militärberater als Interessenvertreter des deutschen Imperialismus und Militärismus in China 1928—1936' (unpublished dissertation, Karl Marx Universität, Leipzig 1961); John P. Fox, 'Max Bauer: Chiang Kai-shek's First German Military Adviser', *Journal of Contemporary History*, V, No. 4, 1970, 21—44; Walter Sommer, 'Zur Rolle deutsche Berater in den Einkreisungs- und Vernichtungsfeldzügen gegen die Südchinesische Sowjetrepublik 1930—1934', *Zeitschrift für Politik*, 18, 1971, 268—304; Jerry Bernard Seps, 'German Military Advisers and Chiang Kai-shek 1927—1938' (unpublished dissertation, University of California, Berkeley, 1972); Billie K. Walsh, 'The German Military Mission in China 1928—38', *Journal of Modern History*, 46, September 1974, 502—13; Adolf Vogt, *Oberst Max Bauer: Generalstabsoffizier im Zwielicht 1869—1929* (Osnabrück 1974); Otto Braun, *Chinesische Aufzeichnungen (1932—1939)* (Berlin 1975); Liang Hsi-Huey, *The Sino—German Connection: Alexander von Falkenhausen between China and Germany 1900—1941* (Assen 1978).
29. *AA*.L1535/L464560—63, von Schubert/Stresemann (at Geneva), 7 March 1929; Fox, art. cit., 32—36.
30. *AA*.K2088/K562106—24, Memorandum by Michelsen, 11 May 1932.
31. Fox, 'Bauer', 44.
32. Wünsche, op. cit., 100—10.
33. *AA*.K2264/K625495—97, Voretzsch/AA, Tokio, 17 February 1932; W. Hoeppener, 'Sind deutsche Offiziere die Führer der chinesischen Shanghai—Truppen? Gerüchte um deutsche Chinakampfer', *Neues Wiener Extrablatt*, 26 February 1932; K2264/K625479—80, Ostasiatischer Verein/AA, Hamburg, 19 February 1932 with enclosure. For further details see Seps, op. cit., 248ff.
34. *AA*.K2264/K625500—03, Voretzsch/AA, Tokio, 26 February 1932; 8587/E602315—16, Trautmann/AA, Peking, 28 July 1932.

35. *AA*.M96/M003271—72, Memorandum by Michelsen, 10 June 1932; K2264/ K625558—59, Memorandum by Michelsen, 2 August 1932, concerning Reichswehr Ministry interest in developing the military strength of the Province of Kiangsi.

36. See Wilhelm Haas, 'Der japanisch—mandschurische Warenaustausch mit Deutschland', *Weltwirtschaftliches Archiv,* XLVI, July 1937, 272—86; F. C. Jones, *Manchuria Since 1931* (New York 1949), 199—200; 'Stellung der neuen japanischen Regierung zur Mandschurei', *OR,* 13, 1 January 1932, 3.

37. Jones, op. cit., 141, 190ff.

38. Yale Candee Maxon, *Control of Japanese Foreign Policy. A Study of Civil— Military Rivalry 1930—1945* (University of California Press 1957), 94.

39. Franz H. Michael and George E. Taylor, *The Far East in the Modern World* (London 1956), 512. See also Herbert P. Bix, 'Japanese Imperialism and the Manchurian Economy 1900—31', *China Quarterly,* No. 51, July— September 1972, 425—43.

40. *AA*.L1780/L517525—41, Trautmann/AA, Peking, 26 February 1932.

41. *AA*.L1780/L517787—836, Trautmann/AA, Peking, 1 June 1932.

42. *AA*.L1780/L518087, Trautmann/AA, Peking, 11 June 1932.

43. See above, p. 14.

44. *AA*.L1780/L517606—08, Czibulinski/Tokio, Peking, 12 April 1932.

45. *AA*.L1780/L517785—86, Köpke/Geneva, 17 June 1932; ibid., L517951—54, Trautmann/AA, Peking, 29 June 1932.

46. *AA*.4620/E199703—09, von Dirksen/von Bülow, Moscow, 5 May 1932; K2264/K625519—20, von Bülow/von Dirksen, 11 May 1932.

47. *AA*.4620/E200225—27, von Bülow/von Dirksen, 14 June 1932.

48. See the two valuable studies by Edward W. Bennett, *Germany and the Diplomacy of the Financial Crisis 1931* (Harvard University Press 1962), and *German Rearmament and the West 1932—33* (Princeton University Press 1979). See also the important series of *Documents on British Foreign Policy 1919—1939,* Second Series, 1929—1938 (London: HMSO, 1947, hereafter cited as *DBFP*), for British Foreign Office documents on these subjects and Far Eastern affairs. German Foreign Office documents up to January 1933 will be found in *ADAP,* Series B (1925—1933).

49. *AA*.L1780/L518245—48, Memorandum by von Bülow, 20 September 1932.

50. Von Hoesch had already reported from Paris on 4 February 1932 on rumours that France was prepared to give Japan a 'free-hand' against China in return for support against Germany over disarmament: *AA*.3088/D624471—73. It also appears that France was playing a similar game *vis-à-vis* the United States emphasising the Far Eastern crisis against the background of serious complications in European relations with Germany connected with such problems as disarmament, reparations and inter-Allied debts: Thorne, op. cit., 325.

51. See above, p. 12, n. 17.

52. *AA*.L1780/L518239—42, Memorandum by Michelsen, 20 September 1932.

53. *AA*.L1780/L518518—20, Memorandum by Meyer, 2 November 1932.

54. R. Bassett, *Democracy and Foreign Policy. A Case History: The Sino— Japanese Dispute 1931—1933* (London 1952, repr. 1968), 296.

55. *AA*.L1780/L518874—75, and L518876—77, Memoranda by Michelsen, 24 and 29 December 1932; 3147/D664273—78, Memorandum by Michelsen, 7 January 1933. Von Bülow also adopted an attitude of reserve when he received the Chinese Minister of Trade and Industry, H. H. Kung, on 9 January 1933: 3088/D624604, Memorandum by von Bülow, 9 January 1933.

56. *AA*.3147/D664258—59, Memorandum by von Bülow, 9 January 1933.

57. *AA*.8933/E626271, Notice of Interpolation, 9 January 1933; ibid., E626253—58, Statement by von Neurath, 20 January 1933; 3147/D664388, Memorandum by von Neurath, 24 January 1933.

58. Willoughby, op. cit., 478—82.

59. *Documents on German Foreign Policy 1918—1945*, Series C, Vol. I, 60—61 (London: HMSO 1957, *DGFP*), Memorandum by Czibulinski, 20 February 1933.

Chapter II

1. Joachim C. Fest, *The Face of the Third Reich* (Pelican ed. 1972), 272. See also Gordon A. Craig, 'The German Foreign Office from Neurath to Ribbentrop', in Gordon A. Craig and Felix Gilbert (eds.), *The Diplomats 1919—1939* (Princeton University Press 1953), 406—36.
2. Hill, art. cit., 569.
3. Paul Schwarz, *This Man Ribbentrop: His Life and Times* (New York 1943), 91.
4. Sir Lewis Namier, *In the Nazi Era* (London 1952), 59—60; Craig and Gilbert, ibid., 478—79.
5. *AA*.2082/450875—77, von Dirksen/Hencke, Moscow, 4 March 1933.
6. Weinberg, op. cit., 65.
7. *FO.646/TWC*, Documents in Evidence, Document Book 11 Erdmannsdorff, Document No. 50, Affidavit of Heinrich Brüning.
8. *AA*.4620/E200268—69, von Bülow/von Dirksen, 6 February 1933. For a full discussion on von Bülow's views and the *Machtergreifung* see Peter Krüger and Erich J. C. Hahn, 'Der Loyalitätskonflikt des Staatssekretärs Bernhard Wilhelm von Bülow im Frühjahr 1933', *VfZ*, 20 October 1972, 376—410.
9. *Foreign Office Correspondence 371*, Public Record Office, London, C8037/478/18, Vol. 17756, Sir Eric Phipps/Orme Sargent, Berlin, 22 November 1934; ibid., C145/145/18, Vol. 19938, Phipps/Eden, Berlin, 7 January 1936 (Hereafter cited as *FO*).
10. Ibid., 22 November 1934; Weinberg, op. cit., 36.
11. John Louis Heineman, 'Constantin Freiherr von Neurath as Foreign Minister 1932—1935: A Study of a Conservative Civil Servant and Germany's Foreign Policy' (unpublished dissertation, Cornell University 1965), 134. This has now been published as *Hitler's First Foreign Minister: Constantin von Neurath* (University of California Press 1980).
12. Hill, art. cit., 559; Craig and Gilbert, op. cit., 418; Jacobsen, op. cit., 30ff.
13. International Military Tribunal. *Trial of the Major War Criminals Before the International Military Tribunal* (Nuremberg 1947—49, 42 Vols. Blue Series. Hereafter cited as *IMT*), XVI, 638. In this connection it is interesting to note that von Neurath wrote an article entitled 'The Work of the Foreign Office in the First Year of the National Socialist Government' which appeared in the *Nationalsozialistische Beamtenzeitung* on 4 February 1934. This article made it appear as though the Foreign Office, and certainly the Foreign Minister, was completely imbued with National Socialist thoughts about the future tasks facing Germany: *Tsingtao Consulate Documents* (filmed at Alexandria, Virginia; National Archives, Washington), T.179/13/4628129—42 (*TC*).
14. Quoted by Paul Seabury, 'Ribbentrop and the German Foreign Office', *Political Science Quarterly*, LXVI, December 1951, 532—55.
15. Watt, 'The German Diplomats', 152, n. 20.
16. Paul Seabury, *The Wilhelmstrasse: A Study of German Diplomats Under the Nazi Régime* (University of California Press, Berkeley and Los Angeles 1954), 14, 88.
17. Ibid., 166.
18. *FO.646/TWC*, Case II, Transcripts Vol. 218, 8087.
19. Sommer, op. cit., 18; Presseisen, op. cit., 45.
20. International Military Tribunal for the Far East, Tokio. *Proceedings*, Vol. 79,

35423—24, Exhibit 3609—A, Memorandum by Togo entitled 'On the Foreign Policy of Japan *vis-à-vis* Europe and America following withdrawal from the League of Nations' (copies of the *Proceedings* are held by the London School of Economics and Political Science, London, and the Imperial War Museum, London, while the latter also has copies of Exhibits. Hereafter cited as *IMTFE*); Presseisen, op. cit., 50.

21. *AA.*5551/E388249—60, Memorandum by Gipperich, 24 February 1933; 8933/E626687—708, Memorandum by Michelsen, 5 July 1933; 8873/E620189—94, von Dirksen/AA, Tokio, 9 January 1934. See also Jones, op. cit., 141—42; Jerome B. Cohen, *Japan's Economy in War and Reconstruction* (University of Minnesota Press 1949), 39; H. F. MacNair and D. F. Lach, *Modern Far Eastern International Relations* (New York 1951), Chapter XVI, 'Manchukuo', *passim.*

22. *Documents diplomatiques français 1932—1939,* 1st Series 1932—1935, Vol. II, 786—87 (Paris 1964—. Hereafter cited as *DDF*).

23. Weinberg, op. cit., 127. It was later confirmed that Heye had not only been involved in the smuggling of drugs but had also been engaged in fraudulent transactions which led to the suicide of one of his partners.

24. *DGFP,* C, I, 104—06, Memorandum by Meyer, 6 March 1933.

25. *AA.*3088/623170—71, Memorandum by von Bülow, 10 March 1934; 8301/E589603—04, von Dirksen/AA, Tokio, 14 March 1934.

26. Herbert von Dirksen, *Moscow, Tokyo, London* (London 1951), 156.

27. *AA.*8794/E612727—30, Memorandum by Michelsen, 20 July 1933.

28. *AA.*6693/H098894, Altenburg/von Dirksen at Moscow, 30 October 1933.

29. *DGFP,* C, II, 9, Memorandum by von Dirksen, 17 October 1933.

30. Dirksen, op. cit., 153.

31. *DGFP,* C, II, 449—50, von Dirksen/von Bülow, Tokio, 4 February 1934.

32. Von Dirksen, op. cit., 129, 153. Weinberg, op. cit., 128—29, n. 36 argues correctly that 'one cannot simply dismiss von Dirksen's repeated insistence that Hitler had authorised recognition in their conversation of 18 October as either a total misunderstanding or a reflection of von Dirksen's confusion about the realities of Far Eastern politics (he thought all the other powers were about to extend recognition)'. Weinberg suggests instead that the fault was perhaps Hitler's who may have linked together Germany's departure from the League of Nations and the League's non-recognition doctrine.

33. The *APA* was established on 1 April 1933, its leader being Alfred Rosenberg who saw himself as a future foreign minister of the Third Reich. On 4 April 1933 the *Völkischer Beobachter* commented: 'with the creation of the *Aussenpolitisches Amt der NSDAP*, the particular desires and the unique aspirations of National Socialism will find expression within the area of foreign policy'. Seabury, *Wilhelmstrasse,* 33—34. Rosenberg made an early attempt to achieve this in Anglo—German relations through his visit to London in May 1933. The visit was a disaster, and consequently, a source of some satisfaction to those in the Wilhelmstrasse. See John P. Fox, 'Alfred Rosenberg in London', *Contemporary Review,* Vol. 213, July 1968, 6—11.

34. DeWitt C. Poole, 'Light on Nazi Foreign Policy', *Foreign Affairs,* 25 October 1946, 130—154; Von Dirksen, op. cit., 156.

35. *AA.*6693/H098910—11, Memorandum by Meyer, 16 November 1933; ibid., H098915—17, Memorandum by Daitz, 9 November; ibid., H098912, Daitz/Meyer, 16 November; ibid., H098918 and H098922, Memoranda by Meyer, 17 November; ibid., H098926—29, Memorandum by Ritter, 21 November 1933.

36. *AA.*8933/E626713—14, Memorandum by Ritter, 21 November 1933; 6693/H098926—29, Memorandum by Ritter, 21 November; ibid., H098932—33, Memorandum by Ritter, 23 November 1933.

37. *AA.*6693/H098924, Büro Reich Minister/State Secretary, 20 November 1933;

ibid., H098925, Memorandum by Meyer, 23 November; ibid., H098932–33, Memorandum by Ritter, 23 November; *DGFP*, C, II, 172, Meyer/Missions in China and Japan, 2 December 1933.

38. *AA*.6693/H099135, Daitz/Ritter, 28 December 1933; ibid., H099136–38, Ritter/Daitz, 3 January 1934.
39. *AA*.8933/E626734–35, Geneva/AA, 21 December 1933; ibid., E626736, Meyer/Geneva, 12 January 1934.
40. *AA*.6693/H098902–07, Balser/AA, Harbin, 31 October 1933; 8933/E626715–16, Memorandum by Meyer, 27 November 1933; ibid., E626718–20, Meyer/Mukden and Harbin, 30 November 1933.
41. Cf. C. W. Guillebaud, *The Economic Recovery of Germany* (London 1939); Hjalmar Schacht, *Account Settled* (London 1949); Edward Norman Peterson, *Hjalmar Schacht: For and Against Hitler, A Political–Economic Study of Germany 1923–1945* (Boston 1954); Earl R. Beck, *Verdict on Schacht: A Study in the Problem of Political 'Guilt'* (Tallahassee 1955); Arthur Schweitzer, *Big Business in The Third Reich* (London 1964); Gustav Stolper, *The German Economy: 1870 to the Present* (London 1967).
42. See Kurt Bloch, *German Interests and Policies in the Far East* (New York 1940), 22–36.
43. Ibid., 33; Jones, op. cit., 201.
44. *AA*.6693/H098946–52, Ritter/Harbin, 4 January 1934.
45. *DGFP*, C, II, 251–52, von Dirksen/AA, Tokio, 19 December 1933; ibid., 287–88, von Dirksen/AA, Tokio, 28 December 1933; von Dirksen op. cit., 156. Von Dirksen's complaint about China employing emigré Social Democratic officials was answered by von Neurath in his instruction of 18 January 1934: 'the principal cases of appointments of Social Democratic officials which were being prepared last summer by the former Minister of Finance (T. V. Soong) have been cancelled by the Chinese Government as the result of German representations and completely satisfactory assurances have been given for the future'., *DGFP*, C, II, 385–86, von Neurath/von Dirksen, 18 January 1934. The cases the Foreign Minister referred to concerned the former Prussian Minister of Public Worship and Education, Adolf Grimme, the former Police President of Berlin, Albert Grzesinski, and the former Police Vice-President of Berlin, Bernhard Weiss. See Herbert E. Tutas, *Nationalsozialismus und Exil. Die Politik des Dritten Reiches gegenüber der deutschen politischen Emigration 1933–1939* (Munich 1975), 25, 143.
46. *AA*.8933/E626729–30, Köpke/Tokio, 21 December 1933; *DGFP*, C, II, 294, von Neurath/Tokio, 1 January 1934; 8933/E626744, von Dirksen/AA, Tokio, 10 January 1934; ibid., E626746, Meyer/Peking, 11 January 1934.
47. *AA*.8933/E626757, Nadolny/AA, Moscow, 16 January 1934. On 22 January 1934 the American Ambassador to Japan, Joseph Grew, reported to Washington that before Knoll left for Manchukuo he had stated to a diplomatic colleague that 'now that Germany has left the League of Nations Germany no longer feels obliged to maintain her former attitude of non-recognition of Manchukuo. It is generally believed here that Germany may extend recognition before the end of the year', *Foreign Relations of the United States,* 1934, Vol. III, 8 (hereafter cited as *FRUS*). In any case, Knoll himself received instructions on the necessity for discretion in interviews: 8933/E626788, Nadolny/AA, Moscow, 5 February 1934; ibid., E626789, von Neurath/Tokio, Harbin, 6 February 1934; ibid., E626792, von Dirksen/AA, Tokio, 7 February 1934.
48. *AA*.6693/H098960, von Dirksen/AA, Tokio, 18 January 1934; ibid., H098961–62, Memorandum by Ritter, 24 January 1934; ibid., H098963, Memorandum by Ritter, 25 January 1934; ibid., H099152–53, Ritter/Far East Missions, 25–26 January 1934.
49. *FRUS*, 1934, III, 22–23, Dodd/Washington, Berlin, 30 January 1934.

50. See below, 83ff.
51. *DGFP*, C, II, 335, von Bülow/von Dirksen, 10 January 1934;ibid., 385—86, von Neurath/von Dirksen, 18 January 1934; ibid., 298—99, von Dirksen/ von Bülow, Tokio, 4 January 1934; ibid., 354—61, von Dirksen/AA, Tokio, 15 January 1934; *AA*.6692/H098750, Memorandum by von Bülow, 8 February 1934; *DGFP*, C, II, 486—87, von Bülow/von Dirksen, 9 February 1934. See also ibid., 449—50, von Dirksen/von Bülow, Tokio, 4 February 1934; ibid., 507—08, von Dirksen/AA, Tokio, 17 February 1934; *AA*.4620/E200298—300, von Dirksen/von Bülow, Tokio, 9 March 1934.
52. *DGFP*, C, II, 450—51, von Neurath/von Dirksen, 5 February 1934; ibid., 454—56, von Dirksen/von Neurath, Tokio, 7 February 1934; *AA*.6693/ H098985, von Neurath/von Dirksen, 8 February 1934. Von Dirksen also informed the Foreign Office of Heye's political activities in Manchukuo during 1933.
53. Von Dirksen's later remarks about Heye, that this 'combination of Party business and Manchukuo did not appeal to me' were probably less an expression of concern at any Party influence in the making of foreign policy than concern for his own claim to be the executor of Hitler's wishes with regard to Japan and Manchukuo. Von Dirksen, op. cit., 156. On the question of von Dirksen's attitudes towards the Nazi Party it is interesting to note that in October 1933 he had written to Ernst Wilhelm Bohle, leader of the *Auslandsorganisation* (*AO*) of the Party that 'a harmonious and intensive cooperation' would be possible between him, his officials in the Embassy at Tokio, and the *Landesgruppe* of the NSDAP in Japan'. Jacobsen, op. cit., 37. On the *AO* in the Far East, see Donald M. McKale, 'The Nazi Party in the Far East 1931—45', *Journal of Contemporary History*, 12 (1977), 291—311.
54. *AA*.6693/H098993, von Neurath/Tokio, 11 February 1934.
55. *FRUS*, 1934, III, 59, Dodd/Washington, Berlin, 28 February 1934; *AA*.6693/H099002, Memorandum by Dieckhoff, 28 February. Shortly afterwards, Daitz again raised the matter at the American Embassy: *AA*.3088/D624764, Memorandum by Meyer, 2 March 1934.
56. *AA*.6693/H098997, von Neurath/Tokio, 17 February 1934; *DGFP*, C, II, 510—11, Memorandum by Ulrich, 19 February 1934. In London it was later noted that 'apart from discovering the possibility in Manchuria for German trade, Heye's task is apparently to organise Nazi cells among Germans resident in the Far East; to establish reliable and discreet communications between these cells and Germany; to get into touch with the Japanese; and to report on all matters of interest, political, military, and economic': *FO*, F2994/720/23, Vol. 18187, Memorandum by Mr Allen, 22 May 1934.
57. This news led to Trautmann complaining to the Foreign Office and von Dirksen that although Mukden was officially within his area of authority, he had had to learn from Japanese press reports that Knoll was to be sent there to organise the new German trade office in Mukden: *AA*.8933/E626861—66, Trautmann/AA, 27 February, von Dirksen/Trautmann, 26 February 1934.
58. On 20 February 1934 the *Financial Times* reported that German efforts to gain an economic foothold in Manchukuo had been rebuffed, despite Hitler's offer of recognition. It was also stated that 'Dr Knoll has just returned, seemingly without having made any progress'.
59. *AA*.6024/H044882—85; *DGFP*, C, II, 785—87, Memorandum by Ritter, 27 April 1934. On 21 February 1934 Grew reported to Washington that Germany intended to obtain all the commercial advantages she could but that recognition was too high a price to pay 'for what may not turn out to be much'. Grew also reported that a member of the German Embassy had stated that he could not recommend his government to do anything drastic with regard to political relations with Manchukuo because of the situation

existing between Japan and Russia, that Manchukuo was 'not master in its own house', while there was also the attitude of China and the position of Germans in China to consider: *FRUS*, 1934, III, 43–44, Grew/Washington, Tokio 21 February 1934.

60. *DGFP*, C, II, 533, Liu Chung-chieh/von Neurath, Berlin 26 February 1934; *AA*.8933/E626818, von Neurath/Liu Chung-chieh, 3 March 1934. On 24 February von Bülow explained to Cerruti, the Italian Ambassador, that although the situation in Manchukuo meant that German firms and businessmen had to deal directly with the authorities, the Japanese, this did not compromise Germany's policy of non-recognition. He also repeated Ritter's standpoint of 4 January, (see above, p. 32) that the Japanese would be making a mistake if they thought they could blackmail or pressurise Germany on the recognition issue on the basis of her supposed 'dependence' on Manchukuoan soya beans. Germany could just as easily obtain these from elsewhere: 3088/D624759–60, Memorandum by von Bülow, 24 February 1934.

61. *DGFP*, C, II, 446–49, Trautmann/AA, Peking 2 February 1934. On 5 March Counsellor Lautenschlager informed Altenburg of Trautmann's 'astonishment' at reading von Dirksen's reports and telegrams of January and February to Berlin. Trautmann therefore wanted von Dirksen to be instructed to keep Peking fully informed as to his intentions:*AA*.6692/ H098766, Lautenschlager/Altenburg, Peking 5 March 1934.

62. *DGFP*, C, II, 539, Keppler/von Neurath, 27 February 1934; *AA*.6692/ H098798, von Bülow/Peking, 8 March 1934.

63. Weinberg, op. cit., 128.

64. *AA*.8933/E626830, Hsieh Chieh-shih/von Neurath, 1 March 1934. Later, the Foreign Office was irritated to learn that Heye and other Germans had attended the coronation celebrations in Mukden: ibid., E626837, Meyer/ Mukden, 14 March 1934; ibid., E626844, Tigges/AA, Mukden 15 March 1934. See also Paul Kramer (ed.), *The Last Manchu: The Autobiography of Henry Pu Yi, Last Emperor of China* (London 1967).

65. *DGFP*, C, II, 354–61, von Dirksen/AA, Tokio 15 January 1934; ibid., 559–61, von Neurath/von Dirksen, 6 March 1934. See also Gerhard L. Weinberg, 'German Recognition of Manchukuo', *World Affairs Quarterly*, XXVIII, July 1957, 149–64.

66. *AA*.6692/H098800–24, von Dirksen/AA, Tokio 21 February 1934, enclosing Knoll's report of 17 February 1934. Meyer sent a copy of the report to Keppler on 16 March, ibid., H098825.

67. *DGFP*, C, II, 582–83, Memorandum by von Bülow, 10 March 1934; *AA*.6693/H099003–04, Memorandum by Strachwitz, 12 March 1934; ibid., H099005–07, Meyer/von Dirksen, 14 March 1934.

68. *AA*.3088/D624757, Trautmann/AA, Peking 22 February 1934; 7072/ E526597, Trautmann/AA, Peking 28 February 1934.

69. *DGFP*, C, II, 609–10, *Ostasiatischer Verein*/von Neurath, Hamburg 13 March 1934.

70. *DGFP*, C, II, 611–13, von Dirksen/AA, Tokio 14 March 1934;*AA*.6693/ H099035, Balser/AA, Harbin 22 March 1934.

71. *AA*.6693/H099388–92, von Dirksen/von Bülow, Tokio 7 April 1934.

72. See above, p. 35.

73. *AA*.6693/H099010, von Bülow/Ritter, 15 March 1934; *DGFP*, C, II, 666–68, Memorandum by Ritter, 23 March 1934. At his trial in 1948 it was said of Keppler that 'in 1933–1934 he frequently visited Hitler and had unlimited access to him; however, he only made use of this privilege in absolutely necessary cases; this changed as early as 1935, and in later years Keppler had no priority over other functionaries in his access to Hitler'. *TWC*, XIV, 130.

74. *AA*.6693/H099319, Daitz/AA, 7 April 1934; ibid., H099323, von Bülow/ Daitz, 24 April 1934.
75. *AA*.6693/H099043, von Dirksen/AA, Tokio 22 March 1934; ibid., H099044, Memorandum by von Erdmannsdorff, 27 March 1934; 8301/E589607—16, Balser/AA, Harbin 6 April 1934, ibid., E589617, von Dirksen/AA, Tokio 6 April 1934; 6693/H099388—92, von Dirksen/von Bülow, Tokio 7 April 1934; ibid., H099372—73, Tigges/AA, Mukden 10 April 1934.
76. Hans Günther Seraphim (ed.), *Das politische Tagebuch Alfred Rosenbergs aus den Jahren 1934/35 und 1939/40* (Göttingen 1956), 39. For the dispute between Heye and Knoll see their correspondence: *AA*.6693/H099027—34, 417—26, 438—52. On 7 June Knoll drew up a memorandum listing Japanese and Manchukuoan complaints against Heye, ibid., H099652—55.
77. *AA*.6693/H099317, Ritter/Thyssen, 11 April 1934; *DGFP*, C, II, 785—87, Memorandum by Ritter, 27 April 1934. There is no mention of the Heye episode in Thyssen's book, *I Paid Hitler* (London 1941).
78. *AA*.6693/H099378, von Bülow/Tokio, 30 April 1934; *DGFP*, C, II, 797—98, von Dirksen/AA, Tokio 5 May 1934. The following day Ritter asked Thyssen to call for a copy of Ott's report: 6693/H099504.
79. *AA*.6693/H099430—32, Memorandum by Strachwitz, on the state of German—Manchukuoan economic negotiations, 30 April 1934; ibid., H099393, Hess/AA, 27 April 1934; ibid., H099379—83, Draft letter to Hess, May 1934; ibid., H099397—400, von Neurath/Hess, 15 May 1934; ibid., H099457, von Neurath/Hess, 29 May 1934 enclosing von Dirksen's telegram of 25 May, ibid., H099455—56.
80. *DGFP*, C, II, 871, von Dirksen/AA, Tokio 5 June 1934; ibid., 883, von Bülow/von Dirksen, 8 June; ibid., 889—90, Memorandum by Ritter, 8 June; ibid., 890—91, Daitz/von Neurath, 8 June; *AA*.6693/H099656—57, Memorandum by von Erdmannsdorff, 9 June; ibid., H099673, von Neurath/ Daitz, 11 June; ibid., H099683—84, Daitz/von Neurath, 15 June; ibid., H099686—87, Ritter/Daitz, 20 June 1934.
81. *AA*.6693/H099664, Trautmann/AA, Peking 10 June 1934; ibid., H099677— 78, *Ostasiatischer Verein*/Hamburg Chamber of Commerce, 11 June; ibid., H099668, von Dirksen/von Bülow, Tokio 11 June; ibid., H099675, von Dirksen/AA, Tokio 12 June; ibid., H099669, Memorandum by Meyer/ Ritter, 12 June; 8301/E589626, Trautmann/AA, Peking 13 June; 6693/ H099604—05, Memorandum by Ulrich, 15 June; ibid., H099676, Memorandum by Erdmannsdorff, 19 June; ibid., H099691—92, Reich Ministry of Food/AA, 19 June 1934.
82. *DGFP*, C, III, 53, von Neurath/von Dirksen, 21 June 1934; ibid., 56—58, von Neurath/Hess, 21 June; *AA*.6693/H099701, Memorandum by Ritter, 21 June 1934.
83. *AA*.6693/H099706, Memorandum by Ritter, 30 June 1934.
84. Seraphim, op. cit., 30, 32—33.
85. *AA*.6693/H099704, von Dirksen/AA, Tokio 29 June 1934; 8301/E589627, von Dirksen/AA, Tokio 29 June 1934.
86. *DGFP*, C, III, 210—11, Memorandum by Ritter, 21 July 1934.
87. *AA*.8987/E630181—85, German—Manchukuo Export/Import Company/ Ritter, 27 July 1934; *DGFP*, C, III, 351—52, Ritter/von Dirksen, 21 August 1934.
88. *AA*.8301/E589628, von Dirksen/AA, 25 July 1934; 6693/H099730—31, von Dirksen/von Erdmannsdorff, Tokio 12 September 1934; 8987/ E630191—92, von Dirksen/AA, Tokio 15 September 1934; *DGFP*, C, III, 424—25, von Dirksen/AA, Tokio 22 September 1934; 8987/E630197—98, Ulrich/von Dirksen, 2 October 1934.
89. *AA*.6693/H099732, Schacht/AA, 12 October 1934; ibid., H099733—34, von Neurath/Hess, 22 October 1934; ibid., H099736, Keppler/Ritter,

29 October 1934; ibid., H099737, Ritter/Keppler, 3 November 1934.
90. *AA*.5647/H002325, von Dirksen/von Erdmannsdorff, Tokio 2 November 1934.
91. *AA*.6693/H099744—46, Trautmann/AA, Peking 30 November 1934, with enclosure from Tigges, Mukden 12 November 1934.
92. *AA*.8987/E630224—33, von Dirksen/AA, Tokio 5 December 1934.
93. Towards the end of November 1934 Zores and Breithaupt arrived in Tokio to negotiate the sale of Zeppelins to the Pacific Air Transport Company, which was to be organised as a joint Japanese—Manchukuoan concern. On 22 November Zores informed von Dirksen that with the agreement of the Reich Air Ministry Heye had been excluded from these negotiations since his participation as Reich Commissar might give the unwelcome impression of official German interference in the discussions. This showed that representations by the Wilhelmstrasse to the Reichswehr Ministry in October 1934 about avoiding any official connotations in such negotiations had had some effect. As it was, strict instructions were issued that Fliegerkommandant Breithaupt from the Air Ministry was only Zores' adviser: *AA*.8986/E630075, Reichswehr Ministry/AA, 11 October 1934; ibid., E630076, Köpke/Reichswehr Ministry, 13 October 1934; 6693/ H099738—39, Noebel/AA, Tokio 20 November 1934; ibid., H099740, Noebel/AA, Tokio 22 November 1934; ibid., H099741, von Bülow/Tokio, 23 November 1934; ibid., H099748—58, von Dirksen/AA, Tokio 8 December 1934. Reports of an exchange of Zeppelins for Manchukuoan soya beans caused great alarm in China: 7072/E526579, Trautmann/AA, Peking 22 November 1934.
94. *AA*.8987/E630199—203, von Dirksen/AA, Tokio 11 December 1934.
95. *AA*.8987/E630237—38, Ulrich/von Dirksen, 25 January 1935; ibid., E630241, Ulrich/von Dirksen, 30 January 1935.
96. *DGFP*, C, III, 904, von Neurath/Hess, 4 February 1935.
97. *AA*.6693/H099775, von Dirksen/von Erdmannsdorff, Tokio 22 February 1935.
98. Von Dirksen, op. cit., 157.

Chapter III

1. See below, p. 59.
2. See above, p. 32, n. 41. For the connection between economics and Germany's rearmament in the 1930s see Burton Klein, *Germany's Economic Preparations for War* (Harvard University Press 1959); Gerhard Meinck, *Hitler und die Deutsche Aufrüstung 1933—1937* (Wiesbaden 1959); A. S. Milward, *The German Economy at War* (London 1965); Georg Thomas, *Geschichte der deutschen Wehr- und Rüstungswirtschaft 1918—1943/45* (Boppard-am-Rhein 1966, ed. Wolfgang Birkenfeld); Berenice A. Carroll, *Design for Total War: Arms and Economics in The Third Reich* (The Hague 1968); Carr, op. cit., *passim*; Deist, Messerschmidt, Volkmann, op. cit., *passim*.
3. *DGFP*, C, III, 761—63, Trautmann/AA, Peking 31 December 1934; Bloch, *German Interests*, 25—26; Causey, op. cit., 239; Mehner, op. cit., 117; Stolper, op. cit., 142—44.
4. Bloch, *German Interests*, 25—27; Causey, op. cit., 234—44.
5. *AA*.3088/D624603, Memorandum by von Neurath, 9 January 1933; ibid., D624604, Memorandum by von Bülow, 9 January 1933; *OR*, 16 January 1933, 42; ibid., 1 February 1933, 64—65.
6. *AA*.8578/E601632, Meyer/Peking, 25 April 1933; ibid., E601635, Trautmann/AA, Peking 26 April 1933; ibid., E601636, von Bülow/Washington, 28 April 1933; ibid., E601650, Trautmann/AA, Peking 10 June 1933;

ibid., E601673—74, Altenburg/Mohr, 17 June 1933; ibid., E601681—82, AA/Ministries and Organisations, 22 June 1933; ibid., E601689—91, Notes of Meeting with Organisations, 22 June 1933; ibid., E601696, Altenburg/ Reichswehr Ministry, 28 June 1933.

7. *AA*.8578/E601651—64, Trautmann/AA, Peking 19 May 1933, with enclosures.

8. Ibid., E601698—701, Memorandum by Kühlborn, 29 June 1933; 8933/ E626687—708, Memorandum by Michelsen, 5 July 1933; 8794/E612739, Renthe-Fink/Michelsen, Geneva 10 July 1933.

9. *AA*.8794/E612736—38, Memorandum by Michelsen, 25 July 1933; ibid., E612745, Dreyse (Reichsbank Vice-President)/Michelsen, 22 July; ibid., E612776—79, Altenburg/Peking, 4 August 1933. Further details on Soong's plans for international cooperation in the reconstruction of China are to be found in Dorothy Borg, *The United States and the Far Eastern Crisis of 1933—1938* (Harvard University Press 1964), 60ff.

10. *AA*.8578/E601716—22, Altenburg/Peking, 31 July 1933; *OR*, 16 July 1933, 288; ibid., 1 August 1933, 319.

11. *TC*, T.179/25/4644845—46, *Peking and Tientsin Times*, 20 May 1933., *Deutsch—Chinesische Nachrichten*, Tientsin, 23 May 1933; *OR*, 16 July 1933, 287—88; ibid., 16 November 1933, 479; *Aus dem Kampf der deutschen Arbeiterklasse zur Verteidigung der Revolution in China* (Berlin 1959), 174.

12. *AA*.K2053/K540747—48, Trautmann/AA, Nanking 16 October 1933; ibid., K540749—52, Wagner/AA, Canton 20 October 1933 with enclosure.

13. *DGFP*, C, II, 676—77, Trautmann/AA, Nanking 26 March 1934.

14. *DGFP*, C, I, 811, Memorandum by von Bülow, 18 September 1933.

15. *DGFP*, C, I, 35—37; Carr, op. cit., 21—22.

16. *AA*.9078/E637456, Trautmann/AA, Peking 20 April 1933. The firms Kinzel acted for included Zeiss, Solothurn, and Rheinmetall, ibid., E637457, Trautmann/AA, Peking 23 June 1933.

17. *AA*.9078/E637458—64, Admiral Kinzel/AA, Shanghai 10 July 1933; ibid., E637465, Altenburg/Peking, 31 August 1933.

18. *DGFP*, C, I, 643—44, Memorandum by Michelsen, 10 July 1933; Weinberg, op. cit., 124.

19. *AA*.8794/E612661—98, Trautmann/AA, Peking 9 June 1933 with enclosures; 9077/E637425—51, Kriebel/AA, Shanghai 23 January 1935 with enclosures. For Kwangsi's role in Nationalist China see Diana Lary, *Region and Nation: The Kwangsi Clique in Chinese Politics 1925—1937* (Cambridge University Press 1974).

20. *DGFP*, C, I, 768—70, Trautmann/von Bülow, Peitaiho 24 August 1933.

21. *AA*.9078/E637465/A, Reichswehr Ministry/AA, 26 September 1933.

22. *AA*.8805/E613635—37, Soong/Krupp von Bohlen, 24 July 1933. The letters were delivered to von Neurath on 16 September by the Chinese Minister: ibid., E613634, Memorandum by von Neurath.

23. *AA*.8805/E613630—33, Memorandum by Michelsen, 25 September 1933; *DGFP*, C, I, 867—68, Memorandum by von Bülow, 27 September 1933.

24. See above, pp. 57—58.

25. *AA*.6691/H098168, Reichswehr Ministry/AA, 15 November 1933; ibid., H098167, Kühlborn/Peking, 17 November 1933; ibid., H098169, Trautmann/AA, Peking 23 December 1933; ibid., H098170, Trautmann/AA, Peking 20 January 1934; 9078/E637473—76, Trautmann/AA, Peking 23 January 1934; 6691/H098171, Meyer/Reichswehr Ministry, 17 February 1934.

26. *AA*.9078/E637469, Trautmann/AA, Peking 27 November 1933; ibid., E637471—72, Trautmann/AA, Peking 6 December 1933; ibid., E637481—82, Chinese Legation/AA, Berlin 23 April 1934; ibid., E637494—96,

Trautmann/AA, Peking 26 April 1934 with enclosure; Clubb, op. cit., 183.
27. *AA*.8933/E626838—39, Poethe—Krupp & Co., Shanghai 8 March 1934, and Krupp/AA, 12 March 1934; ibid., E626841—42, Keppler/von Neurath, 13 March 1934; ibid., E626843, von Bülow/Friedrich Krupp, 16 March 1934.
28. See below, p. 81.
29. *DGFP*, C, II, 760—61, Trautmann/AA, Nanking 21 April 1934; *AA*.6691/ H098270, von Bülow/Nanking, 27 April 1934.
30. *DGFP*, C, II, 825, Trautmann/AA, Peking 17 May 1934.
31. *AA*.6691/H098321, Trautmann/AA, Peking 24 August 1934.
32. *AA*.9074/E637010, Trautmann/AA, Shanghai 10 September 1934; 6691/ Meyer/Reichswehr Ministry, 11 September 1934; ibid., H098316—17, Liese/AA, 15 September 1934 with enclosure from Chinese Legation of 10 September 1934; ibid., H098318, Heye/Peking, 20 September 1934.
33. *AA*.6691/H098334, Trautmann/AA, Peking 18 September 1934; ibid., H098322, Memorandum by Kühlborn, 20 September 1934.
34. For the connection between the *Deutsche Revisions* company and the practice of Reich guarantees for the export trade, and the more general question, see Editors' Note and enclosed document: *DGFP*, C, III, 22—26.
35. *AA*.9270/E657557—61, *Deutsche Revisions-und Treuhand-Aktiengesellschaft*/AA, 21 September 1934; *DGFP*, C, III, 427—28, Memorandum by von Erdmannsdorff, 26 September 1934; 9270/E657553, Ulrich/Ministries of Economics and Finance, 5 October 1934; 7072/E526583—86, Memorandum by Voss, 6 October 1934.
36. *AA*.6691/H098327, Memorandum by Frohwein, 3 October 1934.
37. *DGFP*, C, III, 461, Memorandum by Frohwein, 5 October 1934.
38. *Records of the Oberkommando der Wehrmacht, Wehrwirtschafts- und Rüstungsamt* (filmed at Alexandria, Virginia, National Archives, Washington), T.77/86/810099—103, Thomas/Liese, 16 April 1934 (hereafter cited as *OKW/W-R*).
39. *AA*.7072/E526583—86, Memorandum by Voss, 6 October 1934.
40. *DGFP*, C, III, 489—91, Memorandum by Frohwein, 17 October 1934; *AA*.9074/E637019—20, Memorandum by Frohwein, 19 October 1934.
41. *DGFP*, C, III, 504—05, Memorandum by Frohwein, 19 October 1934; *AA*.9074/E637034, von Reichenau/von Bülow, 19 October 1934; ibid., E637030, von Bülow/von Reichenau, 25 October 1934.
42. *DGFP*, C, III, 666—69, Memorandum by Frohwein, 23 November 1934.
43. *AA*.6691/H098361, Trautmann/AA, Peking 10 November 1934; 6680/ H096021—22, von Bülow/Kühlborn with enclosure, 27 November 1934. See Chapter V below, *passim*, for the complications caused by Klein's armament negotiations with the Canton régime.
44. *AA*.6691/H098424—26, Memorandum by Frohwein, 3 April 1935; ibid., H098418, Memorandum by Rohde, 4 April 1935; ibid., H098419—20, Memorandum by Kühlborn, 4 April 1935. See also *DGFP*, C, III, Document 351, fn. 6.
45. *AA*.6022/H044429—34, Trautmann/AA., Peking 7 May 1935 with enclosure.
46. *AA*.6691/H098422, Meyer/von Neurath, 5 April 1935; ibid., H098435, Soltau/AA, 13 April 1935; ibid., H098440, Meyer/Ministries of Economics and Finance, 18 April 1935.
47. *AA*.6691/H098572—83, Ministry of Economics/AA, 1 November 1935, with enclosure from *Reichskreditgesellschaft* on method of financing Rheinmetall's howitzer transaction with Nanking; ibid., H098588—600, Ministry of Economics/AA, 27 December 1935 with enclosure from Ministry of Economics/*Reichskreditgesellschaft* of 2 December 1935 of the formal guarantee.

48. *AA*.6691/H098650–54, von Falkenhausen/Brinckmann, Nanking 6 January 1936; 5564/E397565, Kamphoevener/Nanking, 20 February 1936; A report from Nanking of 17 March 1936 gave a short survey of Rheinmetall's arms trade with China in previous years: 6691/H098691–93. During 1935 the War Ministry attempted to rationalise the whole question of German arms exports by bringing about the repeal of the Law on War Material of 27 July 1927. Foreign Office opposition delayed the signing of the new law, which referred directly to government responsibility in the export of war material, until 24 September 1935. This was then officially dated 6 November and finally published on 15 November 1935: *DGFP*, C, IV, documents 116, 168, 279, 395, and 402.

The export of arms was further promoted and controlled by the establishment on 16 August 1935 of the Export Consortium for War Material, *Ausfuhrgemeinschaft für Kriegsgerät (AGK)*. The first year's report for November 1935–October 1936 showed that arms exports to China amounted to over 20 million Reichsmarks (only 177,000 Reichsmarks to Japan), and that this represented 57.5% of Germany's total arms exports during that period. To this had to be added what were called 'larger orders' and these amounted to over 71 million Reichsmarks to China. See Editors' Note, *DGFP*, C, IV, 791; *AA*.4795/E236599–640. See also: *DGFP*, D, I, document 576.

49. *AA*.8580/E602010–015, Memorandum by Kühlborn, 24 April 1934.
50. *AA*.8794/E612659–60, Note by Michelsen, 15 June 1933; 8986/E630044–53, Fischer/AA, Peking 12 October 1933; 8800/E613463–70, Trautmann/AA, Peking 14 March 1934; *DGFP*, C, II, 676–77, Trautmann/AA, Nanking 26 March 1934; ibid., 695–96, Trautmann/AA, Nanking 30 March 1934; 8986/E630061, Trautmann/AA, Nanking 31 March 1934; *IMTFE*, Vol. 67, 29570–77, Defence Exhibit 3243, Nanking/Tokio, 20 April 1934. By 1938 the approximate composition of the Chinese Air Force, based on the supply of foreign aircraft, was as follows: American 40%; Soviet 37%; French 10%; British 7%; German 6%: *FO*.F4767/298/10, Vol. 22139, Sir A. Clark Kerr/FO, Shanghai 3 May 1938.
51. *DGFP*, C, II, 708–09, von Dirksen/AA, Tokio 5 April 1934; ibid., 748–49, Meyer/von Dirksen, 14 April 1934.
52. Rumours of other plans and of a contract concluded between Junkers and Yunnan Province for the building of an aircraft factory, a flying training school and ancillary projects caused von Dirksen on 7 May 1934 to request that a denial be published – this was done on 11 May: *AA*.8986/E630065, von Dirksen/AA, Tokio 7 May 1934; ibid., E630068, Press report, 11 May 1934.
53. *AA*.8800/E613472–74, Deutelmoser/von Erdmannsdorff, 23 April 1934; 8580/E602009, Memorandum by von Erdmannsdorff, 27 April 1934; 8800/E613471, Note by Kühlborn, 4 May 1934; ibid., E613462, Meyer/Peking, 9 May 1934; ibid., E613497–498, Trautmann/AA, Peking 22 June 1934; ibid., E613499, von Erdmannsdorff/Peking, 16 July 1934; 6691/H098287–88, Meyer/Peking, 9 August 1934; ibid., H098333, Trautmann/AA, Peking 14 September 1934; 8800/E613507, Memorandum by Kühlborn, 8 August 1934.
54. *AA*.8800/613520, Trautmann/AA, Peking 9 October 1934; ibid., E613529–41, Trautmann/AA, Peking 2 January 1935 with enclosures.
55. *AA*.9074/E637066, Memorandum by Frohwein, 11 May 1935.
56. *AA*.6680/H096293–304, Trautmann/AA, Peking 16 May 1935 with enclosure of Streccius report; ibid., H096308, Memorandum by Frohwein, 8 June 1935. Apart from German military and air advisers in China there was also a German naval adviser to the Chinese government, Lieutenant Commander Rave: L1521/L458185, Trautmann/AA, Peking 24 August 1935.

57. *AA*.8580/E601871, Memorandum by Meyer, 30 March 1933; 3088/ D624737, Note by Völckers, 3 April 1933; *DGFP*, C, I, 288–89, Michelsen/ Trautmann, 11 April 1933; General Friedrich von Rabenau, *Seeckt: Aus seinem Leben 1918–1936* (Leipzig 1941), 676–79; Meier-Welcker, op. cit., 641ff; Mehner, op. cit., 123–27. See also p. 16 above, and Seps, op. cit., *passim*, for the question of the military advisers in China.
58. *AA*.8985/E630033 and E630036, von Seeckt/von Neurath, von Blomberg, 28 March 1933.
59. *AA*.8580/E601879, Voretzsch/AA, Tokio 9 May 1933; ibid., E601881, Michelsen/Tokio, 9 May 1933.
60. *FO*.F5540/753/10, Vol. 17121, Sir Miles Lampson/FO, Peking 22 June 1933; ibid., F2569/771/10, Vol. 18135, Mr Newton/FO, Berlin 2 May 1934.
61. *AA*.8580/E601883, Meyer/Peking, 13 May 1933; ibid., E601887, Trautmann/AA, 22 May 1933; *DGFP*, C, I, 773–76, Trautmann/von Neurath, Peking 26 August 1933; Meier-Welcker, op. cit., 663.
62. *AA*.8580/E601891–92, Wagner/AA, Canton 19 July 1933; Meier-Welcker, op. cit., 658: Rabenau, op. cit., 684–87.
63. *DGFP*, C, I, 773–76, Trautmann/von Neurath, Peking 26 August 1933; *AA*.8580/E601905–25 for von Seeckt's report. See also, Liu, op. cit., 90ff; Meier-Welcker, op. cit., 656–57; Mehner, op. cit., 128–38; Seps, op. cit., *passim*.
64. See Chapter V below, *passim*.
65. *DGFP*, C, I, 768–70, Trautmann/von Bülow, Peitaiho 24 August 1933; ibid., II, 23, Memorandum by Völckers, 19 October 1933; Meier-Welcker, op. cit., 667–68.
66. *AA*.8580/E601933–36, Memorandum by Altenburg, 9 November 1933.
67. *DGFP*, C, II, 84–86, Memorandum by von Bülow, 8 November 1933.
68. The information is contained in a letter from von Bülow to von Blomberg, 29 January 1934: *AA*.8580/E601959–62.
69. *DGFP*, C, II, 113, Memorandum by von Neurath, 11 November 1933.
70. *DGFP*, C, II, 144, Memorandum by Altenburg, 23 November 1933; *AA*.8580/E601944, Memorandum by Altenburg, 6 December 1933; Meier-Welcker, op. cit., 668–69.
71. *DGFP*, C, II, 291–293, Trautmann/AA, Peking 30 December 1933; *AA*.8580/E601973–74, Trautmann/AA, Peking 18 January 1934.
72. See Chapter II above, *passim*.
73. See above, p. 73.
74. *DGFP*, C, II, 387, von Dirksen/AA, Tokio 19 January 1934. A slip occurs in the published document where it is stated that 'in his talk with me in October the Foreign Minister was prepared to do so'. The original document reads; 'Reichswehrminister war hierzu in Unterhaltung mit mir im Oktober bereit'.
75. *AA*.8580/E601959–62, von Bülow/von Blomberg, 29 January 1934; ibid., E601952, von Bülow/von Dirksen, 2 January 1934; *FO*.F1026/771/ 10, Vol. 18135, Mr Newton for Sir Eric Phipps (Berlin), 20 February 1934.
76. *DGFP*, C, II, 457, Memorandum by von Neurath, 8 February 1934.
77. *AA*.8580/E601977 and E601980, von Dirksen/AA, Tokio 8 and 10 March 1934; ibid., E601983, von Bülow/von Dirksen, 10 March 1934; Meier-Welcker, op. cit., 673; *DGFP*, C, II, 607–08, Memorandum by von Bülow, 13 March 1934; 8580/E602007–08, von Dirksen/AA, Tokio 4 April 1934.
78. See below, Chapter IV *passim*.
79. See above, Chapter II *passim*.
80. *AA*.8580/E601988–94, von Dirksen/AA, Tokio 13 March 1934 with enclosures.

81. *AA*.8580/E601996, von Dirksen/AA, Tokio 5 April 1934; ibid., E601997, Erdmannsdorff/Shanghai, Tokio 7 April 1934.
82. See below, Chapter V *passim*.
83. See above, p. 33, n. 45.
84. *AA*.8794/E612872, Ministry of Interior/AA, 26 September 1933; ibid., E612873–74, von Bülow/Ministry of Interior, 5 October 1933; ibid., E612926, Ministry of Interior/AA, 5 February 1934; ibid., E612927, Altenburg/Peking, 15 February 1934; ibid., E612928, Trautmann/AA, Peking 5 March 1934; ibid., E612929–30, von Bülow/Ministry of Interior, 8 March 1934.
85. *AA*.8794/E612950–55, Trautmann/AA, Peking 10 July 1934; ibid., E612957, Meyer/Peking, 17 August 1934. Jaenicke eventually left China in 1935.
86. *AA*.6022/H044359–60, Memorandum by Altenburg, 30 October 1933.
87. *AA*.6022/H044377–79, Memorandum by Altenburg, 15 November 1933.
88. *AA*.6022/H044463, *Deutsches Nachrichtenbüro,* 17 December 1935. At the same time there were a number of public and obviously inspired attempts to reassure the Chinese on the racial question: Martin Otto Johannes, 'Kleine Beiträge: Ostliche Narrheit', *Rasse,* 1934, I, 204–05; H. Hermann, 'Die chinesische Kultur und das Rasseproblem', *Unsere Welt,* XXVII, 10, 1935, 296–98.
89. *AA*.3088/D624772, D624776, Memoranda by von Neurath, 17, 20 May 1935; *DGFP*, C, III, 933–34, Lautenschlager/AA, Nanking 15 February 1935; 3088/D624778–79, Memorandum by von Neurath, 27 June 1935; Meier-Welcker, op. cit., 687, Rabenau, op. cit., 713.

Chapter IV

1. In the summer of 1933 the notion that Japan favoured, or might even pursue, an Asiatic form of the Monroe Doctrine seemed to be gaining ground: *AA*.8873/E620173–76, von Erdmannsdorff/AA, Tokio 22 June 1933.
2. *AA*.8933/E626687–708, Memorandum by Michelsen, 5 July 1933.
3. Cf. above, p. 29ff.
4. *DGFP*, C, II, 696–701, Trautmann/von Bülow, Nanking 31 March 1934, with enclosure of his letter to von Dirksen of 29 March. Three months before, the German Ambassador to Moscow, Rudolf Nadolny, had argued that 'any conspicuous sympathising with the Japanese should be avoided for the time being. As for our choice, when it comes to comparing the concrete advantages of good relations with Soviet Russia and with Japan, it is really not necessary to waste words on the subject.' *DGFP*, ibid., 318–32.
5. *DGFP*, C, II, 446–49, Trautmann/AA, Peking 2 February 1934.
6. Cf. above, p. 71ff.
7. *DGFP*, C, II, 748–49, Meyer/von Dirksen, 14 April 1934.
8. Cf. Walter Hagemann, *Publizistik im Dritten Reich* (Hamburg 1948), 284; Ernest K. Bramsted, *Goebbels and National Socialist Propaganda 1925–1945* (Michigan 1964), 155–56; Presseisen, op. cit., Chapters I and II.
9. *AA*.8887/E621179, Memorandum by Strachwitz, 17 March 1934.
10. *DGFP*, C, II, 640, von Dirksen/von Bülow, Tokio 19 March 1934.
11. *DGFP*, C, II, 750–51, Memorandum by von Neurath, 18 April 1934.
12. Borg, op. cit., 75. Already on 22 February 1934 the Japanese Foreign Minister, Hirota, had spoken to the Japanese Diet on Japan's responsibilities regarding peace in the Far East. One authority has stated that 'the implications of Hirota's pronouncement eluded the attention of diplomats who did not read Japanese until April 17', Crowley, op. cit., 196. It has also

been pointed out that the announcement of April coincided 'with the holding of a conference at Nanchang at which the Chinese political leaders were understood to be engaged in discussing the orientation of Chinese policy towards Japan on the one hand and towards the League of Nations on the other. With the decision between alternative lines of Chinese policy thus hanging in the balance, the choice of this moment for the issue of a Japanese caveat against foreign assistance to China finds a credible explanation', *Survey of International Affairs*, 1934, 649 (hereafter cited as *SIA*). See also Borg, op. cit., 55–92. For British Far Eastern policy at the time see Stephen Lyon Endicott, *Diplomacy and Enterprise: British China Policy 1933–37* (Manchester University Press 1975); Ann Trotter, *Britain and East Asia 1933–1937* (Cambridge University Press 1975).

13. Borg, op. cit., 79–80; *AA*.8873/E620205–11, Memorandum by von Erdmannsdorff, 26 April 1934, and instructions to German Embassy, London, 30 April 1934; ibid., E620213–25, von Erdmannsdorff/Missions, 9 May 1934.

14. *DGFP*, C, II, 756, von Dirksen/AA, Tokio 19 April 1934; *AA*.6024/ H044916–23, von Dirksen/AA, Tokio 23 April 1934.

15. *AA*.8933/E626904–05, von Dirksen/Meyer, Tokio 11 May 1934.

16. *AA*.8572/E600352, Trautmann/AA, Peking 16 August 1934.

17. *DGFP*, C, III, 480, von Bülow/von Dirksen, 12 October 1934; *AA*.4620/ E200319–20, von Dirksen/von Bülow, Tokio 14 December 1934; 6024/ H045005–07, Trautmann/AA, Nanking 30 October 1934.

18. Japanese complaints and concern about Nazi Germany's racial ideologies and practices were complemented by similar expressions by the Chinese: see above, pp. 77–78.

19. This paragraph and much of what follows on the racial question is based on the following: John P. Fox, 'Japanese reactions to Nazi Germany's Racial Legislation', *Wiener Library Bulletin*, Vol. XXII, Nos. 2 and 3, 1969, 46–50; Presseisen, op. cit., 1–13; Sommer, op. cit., 1–11; Ernst L. Presseisen, 'Le Racisme et les japonais (un dilemme nazi)', *Revue d'histoire de la deuxième guerre mondiale*, Vol. 13, No. 51, July 1963, 1–14; Eliahu Ben Elissar, *La Diplomatie du IIIe Reich et les Juifs (1933–1939)* (Paris 1969), 133–55.

20. Hagemann, op. cit., 284; Bramsted, op. cit., 156.

21. Alfred Rosenberg, *Blut und Ehre* (Munich 1934), 347, 377–78; idem, *Krisis und Neubau Europas* (Berlin 1934), 16–17; idem., *Gestaltung der Idee* (Munich 1936), 258–59; Presseisen, op. cit., 7–8.

22. Johann von Leers, 'Aussenpolitische Lage', *Volk im Werden*, 1933, No. 4, 106; idem., *Deutschlands Stellung in der Welt* (Leipzig 1933), 34, 81; idem., 'Japanische Neuformung', *Die Tat*, XXVI, September 1934, 411–23.

23. Norman H. Baynes (ed.), *The Speeches of Adolf Hitler 1922–1939* (London 1942), II, 1157–58; Max Domarus, *Hitler. Reden und Proklamationen 1932–1945* (Wiesbaden 1973), Vol. I, Part 1, 352–62, Introd. by H. R. Trevor-Roper to *The Testament of Adolf Hitler: The Hitler–Bormann Documents* (London 1961), 53. See also *Mein Kampf* (London 1939), 243–44, 521; Introd. by H. R. Trevor-Roper to *Hitler's Table Talk 1941–1944* (London 1953), *passim*.

24. *AA*.6694/H099916–17, Memorandum by Dieckhoff, 1 February 1936.

25. *TC*, T.179/26/464514–47, Lautenschlager/German Missions in China, Peking 24 October 1934. For later Nazi 'defensive' writing on the racial theme see *Germany Speaks* (London 1938); Walter Gross, *Der deutsche Rassengedanke und die Welt* (Berlin 1939), 23–28.

26. Rosenberg, *Blut und Ehre*, op. cit., 378; *AA*.3088/D623165, Voretzsch/ AA, Tokio 20 October 1933.

27. *AA*.3088/D623166, Memorandum by von Bülow, 11 October 1933.

28. *AA*.3088/D623164, Memorandum by Völckers, 20 October 1933; ibid., D623165, Voretzsch/AA, Tokio 20 October 1933.
29. *AA*.8791/E612542—48, Sommer/AA, Leningrad 10 December 1933 with enclosure. One authority has stated that he has been unable to find an official instruction respecting the classification of the Japanese as 'honorary Aryans': Sommer, op. cit., 10, n. 20. But see below, pp. 90—91.
30. It is interesting, and perhaps significant, that no reference was made to any statement by von Neurath on 20 October.
31. *AA*.8930/E625977—79, Memorandum by Altenburg, 25 October 1933.
32. *AA*.8930/E625980—81, Memorandum by Meyer, 30 October 1933.
33. *AA*.8930/E626009—11, Memorandum of 21 November 1933; Arthur Dolman, 'The Third Reich and Japan: A Study in Nazi Cultural Relations' (Unpublished dissertation, New York University 1966), 91—92. Dolman mistakenly refers to 'Ambassador Fujii', but states that his conversation was with Admiral Behncke. On the Foreign Office document the only indication of the author's identity is a pencilled annotation, 'Dr Hack?'. Dr Friedrich Wilhelm Hack, later to be used by von Ribbentrop to contact Hiroshi Oshima, Japanese Military Attaché in Berlin, had been approached at the Association by several Japanese on the general question and about specific instances of racial discrimination.
34. *AA*.8791/E612523—26, Memorandum by Gaus, 20 November 1933.
35. *AA*.4620/E201029—32, von Bülow/Trautmann, 30 November 1933; Elissar, op. cit., *passim*.
36. *AA*.8930/E625987—89, Text of Minister Frick's statement. Cf. *OR*, 16 December 1933, 521, which likewise emphasised the point about there being no intention of passing value judgements on other races. Dr Gross emphasised this point in the *Diplomaten Zeitung* of 30 April 1934, 1136., while the 'defensive' nature of Germany's racial laws was also emphasised by Hans Reepen in 'Kolonialgedanke und Rassenfrage', *Deutsche Kolonial Zeitung*, 1 February 1936, 29—30.
37. *AA*.9451/E666829, Noebel/AA, Tokio 8 December 1933; 8930/E625990, Memorandum by Altenburg, 11 December 1933. Following Noebel's telegram a memorandum entitled 'Brief on the Japanese Attitude towards the Racial Question' was drawn up four days later for President Hindenburg: *DGFP*, C, II, 212—13, Memorandum by Bargen, 12 December 1933.
38. *DGFP*, C, II, 298—99, von Dirksen/von Bülow, Tokio 4 January 1934; *AA*.9451/E666830—35, von Dirksen/AA, Tokio 10 January 1934; *DGFP*, C, II, 486—87, von Bülow/von Dirksen, 9 February 1934.
39. *AA*.8930/E626023—40, Text of Minister Frick's statement.
40. *AA*.8930/E626051—54, Memorandum by Strachwitz, 8 May 1934.
41. *AA*.8930/E626058, Frick/AA, 19 July 1934.
42. *AA*.4923/E257065—67, Memorandum by von Bülow—Schwante, 7 August 1934.
43. *DGFP*, C, III, 367—69, Memorandum by von Erdmannsdorff, 29 August 1934. Although this is clear evidence of von Erdmannsdorff's apparent willingness to adopt Nazi racial standards, a different picture was represented at his post-war examination when defence affidavits emphasised both his anti-Nazi sentiments and attitude of friendliness towards Jews: *FO.646/ TWC*, Documents in Evidence Document Book II, Erdmannsdorff, *passim*.
44. *AA*.4923/E257069—75, von Bülow—Schwante/Ministries, 15 October 1934.
45. *AA*.8930/E626077—90, Admiral Behncke/von Neurath, 26 October 1934 with enclosure.
46. *DGFP*, C, III, 634—37, Memorandum by von Bülow—Schwante, 16 November 1934; *AA*.8930/E626119—23, von Erdmannsdorff/von Dirksen, 30 November 1934.
47. *AA*.8930/E626127—34, Racial Policy Office/AA, 30 January 1935. Although

until September 1935 there existed no formal law forbidding marriages between Aryans and non-Aryans, the German Courts often upheld and justified local officials who had refused to perform such marriages and had granted divorce to the 'Aryan' party on the grounds of the racial principle: Oscar Janowsky and Melvin Fagen, *International Aspects of German Racial Policies* (New York 1937), 196.

48. *AA*.8930/E626056—58, Ministry of Interior/AA, 19 July 1934.
49. *AA*.8930/E626139—45, von Dirksen/AA, Tokio 19 January 1935 with enclosure.
50. *AA*.8930/E626146, Rohde/von Dirksen, 28 March 1935.
51. For the immediate background to the promulgation of the Nuremberg Laws, see Walter Strauss, 'Das Reichsministerium des Innern und die Judengesetzgebung', *VfZ*, Jhg, 9, No. 3, July 1961, 262—313. Cf. also, Dr Wilhelm Stuckhart, 'Die Rassengesetzgebung im Dritten Reich', in Hans Pfundtner, *Dr Wilhelm Frick und sein Ministerium* (Munich 1937); Raul Hilberg, *The Destruction of the European Jews* (London 1961); Karl A. Schleunes, *The Twisted Road to Auschwitz: Nazi Policy Toward German Jews 1933—1939* (University of Illinois Press 1971); Elissar, op. cit., *passim*.
52. See generally: Mary E. Townsend, 'The German Colonies and the Third Reich', *Political Science Quarterly*, LIII, June 1938, 186—206; idem, 'Hitler and the Revival of German Colonialism', in *Nationalism and Internationalism; Essays Inscribed to Carlton J. H. Hayes* (New York 1950); Horst Kühne, 'Zur Kolonialpolitik des faschistischen deutschen Imperialismus (1933—1939)', *Zeitschrift für Geschichtswissenschaft*, 9, 1961, No. 3, 513—37; Wolfe W. Schmokel, *Dream of Empire: German Colonialism 1919—1945* (Yale University Press 1964); Klaus Hildebrand, *Vom Reich zum Weltreich: Hitler, NSDAP und koloniale Frage 1919—1945* (Munich 1969). The legal, as opposed to the political, aspect of Japan's withdrawal from the League and the question of the mandated territories, gave rise to a whole host of articles in German colonial and legal journals.
53. *AA*.6694/H099788, Instructions for the Press, 18 March 1933.
54. *AA*.K240/K070126, Voretzsch/AA, Tokio 23 February 1933.
55. *AA*.6694/H099789, Voretzsch/AA, Tokio 24 March 1933. Solf's views were shared by Heinrich Schnee, President of the Deutsche Kolonial Gesellschaft and Germany's representative on the Lytton Commission; Heinrich Schnee, *Völker und Mächte im Fernen Osten: Eindrücke von der Reise mit der Mandschurei Kommission* (Berlin 1933), 350.
56. *AA*.6694/H099790, Voretzsch/AA, Tokio 25 March 1933; ibid., H099802—13, Voretzsch/AA., Tokio 28 March 1933; ibid., H099794—95, Meyer/Tokio, 29 March 1933; ibid., H099800—01, Voretzsch/AA, Tokio 30 March 1933.
57. *AA*.8587/E602426—30, Trautmann/AA, Peking 3 April 1933 enclosing report from Plaut at Shanghai of 30 March 1933.
58. *AA*.6694/H099798—99, Memorandum by Czibulinski, 5 April 1933.
59. Causey, op. cit., 294.
60. *IMTFE*, Vol. 79, 35423—24, Exhibit 3609—A.
61. *AA*.8925/E625876—77, Unsigned Memorandum, 25 April 1933.
62. *AA*.6694/H099854, Noebel/AA, Tokio 9 November 1934; ibid., H099855, Dieckhoff/Tokio, 10 November 1934.
63. *AA*.9785/E687225—33, Schnee/Hitler, 20 March 1935.
64. *AA*.6694/H099861—62, von Dirksen/AA, Tokio 25 March 1935, with DNB report of 25 March 1935.
65. *AA*.6694/H099863, von Bülow/Tokio, 27 March 1935; ibid., H099877—83, von Dirksen/AA, Tokio 29 March 1935 with enclosures.
66. *DGFP*, C, III, 1043—80, Document No. 555; *DBFP*, 2nd Series, XII,

Document No. 651; The Right Hon the Earl of Avon, *The Eden Memoirs.
Facing the Dictators* (London 1962), 133—38.

67.   *AA*.6694/H099866—68, DNB reports, 29 March 1935.

68.   *AA*.3088/D623173—75, Memorandum by von Neurath, 29 March 1935;
DGFP, C, IV, 131—32, Memorandum by von Neurath, 7 May 1935.

69.   *AA*.6694/H099916—17, Memorandum by Dieckhoff, 1 February 1936;
DGFP, C, V, 264—66, von Dirksen/AA, Tokio 23 March 1936; ibid.,
267—71, von Dirksen/AA, Tokio 23 March 1936; ibid., 1160—61, Memorandum by Dieckhoff, 30 October 1936; Sommer, op. cit., 55, n. 52. See
also Gerhard L. Weinberg, 'Deutsch—japanische Verhandlungen über
das Südseemandat 1937—1938', *VfZ*, Jhg 4, No. 4, October 1956, 390—98.

70.   *OR*, 16 September 1933, 387.

71.   Werner Daitz, 'Die Friedensmission des Nationalsozialismus', *Diplomaten
Zeitung*, November 1933, 1044—46; idem, 'The Economic Problem of
National Socialism', *Der Neue Orient*, January 1934, 7—9; 'Neue Aussen-
handelspolitik', *Diplomaten Zeitung*, February 1934, 1089—90.

72.   *DGFP*, C, II, 750—51, Memorandum by von Neurath, 18 April 1934.

73.   See above, p. 54.

74.   *AA*.6024/H044817—19, von Erdmannsdorff/AA, Tokio 31 August 1933
with enclosure; ibid., H044815—16, von Erdmannsdorff/AA, Tokio
1 September 1933; Dr A. Nagai, 'Bemerkungen zum deutsch—japanischen
Handelsverkehr', *OR*, 16 September 1933, 388.

75.   *DGFP*, C, II, 837—38, von Dirksen/AA, Tokio 24 May 1934; *AA*.8889/
E621306, Ulrich/Tokio, 22 June 1934.

76.   Presseisen, op. cit., 70.

77.   *AA*.8889/E621311—14, von Dirksen/AA, Tokio 7 August 1934.

78.   *AA*.5647/H002334, Benzler/Tokio, 25 August 1934; 3088/D623159,
Memorandum by von Bülow, 31 August 1934.

79.   *AA*.8889/E621315—16, von Dirksen/AA, Tokio 14 September 1934.

80.   Schweitzer, op. cit., 306.

81.   *AA*.8889/E621310, Note by Ritter, 19 September 1934; *DGFP*, C, III,
470—71, Memorandum by von Bülow, 10 October 1934.

82.   *AA*.8889/E621320—22, Nagai/Knoll, Berlin 16 October 1934; ibid.,
E621325—27, Ulrich/Ministry of Economics, 26 October 1934.

83.   *AA*.8889/E621329—31, Knoll/Tokio, 9 November 1934; ibid., E621337—
39, Knoll/Tokio, 29 November 1934; ibid., E621372—74, Memorandum
by Knoll, 14 December 1934.

84.   *AA*.5647/H002310—11, von Dirksen/AA, Tokio 8 February 1935; 8889/
E621393—94, Memorandum by Knoll, 13 February 1935.

85.   *AA*.8889/E621402, Mossdorf, Ministry of Economics/AA, 5 March 1935;
ibid., E621403—04, Knoll/Nagai, 8 March 1935; ibid., E621405, Meyer/
Ministry of Economics, 15 March 1935.

86.   *AA*.8888/E621299—301, Memorandum by Knoll, 15 April 1935; *DGFP*,
C, IV, 127—28, Memorandum by von Neurath, 6 May 1935; 8889/
E621425—26, Meyer/Ministry of Economics, 8 May 1935; ibid., E621436—
38, Memorandum by Mossdorf, 18 May 1935; ibid., E621429, Meyer/
Mushakoji, 16 May 1935.

87.   See Chapter VI, *passim*.

88.   H. Zöller, 'Japans wirtschaftlicher und politischer Auschwung und die
deutsch—japanischen Wirtschaftsbeziehungen', *OR*, 16 December 1936,
659—60.

89.   For a detailed study of German—Japanese military relations during the
Third Reich, see the thesis by John Chapman cited in the bibliography.

90.   *Politisches Archiv des Auswärtigen Amtes (Bonn)*, Po. 13, Japan: Militärangelegenheiten, Band 3, von Bülow/Tokio, 17 March 1933. (*PA*).

91.   *FO*.F1586/720/23, Vol. 18187, Sir Francis Lindley/FO, Tokio 19 February

1934. Ott, a close collaborator of General von Schleicher, was given the Tokio appointment by the army authorities to put him out of the reach of the Nazis. Had he stayed in Germany he would probably have shared von Schleicher's fate in the bloody murders of 30 June 1934.

92. 'Die militärpolitische Lage im Fernen Osten', *Wissen und Wehr*, April 1933, 201–10; *AA*.8887/E621219–23, Trautmann/von Bülow, Peking 17 September 1934 with enclosure.

93. Sommer, op. cit., 20, quoting from his interview with Ott, has this mistakenly as Major-General Köstring. Köstring was Military Attaché at Moscow from 1931 to March 1933, then left on a *Weltreise* and returned to his post in October 1935; see also Hermann Teske (ed.), *General Ernst Köstring: Der militärische Mittler zwischen dem Deutschen Reich und der Sowjetunion 1921–1941* (Frankfurt-am-Main 1966).

94. *AA*.8887/E621181–88, von Dirksen/AA, Tokio 5 March 1934.

95. Presseisen, op. cit., 68–69, 75.

96. *AA*.5892/E432957–64, Moscow 10 January 1934. For other doubts about Japan's possible effectiveness against the Soviet Union, see Hans Thierbach, 'Der Konflikt im Fernen Osten', *Die Tat*, November 1933, 669–72; 'Japan und die Sowjetunion', *Die Tat*, February 1934, 876–83; R. Bauer, 'Gefahrenpunkte Japans', *Volk und Reich*, August 1935, 612–24.

97. See John Erickson, *The Soviet High Command 1918–1941* (London 1962), 357–63.

98. Any stabilisation of the Japanese front with Russia brought to the forefront the debate in Japanese Army and Navy circles of a 'Northern' or 'Southern' strategy. Broadly speaking, there were two main factions in the Japanese Army, the Kodo-ha or Imperial Way School and the Tosei-ha or Control School. From 1934 the continuous struggle between these two was being decided in favour of the latter, its supremacy being assured after the events of 26 February 1936. In the opinion of Prince Konoye, the triumph of the Control Faction after the February Incident marked the beginning of the (southern) Pacific war: 'The ideology of the Kodo generals was exclusively concerned with the Soviet Union. They were, for example, completely opposed to Japan's interference in China or to the advance into South-East Asia. . . . Consequently when these officers were removed in the aftermath of the February rebellion, it furnished the Control Faction with an opportunity to alter Japan's foreign policy, a change which later caused the China Incident and the present war'. Crowley, op. cit., 248. See also: Maxon, op. cit; Richard Storry, *The Double Patriots: A Study of Japanese Nationalism* (London 1957); Alvin D. Coox, *Kogun: The Japanese Army in the Pacific War* (Virginia 1959). Some German commentators pointed out that Japan's policy of expansion was predicated upon her first solving the 'mainland' problem before she could tackle those of the Southern advance and the Pacific. Hartmann stated this in his report of 10 January 1934, while the Soviet spy, Richard Sorge, came to the same conclusion in his excellent analysis of 'Die Japanische Wehrmacht' in the *Zeitschrift für Geopolitik*, August 1935, 479–93. Another writer firmly concluded that Japan's future lay to the South and not to the North: Artur W. Just 'Asien und die Sowjetunion', *Volk und Reich*, February 1934, 102–11.

99. *AA*.5892/E432938–56, Moscow 10 January 1934.

100. DeWitt C. Poole, 'Light on Nazi Foreign Policy', *Foreign Affairs*, 25, October 1946, 130–54.

101. See Hans W. Gatzke, 'Russo–German Military Collaboration during the Weimar Republic', *American Historical Review*, LXIII, 1958, 565–97. For published documents, see Series B (1925–1933) and C (1933–1937) of *ADAP* and *DGFP*.

102. Hans von Seeckt, *Deutschland zwischen West und Ost* (Hamburg 1933),

44–45., quoted in Presseisen, op. cit., 41; Carroll, op. cit., 45. According to British reports, General von Blomberg was hostile towards Russia. The British Military Attaché at Berlin, however, felt that the German General Staff was still under von Seeckt's influence regarding attitudes towards Russia: FO., N.5697/5202/38, Vol. 17277, Chancery, British Embassy, Berlin, 26 July 1933. For an excellent discussion of the factors involved in the final stages of Russo–German military collaboration see Karlheinz Niclauss, *Die Sowjetunion und Hitlers Machtergreifung: Eine Studie über die deutsch–russischen Beziehungen der Jahre 1929 bis 1935* (Bonn 1966) Chapter IX.

103.   This was also the theme of 'Japan und Panasien' by Hansjulius Schepers, *Zeitschrift für Geopolitik*, September 1934, 553—60.

104.   By the Reich Defence Law of 21 May 1935 the Reichswehr became the Wehrmacht, the Reichwehr Minister the Reichskriegsminister etc.

105.   See Ernst L. Presseisen, *Before Aggression: Europeans Prepare the Japanese Army* (Tucson 1965); Georg Kerst, *Jacob Meckel: Sein Leben und Wirken in Deutschland und Japan* (Göttingen 1970).

106.   *AA*.5703/E414030–42, Report by Ott, Tokio 5 July 1935; *FRUS*, 1935, III, 481, Neville/Secretary of State, Tokio 9 December 1935.

107.   *AA*.5703/E414056, Ott/War Ministry, 26 October 1935.

108.   Presseisen, *Germany and Japan*, 100; Harold C. Deutsch, *Hitler and His Generals: The Hidden Crisis January—June 1938* (University of Minnesota Press 1974), 29—32.

109.   *Deutsch—Japanische Gesellschaft* (filmed at Alexandria, Virginia; National Archives, Washington), T.82/180/990685—705, Behncke Correspondence.

110.   *TWC*, The High Command Case, Volume X, 433—65, Document C-156, 'The Fight of the Navy against Versailles 1919—1935', edited by Captain Schuessler (Navy), published by the High Command of the German Navy, Berlin 1937.

111.   Von Dirksen, op. cit., 164.

112.   *IMTFE*, Vol. 62, 26554, Defence Exhibit 2999, Affidavit of Paul W. Wenneker.

113.   *FO*.F959/720/23, Vol. 18187, Sir Francis Lindley/FO, Tokio 20 January 1934; ibid., F1905/720/23, Vol. 18187, Chancery, British Embassy Berlin, 23 March 1934.

114.   *AA*.5703/E413916, Wenneker/Marineleitung, Tokio 23 January 1934; ibid., E413891, Wenneker/Marineleitung, Tokio 6 July 1935; Von Dirksen, op. cit., 164; Poole, art. cit., 136.

115.   *AA*.5703/E413910, Schwendemann/Wenneker, 5 August 1935.

116.   *FO*.F2762/F2763/303/23, Volume 20285, Sir Robert Clive/FO, Tokio 22 and 23 April 1936. These reports are confirmed by the German naval documents used by Chapman, op. cit., 113—14. See idem, 114—15 for the difficulties Wenneker faced when he was finally permitted an 'extended' tour of inspection.

117.   *AA*.7456/H175999, Wenneker/Reichswehr Ministry, Tokio 8 June 1934; ibid., H170642—45, von Dirksen/AA, Tokio 12 June 1934; ibid., H176002, Frohwein/Wenneker, 14 June 1934; *DGFP*, C, III, 58—59, Memorandum by Frohwein, 21 June 1934; 7456/H176037—40, Hoesch/AA, London 26 June 1934.

118.   *AA*.5703/E413919, Wenneker/Marineleitung, Tokio 26 April 1935; ibid., E413920, Wenneker/Marineleitung, Tokio 12 June 1935; ibid., E413898—905, Wenneker/Marineleitung, Tokio 21 June 1935.

119.   See above, p. 50, n. 93.

120.   *AA*.8986/E630100—06, von Dirksen/AA, Tokio 23 December 1934.

121.   *AA*.8986/E630108—10, Köpke/Reich Air Ministry, 28 January 1935; ibid., E630119—24, Reich Air Ministry/AA, 16 March 1935; ibid., E630132—33, Köpke/Tokio 27 March 1935.

122. *AA*.4620/E200319—20, von Dirksen/von Bülow, Tokio 14 December 1934; 5703/E413974, Ott/Reichswehr Ministry, Tokio 6 April 1935; ibid., E413976, Frohwein/Tokio, 11 May 1935; Chapman, op. cit., 86—90; Chalmers Johnson, *An Instance of Treason: The Story of the Tokio Spy Ring* (London 1965), 142. The British Foreign Office believed that Germany was prepared to allow the Japanese extensive aviation information: *FO*.F2994/720/23, Vol. 18187, Memorandum by Mr Allen, 22 May 1934.
123. *AA*.4620/E200319—20, von Dirksen/von Bülow, Tokio 14 December 1934; 5703/E413859—60, Wenneker/Kriegsmarine, Tokio 28 June 1935; ibid., E413861—62, Note by Frohwein, 24 July 1935; Chapman, op. cit., 77.

Chapter V

1. The Arrangement for German—Manchukuo Trade was signed on 30 April 1936, and the Anti-Comintern Pact with Japan on 25 November 1936.
2. Peterson, op. cit., 187.
3. *DGFP*, C, III, 362—65, Trautmann/von Bülow, Peking 28 August 1934.
4. See Chapter III, p. 72. The one-time President of the *Ostasiatischer Verein*, Emil Helfferich, suggests that contact between Klein and von Seeckt had been established some years before and that the latter was instrumental in introducing Klein to China, von Blomberg, Schacht, and even Hitler: Emil Helfferich, *1932—1946 Tatsachen: Ein Beitrag zur Wahrheitsfindung* (Oldenburg 1969), 111—12.
5. *DGFP*, C, I, 812—14, Trautmann/AA, Peking 18 September 1933.
6. *DGFP*, C, II, 154—56, Memorandum by Altenburg, 27 November 1933.
7. *AA*.8580/E601963—65, Memorandum by Altenburg, 29 January 1934.
8. *DGFP*, C, II, 445—46, Memorandum by Altenburg, 2 February 1934. Admiral Kinzel also expressed opposition to the Canton plans: *AA*.8580/E601967, Memorandum by Altenburg, 2 February 1934.
9. *AA*.6680/H095966—67, von Bülow/von Blomberg, 7 February 1934.
10. As early as January 1933 Admiral Raeder, Chief of the German Naval Command in the Reichswehr Ministry, had issued orders to the Navy to support the German armament industry, for the very same reasons as those put forward by General von Reichenau: *TWC*, The High Command Case, Vol. X, 466—68, Raeder Directive of 31 January 1933.
11. Von Reichenau's criticisms of the Nanking Government have been interpreted to mean that the Reichswehr Ministry did not have much confidence in that Government, particularly in view of Japanese activity in North China. Hence its espousal of the Canton projects: Mehner, op. cit., 170.
12. *DGFP*, C, II, 495—97, Minutes by Kühlborn, 16 February 1934; *AA*.6680/H095981, Altenburg/Trautmann, 28 February 1934; ibid., H095978—80, Altenburg/Trautmann, 1 March 1934.
13. *AA*.6680/H095984—86, Trautmann/AA, Peking 1 March 1934; ibid., H095982, Trautmann/AA, Peking 2 March 1934; 8573/E601051—56, Trautmann/AA, Peking 16 March 1934; Mehner, op. cit., 169.
14. *AA*.8580/E602009, Memorandum by von Erdmannsdorff, 27 April 1934; ibid., E602023, Memorandum by Meyer, 7 May 1934; *DGFP*, C, II, 856—57, Hürten/AA, Nanking 29 May 1934.
15. *AA*.9090/E638896—99, Winkler/AA, Peking 8 May 1934, with enclosure from Voskamp at Canton; *DGFP*, C, II, Hürten/AA, Nanking 29 May 1934.
16. See *DGFP*, C, III, 362—65, Document No. 180, n. 4; ibid., III, 575—76, Document No. 301, n. 1.
17. *AA*.8580/E602060—61, Memorandum by Strachwitz, 19 July 1934.
18. *AA*.8588/E602486—87, *APA*/Reichskanzlei, 16 July 1934; 8580/E602065—66, *APA*/AA, 19 July 1934; ibid., E602067, Meyer/*APA*, 25 July 1934; ibid., E602069—71, letter from *APA* to Prussian Police President, and from latter to Foreign Office, 14 July and 8 August 1934.

AA. serial 8588 contains more evidence of the role of the *APA* on this question. See also, Causey, op. cit., 254–56; Mehner, op. cit., 101–02.

19. *AA.*8588/E602488, Memorandum by Thomsen, 18 July 1934; ibid., E602489, *APA*/Reichskanzlei, 21 July 1934; ibid., E602490–91, von Bülow/Reichskanzlei, 23 July 1934; 8580/E602081, Reichskanzlei/AA, 6 September 1934; 8588/E602504–07, *APA*/Reichskanzlei, 20 September 1934; ibid., E602510, Reichskanzlei Note, 13 October 1934.

20. See Chapter II *passim.*

21. *DGFP*, C, III, Documents 153, 157, 168, and 288.

22. *AA.*6691/H098358–59, Trautmann/AA, Nanking 26 October 1934, with enclosure from Voskamp, Canton 20 October 1934.

23. *DGFP*, C, III, 362–65, Trautmann/von Bülow, Peking 28 August 1934. See also Carroll, op. cit., Chapters II and IV; Thomas, op. cit., and Schweitzer, op. cit., 436ff. Thomas's most renowned remark was that 'without export there can be no foreign exchange, without foreign exchange there can be no armament production', ibid., 541. Without foreign exchange, of course, there could be no purchase of foreign raw materials for armament production.

24. *AA.*8580/E602093, Memorandum by von Erdmannsdorff, 3 November 1934; *DGFP*, C, III, 575–76, Memorandum by Meyer, 6 November 1934; *AA.*6680/H096011–12, von Bülow/Peking, 12 November 1934; ibid., H096019, Memorandum by Meyer, 23 November 1934.

25. *AA.*6680/H096021–22, von Bülow/Kühlborn with enclosure, 27 November 1934. See also Chapter III, pp. 64ff.

26. *DGFP*, C, III, 929–30, Memorandum by von Erdmannsdorff, 14 February 1935.

27. *AA.*6680/H096075–77, Memorandum by Endrucks, 23 November 1934 (Aus den Akten der Abteilung Überseeische Ingenieurarbeit Amt für Technik, NSDAP Reichsleitung). Cf. also *DGFP*, C, III, Document No. 258.

28. *DGFP*, C, III, 694–95, Trautmann/AA, Peking 30 November 1934; *AA.*8987/E630204–19, Trautmann/AA, Peking 16 December 1934, with enclosed memorandum by von Seeckt of 21 November 1934.

29. *AA.*6680/H096047–49, Memorandum by von Erdmannsdorff, 14 January 1935; ibid., H096054, Meyer/Canton, 29 January 1935; ibid., H096055, Altenburg/AA, Canton 31 January 1935.

30. *DGFP*, C, III, 893–94, Memorandum by Voss, 31 January 1935.

31. *DGFP*, C, III, 900–01, Memorandum by Voss, 2 February 1935.

32. *DGFP*, C, III, 922–24, Memorandum by von Erdmannsdorff, 11 February 1935.

33. *DGFP*, C, III, 929–30, Memorandum by von Erdmannsdorff, 14 February 1935.

34. *DGFP*, C, III, 959, Trautmann/von Neurath, Shanghai 22 February 1935.

35. *AA.*8229/E585403, Memorandum by von Erdmannsdorff, 15 February 1935; 6680/H096096, Memorandum by Voss, 19 February 1935.

36. *AA.*6680/H096096, Memorandum by Voss, 19 February 1935; ibid., H096095, Memorandum by Voss, 20 February 1935.

37. See Chapter III, pp. 56–57, 60–61.

38. *DGFP*, C, III, 965–68, von Neurath/Reich Finance Minister, 27 February 1935.

39. *AA.*6691/H098398, Plessen/AA, Peking 27 February 1935; ibid., H098451–56, Plessen/AA, Peking 4 April 1935, with enclosure from Altenburg.

40. *AA.*6680/H096251, Trautmann/von Neurath, Shanghai 12 March 1935; 6691/H098395, Trautmann/AA, Shanghai 14 March 1935; ibid., H098399, Trautmann/AA, Shanghai 16 March 1935. For Selmsdorf, see Ruland, op. cit., 184–85, 201–09.

41. *AA.*6680/H096252, von Neurath/von Blomberg, 14 March 1935.

42. *AA.*6680/H096255–60, Memorandum by Voss, 18 March 1935.

43. This referred to January 1935 and a mission from Canton headed by General Tu Yi-tsien: *AA*.8580/E602106–07, Peking/AA, 15 January 1935.
44. *DGFP*, C, III, 1042–43. Von Blomberg/von Neurath, 23 March 1935.
45. *DGFP*, C, IV, 1, Meyer/Kriebel 1 April 1935; 6691/H098409, Meyer/ Trautmann, 3 April 1935.
46. *AA*.8588/E602525–26, Dr Lammers, Reichskanzlei/AA, 5 March 1935.
47. *DGFP*, C, III, 972, Trautmann/AA, Shanghai 1 March 1935; *AA*.8580/ E602115, Trautmann/AA, Shanghai 2 March 1935.
48. *AA*.6691/H098462–66, von Falkenhausen/Lt. Col. Brinckmann, Nanking 13 March 1935; ibid., H098447–49, Lautenschlager/AA, Nanking 2 April; ibid., H098467–70, Lautenschlager/AA, Nanking 23 April; ibid., H098524– 29, von Falkenhausen/Brinckmann, Nanking 26 April; *DGFP*, C, IV, 71, Plessen/AA, Peking 18 April 1935.
49. *AA*.6691/H098475–80, Lautenschlager/AA, Nanking 24 April 1935.
50. Kriebel had already made this point on 12 May 1935, but although Traut- mann discounted this danger he admitted von Falkenhausen's concern on the question: *AA*.6680/H096292, Kriebel/AA, Shanghai 12 May 1935; 3088/624775, Trautmann/AA, Peking 20 May 1935.
51. *DGFP*, C, IV, 167–68, Trautmann/von Neurath, Peking 17 May 1935.
52. See Chapter III, p. 78.
53. *AA*.6680/H096293–304, Trautmann/AA, Peking 16 May 1935, with enclosure. Cf. Chapter III.
54. *DGFP*, C, IV, 192–93, Meyer/Trautmann, 24 May 1935.
55. *AA*.6680/H096308, Memorandum by Frohwein, 8 June 1935.
56. *DGFP*, C, IV, Chinese Finance Minister/Acting Reich Minister of Economics, 7 October 1935; *AA*.6680/H096334, von Erdmannsdorff/Nanking, 13 November 1935; Mehner, op. cit., 179–80.
57. *AA*.6680/H096309–11, Trautmann/AA, Peking 23 May 1935; ibid., H096312, Meyer/Trautmann, 8 June 1935.
58. See Chapter VII *passim*.
59. *AA*.3088/D624778–79, Memorandum by von Neurath, 27 June 1935; Meier-Welcker, op. cit., 687; Rabenau, op. cit., 713; Walter Görlitz, *The German General Staff: Its History and Structure 1657–1945* (London 1953), 295.
60. Crowley, op. cit., 214–17.
61. *DGFP*, C, IV, 864. Trautmann/AA, Canton 28 November 1935.
62. *AA*.6680/H096327–30, von Falkenhausen/Brinckmann, Nanking 13 August 1935.
63. Chiang Kai-shek requested von Seeckt's mediation with the German Govern- ment for this commission: *OKW/W-R*, T.77/81/804746, Wong Wen-hau/ von Seeckt, 4 January 1936; ibid., 804745, von Seeckt/von Blomberg, 8 January 1936. Von Seeckt eventually accompanied the commission when it was received by Hitler on 27 February 1936. Meier-Welcker, op. cit., 692.
64. *DGFP*, C, IV, 1032–33, Memorandum by von Erdmannsdorff, 24 January 1936.
65. *AA*.6680/H096342, Trautmann/AA, Nanking 8 February 1936; ibid., H096350, War Ministry/AA, 14 February 1936; ibid., H096351, von Erdmannsdorff/Trautmann, 19 February 1936.
66. *AA*.6681/H096489, Trautmann/AA, Nanking 26 February 1936; ibid., H096494, Rohde/Nanking, 29 February 1936; Clubb, op. cit., 203; Wein- berg, op. cit., 339.
67. See above p. 126.
68. *AA*.6680/H096369–72, Memorandum by Voss, 4 March 1936.
69. *DGFP*, C, V, 91, Memorandum by von Erdmannsdorff, 10 March 1936.
70. Carr, op. cit., 53–54; Arthur Schweitzer, 'Foreign Exchange Crisis of 1936', *Zeitschrift für Staatswissenschaft*, 118, April 1962, 243–77. For one solu- tion to this crisis and to the underlying problem of the economic bases for

rearmament, the Four Year Plan of 1936, see: Wilhelm Treue, 'Hitlers Denkschrift zum Vierjahresplan 1936', *VfZ*, 3, No. 2, April 1955, 184—210; Dieter Petzina, *Autarkiepolitik im Dritten Reich: Der national-sozialistische Vierjahresplan* (Stuttgart 1968); Carroll, op. cit., Chapter VII *passim*. In his memoirs Schacht refers to his warnings to the armed forces during 1935 'to keep the speed and extent of their rearmament within reasonable bounds . . . owing to the special difficulties of our economic situation. . . .', Schacht, op. cit., 90.

71. *DGFP*, C, V, 202—03, Trautmann/AA, Nanking 19 March 1936.
72. *AA*.6680/H096383—84, Trautmann/AA, Nanking 19 March 1936; ibid., H096387, von Erdmannsdorff/Trautmann, 21 March 1936; 218/147875—77, Kiep/von Erdmannsdorff, Shanghai 25 March 1936. See Chapter VI *passim* for Kiep's Far Eastern mission.
73. See above, p. 129.
74. *DGFP*, C, V, 282—83, von Blomberg/Chiang Kai-shek, 24 March 1936.
75. *DGFP*, C, V, 304, von Blomberg/von Neurath, 25 March 1936; *AA*.6680/H096411—12, von Blomberg/von Falkenhausen, 25 March 1936.
76. *DGFP*, C, V, 341—42, Memorandum by Voss, 30 March 1936.
77. *DGFP*, C, IV, Editors' Note, 941; 1242, footnote 7. Department IV was disbanded by a directive of 21 September 1935. The Far Eastern section with all its officials, under Senior Counsellor von Erdmannsdorff was attached to Department III. Richard Meyer was granted leave from the Foreign Office on 30 September, and was retired on 30 December 1935.
78. *DGFP*, C, V, 347—48, Memorandum by von Erdmannsdorff, 31 March 1936.
79. *DGFP*, C, V, 348—52, Memorandum by Voss, 31 March 1936.
80. *DGFP*, C, V, 384—85, Chiang Kai-shek/von Blomberg, 3 April 1936. See also, p. 131 above.
81. *DGFP*, C, V, 346; von Blomberg/von Neurath, 15 April 1936; ibid., 411—13, copy of Credit Treaty, dated Berlin 8 April 1936; Helfferich, op. cit., 108—10; Mehner, op. cit., 210. Colonel Thomas later claimed that he had signed the agreement on behalf of von Blomberg: Georg Thomas, 'Gedanken und Ereignisse', *Schweizerische Monatshefte*, XXV, December 1945, 538.
82. *DGFP*, C, V, 502—03, Memorandum by von Bülow, 4 May 1936; *AA*.6680/H096424, Colonel Thomas/AA, 6 May 1936; ibid., H096423, Memorandum by von Erdmannsdorff, 11 May 1936; ibid., H096425, von Erdmannsdorff/Nanking, 11 May 1936. In his rather unreliable memoirs, the sycophantic Field-Marshal Keitel records that 'Blomberg had prevailed upon Hitler to despatch Reichenau to China in the winter of 1935—1936', Walter Görlitz (ed.), *The Memoirs of Field-Marshal Keitel* (London 1965), 40. There were even rumours that von Reichenau was being sent to China as a military adviser to Chiang Kai-shek. Reports soon arrived from China expressing the concern of the 'China Firmen' regarding their position after the Klein—HAPRO agreement: *AA*.218/147872—74, Nanking/AA, 26 and 29 May 1936.
83. *AA*.218/147860—61, Memorandum by Voss, 18 May 1936.
84. *DGFP*, C, V, 565—67, Memorandum by von Dirksen, 19 May 1936.
85. See above, Chapter III, p. 72.
86. *DGFP*, C, V, 579—81, Memorandum by von Dirksen, 25 May 1936, with comments by Dieckhoff. The Foreign Office was again reorganised from 15 May 1936, the geographical departments being consolidated into the Political Department: *DGFP*, C, V, appendix I.
87. Carroll, op. cit., 125.
88. *IMT*, XXVII, 144—48, Document 1301-PS.
89. *AA*.218/147957—60, Memorandum by von Erdmannsdorff, 31 July 1936 with enclosure; ibid., 147948—49, Memorandum by von Winterfeldt,

Shanghai 7 July 1936; 211/146026—029, von Falkenhausen/Brinckmann, Nanking 29 June 1936.
90. *AA*.218/147921—22, Helfferich/von Blomberg, Hamburg 7 July 1936; ibid., 147948—49, Memorandum by von Winterfeldt, Shanghai 7 July 1936; Helfferich, op. cit., 116—18.
91. *AA*.218/147997, Göring/Helfferich, 1 August 1936; Helfferich, op. cit., 119.
92. *AA*.218/147896—97, Memorandum by von Erdmannsdorff, 12 June 1936; *DGFP*, C, V, 650—51, Memorandum by von Neurath, 19 June 1936; 218/147927, Memorandum by von Dieckhoff, 17 July 1936.
93. *AA*.218/147925—26, Memorandum by Dieckhoff, 17 July 1936.
94. *DGFP*, C, V, 786—89, Memorandum by Voss 18 July 1936.
95. *AA*.155/130822—34, Trautmann/AA, Nanking 27 January 1937.
96. *DGFP*, C, V, 869—74, Fischer/von Erdmannsdorff, Peitaiho 4 August 1936.
97. *DGFP*, C, V, 842—43, von Neurath/Missions, 30 July 1936.
98. See p. 137 above.
99. *DGFP*, C, V, 890—91, Memorandum by Voss, 10 August 1936; Helfferich, op. cit., 119—20.
100. *DGFP*, C, V, 968—69, Memorandum by Dr Kiep, 15 September 1936.
101. *DGFP*, C, V, 966—67, Fischer/AA, Nanking 14 September 1936.
102. *AA*.218/148002—06, Fischer/von Erdmannsdorff, Peitaiho, 28 August 1936.
103. *AA*.218/148031—37, Fischer/von Erdmannsdorff, Nanking 1 October 1936; ibid., 148030, von Erdmannsdorff/von Weizsäcker, Hans Dieckhoff, 20 October 1936; *FO*.F6483/303/23, Vol. 20285, Sir Robert Clive/FO, Tokio 24 September 1936.
104. See above p. 142 n. 100.
105. *DGFP*, C, V, 886—87, Memorandum by von Neurath, 7 August 1936.
106. *DGFP*, C, V, 1160—61, Memorandum by Dieckhoff, 30 October 1936.
107. *AA*.218/148040—42, Memorandum by von Erdmannsdorff, 4 November 1936.
108. *AA*.2911/D.566171—72, Memorandum by Dieckhoff, with enclosure, 10 November 1936.
109. *AA*.218/148050—51, Memorandum by von Erdmannsdorff, 25 November 1936.
110. *AA*.218/148058—59, Exchange of telegrams between Chiang Kai-shek and von Blomberg, 25 November 1936.
111. *AA*.218/148089—90, Report of Klein, 1 December 1936; ibid., 148088, Memorandum by von Erdmannsdorff, 4 December 1936.

Chapter VI

1. See above, Chapter II, p. 50.
2. *AA*.8987/E630244—45, Memorandum by Knoll, 19 February 1935.
3. See above, Chapter II, pp. 48—50.
4. See above, Chapter II, p. 50. The following documents refer to Japanese and Manchukuoan approaches to Germany on economic matters: *AA*.8987/ E630252—56, Tigges/AA, Mukden 9 February 1935, on his talk with Chang Yen-ching, Manchukuoan Minister of Economics; ibid., E630258— 60, von Dirksen/AA, Tokio 22 February 1935, on Japanese and Man-chukuoan interest in obtaining patents from I. G. Farbenindustrie for hydrogenation plants, a step that von Dirksen supported; ibid., E630264— 68 and E630262, Balser/AA, Harbin 12 and 18 April 1935, regarding Manchukuoan interests in the purchase of Silos from Miag Mühlenbau und Industrie AG. of Brunswick, for use in the bean-export industry.
5. *AA*.8992/E630595/99, Memorandum by Ritter, April 1935.
6. *AA*.8992/E630602—03, Memorandum by Ritter, 25 April 1935. Kiep was

later executed by the Gestapo on 26 August 1944 for anti-Nazi activities. See: Annedore Leber, *Conscience in Revolt: Sixty-four Stories of Resistance in Germany 1933–45* (London 1957), 159–62.

7. Carr, op. cit., 53–54.
8. *AA*.8992/E630600–01, Ulrich/Sarnow, von Dirksen, 9 May 1935; 8987/E630269–70, Ulrich/Harbin, 2 May 1935; 8992/E630611–17, Balser/AA, Harbin 31 May 1935; 8987/E630275–78, Balser/AA, Harbin 2 June 1935, including an assessment of the prospects of several projects under discussion which would involve German participation.
9. *AA*.8992/E630642, von Dirksen/AA, Tokio 8 June 1935.
10. Bloch, *German Interests*, 33–34.
11. On October 1, 2, 5 and 9 1935 *The Times* reported severe fats shortages in Germany. On 13 November 1935 it reported that included in recent export controls were all kinds of edible fats, while a year later, on 4 December 1936 it reported that a rationing system for edible fats was being introduced.
12. *AA*.8992/E630604–05, Memorandum by Ritter, 11 June 1935; 8987/E630274, Ministry of Economics/AA, 15 June 1935; 8992/E630606–10, Memorandum by Knoll, 20 June 1935.
13. *AA*.8991/E630588–91, Memorandum by Kiep, 22 June 1935.
14. *AA*.8991/E630587, Memorandum by von Erdmannsdorff, 28 June 1935; 8992/E630618–19, Knoll/Kiep, 2 July 1935.
15. *AA*.8987–E630283–86, Memorandum by Ritter, 4 July 1935.
16. *AA*.8992/E630643–47, von Dirksen/AA, Tokio 20 June 1935; ibid., E630657–58, von Dirksen/Ritter, Tokio 5 July 1935.
17. *AA*.8992/E630618–19, Knoll/Kiep, 2 July 1935.
18. *AA*.8992/E630634–39, Unsigned Memorandum, 'Wirtschaftliche Studienmission nach Ostasien', July 1935; 8992/E630620–25, Ritter/Far Eastern Missions, 10 July 1935.
19. *AA*.8992/E630679–80, von Dirksen/AA, 16 July 1935; ibid., E630652, von Dirksen/AA, Tokio 19 July 1935; ibid., E630654–55, Trautmann/AA, Peking 23–24 July 1935; ibid., E630656, Ritter/Peking, 30 July 1935.
20. *AA*.8992/E630684–86, Memorandum by Knoll, 9 August 1935; ibid., E630659–61, Ritter/Tokio, 15 August 1935; ibid., E630694, Trautmann/AA, Peking 12 August 1935; ibid., E630698–99, Knoll/Peking, 26 August 1935; *FO*.F5233/3589/10, Vol. 19332, P. D. Butler/FO, Mukden 25 July 1935.
21. See above, p. 150.
22. *AA*.8991/E630577–80, Memorandum by Ritter, 25 July 1935.
23. *AA*.8992/E630669–74, von Bülow/von Neurath, 2 August 1935.
24. *AA*.8992/E630675–78, von Neurath/Schacht, 3 August 1935.
25. *AA*.8992/E630682–83, Memorandum by Ritter, 3 August 1935.
26. *AA*.5703/E414056, Ott/War Ministry, 26 October 1935.
27. *AA*.8992/E630687–88, Schacht/von Neurath, 8 August 1935; ibid., E630689–91, von Bülow/Schacht, 13 August 1935.
28. *AA*.8992/E630706–07, Memorandum by Kiep, 13 August 1935.
29. *AA*.8992/E630659–61, Ritter/von Dirksen, 15 August 1935.
30. *AA*.8991/E630575–76, Memorandum by Knoll, 16 August 1935.
31. *AA*.8992/E630708, Memorandum by Knoll, 22 August 1935.
32. *AA*.8931/E626172–76, Trautmann/AA, Peking 20 August 1935 with enclosure.
33. *AA*.8987/E630293–94 and 295–96, von Bülow/Tokio, Nanking, 18 September 1935.
34. *AA*.8992/E630729–31, Inoue/Dieckhoff, 10 October 1935.
35. *AA*.8992/E630761–62, von Dirksen/von Erdmannsdorff, Tokio 7 November 1935; ibid., E630728, Noebel/AA, Tokio 2 October 1935.
36. *FRUS*, 1935, III, 374, Adams/Washington, Harbin 22 October 1935.

37. *AA*.8992/E630720, Wohlthat/Kiep, 20 September 1935; ibid., E630722—24, Benzler/Ministries, 24 September 1935; 8987/E630301—02, Ministry of Economics/AA, 25 September 1935.
38. *FO*.F111/111/10, Vol. 20246, Wiggin/FO, Tokio 4 December 1935.
39. *AA*.8992/E630804—17, Kiep/Ritter, Tokio 12 November 1935; ibid., E630769—82, Kiep/AA, Tokio 18 November 1935; ibid., E630759, Kiep/AA, Tokio 28 November 1935; ibid., E630850—67, Kiep/AA, Harbin 8 December 1935; *FO*.F111/111/10, Vol. 20246, Wiggin/FO, Tokio 4 December 1935.
40. *AA*.8992/E630764, Kiep/AA, Mukden 1 December 1935.
41. *DGFP*, C, IV, 888—89, Unsigned Memorandum, 6 December 1935.
42. *AA*.6692/H098835, von Grünau/Nanking, 4 December 1935.
43. *AA*.8991/E630566—67, von Dirksen/von Erdmannsdorff, Tokio 28 November 1935.
44. *AA*.8992/E630850—67, Kiep/AA, Harbin 8 December 1935.
45. *DGFP*, C, IV, 948—52, von Dirksen/von Erdmannsdorff, Tokio 1 January 1936.
46. *AA*.8991/E630561—63, Knoll/von Erdmannsdorff, Hsinking 7 December 1935.
47. *AA*.8992/E630879—80, Kiep/AA, Tokio 24 December 1935.
48. *AA*.8992/E630882—83, Dieckhoff/Peking, 31 December 1935.
49. *AA*.8992/E630906—07, Ritter/Kiep, 3 January 1936.
50. *AA*.8991/E630559, Trautmann/AA, Peking 4 January 1936; *DGFP*, C, IV, 895, Memorandum by Ritter, 7 December 1935. See also Chapter VII below.
51. *AA*.8991/E630558, Dieckhoff/Tokio, 7 January 1936.
52. *AA*.8991/E630555—57, Kiep/AA, Tokio 13 January 1936; ibid., E630554, von Dirksen/AA, Tokio 14 January 1936; ibid., E630535—37, von Dirksen/von Erdmannsdorff, Tokio 15 January 1936.
53. *AA*.8991/E630546—47 and 541—45, Ritter/Kiep, 17 January 1936; Bix, op. cit., 438.
54. *AA*.8991/E630496—99, Kiep/Ritter, Shanghai 3 February 1936.
55. *AA*.8991/E630502—28, Kiep/AA, Shanghai 9 February 1936.
56. *AA*.8991/E630529, Knoll/AA, Tokio 31 January 1936; ibid., E630538—39, von Dirksen/von Erdmannsdorff, Tokio 23 January 1936.
57. *AA*.8991/E630532, Trautmann/AA, Nanking 28 January 1936.
58. O. Kiep, 'The Economic Policies of Germany under the New Plan', *Chinese Economic Journal*, XVIII, February 1936, 214—15.
59. *AA*.8991/E630502—28, Kiep/AA, Shanghai 3 February 1936; ibid., E630496—99, Kiep/Ritter, Shanghai 3 February 1936; ibid., E630500—01, Kiep/AA, Shanghai 6 February 1936; ibid., E630465—68, Kiep/von Dirksen, Shanghai 8 February 1936.
60. *AA*.8991/E630450—54, Ritter/Knoll, 18 February 1936.
61. *DGFP*, C, IV, 1157—59, von Dirksen/AA, Tokio 20 February 1936.
62. *AA*.8991/E630434—36, Benzler/Ritter, 24 February 1936; ibid., E630432, von Bülow/Kiep, 27 February 1936; ibid., E630417, Kiep/AA, Nanking 29 February 1936.
63. *AA*.218/147878—79, Unsigned letter to unknown Chinese Minister, Shanghai 24 March 1936, in English in the original.
64. *AA*.9075/E637276—82, von Bülow/Tokio, 6 March 1936.
65. *AA*.7066/E524751—59, Kiep/AA, Tokio 13 April 1936.
66. *AA*.9075/E637261—62, von Dirksen/AA, Tokio 25 March 1936; ibid., E637247, von Dirksen/AA, Tokio 7 April 1936.
67. *AA*.9075/E637243—45, Kiep/AA, Tokio 17 April 1936.
68. *AA*.9075/E637266—28, von Dirksen/AA, Tokio 20 March 1936; ibid., E637253—56, Ritter/Tokio, 3 April 1936; ibid., E637250—51, von Dirksen/AA, Tokio 6 April 1936; ibid., E637248—49, Ritter/Tokio, 7 April 1936;

ibid., E637246, Ritter/Tokio, 9 April 1936; 7072/E526553, Benzler/Nanking, 28 April 1936; 9075/E637177—78, Benzler/Tokio, 29 April 1936.
69. *AA*.9076/E637294—99; Presseisen, op. cit., 152.
70. Commenting on the agreement, the British Ambassador at Tokio, Sir Robert Clive, wrote on 6 May 1936: 'I learn from the German negotiators, Dr Kiep and Dr Knoll, that they are on the whole satisfied with the terms of their Manchukuo agreement. Dr Knoll told me that in Hsinking Mr Ohashi was a rather stupid negotiator, concerned chiefly with appearances rather than realities'. *FO*.F3120/111/10, Vol. 20246, Sir Robert Clive/FO, Tokio 6 May 1936.
71. From Mukden the American Consul General, without wishing 'to comment on the question of "recognition"', drew the attention of the American Ambassador to China to the 'abrupt' inclusion of Japan in Article 3 of the agreement. *FRUS*, 1936, IV: The Far East, 193—94, Ballantine/Johnson, Mukden 4 June 1936.
72. *FO*.F3265/111/10, Sir Eric Phipps/FO, Berlin 5 June 1936.
73. *Manchurian Economic Review*, 15 May 1936, 2.
74. *AA*.7072/E526551—52, Memorandum by Ritter, 30 April 1936.
75. *AA*.9075/E637223, Fischer/AA, Nanking 2 May 1936.
76. *AA*.4602/E190263—64, Memorandum by von Bülow, 4 May 1936.
77. *AA*.1946/435649—50, Memorandum by von Bülow, 15 May 1936. In October 1936 Germany's continued policy of the non-recognition of Manchukuo was repeated to Ciano and Ambassador Mushakoji. *DGFP*, C, V, Document No. 621, 1133; ibid., 1160—61, Memorandum by Dieckhoff, 30 October 1936.
78. Presseisen, op. cit., 91.
79. *FRUS*, 1936, IV: The Far East, 58—60, Johnson/Washington, Nanking 28 March 1936.
80. *AA*.4602/E190265—66, Memorandum by von Bülow, 20 May 1936; 9075/E637184, Fischer/AA, Nanking 8 June 1936; ibid., E637183, Fischer/AA, Nanking 15 June 1936.
81. *AA*.9075/E637205, Fischer/AA, Nanking 16 May 1936.
82. *AA*.4602/E190265—66, Memorandum by von Bülow, 20 May 1936.
83. *AA*.9075/E637180—81, Memorandum by Ritter, 5 August 1936; von Dirksen, op. cit., 132.
84. *AA*.9075/E637176, Noebel/AA, Tokio 5 September 1936; 5647/H002276, Benzler/Tokio, 7 September 1936.
85. *AA*.9075/E637170—75, Memorandum by Knoll, 9 November 1936.
86. *AA*.9075/E637169, von Dirksen/AA, Tokio 18 November 1936.
87. *AA*.9075/E637167—68, Kühlborn/von Erdmannsdorff, Mukden 23 November 1936.
88. *AA*.9075/E637165, Prüfer/Tokio, 23 December 1936.

Chapter VII

1. Cf. Iklé, Presseisen, and Sommer *passim*.
2. *IMT*, XVI, 639.
3. Specifically, part of the charge against von Neurath read: 'he promoted the preparations for war set forth in Count One of the Indictment; he participated in the political planning and preparation of the Nazi conspirators for Wars of Aggression . . . and assumed responsibility for the execution of the foreign policy plans of the Nazi conspirators. . . .' Paragraph F (7) of Count One, The Common Plan or Conspiracy, dealt with Germany's collaboration with Italy and Japan in aggressive war against the United States based originally on the Anti-Comintern Pact of November 1936; *IMT*, I, 40—41, 75—76.

4. See above, Chapter II.
5. *IMT*, X, 240. On another occasion he mentioned that it was in 1934: Sommer, op. cit., 21, no. 18.
6. See above, Chapter II, pp. 28—30.
7. *IMT*, X, 240.
8. Jacobsen, op. cit., 264.
9. Watt, 'Japan in the Anti-Comintern Pact', 46.
10. Schwarz, op. cit., 104; *FO.646/TWC*, Case 11, Transcripts Vol. 217, 7475, Kordt's Testimony.
11. Kordt, op. cit., 61—62; 70.
12. *IMT*, X, 239—40, Defence Examination of von Ribbentrop; *IMTFE*, Vol. 59, 24738—39, Exhibit 2762, Affidavit of von Ribbentrop; Joachim von Ribbentrop, *The Ribbentrop Memoirs* (London 1954, intro. by Alan Bullock), 74—76.
13. See above, Chapter IV, p. 101, n. 98.
14. Chapman, op. cit., 14, 94—95. For Hitler's attitudes and policies towards England in this period see the study by Josef Henke. *England in Hitlers politischem Kalkül 1935—1939* (Boppard am Rhein 1973).
15. *IMTFE*, Vol. 12, 5914, Exhibit No. 477, Oshima's Interrogation; Sommer, op. cit., 25. A recent Soviet study has confused Friedrich Hack with Friedrich Gaus, legal expert in the Wilhelmstrasse and states that it was the latter with whom Oshima spoke: Leonid N. Kutakov, edited with a foreword by George Alexander Lensen, *Japanese Foreign Policy on the Eve of the Pacific War: A Soviet View* (Florida 1972), 4.
16. *IMTFE*, Vol. 76, 33983—84, Exhibit No. 3508, Oshima Affidavit; Chapman, op. cit., 18, 34, 43—44; Heinz Höhne, *Canaris* (London 1979), 244.
17. See *DGFP*, C, III, Documents 153, 157, 168 and 288.
18. *DGFP*, C, IV, 78, Meyer/Reichswehr Ministry, 24 April 1935.
19. See Crowley, op. cit., 211—43.
20. Chapman, op. cit., 45.
21. Presseisen, op. cit., 81.
22. *AA*.5703/E414045—51, von Dirksen/AA, with enclosure, Tokio 2 August 1935.
23. I am indebted to Professor Bernd Martin of the University of Freiburg for very kindly indicating in a letter these and other relevent points from the Hack Papers (hereafter cited as Hack—Martin). See also Professor Martin's chapter in Funke, op. cit., esp. pp. 460—62.
24. Morley, op. cit., 4.
25. Hack—Martin; Funke, op. cit., 461. A recent study of the Anglo—German Naval Agreement emphasises the strategic and naval importance of Japan's role for Britain's position as a European naval power possessing vast overseas interests, especially in the Far East. This was not without significance for Hitler's general attitudes towards Japan since the stronger Japan became the more likely it was that Britain would regard her as a threat to be dealt with at the expense of interest, or even intervention, in central European affairs. On the other hand, the Russians felt particularly threatened by the relative 'freedom' supposedly granted to Japan by Britain under the agreement with Germany since it was argued that Britain would now have to concentrate her attention on European waters to contend with the new German fleet that would soon be in existence. It is also suggested in this book that it was Japan who advised Germany not to retreat from her demands of 35% of the aggregate naval forces of the British Commonwealth countries: Eva H. Haraszti; *Treaty Breakers or 'Realpolitiker'? The Anglo German Naval Agreement of June 1935* (Boppard am Rhein 1974), 149, 151.
26. Hack—Martin, *passim*.

27. *IMTFE*, Vol. 12, 5914—15, Exhibit No. 477, Oshima's Interrogation; ibid., Vol. 75, 33703, Defence Exhibit No. 3492, Wakamatsu Affidavit.
28. Chapman, op. cit., 49.
29. Sommer, op. cit., 28; Von Dirksen, op. cit., 164.
30. Hack-Martin, *passim*. See also von Neurath's statement at the Nuremberg trials, p. 175 above.
31. *DGFP*, C, IV, 829—31, Memorandum by von Erdmannsdorff, 18 November 1935.
32. On 22 and 23 November 1935 this title and a draft of the proposed agreement with Japan was formulated by Hermann von Raumer, another member of the Büro Ribbentrop. Hitler gave his approval to this form of the agreement on 25 November 1935: Sommer, op. cit., 27—28. It is quite likely that von Raumer got his inspiration for the title of the pact from the *Antikomintern* — the Union of German Anti-Communist Societies, founded in the spring of 1933 under the patronage of Reich Minister Goebbels. Its function was to 'combat the Communist International and its allies', Z. A. B. Zeman, *Nazi Propaganda* (London 1964), 87—88. See Jacobsen op. cit., 426, for another suggestion for von Raumer's inspiration.
33. Sommer, op. cit., 28—29 and n. 23. See also: *IMTFE*, Vol. 75, 33707—08, Wakamatsu Cross-examination; ibid., Vol. 76, 34077—78, Oshima Cross-examination.
34. See below, p. 187.
35. Hack—Martin, *passim*.
36. *DGFP*, C, IV, 864—65, von Dirksen/AA, Tokio 28 November 1935.
37. See above pp. 182—183.
38. *IMTFE*, Vol. 75, 33711, Wakamatsu Cross-Examination.
39. *DGFP*, C, IV, 894—95, von Ribbentrop/Kriebel, 7 December 1935.
40. *DGFP*, C, IV, 924—25. Kriebel/von Ribbentrop, Shanghai 16 December 1935.
41. *DGFP*, C, IV, 997, Kriebel/von Ribbentrop, Shanghai 13 January 1936.
42. *DGFP*, C, IV, 895, Memorandum by Ritter, 7 December 1935.
43. *AA*.6024/H045145, Memorandum by von Erdmannsdorff, 30 November 1935.
44. *AA*.6024/H045146—48, Memorandum by von Erdmannsdorff with enclosure, 2 December 1935.
45. *DGFP*, C, IV, 936, Memorandum by Aschmann 27 December 1935. Sommer, op. cit., 29; Weinberg, op. cit., 344.
46. For Karl Haushofer, the theories of geopolitics, and the question of a German—Japanese alignment see Presseisen, op. cit., 14—19, and: Donald Hawley Norton, 'Karl Haushofer and his Influence on Nazi Ideology and German Foreign Policy 1919—1945' (unpublished dissertation, Clark University, 1965).
47. *DGFP*, C, IV, 948—57, von Dirksen/von Erdmannsdorff with enclosure, Tokio 1 January 1936.
48. *AA*.6691/H098650—54, von Falkenhausen/Lt.-Col. Brinckmann, Nanking 6 January 1936; 6024/H045260—63, China-Studien Gesellschaft/von Erdmannsdorff, Berlin 31 January 1936; 9607/E677705, Trautmann/AA, Peking 7 January 1936; 6024/H045207, Memorandum by von Erdmannsdorff, 13 January 1936.
49. *AA*.6024/H045191, von Bülow/Peking, 13 January 1936; 6022/H044468—72, Trautmann/AA, Nanking 15 January 1936.
50. *DGFP*, C, IV, 1011, Memorandum by Dieckhoff, 20 January 1936; *SIA*, 1936, 385; Funke, op. cit., 461.
51. *FO*.C503/4/18, Vol. 19883, Sir Eric Phipps/FO, Berlin 23 January 1936.
52. Kordt, op. cit., 123—24.
53. See below, p. 194.

54. It is interesting to compare the involvement of the Japanese Foreign Office in these negotiations with that of the German Foreign Office. In February 1936 the Chargé d'Affaires at the Japanese Embassy in Berlin, Counsellor Inoue, informed the Gaimusho of the negotiations between the Japanese Army and the Nazi leadership for a defensive alliance between Germany and Japan. Shigenori Togo, Head of the European and American Bureau in the Japanese Foreign Office, then made contact with the Japanese War Ministry and General Staff. In April 1936 Ambassador Mushakoji, absent from Berlin for several months and due to return there, was charged by the new Foreign Minister, Hachiro Arita, to make a study of the matter upon his return to Berlin, particularly 'since it seemed to be necessary to make a political agreement of some kind with Germany'. Following this, and according to his own post-war testimony, Togo endeavoured 'to persuade my superiors as well as the military authorities concerned of the desirability of making the proposed Japanese—German agreement as weak as possible. In other words, I argued that it should be limited strictly to the bare minimum of what had been determined as the national policy to be Japan's needs; and particularly that the matter should be so managed, and the treaty so framed, that it should not injuriously affect our relations with Britain and the United States, as well as with the U.S.S.R. unnecessarily. In this endeavour I was successful in several points. . . . I thus succeeded in making the pact more businesslike.' *IMTFE*, Vol. 79, 35643—47, Exhibit 3646, Shigenori Togo Affidavit. See also Togo's memoirs, *The Cause of Japan* (New York 1956), 30. For the suggestion that the German Foreign Office finally became involved in the formulation of parts of the Anti-Comintern Pact, see below pp. 202—03.

55. *AA*.166/131905—33, von Dirksen/AA, Tokio 3 March 1936; 8886/E620991—98, von Dirksen/AA, Tokio 14 March 1936.

56. *DGFP*, C, V, 271—73, von Dirksen/von Bülow, Tokio 23 March 1936. For von Ribbentrop's visit to London, and the Rhineland crisis as a whole see James Thomas Emmerson, *The Rhineland Crisis, 7 March 1936: A Study in Multilateral Diplomacy* (London 1977), 169—71.

57. See above, p. 176.

58. *DGFP*, C, V, 86—87, von Dirksen/AA, Tokio 10 March 1936; ibid., 264—66, von Dirksen/AA, Tokio 23 March 1936.

59. *DGFP*, C, V, 267—71, von Dirksen/AA, Tokio 23 March 1936.

60. *AA*.6024/H045140—41, von Dirksen/AA, Tokio 31 March 1936.

61. See below, pp. 196—97.

62. Erickson, op. cit., 414—15.

63. See above, Chapter V.

64. See above, pp. 182—83, 193.

65. *DGFP*, C, V, 502—04, Memorandum by von Bülow, 4 May 1936.

66. Cabinet Office, Records of the *Oberkommando der Wehrmacht, Ausland, OKW/991*, Folder 'Akte Stein', Geheime Kommandosachen Japan 1936—1937 (photostat copy).

67. See above, Chapter V, p. 136.

68. F. W. Deakin and G. R. Storry, *The Case of Richard Sorge* (London 1966), 183. See ibid., p. 184 for Richard Sorge's claim to have influenced Ott against any close involvement of Germany with Japan and admission that so far as von Dirksen was concerned 'I could exert no influence'. Sorge, of course, kept the Kremlin informed of all that he knew of the secret negotiations. See also: *AA*.59/39457, Auslandsorganisation der NSDAP, Landesgruppe Japan/AO. Berlin, Tokio Yokohama 10/31 March 1937.

69. See above p. 191, n. 54.

70. *IMTFE*, Vol. 55, 22475, Exhibit 2614, Arita/Mushakoji, Tokio 8 May 1936.

71. *DGFP*, C, V, 603–04, Memorandum by the State Secretary and Head of the Presidential Chancellery, Otto Meissner, 9 June 1936.

72. *IMTFE*, Vol. 68, 29886–94, Exhibit 3267, Japanese Foreign Office memorandum on the problem of the conclusion of a Japanese–German Political Convention, 24 July 1936; *DGFP*, C, V, 899–900, Note by von Ribbentrop, 16 August 1936.

73. *AA*.6567/H490397, Memorandum by von Neurath, 6 May 1936.

74. *DGFP*, C, V, 604–08, Trautmann/Dieckhoff, with enclosure, Berlin 10 June 1936.

75. *AA*.556/241362–63, Prinz zu Wiede/Dieckhoff, Stockholm 11 June 1936; ibid., 241364–65, Dieckhoff/Prinz zu Wied, 16 June 1936. Shiratori, whose name was linked with the 'activist' Army officers in Tokio, had written to Hachiro Arita on 12 November 1935: 'Since the relationship of Germany and Poland with Russia is the same as ours, there is no need for us to make any specific understanding with them. Once the war breaks out they will surely rise', *IMTFE*, Vol. 78, 34839–44, Exhibit 774A, Shiratori/Arita, 12 November 1935.

76. Von Dirksen, op. cit., 182.

77. Dirksen, op. cit., 183.

78. DeWitt C. Poole, art. cit., 137.

79. Ibid., 137.

80. Kordt, op. cit., 155. See also p. 177 above.

81. DeWitt C. Poole, op. cit., 137; Dirksen, op. cit., 184. Von Dirksen thought the reference in the new pact to the activities of the Comintern, 'which had constantly been disowned by the Soviet Union, to be a rather clever device'. Dirksen, op. cit., 182.

82. See above, pp. 194–96.

83. Sommer, op. cit., 33.

84. Ibid., 34–35. For developments at Bayreuth concerning Hitler and German policy towards the Spanish Civil War see Hans-Henning Abendroth, *Hitler in der Spanischen Arena* (Paderborn 1973), 29–31.

85. *DGFP*, C, V, Document No. 490, 853–62, Unsigned Memorandum (Obersalzberg, August 1936).

86. *DGFP*, C, V, 899–900, Note by von Ribbentrop, 16 August 1936; ibid., 1140–41, German–Japanese Exchange of Notes on the Occasion of the Initialling of the Agreement against the Communist International, Berlin 23 October 1936.

87. *FO*.F3523/26/23, Chancery, British Embassy Tokio/FO, 17 May 1937.

88. Sommer, op. cit., 38.

89. Malcolm Muggeridge (ed.), *Ciano's Diplomatic Papers* (London 1948), 55.

90. *DGFP*, C, V, Document No. 621, 1133.

91. *Ciano's Diplomatic Papers*, op. cit., 58.

92. *DGFP*, C, V, 1160–61. Memorandum by Dieckhoff, 30 October 1936.

93. See above, Chapter V, pp. 143–45.

94. Presseisen, op. cit., 104–06; Sommer, op. cit., 41–42.

95. *AA*.43/28684, Unsigned Memorandum of Büro Ribbentrop, 16 November 1936.

96. *AA*.163/131529, Trautmann/AA, Nanking 7 November 1936; ibid., 131530, Dieckhoff/Nanking, 9 November 1936.

97. *AA*.7070/E526094, Trautmann/AA, Shanghai 19 November 1936; 3244/E000007, Trautmann/AA, Shanghai 20 November 1936.

98. See above, Chapter V, p. 145.

99. *AA*.218/148050–56, Memorandum by von Erdmannsdorff with enclosure, 25 November 1936.

100. This refers to the secret German–Italian Protocol of 23 October 1936. *DGFP*, C, V, Document No. 624, 1136–38, and the Rome Protocols of 17 March 1934.

101. *AA*.163/131535, 551, Dieckhoff/Nanking, Tokio 24 November 1936.
102. Gerhard L. Weinberg, 'Die geheimen Abkommen zum Antikominternpakt', *VfZ*, 2, April 1954, 193–201, which published for the first time the secret exchange of letters between von Ribbentrop and Ambassador Mushakoji, dated 25 November 1936 but obviously agreed to on 23 October; see p. 200, n. 86 above. See also Editors' Note, *DGFP*, C, V, 1138–40.
103. Sommer, op. cit., 48. Cf. also the remarks of the American Ambassador to London: 'such safeguarding provisions in the secret clauses if they exist would indicate that the Nazi political leaders did not have an entirely free hand in negotiating the original pact with Japan'. *FRUS*, 1937, III, 668–71, Bingham/Washington, London 9 November 1937.
104. Sommer, op. cit., 45.
105. *AA*.2871/564569–74, Secret Supplementary Agreement to the Agreement Against the Communist International. Berlin 25 November 1936.
106. See above, p. 200, n. 86.
107. Sommer, op. cit., 47–48.
108. Weinberg, 'Die geheimen Abkommen', 198.
109. Sommer, op. cit., 51.
110. Weinberg, 'Die geheimen Abkommen', 196; idem, 'The Foreign Policy of Hitler's Germany', 347; Presseisen, op. cit., 119–23; Sommer, op. cit., 51.
111. Weinberg, 'The Foreign Policy of Hitler's Germany', 347.
112. *AA*.3244/E000011–12, von Dirksen/AA, Tokio 26 November 1936. See also Presseisen, op. cit., 111–16; Sommer, op. cit., 50–52.
113. *AA*.163/131557–58, Trautmann/AA, Nanking 27 November 1936; ibid., 131588–601, Memorandum by Trautmann on his conversation with Chang Chun, Nanking 28 November 1936.
114. *AA*.1702/398193–94, Memorandum by von Pappenheim, 27 November 1936.
115. See above, Chapter V, p. 145.
116. *AA*.163/131559–60, von Weizsäcker/Nanking 30 November 1936.
117. *AA*.3244/E000013, Trautmann/AA, Nanking 1 December 1936; 100/65661, Weizsäcker/Nanking, 2 December 1936.
118. *AA*.1702/398195–96, Unsigned Memorandum, War Ministry, 2 December 1936.
119. *AA*.1702/398197, War Ministry/AA, 7 December 1936.
120. *AA*.163/131567–68, Memorandum by von Neurath, 3 December 1936; ibid., 131564, Trautmann/AA, Nanking 3 December 1936.
121. *OR* 16 December 1936, 674.
122. *AA*.163/131571–86, von Dirksen/AA, Tokio 1 December 1936, a report on Japanese press and public opinion towards the German–Japanese Pact.
123. *OR* did just this on 1 December 1936 when it commented on the Anti-Comintern Pact.
124. *AA*.163/131604, Trautmann/AA, Nanking 17 December 1936; ibid., 131605, von Erdmannsdorff/Nanking, 5 January 1937.
125. See p. 206, n. 122 above.
126. *AA*.161/131246–60, von Dirksen/AA, Tokio 27 December 1936.
127. *AA*.155/130822–34, Trautmann/AA, Nanking 27 January 1937.

Chapter VIII

1. *AA*.163/131559–60, von Weizsäcker/Nanking, 30 November 1936; 919/295109–10, von Hassell/von Weizsäcker, Rome 26 February 1937, Kalrheinz Mack, 'Polen und der Antikominternpakt', *Österreichische Ost-Hefte*, 11 January 1960, 34–40; Sommer, op. cit., 82–93; Presseisen, op. cit., 164–88.
2. *AA*.919/295096–98, von Dirksen/von Erdmannsdorff, with enclosure of

letter to Reichsführer SS Himmler, Tokio 16 December 1936; ibid., 295119—23, von Dirksen/AA, Tokio 14 March 1937. It can be imagined with what mixed feelings the Foreign Office responded to the fact that von Neurath was coopted onto the permanent commission in Berlin established by the Anti-Commintern Pact for the purpose of exchanging information about the Comintern, as well as to investigate defensive measures against the Comintern. In matters connected with this permanent commission, von Erdmannsdorff acted for von Neurath. Others present or represented on the commission were von Ribbentrop, Göring, Goebbels and Himmler: 919/295107, von Raumer/von Neurath, 23 January 1937.

3. *OKW, Wehrmachtamt,* No. 51/37, Chefs. Ausl. 8 July 1937, photostat copy at Foreign and Commonwealth Office, Library and Records Department; F. C. Jones, *Japan's New Order in East Asia: Its Rise and Fall 1937—45* (London 1954), 99; Chapman, op. cit., 151, 154. Chapman's documentation on this whole subject is, of course, much wider, op. cit., 151ff.

4. On 3 February 1937 Trautmann forwarded a report from the Consulate at Tsingtao which included a secret report by the Japanese 'Special Agent' for North China, Major General Matsumoto, on ways and means of strengthening and pursuing Japan's interests in the area: *AA.*184/137554—69, Trautmann/AA, Nanking 3 February 1937 with enclosure.

5. *AA.*211/146030—34, von Falkenhausen/Brinckmann, Nanking 22 March 1937.

6. See Chapter VII, pp. 206—07. Trautmann's report of 27 January 1937 was commented upon by von Dirksen on 2 March: 9148/E643545—48.

7. *AA.*1702/398198—99, Memorandum by Strachwitz, 13 January 1937.

8. *AA.*59/39457, Auslandsorganisation der NSDAP, Landesgruppe Japan/*AO* Berlin, Tokio/Yokohama 10/31 March 1937; ibid., 39458, *AO.* Landesgruppe Japan/*AO* Berlin, Tokio 5 April 1937; ibid., 39465, *AO* Berlin/ Landesgruppe Japan, 30 April 1937; 919/295119—23, von Dirksen/AA, Tokio 14 March 1937.

9. *AA.*7070/E526099, von Hassell/AA, Rome 15 December 1936.

10. The War Ministry continually impressed upon the Foreign Office the economic results of Klein's work in China through the HAPRO contracts: *AA.*6565/E490357—59, Colonel Thomas/AA, 23 January 1937, enclosing a list of Chinese raw materials and agricultural products actually delivered, en route, and planned for the future. A few days before, however, Trautmann forwarded a report from Hankow repeating previous comments on the difficulties arising between Klein and other German trading firms: 218/148114—27, Trautmann/AA, Nanking 18 January 1937 with enclosure. On 13 February Thomas sent von Neurath yet another report: 218/148146—47.

11. *AA.*2910/566123, Trautmann/AA, Nanking 18 February 1937; 3708/ E036579, Schacht/AA, 26 February 1937.

12. *AA.*9142/E642730, von Dirksen/AA, Tokio 6 January 1937; 2898/ D565671, AA/Präsidialkanzlei, 13 January 1937; ibid., 565672, Meissner/ AA, 15 January 1937; 9142/E642731, von Neurath/Tokio, 20 January 1937.

13. *AA.*2898/D565673, Pfleiderer/Strachwitz, 10 February 1937.

14. *AA.*3708/E036580, von Erdmannsdorff/Nanking, 4 March 1937; ibid., E036581, Trautmann/AA, Nanking 6 March 1937.

15. *AA.*9075/E637165, Prüfer/Tokio, 23 December 1936; ibid., E637162—64, Memorandum by Ritter, 6 January 1937. See also Chapter VI, p. 174.

16. *AA.*9075/E637156—57, Memorandum by Voss, 10 March 1937; ibid., E637158, Ritter/Nanking 10 March 1937.

17. *AA.*919/295114, Trautmann/AA, Nanking 11 March 1937; 9075/E637151—52, Memorandum by Ritter 13 March 1937.

18. *AA*.9075/E637153—55, Memorandum by Ritter, 12 March 1937.
19. See above, Chapter VI, p. 166. Von Dirksen also admitted that Ohashi was a difficult person to deal with: *AA*.387/211442—43, von Dirksen/ Dieckhoff, Tokio 27 February 1937.
20. *AA*.9075/E637149—50, Memorandum by Ritter, 30 March 1937.
21. *AA*.3244/E000031, Erdmannsdorff/Nanking, 16 March 1937; ibid., E0032, Trautmann/AA, Nanking 20 March 1937.
22. Following increasing dissatisfaction with his domestic and foreign policies Chiang Kai-shek was arrested on 12 December 1936 by troops under the control of Chang Hsueh-liang while on a visit to Sian in Mongolia. He was released on 25 December 1936 after the intercession of Chinese communist leaders, chief of whom was Chou En-lai. The result was that Chiang Kai-shek gave 'tacit assent to his captors' demands for a cessation of the civil war against the Communists and the formulation of a united front resistance effort against the Japanese': John Hunter Boyle, *China and Japan at War 1937—1945: The Politics of Collaboration* (Stanford University Press 1972), 43; Clubb, op. cit., 202—09. Trautmann's report on the incident was sent on 9 January 1937: *AA*.179/85249—55.
23. See above, p. 204.
24. *AA*.163/131630—36, Trautmann/AA, Nanking 22 March 1937.
25. *AA*.6566/E490380/1—7, von Dirksen/AA, Tokio 16 March 1937.
26. Crowley, op. cit., 316—17.
27. *AA*.2898/D565674, von Dirksen/AA, Tokio 6 March 1937.
28. *AA*.100/65678—87, von Dirksen/AA, Tokio 24 March 1937 with enclosures. Kutakov, op. cit., 12—14, mistakenly dates Dirksen's report to Berlin as 27 March and quotes the Soviet Archives as the source.
29. *AA*.3244/E000033—36, von Dirksen/AA, Tokio 30 March 1937 with enclosures. Already at the beginning of March von Dirksen had reported on the great interest being shown in Japan in the country's policy towards the South Pacific area: 597/246328—31 von Dirksen/AA, Tokio 8 March 1937.
30. *AA*.919/295136, Note by von Neurath, 23 April 1937; Seabury, op. cit., 54.
31. *AA*.919/295124, von Dirksen/AA, Tokio 19 April 1937; 157/131041—42, von Dirksen/AA, Tokio 23 April 1937. A fortnight later Sato again displeased von Dirksen on the matter. In a statement issued to the foreign correspondents in Tokio on 6 May on Japan's foreign policy, Sato only went so far as to remark that the Anti-Comintern Pact with Germany 'has no aims other than those stated by the two Governments at the time of the conclusion of the agreement'. *FRUS*, 1937, III, 83—86, Grew/Washington, Tokio 11 May 1937.
32. *AA*.157/131045, von Dirksen/AA, Tokio 10 May 1937. In von Dirksen's eyes Sato's stock had sunk further when he absented himself, on grounds of 'other business', from a reception given on 5 May by former Minister of War Terauchi to celebrate the Anti-Comintern Pact: 163/131637—40, von Dirksen/AA, Tokio 13 May 1937 with enclosures.
33. *AA*.919/295125—34, 'Cessat' letter with enclosures from Schumberg to von Raumer, April 1937; ibid., 295141, Note by Schumberg (May?) 1937.
34. *AA*.9075/E637145—46, Memorandum by Benzler, 7 April 1937; ibid., E637136—44, Agreement of 21 May 1937 and accompanying documents.
35. *AA*.7072/E526509, Memorandum by Ritter, 7 April 1937.
36. *AA*.9075/E637133—34, Memorandum by Ritter, 20 May 1937.
37. *AA*.1702/398204, War Ministry/AA, 3 April 1937.
38. *AA*.218/148148—53, Trautmann/von Erdmannsdorff with enclosures, Nanking 1 and 3 April 1937. On the question of the role of the private German trading firms in China *vis-à-vis* the Chinese and German organisation of the HAPRO contracts, the Foreign Office adopted an attitude of

reserve and had no wish to interfere. This position served only to underline the fact that the War Ministry's interests were paramount in this aspect of Germany's relations with China: 218/148129—30, Voss/Trautmann, 13 April 1937.

39. *AA*.7070/E526114, von Dirksen/AA, Tokio 6 April 1937.
40. *AA*.9143/E642743, Trautmann/AA, Nanking 30 April 1937; 211/146038— 41, Trautmann/AA, Nanking 30 April 1937. Following a suggestion from Trautmann, von Blomberg sent a congratulatory telegram to von Falken- hausen through the German Embassy at Nanking: 211/146035, War Ministry/AA, 3 May 1937; ibid., 146036 Bismarck/Nanking 11 May 1937. There is no evidence to suggest that von Reichenau returned to China in the summer of 1937, while a few months later War Ministry plans in China were directly affected by the outbreak of the Sino—Japanese war.
41. Anlage 1 to Keitel's memorandum on 8 July 1937: see above p. 210, n. 3.
42. Anlage 2, ibid.
43. Keitel's memorandum of 8 July 1937; Chapman, op. cit., 160.
44. Anlagen 3 and 4, ibid; Chapman, op. cit., 161—62. For details of the con- tinuing consultations between the German and Japanese General Staffs for the exchange of information about Soviet Russia, and military relations in general, see Chapman *passim*. See also Höhne, op. cit., 246—47.
45. See above, p. 216.
46. *AA*.157/131043, von Dirksen/AA, Tokio 10 May 1937; 919/2951474 von Hassell/AA, Rome 26 May 1937; 919/295149—50, Memorandum by Schumberg with comments by von Neurath, 1 June 1937. For the Italo— Japanese negotiations see: Jones, op. cit., 99—101; Presseisen, op. cit., 168—72; Sommer, op. cit., 84—86.
47. *AA*.919/295142—43, von Neurath/Tokio, 4 June 1937; ibid., 295155, von Mackensen/Rome, 16 June 1937; ibid., 295158—59, von Mackensen/ Tokio, 16 June 1937.
48. An element of uncertainty in the situation was how far any improvement in Anglo—Japanese relations would affect German—Japanese relations. Von Dirksen argued that an improvement in relations between London and Tokio would in fact help to stabilise Anglo—German relations and tend to strengthen Germany's own Anti-Comintern role: *AA*.976/303165—77, von Dirksen/AA, Tokio 20 May 1937. Shortly before this, von Reichenau had explained to a British diplomat that Hitler still desired an understand- ing with Britain, and that 'it would not be very difficult to find a pretext for breaking the present liaison between Germany and Italy — as with Japan — if a firm understanding and a pact with Great Britain were defi- nitely in sight; but of course Germany did not wish at present to stand quite isolated in the world': *FO*.C3428/3/18, Vol. 20710, Sir N. Hender- son/FO, Berlin 6 May 1937, enclosing a Munich report of 30 April.
49. *AA*.919/295142—43, von Neurath/Tokio, 4 June 1937; ibid., 295160—61, von Dirksen/AA, Tokio 7 June 1937.
50. *AA*.919/295162, Memorandum by von Schmieden, 2 July 1937.
51. *AA*.919/295163—64, von Mackensen/Tokio, 8 July 1937.
52. *AA*.7071/E526251—52, von Neurath/H. H. Kung, 1 June 1937.
53. *AA*.186/137425—29, Memorandum by von Schmieden, 5 June 1937.
54. *AA*.556/241366—68, Memorandum by von Mackensen, 7 June 1937.
55. *AA*.7071/E526293, Memorandum by von Schmieden, 10 June 1937.
56. *AA*.3708/E036582, Memorandum by von Mackensen, 9 June 1937; 186/ 137425—29, Memorandum by von Schmieden, 5 June 1937.
57. *AA*.7814/E566854—55, Memorandum by Schacht, 10 June 1937.
58. *AA*.3708/E36593—96, Ministry of Economics/AA, 16 June 1937 with enclosure. In connection with Göring's statement of concern to Kung about the usual channels of Sino—German trade, it was in June 1937 that

once again he had shown himself sympathetic to Helfferich's campaign against the activities of Klein and to improve the position of the German businessmen in China *vis-à-vis* the operation of the HAPRO agreements: Helfferich, op. cit., 127—34; 218/148161—63, Helfferich/Schacht, Hamburg 22 June 1937.

59. *AA*.3708/E036585—88, Memorandum by von Schmieden, 15 June 1937.
60. *AA*.3708/E036589—92, Memorandum by von Schmieden, 16 June 1937; 556/241369—71, Memorandum by von Mackensen, 18 June 1937.
61. *AA*.6561/E490199, Memorandum by von Neurath, 6 July 1937.

Chapter IX

1. For the incident and Japanese policy see Crowley, op. cit., 324ff; Jones, op. cit., 30ff. For a partisan account of the ensuing war see: Hsu Longhsuen and Chang Ming-kai, *History of the Sino—Japanese War (1937—1945)*, (Taipei 1971). See also, Lincoln Li, *Japanese Army in North China 1937—41: Problems of Political and Economic Control* (Tokio, Oxford University Press 1976).

2. Von Dirksen, op. cit., 189; *FRUS*, 1937, III, 489—90, Gilbert/Washington, Berlin 28 August 1937. In this connection Ciano indicated to Sugimura, the Japanese Ambassador to Rome, that he hoped that Japan would *not* arrive at a speedy solution of the Amur River incident with Russia because of the crisis in Spain: *AA*.3244/E000041, von Hassell/AA, Rome 7 July 1937. It was towards the end of June that Japanese and Russian forces had clashed at the Amur River: Erickson, op. cit., 468.

3. *AA*.155/130840—41, von Neurath/Meissner, with draft letter, 3 July 1937; ibid., 130844—45, Hitler/Hirota, 10 July 1937.

4. *AA*.178/173215—16, 3888/E048388—89, 7069/E525852—53, Memoranda by von Neurath, 14 July 1937, with Ambassadors Mushakoji, Dodd and Cheng Tien-fong; William E. Dodd Jr and Martha Dodd (eds.), *Ambassador Dodd's Diary 1933—1938* (London 1941), 428; 3888/E048401—03, Memorandum by von Mackensen, 20 July 1937. While there is no evidence to link the two incidents, there can be no doubt that Japan's policy after 7—8 July 1937 was influenced by the events on the Amur River at the beginning of the month. Russia's withdrawal at that time was interpreted as confirming the argument that the Soviet Union was in no position to undertake extended military operations in the Far East: cf. Erickson, op. cit., 468.

5. *AA*.178/137218—20, von Weizsäcker/Tokio, 16 July 1937; cf. Erickson, op. cit., 467.

6. *AA*.6505/E487201—03, Memorandum by von Weizsäcker with enclosures, 16 July 1937; Jones, op. cit., 35—36.

7. *AA*.3888/E048387, von Dirksen/AA, Tokio 12 July 1937; von Dirksen, op. cit., 189.

8. Kordt, op. cit., 167; idem, 'German Political History in the Far East During the Hitler Régime', 7 (Typescript, Nuremberg May 1946; Library of Congress, Washington D.C. — Captured Material, Box 809, Folder 18E-5. Hereafter cited as Kordt, 'Far East').

9. *AA*.3888/E048404—09, von Ribbentrop/von Neurath, London 23 July 1937.

10. When the Japanese discussed the Amur Incident with the Wilhelmstrasse, they did so with specific reference to 'German—Japanese cooperation in Russian questions'. As von Dirksen pointed out on 8 July, the incident with Russia gave the Japanese an opportunity to test Germany out with regard to the Anti-Comintern Pact: *AA*.6561/E490193, von Dirksen/AA, Tokio 1 July 1937; ibid., E490194—96, Memorandum by von Schmieden, 5 July 1937; 156/131000—04, von Dirksen/AA, Tokio 8 July 1937.

11. *AA*.3888/E048392, Memorandum by von Neurath, 16 July 1937.
12. *AA*.3888/E048397—98, von Mackensen/Tokio, 20 July 1937.
13. *AA*.2898/D565679—80, von Mackensen/Tokio, 20 July 1937; Sommer, op. cit., 59.
14. *DGFP*, D, I, 733—35, von Mackensen/Missions, 20 July 1937; *AA*.3888/E048395—96, von Mackensen/Nanking, 20 July 1937.
15. Borg, op. cit., 283ff; Jones, op. cit., 40.
16. *DGFP*, D, I, 735, von Hassell/AA, Rome 21 July 1937; *AA*.178/137221—22, von Dirksen/AA, Tokio 15 July 1937.
17. *AA*.7069/E525856—57, von Weizsäcker/Nanking, 15 July 1937; *DGFP*, D, I, 736, Trautmann/AA, Nanking 21 July 1937; *FO*.F4036/9/10, Vol. 20949, Prideaux Brune/FO, Nanking 12 July 1937; ibid., F4235/9/10, Vol. 20950, Sir Hughe Knatchbull-Hugessen/FO, Nanking 18 July 1937; ibid., F9943/9/10, Vol. 20959, Mr Howe/FO, Nanking 20 November 1937; Presseisen, op. cit., 129. The British Foreign Office thought that von Falkenhausen's views were not only 'dangerous nonsense' but that he had given 'dangerous encouragement to the Chinese Government': comments on Sir Hughe Knatchbull-Hugessen/FO, Nanking 18 July 1937, *FO*.F4259/9/10, Vol. 20950, containing a report by the British Military Attaché who questioned the assumptions of von Falkenhausen's optimism.
18. *DGFP*, D, I, 737, Memorandum by von Weizsäcker, 22 July 1937; *AA*.7069/E525914, von Dirksen/AA, Tokio 22 July 1937; *DGFP*, D, I, 738—39, Memorandum by von Weizsäcker, 24 July 1937 with enclosure.
19. *AA*.7069/E525905, von Dirksen/AA, Tokio 20 July 1937; 153/821136—38, von Dirksen/AA, Tokio 22 July 1937.
20. *AA*.1702/398233—36, von Dirksen/AA, Tokio 30 October 1937, enclosing transcripts of telegrams from Mushakoji and Oshima to Tokio which the Japanese General Staff had given to Ott. Again it is quite remarkable how often von Neurath's records of his conversations omitted certain essential points of the discussion.
21. *DGFP*, D, I, Memorandum by von Weizsäcker, 22 July 1937; ibid., 745—47, Memorandum by von Schmieden, 30 July 1937.
22. *DGFP*, D, I, 740, von Dirksen/AA, Tokio 27 July 1937; *AA*.153/82097—108, von Dirksen/AA, Tokio 31 July 1937; Kordt, 'Far East', 8.
23. *SIA*, 1937, I, 295; Borg, op. cit., 290; *AA*.7069/E525929—31.
24. *AA*.153/82097—108, von Dirksen/AA, Tokio 31 July 1937.
25. *DGFP*, D, I, 744—45, Memorandum by von Weizsäcker, 28 July 1937; ibid., 742—44, von Weizsäcker/Tokio, 28 July 1937; *AA*.3888/E048417, von Neurath's comments *en clair*; *DGFP*, D, I, 748—49, von Dirksen/AA, Tokio 3 August 1937; Ernst von Weizsäcker, *Erinnerungen* (Munich 1950), 141.
26. *DGFP*, D, I, 741, Trautmann/AA, Nanking 27 July 1937; ibid., 748, Trautmann/AA, Nanking 1 August 1937.
27. *DGFP*, D, I, 745—47, Memorandum by von Schmieden, 30 July 1937; *AA*.153/82097—108, von Dirksen/AA, Tokio 31 July 1937.
28. *DGFP*, D, I, 747, von Weizsäcker/Nanking, Tokio 31 July 1937; *FO*.F4610/9/10, Vol. 20951, Sir Eric Phipps/FO, Paris 28 July 1937; ibid., F4724/9/10, Sir Hughe Knatchbull-Hugessen/FO, Nanking 30 July 1937; ibid., F4977/9/10, Vol. 20952, Lord Chilston/FO, Moscow 7 August 1937; *FRUS*, 1937, III, 288—89, Bullitt/Washington, Paris 28 July 1937; *DDF*, 2nd Series, 1936—1939, Vol. VI, 530, Delbos/Nanking, Tokio, Paris 30 July 1937; *DGFP*, D, I, 748, Trautmann/AA, Nanking 1 August 1937; ibid., 748—49, von Dirksen/AA, Tokio 3 August 1937; *AA*.919/295171—73, von Raumer/Schumberg, 21 August 1937 with enclosures from the Japanese Embassy, Berlin.
29. *DGFP*, D, I, 742, von Weizsäcker/Nanking, 28 July 1937; *AA*.1927/432213, Trautmann/AA, Nanking 10 August 1937.

30. *AA*.1702/398213—14, Memorandum by von Weizsäcker, 10 August 1937.
31. *AA*.1702/398215—16, Memorandum on von Blomberg—Kung conversation of 12 August 1937; 3888/E048427, Memorandum by Bracklo, 13 August 1937; 186/137433—38, Memorandum by von Mackensen, 13 August 1937.
32. *DGFP*, D, I, 750, Memorandum by von Neurath, Leinfelden, 17 August 1937; ibid., 753, Memorandum by von Mackensen, 19 August 1937.
33. *AA*.218/148171, Memorandum by Voss, 26 August 1937.
34. *DGFP*, D, I, 852—53, Memorandum by Wiehl, 23 April 1938; ibid., 874—76, Memorandum by Wiehl, with enclosure by von Strachwitz dated 15 June 1938; Drechsler, op. cit., 52—53.
35. Drechsler, op. cit., 55.
36. *AA*.1927/432221, Trautmann/AA, Nanking 13 August 1937; 3888/E048425, von Weizsäcker/Tokio, 13 August 1937; 1927/432226, Bismarck/Tokio, 16 August 1937; 3888/E048470, von Mackensen/Tokio, 2 September 1937; Borg, op. cit., 303—04; Jones, op. cit., 49; Presseisen, op. cit., 127.
37. *DGFP*, D, I, 752—53, Memorandum by von Mackensen, 19 August 1934; ibid., 753—54, Memorandum by von Mackensen, 20 August 1937; Presseisen, op. cit., 128—29.
38. *AA*.153/82093/1—3, Memorandum by von Mackensen, 23 August 1937; 3888/E048444, Trautmann/AA, Nanking 25 August 1937; ibid., E048446, *Ostasiatischer Verein*/AA, Hamburg 26 August 1937; 153/82091, Trautmann/AA, Nanking 26 August 1937; 1927/432265, Trautmann/AA, Nanking 28 August 1937; 185/137456—63, Kung/Hitler, Bad Nauheim 3 September 1937.
39. *AA*.153/82092, Behrend/AA, Shanghai 26 August 1937; 1702/398217, comment by Voss on Trautmann's telegram of 28 August, reporting that the Chinese Propaganda Minister had told him of von Blomberg's statement to the Chinese Ambassador that Germany would no longer deliver arms to China in the event of a Sino—Soviet alliance. This was denied by von Mackensen, and a statement of the current situation regarding arms deliveries to China was given to Trautmann for his personal information only: ibid., 398218—19, von Mackensen/Nanking, 2 September 1937.
40. *AA*.153/82089—90, Trautmann/AA, Nanking 27 August 1937; 187/137392—95, Memorandum by Trautmann, Nanking 27 August 1937; *DGFP*, D, I, 756057, Memorandum by Gaus, 30 August 1937; *AA*.1927/432281, Trautmann/AA, Nanking 3 September 1937; *FRUS*, 1937, III, 499—500, Gilbert/Washington, Berlin 31 August 1937.
41. Liu, op. cit., 167.
42. *AA*.1927/432271—73, Schulenburg/AA, Moscow 31 August 1937; *DGFP*, D, I, 763, Trautmann/AA, Nanking 25 September 1937.
43. *DGFP*, D, I, 761—62, Trautmann/AA, Nanking 23 September 1937; *FRUS*, 1937, II, 481—84, Gilbert/Washington, Berlin 26 August 1937.
44. *DGFP*, D, I, 754—55, von Dirksen/AA, Tokio 23 August 1937.
45. *IMTFE*, Vol. 8, 3605—39, Exhibit 270, Speech by Kenryo Sato, Chief of Press Section, War Ministry, 25—29 August 1938.
46. *AA*.178/137245—46, von Dirksen/AA, Tokio 19 August 1937; 1927/432238, Trautmann/AA, Nanking 21 August 1937; ibid., 432276/1, Memorandum by von Bismarck, 1 September 1937; ibid., 432283, Trautmann/AA, Nanking 3 September 1937; 2911/D566175, von Dirksen/AA, Tokio 6 September 1937; ibid., D566176, Trautmann/AA, Nanking 7 September 1937; ibid., D566177, Prüfer/Tokio, 9 September 1937; *FRUS*, 1937, III, 650—51, Johnson/Washington, Nanking 1 November 1937.
47. *DGFP*, D, I, 759, von Dirksen/AA, Tokio 21 September 1937; *AA*.2911/D566178, von Weizsäcker/Nanking, 22 September 1937; *DGFP*, D, I,

761—62, Trautmann/AA, Nanking 23 September 1937; ibid., 762, von Weizsäcker/Tokio, 24 September 1937; 1927/432336, Trautmann/AA, Nanking 24 September 1937.

48. *FO*.F4472/9/10, Vol. 20951, Sir Hughe Knatchbull-Hugessen/FO, Nanking 24 July 1937; ibid., F6136/1098/10, Vol. 21001, Gage/FO, Nanking 2 September 1937; ibid., F9217/1079/10, Vol. 21001, Foreign Office Minutes, 17 September 1937; ibid., F7595/9/10, Vol. 20957, Howe/FO, Nanking 7 October 1937; ibid., F7911/1079/10, Vol. 21001, Howe/FO, Nanking 11 October 1937; *FRUS*, 1937, III, 650—51, Johnson/Washington, Nanking 1 November 1937. See also Liu, op. cit., 162—63; *SIA*, 1937, I, 215.

49. *AA*.3888/E048487—89, von Dirksen/AA, Tokio 30 August 1937; Oshima/ General Shun Tada, Berlin 20, 25 August 1937 (see above, p. 235, n. 20); 1702/398238—40, von Weizsäcker/von Dirksen, 9 December 1937; *FO*.C7228/3/18, Vol. 20712, Major-General Temperley/Eden, 11 October 1937.

50. *SIA*, 1937, I, 226.

51. *AA*.3888/E048480—82, British Embassy, Berlin/AA, 11 September 1937; ibid., E048483—85, Memorandum by Albrecht of meeting, 13 September 1937. Some of the German military advisers were afraid that the Reich Government would acquiesce in the search of German merchant ships by Japanese warships, thus adding further difficulties to the delivery of German arms to China: *FO*.F6471/130/10, Vol. 20977, Gage/FO, Nanking 11 September 1937.

52. Liu, op. cit., 156—57.

53. *AA*.1927/432241, Behrend/AA, Shanghai 22 August 1937; ibid., 432249, Behrend/AA, Shanghai 23 August 1937; ibid., 432246, Trautmann/AA, Nanking 23 August 1937; ibid., 432254—55, von Dirksen/AA, Tokio 25 August 1937; 178/137271, von Dirksen/AA, Tokio 27 August 1937.

54. *AA*.178/137273, von Bismarck/Tokio, 30 August 1937; ibid., 137287, von Dirksen/AA, Tokio 6 September 1937.

55. *AA*.3888/E048487—89, von Dirksen/AA, Tokio 30 August 1937.

56. Drechsler, op. cit., 50, n. 103.

57. It seems that the Chinese side of the arms trade with Germany was taken more in hand once the conflict with Japan broke out. According to an American report from Paris in September 1938, 'since the beginning of the Sino—Japanese war there has been a Chinese Munitions Purchase Commission in Berlin': *FRUS*, 1938, III, 606, Memorandum by Higgins, Paris 2 September 1938.

58. *AA*.1702/398224—26, von Schmieden/Thomas, 20 September 1937; 1927/ 432312, von Dirksen/AA, Tokio 21 September 1937; ibid., 432311, Memorandum by von Mackensen, 21 September 1937; 224/150507—09, Draft Telegram to Tokio, September 1937; ibid., 150489—90, von Dirksen/ AA, Tokio 24 September 1937. On 9 September Trautmann reported that after an unsuccessful engagement, a torpedo boat purchased by China from Germany had fallen into the hands of the Japanese: 1927/432298, Trautmann/AA, Nanking 9 September 1937.

59. *AA*.219/148252—1/13, von Dirksen/AA, Tokio 27 October 1937; von Dirksen, op. cit., 191.

60. *AA*.185/137456—63, Kung/Hitler, Bad Nauheim 3 September 1937.

61. *Documents on International Affairs*, 1937, 180; Mushakoji/Hirota, Berlin 15 September 1937 (see p. 235, n. 20). Prince Chichibu visited Germany from 7—14 September and was accorded particular attention in the way of receptions and visits.

62. *AA*.2898/D565695—96, von Dirksen/AA, Tokio 28 September 1937.

63. *AA*.1927/432309, Trautmann/AA, Nanking 19 September 1937, ref. his

direct telegram to von Dirksen; *DGFP*, D, I, 761, von Mackensen/Tokio, 23 September 1937; *AA*.1927/432334, von Dirksen/AA, Tokio 24 September 1937; 224/150492, Trautmann/AA, Nanking 25 September 1937; ibid., 150493, von Weizsäcker/Tokio, 28 September 1937.

64. *AA*.7072/E526487, Trautmann/AA, Nanking 23 September 1937; *DGFP*, D, I, 760, Memorandum by von Neurath, 22 September 1937; *AA*.224/ 150505, Benzler/Tokio, 30 September 1937. At the beginning of the month Mushakoji had shown himself agreeable to Trautmann's continued presence in Nanking since it was hoped that he could inform the Japanese authorities of conditions in Nanking and about the Chinese army: 3888/ E048478—79, Memorandum by von Schmieden, 9 September 1937.

65. *AA*.153/82082—87, Memorandum by von Schmieden, August 1937.

66. *AA*.3870/E046499—500, Memorandum by von Weizsäcker, 29 August 1937.

67. *AA*.3870/E046501—03, Memorandum by von Schmieden, 4 September 1937.

68. *AA*.1702/398220, Trautmann/AA, Nanking 10 September 1937; 4422/ E084052, von Neurath/Nanking, 12 September 1937.

69. *AA*.3888/E048495, von Neurath/Geneva, 22 September 1937; 1927/ 432335, Memorandum by von Weizsäcker, 24 September 1937; *SIA*, 1937, I, 279—84.

70. *AA*.160/131168, von Dirksen/AA, Tokio 13 October 1937; *DGFP*, D, I, 764—65, Memorandum by von Strachwitz, 13 October 1937; ibid., von Mackensen/Nanking, 14 October 1937; ibid., 765—66, Memorandum by von Neurath, 14 October 1937; 160/131176, Trautmann/AA, Nanking 14 October 1937; ibid., 131185, Richthofen/AA, Brussels 16 October 1937; ibid., 131181, von Weizsäcker/Tokio, 16 October 1937; ibid., 131183, von Weizsäcker/Rome, 18 October 1937; *DGFP*, D, I, 769—70, von Dirksen/AA, Tokio 21 October 1937.

71. *DGFP*, D, I, 766—67, Memorandum by von Neurath, 15 October 1937; ibid., 767, Trautmann/AA, Nanking 16 October 1937.

72. *FRUS*, 1937, III, 649—50, Johnson/Washington, Nanking 30 October 1937.

73. *AA*.185/137468—71, Trautmann/AA, Nanking 11 October 1937, with enclosure; *FO*.F7911/1079/10, Vol. 21001, Mr Howe/FO, Nanking 11 October 1937; *FRUS*, 1937, III, 547—48, Gilbert/Washington, Berlin 23 September 1937.

74. Sommer, op. cit., 65.

75. *DGFP*, D, I, 750—52, Memorandum for von Ribbentrop by von Raumer, 17 August 1937.

76. *DGFP*, D, I, 758—59, Memorandum for the Führer by von Ribbentrop, 19 September 1937; *AA*.1702/398237, unsigned and undated Note, probably from the Büro Ribbentrop, recording Hitler's observations on the Far Eastern conflict.

77. *AA*.5647/H002217—18, von Dirksen/AA, Tokio 11 September 1937.

78. Presseisen, op. cit., 153; *SIA*, 1937, I, 294.

79. *FO*.F8697/9/10, Vol. 20958, Eden/Henderson (Berlin), 27 October 1937.

80. I am extremely grateful to Dr Meier Michaelis, Research Associate at the University of Jerusalem, for a copy of the relevant parts of the following document: *BA*/MA/PG33612, pp. 1—22, Lecture by Reich Foreign Minister Joachim von Ribbentrop to Admirals and Generals, Berlin, 24 January 1939.

81. Kordt, op. cit., 169.

82. *DGFP*, D, I, 760, Memorandum by von Neurath, 22 September 1937; *AA*.1702/398228, von Dirksen/AA, Tokio 25 September 1937; 4422/ E048053, von Weizsäcker/Tokio, 25 September 1937; *DGFP*, D, I, 15, von Weizsäcker/Rome, 19 October 1937; Presseisen, op. cit., 174.

83. *DGFP*, D, I, 760, Memorandum by von Neurath, 22 September 1937; *Ciano's Diary 1937—1938* (London 1952), 23.
84. Sommer, op. cit., 86.
85. Ibid., 67.
86. Presseisen, op. cit., 175.
87. *DGFP*, D, I, 16—18, von Hassell/AA, Rome 20 October 1937; *Ciano's Diary*, 23; Sommer, op. cit., 67, 86.
88. *Ciano's Diary*, 24; Malcolm Muggeridge (ed.), *Ciano's Diplomatic Papers* (London 1948), 140—41.
89. Kordt, op. cit., 169—70.
90. *DGFP*, D, I, 767—68, Memorandum by von Mackensen, 19 October 1937.
91. *DGFP*, D, VII, 609—10, Appendix III, Oshima/Göring, Berlin 21 October 1937.
92. *FRUS*, 1937, III, 668—71, Bingham/Washington, London 9 November 1937.
93. Mushakoji/Hirota, Berlin 7 October 1937 (see p. 235, n. 20 above).
94. *AA*.3888/E048504, Trautmann/AA, Nanking 10 October 1937; ibid., E048506, Memorandum by Wolf, 11 October 1937.
95. Oshima/General Shun Tada, Berlin 16 October 1937 (see p. 235, n. 20 above).
96. *DGFP*, D, I, 768—69, Memorandum by von der Heyden-Rynsch, 19 October 1937.
97. *DGFP*, D, I, 772, Memorandum by von der Heyden-Rynsch, 22 October 1937.
98. *AA*.218/148175, Clodius/Hankow, 3 December 1937; *FRUS*, 1937, III, 650—51, Johnson/Washington, Nanking 1 November 1937.
99. *FRUS*, 1937, III, 625—26, Gilbert/Washington, Berlin 20 October 1937. The American Ambassador to London, Robert Bingham, also obtained information about the differences of opinion in Berlin about German Far Eastern policy: 'The Nazi Party Leaders . . . are quite prepared to throw German commercial interests in China overboard in order to establish political solidarity with Japan. Which of these two views will finally prevail may still be in doubt. Some indication as to their relative strength may shortly be shown by the result of the present conflict of opinion in Berlin on the withdrawal of German military advisers from China'. Ibid., 668—71, Bingham/Washington, London 9 November 1937. The British also obtained information about the German 'civil war' over Far Eastern policy: *FO*.F8308/9/10, Vol. 20958, Sir G. Ogilvie-Forbes/FO, Berlin 21 October 1937.
100. *AA*.4422/E084054—56, Jannings, Siemssen & Co./von Schmieden, Hamburg 8 October 1937; ibid., E084057, von Schmieden/Jannings, 19 October 1937.
101. See Borg, op. cit., Chapter XV: Japanese Efforts at a Settlement, *passim*; Crowley, op. cit., 340ff.
102. Borg, op. cit., 449. Japanese attempts to arrive at a form of settlement with China were themselves the product of complicated conflicts and manoeuvres within the Japanese Government. Especially acute were the differences of opinion within Army circles as to the desirability of pursuing the war against Chiang Kai-shek to the bitter end or of effecting a compromise solution which would serve to maintain Japan's strength against that of the Soviet Union.
103. Crowley, op. cit., 352.
104. According to a report of 22 September from Krauel at Geneva, this 'special relationship' caused the British some concern since they feared that mediation by Germany and Italy would exclude the League of Nations: *AA*.1687/396336—38, Krauel/AA, Geneva 22 September 1937.
105. *IMTFE*, Exhibit 3268, 11 and 22 October 1937.

106. Presseisen, op. cit., 134. For Ott's trip to Shanghai, see below, pp. 260–63.
107. *AA*.1927/432335, Memorandum by von Weizsäcker, 24 September 1937; ibid., 432374–75, Trautmann/AA, 18 October 1937.
108. *DGFP*, D, I, 769–70, von Dirksen/AA, Tokio 21 October 1937.
109. *DGFP*, D, I, 71, von Mackensen/Trautmann, 22 October 1937.
110. Jones, op. cit., 59, n. 6., from Ott's interrogation, 20 February 1946, *IMTFE*; *AA*.3888/E048532–34, Behrend/AA, Shanghai 31 October 1937.
111. On 4 October von Dirksen had again reported on Japan's dissatisfaction with Germany's supposed lack of a 'positive' approach to the Far Eastern crisis in view of her Anti-Comintern Pact with Japan, especially since the argument was repeated that what Japan was fighting in China was communism. On the other hand, it appeared that the Japanese press had tried to play down the sensitive questions of the German advisers in China and German arms deliveries to that country: *AA*.219/148217–29, von Dirksen/ AA, Tokio 4 October 1937. Nor was Japanese confidence in Germany likely to be increased by reports at the beginning of October that Trautmann had spoken to the German community in Nanking, but principally to the military advisers, on 'the war of resistance waged by the Chinese' and that 'the ability and courage of the Chinese on the battlefield had deeply impressed the Germans at home': *FRUS*, 1937, III, 602, Johnson/ Washington, Nanking, 12 October 1937.
112. *AA*.219/148252–1/13, von Dirksen/AA, Tokio 27 October 1937.
113. Presseisen, op. cit., 132–33; *DGFP*, D, I, 772, Memorandum by von Neurath, 27 October 1937; *AA*.160/131221–23, *Deutsche Diplomatisch Politische Korrespondenz*, 29 October 1937.
114. Jones, op. cit., 55. See also, Borg, op. cit., Chapter XIV *passim*; Tsien Tai, *China and the Nine-Power Conference at Brussels in 1937* (New York 1964).
115. Crowley, op. cit., 388–89.
116. *AA*.3888/E048532–34, Behrend/AA, Shanghai 31 October 1937; ibid., E048523–31, Trautmann/AA, Nanking 6 November 1937.
117. See above, p. 263.
118. *DGFP*, D, I, 773, von Dirksen/AA, Tokio 28 October 1937.
119. *DGFP*, D, I, 774–75, Trautmann/AA, Nanking 29 October 1937.
120. *DGFP*, D, I, 775, von Mackensen/Tokio, 30 October 1937; *FO*.F9796/9/10, Vol. 20959, Mr Howe/FO, Nanking 17 November 1937.
121. *DGFP*, D, I, 776, von Mackensen/Nanking, 30 October 1937.
122. See above, p. 259.
123. *DGFP*, D, I, 777, Trautmann/AA, Nanking 31 October 1937.
124. *AA*.1726/401256–57, Trautmann/AA, Nanking 3 November 1937.
125. *DGFP*, D, I, 778–79, von Dirksen/AA, Tokio 3 November 1937.
126. *DGFP*, D, I, 782, von Hassell/AA, Rome 7 November 1937.
127. *DGFP*, D, I, 779, von Neurath/Nanking, 3 November 1937.
128. *DGFP*, D, I, 780–81, Trautmann/AA, Nanking 5 November 1937. Britain was alarmed at reports that Germany was about to mediate between China and Japan and it was feared in London that this 'would seriously damage British influence in East Asia': Bradford A. Lee, *Britain and the Sino–Japanese War 1937–1939: A Study in the Dilemmas of British Decline* (London 1973), 75. For other recent studies on British policy and the Sino–Japanese war see Aron Shai, *Origins of the War in the East. Britain, China, and Japan 1937–39* (London 1976); Peter Lowe, *Great Britain and the Origins of the Pacific War. A Study of British Policy in East Asia 1937–1941* (Oxford University Press 1977).
129. Sommer, op. cit., 87–93, 98–99.
130. *Ciano's Diary*, 27; Drechsler, op. cit., 63–64; *FRUS*, 1937, III, 668–71, Bingham/Washington, London 9 November 1937.

131. *DGFP*, D, I, 776. Trautmann/AA, Nanking 30 October 1937; *AA*.1726/ 401256—57, Trautmann/AA, 3 November 1937; 1097/318253, Trautmann/ AA, Nanking 4 November 1937; ibid., 318263, Trautmann/AA, Nanking 5 November 1937; Drechsler, op. cit., 66.
132. *AA*.2128/463400—01, von Hassell/AA, Rome 16 November 1937; *Ciano's Diary*, 33. German businessmen were so concerned about their future in China because of what they felt was evidence of a pro-Japanese tendency in the German press that a meeting was called at the Foreign Office on 7 October with Emil Helfferich and representatives of the *Ostasiatischer Verein* of Hamburg. The numerous complaints from those German business-men resident in China were even supported by the China section of the Auslandsorganisation of the NSDAP: 3888/E048501—03, Memorandum by von Schmieden, 8 October 1937; ibid., E048511—14, Lahrmann/*AO*, Shanghai 22 October 1937; 7070/E526182—84, German Chamber of Commerce, Shanghai/*OV*, Hamburg, Shanghai 6 November 1937.
133. Kordt, op. cit., 174; Kordt, 'Far East', 17.
134. Sommer, op. cit., 68, n. 61. See also p. 254 above.
135. Sommer, op. cit., 67—68.
136. *Ciano's Diplomatic Papers*, Muggeridge, (ed.), 143; *DGFP*, D, I, 782, von Hassell/AA, Rome 7 November 1937.
137. On 24 November Kempe wrote from Canton that German businessmen in China were opposed to any German mediation if the result was to be the grant of special advantages and rights to the Japanese to the disadvantage of the Germans: *AA*.2910/D566126—28.
138. Jones, op. cit., 61—62; *SIA*, 1937, I, 219ff.
139. *AA*.1726/401265—66, von Neurath/Tokio, 6 November 1937, informing von Dirksen of Chiang Kai-shek's reply to Trautmann; ibid., 401280, von Dirksen/AA, Tokio 8 November 1937.
140. *DGFP*, I, 783, von Dirksen/AA, Tokio 8 November 1937.
141. *DGFP*, D, I, 777, Memorandum by von Mackensen, 3 November 1937; 5647/H002194, von Dirksen/AA, Tokio 2 November 1937, with comments by Voss relating to the Hitler—von Blomberg conversation; *DGFP*, D, I, 782, Memorandum by von Mackensen, 8 November 1937.
142. *DGFP*, D, I, 784, Trautmann/AA, Nanking 9 November 1937.
143. *AA*.2128/463398—99, Trautmann/AA, Nanking 9 November 1937.
144. *AA*.1726/401275—78, von Neurath/Rome, 11 November 1937.
145. British reports spoke of a rising tide of depression about the military situa-tion among the German military advisers. It seemed that there was a serious rift between von Falkenhausen and Chiang Kai-shek over the general direction of the campaign against the Japanese. Evidently the Marshal had ignored von Falkenhausen's advice not to withdraw troops from the Shanghai and Soochow Creek regions, while von Falkenhausen bitterly opposed Chiang's decision to defend Nanking 'to the last'. He felt that this would not only be 'useless from the military point of view but that it would be madness and could only result in a situation much worse than that of 1927': *FO*.F9498/9595/9943/9/10, Vol. 20959, Nanking/FO, 12, 15, 20 November 1937.
146. Periodically the idea of a joint Anglo—German mediation in the Far Eastern conflict had been mooted, but nothing ever came of what were essentially tentative suggestions anyway. Cf. Lee, op. cit., 150—51.
147. *AA*.219/148239, Trautmann/AA, Nanking 13 November 1937; 1726/ 401290, Trautmann/AA, Nanking 18 November 1937; 210/145968, von Neurath/Hankow, 22 November 1937; *DGFP*, D, I, 781, von Mackensen/ Rome, 6 November 1937; ibid., 782, von Hassell/AA, Rome 7 November 1937; 1726/401275—78, von Neurath/Rome, 11 November 1937; 2128/ 463400—01, von Hassell/AA, Rome 16 November 1937.

148. *AA*.1726/401291, von Dirksen/AA, Tokio 20 November 1937; 210/ 145968, von Neurath/Hankow, 22 November 1937.
149. *DGFP*, D, I, 784—85, Memorandum by von Weizsäcker, 20 November 1937.
150. *AA*.210/145930, Trautmann/AA, Nanking 21 November 1937.
151. *DGFP*, D, I, 785—86, Memorandum by von Neurath 22 November 1937. Hitler did not decline, however, to accept a Japanese invitation to attend an anniversary celebration dinner at the Japanese Embassy on 25 November 1937, thus breaking one of his golden rules never to attend an embassy function.
152. *DGFP*, D, I, 786—87, von Mackensen/Rome, 27 November 1937.
153. *AA*.210/145922, Draft telegram of December 1937, von Weizsäcker/ Mukden.
154. *DGFP*, D, I, 798, Knoll/AA, Hsinking 6 December 1937. Von Neurath's comment was found on another copy of Knoll's telegram by Gerhard Weinberg, 'German Recognition of Manchukuo', 159.
155. *Ciano's Diary*, 35—36.
156. Kordt, 'Far East', 10.
157. *AA*.1726/401296 and 401297, Trautmann/AA, Hankow, 29 November 1937. Like the Chinese Foreign Office and other Western Ambassadors, Trautmann and his staff had removed themselves by this time to Hankow. See also: James T. C. Liu, 'German Mediation in the Sino—Japanese War 1937—38', *Far Eastern Quarterly*, VIII, February 1949, 160.
158. *AA*.1726/401298, Trautmann/AA, Hankow 29 November 1937.
159. *AA*.1726/401297, Trautmann/AA, Hankow 29 November 1937; *DGFP*, D, I, 787, Memorandum by von Neurath, 1 December 1937.
160. Drechsler, op. cit., 45.
161. Liu, 'German Mediation', 161; *FRUS*, 1937, III, 746—47, Johnson/ Washington, Hankow 2 December 1937.
162. Fischer/Trautmann, Shanghai 29 November 1937, quoted in Joachim Peck, *Kolonialismus ohne Kolonien: Der Deutsche Imperialismus und China 1937* (Berlin 1961), 151.
163. *AA*.1726/401307, Memorandum by von Mackensen, 3 December 1937. Oshima had also raised the question of the recognition of Manchukuo with Keitel, indicating that it was high time that Germany acted positively on the matter: 210/145927, Memorandum by von Mackensen, 3 December 1937.
164. *DGFP*, D, I, 787—89, Trautmann/AA, Nanking 3 December 1937. While the East German author, Karl Drechsler (op. cit., 45), is correct in attributing to the Wilhelmstrasse, and even Hitler, more than a slightly passive role and attitude in the whole question of peace negotiations, he is completely wrong in associating von Ribbentrop with the enterprise. At no time was von Ribbentrop involved in the question, and had he been one can be sure that the finesse with which von Neurath, von Mackensen and Trautmann handled the matter would have been thrown to the winds. Furthermore, and despite Drechsler's assertions to the contrary, Hitler at least was aware of the practical disadvantages to Germany of a total Japanese victory over China.
165. *DGFP*, D, I, 789—90, von Dirksen/AA, Tokio 3 December 1937.
166. *IMTFE*, Vol. 65, 33990, Exhibit 3508, Oshima Affidavit.
167. *DGFP*, D, I, 792—93, Memorandum by von Mackensen, 3 December 1937.
168. *DGFP*, D, I, 793—96, von Neurath/von Dirksen, 4 December 1937. Another telegram from von Dirksen urging immediate action by Germany to bring the two parties together crossed Trautmann's report of his talk with Chiang Kai-shek at Nanking: *DGFP*, D, I, 791—92, von Dirksen/AA, Tokio 3 December 1937.

169. *DGFP*, D, I, 797, Trautmann/AA, Hankow 5 December 1937; ibid., 798–99, von Neurath/Tokio, 6 December 1937.
170. While only a bare outline of Germany's actions was given to Attolico, von Neurath refused point blank to consider the Italian Ambassador's suggestion that Germany and Italy should act together to achieve peace in the Far East: *AA*.210/145920–21, Memorandum by von Neurath, 6 December 1937; *DGFP*, D, I, 800, Memorandum by von Weizsäcker, 8 December 1937.
171. *AA*.1928/432521, Trautmann/AA, Hankow 6 December 1937.
172. *DGFP*, D, I, 799, von Dirksen/von Neurath, Tokio 7 December 1937.
173. *DGFP*, D, I, 800–01, von Neurath/von Dirksen, 10 December 1937. Trautmann was also informed of these instructions: *AA*.1726/401360–61, von Mackensen/Hankow, 14 December 1937.
174. Jones, op. cit., 63–65; Crowley, op. cit., 358–60; *FRUS*, 1937, III, 764–65, Grew/Washington, Tokio 5 December 1937.
175. Trautmann/AA, Hankow 10 December 1937, quoted in Peck, op. cit., 127.
176. Ibid., 127–28; *FO*.F10750/9/10, Vol. 20960, Mr Gage/FO, Hankow 9 December 1937; ibid., F959/84/10, Vol. 22106, Mr Blunt/FO, Canton 10 December 1937.
177. A graphic account of the horrors perpetrated by Japanese soldiers on the citizens of Nanking is given in David Bergamini, *Japan's Imperial Conspiracy* (New York 1971), 32–45.
178. *AA*.210/145879–80, Memorandum by von Mackensen, 22 December 1937.
179. *AA*.210/145891, Trautmann/AA, Hankow 13 December 1937; ibid., 145890, von Weizsäcker/Hankow, 16 December 1937.
180. *DGFP*, D, I, 801–02, Trautmann/AA, Hankow 13 December 1937; *AA*.1726/401368–69, von Mackensen/Hankow, 21 December 1937.
181. *SIA*, 1937, I, 245.
182. Trautmann/AA, Hankow 15 December 1937 with enclosure, quoted in Peck, op. cit., 133–35.
183. *AA*.210/145889, von Dirksen/AA, Tokio 16 December 1937; 1726/401370, Trautmann/AA, Hankow 21 December 1937.
184. Crowley, op. cit., 364–65.
185. *IMTFE*, Vol. 72, 37710–11, Exhibit 3788-A, Saionji-Harada Memoirs, 21 December 1937.
186. *DGFP*, D, I, 802–04, von Dirksen/von Neurath, Tokio 22 December 1937.
187. *DGFP*, F, I, 808–09, von Neurath/Tokio, 24 December 1937.
188. *DGFP*, D, I, 805–08, von Neurath/Hankow, 24 December 1937.
189. *DGFP*, D, I, 809, Trautmann/AA, Hankow 26 December 1937.
190. *AA*.210/145854, von Dirksen/AA, Tokio 26 December 1937; 224/150558, von Neurath/Hankow, 26 December 1937; *DGFP*, D, I, 810, Trautmann/AA, Hankow, 27 December 1937.
191. Memorandum by Lautenschlager, Hankow 27 December 1937, quoted in Peck, op. cit., 144–45.
192. *AA*.210/145852, Trautmann/AA, Hankow 28 December 1937.
193. *DGFP*, D, I, 810–11, von Mackensen/Tokio, 29 December 1937.
194. See above, pp. 277–78.
195. *AA*.1726/401407, von Dirksen/AA, Tokio 28 December 1937.
196. *DGFP*, D, I, 811–12, von Dirksen/von Neurath, Tokio 30 December 1937.
197. *AA*.210/145846–47, von Mackensen/Hankow, 29 December 1937; Handwritten comment by Lautenschlager, 30 December 1937, quoted in Peck, op. cit., 149; 210/145838, von Mackensen/Hankow, 31 December 1937.
198. *AA*.210/145844, von Mackensen/Hankow, 30 December 1937; Vermerk by Lautenschlager, Hankow 1 January 1938, quoted in Peck, op. cit., 151.
199. Crowley, op. cit., 366–68.

200. *AA*.210/145841, Trautmann/AA, Hankow 31 December 1937; Trautmann/ AA, Hankow 31 December 1937, quoted in Peck, op. cit., 152.
201. *AA*.210/145835, Trautmann/AA, Hankow 1 January 1938; ibid., 145827– 28, Trautmann/AA, Hankow 2 January 1938; *FO*.F144/16/10, Vol. 22053, Mr Gage/FO, Hankow 3 January 1938; *FRUS*, 1938, III, 2–3, Johnson/ Washington, Hankow 2 January 1938.
202. *AA*.210/145833, von Dirksen/von Neurath, Tokio 1 January 1938. Liu, 'German Mediation', 164, has this wrongly dated as 6 January 1938.
203. Chiang Kai-shek's personal appeal to President Roosevelt of 24 December 1937 proved to be fruitless: Borg, op. cit., 478.
204. *DGFP*, D, I, 812–13, Trautmann/AA, Hankow 31 December 1937.
205. *AA*.224/150566–67, von Dirksen/von Neurath, Tokio 5 January 1937 (sic); Liu, 'German Mediation', 163.
206. *AA*.210/145818, von Mackensen/Hankow, 5 January 1938. Trautmann had in fact requested permission to inform the Chinese of the attitude of the Japanese General Staff as reported from Tokio on 1 January. He thought this would help the discussions in Hankow: ibid., 145825, Trautmann/AA, Hankow 3 January 1938.
207. *AA*.1929/432643, von Dirksen/von Neurath, Tokio 6 January 1938.
208. Memorandum by Lautenschlager, Hankow 7 January 1938, quoted in Peck, op. cit., 163.
209. *AA*.1929/432650, Trautmann/AA, Hankow 7 January 1937 (sic); Peck, op. cit., 163; *AA*.210/145808, Trautmann/AA, Hankow 10 January 1938.
210. *AA*.210/145803, von Dirksen/von Neurath (Trautmann), Tokio 10 January 1938.
211. *AA*.210/145804, Trautmann/AA, Hankow 11 January 1938; ibid., 145802, von Mackensen/Hankow, 11 January 1938.
212. *DGFP*, D, I, 813, Memorandum by von Neurath, 10 January 1938.
213. *AA*.210/145805, von Dirksen/von Neurath, Tokio 11 January 1938.
214. Crowley, op. cit., 368–72.
215. *DGFP*, D, I, 814–15, Trautmann/AA, Hankow 12 January 1938; *AA*.210/ 145793, Trautmann/AA, Hankow 13 January 1938.
216. *AA*.210/145800–01, von Mackensen/Hankow, 12 January 1938; *FO*.F563/ 16/10, Vol. 22053, Sir Nevile Henderson/FO, Berlin 14 January 1938.
217. *DGFP*, D, I, 814, von Dirksen/von Neurath (Trautmann), Tokio 12 January 1938. It is at this point that a certain degree of error has crept into the published series of German Documents and the works of other historians. The published documents are wrong in making it appear that the telegram number 13 from von Dirksen which Trautmann communicated to Wang Chung-hui on the morning of 12 January was that of the *12th* sent direct from Tokio to Hankow under that number and copied to the Wilhelmstrasse as telegram number 16. Von Dirksen's telegram number 13 to Trautmann of 12 January arrived in Hankow during the evening and therefore well after Trautmann's morning interview with the Chinese Foreign Minister. The published volume is in further error in footnote 87, page 814. The Foreign Office's telegram number 10 of 11 January to Hankow only instructed Trautmann to inform the Chinese Government of von Dirksen's telegram number 13 of the 10th; no mention was made of Tokio number 14 of the 11th to Berlin.
218. Memorandum by Lautenschlager, Hankow 13 January 1938, quoted in Peck, op. cit., 169; *AA*.1929/432678, Trautmann/AA, Hankow 13 January 1938. For confirmation of the points concerning von Dirksen's telegram see Peck, op. cit., 164–69. The confusion in the editing of the published volume of documents probably arose because of the closeness of the numbers of von Dirksen's telegrams to the Wilhelmstrasse and of those he sent direct to Trautmann.

219. Liu, 'German Mediation', 165.
220. Iklé, op. cit., 65; Presseisen, op. cit., 140.
221. *DGFP*, D, I, 815—16, Trautmann/AA, Hankow 13 January 1938.
222. *AA*.1929/432677, von Dirksen/AA, (Trautmann), Tokio 13 January 1938.
223. *DGFP*, D, I, 816—17, von Dirksen/von Neurath, Tokio 14 January 1938. Privately, von Dirksen agreed with Hirota's interpretation regarding the information passed to China. He pointed out to the British Ambassador at Tokio, Sir Robert Craigie, that although Hirota's 'additional explanations' had been represented to the Chinese Government as von Dirksen's personal 'impressions', he was convinced that 'the Chinese Government could easily have seen through this transparent device had they so wished': *FO*.F2300/16/10, Vol. 22054, Sir Robert Craigie/FO, Tokio 22 January 1938.
224. It is not clear whether this refers to the nine-point programme which Trautmann certainly did not receive. Jones, op. cit., n. 5, p. 68, suggests that Ott had in fact transmitted the particulars of Japan's new demands to the Chinese authorities.
225. *IMTFE*, Vol. 73, 37722—23, Exhibit 3789-A, Saionji-Harada Memoirs, 14—17 January 1938. This document states that the Liaison Conference took place on 15 January, but although Jones, op. cit., 69 and Crowley, op. cit., 373—75 are correct in placing this meeting on the 14th, neither of them mentions the Cabinet meeting on 15 January when the final text of the Japanese statement was more than likely formulated: *IMTFE*, Vol. 57, 29842, Exhibit 3264, Records Concerning the Imperial Conferences. Crowley, p. 373, quoting the Saionji-Harada Memoirs of 19 January 1938, fails to bring out the important point that the Japanese Government received China's reply from von Dirksen in the middle of its decisive policy discussion on 14 January. He has also confused the date and time when Hirota handed von Dirksen the text of the Japanese statement. Ibid., 375.
226. *AA*.210/145785, von Dirksen/von Neurath (Trautmann), Tokio 15 January 1938.
227. *DGFP*, D, I, 817—18, Trautmann/AA, Hankow 15 January 1938.
228. *FO*.F663/16/10, Vol. 22053, Mr MacKillop/FO, Hankow 15 January 1938; *DGFP*, D, I, 820, von Mackensen/Hankow, 17 January 1938.
229. Von Dirksen, op. cit., 191.
230. *DGFP*, D, I, 819—20, von Dirksen/von Neurath, Tokio 16 January 1938. Both Hirota and Vice-Foreign Minister Horinouchi stated that even if Kung's message had been given to the Japanese authorities before Hirota handed the Cabinet's decision to von Dirksen early on the morning of 16 January it would have had no effect at all on Japanese policy: *AA*.1929/432705, von Dirksen/AA, Tokio 18 January 1938; ibid., 432706, von Dirksen/AA, Tokio 18 January 1938.
231. *DGFP*, D, I, 820, von Mackensen/Hankow, 17 January 1938.
232. *DGFP*, D, I, 822, Trautmann/AA, Hankow 17 January 1938.
233. *DGFP*, D, I, 821, von Dirksen/von Neurath, Tokio 17 January 1938. Although he placed some blame for the failure of the negotiations on Japanese shoulders, privately von Dirksen placed '95%' of the blame on the Chinese Government. He accused that government of failing to take little interest in many of Japan's conditions and accused Chiang Kai-shek of displaying 'lack of interest in the proceedings by failing on one pretext or another to discuss the matter with the German Ambassador [at Hankow] at any time during the final and crucial stage of these discussions': *FO*.F2300/16/10, Vol. 22054, Sir Robert Craigie/FO, Tokio 22 January 1938.
234. *AA*.145/81259, Trautmann/AA, Hankow 18 January 1938.

Chapter X

1. At the beginning of 1938 it seemed that plans were afoot for the reorganisation of the Chinese army under the extended power and authority of the German advisers: *FO.*F217/106/10, Vol. 22111, Gage/Shanghai, Hankow 5 January 1938.
2. Even von Falkenhausen was concerned about the arrival of Russian Military Attachés at the turn of the year in case they prejudiced the position of the German advisers *vis-à-vis* the Chinese and German governments: *FO.*F143/106/10, Vol. 22111, Gage/FO, Hankow 3 January 1938.
3. *DGFP*, D, I, 826—31, von Dirksen/AA, Tokio 26 January 1938. By the time this report arrived in the Wilhelmstrasse on 17 February, events had already moved in the direction hinted at by von Dirksen.
4. *DGFP*, D, I, Document 93, 162—68.
5. See Sommer, op. cit., 94—102; William Carr, op. cit., *passim*.
6. *IMTFE*, Vol. 12, 6051, Exhibit 497, Oshima Interrogation.
7. *IMTFE*, Vol. 68, 35429—30, Exhibit 3618, Kasahara Affidavit.
8. *IMTFE*, Vol. 68, 35391—92, Exhibit 3614, Katsushiro Affidavit. In March 1938 Togo set out for the *Gaimusho* his clear opposition to any pact negotiations with Germany.
9. *AA.*185/137478—82, Trautmann/AA, Hankow 20 January 1938.
10. *DGFP*, D, I, 818—19, von Dirksen/von Neurath, Tokio 15 January 1938; ibid, 822—23, von Neurath/Tokio, 18 January 1938; ibid., 835—39, Unsigned Memorandum, 16 February 1938; Gerhard Weinberg, 'Deutsch—Japanische Verhandlungen über das Südseemandat 1937—1938', 391—92. Apart from its significance in relations with Japan, the importance of the colonial question in Germany's general foreign policy situation was emphasised by von Mackensen's circular to Missions of 11 November 1938: *DGFP*, D, VII, Appendix III, 607—09. See also Hildebrand, op. cit., 511ff.
11. *AA.*100/65693, Unsigned Note of 17 January 1938; 3245/E000110—11, Note for the Führer by von Ribbentrop, 18 January 1938.
12. *DGFP*, D, I, 823—24, von Dirksen/von Neurath, Tokio 24 January 1938; ibid., 825, von Neurath/von Dirksen, 25 January 1938.
13. Ribbentrop, op. cit., 78. Von Ribbentrop's unpopularity in government and Party circles is well described in an aptly titled chapter in Fest, op. cit., 265—82, 'Joachim von Ribbentrop and The Degradation of Diplomacy'. For more pungent remarks about Ribbentrop by his ex-colleagues at the Nuremberg jail see G. M. Gilbert, *Nuremberg Diary* (New York 1947). See also, Eugene Davidson, *The Trial of the Germans: Nuremberg 1945—46* (New York 1966).
14. Deutsch, op. cit., 70—72, 75, 262; Seabury, *Wilhelmstrasse*, 42.
15. *FO.*F761/84/10, Vol. 22106, Minute by Anthony Eden, 18 January 1938; ibid., F1051/84/10, Vol. 22106, Sir Nevile Henderson/FO, Berlin 25 January 1938.
16. *FO.646/TWC,* Documents in Evidence, Document Book Woermann III, Woermann Document No. 92, Affidavit of Andor Hencke; Deutsch, op. cit., 79; Ribbentrop, op. cit., 79.
17. Watt, 'German Diplomats', 157.
18. Hill, art. cit., 563—64; Seabury, op. cit., 540. See also Craig, 'The German Foreign Office', 433—36.
19. See above, p. 255.
20. *FO.*F2610/2/10, Vol. 22043, The Governor/FO, Hong Kong 5 March 1938; ibid., F3322/298/10, Vol. 22138, Air Liaison Officer Hong Kong/Air Ministry, Hong Kong 24 March 1938.
21. *DGFP*, D, I, 832—33, von Dirksen/von Ribbentrop, Tokio 5 February 1938.
22. Sommer, op. cit., 104.

23. Presseisen, op. cit., 152–53; Bloch, *German Interests* op. cit., 37–38: Details of Otto Wolff's negotiations are on AA. Serial 9075 *passim*.
24. *AA*.5647/H002183, Clodius/Tokio, 3 December 1937; ibid., H002175, Clodius/Tokio, 31 December 1937; *DGFP*, D, I, 824–25, Memorandum by von Neurath, 25 January 1938; 5647/H002166–67, Clodius/Tokio, 26 January 1938; Joseph C. Grew, *Ten Years in Japan* (London 1944), 194.
25. Presseisen, op. cit., 154; Bloch, *German Interests* op. cit., 39–40.
26. Japanese assurances that they were 'very much interested in co-operating with Germany in the economic development of China' was a continual part of their efforts to strike a chord of sympathy for Japan in Germany: *DGFP*, D, I, 813, Memorandum by von Neurath, 10 January 1938.
27. *AA*.1702/398275–76, Memorandum by von Schmieden, 9 February 1938.
28. *AA*.145/81202–03, Memorandum by Voss, 8 February 1938; Gerhard Weinberg, 'German Recognition of Manchukuo', 160–61. Voss's memorandum is interesting for another reason since it shows how far the main points of Hitler's analysis of 5 November 1937 regarding the immediate aims of German foreign policy in Europe were common knowledge in the Foreign Office. Cf. the viewpoint of A. J. P. Taylor on the merits and demerits of the November meeting in his *Origins of the Second World War*, 131–34.
29. *AA*.9075/E637116, Undated, unsigned memorandum of three paragraphs covering recognition, colonies, and German–Japanese economic negotiations over Manchukuo and North China; 4422/E084073–74, von Mackensen/Hankow, 10 February 1938; Peck, op. cit., 181–82. Elsewhere the date of von Mackensen's instructions is erroneously given as *12* February: *DGFP*, D, I, p. 833, n. 1; Weinberg, 'German Recognition of Manchukuo', 161. Kordt, op. cit., 191, is mistaken, therefore, in suggesting that the whole question of recognition was a sudden decision and that the relevent department of the Foreign Office had been ignored.
30. *AA*.1702/398280–81, Trautmann/AA, Hankow 9 February 1938.
31. *AA*.145/81226, Trautmann/AA, Hankow 13 February 1938; *DGFP*, D, I, 833–34, Trautmann/AA, Hankow 14 February 1938; ibid., 834–35, Trautmann/AA, Hankow 14 February 1938; *FO*.F2610/2/10, Vol. 22043, The Governor/FO, Hong Kong 5 March 1938.
32. Cf. p. 269 above.
33. *AA*.1702/398289–90, Trautmann/AA, Hankow 16 February 1938. See also the internal Embassy memorandum by von Saucken of 12 February 1938, Peck, op. cit., 182–83.
34. *DGFP*, D, I, 839, Lammers/von Ribbentrop, 17 February 1938.
35. *AA*.1929/432744, Trautmann/AA, Hankow 19 February 1938.
36. Presseisen, op. cit., 144. It appears that the Japanese did indeed read into Hitler's speech Germany's complete abandonment of her former Pacific colonies: Weinberg, 'Verhandlungen über das Südseemandat', 394–95. See also Baynes, op. cit., II, 1376–1409; Domarus, op. cit., Vol. I, Part 2, 792–804.
37. *AA*.185/137498–99, Memorandum by von Schmieden, 14 July 1938.
38. *DGFP*, D, I, 839–40, von Ribbentrop/Hankow, 21 February 1938; *AA*.145/812141, Trautmann/AA, Hankow 21 February 1938; 1929/432746, Trautmann/AA, Hankow 22 February 1938; 1702/398300–01, Memorandum by von Ribbentrop, 22 February 1938; *DGFP*, D, I, 843–44, Memorandum by von Mackensen, 24 February 1938; *FRUS*, 1938, III, 445, Johnson/Washington, Hankow 22 February 1938.
39. *AA*.1702/398291, Trautmann/von Ribbentrop, Hankow 22 February 1938; ibid., 398293, von Ribbentrop/Hankow, 23 February 1938.
40. *AA*.185/137497, Trautmann/AA, Hankow 24 February 1938; Trautmann/AA, Hankow 15 February 1938, quoted in Peck; op. cit., 183.

41. *AA*.145/81215, Memorandum by von Mackensen, 21 February 1938.
42. *AA*.1929/432745, von Mackensen/Tokio, 21 February 1938; 185/1374–92, Noebel/AA, Tokio 22 February 1938. Von Dirksen had left for Germany at the beginning of February and the new Ambassador Eugen Ott, was not officially appointed until April 1938.
43. *AA*.2898/D565714, Memorandum by von Mackensen, 21 February 1938.
44. *AA*.185/137487–90, Memorandum by von Schmieden, 21 February 1938 with enclosure by Voss of 20 February.
45. *DGFP*, D, I, 841–42, Memorandum by von Raumer, 23 February 1938.
46. Weinberg, 'Verhandlungen über das Südseemandat', 395–97. A brief on the colonial question was drawn up for von Ribbentrop in the Foreign Office on 16 February: *DGFP*, D, I, 835–39, Unsigned memorandum, 16 February 1938.
47. Chiang Kai-shek sent Hitler his congratulations over the *Anschluss*, in accordance with the motto 'One people, one Reich', but complained to Trautmann that he 'regretted that Germany had taken a different stand with regard to Manchukuo'. By comparison, the reaction in Japan was enthusiastic: *DGFP*, D, I, 595, Trautmann/AA, Hankow 14 March 1938; ibid., 602, Noebel/AA, Tokio 15 March 1938.
48. *AA*.1702/398283, Keitel/von Mackensen, 12 February 1938. For Keitel's position and role in the Fritsch–Blomberg affair, see Deutsch op. cit., *passim*.
49. *AA*.4422/E084076–77, Memorandum by Voss, 26 February 1938.
50. Sommer, op. cit., 103 and n. 3.
51. *AA*.157/131044, Trautmann/AA, Hankow 5 March 1938. However, the Japanese continued to complain to Moscow of Russia's military help to China: 1929/432780, Tippelskirch/AA, Moscow 4 April 1938.
52. On 31 March Trautmann again warned about exaggerated expectations from economic cooperation with Japan in North China. At the same time, German businessmen in North China rejected any form of official coopera-tion with the Japanese in that region, ideas that were apparently suggested by Dr Woidt. Later in 1938 Dr Woidt was put in charge of special talks with Japanese authorities in North China regarding Germany's economic position there: *AA*.7072/E526410–11, Trautmann/AA, Hankow 31 March 1938; ibid., E526402, Trautmann/AA, Hankow 21 April 1938; Drechsler, op. cit., 108–11.
53. *DGFP*, D, I, 844–50, Trautmann/AA, Hankow 8 March 1938.
54. *AA*.4422/E084076–77, Memorandum by Voss, 26 February 1938. A month later special instructions were despatched to Tokio for transmission to the Consul at Tientsin via Peking. He was asked to discuss the question with German commercial circles in North China and to obtain their views as to what was necessary to secure and promote Germany's economic interests in that region: 5647/H002147–48, Wiehl/Tokio, 21 March 1938. Stoller's answer from Peking was sent on 14 April: 7072/E526403–04. See also n. 52 above.
55. *AA*.9075/E637110–15, Memorandum by Wiehl on meeting of Economic Policy Committee, 25 February 1938.
56. *AA*.9075/E637098–109, Kato/Wiehl with enclosure, 4 March 1938.
57. *AA*.9075/E6370094–96, Memorandum by Voss, 4 March 1938.
58. *AA*.145/81180–81, Memorandum by von Mackensen, 9 March 1938; 9075/E637092–93, Memorandum by Wiehl, 10 March 1938; 145/81165–67, Memorandum by Wiehl, 23 March 1938; ibid., 81163–64, Memorandum by Wiehl, 24 March 1938; 9075/E637079–86, Memorandum by Wiehl with enclosure, 1 April 1938; ibid., E637077, Memorandum by Wiehl, 12 April 1938; 145/81175, Memorandum by von Mackensen, 11 March 1938.

59. *AA*.3888/E048573—74, Trautmann/AA, Hankow 5 April 1938.
60. *AA*.1929/432778, Lietzmann/Commander-in-Chief Navy, Tokio 1 April 1938; Walsh, art. cit., 511.
61. *DGFP*, D, I, 851—52, Memorandum by von Ribbentrop, 8 April 1938.
62. *IMTFE*, Vol. 32, 15983—86, Exhibit 2228A, Extract from pages 353—55 of a book 'Business Reports 1938, Vol. I. Economic Relations In China'. Published by East Asia Ministry, 1 December 1938; Presseisen, op. cit., 158.
63. On Easter Sunday 17 April 1938 von Ribbentrop treated von Weizsäcker, appointed as State Secretary on 1 April 1938, to a long lecture about the future political tasks of Germany. He explained that although Russia was the official enemy of the Reich, in reality Germany's plans were directed against Great Britain. He felt it was essential not to repeat the mistake of opposing Britain, France and Russia at the same time and for this reason Japan had to be won over as Germany's ally. In reply, however, von Weizsäcker thought that in a way Germany could be assured of Japan's support and that it was, therefore, unnecessary in the meantime to have to 'buy' it. In a later memorandum he discounted the kind of help that Japan and Italy could give Germany in any conflict with Britain and France. Yet in a letter to Trautmann dated 30 May 1938, von Weizsäcker virtually confirmed von Ribbentrop's arguments about the role Japan was to play in Germany's foreign policy since he pointed out that.'Russia hardly exists in our calculation today. As long as Stalin makes himself as useful as now, we need not particularly worry about him as regards military policy'. At this time as well von Ribbentrop's attention was directed towards Italy, partly to complement his efforts in the direction of Japan and partly to offset the effects of the Anglo—Italian agreement of 16 April 1938: Von Weizsäcker, op. cit., 154; *DGFP*, D, II, 420—22, Unsigned Memorandum, 20 June 1938; *DGFP*, D, I, 864, von Weizsäcker/Trautmann, 30 May 1938; Presseisen, op. cit., 192; Sommer, op. cit., 116—24.
64. *AA*.1929/432764 Trautmann/AA, Hankow 1 March 1938; ibid., 432765, von Weizsäcker/Hankow, 2 March 1938; 145/81183—84, Memorandum by von Weizsäcker 3 March 1938; ibid., 81172—74, Memorandum by von Mackensen, 11 March 1938.
65. *AA*.7072/E526423, Trautmann/AA, Hankow 16 March 1938; 1929/432771, Trautmann/AA, Hankow 21 March 1938; ibid., 432791—92, Trautmann/ AA, Hankow 12 April 1938; ibid., 432794, von Weizsäcker/Tokio, 14 April 1938; ibid., 432796, Noebel/AA, Tokio 22 April 1938; ibid., 432793, von Weizsäcker/Hankow, 22 April 1938.
66. *DGFP*, D, I, 855—56, Memorandum by von Weizsäcker 27 April 1938. Upon his return from the Far East von Dirksen had complained to Hitler that in Japan 'the tension was increasing substantially' because of this question of the advisers. According to von Dirksen's memoirs, the upshot was that 'Hitler ordered Ribbentrop to have the mission recalled. This instruction was carried out by the Foreign Minister on the same day by means of a rude and tactless telegram': Von Dirksen, op. cit., 207.
67. *DGFP*, D, I, 856, Memorandum by Wiehl, 28 April 1938.
68. *DGFP*, D, I, 856—57, Trautmann/AA, Hankow 29 April 1938; Sommer, op. cit., 111, n. 52. By April 1938 the advisory staff in China was assessed at 24 officers and 9 civilians: *DGFP*, D, I, 854—55, Memorandum on the Advisory Staff in China, 26 April 1938. According to a report by Trautmann on 16 April the high point of the advisory staff was 62 members during 1934, while on 13 August 1937 this number had been reduced to 46: *AA*.211/146051—52, Trautmann/AA, Hankow 16 April 1938 with enclosure.
69. *Reichsgesetzblatt*, 1938, 214, 25 February 1938.

70. *AA*.218/148181–200, Trautmann/AA, Hankow 20 April 1938 with enclosures. Another report setting out the position regarding the HAPRO contracts, deliveries and payments etc, as at 23 March 1938 were received in the Foreign Office on 31 May: 218/148206–14, Trautmann/AA, Hankow 22 April 1938 with enclosure. See also: *DGFP*, D, I, 852–53, Memorandum by Wiehl 23 April 1938, whose analysis of the state of arms contracts with China was taken from the annual report from 1937 of the Association of Exporters of War Material (*Ausfuhrgemeinschaft für Kriegsgerät — AGK*).
71. See above, p. 312, n. 65.
72. Sommer, op. cit., 109, quoting from T. R. Emessen (ed.), *Aus Göring's Schreibtisch* (Berlin 1947), Document No. 35.
73. *AA*.1929/432808, Trautmann/AA, Hankow 5 May 1938.
74. *DGFP*, D, I, 860, Trautmann/AA, Hankow 9 May 1938.
75. See p. 318 below.
76. *AA*.3888/E048578–86, Trautmann/AA, Hankow 9 May 1938 with enclosure.
77. See above, pp. 310–11.
78. *AA*.2898/D565741–43, Memorandum by Voss, 5 May 1938.
79. *Reichsgesetzblatt*, 1938, II, 286–87; *DGFP*, D, VII, Appendix III, 610, Woermann/Hankow, 13 May 1938; Weinberg, 'German Recognition of Manchukuo', 162.
80. Kordt 'Far East', 20 is mistaken, therefore, in stating that the decision to withdraw the advisers from China was taken during the visit to Italy. On the other hand, it is quite likely that the nature of the talks in Rome intensified von Ribbentrop's concern that this particular matter be wound up quickly.
81. At this point it was felt necessary for von Weizsäcker, undoubtedly on von Ribbentrop's instructions, to assure Oshima on 12 May that although Germany was maintaining contact with England over the Czech issue, there were no grounds for believing that negotiations between the two countries would take place: Henke, op. cit., 149–50.
82. *DGFP*, D, I, 861–62, von Ribbentrop/Trautmann, 13 May 1938.
83. *AA*.1929/432818, Trautmann/von Ribbentrop, Hong Kong 15 May 1938. For his talks with Ott, Trautmann utilised a memorandum on the political ramifications of the withdrawal of the advisers drawn up by von Falkenhausen: 3888/E048587–89, Trautmann/AA, Hankow 10 May 1938 with enclosure. In Hong Kong Trautmann also spoke with the Japanese Consul on the question of Sino–Japanese relations, but the latter emphasised that the Japanese Government was adamant that it did not wish to negotiate with the Hankow Government 145/81142, Trautmann/AA, Hankow 3 June 1938.
84. *DGFP*, D, I, 862, von Ribbentrop/Hankow, 17 May 1938.
85. *AA*.1929/432822–24, von Ribbentrop/Hankow, 19 May 1938.
86. *AA*.1929/432821, Lietzmann/Ministry of Marine, Tokio 19 May 1938.
87. *AA*.1929/432825, Trautmann/AA, Hankow 20 May 1938.
88. *AA*.1929/432826, Trautmann/AA, Hankow 20 May 1938; ibid., 432827, von Ribbentrop/Hankow, 23 May 1938; *FRUS*, 1938, III, 191–92, Wilson/Washington, Berlin 2 June 1938. Bloch, op. cit., 43, n. 1 suggests that those advisers who were Jewish or who had Jewish wives remained in China.
89. *DGFP*, D, I, 863, Trautmann/AA, Hankow 21 May 1938.
90. *FRUS*, 1938, III, 182, Johnson/Washington, Hankow 26 May 1938; *AA*.1929/432834, von Weizsäcker/Hankow 31 May 1938; ibid., 432835, Trautmann/AA, Hankow 31 May 1938; ibid., 432836, Trautmann/AA, Hankow 1 June 1938; ibid., 432837, von Ribbentrop/Hankow, 3 June 1938; *FRUS*, 1938, III, 191–92, Wilson/Washington, Berlin 2 June 1938.

91. See above, pp. 315—16.
92. This was also the burden of Oshima's reply to Göring on 18 May: Sommer, op. cit., 109, n. 43.
93. *DGFP*, D, I, 867—68, Memorandum by Wiehl, 2 June 1938; ibid., 865—67, Memorandum by Wiehl, 2 June 1938, with Japanese *Pro Memoria*, 20 May 1938.
94. *IMTFE*, Vol. 69, 35656—57, Exhibit 3646, Affidavit of Shigenori Togo. Togo's evidence refers to the revised *Pro Memoria* submitted by him on 29 June 1938. The German documents make it clear that he was really talking about the memorandum presented on 20 May.
95. *DGFP*, D, I, 868—70, Memorandum by Wiehl, 2 June 1938.
96. *DGFP*, D, I, 870—71, Memorandum by Wiehl, 3 June 1938.
97. Sommer, op. cit., 116—24 and 124ff respectively.
98. *DGFP*, D, I, 851, Keitel/von Ribbentrop, 17 March 1938; Kordt, op. cit., 199. See also Sommer, op. cit., 107—108, n. 31, who brings out the point that the general policy aims of Ott and the German Army *vis-à-vis* Japan were opposed to those of von Ribbentrop. The latter therefore worked through Oshima in Berlin to achieve the strategic parts of his Japanese policy.
99. *DGFP*, D, I, 858—60, Memorandum by Ott with enclosure, Tokio 5 May 1938.
100. Sommer, op. cit., 122; Kordt, 'Far East', 19.
101. *AA*.7072/E526385, Wiehl/Hankow, 4 June 1938.
102. *DGFP*, D, I, 874—76, Memorandum by Wiehl, with enclosure by Strachwitz, 16 June 1938. British records show that during April and May 1938, Germany still maintained her position as the main supplier of arms to China; that according to Shanghai customs figures, in the period January—May 1938 Germany supplied 35% of China's arms imports, and that up to the end of July 1938 more arms were still reaching China from Germany than from Great Britain. See *FO*.F7379/7451/8675/10535/10777/34/10, Vol. 22074.
103. See above, p. 318.
104. *AA*.1929/432843, Trautmann/AA, Hankow 4 June 1938.
105. *AA*.1929/432842, Memorandum by von Weizsäcker, 7 June 1938. Trautmann was also informed that the reports of German advisers in Japan were untrue: ibid., 432844, von Weizsäcker/Hankow, 8 June 1938.
106. *DGFP*, D, I, 872, von Weizsäcker/Trautmann, 10 June 1938.
107. *AA*.145/81147, Trautmann/AA, Hankow 22 May 1938; 1929/432851, Trautmann/AA, Hankow 11 June 1938; ibid., 432854, Trautmann/AA, Hankow 12 June 1938.
108. *DGFP*, D, I, 872, von Ribbentrop/Hankow, 13 June 1938.
109. *DGFP*, D, I, 873—74, Trautmann/AA, Hankow 14 June 1938.
110. *AA*.1929/432859, von Ribbentrop/Hankow 16 June 1938; ibid., 432860, Trautmann/AA, Hankow 18 June 1938; *DGFP*, D, I, 877, Trautmann/AA, Hankow 19 June 1938.
111. *AA*.1929/432867, Trautmann/AA, Hankow 20 June 1938; *DGFP*, D, I, 878—79, von Ribbentrop/Hankow 20 June 1938; *FRUS*, 1938, III, 202, Johnson/Washington, Hankow 23 June 1938.
112. Jones, op. cit., 92; Sommer, op. cit., 114; *FRUS*, 1938, III, 198, Johnson/Washington, Hankow 18 June 1938.
113. *FO*.F6960/106/10, Vol. 22111, Sir A. Clark Kerr/FO, Shanghai 28 June 1938.
114. *DGFP*, D, I, 881—83, Trautmann/AA, Hankow 23 June 1938.
115. *DGFP*, D, I, 883—84, von Ribbentrop/Hankow 24 June 1938; ibid., 884, von Weizsäcker/Hong Kong for Trautmann 29 June 1938.
116. *AA*.1929/432883, Trautmann/AA, Hankow 25 June 1938. Walsh, art. cit.,

512, states that von Falkenhausen forbade the advisers to return to Germany via Japan, and that seven officers, ignoring all threats from Berlin, remained in service with the Chinese.

117. *DGFP*, D, I, 884—86, Memorandum by von Ribbentrop, 29 June 1938.
118. Ibid., XIII, 29—30, Altenburg/AA, Peking 26 June 1941; ibid., 35—36, von Weizsäcker/Tokio, 27 June 1941; ibid., 53, von Weizsäcker Circular, 30 June 1941; ibid., 79—80, Memorandum by von Weizsäcker, 3 July 1941. For Wang Ching-wei's career after 1937 see the studies by Boyle, op. cit., and Gerald E. Bunker, *The Peace Conspiracy: Wang Ching-wei and the China War 1937—1941* (Harvard University Press 1972).
119. For von Ribbentrop's negotiations with the Japanese military authorities from June 1938 and his attempts to draw Germany and Japan closer together as real and practical allies during the course of the European and Far Eastern wars, cf. the published documents in *DGFP*, D, *passim.*, the thesis by Chapman, and the studies by Iklé, Martin, Meskill, Presseisen, and Sommer.
120. Presseisen, op. cit., 161—63.

Bibliography

I. *UNPUBLISHED DOCUMENTS*

1. *Documents of the German Foreign Office*: photostat and microfilm copies at the German Documents Section, Library and Records Department, Foreign and Commonwealth Office, London.

Copies of files from the *Alte- und Neue Reichskanzlei* and the *Dienststelle* Ribbentrop are also held in this collection in London and for the sake of convenience are included in this first category. The figure given is the filmed serial reference number: cf. Georg O. Kent (editor), *A Catalog of Files and Microfilms of the German Foreign Ministry Archives 1920–1945*, Volumes I–IV (The Hoover Institution, Stamford University, California, 1962–1972).

A number of changes occurred in the organisation of the German Foreign Office after the Nazi *Machtergreifung*. Until 1935 Far Eastern affairs were dealt with in the Far East section of Political Department IV by a Deputy Director and officials. During 1935 the three main political departments, II — Western, Southern, and South-East Europe, III — Great Britain, the Americas, the Orient, Navigation, Colonial, and IV — Eastern Europe, Scandinavia, East Asia, were reorganised. Department IV was disbanded by a directive of 21 September 1935, and the Far Eastern section with all its officials was attached to Department III, with the Eastern European and Scandinavian sections moving in turn to Department II. A further change occurred in May 1936 when Departments II and III were consolidated into a Political Department, relinquishing such economic matters as they still handled to the newly-formed and expanded Economic Policy Department. Far Eastern affairs were subsequently dealt with in Section B (Extra-European), sub-section Pol. VIII of the newly constituted Political Department.

Other changes included the revival in 1938 of the title of *Unterstatssekretär* for the Director of the Political Department. The revived (1933) office for questions concerning the relations between foreign and domestic policy, *Referat Deutschland*, was amalgamated in 1940 with the *Referat Partei* (1938) into a new section, *Abteilung Deutschland*. In 1943 this was replaced by *Gruppe Inland I und II*.

For further details of the various schemes of reorganisation and their effects, cf. the relevant appendices in *Documents on German Foreign Policy 1918–1945*, Series C and D, *passim*.

To take account of these changes in organisation and to avoid confusion between the designations for the different political departments and their sections after 1933, the method used in the 'Analysis of the Foreign Ministry Archives' in DGFP has been followed here, i.e. to divide the files into those up to 1936 and those from 1936.

Documents to 1936

Büro des Reichsministers
3088   China. Japan. 1920–1935.
3147   Völkerbund. Juli 1920–October 1933.
8985   Ausstellung von Pässen und Emphfehlungen. Dezember 1925–
          Dezember 1933.

9296   Aufzeichnungen des Herrn Staatssekretär 1934—1935.

Büro des Staatssekretärs
4602   Aufzeichnungen Staatssekretär von Bülow über Diplomaten-besuch. Juni 1930—Juni 1936.
4620   Politischer Schriftwechsel des Herrn Staatssekretär mit Beamten des auswärtigen Dienstes. Juni 1930—Juni 1936.

Handakten Ritter
8991   Mandschukuo. Dezember 1932—February 1936.

Handakten Trautmann
5551   Ostasien. China. Japan. 1924—1931.

Referat Deutschland
8791   Rassenfrage. Juli—November 1933.

Sonderreferat Wirtschaft
8889   Deutsch—Japanische Devisenangelegenheiten. Februar 1933—Mai 1936.
8987   Austauschgeschäfte. Wirtschaftsabkommen mit Mandschukuo. November 1933—Mai 1936.
8992   Wirtschaftskommission für Ostasien. April—Dezember 1935.
9270   Deutsche Exportkreditversicherung Vermittlungsstelle. Deutsche Revisions und Treuhand A. G. Hermes Versicherungsbank. Juli 1933—Dezember 1935.

Geheimakten 1920—36
5564   Kriegsgerät. Ausser—Europa. Januar 1935—Mai 1936.
5703   Marineattache, Militärattache: Tokio. Dezember 1933—April 1936.
5892   Militärattache Moskau. January 1933—Mai 1936.
6680   Ostasien. China. Austausgeschäfte und Wirtschaftsabkommen. Projekte Klein. 1934—Mai 1936.
6681   Ostasien. China: Militärangelegenheiten. Juli 1935—Mai 1936.
6691   Ostasien. Allgemeines. August 1932—Mai 1936.
6692   Ostasien. Die Frage der Anerkennung der Mandschurei. Dezember 1933—Mai 1936.
6693   Ostasien. Fall Heye. 1933—1935.
6694   Ostasien. Ehemals deutsche Kolonien. February 1933—April 1936.
8229   Ostasien. China. Projekte Klein. 1934—1936.
8301   Ostasien. Fall Heye. 1933—1935.
K.240   Ostasien. Ehemals deutsche Kolonien. 1920—1933.

Politische Abteilung II:

II F Luft
8986   Ostasien. Lufverkehr Ostasien. October 1932—Dezember 1936.

II F Militär und Marine
9074   Kriegsmaterial Allgemeines. Dezember 1929—February 1936.

II F Abrüstung
6710   Proklamierung der deutsche Souveränität in der entmilitarisierten Rheinlandzone. 1936.

7456 Marine Konferenz 1935. Januar 1934—Mai 1936.

Referat Völkerbund
8925 Japan. 1921—Dezember 1934.
L.785 Ratstagungen. 1927—1933.

Politische Abteilung IV — Pol.
1946 Äthiopien. Politisches Beziehungen zu Italien. Rückwirkungen auf Deutschland.
6022 China. Politische Beziehungen zu Deutschland. Januar 1931— März 1936.
6024 Japan. Politische Beziehungen zu Deutschland. Januar 1933— März 1936.
8572 China. Politische Beziehungen zu Japan. Januar 1932—Mai 1936.
8573 China. Innere Politik. October 1932—März 1936.
8576 China. Deutsche diplomatische und konsularische Vertretungen. Februar 1933—April 1936.
8577 China. Militärs. Juni 1920—April 1935.
8578 China. Staatsmänner. Juni 1930—April 1936.
8579 China. Diplomatische und konsularische Vertretungen in Deutschland. Januar 1930—März 1936.
8580 China. Militärangelegenheiten. März 1932—Juni 1935.
8587 China. Chinesisch—Japanischer Konflikt. Waffenlieferungen. 1931—1932.
8800 China. Luftfahr im allgemeinen. Juli 1930—März 1936.
8829 Polen. Staatsmänner. October 1929—Dezember 1935.
8873 Japan. Allgemeine auswärtige Politik. Januar 1929—April 1936.
8886 Japan. Innere Politik. October 1932—März 1936.
8887 Japan. Politische Beziehungen zu Russland. 1933—1936.
8930 Ostasien. Nationalitätenfrage. Fremdvölker. Minoritäten. Juli 1921—November 1936.
8931 Mandschurei. Politische Beziehungen im allgemeinen. August— Dezember 1935.
8933 Mandschurei. Allgemeines. Januar 1933—Mai 1936.
9090 China. Militärangelegenheiten. Januar—Juni 1934.
9451 Ostasien. Nationalitätenfrage. Fremdvölker. Minoritäten. 1921— 1936.
K.2053 Ostasien. Zwischenstaatliche aussenpolitische Probleme. Völkerbund. 1921—1936.
K.2073 China. Förderungen aus Anlass des Chinesisch—Japanischen Konflikts. 1931—1932.
K.2088 China. Chinesisch—Japanischer Konflict. 1932—1933.
K.2263 Japan. Allgemeine auswärtige Politik. 1920—1933.
K.2264 Japan. Politische Beziehungen zu Deutschland. 1920—1932.
L.1521 China. Marineangelegenheiten. 1920—1936.
L.1535 China. Militärangelegenheiten. 1920—1932.
L.1780 Mandschurei. Allgemeines. 1930—1932.
M.96 China. Militärangelegenheiten. März 1932.

Politische Abteilung IV — Wirtschaft
8794 Wiederaufbau der chinesischen Wirtschaft nach den inneren

Wirren. Internationale Zusammenarbeit. September 1929–April 1936.
8805   China. Wirtschaft. November 1931–September 1935.
9077   China. Verkehrswesen. Januar–Dezember 1935.
9078   China. Rohstoffe und Waren. September 1921–März 1936.

Documents from 1936

Büro des Reichsministers
F.11   Secretariat.
F.19   Secretariat.

Dienststelle Ribbentrop
43   Vertrauliche Berichte. September 1935–Marz 1939.
1824   Verschiedenes. 1936–1938.

Büro des Staatssekretärs
100   Japan. Russland. China–Japan. Kolonien. Japan, Allgemeine Auswärtige Politik. Deutsch–Japanisches Abkommen gegen die kommunistische Internationale vom 25 November 1936.
111   Chinesisch–Japanischer Krieg. Juli 1938–März 1942.
174   Japan. Juni 1938–März 1941.
191   China. August 1939–Dezember 1942.
224   Chinesisch–Japanischer Krieg. Juli–October 1937.
375   Halifax Besuch und seine Folgen. 1937–1939.
387   Politische Schriftwechsel mit Beamten des auswärtigen Dienstes. August 1936–Dezember 1937.
395   Aufzeichnungen über Diplomatenbesuche. August 1936–Dezember 1937.
597   See also serial 100.
1927   Chinesisch–Japanischer Krieg. Juli–October 1937.
1928   Chinesisch–Japanischer Krieg. October–Dezember 1937.
1929   Chinesisch–Japanischer Krieg. Januar–Juni 1938.
2134   Aufzeichungen über Diplomatenbesuche. August 1936–Juni 1943.
2185   Aufzeichnungen des Herrn Staatssekretär über interne Dienstauswweisungen usw. August 1936–Juni 1943.
2196   Schriftwechsel mit Beamten des auswärtigen Dienstes. August 1936–Juni 1943.

Chef Auslandsorganisation
59   Japan. März 1937–October 1940.

Handakten Hencke
2082   Briefwechsel mit Dirksen. 1933–1942.

Gruppe Inland I und II:

Inland I Partei
4923   Rückwirkung der deutschen Rassenpolitik auf die Beziehungen zu fremden Staaten. 1934–1937.

Inland II Geheim
919   Deutsch–Japanisches und Italienisch–Japanisches Abkommen zur Bekämpfung des Kommunismus. 1936–1938.

Politische Abteilung:

Buro des Unterstaatssekretärs
145   Ostasienkonflikt 1938.
151   Neunmächtkonferenz 1937.
153   China—Japan. I. 1937.
166   Japan. Militärputsch in Tokio. Februar 1936.
210   Neunmächtkonferenz. October 1937—Januar 1938.
3870 China—Japan. Juli—September 1937.
6505 China—Japan. 1937.
6567 Japan. Militärputsch in Tokio. Februar 1936.

Pol. I. Völkerbund
1687 Beziehungen verschiedener Staaten zu einander. Juli 1936—Mai 1940.

Pol. II
976   England. Politische Beziehungen zu Japan. Mai 1936—Juni 1938.
1702 Ostasien. Politische Angelegenheiten. September 1936—März 1938.
1726 Chinesisch—Japanischer Konflikt. 1937. Friedensfühler.
4422 Ostasien. Politische Angelegenheiten. Juni 1936—März 1938.
6565 Ostasien. Politische Angelegenheiten. September 1936—März 1938.

Pol. VIII
155   Japan. Politische Beziehungen zu Deutschland. Mai 1936—November 1939.
156   Manchukuo. Japan. Januar 1938—Juni 1940.
157   Japan. Politische Beziehungen zu Russland. April 1936—Juli 1940.
160   China. Fernostkonferenz 1937.
161   Japan. Allgemeine Auswärtige Politik. Juni 1936—Juni 1940.
163   Japan. Deutsch—Japanisches Abkommen gegen die kommunistische Internationale vom 25 November 1936.
178   China. Chinesisch—Japanischer Konflikt. 1937.
179   China. Innere Politik. Juni 1936—Mai 1938.
184   China. Politische Beziehungen zu Japan. Mai 1936—1940.
185   China. Politische Beziehungen zu Deutschland. Juli 1936—Juni 1939.
186   China. Deutschlandbesuch des chinesischen Finanzministers Dr Kung. 1937.
187   China. Politische Beziehungen zu Russland. September 1936—September 1940.
211   China. Militärangelegenheiten. Mai 1936—Dezember 1938.
219   China. Chinesisch—Japanischer Konflikt. 1937.
556   Japan. Politische Beziehungen zu Deutschland. 1936—1937.
1097 Antikomintern Pakte. October 1937—März 1939.
2898 Japan. Politische Beziehungen zu Deutschland. Mai 1936—November 1939.

2910   China. Politische Beziehungen zu Deutschland. Juli 1936—Juli 1939.
2911   China. Militärangelegenheiten. Mai 1936—Dezember 1938.
3244   Japan. Politische Beziehungen zu Deutschland. Deutsch—Japanische Abkommen gegen die kommunistische Internationale vom 25 November 1936. 1936—1937.
3708   China. Deutschlandbesuch des chinesischen Finanzministers Dr Kung. März—Oktober 1937.
3888   China. Chinesisch—Japanischer Konflikt. 1937—1940.
6561   Manchukuo. Politische Beziehungen zu Russland. Februar 1936—Juli 1940.
6566   Japan. Allgemeine auswärtige Politik. September 1936—Juni 1938.
7066   China. Innere Politik. Februar 1936—August 1938.
7069   China. Chinesisch—Japanischer Konflikt. Juli—August 1937.
7070   China. Politische Beziehungen zu Deutschland. Juli 1936—Dezember 1937.
7071   China. Deutschlandbesuch des chinesischen Finanzministers Dr Kung. März 1937—Oktober 1937.
9142   Japan. Politische Beziehungen zu Deutschland. Mai 1936—Juni 1937.
9143   China. Militärangelegenheiten. Mai 1936—Dezember 1938.

Handakten Wiehl
5754   Mandschukuo. 1938—1944.

Handelspolitische Abteilung:
4795   Handel mit Kriegsgerät. Allgemeines. Mai 1936—Dezember 1939.

Handakten Clodius
5647   Japan. 1929—1938.
7072   China. Dezember 1929—Februar 1939.
9075   Mandschukuo. Juni 1934—Mai 1938.

Ha. Pol. W VII
218   Ostasien. Fall Klein. Mai 1936—April 1938.

Verträge
2871   1936—1944.

Handelspolitische Verträge
9076   Mandschukuo. Handelsabkommen vom 30 April 1936 und Zusatsabkommen. April 1936—September 1940.

Asservate
8133   Nr. 150. Auslandsberichte aus den Jahren 1933—1939.

Nachlass Renthe-Fink
7023   Aufzeichnung Trautmann, 'Deutschland und China', 10 Juni 1936.

Missionen
2128   Deutsche Botschaft Rom (Quirinal). 1937.
9148   Botschaft Moskau. Sonderband: Lage im Fernen Osten. 1937.

Documents Not Originating in the German Foreign Office

Alte Reichskanzlei
8588   China. October 1931—Dezember 1935.
9785   Kolonien. Januar—Dezember 1935.

Neue Reichskanzlei
7814   Bulgarian. China. 1934—1944.

Adjutantur des Führers
3245   Berichte. Notizen für den Führer. Aufzeichnungen und Schrift-
       wechsel. 1936—1939.

2. *Politisches Archiv des Auswärtiges Amt*: Bonn.

Politische Abteilung IV: Po. 13. Japan. Militärangelegenheiten,
    Bd.3.

3. *Oberkommando der Wehrmacht, Ausland*: Foreign and Commonwealth Office, Library and Records Department, London.

OKW/991, Folder 'Akte Stein', Geheime Kommandosachen, Japan
    1936—1937 (photostat copy).
Wehrmachtamt, Nr. 51/37, Chefs. Aus., 8 July 1937 with enclosures
    (photostat copy).

4. *Oberkommando der Wehrmacht, Wehrwirtschafts- und Rüstungsamt*:
   filmed at Alexandria, Virginia: National Archives, Washington.

File Wi./IF.5.370. Correspondence Klein, Blomberg, Seeckt, Chiang
    Kai-shek. T.77/Roll 81.
File Wi./IF.5.383. Rearmament and Foreign Trade Problems.
    T.77/Roll 86.

5. *Deutsch—Japanische Gesellschaft*: filmed at Alexandria, Virginia:
   National Archives, Washington.

GD.3477. Correspondence of Admiral Behncke. T.82/Roll 180.

6. *German Consulate, Tsingtao*: filmed at Alexandria, Virginia: National
   Archives Washington.

Item 256. Allgemeine Politik Deutschlands (Emigranten, Judenfrage).
    1.179/Roll 26.

7. *British Foreign Office*: Public Record Office, London.

Foreign Office Correspondence 371.

8. Max Ilgner: *Bericht über eine Reise nach Ostasien 1934—35* (3
   volumes): Library, Auswärtiges Amt, Bonn.

II. *MILITARY TRIBUNALS*

1. *International Military Tribunal:*

   Trial of the Major War Criminals before the International Military Tribunal (Nuremberg 1947—49). 42 Vols. Blue Series.

2. *Nuremberg Military Tribunals:*

   Trials of War Criminals before the Nuremberg Military Tribunals Under Control Council Law No. 10 (Washington, D.C., 1949—53). 15 Vols. Green Series.

3. *Nuremberg Military Tribunals:*

   Transcript Volumes and Document Books of the Trials of War Criminals (FO.646: Imperial War Museum and Foreign and Commonwealth Office, London).

4. *International Military Tribunal for the Far East:*

   Record of the Proceedings, Documents, Exhibits, Judgement, Dissenting Judgements, Preliminary Interrogations, Miscellaneous Documents (mimeographed, Tokio 1946—49). Copies at the London School of Economics and Political Science and the Imperial War Museum, London.

III. *OFFICIAL SERIES OF DOCUMENTS ON FOREIGN POLICY*

1. *Akten zur deutschen auswärtigen Politik 1918—1945*: Series B, 1925—1933 (Göttingen, Vandenhoeck & Ruprecht, 1966—   ).

2. *Documents on German Foreign Policy 1918—1945*: Series C, 1933—1936; Series D, 1937—1941 (London, HMSO 1949—   ).

3. *Documents on British Foreign Policy 1919—1939*: Second Series, 1928—1938 (London, HMSO 1947—   ).

4. *Documents Diplomatiques Francais 1932—1939*: 1st Series, 1932—1935; 2nd Series, 1936—1939 (Paris, Ministere des Affaires Étrangères, 1963—   ).

5. *Foreign Relations of the United States:* 1933—1938 (Washington: U.S. Government Printing Office, 1939—   ).

IV. *BIOGRAPHIES, DIARIES, MEMOIRS*

AVON, the Rt. Hon the Earl of, *The Eden Memoirs. Facing the Dictators* (London 1962).
BRAUN, Otto, *Chinesische Aufzeichnungen (1932—1939)* (Berlin 1975).
BULLOCK, Alan, *Hitler: A Study in Tyranny* (London 1952).
CIANO, Galeazzo, *Ciano's Diary 1937—1938* (London 1952).

DIRKSEN, Herbert von, *Moscow, Tokyo, London* (London 1951).

DODD, William E., Jr, and Martha (eds.), *Ambassador Dodd's Diary 1933–1938* (London 1941).

EMESSEN, T. R. (ed.), *Aus Göring's Schreibtisch* (Berlin 1947).

FEST, Joachim C., *Hitler* (London 1974).

GÖRLITZ, Walter (ed.), *The Memoirs of Field Marshal Keitel* (London 1965).

GREW, Joseph, *Ten Years in Japan* (London 1944).

HAGEMANN, Walter, *Publizistik im Dritten Reich* (Hamburg 1948).

HELFFERICH, Emil, *1932–1946 Tatsachen: Ein Beitrag zur Wahrheitsfindung* (Oldenburg 1969).

HITLER, Adolf, *Mein Kampf* (London 1939).

HÖHNE, Heinz, *Canaris* (London 1979).

KERST, Georg, *Jacob Meckel: Sein Leben und Wirken in Deutschland und Japan* (Göttingen 1970).

KORDT, Erich, 'German Political History in the Far East During the Hitler Régime' (Typescript. Nuremberg, May 1946. Library of Congress, Washington, D.C., Captured Material, Box 809, Folder 18E-5).

——, *Nicht aus den Akten: Die Wilhelmstrasse in Frieden und Krieg. Erlebnisse, Begegnungen und Eindrücke 1928–1945* (Stuttgart 1950).

KRAMER, Paul (ed.), *The Last Manchu: The Autobiography of Henry Pu Yi, Last Emperor of China* (London 1967).

LIANG, Hsi-Huey, *The Sino–German Connection: Alexander von Falkenhausen between China and Germany, 1900–1941* (Assen 1978).

MEIER-WELCKER, Hans, *Seeckt* (Frankfurt-am-Main 1967).

RABENAU, Friedrich von, *Seeckt: Aus seinem Leben 1918–1936* (Leipzig 1941).

RIBBENTROP, Joachim von, *Memoirs* (London 1954, intro. by Alan Bullock).

SCHACHT, Hjalmar, *Account Settled* (London 1949).

SCHNEE, Heinrich, *Völker und Mächte im Fernen Osten. Eindrücke von der Reise mit der Mandschurei Kommission* (Berlin 1933).

SCHWARZ, Paul, *This Man Ribbentrop: His Life and Times* (New York 1943).

SERAPHIM, Hans-Günther (ed.), *Das politische Tagebuch Alfred Rosenbergs aus den Jahren 1934/35 und 1939/40* (Göttingen 1956).

TESKE, Hermann (ed.), *General Ernst Köstring: Der militärische Mittler zwischen dem Deutsche Reich und der Sowjetunion 1921–1941* (Frankfurt-am-Main 1966).

THYSSEN, Fritz, *I Paid Hitler* (London 1941).

TOGO, Shigenori, *The Cause of Japan* (New York 1956).

VOGT, Adolf, *Oberst Max Bauer: Generalstabsoffizier im Zwielicht 1869–1929* (Osnabrück 1974).

WEIZSÄCKER, Ernst von, *Erinnerungen* (Munich 1950).

V. GENERAL WORKS

ABENDROTH, Hans-Henning, *Hitler in der spanischen Arena. Die deutsch–*

spanischen Beziehungen im Spannungsfeld der europäischen Interessenpolitik vom Ausbruch des Bürgerkrieges bis zum Ausbruch des Weltkrieges 1936–1939 (Paderborn 1973).

(no author), *Aus dem Kampf der deutschen Arbeiterklasse zur Verteidigung der Revolution in China* (Berlin 1959).

BASSETT, R., *Democracy and Foreign Policy. A Case History: The Sino–Japanese Dispute 1931–1933* (London 1952, repr. 1968).

BAYNES, Norman H. (ed.), *The Speeches of Adolf Hitler 1922–1939*, 2 Volumes (London 1942).

BECK, Earl R., *Verdict on Schacht: A Study in the Problem of Political 'Guilt'* (Tallahassee 1955).

BENNETT, Edward W., *Germany and the Diplomacy of the Financial Crisis 1931* (Harvard University Press 1962).

——, *German Rearmament and the West 1932–33* (Princeton University Press 1979).

BERGAMINI, David, *Japan's Imperial Conspiracy* (New York 1971).

BISSON, T. A., *Japan in China* (New York 1938).

BLOCH, Charles, *Hitler und die europäischen Mächte 1933–1934: Kontinuität oder Bruch?* (Frankfurt-am-Main 1966).

BLOCH, Kurt, *German Interests and Policies in the Far East* (New York 1940).

BORG, Dorothy, *The United States and the Far Eastern Crisis of 1933–38* (Harvard University Press 1964).

BOYLE, John Hunter, *China and Japan at War 1937–1945: The Politics of Collaboration* (Stanford University Press 1972).

BRACHER, Karl Dietrich, *The German Dictatorship: The Origins, Structure, and Effects of National Socialism* (London 1971).

BRACHER, Karl Dietrich, Wolfgang SAUER and Gerhard SCHULZ, *Die nationalsozialistische Machtergreifung: Studien zur Errichtung des totalitären Herrschaftssystems in Deutschland 1933/34* (Köln 1960).

BRAMSTED, Ernest K., *Goebbels and National Socialist Propaganda 1925–1945* (Michigan 1964).

BULLOCK, Alan, *Hitler and the Origins of the Second World War* (The Raleigh Lecture on History, British Academy 1967).

BUNKER, Gerald E., *The Peace Conspiracy: Wang Ching-wei and the China War 1937–1941* (Harvard University Press 1972).

BUSS, Claude, *War and Diplomacy in Eastern Asia* (New York 1941).

CARR, William, *Arms, Autarky, and Aggression. A Study in German Foreign Policy 1933–1939* (London 1972).

CARROLL, Berenice A., *Design for Total War: Arms and Economics in the Third Reich* (The Hague 1968).

CARSTEN, F. L., *The Reichswehr and Politics 1918–1933* (London 1966).

CHAMBERLIN, William H., *Japan Over Asia* (London 1938).

CLUBB, O. Edmund, *Twentieth Century China* (Columbia University Press 1964).

COHEN, Jerome B., *Japan's Economy in War and Reconstruction* (University of Minnesota Press 1949).

COOX, Alvin D., *Kogun: The Japanese Army in the Pacific* (Virginia 1959).

CRAIG, Gordon A., *The Politics of the Prussian Army 1640—1945* (Oxford 1955).
——, *From Bismarck to Adenauer: Aspects of German Statecraft* (Baltimore 1958).
——, and Felix GILBERT (eds.), *The Diplomats 1919—1939* (Princeton University Press 1953).
CROWLEY, James B., *Japan's quest for Autonomy: National Security and Foreign Policy 1930—1938* (Princeton University Press 1966).
DAVIDSON, Eugene, *The Trial of the Germans: Nuremberg 1945—46* (New York 1966).
DEAKIN, F. W., and G. R. STORRY, *The Case of Richard Sorge* (London 1966).
DEUTSCH, Harold C., *The Conspiracy Against Hitler in the Twilight War* (University of Minnesota Press 1968).
——, *Hitler and His Generals: The Hidden Crisis, January—June 1938* (University of Minnesota Press 1974).
DOMARUS, Max, *Hitler. Reden und Proklamationen 1932—1945* (Wiesbaden 1973).
DRECHSLER, Karl, *Deutschland—China—Japan 1933—1939: Das Dilemma der deutschen Fernostpolitik* (Berlin 1964).
EASTMAN, Lloyd E., *The Abortive Revolution: China Under Nationalist Rule 1927—1937* (Harvard University Press 1974).
ELISSAR, Eliahu Ben, *La Diplomatie du IIIe Reich et les Juifs (1933—1939)* (Paris 1969).
EMMERSON, James Thomas, *The Rhineland Crisis 7 March 1936: A Study in Multilateral Diplomacy* (London 1977).
ENDICOTT, Stephen Lyon, *Diplomacy and Enterprise: British China Policy 1933—37* (Manchester University Press 1975).
ERICKSON, John, *The Soviet High Command 1918—1941* (London 1962).
FEST, Joachim C., *The Face of the Third Reich* (Pelican edn, London 1972).
FUNKE, Manfred (ed.), *Hitler, Deutschland und die Mächte. Materialien zur Aussenpolitik des Dritten Reiches* (Bonn 1976).
(no author), *Germany Speaks* (London 1938).
GILBERT, G. M., *Nuremberg Diary* (New York 1947).
GÖRLITZ, Walter, *The German General Staff: Its History and Structure 1657—1945* (London 1953).
GROSS, Walter, *Der deutsche Rassengedanke und die Welt* (Berlin 1939).
GUILLEBAUD, C. W., *The Economic Recovery of Germany* (London 1939).
HARASZTI, Eva H., *Treaty Breakers or 'Realpolitiker'? The Anglo—German Naval Agreement of June 1935* (Boppard-am-Rhein 1974).
HEINEMAN, John Louis, *Hitler's First Foreign Minister: Constantin von Neurath* (University of California Press 1980).
HENKE, Josef, *England in Hitlers politischen Kalkül 1935—1939* (Boppard-am-Rhein 1973).
HILBERG, Raul, *The Destruction of the European Jews* (London 1961).
HILDEBRAND, Klaus, *Vom Reich zum Weltreich: Hitler, NSDAP, und koloniale Frage 1919—1945* (Munich 1969).

HILDEBRAND, Klaus, *Deutsche Aussenpolitik 1933–1945. Kalkül oder Dogma?* (Stuttgart 1971).

HILLGRUBER, Andreas, *Kontinuität und Diskontinuität in der deutschen Aussenpolitik von Bismarck bis Hitler* (Düsseldorf 1969).

HOU, Chi-Ming, *Foreign Investment and Economic Development in China 1840–1937* (Harvard University Press 1965).

HSU, Long-hsuen and Chang MING-KAI, *History of the Sino–Japanese War (1937–1945)* (Taipei 1971).

IKLÉ, Frank W., *German–Japanese Relations 1936–1940* (New York 1956).

IRIYE, Akira, *After Imperialism: The Search for a New Order in the Far East 1921–1931* (Harvard University Press 1965).

IRVING, David, *Hitler's War* (London 1977).

——, *The War Path: Hitler's Germany 1935–39* (London 1978).

ISSRAELJAN, V. and L. KUTAKOV, *Diplomacy of Aggression: Berlin–Rome–Tokio Axis. Its Rise and Fall* (Moscow 1970).

JÄCKEL, Eberhard, *Hitlers Weltanschauung: Entwurf einer Herrschaft* (Tübingen 1969).

JACOBSEN, Hans-Adolf, *Nationalsozialistische Aussenpolitik 1933–1938* (Frankfurt-am-Main 1968).

JÄGER, Jörg Johannes, *Die wirtschaftliche Abhängigkeit des Dritten Reiches vom Ausland* (Berlin 1969).

JANOWSKY, Oscar and Melvin FAGEN, *International Aspects of German Racial Policies* (New York 1937).

JOHNSON, Chalmers, *An Instance of Treason: The Story of the Tokio Spy Ring* (London 1965).

JONES, F. C., *Manchuria Since 1931* (New York 1949).

KIMMICH, Christoph, *Germany and the League of Nations* (University of Chicago Press 1976).

KLEIN, Burton, *Germany's Economic Preparations for War* (Harvard University Press 1959).

KUTAKOV, Leonid N. (ed. with foreword by George Alexander Lensen), *Japanese Foreign Policy on the Eve of the Pacific War: A Soviet View* (Florida 1972).

LARY, Diana, *Region and Nation: The Kwangsi Clique in Chinese Politics 1925–1937* (Cambridge University Press 1974).

League of Nations, *Official Journal.*

LEBER, Annedore, *Conscience in Revolt: Sixty-four Stories of Resistance in Germany 1933–45* (London 1957).

LEE, Bradford A., *Britain and the Sino–Japanese War 1937–1939: A Study in Dilemmas of British Decline* (London 1973).

LEERS, Johann von, *Deutschlands Stellung in der Welt* (Leipzig 1933).

LEVI, Werner, *Modern China's Foreign Policy* (University of Minnesota Press 1953).

LI, Lincoln, *Japanese Army in North China 1937–41: Problems of Political and Economic Control* (Tokio: Oxford University Press 1976).

LIU, F. F., *A Military History of Modern China 1924–1949* (Princeton University Press 1956).

LOUIS, William Roger, *Great Britain and Germany's Lost Colonies 1914–1919* (London 1967).

LOWE, Peter, *Great Britain and the Origins of the Pacific War: A Study of British Policy in East Asia 1937—1941* (Oxford University Press 1977).

MACNAIR, H. F. and D. F. LACH, *Modern Far Eastern International Relations* (New York 1951).

MARTIN, Bernd, *Deutschland und Japan im Zweiten Weltkrieg: Von Pearl Harbor bis zur deutschen Kapitulation* (Göttingen 1969).

MAXON, Yale C., *Control of Japanese Foreign Policy: A Study of Civil—Military Rivalry 1930—1945* (University of California Press 1957).

MEDLICOTT, W. N., *The Coming of War in 1939* (Historical Association Pamphlet G.52, London 1963).

MEINCK, Gerhard, *Hitler und die Deutsche Aufrüstung 1933—1937* (Wiesbaden 1959).

MESKILL, Johanna Menzel, *Hitler and Japan: The Hollow Alliance* (New York 1966).

MICHAEL, Franz H. and George E. TAYLOR, *The Far East in the Modern World* (London 1956).

MILWARD, A. S., *The German Economy at War* (London 1965).

MORLEY, James William (ed.), *Deterrent Diplomacy: Japan, Germany, and the USSR 1935—1940. Selected translations from Taiheiyo senso e no michi: kaisen gaiko shi* (New York 1976).

MUGGERIDGE, Malcolm (ed.), *Ciano's Diplomatic Papers* (London 1948).

NAMIER, Sir Lewis, *In the Nazi Era* (London 1952).

NICLAUSS, Karlheinz, *Die Sowjetunion und Hitlers Machtergreifung: Eine Studie über die deutsch—russischen Beziehungen der Jahre 1929 bis 1935* (Bonn 1966).

OGATA, Sadako N., *Defiance in Manchuria. The Making of Japanese Foreign Policy 1931—1932* (University of California Press 1964).

O'NEILL, Robert J., *The German Army and the Nazi Party 1933—1939* (London 1966).

PANG, Bin-Chin, *Der Aussenhandel zwischen Deutschland und China und die deutsch—chinesischen Aussenhandelspolitik* (Erlangen 1937).

PECK, Joachim, *Kolonialismus ohne Kolonien: Der Deutsche Imperialismus und China 1937* (Berlin 1961).

PETERSON, Edward Norman, *Hjalmar Schacht: For and Against Hitler. A Political—Economic Study of Germany 1923—1945* (Boston 1954).

——, *The Limits of Hitler's Power* (Princeton University Press 1969).

PETZINA, Dieter, *Autarkiepolitik im Dritten Reich: Der nationalsozialistische Vierjahresplan* (Stuttgart 1968).

PRESSEISEN, Ernst L., *Germany and Japan: A Study in Totalitarian Diplomacy 1933—1941* (The Hague 1958).

——, *Before Aggression: Europeans Prepare the Japanese Army* (Tucson 1965).

Reichsministerium des Innern, *Reichsgesetzblatt*.

Reichsverbandes der Deutschen Industrie, *Bericht der China Studienkommission des Reichsverbandes der Deutschen Industrie* (Berlin 1930).

REIMERS, Jacobus, *Das japanische Kolonialmandat und der Austritt Japans aus dem Völkerbund* (Quackenbruch 1936).

RICH, Norman, *Hitler's War Aims*. Volume I: *Ideology, the Nazi State, and the Course of Expansion* (London 1973).

ROBERTSON, E. M., *Hitler's Pre-War Policy and Military Plans 1933–1939* (London 1963).

——, (ed.), *The Origins of the Second World War: Historical Interpretations* (London 1971).

ROSENBERG, Alfred, *Blut und Ehre* (Munich 1934).

——, *Krisis und Neubau Europas* (Berlin 1934).

——, *Gestaltung der Idee* (Munich 1936).

Royal Institute of International Affairs, *Survey of International Affairs* (London 1933–   ).

——, *Documents on International Affairs* (London 1932–42).

RULAND, Bernd, *Deutsche Botschaft Peking: Das Jahrhundert deutsch–chinesischen Schicksals* (Bayreuth 1973).

SCHLEUNES, Karl A., *The Twisted Road to Auschwitz: Nazi Policy Toward German Jews 1933–1939* (University of Illinois Press 1971).

SCHMOKEL, Wolfe W., *Dream of Empire: German Colonialism 1919–1945* (Yale University Press 1964).

SCHWEITZER, Arthur, *Big Business in the Third Reich* (London 1964).

SEABURY, Paul, *The Wilhelmstrasse: A Study of German Diplomats under the Nazi Régime* (University of California Press 1954).

SEECKT, Hans von, *Deutschland zwischen West und Ost* (Hamburg 1933).

SHAI, Aron, *Origins of the War in the East: Britain, China, and Japan 1937–39* (London 1976).

SHIRER, William, *The Rise and Fall of the Third Reich. A History of Nazi Germany* (London 1960).

SOMMER, Theo, *Deutschland und Japan zwischen den Mächten 1935–1940* (Tübingen 1962).

STOLPER, Gustav, *The German Economy: 1870 to the Present* (London 1967).

STORRY, Richard, *The Double Patriots: A Study of Japanese Nationalism* (London 1957).

——, *A History of Modern Japan* (London 1967).

SYKES, Christopher, *Troubled Loyalty: A Biography of Adam von Trott zu Solz* (London 1968).

TAI, Tsien, *China and the Nine-Power Conference at Brussels in 1937* (New York 1964).

TAYLOR, A. J. P., *The Origins of the Second World War* (London 1961).

THOMAS, Georg, *Geschichte der deutschen Wehr- und Rüstungswirtschaft 1918–1943/45* (Boppard-am-Rhein 1966, ed. by Wolfgang Birkenfeld).

THORNE, Christopher, *The Limits of Foreign Policy: The West, the League and the Far Eastern Crisis of 1931–1933* (London 1972).

TREVOR-ROPER, H. R. (intro.), *Hitler's Table Talk 1941–1944* (London 1953).

——, (intro.), *The Testament of Adolf Hitler. The Hitler–Bormann Documents* (London 1961).

TROTTER, Ann, *Britain and East Asia 1933–1937* (Cambridge University Press 1975).

TUTAS, Herbert E., *Nationalsozialismus und Exil. Die Politik des Dritten Reiches gegenüber der deutschen politischen Emigration 1933—1939* (Munich 1975).

WALTERS, F. P., *A History of the League of Nations* (London 1965 [repr.]).

WEINBERG, Gerhard L., *Germany and the Soviet Union 1939—1941* (Leiden 1954).

——, *The Foreign Policy of Hitler's Germany: Diplomatic Revolution in Europe 1933—1936* (University of Chicago Press 1970).

WHEATON, Eliot B., *Prelude to Calamity: The Nazi Revolution 1933—1935* (London 1969).

WHEELER-BENNETT, John W., *The Nemesis of Power. The German Army in Politics 1918—1945* (London 1953).

WILLOUGHBY, Westel W., *The Sino—Japanese Controversy and the League of Nations* (Baltimore 1935).

WISKEMANN, Elizabeth, *The Rome—Berlin Axis* (London 1966, rev. edtn.).

ZEMAN, Z. A. B., *Nazi Propaganda* (London 1964).

VI. ARTICLES

BAUER, R., 'Gefahrenpunkte Japans', *Volk und Reich*, XI, August 1935, 612—24.

BIX, Herbert P., 'Japanese Imperialism and the Manchurian Economy 1900—31', *The China Quarterly*, No. 51, July—September 1972, 425—43.

CASPER, Karl, 'Deutschland und China im gegenseitigen Warenaustausch', *Weltwirtschaftliches Archiv*, XLV, March 1937, 409—42.

CAUSEY, Beverley Douglas Jr, 'Why Germany Never Signed the Nine-Power Treaty', *Far Eastern Quarterly*, 1, No. 4, August 1942, 364—77.

(no author), 'The Changing East — Der Werdende Orient', *Der Neue Orient*, X, 1934, Heft 1, 3—4.

CRAIG, Gordon A., 'Totalitarian Approaches to Diplomatic Negotiations', in: A. O. Sarkissian, *Studies in Diplomatic History* (London 1961), 107—25.

DAITZ, Werner, 'Die Friedensmission des Nationalsozialismus', *Diplomaten Zeitung*, November 1933, 1044—46.

——, 'The Economic Problem of National Socialism', *Der Neue Orient*, X, 1934, Heft 1, 7—9.

——, 'Neue Aussenhandelspolitik', *Diplomaten Zeitung*, February 1934, 1089—90.

DIETZEL, Karl, H., 'Das japanische Südseemandat', *Koloniale Rundschau*, August/October 1934, 228—37.

FLEMMIG, Walter, 'Der gelbe Handel droht', *Zeitwende*, IX, July—December 1933, 465—69.

——, 'Japans zweites Schwert: die Wirtschaft', *Zeitschrift für Geopolitik*, X, December 1933, 724—32.

FOMIN, W. T., 'Wahrheit und Legende über die Mitverantwortung der deutschen Diplomaten für die Vorbereitung des faschistischen Aggressionskrieges', in *Probleme der Geschichte des Zweiten Weltkrieges* (Berlin 1958), II, 112—25.

FOX, John P., 'Alfred Rosenberg in London', *Contemporary Review*, Vol. 213, July 1968, 6—11.

——, 'Japanese Reactions to Nazi Germany's Racial Legislation', *Wiener Library Bulletin*, Vol. XXII, Nos. 2 and 3, 1969, 46—50.

——, 'Max Bauer: Chiang Kai-shek's first German Military Adviser', *Journal of Contemporary History*, V, No. 4, 1970, 21—44.

——, 'Adolf Hitler: The Continuing Debate', *International Affairs*, Vol. 55, No. 2, April 1979, 252—64.

FRANK, Elke, 'The Role of Bureaucracy in Transition', *Journal of Politics*, Vol. 28, No. 4, 1966, 725—53.

GATZKE, Hans W., 'Russo—German Military Collaboration during the Weimar Republic', *American Historical Review*, LXIII, 1958, 565—97.

GROTKOPP, Wilhelm, 'Japan's Export offensive — Gefahr oder Schicksal?', *Ruhr und Rhein*, 1934, Heft 20, 332—36.

HAAS, Wilhelm, 'Der japanisch—mandschurische Warenaustausch mit Deutschland', *Weltwirtschaftliches Archiv*, XLVI, July 1937, 272—86.

HENNIG, Richard, 'Das japanische Kolonialmandat', *Deutsche Juristen Zeitung*, 1933, Heft 8, 537—40.

HERMANN, H., 'Die chinesische Kultur und das Rasseproblem', *Unsere Welt*, XXVII, 10, 1935, 296—98.

HILL, Leonidas E., 'The Wilhelmstrasse in the Nazi Era', *Political Science Quarterly*, LXXXII, December 1967, 546—70.

HOEPPENER, W., 'Sind deutsche Offiziere die Führer der chinesischen Shanghai—Truppen? Gerüchte um deutsche Chinakampfer', *Neues Wiener Extrablatt*, 26 February 1932.

HOLLENHORST, N. H., 'Japan stösst vor', *Volk und Reich*, IX, October 1933, 905—10.

(no author), 'Japan und die deutschen Südseeinseln', *Kolonialpost*, 23 March 1933, 28.

(no author), 'Japans Südsee Mandat', *Kolonialpost*, 23 April 1933, 40.

(no author), 'Japans Kolonialpolitik', *Deutsche Kolonial Zeitung*, 1 December 1933, 244.

(no author), 'Die Japanische Wehrmacht', *Zeitschrift für Geopolitik*, XII, August 1935, 479—93.

JOHANNES, Martin Otto, 'Kleine Beiträge: Ostliche Narrheit', *Rasse*, 1934, I, 204—05.

JUST, Artur W., 'Asien und die Sowjetunion', *Volk und Reich*, X, February 1934, 102—11.

KIEP, O., 'The Economic Policies of Germany Under the New Plan', *Chinese Economic Journal*, XVIII, February 1936, 214—15.

KRÜGER, Peter and Erich J. C. HAHN, 'Der Loyalitätskonflikt des Staatssekretärs Bernhard Wilhelm von Bülow im Frühjahr 1933', *Vierteljahrshefte für Zeitgeschichte*, 20, No. 4, October 1972, 376—410.

KÜHNE, Horst, 'Zur Kolonialpolitik des faschistischen deutschen Imperialismus (1933—1939)', *Zeitschrift für Geschichtswissenschaft*, 9, 1961, No. 3, 513—37.

LEERS, Johann von, 'Aussenpolitische Lage', *Volk im Werden*, 1933, No. 4, 1—6.

LEERS, Johann von, 'Japanische Neuformung', *Die Tat*, XXVI, September 1934, 411—23.

LIU, James T. C., 'German Mediation in the Sino—Japanese War 1937—38', *Far Eastern Quarterly*, VIII, February 1949, 157—71.

MACK, Karlheinz, 'Polen und der Antikominternpakt', *Österreichische Ost-Hefte*, January 1960, 34—40.

MCKALE, Donald M., 'The Nazi Party in the Far East, 1931—45', *Journal of Contemporary History*, 12, 1977, 291—311.

MEHNER, Karl, 'Weimar—Kanton: ein Beitrag zur Geschichte der deutsch—chinesischen Beziehungen in den Jahren 1921—1924', *Wissenschaftliche Zeitschrift der Karl Marx Universität* (Leipzig), 8, 1958/59, Heft I, 23—43.

(no author), 'Die militärpolitische Lage im Fernen Osten', *Wissen und Wehr*, April 1933, 201—10.

MOHR, Friedrich W., 'Japans Abschied vom Völkerbund und die Mandatsfrage im Stillen Ozean', *Wirtschaftsdienst*, XX, 12 April 1935, 495—97.

MOHR, Paul, 'Japans Grossraumpolitik und Weltwirtschaftsoffensive', *Deutsche Lebensraum*, December 1933, 135—37.

MÜLLER-ROSS, Dr., 'Die Zukunft des japanischen Südseemandats', *Deutsche Kolonial Zeitung*, 1 February 1933, 30.

NAGAI, A., 'Bemerkungen zum deutsch—japanischen Handelsverkehr', *Ostasiatische Rundschau*, 16 September 1933, 388.

POOLE, De Witt C., 'Light on Nazi Foreign Policy', *Foreign Affairs*, 25, October 1946, 130—54.

PRESSEISEN, Ernst L., 'Le racisme et les Japonais (un dilemme nazi)', *Revue d'histoire de la deuxieme guerre mondiale*, Vol. 13, No. 51, July 1963, 1—14.

REEPEN, Hans, 'Kolonialgedanke und Rassenfrage', *Deutsche Kolonial Zeitung*, 1 February 1936, 29—30.

RETZMANN, Admiral, 'Industrielle Beziehungen zwischen Deutschland und China', *Ostasiatische Rundschau*, 1 April 1931, 177—78.

RIESSER, Dr Hans E., 'Die Diplomaten unter der nationalsozialistischen Diktatur', in the author's *Haben die deutschen Diplomaten versagt? Eine Kritik an der Kritik von Bismarck bis Heute* (Bonn 1959), 47—58.

ROSINSKI, Herbert, 'Der gelbe Exportangriff', *Welt des Kaufmanns*, April 1934, 193—201.

SASSE, Heinz Günther, 'Das Problem des diplomatischen Nachwuchses im Dritten Reich', in Richard Dietrich und Gerhard Oestreich, *Forschungen zu Staat und Verfassung. Festgabe für Fritz Hartung* (Berlin 1958), 367—83.

SCHEPER, Hansjulius, 'Japan und Panasien', *Zeitschrift für Geopolitik*, XI, September 1934, 553—60.

SCHLESING, Heiner, 'Japanische Politik in des Südsee', *Deutsche Kolonial Zeitung*, 1 January 1934, 8—9.

SCHNOECKEL, Paul, 'Japans Handel greift an', *Kolonialpost*, April 1935, 64—65.

SCHULTZE, Ernst, 'Europa und die japanische Exportoffensive', *Erwachendes Europa*, 1934, 211—19.

SCHWEITZER, Arthur, 'Foreign Exchange Crisis of 1936', *Zeitschrift für Staatswissenschaft*, 118, April 1962, 243—77.

SEABURY, Paul, 'Ribbentrop and the German Foreign Office', *Political Science Quarterly*, LXVI, December 1951, 532—55.

SOMMER, Walter, 'Zur Rolle deutsche Berater in den Einkreisungs- und Vernichtungsfeldzügen gegen die Südchinesische Sowjetrepublik 1930—34', *Zeitschrift für Politik*, 18, 1971, 268—304.

SORGE, Richard, 'Die Japanische Wehrmacht', *Zeitschrift für Geopolitik*, XII, August 1935, 479—93.

STRAUSS, Walter, 'Das Reichsministerium des Innern und die Judengesetzgebung', *Vierteljahrshefte für Zeitgeschichte*, 9, No. 3, July 1961, 262—313.

STUCKHART, Dr Wilhelm, 'Die Rassengesetzgebung im Dritten Reich', in Hans Pfundtner, *Dr Wilhelm Frick und sein Ministerium* (Munich 1937).

THIERBACH, Hans, 'Der Konflikt im Fernen Osten', *Die Tat*, XXV, November 1933, 669—72.

——, 'Japan und die Sowjetunion', *Die Tat*, XXV, February 1934, 876—83.

——, 'Um die deutschen Südseeinseln', *Kolonialpost*, 23 January 1935, 10.

THOMAS, Georg, 'Gedanken und Ereignisse', *Schweizerische Monatshefte*, XXV, December 1945.

TOWNSEND, Mary E., 'The German Colonies and the Third Reich', *Political Science Quarterly*, LIII, June 1938, 186—206.

——, 'Hitler and the Revival of German Colonialism', in Edward Mead Earle (ed.), *Nationalism and Internationalism: Essays Inscribed to Carlton J. H. Hayes* (Columbia University Press 1950), 399—430.

TREUE, Wilhelm, 'Hitlers Denkschrift zum Vierjahresplan 1936', *Vierteljahrshefte für Zeitgeschichte*, 3, No. 2, April 1955, 184—210.

VOGELSANG, Thilo, 'Neue Dokumente zur Geschichte der Reichswehr 1930—1933', *Vierteljahrshefte für Zeitgeschichte*, 2, No. 4, October 1954, 397—436.

WALSH, Billie K., 'The German Military Mission in China 1928—38', *Journal of Modern History*, 46, September 1974, 502—13.

WATT, D. C., 'The German Diplomats and the Nazi Leaders 1933—1939', *Journal of Central European Affairs*, XV, July 1955, 148—60.

——, 'Japan in the Anti-Comintern Pact: Dilemmas and Hesitations', *Wiener Library Bulletin*, XIII, Nos. 5—6, 1959, 46, 54.

WEINBERG, Gerhard L., 'Die geheimen Abkommen zum Antikominternpakt', *Vierteljahrshefte für Zeitgeschichte*, 2, No. 2, April 1954, 193—201.

——, 'Deutsch—japanische Verhandlungen über das Südseemandat 1937—1938', *Vierteljahrshefte für Zeitgeschichte*, 4, No. 4, October 1956, 390—98.

——, 'German Recognition of Manchukuo', *World Affairs Quarterly*, XXVIII, July 1957, 149—64.

ZÖLLER, H., 'Japans wirtschaftlicher und politischer Aufschwung und die deutsch—japanischen Wirtschaftsbeziehungen', *Ostasiatische Rundschau*, 16 December 1936, 659—60.

VII. *UNPUBLISHED DISSERTATIONS*

CAUSEY, Beverley Douglas Jr, 'German Policy towards China 1918–1941' (Harvard University 1942).

CHAPMAN, John, 'The Origins and Development of German and Japanese Military Cooperation 1936–1945' (Oxford University 1967).

DOLMAN, Arthur, 'The Third Reich and Japan: A Study in Nazi Cultural Relations' (New York University 1966).

FRANK, Elke, 'The Wilhelmstrasse during the Third Reich: Changes in its Organisational Structure and Personnel Policies' (Harvard University 1963).

HEINEMAN, John Louis, 'Constantin Freiherr von Neurath as Foreign Minister 1932–1935. A Study of a Conservative Civil Servant and Germany's Foreign Policy' (Cornell University 1965).

KINDZORRA, Otto, 'Die Chinapolitik des deutschen Imperialismus der Jahre 1914–1921' (Humboldt University, Berlin 1964).

MEHNER, Karl, 'Die Rolle deutscher Militärberater als Interessenvertreter des deutschen Imperialismus und Militärismus in China 1928–1936' (Karl-Marx Universität, Leipzig 1961).

NORTON, Donald Hawley, 'Karl Haushofer and his Influence on Nazi Ideology and German Foreign Policy 1919–1945' (Clark University 1965).

SEPS, Jerry Bernard, 'German Military Advisers and Chiang Kai-shek 1927–38' (University of California 1972).

WÜNSCHE, Renate, 'Die Haltung des deutschen Imperialismus zum japanisch–chinesischen Konflikt vom 1931–1933 und der Kampf der Kommunistischen Partei Deutschlands gegen die Fernöstliche Kriegsgefahr' (Deutsche Akademie für Staats- und Rechtswissenschaft, 'Walter Ulbricht', Potsdam 1961).

Index

concerned at Japanese reactions on racial question, 89
conversation with Hirota on German-Japanese colonial question, 96
and German-Japanese economic relations, 98
and German-Japanese military relations, 103
positive attitude to Anti-Comintern Pact negotiations, 134
and Sino-German military relations, 135
supports German industrial work in Manchukuo, 146 ff.
and German economic mission to Manchukuo, 152 f.
and Kiep Mission, 153, 156, 158
proposes German Consulate at Hsinking, 161
and Kiep's negotiations in Far East, 162 ff.
informed of AA's views, 164
and appointment of German trade commissioner to Manchukuo, 166 ff., 173
and von Ribbentrop's Anti-Comintern Pact negotiations, 175 f., 182, 185 f., 209
opposes German mediation (1935) on behalf of China, 185
informs AA of Japanese approaches on mutual policy to Russia, 187 f.
informs von Neurath and von Bülow of Pact negotiations, 188 f.
and AA's attitude to Pact negotiations, 190 f., 209, 215
conversations with Hitler and von Ribbentrop (1936) on policy to Japan, 198 ff.
reports Pact's reception in Japan, 198 ff., 204
views on Pact, 205, 211, 376 n. 81
recommends invitation to Prince Chichibu, 212
remonstrates with Sato on Japanese attitudes to Pact, 214 f., 379 n. 31
supports Pact in Tokio, 214 ff.
informs AA of German-Japanese talks on policy to Russia, 223
concerned at outbreak of Sino-Japanese war, 228
instructed to state Germany's neutrality and to emphasise moderation, 233
optimistic on chances of peace, 234
opposes early mediation, 234

reports Japanese criticism of Sino-German military relations, 235, 238
inclined to Japanese viewpoint in Sino-Japanese war, 235–236, 261
instructed to re-emphasise Germany's neutrality, 236
informs AA of Japanese disappointment at Germany's attitudes, 238, 387 n. 111
and Soviet influence in China, 238
instructed to warn Japan of Germany's interests in Shanghai, 241
suggests German mediation, 243 f., 248, 261
and 'Gneisenau' incident, 246 f.
interested in German-Japanese economic cooperation in China, 253
informs AA of Hirota's wish to use Germany as channel of communication to China, 260 ff.
reports Japanese General Staff's use of Ott as channel of communication with China, 261
views on Germany's role in Sino-Japanese war, 268
given Japan's terms by Hirota, urges AA to obtain Chinese acceptance, 265
pressed by Japan on Sino-Japanese peace talks, 269
instructed to establish Japan's position in peace negotiations, 273
warns AA of stronger Japanese terms on China, 274, 276
informs AA of new terms, 277
pressed by Japan for speedy Chinese reply, 278, 281, 283
and final Sino-Japanese exchanges, 288 f.
analysis of Germany and Far Eastern situation (January 1938), 291 f.
and colonial question in German-Japanese relations, 216, 294, 298, 325
informed of Japanese expectations on German policy, 297, 307 f.
informs Hitler of Japanese complaints re German military advisers, 396 n. 66
'Nazi' views on German foreign policy, 331, 336
Disarmament, 19
Disarmament Conference, 20–21, 57
Döberitz, 224
Dodd, William E., American Ambassador to Germany 1933–37, 35 f., 231

exchange of letters with Hitler, 231
informed of German arms trade with China during Sino-Japanese war, 237
informed of Germany's attitude on Sino-German military relations, 256
suggests to von Dirksen German mediation in Sino-Japanese war, 244 ff.
and Germany's role in Sino-Japanese war, 259 f., 277, 282, 287
as spokesman for Japan in final negotiations, 287 ff.
emphasises Germany's responsibility for improvement in German-Japanese relations, 297
opposes special privileges for Germany and Italy in North China, 311 f.
with Ott on German-Japanese relations, 323 ff.
HITLER, ADOLF, Führer and Reich Chancellor, Supreme Commander of the Wehrmacht, 1933–45:
attitudes to AA, 3 ff.
attitude to Sino-Japanese dispute, 1931–33, 13
Chancellor, 23
constitutional position of, 26
political interest in Japan, 3 ff., 26 ff.
positive policy towards Manchukuo, 29 ff.
informed about Heye, 28
talks with von Dirksen on Manchukuo (1933), 29
authorises Heye's negotiations with Manchukuo, 33, 35
authorises statement of Germany's non-recognition of Manchukuo, 36
receives Trautmann's report (February 1934), 36 ff.
rescinds Heye's authority, 50 f.
rearmament policies, 59, 109, 129 ff.
as arbiter in AA-RWM conflict on arms trade with China, 67
and status of Sino-German diplomatic relations, 78
speech on Nazi racial views, 85
orders Nuremberg laws, 93
and colonial question, 93 f.
conversation with Sir J. Simon, 96
concerned over Russo-Japanese military balance, 101

and Russo-German relations, 101 f.
and German-Japanese military relations, 102 f.
receives Chinese mission, 113
and Klein-HAPRO issue, 116 ff.
appealed to by Kriebel over RWM's Canton plans, 124 f.
conversation with von Seeckt on Sino-German military relations, 126, 129
meeting with AA and RWM on arms trade with China, 127 ff.
approves Klein projects, 131
policy towards Japan and position of AA and von Ribbentrop, 136, 175 ff.
concern at Russia's foreign policy, 178, 180
considers agreement with Japan, 178
desires agreement with Great Britain, 178, 181
and Chinese approach (1935) on mediation, 183 f.
warned by von Neurath of effects of agreement with Japan, 185
confirms von Ribbentrop's negotiations, 185
discussion with von Ribbentrop, 190
conversation with Ambassador Mushakoji on German-Japanese relations, 193, 196
given RWM reports on Russo-Japanese military position, 195
conversations with Trautmann and von Dirksen on German-Japanese relations, 197 ff.
receives von Ribbentrop, Oshima at Bayreuth (1936), 200
cautious policy of recognition of Manchukuo (1936), 201
views Anti-Comintern Pact as pressure on Great Britain, 201, 210
policy of reserve to Japan after Pact, 210, 216, 222, 254
and Kung's visit (1937), 212, 224, 226
assures Chiang Kai-shek on Pact, 214
exchanges letters with Hirota (1937), 231
attitude to Sino-Japanese war (1937), 240, 248
appealed to by Kung, 243, 248
reported as considering mediation, 250